JUVENILE THEFT: THE CAUSAL FACTORS

A report of an investigation of the
tenability of various causal
hypotheses about the development of
stealing by London boys.

Prepared by

WILLIAM A. BELSON

on the basis of research by

**William A. Belson, BA, Ph D, (design and direction of the project);
Peter J. Didcott, BA, Dip Crim; Geoffrey L. Millersom, BA, Ph D;
John G. Cleland, BA.**

with programming and analysis by

Vernon R. Thompson

and administrative assistance by

Jean C. Carr.

Harper & Row, Publishers
London, New York, Evanston, San Francisco

Designed by 'Millions'
Typeset by Preface Ltd, Salisbury
Printed by R J Acford Ltd, Chichester

Standard Book Number 06—318026—X

Contents

Preface

This report describes an investigation concerned with the tenability of various hypotheses about causal factors in the development of juvenile stealing. It was itself a part of a wider series of investigations financed by the Home Office and carried out by the Survey Research Centre under the direction of the author.

That wider series of investigations had as its central theme the methodology of criminological research and with Home Office agreement, the present enquiry was focused upon an aspect of criminological investigation which was regarded as important but which it was considered had been neglected because the research procedures necessary for carrying it out had been insufficiently developed. This was the technology of *causal research* and, for social relevance, that class of technology was to be developed and used in the problem area of juvenile stealing.

The decision to attempt to advance causal research technology was admittedly ambitious because of the special difficulties besetting it in the social sciences. The basic trouble is that in the social sciences any causal sequence occurs in the context of a potentially large number of inter-acting processes in, as it were, a deterministic swirl. The identification of any single contributing factor is therefore made very difficult and it is little wonder that many social scientists baulk at that class of causal research. Some of course seek a solution in laboratory type settings or in controlled situations where they attempt to isolate the postulated causal factor in which they are especially interested. Unfortunately this particular strategy can introduce into a study so much atypicality that one must question the meaningfulness of the findings. How, for instance, could one manage to subject a sample of boys to some realistic form of *association with thieves* over some extended time period, keeping some other equivalent sample free of such association? How could one provide *opportunity to steal* to one sample and exclude opportunity from some equivalent sample? In any case, such tactics would be quite unacceptable both ethically and legally. This is not to say that artificial control systems have no place in crime research. Certainly they have an important part to play in studies of the relative efficiency of different remedial systems for boys held in legalistic custody. And obviously there are many other valid uses for artificial control systems in crime research. But for the realistic study of the extent to which and the way in which particular factors contribute to the development of stealing, there is no escaping the multi-determinant social scene as one's research setting.

The research principle adopted was what has been called the Hypo-thetico—Deductive Method. As a method, it is used in investigating hypotheses which are not directly testable. Instead, one deduces from such an hypothesis a series of testable propositions which one could expect to be true if the hypothesis were true. These propositions are made as varied as possible and their testing ordinarily calls for a considerable amount of data collection. If all such propositions are verified by the tests made, then their parent hypothesis is thereby rendered more tenable. If any one of the propositions is not verified, then the parent hypothesis is rendered less tenable. The reader will find this research technique described in principle in Chapter 1 and in practical detail in Chapter 3.

I think it is fair to say that in its application in this enquiry the Hypothetico—Deductive Method worked quite well as a research strategy. In that sense I believe that the criminologist interested in causal research will find it useful to study the method in action in this report. At the same time it must be said that it became clear in the course of investigating the different hypotheses, that the Hypothetico—Deductive Method could with advantage have been taken further than I took it. More particularly, even more propositions could have been derived for most of the hypotheses. And for some of the hypotheses, the propositions derived and tested might have been somewhat different. But having said this, let me restate that I believe that the method has worked and that the causally oriented criminologist will find it useful.

Another methodological feature of this enquiry was the development of a procedure for getting from boys information about the extent and the nature of any involvement they may have had in stealing. The study was of course concerned with boys generally and not simply with that atypical small section of them who have been caught and put into custodial care. This is a necessary feature of any aetiological study of a realistic kind. But it poses major problems for the social scientist. The development of such a technique took over a year in its own right and the procedure in its final form is described in Chapter 1. The method of its development is described in detail in another report within the research project (*The development of a procedure for eliciting information from boys about the nature and extent of their stealing.* W. A. Belson; G. L. Millersom and P. J. Didcott, Survey Research Centre, 1968). The results of using the technique are set out in Chapter 2 of this volume. Here too it is clear now that further development of the method as a procedure is possible and desirable, but the method as it stands should be of use to the quantitatively minded criminologist who seeks to base his work on boys generally. Furthermore, there is no obvious reason why the same kind of technique cannot be adapted for use in studying the incidence of other classes of juvenile delinquency. Indeed this has already been done in a later study, by the author, of juvenile *violence*. But any such conversion calls for a lot of rigorous technique construction and anything less than this will almost certainly produce an invalid measuring procedure.

One feature of this report calls especially for comment. It is not a theoretical document in the sense of dwelling upon competing theories about the aetiology of stealing or in the sense of postulating some alternative theory. Rather it is concerned with the empirical investigation of the tenability of various hypotheses about causal factors. Certainly current theories about causal processes in stealing were represented by some of the hypotheses put to test. But so too were views about causality that, in the world of academic acceptance, fell below the level of theory. In fact, whether a theory or hypothesis or view was chosen for empirical investigation in this enquiry depended upon whether it stood up to the challenge of various scientific criteria as described in Chapter 1. Having said this, let me add that I think it likely, and certainly desirable, that the genuine theorist will want to use the findings presented here for challenging the tenability of the different criminological theories to which those findings appear to be relevant.

It is essential, in considering the findings reported herein, to bear in mind the stipulation, repeated frequently in the book itself, that no single factor has been hypothesised as a sole cause of stealing. Throughout, the basic assumption has been one of *multiple* causality. On the other hand, let there be no mistake about it: causality is being postulated. I make this point because I am aware that some criminologists have virtually denied the concept of causality in relation to deviant behaviour. I profess little sympathy with such a view, my feeling being that it has sprung in large part from frustration at being unable to conduct causal investigations and perhaps a mistaken view that those who take a causal approach are thinking solely in terms of some single cause.

The enquiry began with exploratory work which led on to a lengthy period spent in developing research tactics and in constructing measuring instruments for the enquiry. The fieldwork itself was spread out over a year in the period 1967–68. This was followed by a lengthy phase of complex analyses and the report was passed to the Home Office in 1973. The reader will wish to note that since the period of the fieldwork the Children and Young Persons Act of 1969 has come into force and that its operation could conceivably change the causal scene in some way. Various social changes have also occurred in this period. At the same time, I see no good reason for thinking that events since the end of fieldwork have led to any major upset of the causal scene reported in this book. In this general connection, and in terms of stability of findings, it should be noted that the information gathered in the enquiry referred not just to the period of the fieldwork, but to the whole life of the boys concerned.

The generality of the present findings is another matter that calls for comment. The study reported in this document was carried out in the Greater London area — within its inner 24 miles of diameter. Strictly speaking, it is to that area and to that particular population of boys that the findings apply and this is a position which, from a scientific viewpoint, I must take. Any generalisation beyond that region is at risk. On the other hand, I would regard it as not unreasonable to expect a considerable degree of carry-over to other large conurbations in the United Kingdom say Manchester, Birmingham, Glasgow. If one goes beyond these to large conurbations in other of the English speaking countries (say New York, Philadelphia, Montreal, Sydney) the risks inherent in generalisation grow, particularly because of cultural differences. This is not to rule out any possibility of their applicability there, but I think it would be wiser to regard any transfer of findings simply as constituting strong hypotheses to be tested on the spot. As for transfer to *rural* areas, I would be very wary indeed and would insist that the present findings be regarded as no more than hypotheses and that it would be essential to test them before taking them more seriously.

In this enquiry, my own role has been to design and direct it, to co-ordinate and integrate analysis and to write the report. But many people have contributed to its conduct in varying degrees and I want particularly to acknowledge the contributions of P. J. Didcott, BA, Dip Crim; G. L. Millersom, B Sc, Ph D; J. G. Cleland, BA; V. R. Thompson. Mr. Didcott worked on all phases of the execution of the enquiry and had special responsibility for the control of fieldwork. Dr. Millersom was concerned with searching the literature for hypotheses and theories about the development of stealing and with aspects of the construction of the technique used for eliciting from boys information about their stealing. Mr. Cleland was involved in aspects of the fieldwork and with parts of the analysis of the survey data. Mr. V. Thompson worked as a computer programmer on the extremely complex requirements of analysis and tabulation involved in the project.

The investigation in its early and formative stages had the advantage of critical appraisal and suggestions from an advisory committee of social scientists. In the fieldwork phase, a great deal depended upon the ability and sense of responsibility of those setting up appointments with boys, of the interviewers and of those concerned with quality control and survey administration: Miss V. Booker, Mrs. V. M. Cound-Moreira, Miss A. A. Law, Mrs. B. Jordan, Messrs. N. A. Al-Jibouri, R. M. Alley, N. D. W. Armistead, M. A. S. Cardew, P. A. Fahy, A. V. Fisher, I. J. Piper, J. Rowarth, N. R. Ratledge, F. P. E. Southgate, H. F. Watkins, S. R. G. White, B. D. Willis, G. S. Ben-Tovim, D. A. Robinson, A. M. Varlaam, R. J. Workman.

Thanks are particularly due to the Home Office for its provision of the grant for conducting the enquiry and to Mr. T. S. Lodge, then Director of the Home Office Research Unit, for the support which he gave to the project throughout.

William A. Belson
Project Director.

Summary

AIMS

The study reported herein was designed as an investigation of a large number of hypotheses about causal factors in the development of juvenile stealing. The investigation of an hypothesis was to be of such a character as would either increase or reduce the tenability of that hypothesis. In referring to a causal factor, there is no suggestion that it is a *sole* cause — only that it contributes, as one of many factors, to the development of stealing.

The total number of hypotheses investigated was 45 and these fell into 18 groups, broadly to the effect that contributory factors in the development of juvenile stealing are:

an expectation by the boy that he will not be caught for such stealing as he does;

a non-concern about the consequences of getting caught for stealing;

a strong desire for fun and excitement and a tendency to go out just looking for it;

association with local thieves;

an absence of moral training regarding stealing;

the nature of the boy's nominal religion and his non-attendance at church or chapel or synagogue;

an absence of parental control and discipline;

a home background that a boy finds difficult or unpleasant;

early separation from mother/father;

mother goes out to a job;

the home is or has been broken;

the boy has a permissive attitude towards stealing;

the boy has very few (legal) interests or hobbies;

the boy has no personal ambitions;

the boy dislikes school and/or teachers;

the boy plays truant;

the boy's wants exceed his (legal) financial means;

the boy watches a great deal of television.

The sub-hypotheses linked to the above classes of hypothesis are detailed in the relevant chapters of this report.

It was intended that in addition to investigating the hypotheses themselves, information would be derived about the distribution of both the dependent and the independent variables referred to in the different hypotheses.

METHODS

The methodology of this enquiry is best considered as made up of two parts, namely: (i) the preparation of techniques or tactics to be used in the causal enquiry and (ii) the use of these in a large scale enquiry based on 1425 London boys.

Preparation of research techniques and tactics

The preparation of techniques and tactics principally involved:

a) the use of intensive interviewing methods for developing a large number of hypotheses about the causes of stealing;

b) the construction of techniques for measuring the variables named in the different hypotheses, including (i) the technique for getting from boys reliable information about such stealing as they have done, (ii) questioning procedures for determining whether boys qualified or not in terms of the many different hypotheses to be investigated;

c) the design of challenging tactics for investigating hypotheses about causal processes (in fact a development of what has been called the Hypothetico—Deductive Method);

d) the development of an interviewing context and of extraction procedures in and through which boys would provide workably accurate information.

It is strongly suggested that the reader examine the descriptions, in Chapter 1, of the techniques referred to above, particularly the descriptions of (i) the research strategy and (ii) the procedure for getting boys to provide reliable information about such stealing as they may have done.

Conducting the enquiry

The investigation of the hypotheses was based on long interviews with 1425 London boys, representing 86% of the total target sample of 1655 boys. These boys were in the age range 13—16 years* and all were drawn from Greater London. The target sample of 1655 boys was drawn on the random principle from a universe of boys established through an enumeration survey based on approximately fifty-eight thousand homes in 40 polling districts.

All the interviewing was done at an interviewing centre in mid-London, the interviewing rooms being small, soundproofed and specially equipped with apparatus for the interview. The interviewers were male graduates who had undergone a preliminary two weeks selection-training course and who were thereafter subject to continuing quality control. Interviewing was spread over a twelve month period.

In getting the boys to the interviewing centre, a system of appointment-making and collection was used. An Appointment Maker went to the home of each boy to convince him and his parents that he should come to the Centre for interview. Inducements (including a fee of £1, choice of a pop record and the promise that the evening would be an interesting one) were used. A Collector called at the agreed time to collect the boy and take him to the Centre by car. When an appointment was not kept by a boy, the Appointment Maker would attempt to make a new appointment and was prepared to go on doing so until the boy was secured.

At the interviewing centre, each boy was given a false name, was fed on arrival and was taken to an interviewer. In the interview, the boy was assured of his anonymity and was processed through: a questioning procedure for establishing whether he qualified or not in relation to each of the many hypotheses; the technique which had been designed for eliciting from boys details of any stealing they may have done; a large number of questions that had been included for matching purposes. This total procedure was broken by pauses for rest and for food, by card sorting, by movement round the room to different kinds of equipment, by variation in the form of the procedure itself, by periodic chats between boy and interviewer.

*Though a limited number of 12 year olds and 17 year olds were included.

An analysis was made of the age and class characteristics of the 14% of boys who were not secured for interview (these being known from the enumeration survey) and it was estimated that their inclusion would not have changed, to any appreciable degree, the overall distribution of age and class characteristics of the boys actually interviewed. Similarly, the available evidence strongly suggested that inclusion of the *theft* details of the remaining 14% would not have made any appreciable difference to the theft level established for the 86% actually interviewed.

Several kinds of analysis were used for investigating or challenging the hypotheses. The first of these, preliminary and ambiguous* in character, involved assessing the correlation between amount of thieving done and whether boy qualified in terms of the hypothesis. A second challenging procedure, known as the 'matching' technique, involved; (i) classifying boys as qualifying on a given hypothesis or as not qualifying; (ii) matching the latter to the former group in terms of a large composite of the *correlates* of stealing; (iii) interpreting a significant residual difference in theft score of the two groups as supporting the hypothesis. A third approach, insufficient in itself but useful in a combination or battery of checks, included the use of the challenged testimony of boys.

As background to the investigation of each hypothesis, tabulations were prepared of the distribution of 'scores' in terms of the hypothesized causal factor and of how that distribution varied with other aspects of the boys' backgrounds. For example, as background to the study of an hypothesis that unpleasant home conditions help to produce thieving in boys, details of the following kind were presented: family composition; crowdedness of the home; the incidence and nature of family rows; boys' feelings about being at home; whether there is anything interesting to do at home; and so on.

For a fairly detailed description of methods, the reader should study Chapter 1.

FINDINGS

A summary of the findings from the enquiry is best presented under three heads:

1) the extent and nature of stealing committed by London boys;

2) getting caught for stealing;

3) the tenability of the hypotheses that were investigated.

I Extent and nature of stealing by London boys

The evidence about the nature of stealing is presented mainly in Chapter 2. It is based upon the responses of boys, under conditions designed to promote accuracy, to questions about 44 categories of theft behaviour which are listed in full on pp. 102–103 of Chapter 2. Some examples of the matters covered by the complex of 44 types are set out below.

getting out of paying one's fare   stealing from a bike or motor bike
stealing from a cafe   stealing from a meter
stealing from work   stealing money
stealing by stripping things   buying things known to be
from buildings   stolen
stealing for a dare   getting into a place and stealing

---

*Ambiguous in the sense that a correlation does not in itself establish a *causal* relationship.

The main indications of the collected evidence are as follows.

1) All of the 1425 London boys in the sample admitted to at least some stealing and there was no class of theft behaviour amongst the 44 that was endorsed by less than 5%. Some examples follow: 88% had at some time stolen something from school; 70% from a shop and 33% from a stall or barrow; 30% had at some time got something by threatening others; 25% had stolen from a car or lorry or van, 18% from a telephone box, 17% a letter or parcel and 11% from a meter; 5% had taken a car or lorry or van. The average for the whole 44 classes of theft behaviour was 42%.

2) Whereas there is a tendency for the incidence of stealing to fall off in going from the sons of the unskilled to the sons of the professionally occupied, that fall-off is not especially sharp (34% at one extreme to 22% at the other) and it is clear that stealing is widely spread through the different occupational strata, with the sons of the professionally occupied sector being quite substantially involved. The pattern is broadly similar with respect to school background.

3) Some types of theft behaviour tended to occur more amongst the sons of the less skilled, for example: stealing food, sweets; taking things from a bike or motor bike; stealing from work; from a stall or a barrow, from a goods yard; getting into a place and stealing; stealing from a meter. For others, however, the theft level is much the same across the 'social gradient', for example: cheating someone out of money; fare evasion; taking something for a dare; pinching from one's own family or relations; stealing from a changing room; stealing from a telephone box.

4) With respect to occupational background, one finding worth noting is that the tendency for stealing to increase in going down the social scale is broken in going from the sons of the semi-skilled to the sons of the unskilled: the latter do somewhat *less* stealing than the sons of the *semi*-skilled.

5) Theft level varies also with other aspects of boys' behaviour or background. Thus boys who go out just looking for fun and excitement engage in much more stealing than those who don't. Jewish boys in the sample did markedly less stealing than other boys; boys born outside of the United Kingdom did somewhat less stealing than boys born *in* the United Kingdom.

6) The accumulated amount of stealing by boys may be expected to, and does, increase with the age of the boy. But the evidence does not suggest that there is any fall-off in theft level in going from age 14 to age 15 to age 16. On the other hand, there are *some* kinds of theft behaviour that *do* tend to fall-off after the age of 13 or 14, for example: stealing from a building site; stealing by threatening; stealing a letter or a parcel; stealing from a park or playground.

7) The age at which boys commit their first 'serious' theft is very varied, but 18% have done so by the age of 7 years and 42% by the age of 10 years. Furthermore, serious stealing is widely distributed amongst London boys of all social backgrounds.

8) The proportion of the 44 types of theft behaviour that the boy has *ever* committed may be regarded as an index of the *variety* of his stealing. Many boys have a high variety index, with about a quarter of the sample having committed 25 or more of the listed 44 acts at least once and the average boy about 18 of them. 'Variety' of stealing is associated with the boy's background in much the same way as is his 'total amount' of stealing.

II Getting caught for stealing

1) Thirteen percent (13%) of the boys in the sample claimed they had at some time been caught by the police for stealing. A further 37% said they had been caught by someone other than the police and 50% denied ever having been caught for stealing by anyone.

2) The 13% who claimed they had been caught by the police had been much more heavily involved in stealing than other boys. On the other hand, many of the boys who said they have never been caught by anyone for stealing had in fact been heavily involved in theft: 14% of them were in the top scoring quarter of the boy population with respect to stealing. In other words, (i) the boys caught by the police (for stealing) tended to be the ones most heavily involved in stealing; (ii) many boys who have been substantially involved in stealing have not been caught by anyone.

3) The likelihood of a boy being caught by the police for the stealing he commits varies with his background, being lower for those boys: whose fathers are in the upper professional bracket; who are Jewish; who attend Grammar or Public School; who are younger. The evidence does not support the view that coloured boys are more likely to be caught (by police) for the stealing they do than are white boys.

4) What happens to a boy on first being caught by the police for stealing appears to vary with the background of the boy, some boys being more likely to be sent to Court than others, for example: older boys, the sons of the less skilled.

III The tenability of the hypotheses that were investigated

Forty-five hypotheses, classifiable into the 18 groups listed under AIMS, were investigated. Since they could not be tested directly, the investigation of them involved testing the validity of propositions derived from them and, in general, challenging the hypotheses with a multiplicity of relevant facts which the present enquiry was made to provide. If an hypothesis withstood this challenging process, it was regarded as being made more tenable. If it did not do so, it was regarded as being made less tenable.

1) This class of investigation suggested that certain of the 18 groups of hypotheses may be regarded as much more tenable than others. The particular causal factors involved in these more tenable hypotheses were:

permissiveness on the part of the boy in relation to stealing;

association with boys who are already engaged in stealing;

a desire for a lot of fun and excitement and a tendency to go out 'just looking for fun and excitement';

truancy from school;

a belief on the part of the boy that the police will not catch him for stealing.

See summary item III.6 for elaboration of some of these factors.

2) Other of the hypotheses were also rendered more tenable — but to a lesser degree — than those listed above. The factors or conditions postulated in these as causal were of the following kinds:

the existence of home conditions that make of the home a place that boys find unpleasant or otherwise unattractive;

a situation in which the boy's mother has always gone out to work;

frequent boredom on the part of the boy;

having wants that exceed his legal means;

early separation from mother.

3) Several factors that appear to work appreciably *against* the continuance or the development of stealing were:

getting caught (for stealing) by the police or knowing about mates getting caught;

frequent church attendance;

Jewish denomination;

having a grandparent living in the home.

4) Findings relating to certain of the other hypotheses are especially noteworthy in that the hypothesis concerned is either not borne out at all or is supported by the evidence to only a minor degree.

a) The existence of a *broken* home did not emerge as an appreciable causal factor in its own right — though a miserable or uninteresting home *did*. The wide acceptance of a broken home as a causal factor may have part of its origin in a tendency of law-keeping agencies to regard boys from such homes as especially warranting full legal processing. It may also be that boys from broken homes are less likely to be guarded against detection or against initial legal processing than are boys who have two parents looking after their interests.

b) Parental control (during the boy's first 10 years) over where the boy went in his spare time and with whom, did not emerge as a causal factor of any weight — though control over whether the boy went out at all appeared to be marginally causal. Part of the reason for this sort of finding appears to be that control over where the boy goes and with whom he associates cannot be anything like complete. To start with, the boy has to go to *school* where he may well mix with boys who are engaged in a considerable amount of stealing. Over and above this, parental control over boys appears to operate at a relatively low level for the majority of boys.

c) The punishment of boys for misbehaviour does not appear to operate as a deterrent in relation to stealing. This finding has of course to be related to the *forms* that present-day punishment of boys does or can take. Thus it may well be that a study of the effectiveness of *different forms* of parental punishment will identify some of these as more preventive than others.

d) The causal association between *viewing behaviour* and stealing is complex. At the level merely of numerical association, a feeling of non-interest in watching television went along with a greater than average involvement in stealing. In terms of actual *viewing behaviour*, there was an overall tendency for less than average viewing to go along with greater than average involvement in stealing. In other words, the evidence in the form of mere association went against the hypothesis that watching television increases stealing. However, when extraneous differences between the heavier and the lighter viewers were removed by empirical matching, differences in terms of theft behaviour also virtually disappeared. In other words, the evidence suggested that exposure to television had virtually no effect on boys' involvement in stealing.

e) The extensiveness of a boy's (legal) interests, at either the active or the passive level, does not appear to be causally associated with the level of thieving. At the same time, it is noteworthy that at the level of mere numerical association, some classes of interest have a greater correlation with stealing than others and that some of these correlations are negative and some positive. The possibility therefore exists that the original hypothesis applies only to certain kinds of interests. But it does *not* hold for interests considered generally.

5) Boys had been asked to indicate from which of several sources (if any) they had in the past received instructions about 'not stealing'. The three sources were home, school and church, the hypothesis being that

where anti-theft teaching was received from only one or none of these three sources, boys would become involved in a greater amount of stealing than would boys who had received instruction from two or three of those sources. The hypothesis was *not* supported by the evidence collected. What we don't know in this case is the form taken by such instruction as was received. On the other hand, the evidence does provide grounds for the formulation of an hypothesis that the level of theft is reduced when anti-theft teaching is received *at a relatively intense level* from *all three* sources.

6) Some extension of presentation is called for with respect to summary items 1 and 2 which deal with the several hypotheses which most effectively came through the challenging procedure.

a) *Permissiveness in relation to stealing.* Permissiveness towards stealing was defined in terms of how right or wrong boys felt it would be to commit various forms of theft, 25 in all and including things like: pinching from someone who is rich, taking things from where you work, pinching from a shop, robbing a bank, pinching from an old lady, taking things just left lying around. A boy's permissiveness score was a weighted mean based on all his 25 ratings. There was a tendency for the more permissive boys to have been involved in much more stealing than had the less permissive boys and this still applied after close matching of the less permissive to the more permissive.

A related hypothesis, to the effect that boys who engage in stealing are lacking in remorse over acts of theft, was also rendered highly tenable by the challenging procedure administered.

Neither finding can be considered startling, but the two of them do identify a potent factor in the development of juvenile stealing and one that calls for careful consideration in any programme designed to reduce the incidence of stealing.

b) *Association with thieves.* The evidence indicates that association with boys who already steal is a very influential factor in the development of stealing by the individual boy. The causal link between mixing with thieves and committing thefts oneself is the stronger where: the associates are doing a *lot* of stealing (as against a little); the association with thieves began at an early age (as against later); the association is one of long standing (as against short term).

The ways in which association leads to greater stealing by the boy include: wanting to be accepted by other boys or to look good in their eyes; copying mates; being actively encouraged by mates to steal; being threatened or bullied or dared to steal; being encouraged by the stealing experiences of mates (e.g. by their getting away with it, by the kinds of things they steal). Some boys, on the other hand, claim that association with thieves eventually deterred them because: they were worried by the fact that some members of their group *did* get caught; seeing others stealing made it seem wrong.

Reasons for getting round with thieves were principally that: the boys concerned were friendly, lively, easy to get on with, fun; they had his own sorts of interests (other than stealing) and were of his own type; they went to the same school as he did; there was no-one else to get around with; they were tough and he wanted to be tough too.

c) *Desire for fun and excitement.* The first of the two hypotheses dealing with fun and excitement seeking was that: 'A desire for a lot of fun and excitement is a contributing factor to the initiation and maintenance of juvenile stealing'. The extensive evidence developed for the investigation of this hypothesis gave it considerable support and rendered it more tenable. Furthermore, this particular causal variable appears to apply for a very wide range of different types of stealing. A second hypothesis, involving the causal factor 'going out just looking for fun and excitement', was also strongly supported by the evidence.

The importance of the 'fun and excitement seeking' variable as a causal factor is emphasised by the demand amongst London boys of all social sectors for fun and excitement and by the fact that about half the boys in the sample claimed they didn't get enough of it.

d) On the evidence gathered, *truancy* is a potent factor in the development of stealing. Furthermore, truancy appears to be very common, with 11% of boys saying they do it once a week and 8% more saying they do it about once a month. Truancy is much more prevalent amongst secondary modern and comprehensive school boys and, not surprisingly, amongst those who say they dislike school (and teachers) and who like lots of fun and excitement.

e) *An expectation that one would not get caught for stealing, and related factors.* Approximately 30% of London boys felt that they would not get caught by the police if they engaged in stealing, and a further 40% felt only that they *might* get caught. The evidence collected in this enquiry strongly indicates that such a belief contributes causally to the development of juvenile stealing.

A small proportion of boys claim that they would not care if caught by the police for stealing and, on the evidence of this enquiry, this attitude is causally linked to stealing.

The evidence also indicates that 'actually getting caught by the police for stealing' operates as a deterrent in relation to future stealing. It also indicates that boys who were subsequently processed through the Courts were no more deterred by that than boys who were not taken through the Courts. This finding must be interpreted warily because (a) much depends upon the character and consequences which Court processing happened to have at that period and (b) the boys processed through the Courts may have been the more entrenched in their stealing behaviour. Nonetheless the evidence is challenging and invites the tentative conclusion that in the circumstances operating at the time of the enquiry, what mattered was not so much the processing of the boy through Court as the fact that he was apprehended by the police.

Recommendations

The findings of this enquiry provide various pointers or guide lines for remedial or preventive action against the development of stealing in boys. I have set out hereunder a number of recommendations for such action. Each recommendation is based directly upon findings reported in this book.

1) *Providing legal outlets for fun and excitement seeking* (see also 'Comments and possible action' in Chapter 4). The evidence indicates that 'fun and excitement seeking' is a powerful catalyst in the development of stealing. It leads boys into forms of behaviour that in turn lead to stealing — which then becomes an effective outlet in its own right for the 'fun and excitement' need.

The preventive or remedial action required in this case is the development of alternative outlets for fun and excitement seeking. Such outlets should be forms of activity which are not only socially acceptable but are attractive to the kinds of boys already engaged in stealing or in the excitement seeking activities that put them at risk. If such outlets can also satisfy other of the needs that lead boys to steal (e.g. money needs), they are the more likely to be adopted and maintained.

The identification and development of such alternative outlets for fun and excitement seeking will call for a considerable amount of searching enquiry and for close liaison with both delinquent boys and local authorities. *A proposal for such work has been developed and is available for study.*

2) *Concerning association with thieves* (see also 'Comments and possible action' in Chapter 6). A concerted effort should be made to discover ways of reducing the degree to which honest boys fall into association with boys who are engaged in stealing. In seeking such a solution it will be useful to keep certain considerations in mind.

a) In the first place, it seems most unlikely that a *simple appeal* to parents to keep their sons away from boys who steal will be very effective — if for no other reason than that once boys start to go to school, parents have incomplete control over which boys their sons mix with. On the other hand, widespread and intensive publicity about the dangers of such association should alert many parents to those dangers and lead them to take whatever preventive steps seem possible for them. These steps may include warning their sons about the dangers of association with thieves, trying to learn more about the boys with whom their sons associate, having their sons bring their friends home; increasing the degree to which home is the sort of place boys want to be in and care to bring their friends to. But *easy* success should not be expected from this approach and, generally speaking, publicity aimed at parents will have to be well designed and dramatic and will need to involve repeated mass media presentation if substantial success is to be achieved.

b) Such publicity should also be aimed at school teachers and local authorities so that they too are better prepared to take the preventive steps open to them.

c) The safeguarding of boys against undesirable association could gain considerably from teacher—parent liaison (perhaps in the context of Teacher—Parent Associations). The teachers might pass into that liaison such information as they have about undesirable associations at school. Parents might then be in a position to take some form of appropriate action. Local police officers, with their special awareness of boy-associations and of juvenile stealing in their areas, may on occasions be well positioned to discourage certain associations and to alert parents to developing dangers for their sons. Social workers likewise have much to offer in helping parents to be selective in relation to the association of their sons with local boys.

d) Another important avenue for action appears to be the development of encouragement of acceptable goals in terms of which boys may shine in the eyes of their associates. At present, successful thieving is one such goal. But many alternatives of an effective kind may be discerned in our youth society: soccer, pop music, motor cycles, hair styles, athletics. The development of a sufficient array of effective success symbols may well call for initial research to discover wants and needs that the new goals will have to satisfy. Readily available training facilities, perhaps on a large scale, will almost certainly be needed where the new goal or activity calls for the development of special skills. Promotion through the mass media will also be required where it is necessary to present the new activity in a realistic and appealing way to large populations of boys.

e) The search for further means of reducing association with boys who engage in stealing should be regarded as urgent. That search should be guided by an understanding of how boys fall into association with thieves, or avoid doing so, or eventually break the association. This report provides evidence that should advance such understanding, but much more is needed.

3) *Permissiveness in relation to stealing* (see also 'Comments and possible action' in Chapter 5). There is amongst boys a very considerable degree of permissiveness towards stealing — a situation which the enquiry indicated is very strongly associated, in a causal sense, with participation in stealing itself. The reduction of permissiveness towards stealing does not seem likely to be achieved in any short period of time or through some simple or single line of action. It will require long-term action on a broad front. Certainly an attack on 'permissiveness towards stealing' is essential because it is, in a sense, a broad underlying support for all the other causal factors: its reduction would automatically limit the power of those other factors.

It is not my purpose at this point to propose in any detail what type of campaign should be launched against 'permissiveness towards stealing'. That would be premature. But it does seem essential that any campaign designed to reduce permissiveness towards stealing should include: very early school training in honesty as part of the curriculum and taught as a *social* subject rather than as a religious one; the mounting of enduring publicity campaigns against stealing, just as campaigns may be mounted against careless driving or other socially undesirable behaviour; the active discouragement of those who entice stealing by providing the glaring opportunity for it. Such campaigning should also involve encouraging the formation of voluntary associations of parents and other citizens for the long-term maintenance and development of the campaign itself.

Doubtless many different people have an important part to play in the recommended campaign, each in his or her own way: police officers, social workers, teachers, local tradesmen and merchandising organisations, mass media proprietors, existing voluntary organisations, members of local government. It may even be that some form of council for social education would help in catalysing the many different elements and lines of action of the campaign.

Whatever is done, there must be no misunderstanding about the situation: permissiveness by boys towards stealing is widespread and if it is to be reduced to any appreciable degree, the attack on it will have to be well planned and widely based. Nor should we be unaware that an effort of the kind advocated will be undermined by some and abused by others. But nonetheless the effort will have to be made — carefully guarded and vigorously made.

4) *Concerning truancy.* Another major factor in the development of stealing is truancy from school and its reduction should be regarded as a

matter of urgency. There is a sense in which the reduction of truancy may be open to management in that truancy involves boys in breaking a specific rule within a particular establishment. On the other hand, this enquiry has shown that truancy is associated to a major degree with poor performance in school work and with poor relationships with teachers, and obviously any improvement in those two situations is likely to be difficult to bring about. But truancy is also associated with a desire for fun and excitement — about which something might well be done in association with schools (see Recommendation 1).

Whatever the difficulties to be overcome in reducing truancy, those difficulties must nonetheless be tackled, for truancy is a major causal factor in the development of stealing. There is urgent need for discussion of the action that should be taken. Clearly any such discussion must include teachers and parents and truanting boys — especially truanting boys. The detailed findings reported in this document provide useful information about the background, the reasoning and the behaviour of truants and they are highly relevant to the consideration of preventive action.

5) *Concerning the expectation of getting caught and fears of the consequences of getting caught.* Two of the findings of this enquiry will probably lead to little in the way of surprise, namely that stealing tended to be lessened (i) where boys expected to be caught if they stole or continued to steal; (ii) where boys feared the consequences of getting caught for stealing. However, these findings have important implications: *any policy that gives boys the idea that they can 'get away with' stealing or that reduces their fears of the consequences of getting caught for stealing is likely to lead to an increase in the incidence of stealing.* The possible effects of the 1969 'Children and Young Persons Act', as implemented, might be considered in this context.

At the level of positive action, it may well be possible in the context of a programme of social education and with the aid of film and other media, to communicate to young school children realistic impressions of the adverse consequences of getting caught for stealing, including hurt to parents and damage to family relationships. It may be too that publicity could with advantage be given to police success in catching young thieves. Any such steps would of course call for great care lest they inadvertently produce side effects of a damaging kind. However, the evidence provides a case for the suggested class of action.

William A. Belson

Chapter one
The background, aims and methods of the inquiry

CONTENTS

1 BACKGROUND TO THE INQUIRY

During the 1960s the Home Office made a series of grants to the Survey Research Centre of the London School of Economics for the study of various aspects of delinquency, primarily from a methodological point of view. More specifically, the programme of work was to be concerned with testing and with developing a range of research techniques on which criminological inquiries are based or might be based. Whereas the emphasis was thus strongly methodological, it was hoped nonetheless that the programme of research would produce findings about criminological phenomena in their own right.

The fact that the project had a strong methodological character sprang jointly from two considerations. One was the general concern of the Home Office Research Unit for the continuing development of the technology of crime research. The other was the fact that the Survey Research Centre was known to have a primary concern with testing and developing the techniques of social and business research.

The first study in this series dealt with the research potential of the case records of approved-school boys. Since many researchers use this source from time to time as a basis for analytical work, it seemed most important to assess its strengths and weaknesses from a scientific viewpoint. The findings were reported in a two-volume document passed to the Home Office[1].

The case records study was followed by a tightly-integrated composite of inquiries[2,3,4,5] conducted in preparation for the study reported in this volume. This study, a major one, was an investigation of a large number of hypotheses about causal factors entering into the development and continuation of juvenile stealing. It was based upon a representative sample of London's boys in the age range twelve to seventeen years.

Reasons for deciding to study stealing and its causes

There were several reasons for making this particular choice of topic:

The choice of causal research as a central theme In the opinion of the research team and their advisers, one of the most serious gaps in the technology of criminological inquiries concerns causal research. Techniques for identifying and evaluating the various causes of some specified form of delinquency — as distinct from finding its correlates — have tended not to be used in delinquency research. Correlational research can be useful and informative, but inevitably it does not establish *causal* relationships. After all, the existence of a correlation between a given variable and some form of delinquency leaves wide open the possibility that some other variable altogether lies behind or supports that correlation. It also leaves open the possibility that the *delinquent condition* itself partly controls that correlated variable.

On the other hand, the taking of crime research beyond mere correlational work is no simple matter and one can understand why it tends not to be done. Faced with the need to derive unambiguous findings, the criminologist might consider conducting tightly-controlled experimentation. If he does this on the pattern of laboratory experimentation with simulated models of even a subtle kind, it is most unlikely that the extrapolation of his findings to real-life delinquency will meet with much acceptance. If he attempts to set up local experiments with real-life delinquency as his dependent variable and with real-life representation of his hypothesized causal factor(s), he faces not only major expense but serious problems in ensuring that his experimental design is maintained. He also faces the hard fact that he cannot, from an ethical or a legal stand-point, easily justify the inclusion in his experiment of any factors hypothesized as *increasing* delinquency.

Confronted by this forbidding set of problems, the researcher may perhaps feel defeated because his only other choice appears to be the formidable one of teasing-out cause and effect from the great mix of factors ordinarily operative within a society. However there are in use in other branches of the social sciences, particularly in media research, techniques which can be adapted fairly readily to causal research in criminology.

It was against this background that the decision was taken to proceed with a causal enquiry in the expectation that: (*a*) it would provide a much-needed class of information about delinquent behaviour; and (*b*) it should provide additional methodological strategies for research into the *causes* of delinquent behaviour.

The choice of stealing by boys' as a central theme The focusing of the study on stealing by boys was governed by utilitarian considerations. It was our aim to base this obviously expensive programme of research upon the most prevalent class of juvenile delinquency. Clearly, this was stealing. Moreover, crime statistics marked it out as a primarily male class of behaviour.

The decision to base the study on boys in the general population A distinctive feature of the inquiry is that it was based upon a general population of boys rather than upon some population of detected delinquents. There was an important reason for doing this. If, as seemed likely, those who get caught for stealing are different from those who *do not* get caught (e.g. in terms of educational background, quality of home life, area of residence), this distinction could be crucial. Certainly, it could mean that findings based upon a sample of detected thieves could not be projected to boy thieves generally.

Principally for these reasons, the basing of the study upon boys in the general population was regarded as essential for any properly balanced understanding of how stealing by boys originates and continues.

It was also clear, in making this decision, that there was a pressing need for the development of a technique for providing reliable information about the incidence of juvenile stealing in the general population. It is the absence of eliciting techniques in the general area of delinquency that has helped to drive many researchers to the sometimes unsatisfactory practice of basing studies of delinquency solely upon boys who happen to have been caught and detained and who thereby have records of some kind to which the researcher may go. If research is to be based upon representative samples of delinquents, valid methods must be developed for eliciting evidence of delinquent behaviour from boys *generally*.

The construction of such a technique with respect to stealing was therefore seen as a methodological by-product of considerable relevance to the purpose of the Home Office grant.

There was one other methodological issue that helped to shape the purpose and the direction of the present inquiry. This was the need to draw the attention of the young social scientist in criminology to the ease with which the intensive interviewing of boys and of others can be used to help in the development of insightful hypotheses about factors that enter causally into the aetiology of juvenile stealing. The hypothesis development process did of course also involve close study of the literature of delinquency and of the views of people connected with delinquent or non-delinquent boys. But the intensive interviewing technique, applied to boys, proved to be particularly rewarding.

To sum up, the choice of problem for investigation was in this case influenced by two classes of consideration: (*a*) the need to identify for investigation a problem of social importance in its own right; (*b*) the need to develop or promote certain classes of methodology for use in delinquency research.

A preliminary note about the limitations of causal research into juvenile delinquency

In presenting the background to this inquiry, it is most important that two aspects of the approach be made clear from the outset. They relate respectively to the concept of 'cause' and to the proper interpretation of the results of the investigations made of causal hypotheses.

In the first place, the approach to causality adopted here is *multiple* in character. It is multiple in the sense that the specific variables named in the hypotheses as causal (e.g. 'fun and excitement-seeking', association with thieves, truancy) were from the outset regarded as no more than contributory in character. Certainly there was no expectation that one or another of them might somehow turn out to be a sole explanatory factor. It was also fully recognized that there is likely to be complex interaction between the different factors that turn out to be contributory.

Secondly, by 'investigating' a causal hypothesis, was meant subjecting that hypothesis to such study and challenge as is necessary either to reduce or to increase its tenability as an hypothesis. For the approach adopted, strictly controlled experiments were out of the question: an attempt was to be made to study each postulated 'causal process' in its normal social setting — i.e., in a setting involving the inevitable intrusion of a multiplicity of other variables. Later in this chapter* I

*See also the description of these tactics in *Causal factors in the development of stealing by London boys: Methods of research.* W. A. Belson and P. J. Didcott. Survey Research Centre, 1969.

will deal at length with the complex investigatory tactics that were designed to meet this problem, but for the present it is important that I warn the reader that the extensive evidence gathered cannot, by the nature of the problem, provide final *proof* or *disproof* of any particular hypothesis. The investigatory tactics served — and were meant to serve — either to increase or reduce the tenability of the hypotheses. At the same time it should be noted that this does not preclude a *marked* increase or decrease in tenability.

2 AIMS OF THE INQUIRY

The present inquiry had, then, more than one orientation. It was a social investigation heavily featured by methodological developments in what was judged to be an important area of delinquency research, namely the identification and evaluation of contributory factors behind one of the more prevalent forms of juvenile delinquency, stealing.

More specifically, the inquiry had the following aims.
1 To originate empirically, and then to investigate, a wide range of hypotheses concerning causal factors in the initiation and the development of juvenile stealing.

2 In preparation for this work, and in its process:
a To provide a working example of the use of the intensive interviewing method with boys as an aid in developing hypotheses in the criminological area.
b To develop a procedure for getting from boys in the general population reliable information about the extent and the nature of such stealing as they may have committed; to open the way for the use of this technique as an aid in providing statistics of juvenile theft.
c To provide a detailed working example of the use of certain research techniques for investigating *causal* hypotheses in the criminological area.
d To provide a wide body of information about the extent and nature of juvenile stealing in London.
e To provide a wide range of background information about those factors and situations found through the inquiry to be causally linked with stealing.

Aim **2b** has already led to the presentation of a major report[6] and the present volume is concerned primarily with presenting the results of work geared to the other aims. More specifically, this volume presents evidence about:

  i The nature and the extent of stealing by London boys.

  ii The methods used for the investigation of causal hypotheses.

  iii The results of such investigation.

  iv Background information about each of the factors involved in the causal hypotheses.

3 THE METHODS OF THE INQUIRY
Preparatory work in the form of instrument development and the formulation of research strategies

Preparatory work was both extensive and demanding. It involved several distinct phases.

1 The first of these was the derivation of hypotheses about the causes of stealing. This process was based jointly upon an extensive analysis of the literature of criminology and a large number of intensive interviews with boys and others including many detected delinquents. This part of the preparatory work is described in broad terms in this chapter.

2 After this came the development of a questioning procedure for getting from boys information about the nature and the extent of such stealing as they may have committed. This was a major operation, extending over a period of more than a year. It has been fully documented in a separate report[7] and the procedure itself is presented as an appendix to this chapter.

3 A third important preparatory operation was the formulation and piloting of the wider questioning procedure in the context of which the hypothesis testing was to be done. This wider array of questions was concerned with: (a) the formulation of questions to separate out the boys who qualified on a given hypothesis and those who were to be used as controls; and (b) the gathering of a lot of background information relevant to the hypotheses, e.g. the attitudes of boys towards being at home as background to an hypothesis about hostile home environment (as a causal element in the initiation of stealing).

With the completion of these three preparatory steps, the main causal inquiry could be set going, starting with an enumeration survey referred to in the section on sampling.

The development of causal hypotheses

It was essential that the hypotheses tested as causal elements should be both realistic and comprehensive. Accordingly, a major search for possible causal elements was conducted in two broad but overlapping areas: the ideas of the boys themselves; the literature of criminology.

Throughout this search there was no question of any *single* or predominant causal factor being sought. Rather, the search was based upon an assumption of multiple causality. This approach does not rule out a subsequent discovery that some one factor is a very important one in the causal 'mix'. But it would be most unwise to design an inquiry on the assumption that such a discovery would be made.

The search of the literature and the intensive interviewing of boys went on in parallel.

The sample of boys interviewed in the context of hypothesis development

The boys interviewed came from three different sources: Stamford House Remand Home and Classifying Centre in London (thirty-seven boys); four approved schools (fifty-eight boys) whose boys were drawn from the Greater London area; boys from the general population in London (103 boys).

Whereas the boys from the approved schools and the remand home were interviewed in their respective establishments and with the approval of the appropriate authorities, the interviewing of boys in the London population at large called for special contact procedures. An enumeration survey was conducted in four London areas selected on the basis of police ratings of area delinquency levels. A 120-boy sample was drawn on random principles from the names yielded by the enumeration survey. These boys were approached by special interviewers and arrangements were made for 103 of them to be interviewed at a mid-city centre. In agreeing to take part, the boys understood that they would be brought to the centre by car, would receive a fee for taking part and would be given the fare home. In line with what was expected from the selection of the enumeration areas, it turned out that the involvement of these boys in stealing ranged from being very heavy to negligible. In other words, they together provided a basis for intensive interviews not only about how some boys thought they got *into* stealing, but about how other boys felt they had kept out of it.

The method of interviewing boys for the derivation of causal hypotheses

Inevitably there were some differences between the methods used for interviewing the three samples of boys and these different methods are detailed elsewhere.[8] In broad terms, however, the aims and procedures were as follows.

Aims For all boys who had been engaged in an appreciable amount of stealing, the aim was to secure their ideas about what started them stealing and what it was that led them to keep on stealing. For non-thieves (available within the sample of 'free' boys), the aim was to secure ideas about what it was that had kept them out of stealing or had led them to give it up.

Interviewing procedures

1 All boys worked under promise of anonymity and with a firm assurance that nothing they revealed would ever be connected with them personally.

2 After a preliminary phase, the boys were taken through various of their own thefts, either as revealed in their records or as elicited through a form of intensive

interviewing*. For each of these, the boy was asked for the circumstances of the theft or how he came to commit it†.

3 Each boy who had done a lot of stealing was asked to think back over what he had done and to talk about what it was that got him started in stealing — and what kept him at it once started. In the case of boys who had done very little stealing, the questions were focused on what it was they thought had helped to keep them *out* of stealing‡.

Analysis of the leads derived from boys

The technique of *content analysis* was used to derive from the statements of boys the different factors and circumstances which they claimed entered into their involvement in stealing or their non-involvement in it. This method protects data of this kind from selective screening by the analysts and from the imposition of an analyst's ideas upon the data.

Leads from those working with delinquents

To broaden the source of ideas to be used in developing hypotheses, intensive interviews were carried out also with a number of adults closely associated with boys, particularly delinquent boys. These adults were: four house masters, two teachers and one psychologist (all from a London remand home) and three youth leaders. These people were intensively interviewed at length in an effort to get from them their ideas about causal factors in the development of juvenile stealing. The interviews were tape-recorded and the results fed into the content analysis of the material derived from the boys.

Leads from the literature

A major search for tenable hypotheses about causal factors in stealing was made in the literature of criminology. There were four steps in deriving hypotheses from this source.

1 An examination was made of twelve standard textbooks on criminology available at that time[9]* in order to identify the main theories, hypotheses and ideas about causes of juvenile delinquency (particularly of theft) put forward in them and to provide a guide to primary sources.

2 An examination was made of primary sources when the main text gave too little information.

3 An evaluation was made of the ideas, hypotheses and theories derived from 1 and 2 above.

4 A content analysis was made of the yield from 1 to 3 above.

For each idea, hypothesis or theory put forward, the following were sought: (a) a clear statement of the idea or hypothesis or theory; (b) an explanation of the mechanism behind the theory or hypothesis (i.e. *how* the hypothesized causal factor was supposed to contribute to the delinquent condition concerned); and, (c) reference to any *other* books, articles, reports where these seemed likely to throw up relevant information not included in the text book being examined.

This class of evidence was scrutinized with a view to answering questions of the following kinds: (a) was the hypothesis or lead based upon a properly-conducted causal inquiry or upon a correlation, or was it just speculation? (b) did some apparent theory qualify as a theory in the proper sense of that term? (c) did the causal hypothesis or statement postulate the sort of delinquency that was being 'caused' (e.g. larceny, offences against persons ....) or did it just refer generally to delinquency? (d) what sort of people were concerned in the causal statement (e.g. adults, boys, the mentally unstable)? (e) is there an account of the process whereby the hypothesized factor is said to contribute to the dependent condition and if so what is

---

*The methods used for getting from 'free' boys admissions about thefts committed was a very early form of the technique eventually developed for the final survey. At this early stage, it involved preliminary sorting of a set of cards on each of which was some broad class of stealing. A challenging and defining process then followed with a view to securing relatively firm instances of thefts on which to work further with the boy. For the boys in the remand home and the approved schools, the acts of theft dealt with were those entered in their case files.

†For each of a number of his admitted or recorded thefts, the boy was asked for the circumstances of the theft and/or how he came to do it. This rather lengthy part of the interview was intended to set the boy thinking, in a realistic context, about how he came to get involved in his thieving activities. This in turn was intended to prepare him for thinking, in the next stage of the interview, rather more generally about causal and precipitating factors.

‡If the boy had done a lot of stealing, he was reminded of this and asked what it was that got him started in stealing. His replies were probed and the question was re-put in various ways. After this open approach, the boy was taken through various broad groupings of social, environmental and personal factors frequently postulated in the literature as contributing to the development of delinquency (e.g. family life and conditions at home, his associates, his neighbourhood, his school, his spare-time activities, his religion, the mass media, his own ideas about honesty). In all cases the approach was indirect and any claim made by the boy was challenged in order to discourage a too-easy agreement with any of the possibilities discussed with the interviewer. In this general connection, it must be remembered here that what were being sought were leads and possibilities on the basis of which hypotheses might be developed.

If the boy had done very little stealing, the interviewer summed up by saying this. He then asked the boy to help him understand how it was that he had kept out of stealing, whether he ever came close to stealing but drew back — and why; whether he ever felt tempted to steal and, if so, what stopped him.

---

*Use was also made of the valuable contribution by O. Moles, R. Lippitt, S. B. Withey, (1959), *Selective Review of Research and Theories Concerning the Dynamics of Delinquency*. (Inter-Center Program of Research on Children, Youth and Family Life, Ann Arbor, Michigan). As the title indicates, the review is selective and there is, in particular, a dearth of information about English studies. It is, however, a very well organized presentation of many major contributions.

this? (f) is the information on which the causal statement rests scientifically adequate in its own right (e.g. with regard to sample size, the possible existence of bias in the way the data were collected, the size of the correlation on which the causal statement rests)?

Causal statements tended to be disregarded where they related specifically to a kind of delinquency which was other than stealing (e.g. offences against persons) or where the evidence on which they rested was of a grossly inadequate kind.

A pool of hypotheses

The hypotheses and the suggestions stemming from the interviews with the boys were brought together, in a general pool, along with the yield from the search of the literature and the interviews with those in working contact with delinquents. From this pool were drawn sixteen groups of hypotheses (or theories or ideas) for investigation in the causal inquiry. This selection was guided by several considerations: (a) the frequency with which the different factors or conditions came up in testimony; (b) the adequacy of the evidence on which published hypotheses rested; (c) the feasibility of investigating particular hypotheses; (d) the degree of overlap between hypotheses; (e) the total length of interview that it was feasible to conduct.

No doubt there are gaps in the list of hypotheses selected for inquiry, some of which may be deemed important. Gaps are in large part due to the selective criteria listed above. On the other hand, the total number of hypotheses selected for testing, and their range, is quite large.

The hypotheses selected for investigation

The large pool of hypotheses built-up in this way was sorted in terms of the variable or condition hypothesized as contributing to the development of juvenile stealing. Sixteen broad classes of proposed causal factors emerged and thirteen of these were selected for investigation through this inquiry. These thirteen were concerned with the groups of factors set out below*.

1 *Concerning the possibility of getting caught:*
a An expectation of being caught by the police if he steals/continues to steal (−)†.
b An expectation of being caught by someone (not necessarily the police) if he steals (−).
c The experience of being caught by the police (−).
d Fear of the consequences of being caught by the police (−).
e Concern at the thought of parents finding out (−).

2 *Concerning the desire for fun and excitement:*
a Wanting a lot of fun and excitement (+)‡.

*Unless otherwise indicated, the postulated causal factor refers to a condition in or a circumstance of a *boy*. For example, 'an expectation of being caught by the police if he steals/continues to steal' refers to an expectation in the *boy*.
†(−) = The hypothesis is that this factor makes for *less* stealing
‡(+) = The hypothesis is that this factor makes for *more* stealing

b Going out just looking for fun and excitement (+).

3 *Concerning association with thieves:*
a Having mates/friends who steal (+).
b Having amongst their associates a majority who steal (+).
c Association with thieves at an early age (+).
d Lengthy association with boys who steal (+).

4 *Concerning personal ambition:*
a An absence of personal ambition (+).

5 *Concerning school and truancy:*
a Involvement in truancy (+).
b Being backward at school (+).
c Disliking school (+).

6 *Concerning interests and hobbies and spare-time activities:*
a A paucity of (legal) interests (+).
b A paucity of (legal) interest at the active level (+).
c Not knowing what to do in his spare time (+).
d A tendency to get bored or fed-up (+).
e Spending a lot of time watching television (+).

7 *Concerning religion and religious attendance:*
a The nominal religion of the boy (no *particular* religion hypothesized as + or −).
b High frequency of attendance at church or chapel or synagogue (−).

8 *Concerning parental control or discipline:*
a Tendency of parents to exercise early (e.g. at ten years or less) control over boy's choice of associates (−).
b Tendency of parents to exercise early (at ten years or less) control over where he spends his spare time (−).
c Tendency of parents to exercise early (at ten years or less) control over boy's 'going out' (−).
d Parents tend not to punish boy for misdemeanours (+).
e Inconsistency of parental punishment (+).

9 *Concerning teaching or training in honesty:*
a The boy has received direct instruction about 'not stealing' (−).
b A belief by the boy that stealing is wrong (−).

10 *Concerning conditions at home:*
a A high frequency of rows between family members (+).
b Boy's dislike of or boredom with 'being at home' (+).

11 *Concerning separation from parents, 'broken homes' and family composition:*
a Early separation of boy from mother/father/both parents (+).
b Later separation of boy from mother/father/both parents (+).
c The home is broken by the permanent absence of one or both parents (+).
d The presence of grandparents in the home (−).

12 *Concerning mother's absence at work:*
a During the boy's early childhood the mother went out to work (+).
b The mother tended not to be at home when the boy got home from school (+).

13. *Concerning money matters:*
The boy has wants which go beyond his (legal) means (+).

The development of a procedure for getting boys to provide information about their involvement in stealing:

A major inquiry, spread over approximately a year, was conducted in order to develop techniques capable of yielding workably accurate information about the degree to which boy informants had been involved in stealing. The development of this procedure is described in detail in a report by the Survey Research Centre[10] and the procedure itself is presented in working detail in Appendix 1.1.

The eliciting procedure was developed through what I have called the Progressive Modification Technique. This technique principally involved:

1 Identifying difficulties and facilitating factors in getting information from boys about their stealing[11].

2 Developing a 'best try' procedure keyed to overcoming the difficulties and making the most of the facilitating factors.

3 Testing that method to find out how well it works and in particular which of its features are *not* working and which are.

4 Modifying the procedure with a view to overcoming its weaknesses and making the most of its strengths.

5 Proceeding through further cycles of test and modification till the final test indicates that the method is sufficiently accurate and workable for use.

In fact, a total of six cycles was necessary before the procedure was regarded as potentially acceptable for the inquiry. It was then subjected to a reliability check.

The form and the administration of the eliciting procedure

The eliciting procedure in its final form is a complicated technique and is presented in full working detail in Appendix 1.1. The following description of its main operational features is meant both to indicate its general form and to emphasize the importance of certain of its procedures. It is essential that the reader who wishes to *use* the technique should both study the detailed report on its construction[12] and should adopt the technique in its entirety. Above all, he should not try to strip it down to what he believes are its fundamentals. Like the

psychological test, it is a total package and must be used fully as instructed.

The place of interview

The eliciting technique is to be used in a room properly set-up for its administration. The room must be in a building away from the interviewee's own home, must be of a structure that will prevent conversations being overheard outside the room and must have in it the necessary interviewing equipment. This consists principally of a large sorting screen (see Figure 1.1), three booklets to be used in a card-sorting operation (see Appendix 1.1), a tape recorder, table and seating facilities. For large-scale work in an urban region, based on a representative sample, central interviewing premises are needed because in practice it is not possible to secure adequate premises in all or most of the sampling sub-areas. One can try to make do, as was attempted in the *preparatory* phase of this inquiry, with the sometimes available school premises, the sometimes available rooms in town halls, occasionally available space at community centres, and even church crypts. But rarely are the interviewing conditions which are available on an ad hoc basis in such premises anything like sufficient for the interview. And in most sampling sub-areas, premises for the required fortnight or so are not available at all. Above all, the homes of boys are unsuitable, the possibility of being overheard by parents being sufficiently serious to inhibit most boys. Nor can a stranger in a home closet a boy alone in one of the family rooms for the necessary duration of the long eliciting procedure.

Central interviewing premises are, then, necessary for the large-scale representative study. Furthermore, to secure a high level of success in interviewing the sampled boys, it is necessary that they be *brought to* the interviewing centre by an agent of the research organization. Almost always this means that boys should be collected from home by car. Some form of inducement to take part is also necessary, preferably a small fee at the end of the interview (plus fare or transport home).

Conditions of the interview

It is essential that boys taking part should be made aware and should accept that admissions by them will not and cannot go beyond the interviewer to whom they are made — just as in a religious confessional system. To this end special steps are taken to give each boy genuine and full anonymity and to convince him of his real safety in 'talking'.

In the first place, each person collecting boys from their homes must, of course, have the name of each boy she is to collect. But she collects between three and six on the one collection 'round', tells them in the car not to exchange names because for the interview they have to be nameless, and passes them over to the receptionist at the interviewing centre with only the *collective* list of their names. She then makes a point of driving off without further verbal contact with the receptionist. Within the interviewing centre, the receptionist asks each boy to choose a 'false name' card from an array available

Figure 1.1
The sorting screen in use

and to regard this false name as his only identity throughout his stay at the centre. On being taken to his interviewer by the receptionist, he is introduced by that false name and is so referred to by the interviewer throughout their period together. The interviewer is required to make a special point of this arrangement and to ask the boy to make no mention of his *own* name at any time.

To give the boy further assurance that it is safe to 'talk', a carefully-programmed verbal procedure is administered by the interviewer. The detail of this system can be seen in working detail in Appendix 1.1, but in general terms it involves: the use of a confessional-type screen between boy and interviewer during the early stages of the interview, a non-censuring manner in the interviewer, discussion of the boy's reasons for being willing or unwilling to make admissions, the administration of a conditioning process for temporarily reducing the boy's individual resistances to 'talking'.

It is important to add at this point that these varied conditions, along with others that were imposed to secure accurate information from boys, were not devised simply through some inspirational hunch, but were progressively developed on the basis of evidence secured through the six cycles of modification and test through which the eliciting procedure was constructed.

The basic steps in the eliciting procedure
There are four fairly distinct stages in the eliciting procedures.

1 An extended introductory phase designed to lead the boy up to the issue of stealing and to teach him certain rules of procedure.

2 The administration of a 'web of stimuli' (involving card sorting) designed to take the boy deep into the concept of theft as defined by the inquiry and to get preliminary evidence of his own involvement in stealing.

3 The use of conditioning and checking techniques to increase the boy's willingness and ability to provide accurate information.

4 Securing detailed information about broad classes of stealing admitted by the boy.

These four stages are described in general terms hereunder and may be seen in full working detail in Appendix 1.1.

8

Stage 1 An extended introduction to the eliciting procedure

The part of the eliciting procedure that is directly concerned with stealing is preceeded by a sequence designed partly to put the boy at ease and to establish good rapport and partly to introduce him to the concepts and the techniques which would be used in securing information about stealing.

Early in the interview, the boy is told that the first part of the interview will deal with the kinds of things he might do in his spare time. The interviewer explains that the purpose of all his questions is to help prepare a book on boys and their activities. The interviewer also explains the presence of a tape recorder, namely that it will save writing lots of notes during the interview. This is indeed so, but it is also essential as a means of scrutinizing and controlling interviewer performance throughout the interview. The boy is next shown the sorting screen which will be used in this introductory phase (and of course in the phase concerned specifically with stealing, though no reference is made to stealing at the introductory stage). This screen, which is shown in Figure 1.1 is approximately three feet wide and two-and-a-half feet high and is designed for placement on a table between the seated boy and the seated interviewer. On the boy's side are fixed two sorting boxes labelled 'YES' (meaning 'Yes, I have done that at some time in my life') and 'NEVER' (meaning 'No, I have never done that'). Along the bottom edge of the screen is a slot through which the interviewer is to pass the boy a series of cards on each of which is printed a reference to some spare-time activity (e.g. I have been fishing, I have made models, I have played football, I have been to a funfair or amusement arcade). If the boy believes he has *ever* done what is on the card, he is to put it into the YES box. If he believes he has never done it, he is to put it into the NEVER box.

So far, then, the boy has been introduced to the procedure and to a basic item of equipment in a non-threatening manner and situation. The introduction is now furthered by using the sorting of spare-time activity cards to introduce the boy to certain rules that he will need in the next stage of the interview. Thus he is taught, through a combination of instruction and questioning, that:

1 A card is to be sorted as 'YES' even if the act concerned had been done *only once* in all the boy's life, had been last done *a long time ago* or when he was *very young*, had been *only a 'try out'* in character.

2 If he does not know where to put a particular card, he should ask the interviewer to help him, but if this does not clear up his problem, he should put the card face down in front of him.

The first few cards are also used to find out if the boy has reading difficulties — in which case the interviewer will have to read out the detail on *all* cards and take various other steps throughout the interview.

At the end of this sorting procedure (with twenty cards) the interviewer is to clear-up any outstanding 'NOT SURE' cards, coming round from behind the screen to do so. When this is done, the NEVER, the YES and the remaining NOT SURE cards are banded into two/three separate bundles.

Stage 2 Administering the 'Web of Stimuli'

The way is now open for introducing the boy to the questions about stealing, the rules and the methods so far taught being directly transferable to this next part of the procedure. This vital sequence is fully detailed in Booklet B in Appendix 1.1.

Once more separated from the boy by the screen, the interviewer says that he has some more cards to be sorted in the same way, this time about some of the *mischief* boys get up to in their spare time — some of the things they pinch or borrow or steal. The boy is reminded that he has a false name and special emphasis is now put upon the fact that the interview is private, that the boy will not meet the interviewer again, that it is essential for the research that the boy tell the interviewer of *everything* he has ever pinched.

At this stage in the interview, the sorting screen becomes vital. Its use had sprung directly out of the indications of the exploratory study preceding the development of the eliciting procedure. This study had shown that many boys felt ashamed, nervous or embarrassed when asked by a stranger about their involvement in stealing. It was hoped that the screen would give the boy a sense of privacy when sorting the cards and would take out of the situation something of his feeling of personal confrontation. The testing of this expectation in the first cycle of construction work had been favourable in that most of the boys confirmed that they wanted the screen *up* at this stage of the interview.

In Stage 2 of the procedure there are forty-five cards to be sorted, the reference on each card being to some broad class of theft (e.g. 'I have pinched sweets'), or to the place of the theft (e.g. 'I have stolen something from a stall or a barrow'), or to the reason for the theft (e.g. 'I have stolen something just for fun'), or to the circumstances of the theft (e.g. 'I have got into some place without paying the money to get in'). These forty-four items were by no means some *intuitively*-developed set. They were designed as a *web of stimuli* in the sense that together they tended to evoke in boys recall of all the different things that the research team had, for the purposes of this inquiry, defined as 'stealing'. The development of the web is described in detail in a separate report[13]. In very general terms, the construction stages were as follows: (*a*) an *initial* broad reference system was formulated on the basis of exploratory interviews with boys about the kinds of stealing they had done; (*b*) this web was used on a sample of boys by means of a card-sorting technique but immediately after this, each boy was intensively questioned and prompting methods were used in order to find out what sorts of stealing the web of stimuli had failed to bring out and what sorts of misunderstanding of web items had been involved; (*c*) the web of stimuli was then amended both by modifying specific items and by adding others with a view to making the web more efficient and more comprehensive; (*d*) this process was continued through further samples until the evidence from the intensive follow-up interviewing indicated that the web of stimuli was in general fairly highly effective in evoking relevant recall. The forty-four items in the final form of the web of stimuli are presented in Appendix 1.2.

For the sorting operation, the forty-four theft cards are inserted in a particular order into an instruction booklet (see Figure 1.2). These instructions are for the interviewer, who is required to follow them faithfully. The tape recording of the interview is meant to pick-up any interviewer deviation in this regard.

Teaching the boy the rules of sorting The first seven cards in the set of forty-four had been selected as the more suitable of the forty-four for reminding the boy of the rules already taught and for teaching him several new rules. Here, too, teaching is through the method of questioning. Thus, the delivery of Theft Card 1, which is to be used to teach the boy that 'finding and keeping even a *very small* amount of money still counts as stealing', is preceded in the instruction booklet by the directions set out below.

PASS CARD 1 (dealing with 'keeping things he found'),

Figure 1.2
The interviewer preparing to take a theft card out of his book of instructions and to pass it to the boy for sorting

SAYING:
'I'll hold it while you read it out aloud for me.'
THEN SAY:
'Suppose a boy kept 6d he had found: what box should he put this card in?'
CORRECT HIM IF WRONG (RIGHT ANSWER IS 'THE YES BOX')
'So the rule is: It counts even if the amount is very small.'
SAY:
'Now look at this card again and decide whether or not you've *ever* done what it says on the card *yourself*. Then put it in the box where it ought to go.'
PUSH THE CARD RIGHT THROUGH THE SLIT SO THAT HE CAN TAKE IT AND SORT IT.

After the sorting of Theft Card 1, there follow six more practice cards, each preceded by a similar form of instruction. Together, the seven practice cards are used in teaching the following seven rules or arrangements.

1 An act counts (as 'yes') even if the amount or the thing taken was very small.

2 An act counts even if the boy did it only once in all his life.

3 An act counts even if the boy did it only a long time ago.

4 An act counts even if the boy did it just for fun or just to try it out.

5 An act counts even if the boy was just helping others to do it or just acting as a look-out.

6 If the boy cannot remember if he did it or not he is to put the card face down in front of him.

7 The boy is to ask the interviewer for help at any time this is needed (e.g. if the statement on the card is not clear, if the boy is not sure about some rule, if he simply doesn't know what to do).

After this comes the main sorting procedure, though this is featured by interruptive reminders of the rules and by appeals for frankness and for care. For the most part, these reminders, appeals, etc. precede cards which the construction procedure had identified as sources of trouble. For example, just before the delivery of theft card 22 ('I have stolen toys'), the interviewer's instructions read as follows.

BEFORE PASSING IT, SAY:
'The next one is about pinching toys. This could be from anywhere at all — from a shop, in a park, off kids, . . . anywhere at all.'
PASS CARD

Then again, card 41 ('I have stolen money from a meter') was quite often interpreted narrowly (e.g. as money from a gas meter only). Accordingly it was preceded by the following instruction card (to be administered by the interviewer):

SAY, BEFORE PASSING CARD:
'This is about stealing money from a meter. This could be any sort of meter at all: a gas meter, a light meter, a parking meter — any meter at all.'

The full set of the interruptive instruction cards can be identified within Booklet B in Appendix 1.2.

At the end of this initial sorting operation, the interviewer attempts to help the boy resolve the difficulties associated with the theft cards he has sorted as 'NOT SURE'.

Stage 3 Conditioning and checking techniques to increase the willingness/ability of boys to give accurate information

At this point, the interviewer begins the administration of what has been called 'the pretending game'. This is a procedure designed to identify and to overcome such resistances as the boy has to making open admissions and to strengthening his existing reasons for being willing to do so. It culminates in the resorting of the cards originally put into the 'NEVER' box.

The interviewer starts this procedure 'out from behind' the sorting screen in order to work face-to-face with the boy. He tells the boy that the first part of the interview is over and that now something different is to be done — in fact that he needs the boy's help in finding out if there is anything at all that might stop boys from telling 'us' of *everything* they have pinched. In this context the boy is asked 'just to pretend' that he had stolen £5. In that case, would he have admitted this in his interview? If the boy says 'Yes', he is asked to explain why. His reasons are then repeated back to him with a statement that he is right. This is done in order to reinforce the boy's existing willingness to make such an admission. If he says 'No', he is asked *why* he would not do so. His reasons are discussed with him with a view to explaining why they are ungrounded. Into this discussion are brought certain prepared counter-arguments. These counter-arguments and their respective targets are listed in Appendix 1.3. For instance, if the boy expresses concern that the interviewer *may tell someone else* what the boy admits, the interviewer is to answer in the vein:

'If we did a thing like that, boys would not help us any more . . . we'd be finished. If we talked, other boys in your area would get to know and we'd be finished. . . . Anyway there were four boys came in here together. I don't know their names. Even if I did, I don't know which one you *are. . . . I wouldn't do a thing like that. Anyhow, it would only be my word against yours. There are no witnesses are there. And you could deny the whole thing.'*

If a boy offers no reason either way, he is to be given two standard counter-arguments in any case, namely: 'Remember that nothing goes further than this room. It's just between the two of us', and: 'Remember you've got a false name and anything you say is absolutely private'.

The whole procedure is then repeated with a second 'supposed' theft of a more serious kind: 'I have stolen a bike or a motor bike'. It may perhaps be argued by some that this second application of the pretending game is 'too much' and will alienate the boys. However, experience with the procedure (and with testing it) has strongly indicated that the repeat operation is necessary for most boys and that any objections to it come principally from the interviewers rather than from boys. Certainly it is most important that the second application of the 'pretending game' be retained.

After making the two applications of the pretending game, the interviewer raises again with the boy the question of how he feels about fully admitting what he has done. In the course of the discussion that ordinarily follows, the interviewer asks specifically about the following if they have not already been raised: (*a*) does the boy fear that someone may link him with his admissions in the interview?; and, (*b*) is he embarrassed in any way over speaking about his stealing? Counter-arguments are delivered as necessary in the course of this exchange.

The boy is now asked to re-sort the cards which he had originally placed in the 'NEVER' box or sorted as 'NOT SURE' — with the explanation that he may have forgotten something the first time or perhaps didn't want to 'tell us' that first time. The interviewer goes back behind the screen with these cards and re-sorting is begun with stress on the need for *care* and for 'taking your time over it'. Reminders of the privacy of the interview are also administered.

Stage 4 Securing detailed information about the broad classes of stealing admitted by the boy

The interviewer is now required to concentrate upon securing certain classes of information with respect to each of the cards sorted by the boy as 'YES'. He takes down the sorting screen and conducts the rest of the interview face-to-face with the boy – a step clearly indicated as *now* desirable by the tests conducted in the course of constructing the eliciting procedure. Thus, though boys had 'voted' strongly in favour of having the board *up* in the early stages of the interview (when the interviewer was a total stranger), they wanted it *down* at this later stage (when they felt they knew the interviewer better and could trust him).

Three types of information are needed about each of the admitted 'categories' of theft: the biggest thing of this type taken or done; how often the boy had ever done this class of thing; his age when he first did it and his age on the last occasion he did it.

This sequence is begun with a fairly innocuous item, e.g. 'I have kept something I have found'. In this case, the interviewer would ask: 'What is the biggest thing you have ever kept or found? I mean the biggest thing or the most valuable thing. Think carefully.'

The boy's reply is entered on the back of the card concerned, but there now follows a phase of probing, reassurance and re-conditioning designed to detect and to deal with any residual or resurgent worries on the part of the boy and to get him to include his more recent acts when considering 'the biggest thing'. After this, the boy is asked again for the 'biggest thing' he ever found or kept and the original entry on the card is modified if necessary. The details of these procedures are given in Booklet C in Appendix 1.1.

The same class of information is now sought with respect to each of the boy's 'YES' cards, the boy's responses being automatically subjected to the intensive probing, challenging and checking designed to keep the boy alert and 'trying hard'. Entries are made on the back of the respective 'YES' cards.

After this has been done for all the 'YES' cards, the boy is taken right through them once more for the rest of the required information, namely: how often the boy had committed the class of theft on the card; how long ago it was that he last committed this act of theft; how old was he when he *first* did it?

The first card dealt with in this way is subject to special treatment because it is used for rule teaching and for introducing the boy to something new. Thus, in getting information about frequency of committing an act, the boy is progressively constrained by the following rules or reminders: that the count must include the little things as well as the big things; that his recent thefts must be included in the count; that the count should include occasions when he 'just helped'. In addition, the

boy's response is subject to challenging, to probing and checking. Similarly, in asking the boy how long ago it was when he last did the class of theft on the card, the interviewer periodically challenges the boy on the following counts. First, was he including the little things as well? Was he offering a very careful reply or just a rough idea? If 'careful', his approach is acknowledged as correct; but if 'rough' he is told that careful thought is essential. The same approach is used with respect to information about the boy's age on the very first occasion of committing the act.

The rest of the boy's 'YES' cards are now dealt with (to secure the same items of information about each). There is a printed instruction (Booklet C) to the interviewer to probe and challenge these replies along certain lines and to do so with a frequency that will entail at least one probe or challenge for every two cards. Interviewers are repeatedly told in their quality-control sessions that the whole purpose of the demanding system of probing and challenging is to keep the boy alert and 'trying hard'. The use of the tape recorder makes it possible to keep a close watch on the rigour of the interviewer's work at this vital stage of the procedure.

Some noteworthy features of the eliciting procedure

Concerning the use of a tape recorder in the interview[14]

In the development of the eliciting procedure, a tape recorder had been used extensively as a tool of construction, its special advantages being that it revealed *how* the interviewer went about some newly-formulated conditioning or training procedure and that it allowed the interviewer to concentrate upon his administration of procedure rather than giving a lot of his time and attention to note taking. During its use in the construction stage, a series of checks had been made to find out how boys reacted to its use. In fact, the evidence strongly indicated that boys came to accept the presence of a tape recorder – indeed to overlook its presence – in the special circumstances of this interview. Thus, the tape recorder was introduced during the innocuous 'spare-time activities' phase, the boy had a false name, he was told *why* the tape recorder was being used, he was told that he could wipe it clear at the end of the interview if he so wished. In these circumstances, it was retained during parts of the eliciting procedure in its final form, primarily as a means of exercising supervisory control over the interviewers' administration of certain difficult parts of the interview, especially the pretending game. The importance of exercising such control over interviewer performance cannot be over-stated: it was the constant experience of the research team that interviewers tended to reduce the required amount of probing, challenging, reassurance and conditioning and that only the most careful control over this part of the procedure could maintain it at the necessary level of rigour.

On the matter of tape recording, one thing is most

important. There can be no question of tape recording an interview without the boy concerned being made aware of this. To do so would be a gross breach of ethics and in any case would be courting disaster in the interview itself.

Concerning the reliability and the validity of the eliciting procedure

The eliciting procedure in its final form had been subject to reliability testing. The one sample of boys (146 in all) went through the eliciting procedure twice, with approximately a week between administrations. They did not know that the second interview would be a repeat of the first interview. The results from the two administrations of the procedure were compared. There was an 88 per cent consistency in the way the cards were sorted into YES and NEVER boxes. The consistency level was 80 per cent with respect to boys' estimated value of the biggest thing (in a specific class of theft) that they had ever taken. For 'total number of YES responses' for the forty-four cards, the correlation between scores on the two occasions was +0.86.

It can reasonably be argued that only the most clever and systematic lying could have nullified the evidence secured to the effect that the eliciting procedure has an acceptably high level of reliability. At the same time it must be borne in mind that reliability is not the same thing as validity — and that so far the eliciting procedure has not been subjected to validity testing in the proper sense of that term. Thus, in the present case, a boy's memory of how many times he has ever done various things during his lifetime may be quite unconsciously distorted in the direction of over-statement or under-statement, so that he tends to give the *same* under-statement each time he is questioned (or the *same* over-statement). It is quite possible that this could happen when boys think back towards the limits of their memories[15]. The same objection applies when it comes to recall of 'the biggest thing' (in some class of theft) the boy ever took. His memory may well have become fixed upon some item other than the biggest, so that he gives the same answer each time but is somewhat wrong each time. In other words, a successful reliability test is in the present case markedly reassuring, but it does not in itself guarantee accuracy.

In fact, careful consideration was given to conducting a validity test. But what has to be remembered here is that the evidence of stealing which has to be checked for accuracy relates to the whole life of the boy and not just to what he did, say, last week or in the last twelve months. This makes validation of this particular procedure virtually impossible — in that we cannot bring together precise facts about the boy's conduct in relation to stealing over his whole life-time. In any case, the realistic validation of even very recent thefts raises major problems in terms both of technology and of ethics.

The absence of a validity test means that we must at all times maintain a certain degree of reservation about the meaningfulness, in absolute terms, of the figures which stem from the use of the eliciting procedure, the reservation being that some form of bias may be distorting the results to some degree. On the other hand it is right to bear firmly in mind:

1 That strenuous efforts were made in each construction stage to eliminate error-producing elements from the eliciting procedure and that this was done progressively over six construction cycles.

2 That high reliability figures were obtained for scores of the kind on which the tests of hypotheses were to be based.

In the circumstances, it was thought desirable to regard the 'scores' produced by the eliciting procedure as being meaningful *indices* of the level of boys' involvement in stealing, suitable for use as discriminants in testing hypotheses, but nonetheless open to some degree of over-statement or under-statement in their own right.

Concerning residual sources of error

Though there is evidence that resistance to making admissions was progressively reduced during the six cycles of the construction procedure, some degree of resistance was still operative in the later cycles of construction. In addition, in the later cycles:

1 Some boys were still experiencing embarrassment at telling someone about their stealing.

2 There were still problems of recall, particularly with respect to the detail required for the YES cards.

3 Problems of definition were still marginally present.

Whereas there is no good reason for thinking that these weaknesses seriously impair the functioning of the method in producing an *index* of involvement in stealing, obviously it is sensible to keep them in mind.

Concerning the possibility of over-claiming by boys

It has been said that in securing theft information of the kind here involved, it would be all too easy to be misled by sheer invention (of thefts) by the boys being interviewed. Certainly, one should not rule out the operation on a limited scale of such a process in using the final form of the present eliciting procedure. On the other hand, the following points should be noted.

1 In the exploratory study there was abundant evidence of factors operating to produce substantial understatement of thefts (e.g. resistance to telling, embarrassment, forgetting ...), but relatively little evidence of factors operating to produce any substantial degree of *over*-claiming. Accordingly, eliciting efforts became focused upon reducing the operation of the understatement factors.

2 Throughout the construction process — and this included six cycles of 'test and modification' — the evidence continued to point to under-statement rather

than over-statement as the major problem to be overcome. Nonetheless, the eliciting procedure is featured by a persistent challenging and probing of boys' claims about *what* they stole, and how often they stole.

3 If, nonetheless, there remains an over-statement factor operative in the eliciting procedure, its total effect should be to balance out at least some of the influence of the method's residual under-statement factors*. This argument would apply less if the concern of the inquiry was *solely* to assess the extent of stealing for some individual boy. But the balancing-out process is normally an important safeguard where, as in the present situation, the ultimate concern is to develop average 'scores' for the comparison of large sub-groups.

The strategy for investigating causal hypotheses

The technique or strategy used in investigating the hypotheses was derived from the Hypothetico-Deductive Method. This is a technique which is used for the investigation of hypotheses which are not open to direct experimental inquiry as, for example, the hypothesis that attitudes are related to values in certain ways, or that the core of the earth has certain qualities. In such cases, one deduces from the hypothesis certain propositions which: (*a*) are themselves testable; and, (*b*) are of a kind that one would expect to be verified if the hypothesis were true and shown to be wrong if the hypothesis were untrue.

In the present case, the causal process involved in the hypotheses will have been operative within a multi-factor social setting and it was considered that no simulation technique could be developed sufficiently to recapture the realities of the hypothetical process and, at the same time, exclude the operation of confounding and competing extraneous factors. Indeed, to exclude them might well render the inquiry fairly unrealistic.

In the context of this inquiry, calling as it did for realistic assessments, the techniques of simulation, the strategy of factor isolation, the direct testing of hypotheses . . . these were all either unsuitable or impossible to apply. On the other hand, the Hypothetico-Deductive Method was both suitable and possible. Through this method was derived a series of testable propositions or expectations with respect to each of the hypotheses under investigation.

This procedure is best illustrated through an example. Suppose that the hypothesis to be investigated was:

'A desire for fun and excitement is a contributory factor in the initiation and maintenance of juvenile stealing'.

One possible, but obviously unsatisfactory, expectation in relation to that hypothesis might be that boys who want a lot of fun and excitement will have committed

more stealing than boys who want relatively little fun and excitement (= Expectation 1).

However, a test of that expectation cannot possibly be regarded as a crucial test of the hypothesis. This is because a difference in the theft level of boys who want different amounts of fun and excitement could arise out of three different types of situations. Thus, that difference could be due to:

1 The influence of fun and excitement seeking.

2 Original differences, between the two groups of boys concerned, of kinds that are correlated with stealing.

3 The influence of different amounts of stealing upon the amount of fun and excitement desired.

A meaningful investigation of the hypothesis would have to take all three possibilities into consideration, perhaps through expectations of the following kind.

Expectation 2 When boys who want relatively little fun and excitement are closely and empirically matched to those wanting a lot of fun and excitement, a residual difference in theft level will still be found and will be statistically significant in size.

Expectation 3 Boys will neither volunteer, nor admit when directly asked, that it was stealing that led them to want fun and excitement.

The testing of such expectations — especially expectation 3 — cannot prove or disprove the hypothesis. But such tests can add usefully to the total body of evidence that is brought to bear on the tenability of the hypothesis. In fact, a total of nine expectations was derived for testing in the case of this hypothesis, the remaining six being as follows.

4 Expectation 2 applies separately for most classes of theft, as encompassed by the forty-four items used in the eliciting procedure.

5 Boys will volunteer/admit that they steal in order to get fun and excitement; the more fun and excitement they want, the more they will tend to volunteer/admit that they steal to get it.

6 Boys will admit that stealing *gives* them fun and excitement; and the more fun and excitement they want the more they will tend to admit that stealing gives them that fun and excitement.

7 A large number of boys will endorse the statement that they have at some time stolen in order to get fun and excitement.

8 The greater the claimed frequency of stealing in order to get fun and excitement, the greater will be the boy's involvement in stealing.

9 Those who say they do in fact get fun and excitement

---

*The writer takes no credit for this situation. Nonetheless, the balancing of over- and under- claims is a matter of basic importance in the construction of any technique which is to be used to derive group scores or group averages.

from stealing will have done more stealing than other boys.

All the above expectations are open to being tested and the verification of all of them would serve to make the hypothesis more tenable. The non-verification of one or more of them would reduce the tenability of the hypothesis.

Expectation Testing Involving Matching (Expectation 2 in this case)*

The most important of the expectations detailed above is that which involves the empirical matching of boys wanting little fun and excitement to those wanting a lot of fun and excitement. As this class of expectation is involved in relation to most of the hypotheses studied in this inquiry, I intend to describe in fairly full detail the method of testing it*, using the fun and excitement hypothesis as an example and drawing on the response distributions secured through the inquiry and reported in Chapter 4.

The first step in testing Expectation 2 was to divide the 1425 boys in the overall sample† into a 'qualifying' and a 'control' group. The qualifying group consisted of boys who *qualified* in terms of the hypothesis, in the sense that they gave evidence of wanting a lot of fun and excitement. The control group consisted of boys who gave evidence of wanting some lesser amount of fun and excitement. The distribution of responses on the basis of which the two groups were identified was as shown in the following table.

Boy claims that he wants	No. of boys
'A terrific amount of fun and excitement'	219
'Quite a lot of fun and excitement'	521
'A fair bit of fun and excitement'	433
'Some fun and excitement'	226
'Not much fun and excitement'	22
'None'	1
'No information'	3
All	1,425

The top two categories of response were allocated to the qualifying group (740 boys) and the others (682 boys) became the control group.

*This technique was developed by the writer during the early 1950s, used in his BBC studies of programme effects, and published in 1959 as 'Matching and prediction on the principle of biological classification' (*Applied Statistics*, Volume VIII, No. 2). It is referred to in general practice as 'the Stable Correlate Technique'. Its procedure for identifying matching variables was adopted almost in its entirety by Morgan and Sonquist as the basis of their A.I.D. computer program J. N. Morgan, and J. A. Sonquist. Problems in the Analysis of Survey Data and a Proposal. *Journal of the American Statistical Association*, Volume 58, No. 302, 1963).

†The techniques described in this chapter were built into an hypothesis testing operation involving a 1,425-boy sample of London's boys.

The next step in this particular type of test is to equate the control group to the qualifying group in terms of the correlates of stealing. If the control group could be re-weighted so that it was the same as the qualifying group in terms of all the variables (with the exception of the causal variable named in the hypothesis) which are correlated with stealing, then any residual difference in theft level between the control group and the qualifying group could be attributed to the hypothesized causal factor*. In fact, it is unlikely that we could ever get guaranteed complete equality of this sort. But we *can* go a very useful way towards it if we use the technique of *empirical* matching. Stated in summary form the method of empirical matching is as follows.

1 A large pool of *possible* correlates of stealing is built up from the indications of previous research and from observational, speculative and other sources (e.g. age of boy, educational background, occupational level of father, whether the boy is working or at school, family composition, whether the mother goes out to work, physical strength of boy, boy's nominal religion, and so on). The total number of items in this 'pool' might be as many as 200 or even more. It is essential that all pool items be 'stable' in the sense that they are not open to being changed through the factor named in the hypothesis as causal.

2 Correlational techniques are used to identify that combination of the pool items which maximizes the multiple correlation with stealing which is available from the total pool. This is the combination or composite of variables to be used in the matching process†.

3 The control group is then equated or matched to the qualifying group in terms of this composite of matching variables. The method of matching is through the weighting of individual cards and not through any form of 'throwing out' of data.

Deriving the pool of possible correlates of stealing

Many of the items in the pool of possible matching variables (i.e. possible correlates of stealing) are set out in Appendix 1.4. These items were accumulated in various ways: from the reported results of studies which related characteristics of boys to the extent of their known stealing; from theoretical publications of various kinds in the literature of criminology; from non-criminological correlational studies‡. To the yield from these sources were added the ideas of members of the research team and of others, based on observation, discussion and speculation.

*Unless, as already stated, the hypothesis really works in reverse or does so in part.

†See footnote * in left hand column.

‡Some of these sources have thrown up variables which have shown correlations with a wide variety of dependent variables and hence possibly with stealing (e.g. length of residence in a district, certain childhood achievements and memberships, goods owned by the family, household composition).

Table 1.1
Power of 'birth order' as a predictor of theft score

Theft Score	Birth order				
	First	Intermediate	Last	No information	All cases
Higher score	252	215	238	9	714
Lower score	321	166	218	6	711
All	573	381	456	15	1,425
Number of cases 'expected' in higher scoring sector	287	191	228	8	714
Difference between 'expected' and 'actual' number in higher scoring sector (= predictive power)	−35	+24	+10	+1	0

Calculating the predictive power of variables in the pool

The method of selecting variables from this pool is through a correlational technique. For each variable in the total pool, a calculation is made of its degree of numerical association with *amount of stealing*. The amount of stealing will be referred to in this section as the 'criterion' against which the matching variables (or correlates) are to be selected. The higher the degree of numerical association between a pool item and the criterion score, the more relevant will that pool item be for matching purposes. Thus, if the qualifying group and the control group are even sharply different in terms of a variable which is *unrelated* to the amount of stealing, then that difference will be of no practical importance to the testing of the expectation concerned. If on the other hand, the qualifying and control groups are appreciably different in terms of a variable which is *highly related* to theft level, then it will be most important that any such difference be 'matched out'. And the higher the correlation, the more important it will be to match out that difference.

Let us imagine that this procedure is being used to assess the predictive power of 'birth order' of boys. The first step is to split the *total sample* of boys into two fairly equal groups, those with higher theft scores and those with lower theft scores. The split should be made along the theft score continuum at a point which comes nearest to dividing the boys 50:50. Each of these groups is next split three ways, namely according to whether first born, last born, or intermediate birth order. For the sample used in the causal inquiry, this splitting process led to the distributions shown in the top three rows of Table 1.1.

A calculation is then made of the proportion of boys who would fall into the higher scoring sector *if* birth order was quite unrelated to level of theft. Thus, for the 'first in birth order' sub-group, this figure would be:

$$\frac{714}{1425} \times \frac{573}{1} \fallingdotseq 287$$

The difference between this figure and the *actual* figure is $252 - 287 = -35$. A similarly-calculated figure is entered in each of the four cells at the bottom of Table 1.1 and their sum total *excluding signs* is the predictive power of the variable 'birth order' (=70 in this case). Had there been *no* numerical association between 'birth order' and the amount of stealing, this total would, of course, have been zero.

Selecting a combination or composite of matching variables, using the selection system described above

In selecting a combination or composite of matching variables, the method deliberately departs from the more usual multiple correlational techniques — as embodied in the Wherry-Doolittle[16] and similar systems. This is done in order to better the predictive or matching power available from such methods. The method used was the Belson Stable Correlate Technique[17]. It involves the following selection stages.

In Stage 1 the predictive power of each variable in the pool is calculated (using the method already described) and that one with the highest predictive power* is

*Unless it was judged as 'probably unstable'.

chosen as the first stage predictor (or matching variable). Let us suppose that it is pool variable no. 24. The sample of boys (1425 cases) is then split in *two* ways in terms of Variable 24, namely those with 'Variable 24 characteristics' (e.g. YES on Variable 24) which are associated with *higher* theft score, and those with 'Variable 24 characteristics' (e.g. NO on Variable 24) which are associated with *lower* theft score.

a consideration of the predictive power which is thereby added to the total composite of predictive variables. In this way, unnecessary and unmanageable sub-division of a sample can be avoided. It can be seen from this account that *initial two-way splitting is both the most economical and the most powerful developmental principle.*

In *Stage 2* of the selection of the predictive com-

Figure 1.3
Stage 1 split

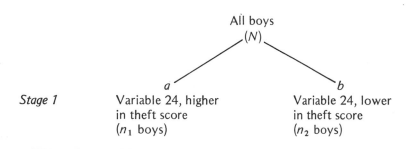

All boys
(N)

Stage 1

a
Variable 24, higher
in theft score
(n_1 boys)

b
Variable 24, lower
in theft score
(n_2 boys)

Where a variable has to it only two alternatives (e.g. YES or NO), then a two-way split is quite simple, the total sample being split respectively into boys who answer 'Yes' on the variable concerned and those who answer 'No'. If those who answer 'Yes' on the variable concerned have a 'plus' difference between 'expected' and 'actual' scores, then those answering 'No' will inevitably have a minus difference between expected and actual scores. The YES response will then be regarded as 'generally associated with higher theft score' and the NO response will be 'generally associated with lower theft score'.

A special difficulty arises where a variable is ordinarily split into more than two parts. Thus, in the example, birth order happened to be expressed in terms of three categories: first, intermediate, last. It might have been expressed in more than that number of categories. But with three categories, the two-way split is achieved by bringing together the 'intermediate' and the 'last born' sub-groups into one group because both are associated with *higher* theft scores. The second sub-group will then be made up of the 'first born' boys.

The same type of grouping is used with variables expressed in terms of a larger number of intervals or sub-groups. Thus it may be, in a given case, that both the upper and the lower age-groups in some population have a negative predictive score while the middle range members of the population have a positive predictive score. In such a case, the middle-range people will constitute one of the two required sub-groups and the extreme groups will be combined to form the other group.

Where two sub-groups are combined in this way, it still remains possible that they will be separated at some later stage in the selection of the composite of predictors, but this will happen only if the predictive power added to the composite through such a split is greater than that which would be added through dichotomizing some other competing variable. *In other words, the extent to which a variable is split is strictly controlled by*

posite, the whole selection procedure is repeated for each of the two groups of boys separated through Stage 1. Thus, for the n_1 boys in Group *a* (=Variable 24, higher), an assessment is made of the predictive power of each variable in the total pool of proposed matching variables. That one with the highest predictive power is selected and Group *a* is sub-divided dichotomously in terms of it. For the n_2 boys in Group *b*, the predictive power of each pool item is calculated afresh and the topmost predictor for Group *b* is selected for dichotomizing group *b*.

The thing to notice here is that the best predictor (or matching variable) for boys in the *a* group is not necessarily the same as the best one for boys in the *b* group. It is worth contrasting this outcome with the process in which one variable only is chosen at each selection stage*. Thus, it is possible that Variable 15 may have a large degree of positive association with stealing in Group *a* above, and a large degree of *negative* association with stealing in Group *b* above. But, for the sample *as a whole* (i.e. *a* and *b* taken together), Variable 15 is quite likely to have relatively little (total) predictive power because of a cancelling-out effect and so would not compete successfully for inclusion in a matching composite derived in the traditional manner. On the segmentation system actually used, Variable 15 could well win its way into a major sector of the matching composite.

In *Stage 3* of the development of the matching composite, the whole process of Stage 2 is repeated, though in this case, *four* separate selection operations are necessary.

Further stages of splitting or *segmentation* are derived in the same way so long as the numerical size of the sub-groups warrant it. In the present inquiry, the splitting process was discontinued once the sub-group size fell below fifty.

---

*That is, as applying for the whole sample rather than for some *part* of the sample.

Figure 1.4
Stage 2 split

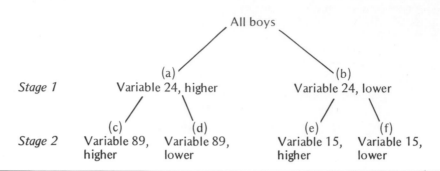

A limitation which must be imposed upon the selection of matching variables

One important limitation must be set upon the selection of high-powered predictors from the pool. A predictor should not be used if it is *unstable* in the sense that the hypothesized causal factor could itself change a boy's situation with respect to the pool item concerned. Thus, a boy's chronological age could not be affected by the suggested causal factor 'desire for fun and excitement'; but 'frequency of attendance at church' might well be affected by the boy's desire for fun and excitement. In other words, frequency of church attendance must be suspected of being unstable with respect to the hypothesized causal factor and 'age' must be regarded as *stable* in terms of it. If an unstable variable was, in fact, used for matching purposes, the effect of so using it could be to reduce such legitimate evidence as there was of the hypothesized variable producing a difference in theft level.

In practice, it is sometimes very hard to judge whether a particular variable is stable or unstable in relation to the hypothesized causal factor. In attempting to meet the requirement that matching variables be stable, there has been a deliberate tendency in this inquiry to err on the side of safety, eliminating pool items whose stability (in relation to the hypothesized causal variable) was perhaps arguable.

In spite of this policy one may accidentally include a variable which is to some degree unstable. It is therefore important to consider the implications of the inclusion amongst the matching variables of one or more with some degree of instability. The effect of any such instability is of course to reduce the legitimate evidence of a causal process. In other words, the effect of this is to make the test of the causal hypothesis *more stringent* than it really should be. Accordingly, an hypothesis which passes a test involving the use of an unstable matching variable is probably somewhat stronger than appears to be the case. On the same argument, a relatively weak hypothesis might wrongly appear to have been eliminated by the matching challenge.

A matching composite actually used in the causal inquiry

The outcome of the segmentation or splitting procedure described above can be illustrated by one of the predictive composites developed for use in the present causal inquiry. It is set out in full in Figure 1.5. It involved segmenting the total population into sixteen groups on the basis of eleven discriminating (or predictive) variables.

Because the criterion in all the hypotheses featured in this inquiry was the same (i.e. the amount of stealing done by boys) it was expected that the one matching composite – the one shown in Figure 1.5 could be used in testing all the expectations in this inquiry that called for matching. In fact, a second composite was needed because one correlate in the first composite was thought to be unstable with respect to one of the hypothesized causal factors.

It may be wondered why one or another characteristic known to be correlated with stealing does not appear in the composite of matching variables shown in Figure 1.5. This *may* be because the characteristic concerned was considered unstable in relation to the hypothesized causal factor. On the other hand, its exclusion could well be the consequence of its being highly correlated with one or more of the variables already in the composite. Suppose, for example, that at the first selection stage (see Figure 1.3), Variable 20 is second only to Variable 24 in predictive power. In that case, Variable 24 is selected and Variable 20 remains in the pool for consideration at the *next* selection stage. If Variable 20 is largely *un*correlated with Variable 24, the likelihood of its being selected in the next selection stage is very high. On the other hand, if Variable 20 is *highly correlated* with Variable 24, then the likelihood of its being selected in that next stage is low to negligible: this is simply because in this case much of the predictive power latent in Variable 20 would already have been tapped through Variable 24. Variable 20 is, as it were, in the same family of predictors as is Variable 24 and hence partly duplicates its predictive power.

Using the composite of matching variables in equating the control group and the qualifying group

The whole purpose of the matching process is to reconstitute the control group so that its different matching sub-groups contribute to overall 'score' on the same numerical basis as the equivalent sub-groups in the qualifying group.

Figure 1.5
Matching composite

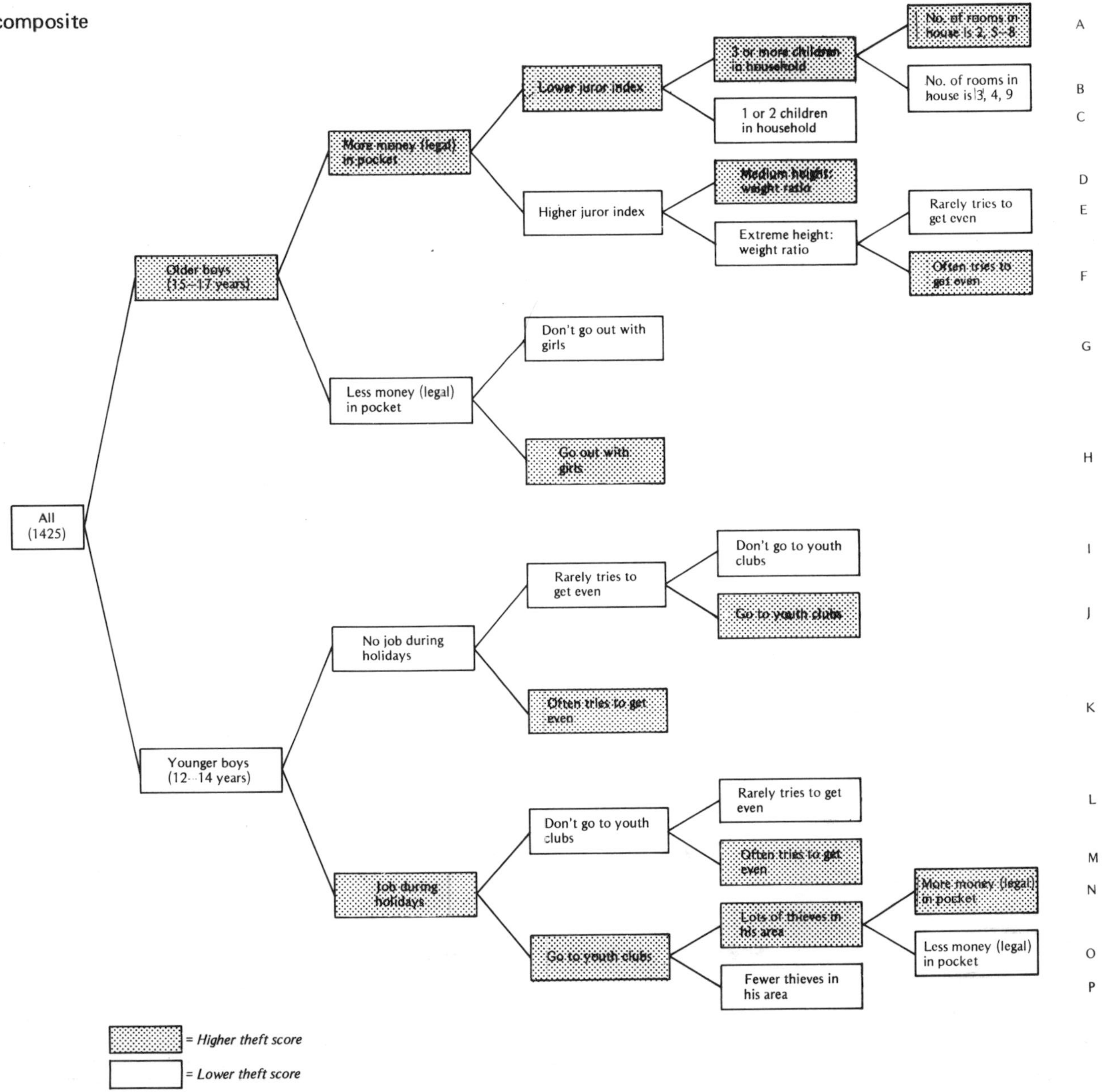

A No. of rooms in house is 2, 5–8

B No. of rooms in house is 3, 4, 9

C

D Rarely tries to get even

E Often tries to get even

F

G

H

I

J

K

L

M More money (legal) in pocket

N Less money (legal) in pocket

O

P

3 or more children in household

1 or 2 children in household

Median height: weight ratio

Extreme height: weight ratio

Lower juror index

Higher juror index

Don't go to youth clubs

Go to youth clubs

Rarely tries to get even

Often tries to get even

Lots of thieves in his area

Fewer thieves in his area

More money (legal) in pocket

Less money (legal) in pocket

Don't go out with girls

Go out with girls

Rarely tries to get even

Often tries to get even

Don't go to youth clubs

Go to youth clubs

No job during holidays

Job during holidays

Older boys (15–17 years)

Younger boys (12–14 years)

All (1425)

= Higher theft score

= Lower theft score

19

To start with, the control and qualifying groups are separately sorted into those sub-groups defined by the matching composite. Let us *imagine* that they were constituted, in terms of the sixteen sub-groups, as shown in the following fictitious case.

	A	B	C	D	E	F	G	H	I	J	K	L	M	N	O	P	All
Qualifying group	42 6%	32 4%	43 6%	36 5%	53 7%	33 5%	42 6%	55 8%	33 5%	33 5%	74 10%	52 7%	27 4%	62 9%	25 4%	66 9%	712 100%
Control group	61 9%	51 7%	38 5%	73 10%	28 4%	36 5%	26 4%	60 8%	62 9%	37 5%	44 6%	29 4%	47 7%	31 4%	34 5%	56 8%	713 100%

Obviously the control group is different from the qualifying group in terms of the proportion of their members falling into the different matching sub-groups.

In the example with which we are working, each card in Control Sub-Group A is given a weight of 42/61, the overall effect of which is to give that sub-group a weight of 42 instead of 61 (i.e. 42/61 x 61). For Control Sub-Group B, the weight applied would be 32/51, and so on as indicated below.

This system achieves the purpose of making the control group equivalent to the qualifying group in terms of the numerical bases of the sixteen matching sub-groups. In other words, the control group has been matched to the qualifying group in terms of the total composite of correlates of stealing.

Other matching methods available for use are: (*a*) the system in which the average number of thefts from each control group is multiplied by the weighting factor; and, (*b*) replication of randomly-selected cards in the control group. However, the method chosen has the advantage of: being well suited to computer usage; allowing weighted *distributions* to be produced; avoiding the problem of accidentally-biased card replication; flexibility at the stage of cross-analysis.

The scores for the *modified* control group and the qualifying group are now ready for direct comparison in terms of involvement in stealing: a statistically-significant difference between them would be regarded as rendering the hypothesis more tenable.

When the full matching procedure was applied to Expectation 2 for the second 'fun and excitement' hypothesis the outcome was as in Table 1.2.

What Table 1.2 means is that for both variety and amount of stealing, there is a statistically-significant difference between the qualifying group and the modified or adjusted controls. And this, in turn, means that the *expectation* is verified.

This class of test was made with respect to a class of expectation derived from most of the hypotheses dealt with in this inquiry. As a test of an expectation, it does not verify its parent *hypothesis* because in each case there are further expectations to be tested. But the verification of this class of expectation does serve to increase the *tenability* of the parent hypothesis.

Testing expectations relating to testimony

Another type of expectation involved the nature of the testimony of boys about the causal processes specified in the hypothesis. For instance, boys were asked, late in

	A	B	C	D	E	F	G	H	I	J	K	L	M	N	O	P
Qualifying group	42 6%	32 4%	43 6%	36 5%	53 7%	33 5%	42 6%	55 8%	33 5%	33 5%	74 10%	52 7%	27 4%	62 9%	25 4%	66 9%
Control group	61 9%	51 7%	38 5%	73 10%	28 4%	36 5%	26 4%	60 8%	62 9%	37 5%	44 6%	29 4%	47 7%	31 4%	34 5%	56 8%
Weighting factor	$\frac{42}{61}$	$\frac{32}{51}$	$\frac{43}{38}$	$\frac{36}{73}$	$\frac{53}{28}$	$\frac{33}{36}$	$\frac{42}{26}$	$\frac{55}{60}$	$\frac{33}{62}$	$\frac{33}{37}$	$\frac{74}{44}$	$\frac{52}{29}$	$\frac{27}{47}$	$\frac{62}{31}$	$\frac{25}{34}$	$\frac{66}{56}$
Modified composition of control group	6%	4%	6%	5%	7%	5%	6%	8%	5%	5%	10%	7%	4%	9%	4%	9%

Table 1.2
Differences between qualifiers and controls before and
after matching: variety and amount of stealing

Theft score*	Unadjusted average score for qualifierst a	Unadjusted average score for controls b	Adjusted average score for controls c	Differences between qualifiers and adj. controls a−c P‡	Difference a−c as percentage of c
Averaged indices of variety* of stealing	16.29	9.23	11.09	5.20 (0.01)	46.89
Averaged indices of amount* of stealing	120.78	59.45	75.63	45.15 (0.01)	59.70

*The eliciting procedure yielded two types of score. One was the number of acts committed out of the forty-four included in the web of stimuli (see earlier section of chapter). The other was the total score over the whole forty-four taking into account the number of times each act was said to have been done. The first is referred to as an index of 'variety' score and the second as an index of amount.
†Boys who tend to 'go out just looking for fun and excitement'.
‡Probability that this difference is a product of chance difference between the two samples.

the sub-questionnaire on 'atmosphere at home' (see Chapter 7):

At present you LIKE/DON'T LIKE being at home'.
(SAY WHICH HE CHOSE IN RESPONSE TO QUESTION IQ.1c)
Exactly what difference does this make to *where* you spend your spare time?

This question was followed by *probing* in order to activate the boy's thinking about his behaviour in relation to his 'at home'/'away from home' activities. The next question was meant to channel that thinking directly into the area of stealing.

Exactly what difference does it make to the amount of pinching you do?'
SHOW CARD (NO DIFFERENCE/IT MADE ME STEAL LESS/IT MADE ME STEAL MORE/IT STARTED ME OFF)
CIRCLE HIS CHOICE OF RESPONSE*.

*This pair of questions had, in fact, been preceded by others intended to identify any occasions in the past when the boy felt *differently* about being at home. Such preceding questions had two purposes: (a) to ensure that boys who were put into the qualifying or the control groups were thus classified on the basis of a long-standing condition rather than a recently-developed one; (b) to find out where the boy spent his time during any such periods of difference and to get his impressions about the influence of that changed condition upon the general level of his honesty.

Obviously, this type of check cannot be regarded as remotely approaching a crucial test of an hypothesis of the kind here involved. Boys certainly *could* be mistaken in their replies. But I have taken the view that a boy's statement that some event or circumstance has influenced the extent of his stealing — and particularly if he *volunteered* a statement to this effect — can be taken as somewhat more likely to be true than false, and may thus be regarded as a pointer to the situation in that boy's case. If, as a pointer, it is in line with the results from the association and the matching tests, it should be regarded as strengthening the indications of those two. If it is not in line with them, then it should be regarded as weakening their indications.

A check on the direction of the causal process

An important consideration throughout this inquiry was the possibility that the hypothesized causal factor was in fact an *effect* — an effect of the boy's stealing rather than a cause of it. In other words, there exists a theoretical possibility that the hypothesis would have been better stated in reverse. The results of the preliminary intensive interviews had suggested otherwise, e.g. that association with thieves led the associating boy to adopt thieving behaviour as a requirement for continuing the association. Nonetheless, one must face the possibility that boys' association with thieves tends to develop out of their personal and prior involvement in stealing.

However arguable or otherwise this class of supposition may be, it cannot be ignored. Accordingly, a special check was made with respect to most of the hypotheses. For example, in the questionnaire broadly concerned with 'association with thieves', boys were asked at the end of the sub-questionnaire: (a) to volunteer an explanation of *why* they mixed with the particular boys concerned; and, (b) to say if the reason was in fact 'just because those boys were pinching things'. In the same way, in the sub-questionnaire dealing with parental control and punishment, it seemed theoretically possible that an increase in parental control and punishment arose largely out of parents' realization that their sons were stealing. The question asked in this case was as follows:

'The sort of control they kept over you ... the sort of punishment they gave you ... was this *because* they knew you were pinching?'
    YES/NO/DON'T KNOW

Just as for the testing of expectations following directly from the hypothesis, such checks or challenges must be regarded as providing pointers rather than crucial evidence. But a virtual absence of reference to stealing as a source of the hypothesized causal condition was regarded as strengthening the hypothesis rather than as weakening it. On the other hand, a large number of references to stealing in this class of context would be regarded as weakening the hypothesis.

The questionnaire: a summary
The questioning procedure used in this inquiry was based upon a large number of different questionnaires, referred to here as 'sub-questionnaires'. A sub-questionnaire was prepared for each of the main groups of hypotheses. It was designed to provide assessments in terms of, and background information about, each of the independent variables featured in it. It also included questions about matters that it was thought might possibly emerge as matching variables or items. In addition, there was one questionnaire that was concerned solely with possible correlates of stealing (for use in the matching operation).

The different sub-questionnaires are presented as appendices to the chapters based upon them.

4 SURVEY METHODS

An overview of strategy
The survey area was a region within a radius of approximately twelve miles from the centre of London as indicated by the map in Figure 1.6. The population to be sampled within this region was made up of boys in the age range thirteen to sixteen, with an allowance for some spread into the twelve and seventeen year olds*.

---

*Although the survey was to be confined principally to boys aged between thirteen and sixteen years, details were collected at the enumeration stage about twelve and seventeen-year olds as a safety measure — their ages being subsequently checked against date of birth to ensure that the informants had not slightly miscalculated.

The sample was complex in design, involving two stages of weighting. It was drawn on random principles within a system of stratification, but preliminary enumeration on a stratified basis was called for in developing the sampling frame itself. A total of 1,425 boys out of a target sample of 1,655 boys was interviewed on Survey Research Centre premises, the average length of interview being three hours. In this period, each boy went through extensive questioning to establish the nature and the degree of his involvement in stealing, his position in relation both to the many hypotheses being investigated and to the variables proposed as possible matching criteria. Throughout the interview each boy had a false name and a considerable effort was made to maintain his awareness of his anonymity and of the confidential character of the interview.

The Sampling Methods Used

The region and the population on which the inquiry was to be based
The area chosen for the inquiry was Greater London. It was chosen mainly because it constituted the largest single concentration of population in the United Kingdom and because the amount of detected juvenile stealing there was relatively high. A supporting consideration was that the Survey Research Centre had available excellent interviewing facilities in the form of a mid-city building containing a reception room, interviewing-rooms and space suitable for briefing and control of interviewers.

It was considered desirable to exclude from the survey area certain of the outer suburbs of London, namely districts situated more than twelve miles from the interviewing centre. This was because bringing boys in from these areas and getting them back again raised major problems in terms of timing and of transport. The effect of this decision was to eliminate from the survey the homes of about one quarter of the 'electors' in the Greater London conurbation leaving a total of 4,491,076 electors.

The location of the excluded areas is shown in the map on p. 24, as is the location of the stratified sample of sub-areas from which the sample of boys was drawn.

A further limitation to sampling was the restriction of interviewees principally to those aged thirteen to sixteen. This was because: (a) interviewing of boys of below thirteen was expected to raise special problems concerning their attendance (alone) at the centre and also to call for additional interviewing procedures (e.g. for ten-year olds, for six-year olds); (b) since the inquiry was to be about *juvenile* stealing, the upper limit to the 'juvenile' age was used. At the same time, it was regarded as inevitable that some boys who fell or appeared to fall into the range thirteen to sixteen years at the time of the enumeration survey would turn out to be twelve or seventeen when interviewed in the final survey.

The age limitation upon the sample must tend to restrict the interpretation of the findings, but nonetheless it should be noted that for each boy information was to be sought about his theft behaviour and his background over a period going back as far as possible.

The sampling of area units within the total region of the survey

A basic sampling requirement for investigating the hypotheses A basic requirement of the ultimate sample was that it should yield, for each hypothesis, a sufficient number of qualifying boys. Thus, for the hypothesis:

Boys who associate with thieves at an early age are thereby rendered more likely to engage in stealing themselves

it was essential that there be in the final sample a statistically-adequate number of boys who qualified as 'associating with thieves at an early age'. Similarly for each of the other hypotheses. With unlimited funds, this requirement could be met by using a very large sample of boys — well beyond the maximum of 1,500 which the available funds could support. Accordingly the following economy tactic was used.

Since the available correlation evidence indicated that 'qualifiers' would be more numerous in the more economically-depressed sections of the community, it was decided *initially* to skew the sample downwards in terms of economic level (and so to over-represent the 'less well-off'), *but with the intention ultimately of re-weighting the sample to restore representativeness in terms of economic level.* In this way, an adequate number of qualifiers could be secured without having to lift total sample size to a very costly level and at the same time it would be 'possible, *with the restored sample,* to secure meaningful descriptions of London boys in terms of the extent and nature of their thieving and in terms also of their general background. The details of this weighting and re-weighting process are given on pp. 23 to 24 and 30 to 32.

The initial skewing 'downwards' of the sampling units This process was geared to the juror index system[18], wards with lower juror percentages being regarded as of lower economic level. Since the available juror percentage counts were all in terms of *wards* it was necessary to introduce the skew towards districts of lower economic level through the selection of *wards* rather than of any type of area unit.

The selection of wards was made as follows.

1 All wards in the survey area were listed in descending order according to their 'juror percentages'.

2 This full list was then separated into ten divisions which were approximately equal in terms of the number of electors in them. These were regarded as 'decile' divisions.

3 To secure the required systematic bias towards areas of lower economic level, the number of wards selected for each decile group was increased in going from the top towards the bottom decile division, as shown in Table 1.3. A total of forty wards was selected in this way. For *re*-weighting, it was planned that a reverse system be used, results from the districts in the bottom decile division being rated as 1.0 and those from districts in the top decile division getting a weight of 9.0. The purpose of this proposed form of re-weighting was to bring the sample back to representativeness in terms of economic level. Full details of the re-weighting actually carried out are given on pp 30—32.

4 The sampling of wards from within decile groups was itself controlled by juror percentage level. Thus, each decile list was split into a number of sections corresponding to the number of wards to be drawn from that decile group, these several sections being approximately equal in terms of the number of electors living in them. Within each section, a ward was drawn at random.

Table 1.3 Some characteristics of decile groups and the number of wards selected from each group	Decile groups in the Greater London population*	No. of wards*	No. of electors	Range of juror indices	No. of wards drawn
	1 High-juror index	72	445,701	26.29—12.62	1
	2	53	451,429	12.61—9.69	2
	3	58	450,205	9.68—7.28	2
	4	59	451,201	7.27—5.46	2
	5	54	449,424	5.45—4.27	3
	6	57	449,530	4.26—3.27	3
	7	62	446,866	3.26—2.52	5
	8	59	444,125	2.51—1.72	6
	9	73	453.783	1.71—1.03	7
	10 Low-juror index	81	448,812	1.02—0.03	9
	Total	628	4,491,076	—	40

*Using the reduced area bounded by a 'circle' with a radius of twelve miles from city centre

23

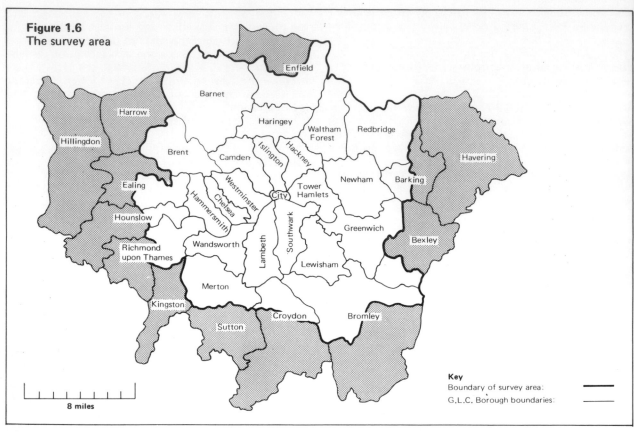

Figure 1.6
The survey area

Key
Boundary of survey area: ▬▬▬
G.L.C. Borough boundaries: ─────

8 miles

Take, for example, the selection of the required nine wards from the bottom decile division. The wards in this division had already been listed in descending order of juror percentage. The total list of them was split into nine sections, in each of which the number of electors was approximately the same. From each of these nine sections, a ward was drawn at random.

5 Control was exercised over the geographic location of each selected ward in order to ensure a wide scatter of the sampling units throughout the total survey area. When a selected ward proved to be very close to one already drawn, that particular ward was rejected and a substitute for it randomly drawn from the same section of the decile division concerned. This was also done where a ward was drawn which had already been used in one of the preparatory phases of the inquiry. The geographic distribution of the wards eventually included in the sample is given in Appendix 1.5.

Drawing polling districts within the wards For financial reasons, the development of ⌐ sample of boys had to be geared to area units *smaller than wards*. This was because the sampling of boys in any area had to be preceded by an enumeration survey to establish a 'universe' from which to draw a sample, there being available no listing of the universe of London boys. To conduct an enumeration survey in each of the forty wards would have been enormously expensive, involving data collec-

tion at over 200,000 homes. To be financially feasible, an area unit smaller than the 'ward' would have to be used, and the natural choice appeared to be the 'polling district'. As it was, conducting enumeration surveys in each of the forty polling districts was obviously going to be a major task.

Accordingly, the next step in the sampling procedure was to draw a polling district at random from each of the selected forty wards. Where a polling district had in it less than 1,500 electors*, the polling district adjacent but nearest to it in juror percentage level was also drawn, the two polling districts to be treated as one sampling area. Where their joint number of electors was still less than 1,500, a third polling district was included on the same principle. In fact, in twenty-four of the forty wards only one polling district was drawn; in a further fifteen wards, two polling districts had to be drawn; in one ward three polling districts had to be drawn.

An additional control was exercised over the drawing of polling districts. A drawn polling district was rejected (and a substitute for it randomly drawn within the limits already outlined) if it was found to contain large areas of property in process of demolition or if it was made up primarily of business rather than residential property. Substitution on these grounds occurred in two instances.

*Experience in the developmental stages of the research project indicated that on average, an electorate of 2,000 could be expected to yield approximately sixty boys aged thirteen to sixteen years.

24

The enumeration surveys in the polling districts drawn in the area sample

The reasons for conducting an enumeration survey An important factor in this inquiry was the unavailability of anything like a complete list of London boys from which to draw a sample*. A 'universe' from which to draw the sample had therefore to be specially prepared. It would not have been possible, in terms of the money or the time available, to compile a full list of all London boys in the target age range. What could be done, however, was to compile a 'universe' in each of the polling districts drawn in the sample and to draw the sample of boys from these (i.e. forty boys aged thirteen to sixteen from each of the forty sampling areas).

The methods used in conducting the enumeration survey For each sampling area, the following procedures were used in the enumeration survey.

1 Each household in the polling district was recorded on the enumeration inventory together with its address, the list of households being obtained from electoral registers. Amendments and additions to this enumeration inventory were subsequently made by the enumerators to take account of changes since the completion of the records on which the electoral registers were based.

2 The enumerator was to visit each household on the inventory, making repeat calls as necessary in an effort to contact at least one of its members. On making such contact, she was to introduce herself as from 'the university' and was to explain that she was 'carrying out a youth survey in this area to find out what boys do in their spare time', and that, 'to start with we are getting the ages of all boys in this district'. She then attempted to find out if there were any boys living in the informant's home or ordinarily resident there, and if so what their ages were. If there were not any boys there or if there were none in the age range twelve to seventeen†, the interview was to be terminated. If not, the following details were sought about each boy aged twelve to seventeen: the boy's first name; the date of his birthday; whether he was living at home or away from home;

whether he was at school or at work; date of his next return home if he was living away; whether he was handicapped (i.e. physically or mentally). The informant was then asked for the occupation of the head of the household and was told by the interviewer that if the boy was selected for interview, someone would call to arrange an appointment. The respondent was thanked for the interview just given.

3 Enumerators were instructed to make at least three recalls on three separate days and, if possible, at different times of day before giving-up the attempt to contact some member of a household. If such contact had not been made by this time, information was sought from neighbours and recorded on the enumeration sheets. In this way direct contact was made with 94 per cent of the households, and indirect contact with an additional 4.5 per cent of them (i.e. information was secured about a total of 98.5 per cent of the households in the inventory).

4 Enumerators worked mainly in the afternoons and evenings and were required to make daily telephone contact with the survey controller.

5 The work of enumerators was subject to vigorous personal check by a full-time supervisor/checker.

6 The enumerators worked steadily through the sampling sub-areas, with the survey itself following two to three polling districts behind. The reason for this was to keep the derived sample of boys for use in the survey as 'current' as possible and so to reduce sample loss through families moving away. Both the enumeration and the fieldwork for the causal enquiry were spread over a full year.

Success rates in the enumeration survey

Over the whole forty polling districts, successful calls were made with respect to approximately 57,650 of the 58,550 households in the enumerators' inventories (= 98.5 per cent). Between them, these households yielded a total of 3,878 boys said to be aged from thirteen to sixteen and distributed as follows:

Age	No.
13 yrs	910
14 yrs	952
15 yrs	974
16 yrs	1,042
	3,878

This yield is very close to what would be expected on the basis of census data. It represents an average of ninety-seven boys per sample area, the range being from fifty in the area with fewest boys to 276 in the area with most. The distribution of boys by age in each of the forty sampling areas is given in Appendix 1.5.

*The following sources were carefully considered, but rejected on the grounds indicated:

i *Schools.* Permission could not be obtained in all cases. Some boys attended schools well away from the area in which they lived and any sampling would have to be based on *schools*, not on place of residence.

ii *School attendance lists.* These were available only for certain areas. Moreover, these did not include details of boys who had left school.

iii *Lists of National Health Service patients.* Official permission for access was known to be very difficult to obtain; in any case, these lists tended to be much out of date.

†Although initially the survey was to be confined to boys aged between thirteen and sixteen, details were collected at the enumeration stage about twelve- and seventeen-year olds to provide a margin of safety — their ages being subsequently checked against date of birth to ensure that the informant had not slightly miscalculated.

Drawing a sample from the total list of boys

The elimination of certain boys from the enumeration lists Prior to sampling, certain types of boys were eliminated from the lists built up through the enumeration survey. Firstly, where more than one boy in the relevant age range came from the one household, all but one of these was eliminated by random methods. This was done to avoid the influencing of boys yet to be interviewed by brothers already interviewed. Secondly, boys reported by the enumerators to be seriously disabled or handicapped, so as to make them unfit for being interviewed (e.g. spastic, deaf, chronically ill), were also removed from the lists. So, too, were boys whom the enumerators reported to be currently in approved schools* and those living permanently away from home.

Reasons for Elimination	No. of boys eliminated
Brothers	330
Disabled or handicapped	31
At approved school	12
Living permanently away from home	21
Total	394

This process led to the elimination of 394 boys as indicated in the above table, leaving a total of 3,484 boys. It should be noted that certain other types of boys quite likely to present difficulties with respect to interviewing were not removed from the lists: boys living temporarily or periodically away from home but not at approved school (e.g. at boarding school); moderately handicapped boys such as illiterates, the partly crippled, the chronically shy. The 3,484 boys left in the lists were distributed, with respect to age and area, as shown in Appendix 1.5.

Drawing a sample for each of the forty (enumerated) polling districts For each of the forty sampling areas, the remaining boys were separated into four age-groups: thirteen-, fourteen-, fifteen- and sixteen-year olds. For each such age group, ten boys plus one potential substitute were drawn on random principles. These substitutes were to be used where necessary to replace boys who were completely unavailable for interview throughout the period of the survey (e.g. boy permanently away from home, spastic, very low intelligence). A given polling district thus yielded a sample of forty boys plus four potential substitutes. This selection process was carried out progressively as each new sampling area was enumerated, but over the whole forty sampling areas, the derived sample aggregated to 40 x 40 (= 1,600) boys plus 40 x 4 (= 160) potential substitutes†.

*Some of these boys nonetheless were unintentionally included and these account for some of the eventual sample loss.

Securing Interviews with Boys in the Sample

The requirement that the interview be done away from home

A considerable amount of preliminary inquiry had firmly established the necessity of conducting the interviews *away* from the homes of the boys. Thus, it had been found that in many homes the quiet and privacy necessary for conducting the very specialized interview were far from being available. Boys tended markedly to be unwilling to talk about their stealing or about home conditions when their parents were within hearing. Furthermore, the home tended not to be conducive to establishing the rapport and the considerable control which was essential for the proposed interview. Nor could interviewers readily carry into homes the equipment which was an integral part of the questioning procedure: an interviewing screen; sorting bags and sorting boxes; tape recorder; food.

Nor was it feasible to conduct the interview at some *local* headquarters, for preliminary work had clearly shown: (*a*) that it was virtually impossible in many areas to secure any such headquarters for short-term occupation; and, (*b*) that where a headquarters site *did* become available, it was likely to be ill-suited to our specialized purposes — insufficient interviewing-rooms, insufficient privacy for boys during interview, dirty or dismal conditions.

Because of these circumstances, it had been decided to carry out all interviews in a mid-city building designed for such work. This necessary decision did, however, raise problems of its own — problems which though surmountable, called for special measures. Thus, parents had to be persuaded to let boys go to the centre for interview; the boys, too, had to be persuaded to make this journey; the time of arrival of boys at the interviewing centre had to be tightly geared to the availability of members of the interviewing team; special steps had to be taken to get the younger boys home again.

This operation was, in fact, a highly specialized one, featured by a number of innovations in recruitment tactics and aimed at securing interviews with not less than 90 per cent of the sample. The full recruitment procedure is briefly described below. It is given in full in a separate document.[19]

The recruitment system used

In broad outline, the system used was as follows. A special member of the survey team (called an 'appointment maker') would call at the home of a boy and get from him, with the agreement of his parents, a promise to take part. Boys were made aware that they would receive a fee of £1 if they took part. The appointment

†In four of the 160 age lists, the number of names available from the enumeration survey was less than the required forty-four. In the one case where this affected the main sample, a suitably-aged respondent was drawn from an adjacent polling district. In the other cases, where only the potential substitutes were affected, a respondent was drawn from an adjacent age-group in the same area. Details of distribution are given in Appendix 1.5.

maker fixed with the boy the evening on which he would come for interview and the time at which another member of the research team (called a 'collector') would call by car to collect him and take him to the interviewing centre. There he would be met at reception and allocated to one of the interviewers. After being interviewed, the boy would be given his fare home or, as for some of the younger boys, would be sent home by taxi.

Appointment making Two appointment makers were engaged on a full-time basis, working in the afternoons and evenings. They worked quite separately, each to an assigned sampling area, and they moved progressively through twenty sampling areas each. Each appointment maker was responsible for securing four firm appointments for interview per evening from Monday to Friday inclusive.

From the point of view of arranging appointment times, the sample divided conveniently into two halves: the younger boys, all of whom were at school during the day; the older boys, many of whom were in full-time jobs. This meant that at least two interviewing times had to be arranged. For the younger boys, the appointment time was, wherever feasible, geared to the commencement of interviewing at 5.15 p.m., whereas for the older boys the appointment for collection was geared to a commencement time of 7.15 p.m. There was, of course, room for some degree of variation from this pattern. Appointments for interview were not usually made for more than three or four days in advance because it had been found that with longer intervals boys tended either to forget or to lose interest. Here too, however, there was room for the occasional long-term appointment, though in such cases the boy was re-contacted within a few days of the actual appointment time.

In attempting to fix an appointment for a boy to be taken to the centre for interview, the first approach was made to the parents whenever this was feasible. On meeting them, every effort was made to enlist their support for the project so that they could use their influence to help the boy agree to take part and to help him keep to his appointment.

The appointment makers were both women, one of whom had done a lot of this class of work in the preparatory stages of the inquiry. An appointment maker would begin by introducing herself as working for the university (showing an official card of the centre) and explaining that she was helping to conduct a survey of some of the activities of boys. She explained to the parents that many boys in London were being interviewed in this survey and that their son had been selected at random* as one of the boys from this district to be asked to take part. The interview was to be on university premises and the boy would be paid a fee of £1 for giving the interview.

The social importance of the survey was emphasized. Parents were told that if the boy would agree to take part, she (the appointment maker) would arrange a convenient date and time for him to be collected from

*The term 'random' was elaborated where it seemed necessary.

his home and driven to the centre for the interview. Arrangements for getting him home were explained.

Either during the interview with a parent or after it this explanation was repeated in full to the boy, and the payment of £1 was stressed, as were certain other rewards for taking part (see below).

When a date for the collection time had been fixed, the appointment maker gave the boy an appointment card on which was written the time at which he would be called for, the fact that he would be paid £1 for the interview and the fact that light refreshments would be served at the centre. At this stage the parent was given a letter signed by a senior research officer of the Survey Research Centre thanking him for giving permission for the boy to be interviewed and re-stating the point that the boy would be called for by a member of the research team.

The incentives offered to the boy An important element in persuading boys to take part was the use of incentives. Thus as already stated boys were told beforehand that they would be paid £1 for taking part, would be called for by car, would receive light refreshments at the centre. With some of the hard-to-recruit boys, the fee for taking part was raised to £2, but only when most of the other boys in the sample for that district had been dealt with. On occasions, a second appointment maker — e.g. a male member of the research team or, for some older boys, an attractive young female appointment maker — was sent to try to get the boy to agree to come for interview. In addition, certain other benefits were provided in the course of the boy's stay at the centre, these being intended to serve both to heighten rapport and to encourage other sample members to take part once the interviewees got talking to them later on. Thus, on arrival at the centre, the boy found the reception-room stocked with a wide range of publications for his age-group; at several points during the interview, a halt was called for refreshment; about two-thirds of the way through the interview, the boy was told that at the end of the interview he would receive, in addition to his £1 fee, either a Churchill Memorial Crown or a choice of a pop record, whichever he wanted.

Overcoming parents' reluctance to let their sons take part Quite understandably, some parents were reluctant to have their young sons taken off for interview. It was for this reason that the appointment maker, a woman, talked first to the parents, establishing the survey as genuine, respectable and socially useful and making it clear that the boy would be taken to the centre by car and that proper arrangements would be made for getting him home — by car if the boy was young or if the parents were especially anxious. In some instances, parents of a shy or disabled child who felt that he could not go alone were told that their son could if he so wished go with a friend (though the friend was not interviewed unless he, too, happended to be in the sample).

Parental support for boys' attendance was obviously vital and this was always regarded as a primary target for the appointment maker.

Dealing with boys who broke appointments A total of eighty-nine boys out of the target sample* broke their appointment arrangement, though fifty-one of these were subsequently interviewed. Appointment breaking appeared to occur: (*a*) where the boy was genuinely prevented from taking part through illness or some other pressing circumstance; and (*b*) where the boy made the initial appointment without really intending to keep it. In the former situation, a second appointment could usually be arranged and it tended to be kept. The other class of boy was pressed for a second appointment and, if that failed, for a third. With some of these boys, special tactics were used, such as making appointments for immediate interview, collecting them from outside school or their place of work.

Dealing with boys who had moved away from the district since the enumeration survey The appointment makers found that about fifty boys had changed address since the enumeration survey — which in a given case may have preceded appointment making by anything from a few weeks to several months.† Of these boys, nearly half were traced and contacted either by consulting local authorities (in the case of families living in council dwellings) or by asking neighbours. Any boy who could not be traced or whose new address was outside the London area was replaced by a substitute drawn from the supplementary list of 160 (see details in Appendix 1.5).

The collection and transport of boys to the interviewing centre The names and addresses of boys for whom appointments had been arranged were given to a female member of the research team, referred to here as the 'collector'. On a typical evening, she would first collect from their homes all the boys whose appointments were for the earlier interviewing session and would take them by car or taxi to the interviewing centre. These boys would tend to be all in the thirteen to fourteen age-group due to start their interview at 5.15 p.m. She would next prepare to collect the remaining four boys due for the interview to commence at 7.15 p.m. Inevitably, there were instances on a given night when a single boy had to be collected from a district well away from that in which the other boys lived. In such cases, a second collector was called in to bring the boy to the centre. This happened more and more towards the end of the survey when quite a lot of 'clearing-up' had to be done.

The collector would introduce herself to the boy and his parents, showing an official card. In most cases the boy was ready and eager to accompany her. On some occasions, however, the boy would not be available when the collector called and when this happened, it was her task to find out the reasons why and to pass these on to the appointment maker for action.

*The target sample consisted of 1,600 boys in a primary sample and 160 in a pool of potential substitutes (of whom fifty-five were actually drawn for interview).

†As when the boy was contacted well after the appointment maker had dealt with most of the other boys in the district.

Table 1.4

Reasons for failure to interview

	n	Percentage on 230	Percentage on 1,655
Boy's family had moved and could not be traced or had moved to new address too far away	27	11.7	1.6
Boy had moved permanently away from home	4	1.7	0.2
Boy away at school or work for a long period	8	3.5	0.5
Boy committed to approved school or similar institution	9	3.9	0.5
Family not contacted after repeated calls	6	2.6	0.4
Boy very seriously handicapped (physically or mentally)	2	0.9	0.1
Boy actually interviewed but results discarded because boy completely uncommunicative or mentally sub-normal	3	1.3	0.2
Boy a recent immigrant and cannot speak English	2	0.9	0.1
Boy unknown at address	3	1.3	0.2
Recorded age grossly inaccurate	2	0.9	0.1
Boy deceased	1	0.4	0.1
Boy dropped because father a public figure (i.e. to avoid publicity)	2	0.9	0.1
Boy refused and could not be persuaded to change his mind	123	53.5	7.4
Boy broke first appointment *and* either broke a second appointment or refused a second appointment	38	16.5	2.3
All	230	100.0%	13.8%

The success rate achieved

It will be recalled that 1,600 boys had been drawn in the primary sample and a further 160 had been placed in a pool for use as substitutes if necessary. Of these 160, a total of fifty-five were in fact drawn, bringing the effective target sample to 1,655.

Substitutes were drawn only under stringent conditions – e.g.: family had moved and boy could not be traced to new address or new address was too far away; boy had been committed to an approved school or some similar institution; boy was mentally sub-normal to a degree that would have made his result unusable.

Of the total sample of 1,655 boys, 1,425 completed the interview at the centre, representing an 86 per cent success rate. The reasons for loss are set out in Table 1.4.

Comparing those interviewed with those not interviewed

In a study of this kind, it is essential that consideration be given to the possibility that the 14 per cent of boys not interviewed were appreciably different from those who *were* interviewed.

The enumeration survey had produced certain background information about all the boys in the target sample, namely the age of each boy and the job or each boy's father. The 230 non-interviewed boys and the other 1,425 are compared in these terms in Tables 1.5 and 1.6. This comparison indicates that the un-interviewed boys were somewhat the older and of somewhat lower socio-economic level.

What matters, of course, is how these differences affect the findings, especially the findings related to amount of stealing done. The information available from the study as a whole allows us to attempt an estimate of

Table 1.5

A comparison of boys interviewed with those not interviewed, in terms of social class.

	a Boys interviewed (1,425)		b Not interviewed (230)		c All boys (1,655)	
	(No.)	(%)	(No.)	(%)	(No.)	(%)
Social class rating of boy's father (*Registrar General's classification*)						
Professional and semi-professional	232	16.3	23	10.0	255	15.4
Skilled, non-manual	170	11.9	17	7.4	187	11.3
Skilled, manual	628	44.1	91	39.5	719	43.4
Semi-skilled	249	17.5	39	17.0	288	17.4
Unskilled	143	10.0	26	11.3	169	10.2
Not classified	3	0.2	34	14.8	37	2.2
All	1,425	100.0	230	100.0	1,655	99.9

Table 1.6

A comparison of boys interviewed with those not interviewed in terms of age

	a Boys interviewed* (1,425)		b Not interviewed† (230)		c All boys (1,655)	
	(No.)	(%)	(No.)	(%)	(No.)	(%)
Boy's age						
13	329	23.1	25	11.1	354	21.4
14	369	25.9	38	16.8	407	24.7
15	338	23.7	62	27.4	400	24.2
16+	389	27.3	101	44.7	490	29.7
All	1,425	100.0	226	100.0	1,651	100.0
Average age	14.6		15.1		14.6	

*Age at time of interview

†Ages for non-interviewed boys are estimates of their ages at the time when the other boys were interviewed, namely three months (on average) after enumeration

Table 1.7
Theft Level By Class and Age

Social class† of boy's father	Averaged index of amount of stealing*	Age of boy	Averaged index of amount of stealing*
Professional and semi-professional	76.6	13	64.9
Skilled, non-manual	91.5	14	83.4
Skilled, manual	102.2	15	108.0
Partly skilled	95.3	16	122.6
Unskilled	103.8		

*Based on scores of *interviewed* boys at time of that interview
†Registrar General's classification

that kind. Thus, we know that class and age made certain differences to the theft level of the interviewed boys. See Table 1.7.

If we assume the same relationship to apply to the non-interviewed boys, then we can derive the estimates set out below. Table 1.8

Table 1.8
Actual and estimated theft scores

Averaged index of amount of stealing based upon:	Scores for boys actually interviewed	Estimated scores for boys not interviewed	Estimated scores for all boys in target sample
Social class	95.7	97.1	95.9
*Age**	95.7	105.6	97.0

*Age at time of interview (or attempted interview)

These data suggest relatively little effect, on total theft score, of losing the 230 non-interviewed boys — though this suggestion involves an assumption that variation in theft 'score' with age and father's job level are the same in the achieved and the non-achieved section in the target sample.

Another way to consider the effects (on the results) of failing to interview 14 per cent of the sample is to compare the results from the 'easier-to-contact' boys with those from the 'harder-to-contact', and then to extrapolate to the 14 per cent who were total failures as far as securing an interview is concerned.

Direct extrapolation of these findings to the missing 14 per cent would suggest averages for the latter of approximately 14.0 and 101.3 respectively. Even if these averages were as high as 15 and 120 respectively — which seems most unlikely — their addition to the sample would make relatively little difference to the results based solely on the achieved 86 per cent.

Re-weighting the sample

It will be remembered that the sample had been skewed towards the lower socio-economic levels in order to meet the primary purpose of the inquiry, namely to investigate various causal hypotheses. This had been achieved

Table 1.9
Comparing theft 'scores' for the 'easier' and the 'harder' to contact

Type of theft score	Average theft score for boys who were:	
	Easier to secure for interview (51%)	Harder to secure for interview (35%)
No. out of 44 types of theft committed at least once	13.1	13.7
Total no. of thefts claimed to have been committed	93.6	98.7

by over-representing the number of wards in the lower socio-economic decile groups in the population. However it was at all times intended that this skew should be removed for the *other* purposes of the inquiry, namely for the purposes of establishing: (*a*) the extent and nature of stealing by London boys; and, (*b*) the distribution of the boy population of London in terms of the many variables hypothesized as causal.

What, in effect, this meant was that there were two samples in use: (*a*) a sample skewed towards the lower socio-economic (decile) sectors as a pre-requisite for investigating the hypotheses; and (*b*) a sample with its initial socio-economic skew removed from it.

To remove the socio-economic skew from the sample, re-weighting methods were used. The case cards were to be differentially weighted so that the number in each of the original decile groups became equal. This process was not to involve any casting out of cases: since the decile group with the largest number of cases was Group 10 (based on 312 cases from nine wards), all the different decile groups were to be brought up to *its* numerical level (i.e. 312). The weighting system proposed for doing this took the form shown in columns *d* and *e* of Table 1.10.

However, on later discussion of the statistical problems raised by the heavy weighting of small sub-groups of a sample (in this case, of the sub-group of boys from

Table 1.10
Proposed and actual
re-weighting systems

Decile Group	Number of Wards Included	Actual Number of Cases Yielded	Weighting Index Initially Proposed	Planned Yield of Cards	Actual Weighting Index Used	Actual Yield of Cards
a	b	c	d	e	f	g
1	1	38	8.21	312	4.98	189
2	2	76	4.11	312	4.98	378
3	2	74	4.22	312	4.98	369
4	2	67	4.66	312	3.69	247
5	3	102	3.06	312	3.69	376
6	3	101	3.09	312	2.23	225
7	5	179	1.74	312	2.23	399
8	6	217	1.44	312	1.44	311
9	7	259	1.20	312	1.20	311
10	9	312	1.00	312	1.00	312
		1,425		3,120		

decile Group 1) and on the advice of statistical colleagues, a less extreme system of re-weighting was used. Thus the economic-decile-Groups 1 to 3 (including five wards in all) were grouped together and given a joint weighting index sufficient to lift their combined total of 188 cases to a weighted total of 3×312 (= 916/188 = 4.98). Similarly, economic-decile-Groups 4 and 5 were combined and given a joint weighting index of 3.69 (= 624/169). Economic-decile-Groups 6 and 7 were given a combined weighting index of 2.23 (= 624/280). Decile Groups 8, 9 and 10 were weighted as originally planned.

The result of this 'precautionary' measure is shown in Columns f and g of Table 1.10. Clearly it was to under-represent boys from Groups 1, 4 and 6 and to over-represent boys from decile Groups 2, 3, 5 and 7.

Inevitably, this type of arrangement leaves the way open to disagreement of some kind. At the same time, it is important to take note of the very small difference in the estimated (all sample) theft level yielded by the above re-weighting system and, on the other hand, by the re-weighting system which was initially planned and which is shown in Column d of Table 1.10. This comparison is presented in Table 1.11. In fact, the difference is remarkably small. The reason for this is simply that the economic level of a ward, as indicated by the juror figure, proved to have a linear correlation with theft level of less than -0.1. This was fully recognized at the time the compromise decision about weighting was reached.

Moreover, it is very much worth noting that the completely unweighted distributions of theft score are remarkably similar to the distributions yielded by either of the two weighting systems.

Had the initial skewing and the subsequent re-weighting been based, not on the economic-decile level of wards, but upon the occupational level of the fathers of boys, the outcome would have been much the same, for the linear correlation between occupational level of father and total amount of stealing by boys is approximately -0.2[20]

Interviewing
The total interviewing procedure is described in full in Section I of this chapter and what follows here is a summary of that detail.

The place of interview
Interviewing was conducted in a mid-city centre especially equipped for interviewing. The reasons for this choice of interviewing venue were: (a) the necessary degree of privacy was rarely available in boys' homes; (b) it was virtually impossible to get local interviewing centres in each of the districts drawn in a random sample; (c) even when such premises became available in some districts, they did not provide anything like desirable interviewing conditions.

The mid-city centre used was a small self-contained building, the internal structure of which had been adapted to provide eight interviewing-rooms, a reception room and two additional offices for members of the research team in charge of the day-to-day running of the project. The interior of the building was decorated to provide an informal atmosphere and to avoid possible association with school or officialdom. Each of the eight interviewing rooms was sound-proofed to prevent anyone outside a room hearing what was said by boys being interviewed there, to protect the interview from outside noises and distractions and to impress the boy with the privacy of the interview. Each room was furnished with two tables, chairs and various items of equipment connected with the interview and described later on in this section.

Table 1.11
The effect upon score
distribution of using a
modified weighting system

'Amount'* scores	Using weighting system as initially planned (see col. *d* of Table 1.10)		Weighting system actually used (see col. *f* of Table 1.10)		Completely unweighted system (see col. *c* of Table 1.10)	
	(*n*)	(%)	(*n*)	(%)	(*n*)	(%)
0— 10	375	12	370	12	159	11
11— 20	213	7	222	7	105	7
21— 30	290	9	300	10	136	10
31— 40	223	7	216	7	88	6
41— 50	193	6	204	7	92	6
51— 60	128	4	132	4	60	4
61— 70	159	5	157	5	70	5
71— 80	166	5	157	5	71	5
81— 90	128	4	138	4	60	4
91—100	157	5	141	5	59	4
101—110	100	3	99	3	48	3
111—120	89	3	89	3	38	3
121—130	96	3	96	3	43	3
131—140	69	2	69	2	34	2
141—150	109	4	107	3	50	4
151—200	275	9	266	9	127	9
201—250	125	4	119	4	66	5
251—300	92	3	90	3	42	3
301+	132	4	138	4	77	5
	3,119	99%	3,110	100%	1,425	99%

*As assessed by the technique described in this chapter

The interviewers

For a number of reasons the interviewing procedure was a difficult and demanding one: matters being investigated were of a distinctly delicate kind; the administration of the interview was complex and lengthy; a high quality of intensive probing was required.

For these and other reasons it was essential that interviewers should be carefully selected and trained and that their work should at all times be subject to quality control.

The interviewers were all young men (aged under thirty) and had been selected against the ideals of: above-average intelligence; friendliness coupled with firmness; an unshockable outlook; a tendancy to use simple language. There was also a tendancy for the selection team to avoid young men whose appearance or demeanor might suggest that they were policemen.

Selection of these interviewers was done through a week-long training-selection course through which an initial twenty or so applicants were reduced to ten men who then underwent further training as interviewers for this particular project. Over and above teaching the interviewers how to handle the particular questions and procedures, there was special instruction: in sticking to the required wording of questions and to procedural instructions; in probing techniques.

The selected interviewers expected to work for a year on the project and this helped to keep them together as a team. Where there were replacements the new man went through the same training process.

The organization of the interviewing

Appointments for interview were made by 'appointment makers' who went out to the homes of sampled boys and persuaded them to agree to attend the centre for interviews. They were then collected by car and brought to the centre. At the centre they were met by a receptionist who checked them in, allowed each to choose a false name (e.g. Peter, Charlie, Bert), offered them food and then sent each off to the room in which he would be interviewed.

During the late morning or early afternoon of each day, the interviewers finalized their reports on the previous evening's interviews, making full use of the tape recordings made of their interviews. Time was also available for meetings and discussion with a quality control officer whose role is detailed below. In the late afternoon and evening, the interviewers conducted further interviews.

The interviewing was spread over a full year partly to spread the load but also to guard against seasonal influences. In the course of that year, fourteen interviewers were employed, though the number operating any one evening did not exceed eight. The number of interviews conducted per interviewer varied from 167 to 44.

Continuing quality control was exercized over the performance of the interviewers by quality control staff who used the tape recordings of the interviews as evidence of the way in which interviews were carried out. Deficiencies in performance were straightaway communicated to the interviewer responsible. In addition, daily meetings between the quality control officer and the interviewers were held for the discussion of recurrent points of failure and of methods of controlling these.

After the interview
After the interview, each boy was brought back to the reception room by his interviewer, where the receptionist measured his height, weight, strength of grip (with apparatus in the reception room). She then gave each boy his promised payment of £1 and offered the boy a choice of a Churchill Memorial Crown, a pop record or five shillings. The boy was also given his fare home by public transport or, if a boy was quite young or if the interview had finished very late, was sent home in a taxi.

The sequence and the content of the interview
The interview itself was conducted in three stages.

1 The first was an introductory stage designed to put the boy at ease and to prepare him for the second stage.

2 Then came the administration of a specially-constructed questioning technique for getting from boys information about the nature and the extent of such stealing as they had ever done — a technique referred to already in this document as the eliciting procedure.

3 A third and major stage was concerned with the administration of ten sub-questionnaires geared to: (*a*) the informational needs of the investigation of the numerous causal hypotheses; and, (*b*) the provision of general background information relevant to the different hypotheses.

The introductory stage In this stage of the interview, which is described fairly fully earlier in this chapter, the boy to be interviewed was taken to one of the interviewing rooms by the receptionist and introduced by his false name to the interviewer assigned to that room. The interviewer welcomed him warmly by that false name and offered his own first name (e.g. Jack) in return. He then began to work through the instructions set out in Booklet A which has already been described in this chapter as part of the eliciting procedure and which deals with the interests of boys.

The reader may study this part of the procedure in its full working detail in Appendix 1.1, giving special thought to the psychological position into which it was intended to lead the boy. Thus it was the purpose of Booklet A:

1 To establish a serious but friendly working relationship between boy and interviewer.

2 To help the boy settle into the false-name situation and to develop a degree of normality and an acceptance with regard to the interviewing operation.

3 To familiarize the boy with the process of sorting cards into boxes as a means of registering his own position in relation to what is printed on the cards.

4 To teach the boy that he must operate to rules and to communicate two of the several rules to which he would be working when providing information about his stealing behaviour.

5 To let him get used to and accept the presence of the tape recorder.

Securing information about the boy's involvement in stealing
The interviewer now proceeded through Booklet B of the eliciting procedure which, like the introductory stage, is described in earlier parts of this chapter and is presented in full working detail in Appendix 1.1. Accordingly, all that need be said here is that: (*a*) as a procedure it took about an hour to deliver; and, (*b*) in general, boys seemed to work hard and conscientiously at it and to accept it for what it was said to be and what in fact it was. In terms of its function, this procedure yielded the body of information which was central to the whole inquiry — information of a quantitative kind about the nature and the extent of the accumulated involvement in stealing of London boys principally in the age range thirteen to sixteen years.

Securing information about the distribution of factors hypothesized as causal and of various background variables
In the third stage of the interview, boys were taken through a series of ten sub-questionnaires, each providing information relevant to the investigation of some group of causal hypotheses. An eleventh sub-questionnaire dealt principally with variables included as items in a pool of possible matching criteria — a central requirement of the strategy of investigation.

These sub-questionnaires are presented mainly in the appendices of the chapters that draw upon the information yielded through them. Thus, the sub-questionnaire dealing with 'association with thieves' is presented in the Appendix 6.1, which is directly concerned with that issue. In addition there is an early outline in each of the chapters, reporting on the investigation of hypotheses, and on the coverage and the purposes of its sub-questionnaire.

The principal 'causal' variables dealt with in the sub-questionnaires follow directly from the list of hypotheses set out on pp. 6—7 and are as follows:

1 Whether the boy has ever been caught by the police or others for stealing and his views about the likelihood of his getting caught if he continues stealing; his views about the consequences of getting caught.

2 The extent of the boy's desire and search for fun and excitement.

3 The extent, nature and duration of the boy's association with boys who steal.

4 The existence in the boy of personal ambitions and the nature of these.

5 The boy's achievements, position and attitudes in relation to school; the extent of his involvement in truancy.

6 The boy's present day (legal) interests and hobbies and the nature of his (legal) spare-time activities.

7 The boy's religious denomination and the extent of his attendance at church, chapel or synagogue.

8 The nature and the degree of parental control over the boy's choice of associates, where he spends his spare time, his 'going out'; the nature and degree of the punishment he has received from his parents.

9 The extent and sources of teaching or training directed at the boy with respect to personal honesty.

10 The satisfactoriness, in the eyes of the boy, of his home environment; the frequency of family rows there.

11 The composition of the boy's family, including whether it is 'broken'.

12 Various aspects of family composition and continuity, including evidence of boy's separation from parents and of the home being 'broken'.

13 Whether the boy's mother goes out to work and the proportion of his life for which she has done so.

14 The relationship of the boy's wants to his (legal) financial means.

General background information was collected both as possibly bearing on the factors hypothesized as causal and as relevant to the cross-analysis of various of the findings. Amongst the variables included for this purpose (and not listed above) were the following: age of boy; occupational level of boy's father; type of school last attended; country of birth/colour of skin; whether still at school; family possession of certain goods and facilities; additional aspects of family composition; size and nature of household; length of residence in present district; whether the boy has a girl friend.

Variables included as potential matching criteria These were numerous and many of them are listed in Appendix 1.4. The general form of the sub-questionnaires can readily be seen in the appendices to the various chapters. It may be useful, however, to pinpoint and comment upon certain of their features.

1 Much use was made of 'signposts' throughout the sub-questionnaire. These were intended to help the interviewer 'know where he was' at any time and to give him direction in his probing activities. A typical 'signpost' was as follows:

Q1 Does he like being at home/Does he want to spend spare time there?

This signpost was not meant to tell the interviewer to find out about this in his own way, but simply to indicate that all the questions presented under this signpost were directed at establishing this sort of information.

2 Under each such signpost came a sequence of instructions to the interviewer and of specific questions to be put to the respondent. The instructions to interviewers were always in full capitals and were indented, whereas the questions to be asked of boys were in lower-case type, were set out to the margin and were shown in full quotes. This system was also meant to help the interviewer know just what the page of instructions was all about and to help him preserve the verbatim character of those parts of the sub-questionnaire which were to be presented verbatim.

3 Some of the questions asked were not intended to be analysed but were asked simply to get boys thinking about chosen subject matter prior to their making a rating of some kind. Thus in Question 1a in the 'atmosphere at home' questionnaire, the boy was asked:

What are the things you *like* about being at home?

and in Question 1b:

What are the things you *don't* like about being at home?

The responses to these questions were meant to bring to the forefront of his awareness the boy's feelings about being at home and so help to secure from him a meaningful rating in answer to Question 1c — which was an important one for hypothesis testing and which went as follows:

Now I want you to read out all the things on this card. (*PASS CARD*) Read them all aloud for me please

   THEN SAY:
Now here is the question. Think carefully about it before you answer. Which of those (POINT) is nearest to the way *you* feel about being at home? (REPEAT)

DISLIKE IT VERY MUCH
DISLIKE IT
LIKE IT
LIKE IT VERY MUCH   *RING THE*
LIKE IT TREMENDOUSLY   *ONE CHOSEN*
BETWEEN LIKING AND
DISLIKING

4 Considerable use was made of cards on which were printed all the answers from which the boy was to choose his reply. To have required the interviewer to *read out* to the boy the choice of answers would have been to risk biased presentation of those possible answers and a muddled choice between those of them that happened to 'stick' in the boy's memory.

5 Where a lot of statements had to be judged by the boy, a *sorting technique* was used. In one sub-questionnaire, for example, this was done in trying to find out how boys reacted to forty different statements about aspects of their home life (e.g. 'I have been told off by one of my parents'; 'There would be a row if I brought my friends home'). Each statement was entered on a single small card and the boy was required to study each in turn and to sort it into one of four bags labelled respectively 'TRUE', 'PARTLY TRUE', 'NOT TRUE', 'QUERY'. To do this, the boy had to get up from the interview table and walk across the interviewing room to a screen on which four sorting bags were hung.

This sort of procedure was regarded as adding variety and interest to the interview and generally increasing the validity of the information yielded.

6 Probing and challenging sequences were built into certain of the open-ended questions asked. Thus where boys had answered an open-ended question they were, on selected occasions, asked: What else? or Who else? Where boys laid claim to something, they were asked for detail or to think again about some quantity claimed. In some of the sub-questionnaires, a more thoroughgoing probing system was applied to encourage the boy to give more information. Such probes included: Uhuh?; What else?; Yes?; the use of a 'waiting silence'.

5 ANALYSIS AND PRESENTATION OF FINDINGS

The form of analysis, which was extremely complex, was the same with regard to each hypothesis. It involved the following operations.

1 The testing of the various expectations derived from the hypothesis, usually with the matching of a control group to a qualifying group on the lines detailed under 'The Strategy for Investigating Causal Hypotheses'.

2 The derivation of a population distribution with regard to the variable hypothesized as causal.

3 Various cross-tabulations of the distribution of the 'causal' variable (e.g. 'fun and excitement seeking' analysed by boy's age, nominal religion, family composition, occupational level of his father). Where appropriate, these cross-analyses were extended to include variables which, though not hypothesized as themselves *causal* variables, appeared to be *associated* with such variables.

The decisions about the particular cross-analyses to be made were in all instances subject to extensive discussion within the research team.

The order and the form of the presentation in each of Chapters 3 to 12 is the same, namely:

1 A statement about the coverage of the chapter and the nature of the hypothesis or group of hypotheses dealt with in it.

2 A brief statement about the research procedures common to all the hypotheses dealt with in the inquiry.

3 A brief statement about the research procedures specific to the hypothesis (or hypotheses) dealt with in the chapter concerned.

4 A description of the methods and findings relating to the hypothesis(es) under investigation, starting with
a The distribution of boys in terms of the variable (or variables) hypothesized as causal within the London population as a whole and within various sectors of the London population.
b The results of testing the various expectations derived from the hypothesis(es) dealt with in the chapter.

5 A summary of the results of investigating the hypothesis(es) featured in this chapter.

6 Comments on the findings and suggestions for possible action.

6 APPENDIX 1.1

The questioning system for getting information about the nature and extent of stealing by boys

BOOKLET A Dealing with spare-time activities

Through this booklet we planned: to set the boy at ease; to orient him to the sorting of cards; to give him easy familiarity with certain of the rules of the procedure which were to apply in the sorting of theft cards (see Booklet B).

```
A.

SPARE-TIME
ACTIVITY
CARDS
```

---

page 1

THE FIRST PREPARATION OF BOY FOR THE INTERVIEW.

1 TELL BOY THAT THE INTERVIEW IS ABOUT WHAT HE DOES IN HIS SPARE TIME.

2 TELL HIM YOU DON'T KNOW HIS REAL NAME AND YOU DON'T WANT TO KNOW IT.

3 TELL HIM WHY HE HAS A FALSE NAME (i.e. TO HELP HIM TELL US ABOUT ALL THE THINGS HE HAS DONE).

4 TELL HIM THAT WE WANT TO KNOW ALL THIS BECAUSE WE ARE WRITING A BOOK.

5 ASK HIM IF HE HAS HEARD ABOUT THIS FROM ANY OTHER BOYS.

6 TELL HIM YOU WANT TO USE THE TAPE RECORDER TO SAVE TAKING NOTES.

Card fixed
in booklet
(pink)

---

page 2

THE SPARE-TIME ACTIVITY CARDS.

1 TELL HIM YOU WANT HIM TO SORT CARDS ABOUT THINGS BOYS MAY DO IN THEIR SPARE TIME.

2 SHOW HIM A CARD AS AN EXAMPLE (SO THAT HE CAN READ IT.)

3 TELL HIM YOU WILL USE 'THIS' BOARD TO SORT THE CARDS. GET THE BOARD ONTO THE TABLE.

4 EXPLAIN WHAT BOY HAS TO DO. EXPLAIN ABOUT:
(1) THE SLIT
(2) THE YES BOX
(3) THE NEVER BOX
(4) THE NOT SURE CARDS [THESE GO FACE-DOWN IN FRONT OF BOY]

5 ASK BOY WHAT THINGS GO INTO THE YES BOX.
ASK BOY WHAT THINGS GO INTO THE NEVER BOX.
ASK BOY WHAT TO DO IF HE IS NOT SURE.

Card fixed
in booklet
(pink)

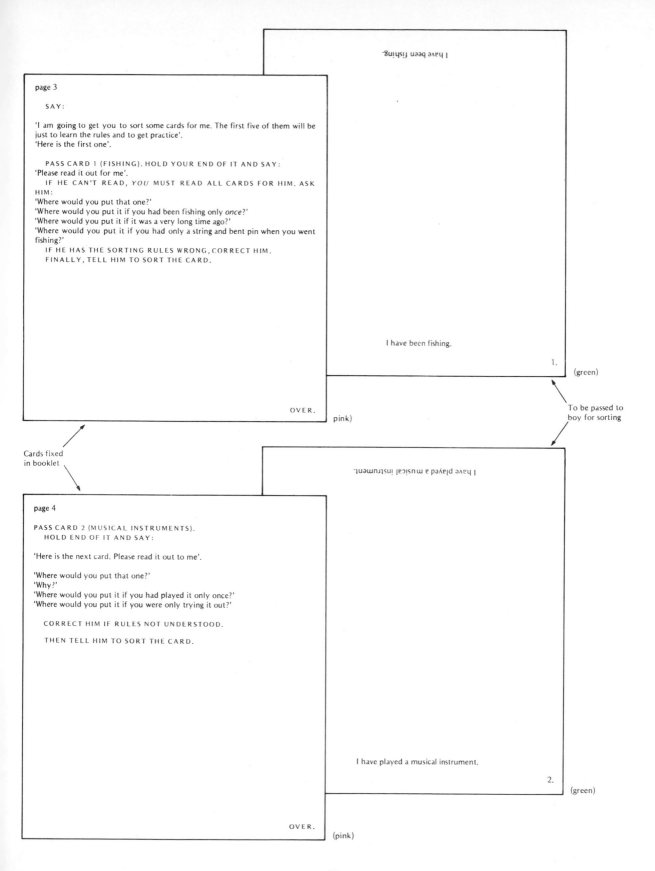

I have been fishing.

page 3

SAY:

'I am going to get you to sort some cards for me. The first five of them will be just to learn the rules and to get practice'.
'Here is the first one'.

PASS CARD 1 (FISHING). HOLD YOUR END OF IT AND SAY:
'Please read it out for me'.
IF HE CAN'T READ, *YOU* MUST READ ALL CARDS FOR HIM. ASK HIM:
'Where would you put that one?'
'Where would you put it if you had been fishing only *once*?'
'Where would you put it if it was a very long time ago?'
'Where would you put it if you had only a string and bent pin when you went fishing?'
IF HE HAS THE SORTING RULES WRONG, CORRECT HIM.
FINALLY, TELL HIM TO SORT THE CARD.

I have been fishing.

1.

(green)

OVER.

pink)

To be passed to
boy for sorting

Cards fixed
in booklet

I have played a musical instrument.

page 4

PASS CARD 2 (MUSICAL INSTRUMENTS).
HOLD END OF IT AND SAY:

'Here is the next card. Please read it out to me'.

'Where would you put that one?'
'Why?'
'Where would you put it if you had played it only once?'
'Where would you put it if you were only trying it out?'

CORRECT HIM IF RULES NOT UNDERSTOOD.

THEN TELL HIM TO SORT THE CARD.

I have played a musical instrument.

2.

(green)

OVER.

(pink)

I have made models.

page 5

PASS CARD 3 (MODEL MAKING).
HOLD IT AND SAY:

'Here is the next one. Please read it out'.

'Where would you put this one?'
'Why?'
'Where would you put it if you had only made it once?'
'Where would you put it if it was a long time ago that you did it?'

CORRECT IF RULES NOT UNDERSTOOD.

THEN GET HIM TO SORT IT.

I have made models.

3.

(green)

To be passed to
boy for sorting

OVER.

(pink)

Cards fixed
in booklet

I have been train-spotting.

page 6

PASS CARD 4 (TRAIN SPOTTING).
HOLD IT AND SAY:

'Here is another. Please read it out'.

'Where would you put that one?'
'Why?'
'Where would you put the card if you did this only when you were very young?'
'Where would you put the card if you just tried out doing train-spotting?'
and
'Where would you put it if you don't know whether you did it?'

CORRECT IF NECESSARY.

THEN GET HIM TO SORT IT.

I have been train-spotting.

4.

(green)

OVER.

(pink)

I have been skating.

page 7

PASS CARD 5 (SKATING). HOLD IT AND SAY:

'Here is a last one for practice. Read it out'.

'Where would you put that one?'
'Where would you put it if you *had a go at* skating?'
'Where would you put the card if it was *roller* skating you did?'
'Where would you put the card if you could not make up your mind about it?'

CORRECT IF NECESSARY.

THEN GET HIM TO SORT IT.

I have been skating.

(green)

Passed to boy
for sorting

OVER

(pink)

Cards fixed
in booklet

page 8

SAY:

'That's the end of the practice. I'll give you the rest, one at a time. Think carefully and then sort into *YES* or *NEVER*'.

PASS CARD 6. THEN SAY:

'Don't read it out. Just think about it carefully and sort it'.

AFTER HE SORTS IT SAY:

'Do all the other cards in the same way — don't read them out.'
'And I won't be asking questions about them'.

NOW PASS REST OF CARDS, ONE AT A TIME AND SLOWLY.

(pink)

Next came cards 6—20, as follows:

6 I have played table tennis.

7 I have collected stamps or coins.

8 I have collected gramophone records.

9 I have been a cub or a scout.

10 I have done some photography.

11 I have looked after a pet.

12 I have played football.

13 I have played billiards or snooker.

14 I have been a member of a club.

15 I have been to a museum.

16 I have been to a fun fair or an amusement arcade.

17 I have been to a school dance.

18 I have borrowed books from a public library.

19 I have been to a theatre to see a play.

20 I have gone specially to see some famous buildings.

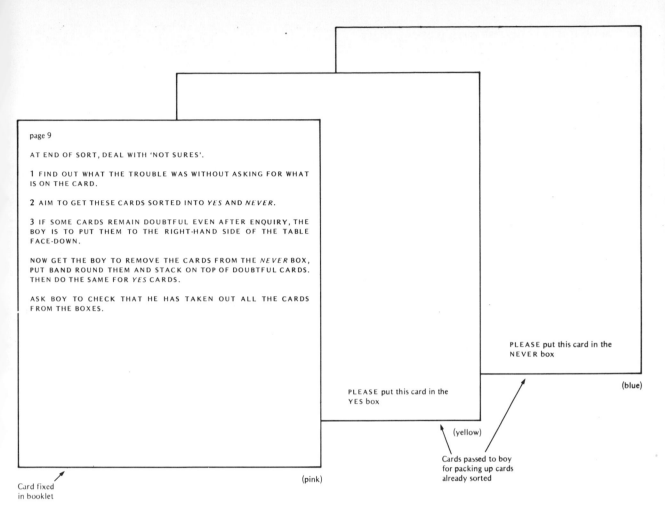

page 9

AT END OF SORT, DEAL WITH 'NOT SURES'.

1 FIND OUT WHAT THE TROUBLE WAS WITHOUT ASKING FOR WHAT IS ON THE CARD.

2 AIM TO GET THESE CARDS SORTED INTO *YES* AND *NEVER*.

3 IF SOME CARDS REMAIN DOUBTFUL EVEN AFTER ENQUIRY, THE BOY IS TO PUT THEM TO THE RIGHT-HAND SIDE OF THE TABLE FACE-DOWN.

NOW GET THE BOY TO REMOVE THE CARDS FROM THE *NEVER* BOX, PUT BAND ROUND THEM AND STACK ON TOP OF DOUBTFUL CARDS. THEN DO THE SAME FOR *YES* CARDS.

ASK BOY TO CHECK THAT HE HAS TAKEN OUT ALL THE CARDS FROM THE BOXES.

PLEASE put this card in the NEVER box

(blue)

PLEASE put this card in the YES box

(yellow)

Cards passed to boy for packing up cards already sorted

Card fixed in booklet

(pink)

End of Booklet A.

41

BOOKLET B The initial sorting of the theft cards as YES or NEVER (a section of Part I of the eliciting procedure)

Through this booklet, the forty-four theft cards are sorted into two boxes, YES and NEVER. This sorting process is governed by various rules and definitions which are to be taught through the earlier parts of the booklet and thereafter reinforced (through instructions built into the booklet).

B.

THEFT CARDS

---

page 1(a)

THEFT CARDS

1 *TELL HIM YOU WANT HIM TO SORT SOME MORE CARDS AND THESE ARE ABOUT SOME OF THE MISCHIEF THAT BOYS MAY GET UP TO IN THEIR SPARE TIME.*

2 SHOW HIM CARD 1 AS AN EXAMPLE (SO THAT HE CAN READ IT)

3 TELL HIM YOU WILL USE 'THIS' BOARD TO SORT THE CARDS. GET THE BOARD ON TO THE TABLE.

4 EXPLAIN WHAT BOY HAS TO DO, EXPLAIN ABOUT:
(1) THE SLIT
(2) THE YES BOX
(3) THE NEVER BOX
(4) THE NOT SURE CARDS
(THESE GO FACE-DOWN IN FRONT OF BOY)

5 ASK BOY WHAT THINGS GO INTO THE YES BOX
ASK BOY WHAT THINGS GO INTO THE NEVER BOX
ASK BOY WHAT TO DO IF HE IS NOT SURE

OVER

(pink)

---

page 1(b)

THEFT CARDS

TELL BOY YOU HAVE MORE CARDS TO SORT IN JUST THE SAME WAY.

TELL BOY WHAT THESE CARDS ARE ABOUT. SAY:
'The only difference is that these cards are about some of the *mischief* that boys get up to in their spare time — some of the things they pinch or borrow or steal. This is something a lot of boys do in their spare time. We want to know how much of it boys do. Remember we are writing a book about it and we depend on you for help.'

REMIND BOY WE DON'T KNOW HIS REAL NAME.
'You have got a false name and I don't want to know your real name. This is so that you can tell us *all* that you have ever done. Is that all right?'
'We want to know *everything* you have ever done — every single thing — if you don't tell us everything it is really just a waste. So we need to know everything. O.K.?'
'And remember you have got a false name. I will be calling you
I don't know you, you don't know me . . . and I don't suppose we'll ever meet again'.
'And everything you say is absolutely private'.

OVER.

(pink)

42

TELL BOY THAT BEFORE HE DOES
ANY SORTING WITH THE CARDS,
YOU WANT TO MAKE SURE HE
KNOWS THE RULES.

ASK HIM:

'If you have done the thing only *once* in your whole life, what box would you put it in?'

'If it was a very long time ago when you did it, what box would you put it in?'

'If you don't know what box to put it in, what would you do?'

SAY:

1 'If there's anything you don't understand, tell me and I'll try to help. O.K.?'

2 'If you still can't work out where it goes, just put it face down in front of you'.

OVER

(pink)

PASS CARD 1 (KEPT THINGS FOUND),
SAYING:

'I'll hold it while you read it out aloud for me'.

THEN SAY:

'Suppose a boy kept 6d. he had found: what box sould he put this card in?'

CORRECT HIM IF HE IS WRONG.
(RIGHT ANSWER IS 'THE YES BOX').

'So the rule is: it counts even if the amount is very small'.

SAY:

'Now look at this card again and decide whether or not you've *ever* done what it says on the card *yourself*. Then put it in the box where it ought to go'.

PUSH THE CARD RIGHT THROUGH THE
SLIT SO THAT HE CAN TAKE IT AND
SORT IT.

OVER.

(pink)

I have kept something I have found.

I have kept something I have found.

1

Card passed to boy for sorting.

(blue)

43

I have stolen something just for fun. (upside down text at top of first blue card)

page 2(a)

PASS CARD 2 (JUST FOR FUN), SAYING:

'I'll hold it while you read it out aloud for me'.

THEN SAY:

'Suppose a boy did that just once in his life: what box should he put the card in?'

CORRECT HIM IF HE IS WRONG.
(RIGHT ANSWER IS 'THE YES BOX').

'So it counts even if you did it just once'.

SAY:

'Now look at the card again and decide whether or not you've *ever* done what it says *yourself*. Then put it in the box where it ought to go'.

I have stolen something just for fun.

2.

(blue)

(pink)

Cards passed to boy for sorting

Instruction cards fixed in booklet

I have taken something just for a dare. (upside down text at top of second blue card)

page 3(a)

PASS CARD 3 (JUST FOR A DARE),
HOLDING IT AND SAYING:

'Will you please read it out aloud for me?'

THEN SAY:

'If a boy did that *a long time ago*, what box should he put the card in?'

CORRECT IF WRONG,
(RIGHT ANSWER IS 'THE YES BOX').

'So it counts even if you did it a long time ago'.

SAY:

'Now look at the card again and decide whether or not you've *ever* done what it says *yourself*. Then put it in the box where it ought to go'.

I have taken something just for a dare.

3.

(blue)

(pink)

(pink)

page 5(a)

PASS CARD 5 (STALL OR BARROW),
HOLDING IT AND SAYING:

'Will you please read this one out for me?'

SAY:

'Suppose that a boy did this *just for fun or just to try it out*. What box should he put the card in?'

CORRECT IF WRONG,
(RIGHT ANSWER IS 'THE YES BOX').

SAY:

'So you would put it into the YES box even if you were just trying it out or doing it for fun.'

SAY:

'Now look at the card again and decide whether or not you've *ever* done what it says *yourself*. Then put it in the box where it ought to go.'

5.

I have stolen something from a stall or a barrow.

(blue)

I have stolen something from a stall or a barrow.

Instruction cards
fixed in booklet

Cards passed to
boy for sorting

(pink)

page 4(a)

PASS CARD 4 (JUNK OR SCRAP),
HOLDING IT AND SAYING:

'Please read it out aloud for me.'

THEN SAY:

'Just suppose a boy couldn't remember if he'd done it or not. Where should he put this card?'

CORRECT IF NECESSARY, SAYING:

'He'd put it face down in front of him, because that would mean he was *not sure*. *Face down in front of you if you are not sure*.'

SAY:

'Now look at the card again and decide whether or not you've *ever* done what it says *yourself*. Then put it in the box where it ought to go.'

4.

I have taken junk or scrap without asking for it first.

(blue)

I have taken junk or scrap without asking for it first.

I have stolen something from a shop.

page 6(a)

PASS CARD 6 (SHOP), HOLDING IT
AND SAYING:

'This is the last example. Just once more will you please read it out aloud for
me?'

SAY:

'Let's suppose that a boy acted as a *look-out* for someone who was doing the
stealing. Suppose he was just keeping watch. Where should he put this card?'

CORRECT IF NECESSARY.
(RIGHT ANSWER IS 'THE YES BOX').

SAY:

'So it would count if you were just helping' . . . (Repeat) . . . *It would count
even if you were just helping.*'

SAY:

'Now look at the card again and decide whether or not you've *ever* done what
it says *yourself*. Then put it in the box where it ought to go'.

I have stolen something from a shop.

(blue)

Card passed to
boy for sorting

(pink)

Card fixed
in booklet

page 7(a)

SAY:
'That's the end of the practice. Let's just make sure we've got *all* the rules'.
1 'If it was *just a small thing* you took — something that was *not* important —
what box would you put the card in?' (YES box) (Praise if right).
PAUSE AND SAY:
2 'If it was *a long time ago* that you took something, what box would you put
the card in?' (YES box) (Praise if right).
PAUSE AND SAY:
3 'If you did the thing on the card *just once in your life*, what box would you
put the card in?' (YES box) (Praise if right).
PAUSE AND SAY:
4 'If you did the thing on the card *just for fun* or if you were *just trying it out*,
what box would you put the card in?' (YES box).
PAUSE AND SAY:
5 'If you were just helping someone else to do what was on the card, where
would you put the card?' (YES box).
PAUSE AND SAY:
6 'If you can't remember whether you did it or not, where would you put the
card?' IF THE BOY IS WRONG TELL HIM THAT: 'You put the card face
down in front of you'.
PAUSE AND SAY:
7 'Are you allowed to ask me any questions to help you sort the cards?' IF
THE BOY IS WRONG, EXPLAIN: 'Of course you are — ask as much as you
like. *But if that doesn't help you*, put the card face down in front of you'.
'Please ask me questions every time it's not clear'.

(pink)

46

I have stolen a book or a newspaper or a magazine or a comic.

page 7(b)

SAY:

'Now I'll pass you the rest of the cards, one at a time. Think about each one carefully'.

'And one other thing. Please don't hold anything back. We need to know *all* you've done. *You've got a false name and everything is absolutely private*'.

'Here is the first card'.

PASS CARD 7.
TELL BOY THAT HE DOES NOT HAVE
TO READ OUT ANY MORE CARDS.

SAY:

'Any troubles at all about that one?'

IF NO TROUBLE, LET HIM SORT IT.

ALL HIS DIFFICULTIES SHOULD BE
LINKED TO THE SPECIFIC CARDS
WHICH GAVE RISE TO THEM.

I have stolen a book or a newspaper or a magazine or a comic.   7.

(white)

(pink)

Cards passed to
boy for sorting

Card fixed
in booklet

I have pinched something from my family or relations.

page 8(a)

SAY:

'Tell me each time you want the next card. Then I'll pass it through to you'.

I have pinched something from my family or relations.   8.

(white)

(pink)

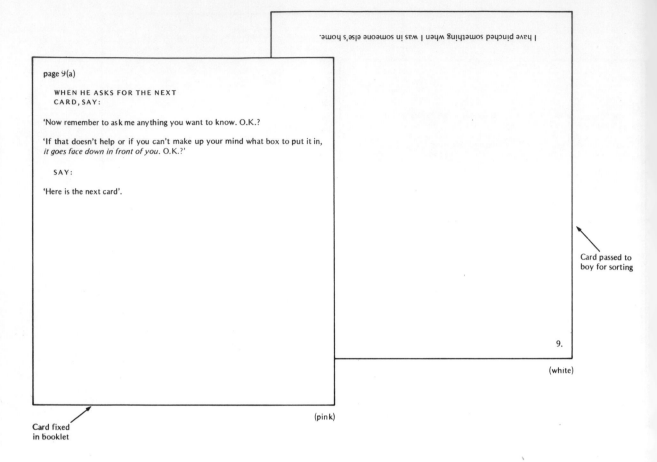

page 9(a)

WHEN HE ASKS FOR THE NEXT
CARD, SAY:

'Now remember to ask me anything you want to know. O.K.?

'If that doesn't help or if you can't make up your mind what box to put it in,
it goes face down in front of you. O.K.?'

SAY:

'Here is the next card'.

I have pinched something when I was in someone else's home.

Card passed to
boy for sorting

9.

(white)

Card fixed
in booklet

(pink)

Next came theft cards 10, 11, 12 as follows:

10 I have got away without paying the fare or the proper fare.

11 I have taken things belonging to children or teenagers.

12 I have got something by threatening others.

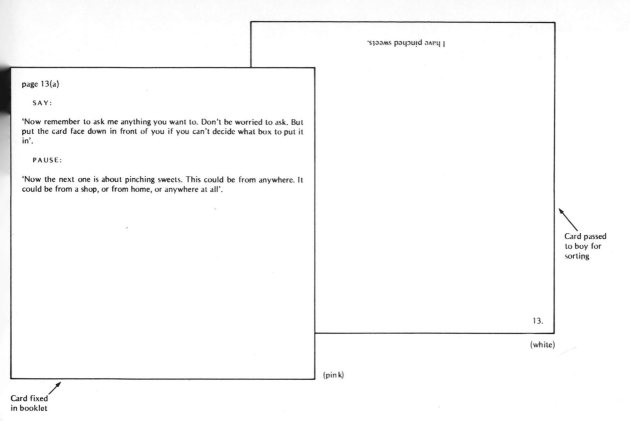

I have pinched sweets.

page 13(a)

SAY:

'Now remember to ask me anything you want to. Don't be worried to ask. But put the card face down in front of you if you can't decide what box to put it in'.

PAUSE:

'Now the next one is about pinching sweets. This could be from anywhere. It could be from a shop, or from home, or anywhere at all'.

Card passed
to boy for
sorting

13.

(white)

(pink)

Card fixed
in booklet

Next came theft cards 14 and 15 as follows:

14 I have stolen cigarettes.

15 I have stolen something from a changing room or a cloakroom.

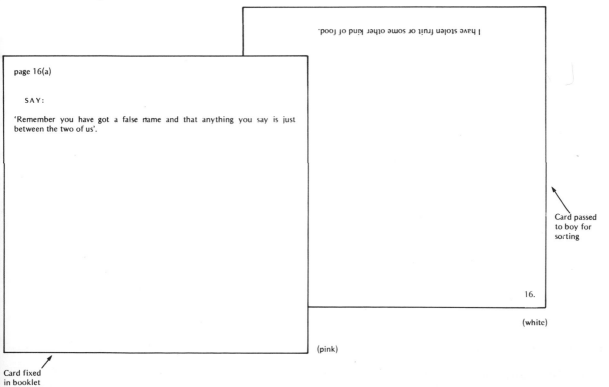

I have stolen fruit or some other kind of food.

page 16(a)

SAY:

'Remember you have got a false name and that anything you say is just between the two of us'.

Card passed
to boy for
sorting

16.

(white)

(pink)

Card fixed
in booklet

Then came card 17:

17 I have got into a place and stolen.

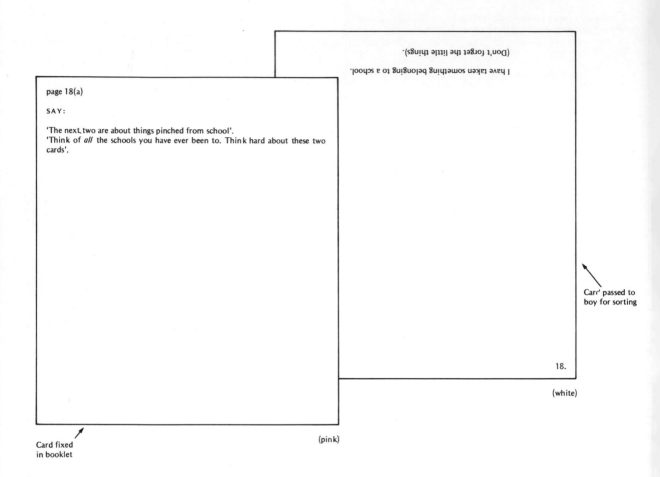

page 18(a)

SAY:

'The next two are about things pinched from school'.
'Think of *all* the schools you have ever been to. Think hard about these two cards'.

Card fixed
in booklet

(pink)

I have taken something belonging to a school.

(Don't forget the little things).

18.

(white)

Card passed to
boy for sorting

Then came cards 19, 20, 21 as follows:

19 I have stolen something from someone at school.

20 I have pinched something when I was on holidays.

21 I have stolen from a park or a playground.

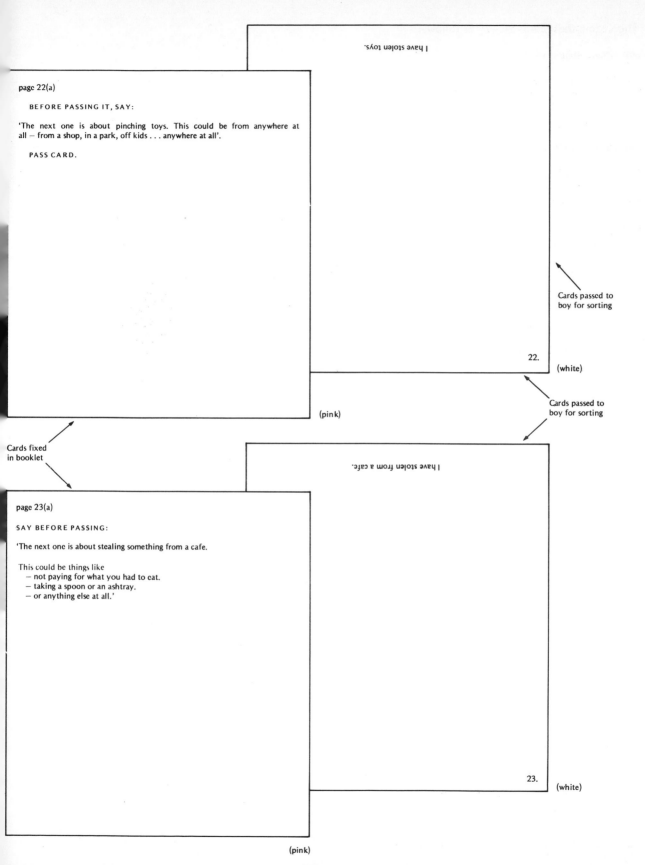

I have stolen toys.

page 22(a)

BEFORE PASSING IT, SAY:

'The next one is about pinching toys. This could be from anywhere at all — from a shop, in a park, off kids . . . anywhere at all'.

PASS CARD.

22.

(white)

Cards passed to
boy for sorting

(pink)

Cards passed to
boy for sorting

Cards fixed
in booklet

I have stolen from a cafe.

page 23(a)

SAY BEFORE PASSING:

'The next one is about stealing something from a cafe.

This could be things like
— not paying for what you had to eat.
— taking a spoon or an ashtray.
— or anything else at all.'

23.

(white)

(pink)

Then came theft cards 24—29 as follows:

24 I have stolen milk.

25 (Read this one very carefully)
I have stolen coal or wood or paraffin or something else
that is used for burning.

26 I have stolen from a building site.

27 I have stolen by stripping something from a building.

28 I have stolen from *a goods yard*
or from *the yard of a factory*
or from *the docks*
or from *a timber yard.*

29 I have stolen a letter or a parcel.

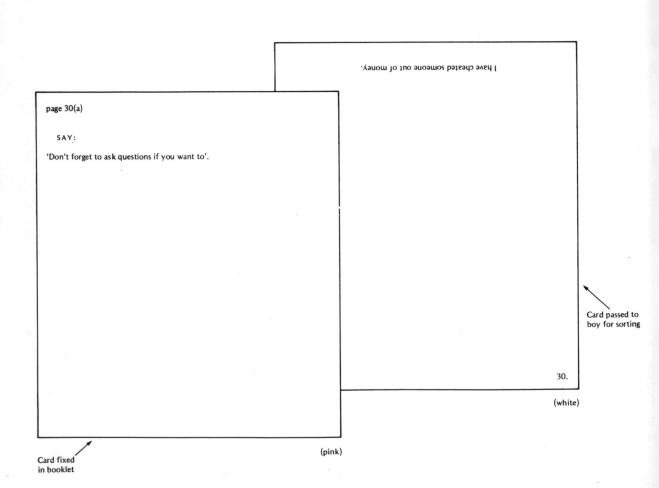

I have cheated someone out of money.

page 30(a)

SAY:

'Don't forget to ask questions if you want to'.

Card passed to
boy for sorting

30.

(white)

(pink)

Card fixed
in booklet

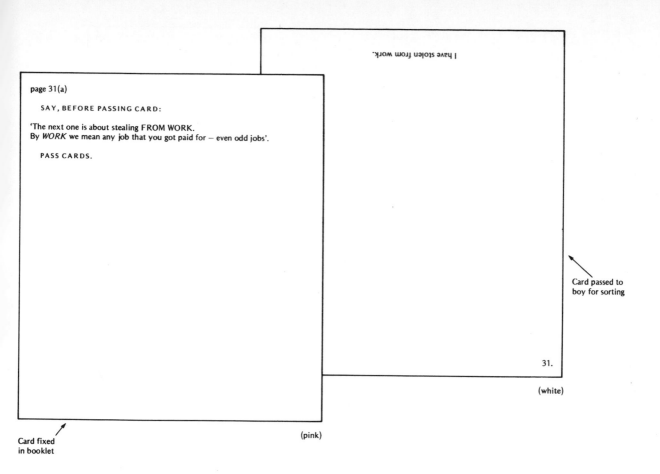

I have stolen from work.

page 31(a)

SAY, BEFORE PASSING CARD:

'The next one is about stealing FROM WORK.
By *WORK* we mean any job that you got paid for — even odd jobs'.

PASS CARDS.

31.

Card passed to
boy for sorting

(white)

Card fixed
in booklet

(pink)

Then came theft cards 32—40 as follows:

32 I have stolen *from someone* at work.

33 I have had something that I knew was stolen.
(Someone else did the stealing and passed it on to me.)

34 I have stolen something out of a garden or out of the
yard of a house.

35 I have stolen a bike or a motor bike.

36 I have stolen something *from* a bike or a motor bike.

37 I have stolen a car or a lorry or a van.

38 I have stolen something *from* a car or a lorry or a
van.

39 I have stolen from a club.

40 I have got into some place without paying the
money to go in.

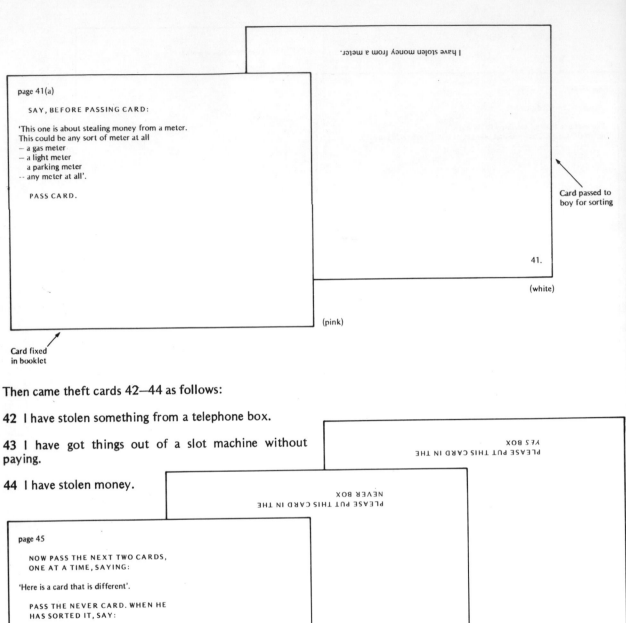

page 41(a)

SAY, BEFORE PASSING CARD:

'This one is about stealing money from a meter.
This could be any sort of meter at all
— a gas meter
— a light meter
  a parking meter
-- any meter at all'.

PASS CARD.

I have stolen money from a meter.

41.

(white)

Card passed to
boy for sorting

(pink)

Card fixed
in booklet

Then came theft cards 42—44 as follows:

42 I have stolen something from a telephone box.

43 I have got things out of a slot machine without paying.

44 I have stolen money.

PLEASE PUT THIS CARD IN THE
YES BOX

PLEASE PUT THIS CARD IN THE
NEVER BOX

page 45

NOW PASS THE NEXT TWO CARDS,
ONE AT A TIME, SAYING:

'Here is a card that is different'.

PASS THE NEVER CARD. WHEN HE
HAS SORTED IT, SAY:

'Here is another'.

PASS THE YES CARD.

BUNDLE UP THE YES AND THE NEVER
CARDS AND PUT EACH TO ONE SIDE.

MAKE SURE ALL THE CARDS HAVE
BEEN TAKEN OUT OF THE BOXES.

NEVER, FIRST SORT (A)

(blue)

(yellow)

Cards passed to
boy for sorting

(pink)

Card fixed
in booklet

SAY:

'Now the next thing I want to do is to help you with any cards you were *NOT SURE* about'.
'Have you got any cards face-down in front of you — ones you were not sure about?'

IF YES, SAY:

'Pick up the first one and look at it. Don't tell me what is on it, but just tell me why you were not sure'.

HELP HIM SOLVE THE PROBLEM AND THEN GET HIM TO SORT IT.
IF YOU CAN'T GET IT RESOLVED AND THERE IS STILL DOUBT, GET HIM TO PUT IT FACE-DOWN AGAIN.
THEN DO THE SAME FOR ALL THE OTHER *NOT SURE* CARDS.
BUNDLE UP THE THREE PILES WITH CORRECT TERMINAL CARDS AND PUT TO ONE SIDE.

Card fixed in booklet

(pink)

THE DIFFERENT SETS OF CARDS

There will be different sets of cards to be bundled together, the numbers of these to be entered in your report form. The following diagram will show you which they are and how they are to be derived.

First sort

YES (FIRST SORT)
(Put on the terminal card, put on band, place to one side)

NEVER (FIRST SORT) (A)
(Put on terminal card, put on band, place to side)

NOT SURE (FIRST SORT)
(To be sorted after YES and NEVER cards have been removed from sorting boxes)

YES (NS RESORTED)
(Put on the terminal card, put on band, place to side)

NEVER (NS RESORTED) (B)
(Put on the terminal card, put on band, place to side)

NOT SURE (RESIDUAL)
(Put on the terminal card, put on band, place to side)

Pick up (A) and (B), enter card numbers in the (B) pack in your notebook, then pass each card of (A) + (B) to boy to RESORT

NEVER—YES
(At end of interview, put a terminal card on this pile, put on band, and put to one side)

NEVER—NEVER
(At end of interview, put a terminal card on this pile, put on band, and put to one side)

NEVER—NOT SURE
(At end of interview, put a terminal card on this pile, put on band, and put to one side)

Fold-out page fixed in booklet

(white)

End of Booklet B.

BOOKLET C dealing with The 'pretending game' and the re-sort of cards originally sorted as NEVER (both are sections of Part One of the eliciting procedure) and with the eliciting of details for cards sorted as YES (= Part Two of the eliciting procedure)

Through this booklet, the pretending game is used to prepare the boy for a re-sort of the cards he originally sorted as NEVER. After the re-sort comes a questioning, probing and challenging procedure designed to elicit from each boy certain details of the cards he sorted as YES (either in the first sorting of cards or in the re-sort of his NEVERS)

C.

'Pretending Game'

Re-sort of NEVER cards

Details of YES cards

page 2

COUNTERING BELIEFS THAT STOP BOYS FROM TELLING

1 SWITCH THE TAPE RECORDER ON
Explain to the boy that you are now using the tape recorder to save you making notes. If he is worried at all, he can wipe the tape at the end of the interview. We hope he won't wipe the tape because we need the information for our work.

2 Come out from behind the board by moving to one side (but leave the board up).

3 Explain to the boy that the first part of the interview is over and that now you want to do something different.

4 (SLOW AND CAREFUL) Tell this boy that you want to know if there is anything at all that might stop boys from telling us *everything* they pinched. Explain that if we know this we can improve the way we ask our questions. Boys like him are the only ones who can help us.
(Elaborate if necessary.)

(pink)

56

I have stolen a £5 note

page 3

    SAY: (CARD A: £5 note)
'So I want to find out if there is anything that might stop boys from telling us *everything* they have done.'
'So let's just *pretend* that you had pinched a few things. Let's just *pretend* that you had done *this* one. I'm not saying you *have* done it, I just want you to pretend you've done it'. SHOW CARD AND WAIT TILL HE READS IT.
    SAY: 'Just *pretend* that you had done *this* or that. Would you have told me about it? I mean would you have put it into the YES or the NEVER box?' ASK P or Q or R.

    IF YES, ASK: 'Why would you have told me?'
IF HE GIVES *OUR* REASONS FOR ADMITTING: (*a*) tell him he is quite right; *and*, (*b*) repeat his own reasons back to him *with all necessary elaborations*.

    IF NO, OR *NOT SURE*: 'Why not?' Why wouldn't you tell me?' WHATEVER HE SAYS: (*a*) *Meet his reasons with the prescribed counter-arguments*; and (*b*) *Make a big thing of this and if at all necessary have a discussion about it with the boy*. In this discussion, let the boy see that you are completely sincere and that you are friendly and someone he can trust.

    IF HE OFFERS NO REASONS EITHER WAY, GIVE HIM THE following counter-arguments:
'Remember that nothing goes further than this room. It's just between the two of us.'
'Remember you've got a false name and anything you say is absolutely private.'

    NOW DEAL WITH CARD B

(Card A)   (blue)

(pink)

Card A passed to boy

Card fixed in booklet

I have stolen a bike or a motor-bike

page 4

    (CARD B: Stole bike or motor bike)
    SAY: 'Now let's do the same with *this* card'.
    PASS IT. WHEN HE READS IT SAY:
'Let's just *pretend* you really did that. I'm not saying you *have* done it, I just want you to pretend you've done it. Would you have told me about it? I mean would you have put it into the YES box or the NEVER box?'
    NOW DO P or Q or R AS APPROPRIATE

    IF YES, ASK:
'Why would you have told me?'
    IF HE GIVES *OUR* REASONS FOR ADMITTING: (*a*) Tell him he is quite right *and* (*b*) repeat his own reasons back to him *with all necessary elaborations*.

    IF NO, ASK:
'Why not? Why wouldn't you tell me?'
    WHATEVER HE SAYS: (*a*) *meet his reasons with the prescribed counter-arguments;* and (*b*) *make a big thing of this and if at all necessary have a discussion about it with the boy*. In this discussion, let the boy see that you are completely sincere and that you are friendly and someone he can trust.

    IF HE OFFERS NO REASON EITHER WAY, SAY:
'Remember that everything we say is private. It won't go further than this room. You've got a false name and you don't have to hold anything back.'

(Card B)   (blue)

(pink)

Card B passed to boy

AFTER DEALING WITH CARDS A AND B, SAY:

'Now is there anything at all that still makes you want to hold things back? Tell me so I can clear it up'.

IF NO REPLY, ASK:

'Is there anything which might make it difficult for you to tell me about things?'

USE COUNTER-ARGUMENTS TO MEET HIS REASONS.
Make it a discussion. Get his confidence.

IF IN THE DISCUSSION SO FAR, HE HAS NOT RAISED the following issues, raise them yourself and give the boy the answers. The issues are: (*a*) will anyone else find out?, and, (*b*) is the boy embarrassed at talking about these things?

ASK THE BOY:

'Did you feel shy or embarrassed about anything I asked you? The reason I ask is that some boys feel a bit embarrassed or shy when they tell us about these things. Do you feel that way at all?'

PROBE AS NECESSARY

OVER

(pink)

RE-SORTING THE NEVERs

NEXT SAY:

'Now I want to go through the cards you put into the NEVER box once more I'll tell you why. It's because you might have forgotten something the first time you went through (PAUSE) or perhaps you didn't want to tell me the first time. Boys like you are the *only* ones who can help us. That's why we asked you to come.'
SAY:
'Do you mind if I collect your NEVERs from the heap over there and pass them through to you one at a time?'
GET THE NEVERs, AND ANY NOT SURE CARDS.
THEN SAY:
'So I'll pass them to you one at a time and I want you to sort them SLOWLY AND CAREFULLY. Think HARD and CAREFULLY about each one. Then put it in the YES box or the NEVER box.'
PAUSE AND SAY:
'And remember it's absolutely private. I don't know you . . . You don't know me . . . And I don't suppose you'll ever see me again. And it's private.' GO BACK BEHIND THE BOARD. START WITH
THE HIGH-NUMBERED CARDS AND WORK BACK. SAY:
'Here's the first one. Don't rush it . . . take your time with it . . .' SAY:
'Here's the next one . . . Ask me about any you have trouble with. Ask me if you need help.'
AFTER HE SORTS IT, BUT JUST BEFORE YOU PASS THE NEXT ONE, SAY: 'By the way, where would you put a card if you were just *helping* someone to do a bit of pinching?' (= YES box).
TURN OFF THE TAPE RECORDER

OVER

(yellow)

---

1 KEEP PASSING THE CARDS SLOWLY. IF HE STARTS to speed it up, say one or another of the following:
'Take your time . . . Don't rush it . . . Think carefully.'

---

2 THROUGHOUT, ENCOURAGE THE BOY TO ASK QUESTIONS about any cards which he finds difficult

---

3 AFTER A THIRD OF THE CARDS HAVE BEEN RE-SORTED, remind the boy:

'Please don't hold anything back. Everything you say is absolutely private.'

DO THIS AGAIN AFTER TWO THIRDS OF THE CARDS have been re-sorted.

'Remember that all this is private. It's just between the two of us. So please don't hold anything back.'

---

4 THEN GET BOY TO PUT ALL THE CARDS FROM THE NEVER box face-down in front of him in one pile and all the cards from the YES box face-down in another pile.

PUT TERMINAL CARDS ON THESE (+ BAND) AND PUT TO SIDE

OVER

(yellow)

THE YES CARDS

A *PREPARING FOR THE 'YES' CARDS*

TAKE DOWN THE SCREEN. LET THE BOY SETTLE. OFFER HIM A DRINK, THEN GUM OR CIGARETTES

TURN THE TAPE RECORDER ON AGAIN

SAY:

'Now I want to ask you a few questions about the cards you put in the YES box. Is that alright?'

COLLECT THEM. WHILE BOY DRINKS, enter numbers of the NEVER-YES cards on back page of report form.

THEN SAY:

'Now do you mind my asking you some questions about these cards?'

IF YES, FIND OUT *WHY* AND REASSURE IN same way as before. *This is most important.*

OVER

(purple)

page 9

B ESTABLISH HOW SERIOUS IT WAS

1 SAY:

'So the next thing I want to do is to ask you about some of the cards you sorted as YES.'

PREPARE TO SORT THE YES CARDS INTO THREE GROUPS.

TAKE CARD 1 (THINGS FOUND) FROM HIS ORIGINAL YES PACK AND SAY:

'Let's take this one for a start.'

PASS IT TO BOY, PAUSE, THEN SAY:

'What is the biggest thing you have ever found and kept? I mean the biggest thing or the most valuable thing? Think carefully.'

ENTER HIS REPLY ON CARD

(purple)

---

page 10

2 Now tell boy the rest are done in the same way.

- -

3 But first ask him if he has any worries at all about these questions. *This is important.* Probe for any worries. Reassure him. Also tell him that if he wants to do so later on, he can tear up what you have written down. If he has not mentioned embarrassment raise it yourself and explain why he should not be embarrassed. Reassure him, even if he says he is not embarrassed. *Stress* to him that he will have to think hard when he tells us about the biggest thing.

- -

4 Deal with the NEVER-YES cards first, (if any). Now for the first of the NEVER-YES cards ask the boy what was the biggest thing/biggest amount he ever took. Probe his reply with the following questions/instructions:
4a 'Were you embarrassed about telling me that?'
    Reassure.
4b 'When you answered . . . were you thinking of things you have only just done as well?'
IF NO, correct him. IF YES, tell him that he is right and repeat the rule. (On all these cards, I want you to think about the biggest thing ever — whether it was a long time ago or very recently.)
Enter item on the front of the card.

- -

5 For the second NEVER–YES, ask boy what was the biggest thing he took. Follow this with: *'Remember* on all these cards it counts even if you were only just helping.'
Enter the item on the front of the card.

- -

6 After the third card, say: 'By "biggest thing" I mean the thing which costs the most money or is the most valuable'.

- -

7 Now ask about the rest of the NEVER–YES cards and about the original YES cards. For each get the most valuable thing or largest amount of this kind ever taken.

---

page 10a

Systematically probe these replies along the lines indicated below.
Don't do these on every card, but use them to keep the boy alert and trying.
We suggest at least one probe on every other card.
Enter most valuable thing on front of card.

GENERAL INSTRUCTIONS
1 Encourage him to take time enough to think carefully.
2 Watch for embarrassment and reassure.
3 Make sure he means the most valuable things pinched *at one time.*

PROBES
1 Was there something a bit more valuable than that?
2 Are you thinking about the very recent things as well?

59

C *ESTABLISHING HOW OFTEN AND WHEN FOR SERIOUS ACTS*

1 NOW DEAL WITH THE FIRST OF THE CARDS IN THE *SERIOUS* GROUP. READ IT OUT. NOW ASK:

'How many times *altogether*, have you ever done this sort of thing?'
'Just before you answer me, remember that I'm asking about everything of this sort that you've ever done – the little things as well as the big things – about everything.'
'So how many times altogether have you ever done this sort of thing?'
    WHEN HE REPLIES, ASK HIM:
'Are you counting all the *little things* as well?'
    IF NO, correct him.
    IF YES, agree that this is what you want for all questions. THEN ASK:
'And were you counting anything you did very recently, too?'
    IF NO, correct him.
    IF YES, agree that this is what you want for all questions. THEN ASK:
'And were you counting any times where you were *just helping*?'
    IF NO, correct him.
    IF YES, agree that this is what you want for all questions. THEN SAY:
'Think about it again for me and tell me how many times *altogether* you have *ever* done this sort of thing'.
'I'll read it out again.'
    READ OUT CARD AGAIN, THEN ASK:
'Now how many times *altogether* have you *ever* done this sort of thing?'
    ENTER NUMBER OF TIMES ON FRONT OF CARD
    (e.g. 7x)

---

2 IF MORE THAN ONCE, REMIND BOY OF WHAT IS ON THE CARD AND THEN ASK:
'How long ago was *the very last time* you did this sort of thing?'
    BEFORE ENTERING REPLY ON FRONT OF CARD, ASK:
'Are you thinking about the *little things* as well?'
    IF NO, correct him.
    IF YES, agree that this is what you want for all questions. THEN ASK:
'Did you think *very carefully*, when you said . . . or was it only a rough idea?'
    If 'thought carefully' agree and *stress* importance of this.
    If 'rough idea only' correct him and *stress* importance of thinking hard.
    ENTER REPLY
– –
THEN SAY:
'And now I want to ask you *exactly* how old you were *the very first time* you did anything of this sort – the very first time. Exactly how old were you the very first time you did it?
    READ OUT CARD
    BEFORE ENTERING REPLY ON FRONT OF CARD ASK:
'Were you thinking of all the *little things* too?'
    IF NO, correct him.
    IF YES, agree that this is what you want for all questions. ENTER REPLY
– –
IF *ONLY ONCE*, ASK:
'Exactly how long ago was it that you did this?'
    WHEN HE REPLIES, SAY:
'Are you sure that's how long ago it was?'
    ENTER REPLY ON FRONT OF CARD

> If first card is 'once only', go back to the rule-teaching on p. 12 with the *second* card

4 Now ask about the rest of the NEVER–YES cards and the original YES cards.
For each get:
a How many times altogether he has done that sort of thing.
b How long ago was the very last time.
c How old he was the very first time.

Systematically probe these replies along the lines indicated on the right. ———
Don't do these on every card, but use them to keep the boy alert and trying. We suggest at least one probe in every two cards. Enter details on the front of cards.

– – – – – – – – – – – – – – – – – – – –

5 Use the challenges shown opposite *whenever* you think the boy is getting a bit careless.

IN THE COURSE OF THIS WORK ON SERIOUS CARDS, *BREAK* THE BOY's BOREDOM AS SOON AS YOU SUSPECT IT IS PRESENT. DO THIS BY:
(a) Getting/letting the boy tell you about how he did some theft.
(b) Give him a drink/sandwiches/smoke.

PROBES
(a) Ask the boy to tell you how he worked out that the number was *X*. Tell him the number is very important and that you want it as close as he can get it.
(b) Ask him how he worked out how long ago the first/last occasion was and try to get him to think again about it.

CHALLENGES
TO BE USED WHENEVER THE INTERVIEWER THINKS THE BOY IS BECOMING CARELESS IN ANY WAY.
(a) 'Do you mean *exactly* that many/that long ago/or that age?'
(b) 'How did you manage to work it out so quickly?'
(c) 'That is the same number/time ago/that age you gave for another card. How come it is just the same?'

APPENDIX 1.2

The forty-four theft cards used in the final form of the eliciting procedure

1 I have kept something I have found.

2 I have stolen something just for fun.

3 I have taken something just for a dare.

4 I have taken junk or scrap without asking for it first.

5 I have stolen something from a stall or a barrow.

6 I have stolen something from a shop.

7 I have stolen a book or a newspaper or a magazine or a comic.

8 I have pinched something from my family or relations.

9 I have pinched something when I was in someone else's home.

10 I have got away without paying the fare or the proper fare.

11 I have taken things belonging to children or teenagers.

12 I have got something by threatening others.

13 I have pinched sweets.

14 I have stolen cigarettes.

15 I have stolen something from a changing room or a cloakroom.

16 I have stolen fruit or some other kind of food.

17 I have got into a place and stolen.

18 I have stolen something belonging to a school.

19 I have stolen something from someone at school.

20 I have pinched something when I was on holiday.

21 I have stolen from a park or a playground.

22 I have stolen toys.

23 I have stolen from a cafe.

24 I have stolen milk.

25 I have stolen coal or wood or paraffin or something else that is used for burning.

26 I have stolen from a building site.

27 I have stolen by stripping something from a building.

28 I have stolen from a goods yard, or from the yard of a factory, or from the docks, or from a timber-yard.

29 I have stolen a letter or a parcel.

30 I have cheated someone out of money.

31 I have stolen from work.

32 I have stolen from someone at work.

33 I have had something that I knew was stolen.

34 I have stolen something out of a garden or out of the yard of a house.

35 I have stolen a bike or a motor bike.

36 I have stolen something *from* a bike or a motor bike.

37 I have stolen a car or a lorry or a van.

38 I have stolen something *from* a car or a lorry or a van.

39 I have stolen from a club.

40 I have got into some place without paying the money to go in.

41 I have stolen money from a meter.

42 I have stolen something from a telephone box.

43 I have got things out of a slot machine without paying.

44 I have stolen money.

8 APPENDIX 1.3

The counter-arguments used in the pretending game

I If a boy is ashamed of his act
   SAY:
1 'I'm not judging anyone. I'm just finding out.'
2 'You don't know me . . . I don't know you . . . and I don't suppose we'll ever meet again.'

II You might tell someone
   SAY:
1. 'Do you really think this is so?'
   WHATEVER HE REPLIES, TELL HIM:
2 *'If we did a thing like that, boys would not help us any more . . . we'd be finished.'*

If we talked, other boys in your area would get to know and we'd be finished.'
3 'Anyhow there were four boys who came in together. I don't know their names. Even if I did, I don't know which one you were.'

IF HE HAS DOUBTS STILL, SAY:
4 'I wouldn't do a thing like that. Anyhow, it would only be my word against yours . . . There are no witnesses, are there? . . . And you could deny the whole thing.'
'I'll tell you something else: Nobody can tell from what you said *where* you pinched from or how you got it. So they couldn't do a thing about it.

IIIa They really know my name
SAY:
'I don't know your name. There were four boys came this evening. Even if I knew any names, I wouldn't know which one you were. You've got a false name. I don't know who you are.'

b The lady knows my name
SAY:
'Yes, but she didn't tell the receptionist who was who, did she? And nobody's told me.'
'There will be no leak. You've got my word for that. It's private.'

IV It's going down in a book
Explain that there are no real names in this sort of book. Explain that it is all figures and show the boy a page of such a book as an example.
SAY ALSO:
'You could just deny it and you could sue me. Anyway, nobody is allowed to give names in this sort of book. That's one of the rules. The people who publish these books don't allow it because they know they'd be sued.'

V He does not believe it is for a book
Show him the cover of a criminological book. Show him pages of *tables*.

VI It's on that tape
SAY:
'Yes, but your name is not on it . . . it's just . . . (e.g. Ringo).'
SAY ALSO:
'If you really want me to, I'll wipe it off the tape at the end. I hope you won't ask me to do that, but I will if you really want me to. That's a promise.'

VII Some general arguments
1 'Nobody knows who you got it from, do they? So they couldn't do anything about it, could they?'
2 'Nobody will find out — it's just between the two of us.'

9 APPENDIX 1.4

Some of the items (in the form of questions) in the pool of possible predictors of stealing
This list includes some of the questions asked as a basis for identifying boys as qualifying or not in relation to

certain of the hypotheses. This is because it is conceivable that these questions might be usable for matching purposes in dealing with *other* hypotheses — though in the event they were ruled out on the grounds of instability in relation to the hypotheses concerned.

Was the boy illiterate, as judged by the interviewer? (Rated as Yes, Possibly, No.)

How much stealing is going on in the area in which the boy lives? (Rated as higher-theft area or lower-theft area, according to the average for the area based on theft scores for area boys interviewed.)

What is the ethnic grouping of the boy? (West Indian, African, Other Negro or coloured, Pakistani, Greek or Greek Cypriot, United Kingdom White (assumed), other White (assumed), Others.)

Does the boy like to do things 'in bits and pieces' or 'all at once'?

Has the boy got a religion? (Yes/No.)
If so, what is his religion? (C. of E./Methodist/ Presbyterian/Protestant/Roman Catholic/Catholic (only) /Christian/Greek Orthodox/Jew/Other/none/no information.)

How often does the boy go to church? (Never/hardly ever/once a month/each week/no information.)

Is the boy still at school full-time? (Yes/No.)
If he has left school, at what age did he leave? (14—15/16—17/age not given.)

What type of school did he last attend? (Secondary modern/technical college/grammar/public school/comprehensive school/approved school/special school/other/ no information.) *If comprehensive*, what sector was he in? (Secondary modern/technical college/grammar/other/ no information.)

Did the boy 'pass' the 11-plus 'examination'? (Yes/no/ didn't take it/no information/not applicable.)

What is the economic level of the district in which the boy lives (as indicated by the juror index)? (Top decile group economically/next decile group down/ . . . /bottom decile group.)

What is the occupational level of the boy's father? (Professional, semi-professional or higher executive/ lower professional/highly skilled/skilled/moderately skilled/semi-skilled/unskilled/no information.)

How many boys were there in his last class at school? (Below 10/11—15/15—20/ . . ./ 41—45/46 or over/no information.)

Did he like or dislike his school work? (Disliked it very much/disliked it/liked it/liked it very much.)

How did he get on with his teachers at school? (Well/average/not very well/badly.)

Was he ever a prefect or head boy or 'anything like that' at school? (Yes/no.)

Where did he usually come in his class? (In first quarter/second/third/in fourth quarter/no information.)

Did he ever play truant from school? (Yes/no.)
If 'Yes', how often? (Once a week/once a month/hardly ever/not at all.)

Has he got a girl friend? (Yes/no.)

How often does he go out with girls? (Each week/once a month/less than that.)

How many rooms are there in the boy's house? (1/2/ . . . /9 or more/no information.)

Has he ever done any of the following? (Each answered as 'Yes' or 'No'). Been a cub or scout/played a sport/won a prize/belonged to a library/gone to a youth club/passed an examination/did some welfare work/been baptised/been to Communion/taken a trip out of England/had a fist fight/had a job during school holidays/played in the street a lot/delivered newspapers/been in a team for sports/had a talk with someone about 'what you want to do in life'.

Does he ever try to get his own back on boys? (Yes/no.)
If 'Yes', how often? (Often/now and then/hardly ever/never.)

How many times has his family moved house? (Never/once/twice/three times/four or more/no information.)

Was the boy born in the United Kingdom or not? (United Kingdom/not United Kingdom.)

What was the birth order of the boy in his family? (First/intermediate/last/no information.)

What is the social class of the boy according to the Registrar General's classification of his father's occupation? (Professional/semi-professional/skilled, non-manual/skilled manual/semi-skilled/unskilled.)

Does the boy earn money by working? (Yes/no/no information.)

How much money per week does the boy have for his own pocket? (Graded by amount.)

Does he ever do any saving up? (Yes/No.)

Does he ever borrow in order to pay for the things he wants? (Yes/no.)

Does he ever want things he can't afford? (Yes/no.)

Certain details about the boy's mother or mother substitute. (Real mother alive/real mother dead/real mother at home/real mother absent/woman at home his real mother/woman at home is not real mother.)

Certain details about the boy's father or father substitute. (Real father is alive/real father dead/real father at home/real father absent/man at home is real father/man at home is not real father.)

Number of people in the boy's household? (1/2 . . . /8 or more/no information.)

Number of people per room in the boy's house (i.e. crowdedness index)? (0.5 or less/ . . . /2.0 or more/no information.)

Number of living siblings? (None/1/ . . . /9 or more/no information.)

Other people living at home (apart from parents and siblings)? (Grandparents/other relatives/lodgers/no one else/no information.)

Occupational status of father? (Full-time/part-time/self-employed/shift-work/two or more jobs/out of work/retired/not applicable/no information.)

Occupational status of mother? (Full-time/part-time/self-employed/shift-work/housewife/not applicable/two or more jobs/no information.)

Has his mother ever gone out to work? (Yes/no/don't know/not applicable/no information.)

When he was smaller, were there times when he got home before his mother got back from work? (Yes/no/don't know/no information.)

If 'Yes', how often did this happen? (All the time/often/now and then/hardly ever/no information.)

The boy's own occupational status? (Still at school/full-time/part-time job/on shift-work/out of work/no information.)

If the boy is at work, what is his occupational level (Belson index)? (1/2 . . . /7/unclassifiable/no information.)

If the boy is at work, what is his job level according to the Registrar General's classification? (I,II/III non-manual/III manual/IV/V/unclassifiable/no jobs given.)

If the boy has left school, has he ever been out of work? (Yes/no/no information.)

Has he got a room all to himself at home? (Yes/no.)

How often are there rows in his family? (Every day/most days/once a week/once a month/hardly ever/never/no information.)

Which of the following ever tried to teach him about not pinching: (parents, teachers, Church?) (All three/two/one/none of them.)

From how many of the above three sources (i.e. home, school, Church) did he get 'a lot of teaching about not pinching'? (All three/two/one/none of them.)

How pervasive was the control which his parents exercised over him when he was smaller? (Various ratings of pervasiveness.)

When he was smaller did his parents punish him if he misbehaved? (Yes/no/no information.)

How much punishment did his parents give him when he was smaller? (A lot/a fair bit/ a little/none/no information on how much.)

What is the boy's age? (12/13/14/15/16/17/no information.)

To what extent has the boy got interests (other than thieving)? (Various indices of extent of his interests.)

Does the boy come from a high or a low theft area (various indices of theft level in boy's district)?

What is the 'ponderal' index for the boy? (Various indices.)

Has the boy ever been caught by the police for stealing? (Yes/no.)

What was the boy's score for strength of grip? (Various strength ratings based upon dynamometer score.)

What is the height of the boy? (As measured at Centre.)

What is the boy's weight? (As measured at Centre.)

10 APPENDIX 1.5

Basic sampling details: numerical distributions for enumeration and causal surveys

Sampling areas in ascending order of juror index			Juror index for ward	No. of polling districts selected	Total *electorate* of polling districts selected	No. of boys enumerated in each age-group				
London borough*	Constituency	Ward				13	14	15	16	Total 13–16
Lewisham	Lewisham S.	Bellingham	0.10	1	1,982	20	25	25	34	104
Tower Hamlets	Poplar	Bromley	0.24	1	1,689	15	20	22	17	74
Brent	Willesden W.	St Raphael's Stonebridge	0.36	2	4,681	39	33	37	43	152
Enfield	Enfield E.	Ordnance	0.49	1	2,107	12	20	12	18	62
Greenwich	Greenwich	Kidbrooke	0.64	2	3,038	25	22	39	33	119
Barking	Barking	Manor	0.74	1	1,589	17	18	15	20	70
Greenwich	Greenwich	Trafalgar	0.77	2	2,395	16	19	23	25	83
Wandsworth	Battersea N.	Queenstown	0.88	1	1,796	36	33	33	52	154
Greenwich	Woolwich E.	St Margaret's	0.96	2	3,452	27	24	28	26	105
Southwark	Camberwell– Peckham	Brunswick	1.08	2	2,930	24	25	32	26	107
Wandsworth	Wandsworth C.	Graveney	1.21	1	3,862	28	25	31	30	114
Greenwich	Woolwich W.	Coldharbour	1.25	1	3,016	36	53	45	61	195
Southwark	Bermondsey	Dockyard	1.36	1	1,944	19	22	20	16	77
Tower Hamlets	Stepney	Limehouse Shadwell	1.51	2	3,206	34	30	22	20	106
Haringay	Tottenham	S. Tottenham High Cross Tottenham C.	1.56	1	2,144	21	13	13	22	69
Lambeth	Lambeth Vauxhall	Bishop's	1.69	2	3,859	26	22	31	21	100
Brent	Wembley N.	Kingsbury Queensbury	1.74	1	3,247	20	15	20	23	78

Universe of boys in each age-group (after elimination of certain types)†					Total in *drawn* primary‡ sample (data from enumerator)					Substitutes *drawn*	Total in interviewed sample (including substitutes)					Success rate (%)
13	14	15	16	Total 13–16	13	14	15	16	Total		12/13	14	15	16/17	Total	
16	24	24	30	94	10	10	10	10	40	0	9	8	9	7	33	82.5
12	18	20	15	65	10	10	10	10	40	2	9	10	9	6	34	81.0
36	30	33	39	138	10	10	10	10	40	1	10	9	9	10	38	92.7
11	19	12	17	59	10	10	10	10	40	1	10	9	8	9	36	87.8
21	21	37	26	105	10	10	10	10	40	1	9	7	8	4	28	68.3
16	18	15	15	64	10	10	10	10	40	0	9	10	10	8	37	92.5
14	16	21	23	74	10	10	10	10	40	0	9	8	7	7	31	77.5
30	29	26	48	133	10	10	10	10	40	3	10	11	8	8	37	86.0
24	21	27	22	94	10	10	10	10	40	1	10	10	9	9	38	92.7
20	24	30	21	95	10	10	10	10	40	0	10	10	9	10	39	97.5
25	23	27	25	100	10	10	10	10	40	4	10	10	9	9	38	86.4
32	48	40	57	177	10	10	10	10	40	1	10	10	7	9	36	87.8
19	20	20	14	73	10	10	10	10	40	1	9	10	10	10	39	95.1
30	27	19	17	93	10	10	10	10	40	3	9	9	8	9	35	81.4
20	11	12	18	61	10	10	10	10	40	1	7	10	9	8	34	82.9
21	22	30	20	93	10	10	10	10	40	1	9	10	9	10	38	92.7
19	15	19	21	74	10	10	10	10	40	0	10	9	8	10	37	92.5

Sampling areas in ascending order of juror index			Juror index for ward	No. of polling districts selected	Total *electorate* polling districts selected	No. of boys enumerated in each age-group				
London borough*	Constituency	Ward				13	14	15	16	Total 13–16
Camden	Holborn—St Pancras	Holborn	1.90	1	2,443	14	10	19	17	60
Southwark	Camberwell—Dulwich	Waverley	2.04	2	3,346	16	27	29	27	99
Camden	Holborn—St Pancras St Pancras N.	St Pancras (pt) St Pancras (pt)	2.21	1	3,200	22	28	23	19	92
Kensington & Chelsea	Chelsea	South Stanley	2.37	1	3,328	15	23	27	25	90
Hackney	Hackney C.	Downs	2.51	1	2,545	17	21	22	26	86
Waltham Forest	Leyton	Leyton (E)	2.58	2	5,155	25	34	20	30	109
Waltham Forest	Walthamstow W.	St James St	2.69	1	2,599	21	19	15	23	78
Newham	Eastham S.	Greatfield	2.87	2	4,616	29	29	26	22	106
Hammersmith	Hammersmith N. Barons Court	Addison (pt) Addison (pt)	3.04	1	2,910	15	17	14	18	64
Ealing	Acton	Acton	3.20	2	3,223	28	22	24	44	118
Newham	West Ham N.	Stratford	3.40	2	2,457	19	21	14	22	76
Hackney	Shoreditch & Finsbury	Moorfields	3.73	3	2,633	17	20	25	19	81
Croydon	Croydon N. W.	Whitehorse Manor	4.20	2	4,120	31	31	24	33	119
Westminster	Paddington N.	Maida Vale	4.42	1	2,826	17	20	14	19	70
Islington	Islington N.	Highview-Hillrise-Parkway	4.57	1	3,952	27	30	31	21	109
Westminster	St Marylebone	Cavendish	5.42	1	5,688	12	12	12	11	47
Lambeth	Wandsworth—Streatham	Streatham Wells St Leonards Streatham South	5.58	1	1,814	18	11	18	24	71
Bromley	Bromley	Bromley Common	7.08	1	3,258	22	18	16	22	78
Southwark	Camberwell—Dulwich	The College	7.59	1	4,567	70	71	78	57	276
Brent	Willesden E.	Cricklewood	8.40	1	2,426	13	22	11	15	61
Barnet	Finchley	West	10.37	1	2,295	17	25	31	32	105
Haringay	Wood Green	Alexandra-Bowes	11.24	2	1,850	17	15	19	13	64
Richmond	Richmond	Kew	17.07	2	2,779	13	7	14	16	50
		Totals				910	952	974	1,042	3,878

*Greater London Council naming system used
†See p. 18.
‡Exclusive of substitutes
**One boy drawn from extension of area

Universe of boys in each age-group (after elimination of certain types)†					Total in *drawn* primary‡ sample (data from enumerator)					Substitutes *drawn*	Total in interviewed sample (including substitutes)					Success rate (%)
13	14	15	16	Total 13–16	13	14	15	16	Total		12/13	14	15	16/17	Total	
14	10	18	16	58	10	10	10	10	40	1	9	10	10	5	34	82.9
12	21	26	25	84	10	10	10	10	40	1	10	10	10	8	38	92.7
20	22	16	18	76	10	10	10	10	40	3	11	9	6	10	36	83.7
13	20	24	25	82	10	10	10	10	40	4	10	8	9	9	36	81.8
16	18	20	25	79	10	10	10	10	40	1	10	10	8	8	36	87.8
23	32	18	27	100	10	10	10	10	40	1	9	10	8	9	36	87.8
19	18	12	19	68	10	10	10	10	40	1	10	10	8	8	36	87.8
29	27	26	20	102	10	10	10	10	40	0	8	10	8	7	33	82.5
12	16	12	16	56	10	10	10	10	40	1	9	10	9	10	38	92.7
22	16	20	41	99	10	10	10	10	40	1	10	9	9	8	36	87.8
16	21	13	20	70	10	10	10	10	40	1	10	9	9	9	37	90.2
15	19	23	17	74	10	10	10	10	40	3	10	9	5	7	31	72.1
26	30	22	29	107	10	10	10	10	40	0	10	9	6	8	33	82.5
16	19	13	19	67	10	10	10	10	40	0	10	9	7	9	35	87.5
23	26	26	19	94	10	10	10	10	40	4	9	9	10	9	37	84.1
12	10	12	11	45	10	10	10	10	40	2	6	8	10	6	30	71.4
16	11	15	19	61	10	10	10	10	40	3	11	7	6	7	31	72.1
20	17	16	19	72	10	10	10	10	40	1	8	10	8	10	36	87.8
62	66	70	48	246	10	10	10	10	40	0	9	10	10	7	36	90.0
11	19	10	14	58	10	10	10	10	40	2	10	9	10	9	38	90.5
15	22	27	29	93	10	10	10	10	40	1	10	10	10	9	39	95.1
15	14	17	10	56	10	10	10	10	40	2	8	11	10	8	37	88.1
11	9	14	15	49	10	10**	10	10	40	2	10	8	10	10	38	90.5
804	869	882	929	3,484	400	400	400	400	1,600	55	375	374	342	334	1,425	86.1

Note: All figures to the left of the arrow (at top of page) relate to age at time of enumeration survey. Figures to the right of this arrow relate to age at time of interview. The average length of time between enumeration survey and interview is three months. This fact has been taken fully into consideration in the sections of the report which are concerned with success rate, sample bias, estimating the 'theft level' of uninterviewed boys.

REFERENCES TO PUBLICATIONS

1 W. A. Belson and R. Hood. *The research potential of the case records of Approved School boys.* Survey Research Centre, 1967.

2 W. A. Belson and M. Beeson. *Identifying difficulties and facilitating factors in getting information from boys about their stealing and about associated matters: an exploratory study.* Survey Research Centre, 1968.

3 W. A. Belson and G. L. Millerson. *The development of hypotheses about causal factors in the aetiology of juvenile stealing.* Survey Research Centre (unpublished), 1967.

4 W. A. Belson. *The development of strategies for testing causal hypotheses relating to stealing.* Survey Research Centre (unpublished), 1966.

5 W. A. Belson, G. L. Millerson and P. J. Didcott. *The development of a procedure for eliciting information from boys about their stealing.* Survey Research Centre, 1968.

6 See 5 above.

7 See 5 above.

8 W. A. Belson. Causal Factors in the development of stealing by London boys: Methods of research. Survey Research Centre, 1969.

9 H. E. Barnes, and N. K. Teeters, (1959): *New Horizons in Criminology*; Prentice-Hall, New Jersey.
E. H. Johnson, (1964): *Crime, Correction and Society*; Dorsey Press, Illinois.
H. Jones, (1965): *Crime and the Penal System*; University Tutorial Press, London.
R. R. Korn, and L. W. McCorkle, (1961): *Crime and Penology*; Holt, Rinehart and Winston, New York.
M. H. Neumeyer, (1961): *Juvenile Delinquency in Modern Society*; Van Nostrand Co., Inc., New York.
S. M. Robinson, (1960): *Juvenile Delinquency — Its Nature and Control*; Holt, Rinehart and Winston, New York.
H. M. Shulman, (1961): *Juvenile Delinquency in American Society*; Harper, New York.
E. H. Sutherland, and D. R. Cressey, (1960): *Principles of Criminology*; J. B. Lippincott Co., New York.
D. R. Taft, (1956): *Criminology*; Macmillan, New York.
P. W. Tappan (1960); *Crime, Justice and Correction*; McGraw-Hill, New York.
G. B. Vold, (1958): *Theoretical Criminology*; Oxford University Press, New York.
N. Walker, (1965): Crime and Punishment in Britain; Edinburgh University Press.

10 See 5 above.

11 See 2 above

12 See 5 above.

13 See 5 above.

14 W. A. Belson. 'Tape recording: Its effect on accuracy of response in surveys'. *Journal of Marketing Research*, Vol. 4, 1967.

15 See for example: R. S. Woodworth, and H. Schlosberg. *Experimental Psychology*. Methuen, London, 3rd Ed., Reprinted 1966. W. A. Belson. *Studies in Readership*, Business Publications, London, 1962.

16 See H. E. Garrett. Statistics in Psychology and Education; Longmans, Green & Co., New York, 1947.

17 W. A. Belson. "Matching and prediction of the principle of biological classification", Applied Statistics, Vol. 8, No. 2 (1959).

18 See P. G. Gray, T. Corlett, C. P. Jones. "The proportion of jurors as an index of the economic status of the district". Govt. Social Survey, M60, September, 1951.

19 P. J. Didcott. *Field strategies used in securing a high rate of success in interviewing boys.* Survey Research Centre, 1969.

20 W. A. Belson. 'The extent of stealing by London boys and some of its origins'. *The Advancement of Science*, Vol. 25 (124), December, 1968.

Chapter two
The nature and extent of stealing by London boys

CONTENTS

1. INTRODUCTION

In this chapter are presented various details of findings from the inquiry which bear directly upon the nature and the extent of the stealing done by London boys*. These findings stem from the use of the techniques summarized in Chapter 1.

It is essential that the information presented in the present chapter be seen as a by-product of the causal inquiry and not as a primary result of the inquiry. *Because* it is a by-product, it has certain limitations and these have been set out hereunder. Nonetheless, I believe that, if it is carefully interpreted, this by-product material can be of considerable value in its own right. A guide to such interpretation is given on pp. 70-71 under 'Legitimate interpretation of the findings about the nature and extent of stealing'.

Limitations of the findings about the nature and the extent of stealing

The present findings about the nature and extent of stealing relate specifically to *London†*. The reader may feel that the findings could quite possibly apply elsewhere, but in the end he must recognize that as presented here they relate to London and that no claim is being made by the writer that they necessarily apply elsewhere. Moreover, the findings relate principally to *boys* in the age range 13 to 16 years‡.

A second limitation of this by-product of the inquiry relates to the *elicitation technique* used in extracting theft details from boys. It is true that a major effort went into the construction of the elicitation technique§ and that for the main body of data presented in this chapter, a high degree of reliability was established‖. On the other hand:

1 The forty-four 'types of theft' featured in the elicitation technique and in this report are not so much categories of theft as a 'web of stimuli' designed to set the respondent thinking about all aspects of his behaviour which fit the definition of theft adopted in this inquiry. (In addition to its defining function, the web of stimuli was, of course, intended to function as a memory aid for the respondents.)

2 The forty-four stimuli involve some degree of 'overlap'. This arose through the team's efforts to ensure that no act of theft could, in principle, slip through the 'web'. But this feature of the web means that a boy who says 'yes' to twenty of the forty-four stimulus statements has not necessarily committed twenty quite different types of theft — because one single act may conceivably have qualified under each of two overlapping 'types'. This in turn means that whereas we may derive quantitative results about any one 'type' amongst the forty-four, we cannot treat their accumulation in a strictly quantitative fashion. On the other hand, there is much we *can* do with such accumulations and to this point I will come under the heading: 'Legitimate interpretations of the findings about the nature and extent of stealing'.

3 For each of his admitted 'types of theft', each boy was asked for further information: how often he had ever done that type of thing; the value of the 'biggest thing' of that sort ever taken; his age on the first (and last) occasions of such a type of theft. Quite apart from the problem of overlap between types of theft (see 2 above), it is feasible that boys will under-estimate or over-estimate the *number of times* they have done any one admitted type of theft. A major effort was made, at the techniques development stage, to limit such error and in this respect a reliability index of approximately +0.95 was achieved. Nonetheless, that finding still leaves room for error and in all the circumstances it is undesirable to interpret at face value the accumulation of frequencies based on all forty-four 'types' of theft. On the other hand, there is much that *can* legitimately be done with such accumulations and to this I will come in the next section.

Legitimate interpretation of the findings about the nature and the extent of stealing

1 Part of this chapter is based upon findings about the proportion of boys who have committed a particular type of theft at least once — e.g.:

I have stolen money	58 per cent
I have stolen from work	32 per cent
I have taken a letter or a parcel	17 per cent

Such information was subject to major checking and challenging at the collection stage, has an average reliability index of +0.95 and is not subject to exaggeration through overlap with another 'type'. Accordingly, this class of information may be regarded as being fairly meaningful in its own right (and not solely at the comparative level).

2 In presenting information about the total number (out of forty-four) of types of theft a boy has done at least once, the writer was sharply aware of the fact that a boy could qualify for two types of theft on the basis of the one act. Thus the boy who 'steals money from a meter' (see theft Type 41), should automatically qualify

*These findings should be considered in relation to official publications of criminal statistics and to the results of various studies of undetected and of self-reported delinquency.(See Appendix 2.4.)

†The survey area was Greater London less districts more than twelve miles from the centre of London. The reason for this exclusion was that boys had to be brought into a mid-city interviewing centre, the expenses and the problems of timing being prohibitive beyond the twelve-mile limit. A map of the survey area is given in Chapter 1.

‡The sample included a small number of the boys aged twelve or seventeen.

§"The development of a procedure for eliciting information from boys about the nature and extent of their stealing", 1968, W. A. Belson, G. L. M. Millerson, P. J. Didcott, Survey Research Centre, London.

‖ibid, pp. 262—271.

also as having 'stolen money' (see theft Type 44). This means that we cannot regard total score out of forty-four as a direct measure of the number of different types of theft committed by the boy. We may, however, regard that total as an 'index of the variety of his stealing', referred to hereafter by that name. This form of interpretation of 'score out of forty-four', may be bettered by using the index in a purely comparative way, as in the following table. In this way it is possible to

Index of variety of stealing
(3,113 cases, weighted)

Type of school last attended	Lowest quarter in terms of variety score			Top quarter in terms of variety score
	Q1 (%)	Q2 (%)	Q3 (%)	Q4 (%)
Grammar	32	33	20	15
Secondary modern	19	20	31	30
All	25	25	26	24

make meaningful comparisons, in terms of variety of stealing, of boys with different backgrounds. The *comparative* is the only type of use to which the 'variety' score should be put. The method of computing quartile scores is given later (pp. 82-83).

3 The position with regard to 'total *amount*' of stealing is very similar to that for 'total number of types' of theft committed: accumulations of frequencies were interpreted as indices of amount and were used solely in a comparative context, as in the following illustration:

Index of amount of stealing
(3,113 cases, weighted)

Type of school last attended	Lowest quarter in terms of amount score			Top quarter in terms of amount score
	Q1 (%)	Q2 (%)	Q3 (%)	Q4 (%)
Grammar	30	30	23	17
Secondary modern	20	25	27	28
All	24	28	25	23

Here, too, it was thus possible to make meaningful comparisons, in terms of amount of stealing, of boys with different social or psychological backgrounds. This is the only type of use to which the 'amount scores' should be put. The method of computing 'amount' and quartile scores is given later (pp. 82-83).

4 In the general context defined by 2 and 3 above, the reader should note that the *comparative use* of 'variety' and 'amount' scores was from the beginning planned as an essential feature of the investigation of hypotheses to which the total inquiry was directed. The arguments for the comparative use of these two scores in the present (more limited) context are the same as those for their *comparative* use in investigating *hypotheses*, namely as protection against possible inadequacies in the amount and variety scores when interpreted as absolutes. At the same time, the reader who wants 'amount' and 'variety' data in that absolute form will find it available to him, with appropriate warnings in different parts of this volume.

2. THE DIFFERENT TYPES OF STEALING DONE BY LONDON BOYS

The different types and levels of stealing studied
In the present inquiry, 1,425 boys were asked, through a procedure hereafter called 'the elicitation technique', for information about whether or not they had ever committed certain types of theft. There were forty-four of these listed on p. 72. For each of them that he had 'ever done', the boy was asked (among other things) what was the biggest thing of that kind he had ever taken and, after that, what he thought its value to be. On the basis of that latter information, that type of theft was later allocated a 'level' according to the following criteria.

Level 1 or over Any theft counts, irrespective of its value or seriousness. For example, if the boy has stolen from home at some time or other, he qualifies with regard to that type of theft, no matter how small the value of what was taken.

Level 2 or over The qualifying value is small, being set at 1/6d or over*. For example, if the boy has 'stolen from work' at some time, he qualifies with regard to that type of theft only if the value of the biggest thing ever 'stolen from work' is 1/6d or over. Similarly with regard to the value of the biggest thing ever stolen 'from a car or lorry or van'. Similarly for each of the other forty-two types of theft.

Level 3 or over The qualifying value is set at 4/6d* for each of the forty-four classes of theft.

Level 4 or over The qualifying value is set at £1* for each of the forty-four classes of theft.

*These limiting values are in terms of pre-decimalization currency. Furthermore, money at that time had considerably more value than at the time this report was published. Some examples of stolen goods at these limited values are given in Appendix 2.5 on page 104.

Types of Theft Presented to Boys in the Form of a Web of Stimuli

1 I have kept something I have found.

2 I have stolen something just for fun.

3 I have taken something just for a dare.

4 I have taken junk or scrap without asking for it first.

5 I have stolen something from a stall or a barrow.

6 I have stolen something from a shop.

7 I have stolen a book or a newspaper or a magazine or a comic.

8 I have pinched something from my family or relations.

9 I have pinched something when I was in someone else's home.

10 I have got away without paying the fare or the proper fare.

11 I have taken things belonging to children or teenagers.

12 I have got something by threatening others.

13 I have pinched sweets.

14 I have stolen cigarettes.

15 I have stolen something from a changing-room or a cloakroom.

16 I have stolen fruit or some other kind of food.

17 I have got into a place and stolen.

18 I have stolen something belonging to a school.

19 I have stolen something from someone at school.

20 I have pinched something when I was on holiday.

21 I have stolen from a park or a playground.

22 I have stolen toys.

23 I have stolen from a cafe.

24 I have stolen milk.

25 I have stolen coal or wood or paraffin or something else that is used for burning.

26 I have stolen from a building site.

27 I have stolen by stripping something from a building.

28 I have stolen from a goods yard, or from the yard of a factory, or from the docks, or from a timber yard.

29 I have stolen a letter or a parcel.

30 I have cheated someone out of money.

31 I have stolen from work.

32 I have stolen from someone at work.

33 I have had something that I knew was stolen.

34 I have stolen something out of a garden or out of the yard of a house.

35 I have stolen a bike or a motor bike.

36 I have stolen something *from* a bike or a motor bike.

37 I have stolen a car or a lorry or a van.

38 I have stolen something *from* a car or a lorry or a van.

39 I have stolen from a club.

40 I have got into some place without paying the money to go in.

41 I have stolen money from a meter.

42 I have stolen something from a telephone box.

43 I have got things out of a slot machine without paying.

44 I have stolen money.

The proportion of boys who have ever committed the different types of theft at specific levels

Table 2.1 presents the percentages of London boys, aged thirteen to sixteen, who say they have *ever* committed the different types of theft listed in that table. In this table there are four columns of percentages, based on the four theft levels defined on p. 71. Thus, 98 per cent of London boys have at some time kept something they have found, whereas if we exclude 'finds' of value less than £1, that figure reduces to 40 per cent. The order in which the forty-four types of theft are presented in Table 2.2 is geared to the percentages in the first column of figures and this order is maintained in all future tables featuring the list of thefts.

Concerning Column 1 in Table 2.1 Perhaps as is to be expected, there is a great deal of variation, in Column 1, in the percentage who have at some time committed the different acts of theft about which questions were asked.

Table 2.1
Percentage of boys who have ever committed certain
acts of theft, according to level of seriousness*
(*3,113 cases, weighted*)

Identification no. of theft	Nature of theft	Percentage who have ever done it			
		At Level 1* or over (%)	At Level 2* or over (%)	At Level 3* or over (%)	At Level 4* or over (%)
1	I have kept something I have found	98	89	71	40
10	I have got away without paying the fare or the proper fare	97	39	16	2
18	I have stolen something belonging to a school	88	63	43	13
13	I have pinched sweets	81	37	15	5
40	I have got into some place without paying the money to go in	73	64	21	1
6	I have stolen something from a shop	70	53	37	16
33	I have had something that I knew was stolen	69	60	52	33
30	I have cheated someone out of money	68	47	27	7
43	I have got things out of a slot machine without paying	66	28	15	5
2	I have stolen something just for fun	64	50	36	18
16	I have stolen fruit or some other kind of food	61	40	22	6
44	I have stolen money	58	51	39	22
4	I have taken junk or scrap without asking for it first	57	51	39	17
7	I have stolen a book/newspaper/magazine/comic	56	40	24	6
3	I have taken something just for a dare	52	38	28	13
19	I have stolen something from someone at school	49	35	27	8
8	I have pinched something from my family or relations	47	35	21	8
11	I have taken things belonging to children or teenagers	44	36	28	11
22	I have stolen toys	42	38	23	8
34	I have stolen something out of a garden or out of the yard of a house	37	31	22	10
23	I have stolen from a cafe	34	21	10	2
20	I have pinched something when I was on holiday	34	29	21	9
24	I have stolen milk	34	11	3	1
25	I have stolen coal or wood or paraffin or something else that is used for burning	33	22	13	3
5	I have stolen something from a stall or a barrow	33	20	12	4
31	I have stolen from work	32	25	18	8
36	I have stolen something *from* a bike or a motor bike	31	28	25	12
26	I have stolen from a building site	31	27	21	11
12	I have got something by threatening others	30	15	9	4
14	I have stolen cigarettes	28	22	17	8
38	I have stolen something *from* a car or a lorry or a van	25	23	19	13
39	I have stolen from a club	22	17	12	6
28	I have stolen from a goods yard, or from the yard of a factory, or from the docks, or from a timber-yard	21	20	15	8

Table 2.1 (continued)

Identification no. of theft	Nature of theft	Percentage who have ever done it			
		At Level 1* or over (%)	At Level 2* or over (%)	At Level 3* or over (%)	At Level 4* or over (%)
9	I have pinched something when I was in someone else's home	20	16	10	4
27	I have stolen by stripping something from a building	20	18	15	9
42	I have stolen something from a telephone box	18	11	8	3
17	I have got into a place and stolen	18	17	15	11
15	I have stolen something from a changing-room or a cloakroom	18	15	12	5
29	I have stolen a letter or a parcel	17	7	6	4
21	I have stolen from a park or a playground	15	12	8	4
35	I have stolen a bike or a motor bike	14	14	14	14
41	I have stolen money from a meter	11	9	8	4
32	I have stolen from someone at work	8	7	5	2
37	I have stolen a car or a lorry or a van	5	5	5	5
	Average item of theft	42%	30%	21%	9%

*At Level 1 or over: any theft counts irrespective of its value or seriousness. For example if the boy has stolen from home at some time or other, he qualifies with regard to that type of theft, no matter how small the value of what was taken
At Level 2 or over: the qualifying value is small, being set at 1/6d or over. For example, if the boy has 'stolen from work' at some time, he qualifies with regard to that type of theft only if the value of the biggest thing 'stolen from work' is 1/6d or over.

Similarly with regard to the value of the biggest thing ever stolen 'from a car or lorry or van'. Similarly for each of the other forty-two types of theft
At Level 3 or over: the qualifying value is set at 4/6d for each of the 44 classes of theft
At Level 4 or over: the qualifying value is set at £1 for each of the 44 classes of theft

1 98 per cent had at some time kept something found.

2 70 per cent had at some time stolen something from a shop.

3 42 per cent had at some time stolen toys.

4 31 per cent had at some time stolen from a building site.

5 18 per cent had at some time stolen from a telephone box.

6 8 per cent had at some time stolen from someone at work.

7 5 per cent had at some time taken a car or a lorry or a van.

What seems especially noteworthy, however, are the percentage figures for certain of the listed types of theft: 88 per cent had at some time stolen something from school; 70 per cent had at some time stolen something from a shop, 33 per cent from a stall or a barrow; 30 per cent had at some time got something by threatening others; 25 per cent had stolen from a car or lorry or van; 18 per cent had at some time stolen from a telephone box; 17 per cent a letter or parcel, 11 per cent from a meter; 5 per cent had taken a car or lorry or van. The average for the whole forty-four types was 42 per cent.

Concerning Columns 1 to 4 in Table 2.1 Naturally enough, there is (for practically all the types of theft) a falling-off in percentage as the seriousness of the qualifying level increases, the averages in going from Columns 1 to 4 being: 42, 30, 21 and 9 per cent respectively. Clearly, there are exceptions to this trend, though these exceptions tend to be related to the minimum value of the items likely to be involved. Thus, in the case of taking a car or a lorry or a van, the figure 5 per cent all the way across the four columns arises from the fact that the minimum value of a car etc. is not likely to be less than £1! By contrast, the percentage stealing sweets falls off *very* sharply as the qualifying value reaches £1 — an amount that would involve something rather different from casual 'lifting' from the sweet counter.

Concerning Column 4 in Table 2.1 The figures in Column 4 may be taken as indices of relatively serious stealing. What is important about the Column 4 evidence is that some of its figures are quite high: 33 per cent for 'receiving items known to be stolen', 22 per cent for stealing money; 14 per cent for stealing a bike or a motor bike; 13 per cent for stealing *from* a car or lorry or van; 13 per cent for a school theft; 11 per cent for getting into a place and taking something. The Column 4 figures for some of the other types of theft, though small, are also noteworthy: stealing from work, 8 per cent; stealing from someone at school, 8 per cent; taking a car or lorry or van, 5 per cent; stealing from a meter, 4 per cent; stealing from a changing-room or cloakroom, 5 per cent; stealing by threatening others, 4 per cent.

The total indication of Table 2.1 seems to be that theft is or has been carried out on a large scale by London boys aged thirteen to sixteen years and that its extent is still quite considerable when we consider only thefts involving values of £1 or over. However, it is feasible that the bulk of the thefts reported in Table 2.1 have been committed by a fairly limited proportion of the boy-population concerned, with a large proportion of boys doing little or nothing at all. Table 2.2 presents evidence on this matter.

Table 2.2
Index of Variety of Stealing

| Variety score | Level of theft | | | |
	L 1+ (%)	L 2+ (%)	L 3+ (%)	L 4+ (%)
0	0	2	7	30
1— 2	1	5	14	28
3— 4	3	8	16	14
5— 8	10	20	21	12
9—12	12	19	15	6
13—16	19	15	10	5
17—20	17	11	7	2
21—24	15	9	4	2
25—28	11	5	3	1
29—32	6	3	2	—
33—36	4	2	1	—
37—40	1	—	—	—
41—44	1	—	—	—
Totals	100%	99%	100%	100%
Average score on 44	18.1	12.9	9.2	4.6

— = Less than 0.5 per cent

If we ignore altogether the values of what was taken (i.e. if we consider stealing at Level 1 or over), we find that all the boys have committed at least one of the forty-four acts of theft, 86 per cent of them at least nine of the forty-four, and 23 per cent of them at least twenty-five of the forty-four types of theft. This suggests a high degree of pervasiveness of dishonesty of at least some degree of seriousness. It could still be the case of course that: (*a*) wherever thefts involve items of appreciable value, relatively few boys are involved; and, (*b*) the bulk of the thefts are committed by a relatively small number of boys. In fact, at Level 4 or over, 70 per cent of the boys in this sample had committed at least *one* of the forty-four types of theft, 42 per cent had committed at least three and 16 per cent had committed at least nine of the forty-four types of theft. What this evidence means then is that the more serious theft dealt with in Table 2.1 is contributed to in a substantial way by a fairly wide spread of the boys in the sample.

The different types of theft compared in various ways

The characteristics of boys who commit the different types of theft
Various sub-analyses were made to determine the percentage or incidence of different types of theft in different population sectors. In Table 2.3 these percentages are given in terms of occupational level of boy's father, type of school last attended, present age of boy. In addition they have been presented separately for boys who do (or do not) go out 'just looking for fun and excitement'.

Table 2.3 data are in terms of thefts at Level 2 or over, though similar tables based on each of the four levels are given in Appendix 2.1 (Tables A2.1 to A2.4). The reason for choosing 'Level 2 or over' for inclusion in the main text was that it seems to deal with the main bulk of thieving without the trends within it being obscured by really trivial acts, namely acts that do not go beyond Level 1 in their seriousness. On the other hand, the reader's attention will later be drawn to any noteworthy difference in going from 'Level 2 or over' findings to findings at the other levels (see pp. 78-79 and Table 2.4).

Involvement in stealing analysed by occupational level of boys' fathers It is frequently asserted that social class is a major correlate of involvement in delinquent activity. Such assertions tend to be based upon comparisons of *apprehended* delinquents on the one hand and boys of the general population on the other. One difficulty about such a comparison is that the apprehended boys may quite conceivably be merely the duller or less alert of the practising delinquents. The present results, shown in Table 2.3, provide a comparison of boys in terms of level of *actual* stealing — as distinct from *detected* stealing. The main indications of this evidence with respect to occupational level are set out below.

1 Taking all forty-four types of theft together, the average percentage increases with each step down the occupational scale, with the exception of the sons of the unskilled. Boys in this group have a lower average percentage than boys whose fathers are one step up the occupational scale — a finding that may be contrary to some expectations. Another challenging feature of the above findings is the shallowness of the trend they exhibit: the sons of the professional and the highly skilled are not all that much different from the sons of the less skilled. Whereas this information does not relate to the *frequency* with which the different acts are committed, it is not inconsistent with the view that stealing occurs to a substantial degree right across the occupational spectrum.

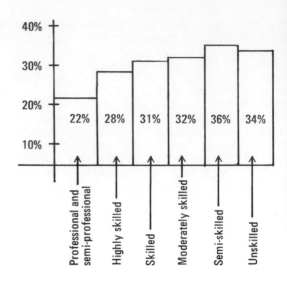

Table 2.3

The percentage of boys who have ever committed certain types of theft† analysed by occupational level, age, type of school last attended, tendency to seek fun and excitement

Identification no. of type of theft (see Appendix 2.3 for these)	All cases (3,113 wt'd)	Occupational level of boy's father*						Type of school last attended				Age of boy				Goes out 'j looking for fun and excitement	
		A	B	C	D	E	F	Secondary modern	Compre-hensive	Grammar	Public	12/13 yrs	14 yrs	15 yrs	16/17 yrs	Yes	No
	(%)	(%)	(%)	(%)	(%)	(%)	(%)	(%)	(%)	(%)	(%)	(%)	(%)	(%)	(%)	(%)	(%)
1	89	83	90	92	87	92	93	91	92	88	83	79	90	93	94	93	87
10	39	45	36	40	35	40	38	41	36	36	48	16	35	47	55	42	37
18	63	56	62	61	66	64	71	66	63	60	58	43	57	69	79	65	61
13	37	22	30	43	40	46	46	45	37	28	18	28	36	40	44	46	31
40	64	57	67	65	64	64	66	66	70	58	57	53	61	66	73	71	59
6	53	37	56	54	54	65	54	60	55	46	35	44	54	53	62	63	46
33	60	41	56	67	65	67	64	67	70	50	29	48	58	63	70	69	54
30	47	46	39	50	45	52	48	49	45	43	51	29	38	53	64	54	42
43	28	18	25	33	30	35	26	30	34	25	14	24	22	29	38	34	24
2	50	33	46	58	50	57	55	55	51	43	33	40	49	50	59	58	43
16	40	24	37	39	45	50	55	50	40	31	15	35	39	38	49	48	35
44	51	42	46	49	55	58	59	59	53	39	36	42	46	55	59	61	43
4	51	43	56	55	49	55	49	55	50	48	43	46	49	56	54	57	47
7	40	28	43	41	43	45	40	42	46	35	29	31	35	42	50	47	35
3	38	26	40	42	39	42	36	45	36	28	30	30	36	39	46	47	32
19	35	34	28	33	40	37	41	36	36	31	35	29	32	37	42	41	31
8	35	44	36	30	34	32	34	36	27	34	49	32	31	37	39	37	33
11	36	28	36	36	35	44	37	39	39	32	26	33	31	39	40	44	30
22	38	24	36	35	44	47	42	44	37	32	23	39	35	36	41	45	33
34	31	20	31	35	29	32	41	36	30	25	16	30	28	35	31	39	25
23	21	18	18	23	22	23	22	22	24	18	17	10	15	22	34	24	19
20	29	18	27	32	24	41	33	31	32	27	16	26	22	29	36	33	26
24	11	2	8	11	11	18	17	14	13	4	3	8	10	10	14	15	8
25	22	13	17	23	23	28	28	24	25	16	20	21	19	21	26	24	20
5	20	11	16	18	26	25	29	26	22	11	8	18	19	18	25	24	17

Table 2.3 (continued)

Identification no. of type of theft (see Appendix 2.3 for these)	All cases (3,113 wt'd)	Occupational level of boy's father*						Type of school last attended				Age of boy				Goes out 'just looking for fun and excitement'	
		A	B	C	D	E	F	Secondary modern	Compre-hensive	Grammar	Public	12/13 yrs	14 yrs	15 yrs	16/17 yrs	Yes	No
	(%)	(%)	(%)	(%)	(%)	(%)	(%)	(%)	(%)	(%)	(%)	(%)	(%)	(%)	(%)	(%)	(%)
31	25	9	20	27	29	38	28	32	29	17	7	11	20	23	44	33	20
36	28	15	24	25	34	43	33	37	27	19	9	27	28	26	34	39	22
26	27	18	19	33	31	34	28	31	34	18	26	27	27	28	27	37	21
12	15	11	12	16	14	23	16	19	17	10	10	10	17	16	18	18	14
14	22	8	20	23	27	31	24	29	22	14	7	11	21	22	33	32	16
38	23	12	21	19	28	34	24	29	27	13	8	19	21	25	27	29	19
39	17	12	13	13	22	19	28	18	20	14	10	11	17	18	21	20	15
28	20	11	14	18	25	26	29	25	19	14	8	16	18	19	24	21	18
9	16	14	11	15	18	18	18	16	15	14	16	15	12	17	18	19	13
27	18	10	15	20	18	24	21	22	19	12	14	14	14	24	20	22	15
42	11	10	6	12	12	14	11	12	14	9	8	8	12	13	10	14	9
17	17	6	10	16	23	23	26	23	19	6	7	15	13	19	20	24	12
15	15	16	10	14	17	20	14	17	16	10	16	11	15	15	20	22	11
29	7	4	4	8	10	8	11	10	8	4	0	9	5	9	6	10	5
21	12	6	9	9	14	16	18	13	13	10	10	14	11	11	11	14	10
35	14	2	6	15	19	25	19	21	16	4	0	9	12	14	22	21	10
41	9	3	6	8	12	10	16	12	9	3	4	7	7	10	10	11	7
32	7	3	3	7	9	11	8	9	8	3	3	6	5	7	8	9	5
37	5	1	4	4	5	9	4	7	4	2	0	1	2	6	8	7	3
For the average theft type†	30%	22%	28%	31%	32%	36%	34%	34%	32%	25%	22%	24%	28%	32%	36%	36%	26%

*A, professional, semi-professional and executive; B, highly skilled; C, skilled; D, moderately skilled; E, semi-skilled; F, unskilled

†At Level 2 or over (i.e. disregarding only instances where the biggest thing ever taken was less than 1/6d). See appendices for equivalent tables for Level 3 and above, Level 4 and above and Level 1 and above

2 For some of the individual acts in the list of forty-four, there is a fairly consistent tendency for the percentage figure to increase in going from high to low occupational rating and these acts are listed on page 78 in the column on left hand. On the other hand, there are many acts in the list of forty-four where any such tendency is by no means marked and some where it does not exist at all. The latter are listed on page 78.

In other words, in spite of *an overall moderate tendency* for the percentage of those who have ever committed an act of theft to increase in going down the occupational scale, there are many exceptions to this at the specific level.

Involvement in different types of theft analysed by educational level of boys Table 2.3 provides evidence of differences in theft level between boys of different educational backgrounds.

1 Taking all forty-four types of theft together, the average percentage increases as we go from boys with public school education to those with a background of secondary modern schooling.

Public school	22 per cent
Grammar school	25 per cent
Comprehensive school	32 per cent
Secondary modern	34 per cent

2 Just as for occupational level, the *trend of the averages* is subject to exception at the level of the individual type of theft. Thus for the following types of theft, there is no clear evidence of stealing falling off in incidence in going up the educational scale: getting away without paying the fare or proper fare; cheating someone out of money; stealing something from someone at school; pinching something from my family or relatives; pinching when in someone else's home; stealing from a changing-room or a cloakroom. In other words, there are types of theft that are no less prevalent amongst boys of public-school background than amongst those of grammar school, comprehensive or secondary-modern school background. In fact, for several of these

Negative association with occupational level

16 I have stolen fruit or some other kind of food
13 I have pinched sweets
36 I have stolen something from a bike or a motor bike
31 I have stolen from work
5 I have stolen something from a stall or barrow
28 I have stolen from a goods yard or yard of a factory or from docks or from a timber yard
17 I have got into a place and stolen
35 I have stolen a bike or a motor bike
24 I have stolen milk
41 I have stolen money from a meter

Little or no negative association with occupational level

30 I have cheated someone out of money
10 I have got away without paying the fare or proper fare
3 I have taken something just for a dare
8 I have pinched something from my family or relations
15 I have stolen from a changing room or cloakroom
42 I have stolen something from a telephone box

of theft appear to 'cut out' after the age of thirteen or fourteen.

Involvement in different types of stealing, analysed by tendency of boy to seek fun and excitement This particular variable — 'going out just looking for fun and excitement' — was included because other evidence from this enquiry had marked it out as substantially correlated with both variety and amount of stealing. This relationship is reflected in the average at the foot of Table 2.3.

Yes, go out just looking for fun and excitement
36 per cent average
Don't go out just looking for fun and excitement
26 per cent average

The principal purpose of cross-analysing the survey findings on this variable was to see if any of the different types of theft were exceptions to the overall trend. Below on the left, are types of theft *more* associated with fun and excitement seeking and on the right (below) are types which are less strongly associated with fun and excitement seeking.

More strongly associated with fun and excitement seeking

42 Stealing from a telephone box
17 Getting into a place and stealing
15 Stealing from a changing-room or cloak-room
35 Stealing a bike or motorbike
37 Stealing a car or a lorry or a van

Less strongly associated with fun and excitement seeking

1 Keeping something found
18 Stealing something belonging to a school
8 Stealing from family or relations
28 Stealing from a goods yard or yard of a factory, or from docks or from a timber yard.

types of theft, public-school boys have the highest score: getting away without paying the fare or proper fare; cheating someone out of money; pinching from my family or relations.

On the other hand, some types of theft show a marked tendency to be committed more as one goes down the educational scale: pinching sweets; stealing fruit or other food; stealing from a garden or from the yard of a house; stealing from work; stealing from a bike or a motorbike; stealing cigarettes; stealing from a goods yard, etc.; stealing a letter or a parcel.

So here, too, just as with parental occupational level, the overall trend masks a lot of variability in going from one type of theft to another and certainly there are types of theft which are at least as prevalent amongst public-school boys as amongst others.

Involvement in different types of theft analysed by boys' ages Since boys were asked if they had *ever* committed the different types of theft, we must expect the theft level to rise with each step upwards in age. In other words, boys aged sixteen had had three more years than thirteen-year olds in which to commit any given type of theft. The averages at the foot of Table 2.3 show the overall trend:

Age	12-13	14	15	16-17
Average	24%	28%	32%	36%

However, not all theft types are subject to this steady upward trend, some of the most noteworthy exceptions being: stealing from a building site; getting something by threatening others; stealing a letter or a parcel; stealing from a park or playground. In other words, such types

There seems little here that is surprising, the extreme cases on the left seeming to call for somewhat more in the way of daring.

Characteristics of boys stealing at different levels of seriousness

So far, this report of how theft varies with the characteristics of boys has been limited to theft at Level 2 or over (i.e. excluding trivial thefts as defined on p. 71). Parallel information is in fact given in Appendix 2.1 (Tables A2.1, A2.3, A2.4) for each of the other levels, and this information is summarized in Table 2.4.

Table 2.4 indicates:

1 That the trends found at Level 2 or over are repeated for each of the other levels of seriousness.

2 That at each level — even Level 4 — thieving is by no means limited to any one section of the population.

Table 2.4

Percentage committing the 'Average theft', analysed by characteristics of boys and by seriousness of theft

Theft Level	All (%)	Occupational level of boy's father						Type of school last attended				Age of boy				Goes out 'just looking for fun and excitement'	
		A (%)	B (%)	C (%)	D (%)	E (%)	F (%)	Secondary modern (%)	Comprehensive (%)	Grammar (%)	Public (%)	12/13 yrs (%)	14 yrs (%)	15 yrs (%)	16/17 yrs (%)	Yes (%)	No (%)
At Level 1 or over*	42	34	39	42	43	46	46	45	43	37	33	39	40	42	45	47	38
At Level 2 or over	30	22	28	31	32	36	34	34	32	25	22	24	28	32	36	36	26
At Level 3 or over	21	14	17	21	22	26	24	24	22	15	14	15	17	22	27	25	17
At Level 4 or over	9	5	7	9	11	12	12	12	9	6	6	6	7	10	14	12	7

*At Level 1 or over: any theft counts irrespective of the value of what was taken or seriousness. For example, if the boy has stolen from home at some time or other, he qualifies with regard to that type of theft, no matter how small the value of what was taken.

At Level 2 or over: the qualifying value is small, being set at 1/6d or over. For example, if the boy has 'stolen from work' at some time, he qualifies with regard to that type of theft only if the value of the biggest thing ever 'stolen from work' is 1/6d or over. Similarly with regard to the value of the biggest thing ever stolen 'from a car or lorry or van'. Similarly for each of the other forty-two types of theft

At Level 3 or over: the qualifying value is set at 4/6d for each of the 44 classes of theft

At Level 4 or over: the qualifying value is set at £1 for each of the 44 classes of theft

79

Ages of boys on first committing the different types of theft

For each type of theft committed, a boy was asked how old he was on the first occurrence of such a theft. The figures given in the third column of Table 2.5 relate to types of theft committed at Level 2 or over and they are averages of the ages of boys at the time of the first offence of this type.

Several points about this body of evidence seem noteworthy:

1 Table 2.5 clearly indicates that there is a lot of variation in 'starting age' in going from one to another of the forty-four types of theft. In the left-hand column below are given the four types of theft which tend to start earliest in the boy's life and on the right the four types that tend to start latest in his life.

Start earlier		Start later	
	yrs		yrs
1 Keeping some-thing found	(8.7)	37 Stealing a car or lorry or van	(14.2)
22 Stealing toys	(9.1)	31 Stealing from work	(14.0)
13 Pinching sweets	(9.2)	32 Stealing from someone at work	(13.7)
16 Stealing fruit or other food	(9.7)	23 Stealing from a cafe	(13.2)

2 There is some tendency for the 'later starting' types of theft: to be of the more serious kind; to involve behaviour and situations common to older boys (e.g. going to work, going to a cafe, being able to drive a car, being a member of a club); to be related to older-boy interests.

3 One of the 'early starting' types of theft may be surprising: stealing by threatening others.

Frequency with which different types of theft are committed and tendency for boys to specialize

In interpreting findings about the frequency of occurrence of different types of theft behaviour, it is desirable to repeat a warning given earlier. Thus, certain errors are likely to condition estimates of the total number of times a given type of theft has been committed. *In the first place*, some respondents make extravagant claims about how often they have committed certain types of theft — a practice that could upset any estimate of the sample average. Because of this, the computation of averages had involved the imposition of a ceiling of twenty times upon any one type of theft. This serves to protect the average from wild estimates, but it must also serve to depress the level of the averages generally. In the *second place*, even careful estimates by individual boys about the number of times they committed any one type of theft must be suspected of at least some degree of error. It is true of course that the reliability tests on this particular matter indicated a 90 per cent degree of consistency for the average type of theft. But reliability is not the same thing as validity and though major work was done in order to secure validity, a meaningful test of it could not be made. In the circumstances, it is important that all the averages presented in Table 2.5 be regarded *comparatively* and not as absolutes.

The frequency data in Table 2.5 appear to exhibit the following tendencies.

1 As one goes from Level 1 (or over) to Level 4 (or over), the frequency of theft increases. This finding requires careful interpretation. Take, for instance, theft Type 18 which is 'stealing something belonging to a school'. Some 88 per cent of the boys had admitted committing this type of theft at least once and for *these* boys the average number of times they had done it was 8.5. If now we consider only the boys whose biggest theft of this kind exceeded 1/6d the total number of them falls to 63 per cent and for these more serious 'school thieves', the average number of thefts goes up, to 9.4. In other words, as we eliminate the less serious thieves of this kind, the average frequency of theft goes up. This trend, for school stealing, is continued through Level 3 or over to Level 4 or over:

8.5	9.4	10.0	11.8

The same trend emerges for the *average* type of theft (see row at bottom of Table 2.5) and is fairly consistently present for the individual types of theft. Thus, the more serious the level of stealing ever reached by a boy, the more *frequently* he commits the type of theft concerned. In Table 2.5, the only apparent exception to this trend is for theft Types 35 and 37: in these cases, any item that qualifies at Level 1 or over will also qualify at Level 4 or over, simply because any such items are costly.

2 The other indication of the four right-hand columns in Table 2.5 is that boys who ever commit a given type of theft *tend to repeat it* a number of times, the average over all forty-four types being:

a For those who have ever committed it at Level 1 or over: 5.7.
b For those who have ever committed it at Level 2 or over: 6.1.
c For those who have ever committed it at Level 3 or over: 6.6.
d For those who have ever committed it at Level 4 or over: 7.4.

3 As the total number of boys who have ever committed a specific type of theft *falls*, so does the *frequency* with which the average 'offender' commits it. In other words, types of theft in which only a small proportion of boys ever involve themselves, are not subject to much repeat performance by the boys concerned. One might have thought that such boys

Table 2.5

For each theft studied: age of first offence at Level 2 or over*; length of period between first and last offence; frequency of offence at Levels L1+, L2+, L3+, L4+

Indication No. of theft	Percentage who have ever done it at Level 2 or over %	Average age when first committed at Level 2 or over (see Table A2.5) yrs	Average period of years between first and last act of this kind (at Level 2 or over) (see Table A2.6) yrs	Level 1 or over (See Table A2.7)	Level 2 or over (See Table A2.8)	Level 3 or over (See Table A2.9)	Level 4 or over (See Table A2.10)
				For boys who have done it at all, average no. of times committed at:			
1	89	8.7	5.4	9.7	10.1	10.3	11.1
10	39	10.7	4.1	12.7	14.9	16.0	16.1
18	63	10.6	3.9	8.5	9.4	10.0	11.8
13	37	9.2	4.9	10.2	12.7	13.3	13.4
40	64	11.6	3.0	6.4	6.9	8.9	14.1
6	53	10.0	4.2	9.7	11.1	12.4	14.3
33	60	12.2	2.6	4.6	4.7	4.8	5.5
30	47	12.2	2.8	6.1	6.6	7.2	8.8
43	28	11.9	3.0	5.4	6.1	6.3	7.4
2	50	11.1	3.2	6.1	6.5	6.8	7.7
16	40	9.7	4.2	9.8	11.4	12.9	14.3
44	51	10.2	4.1	8.4	9.0	9.8	10.8
4	51	11.5	2.9	4.8	5.0	5.3	5.2
7	40	11.6	3.0	6.5	7.4	8.6	9.6
3	38	11.1	3.3	4.7	5.1	5.2	5.8
19	35	11.0	3.4	6.2	6.4	6.9	8.8
8	36	10.0	4.2	7.2	7.7	8.5	8.5
11	36	10.5	4.1	6.2	6.6	7.0	7.9
22	38	9.1	3.5	6.1	6.3	7.4	7.6
34	31	10.8	3.4	6.2	6.1	6.2	4.9
23	21	13.2	2.2	4.6	4.2	4.6	5.6
20	29	12.0	2.5	4.3	4.4	5.0	5.9
24	11	11.8	3.0	5.9	7.2	7.4	7.1
25	22	11.2	2.9	5.3	5.7	5.8	7.6
5	20	11.1	3.4	5.4	6.3	6.6	6.4
31	25	14.0	1.3	6.5	7.0	7.9	9.5
36	28	12.5	1.9	4.4	4.6	4.9	6.1
26	27	11.9	2.3	3.6	3.7	4.0	4.4
12	15	12.0	2.4	5.5	5.8	6.7	8.2
14	22	12.6	2.2	7.7	8.1	9.0	10.2
38	23	12.6	2.1	3.9	3.9	4.0	5.0
39	17	13.1	1.6	3.4	3.5	3.8	4.1
28	20	11.9	2.3	4.0	4.1	4.3	4.6
9	16	11.4	3.0	3.1	3.2	3.4	4.0
27	18	12.6	2.1	3.4	3.6	3.7	4.7
42	11	13.0	1.6	3.2	3.0	2.6	3.6
17	17	12.1	2.2	5.3	5.6	5.8	6.2
15	15	11.8	2.6	4.3	4.4	4.6	5.6
29	7	12.4	2.7	2.9	3.2	3.3	3.4
21	12	11.0	3.2	3.8	4.0	4.6	4.6
35	14	13.0	1.8	3.7	3.7	3.7	3.7
41	9	12.7	1.8	4.0	4.2	4.4	4.4
32	7	13.7	1.2	3.7	3.8	4.4	6.0
37	5	14.2	1.2	2.4	2.4	2.4	2.4
Average	30%	11.6	2.9**	5.7**	6.1**	6.6**	7.4**

*Level 2 or over: disregarding only instances where the biggest thing ever taken was less than 1/6d

**The overall averages should not be regarded as absolute figures. They are for comparative purposes only

might become specialists in this type of 'rare theft', but this does not appear to be so.

The numerical association of different types of stealing

The information collected in this inquiry made possible the development of a correlation matrix based on the full forty-four 'types of theft' about which this chapter has so far been written. This correlational matrix is set out in Appendix 2.2 and it is presented here more for the record and for completeness than for anything like detailed analysis and comment. A factor analysis of the matrix of data will be made and presented in due course.

For the present, some of the things which the reader may care to note about the matrix are: (a) that all the correlations are positive; (b) that the great majority of them are below the level of +0.30; (c) that the types of theft with the highest correlation with 'score out of forty-four' are: 'I have stolen something from a shop' ($r = +0.60$), 'I have pinched sweets' ($r = +0.60$), 'I have stolen money' ($r = +0.60$), 'I have stolen something *from* a bike or motor bike' ($r = +0.58$); (d) that the types of theft with the lowest correlation with score out of forty-four are: 'I have pinched something from my family or relations' ($r = +0.26$), 'I have kept something I have found' ($r = +0.34$), 'I have taken junk or scrap without asking for it first' ($r = +0.34$), 'I have stolen from someone at work' ($r = +0.34$).

3. THE OVERALL INCIDENCE AND VARIETY OF STEALING BY LONDON BOYS

Developing indices of amount and variety of stealing

So far the results considered have been mainly those relating to the percentage and the type of boys who commit specific types of theft and to the association of different types of thieving. However, findings are also available in terms of an index of *variety* of stealing and of an index of *amount* of stealing.

The index of variety

The index of variety adopted here is the number of thefts out of the total of forty-four which the respondent says he has ever committed. Comparison of the different sub-sections of the population could, of course, be made directly in terms of the averaged score out of forty-four. But this does offer some encouragement to the interpretation of such figures in an absolute sense. Accordingly, such comparisons have been made only in terms of quartile distributions of the variety scores.

The quartile cutting points (which are derived from the detail in Table 2.2) are set out in Table 2.6.

Obviously, one cannot expect to secure cutting points at precisely 25 per cent, 50 per cent, and so on, but it was possible to get fairly near to this situation. Thus, we see that, at Level 1 or over, the score of twelve out of forty-four came nearest to cutting off the bottom-scoring 25 per cent — in fact, 26.4 per cent. Similarly, the second quartile cutting point, instead of being at 50 per cent, had to be made at 53.9 per cent.

The index of amount

Approximate quartile break points were also established for 'index of amount' scores — in fact, from the detail in Table 2.7. The approximate quartile cutting points derived from Table 2.7 are shown in Table 2.8. Here, too, it was possible to bring these cutting points quite close to the ideal 25, 50, 75 and 100 per cent levels.

Amount and variety of stealing analysed by characteristics of boys

Amount and variety analysed by occupational levels of fathers

The quartile distribution of variety and amount indices for the different occupational sectors are shown in Tables 2.9.1 to 2.9.3. In Table 2.9.1 the distributions are related to stealing at Level 2 or over (i.e. excluding only

Table 2.6
Approximate 'Quartile'* Break Points for Variety Scores

Approximate 'quartile' break points	Level of theft							
	L1+		L2+		L3+		L4+	
	Variety score	Percentage cut off	Variety score	Percentage cut off	Variety score	Percentage cut off	Variety score	Percentage cut off
First 'quartile'	0–12	26.4	0– 6	24.8	0– 3	30.2	0	29.9
Second 'quartile'	13–18	53.9	7–11	49.5	4– 8	57.5	1–2	57.7
Third 'quartile'	19–24	77.0	12–18	75.9	9–14	79.0	3–6	80.1
Fourth 'quartile'	25+	100.0	19+	100.0	15	100.0	7+	100.0

*Properly speaking, the quartile break points should have been at: the point in the variety score distribution marking off the lower scoring 25 per cent of boys; at the point marking off the lower 50 per cent of boys; at the point marking off the lower 75 per cent of boys; at the 100 per cent level. However, in practice all that can be done is to make the break at points in the distribution which come as near as possible to these requirements and this has been done

Table 2.7
Index of amount scores

Amount score*	Level of theft			
	L1+ (%)	L2+ (%)	L3+ (%)	L4+ (%)
0	0.4	2.4	7.5	29.5
1— 5	1.0	4.4	8.3	13.2
6—10	1.4	5.3	8.9	10.1
11—15	1.8	4.5	5.3	4.2
16—20	2.0	2.7	5.0	6.4
21—25	2.9	4.8	5.5	6.0
26—30	2.8	4.9	3.7	3.6
31—40	6.1	6.8	8.9	5.1
41—50	4.9	6.5	5.7	4.4
51—60	6.3	4.3	5.3	1.8
61—70	6.7	5.1	4.1	2.8
71—80	5.9	4.8	4.0	1.8
81—90	4.5	4.4	3.4	1.6
91—100	4.9	4.5	3.1	1.1
101—110	4.1	3.1	2.4	1.7
111—120	4.0	3.0	2.0	0.7
121—130	3.6	3.1	1.7	0.4
131—140	2.9	2.1	1.1	1.0
141—150	3.6	3.5	1.4	0.4
151—200	13.5	8.7	5.7	2.2
201—250	6.9	3.8	3.1	0.9
251—300	4.0	2.8	1.7	0.3
301+	5.8	4.5	2.3	0.9
Total (%)	100	100	100	100
Average amount score	117.6	90.4	64.2	30.2

*With a ceiling of 20 per cent upon the allowable claims of any boys for any single type of theft (with the purpose of protecting results from extravagant claims)

classes of theft committed at a trivial level), whereas in Table 2.9.2, the distributions are related to stealing at Level 4 or over (i.e. stealing at a fairly serious level).

In Table 2.9.1 the trends for *variety* and *amount* of stealing are broadly similar:

1 There is a clear tendency for involvement in theft to increase as we go down the parental occupational scale.

2 This tendency is not maintained for those in the *bottom* occupational group (the sons of the unskilled), their theft level being lower than for the semi-skilled.
3 In spite of the difference in theft level of boys according to occupational level of father, stealing is substantially present in all the occupational sectors.

At the more serious level of stealing, as presented in Table 2.9.2, the occupational trends in going from higher towards lower are somewhat more marked, but nonetheless are similar in direction and in character to those presented in Table 2.9.1. Here, too (i.e., at this more serious level) it is clear that stealing by boys is well spread throughout the different social sectors of the London population. One should note of Table 2.9.2 that the trends *across* the table are somewhat exaggerated for the upper occupational sectors because it was not possible to split the sample at precise quartile points. In Table 2.9.3, I have attempted a redistribution of Table 2.9.2 findings for sample sectors split at 25 per cent points. When this is done, one can compare more readily the results in Table 2.9.1 and those for more serious stealing.

The reader may wish to compare the evidence in Table 2.9.1 with that in the bottom row of the occupational section of Table 2.3, where the same trends are present.

Table 2.8
Approximate 'quartile'* break points for amount scores

Approximate 'quartile' break points	Level of theft							
	L1+		L2+		L3+		L4+	
	Amount score	Percentage cut off	Amount score	Percentage cut off	Amount score	Percentage cut off	Amount score	Percentage cut off
First quartile	0—55	25.4	0—25	24.1	0—13	27.7	0	29.5
Second quartile	56—101	51.9	26—70	51.8	14—41	53.8	1—10	52.8
Third quartile	102—172	76.4	71—140	76.8	42—101	78.9	11—36	78.0
Fourth quartile	173+	100.0	141—000	100.0	102	100.0	37+	100.0

*Properly speaking the quartile break points should have been at: the point in the amount score distribution marking off the lower scoring 25 per cent of boys; at the point marking off the lower 50 per cent of boys; at the point marking off the lower 75 per cent of boys; at the 100 per cent level. However, in practice all that can be done is to make the break at points in the distribution which come as near as possible to these requirements and this has been done

Table 2.9.1
Distribution of variety and amount of stealing according
to occupational level of boy's father at Level 2 or over
(see Table A2.11)

Occupational level of boy's father	Index of variety of stealing				Index of amount of stealing			
	Low score quartile Q.1 (%)	Q.2 (%)	Q.3 (%)	High score quartile Q.4 (%)	Low score quartile Q.1 (%)	Q.2 (%)	Q.3 (%)	High score quartile Q.4 (%)
Professional, semi-professional and executive	35	35	17	12	28	40	19	14
Highly skilled	26	30	27	17	25	24	32	19
Skilled	23	20	33	25	23	25	28	24
Moderately skilled	24	23	24	29	27	26	21	26
Semi-skilled	20	16	28	36	20	23	25	32
Unskilled	16	27	30	27	18	31	28	23
All boys	25	25	26*	24*	24*	28*	25	23*

*Some of these base figures are not 25 per cent as ideally required

Table 2.9.2
At Level 4 or over (See Table A.2.12)

Occupational level of boy's father	Index of variety of stealing				Index of amount of stealing			
	Low score sector Q.1 (%)	Q.2 (%)	Q.3 (%)	High score sector Q.4 (%)	Low score sector Q.1 (%)	Q.2 (%)	Q.3 (%)	High score sector Q.4 (%)
Professional, semi-professional and executive	44	31	17	8	44	21	21	14
Highly skilled	37	33	17	13	35	25	24	16
Skilled	29	24	26	21	29	21	27	23
Moderately skilled	27	26	22	25	27	24	24	25
Semi-skilled	19	27	27	27	18	24	27	31
Unskilled	21	24	28	27	21	25	29	25
All boys	30*	28	22	20*	30*	23	25	22*

*Note that the effort to establish *quartile* sectoring tended to fail here and that the sectoring points actually established (30:28:22:20) tend to exaggerate the trends running *across* this table. Trends should be read *vertically*

84

Table 2.9.3
At Level 4 or over, converted to quartile bases
(for comparison with Table 2.9.1)

Occupational level of boy's father	Index of variety of stealing				Index of amount of stealing			
	Low score quartile Q.1 (%)	Q.2 (%)	Q.3 (%)	High score quartile Q.4 (%)	Low score quartile Q.1 (%)	Q.2 (%)	Q.3 (%)	High score quartile Q.4 (%)
Professional, semi-professional and executive	37	29	22	12	37	26	21	16
Highly skilled	31	30	22	17	29	27	25	19
Skilled	24	22	27	27	24	23	27	26
Moderately skilled	22	23	25	30	23	25	25	27
Semi-skilled	16	22	29	33	15	24	27	34
Unskilled	18	21	28	33	18	25	29	28
All boys	25	25	25	25	25	25	25	25

'Amount' and 'variety' analysed by other characteristics

In Table 2.10 are presented the quartile distribution scores of boys according to social class (Registrar General's classification), place of birth, whether born in United Kingdom or not, nominal religion, type of school last attended. These particular figures relate to all thieving excluding trivial thefts (i.e. Level 2 or over). In Appendix 2.1 (Table A2.12) parallel details are available for more theft behaviour at a more serious level. The reader will find that the trends in Table A2.12 are broadly similar to those evident in Table 2.10, though in doing this he will need to note that quartile splits were not achieved for Table A2.12.

Bearing in mind the number of cases in the different sub-groups, several of the notable indications of Table 2.10 are as follows.

1 Variation in theft score according to the Registrar General's 'social class' categorization is more or less in line with the variation by occupational level (of fathers) shown in Table 2.9.

2 Boys from (or at) public schools tend to do less stealing than boys from other types of school backgrounds, the 'scoring order' being: public school (lowest theft rate); grammar school; comprehensive school; secondary modern school (highest theft rate).

At the same time, the public- and grammar-school boys are by no means clear of substantial thieving. They do less than the other boys but still quite a lot.

3 The boys who said they were Jewish had lower theft scores than had Protestant and Catholic boys. The small number of boys in the Jewish sub-group makes it necessary to interpret this finding warily, but the extent of the difference is, in fact, highly significant in statistical terms.

4 Boys born outside the United Kingdom had lower theft scores than United Kingdom-born boys. Here, too, the numbers are small and the differences suggested above must be treated warily.

5 Boys who go out 'just looking for fun and excitement' do appreciably more stealing than those who do not go out 'just looking for fun and excitement'.

There are other differences in Table 2.10 which the reader may care to study. However, the overall indication of this table is, like that of Table 2.9, that stealing is present to a substantial degree throughout the social spectrum.

Another of the analyses made was in terms of the *ages* of the boys. Each boy, whatever his age, was reporting his thefts over his whole lifetime. Thus, those aged thirteen were reporting thefts right up to their present age of thirteen while those aged sixteen were reporting on their thefts right up to *that* age. Accordingly, one must expect that with each step up the age scale, the total theft score will rise. This is in fact what shows up in Table 2.11. The figures here do, of course, relate to variety and amount scores when theft types involving *only* units of small value are excluded.

But what is particularly challenging about this table is that it provides no sign of fall-off in the *amount* of stealing of this more serious kind, or in the variety of it, as boys go from the age of fifteen towards sixteen years. If anything, *the evidence suggests an increasing rate*. This, of course, is not in line with the indications of the

Table 2.10

Quartile distributions of variety and amount of stealing according to other characteristics of the boys (Level 2 or over) *†

Characteristics of boys	Index of variety of stealing				Index of amount of stealing			
	Low score quartile Q.1 (%)	Q.2 (%)	Q.3 (%)	High score quartile Q.4 (%)	Low score quartile Q.1 (%)	Q.2 (%)	Q.3 (%)	High score quartile Q.4 (%)
Social class								
Professional, semi-professional	33	33	19	15	28	35	23	15
Skilled, non-manual	20	27	29	24	20	27	27	26
Skilled, manual	24	20	29	27	24	24	26	26
Partly skilled	22	24	27	27	23	28	23	26
Unskilled	19	20	29	32	19	27	29	26
Born in UK or not								
Yes	24	25	26	24	23	28	25	23
No	31	21	27	21	31	24	22	23
Religion								
Protestant	23	25	28	24	23	28	22	27
Catholic	21	27	25	27	23	22	29	26
Christian	25	13	27	35	21	22	34	23
Jewish	44	33	16	7	33	35	29	3
None	20	26	26	28	22	27	26	25
Type of school last attended								
Secondary modern	19	20	31	30	20	25	27	28
Comprehensive	24	25	24	27	23	26	26	25
Grammar	32	33	20	15	30	30	23	17
Public	39	29	24	8	28	43	15	14
Does he go out 'just looking for fun and excitement'?								
Yes	15	21	32	32	15	28	28	29
No	31	27	22	19	31	27	23	19
All	25	25	26	24	24	28	25	23

*Level 2 or over: disregarding only instances when the biggest thing ever taken was less than 1/6d. See footnote to Table 2.1 for further information about theft *levels.*
†Percentages have been rounded up or down and in some cases their totals are either 99 or 101 per cent

Table 2.11

Quartile distributions of variety and amount scores
according to ages of boys at interview

Age of boy	Index of variety of stealing				Index of amount of stealing			
	Low score quartile Q.1 (%)	Q.2 (%)	Q.3 (%)	High score quartile Q.4 (%)	Low score quartile Q.1 (%)	Q.2 (%)	Q.3 (%)	High score quartile Q.4 (%)
12/13 yrs	38	25	20	16	36	32	20	12
14 yrs	26	28	27	19	26	30	25	19
15 yrs	23	22	33	22	19	29	27	26
16/17 yrs	14	23	26	37	17	20	28	35

official crime figures and it raises the possibility that the older boys, rather than reducing the amount of their stealing, are simply getting away with it more. This would certainly be in line with an assumption of increasing expertise in thieving amongst the older and more experienced boys.

4 SUMMARY

1 All the 1,425 London boys in the sample admitted to at least some stealing and there was no class of theft amongst the forty-four studied that was endorsed by less than 5 per cent of the boys. In general, the percentages of boys admitting ever committing the different types of theft was high, e.g.: 88 per cent had at some time stolen something from school; 70 per cent had at some time stolen something from a shop, 33 per cent from a stall or barrow; 30 per cent had at some time got something by threatening others; 25 per cent had stolen from a car or lorry or van; 18 per cent had at some time stolen from a telephone box, 17 per cent a letter or parcel, 11 per cent from a meter; 5 per cent had taken a car or lorry or van. The average of such percentages for all forty-four types of theft was 42 per cent. With the discounting of thefts involving trivia, this overall average stands at 30 per cent. For thefts of money or goods involving £1 or more, the average over all forty-four types of theft was 9 per cent.

2 Whereas the incidence of stealing falls off in going from the sons of the unskilled to the sons of the professionally occupied, that fall-off is not drastic and it is clear that stealing is widely spread through the different occupational sectors, with the sons of the professional sector being quite substantially involved in stealing. The position is broadly similar with respect to school background: boys with secondary-modern or comprehensive schooling are more involved in stealing than are boys with grammar-school or public-school backgrounds, but even the latter are quite substantially involved in stealing.

3 Other differences in theft level should be noted: boys born outside the United Kingdom had done somewhat less stealing than other boys; Jewish boys had done less stealing than others and boys who go out just looking for fun and excitement had done more.

4 The evidence does not suggest that boys reduce the extent of their stealing in going from ages fourteen to sixteen.

5 There is a lot of variation in the age at which boys first carry out different kinds of stealing. Types of stealing subject to an early start include: keeping something found, stealing toys, pinching sweets, stealing fruit or other food. Types of theft subject to a late start include: stealing a car or lorry or van, stealing from work, stealing from someone at work, stealing from a cafe.

6 The more serious the level of stealing of a given kind at which a boy operates, the more frequently he commits that type of theft.

7 The forty-four types of theft featured in the inquiry are all positively inter-correlated, those with the highest correlation with 'score' on all forty-four types being: stealing from a shop, pinching sweets, stealing money, stealing from a bike or motor bike.

5 APPENDIX 2.1

Table A2.1
Percentage of boys who have ever committed certain types of theft, irrespective of the value of what was taken (i.e. Level 1 or over). Analysed by characteristics of boys: occupational background of parents; school; age; excitement seeking

Identification no. of type of theft (see p. 72)	Percentage who have done it (Level 1 or over)	Occupational level of boys' fathers*						Type of school last attended				Age of boy				Boy goes out 'just looking for fun and excitement'	
		A (%)	B (%)	C (%)	D (%)	E (%)	F (%)	Secondary modern (%)	Comprehensive (%)	Grammar (%)	Public (%)	12/13 (%)	14 (%)	15 (%)	16/17 (%)	Yes (%)	No (%)
1	98	99	98	98	96	98	98	98	99	97	98	97	98	98	98	98	98
10	97	97	99	95	95	97	98	95	100	98	100	94	98	98	97	98	96
18	88	83	90	88	89	87	91	87	93	88	80	84	86	87	92	90	86
13	81	75	81	80	84	84	86	84	86	76	73	79	85	79	82	87	78
40	73	69	74	72	73	76	76	75	75	69	70	65	70	76	79	79	69
6	70	54	72	67	74	78	74	74	76	60	56	66	72	69	71	80	62
33	69	54	65	76	71	74	69	72	75	65	43	59	68	71	74	75	64
30	68	71	64	69	64	72	69	67	67	71	73	65	63	68	75	72	65
43	66	58	71	69	67	70	59	66	71	71	51	67	60	68	71	69	65
2	64	51	59	70	65	69	72	70	66	56	51	57	63	63	72	75	57
16	61	54	54	59	61	69	78	67	59	53	48	61	59	55	67	68	56
44	58	51	56	56	62	62	65	65	58	50	44	55	52	64	61	68	51
4	57	49	60	61	56	59	56	60	55	55	51	56	54	60	59	43	53
7	56	39	54	57	60	65	60	60	59	49	41	50	56	55	60	63	51
3	52	42	52	56	55	54	52	59	50	41	46	47	52	51	58	62	45
19	49	47	40	47	51	50	61	51	48	44	48	47	48	49	50	55	44
8	47	60	51	42	45	39	48	46	37	48	69	49	45	50	45	47	47
11	44	35	43	45	44	50	47	46	45	39	34	43	40	46	46	51	38
22	42	27	40	40	49	51	46	48	43	36	26	46	38	41	45	50	37
34	37	25	39	42	35	35	47	42	36	32	16	35	35	41	36	44	31
23	34	35	36	36	29	37	33	35	38	31	30	23	30	36	47	38	32
20	34	23	35	36	30	44	37	36	36	33	24	33	28	33	41	39	31
24	34	16	28	34	35	47	48	43	31	24	10	32	32	34	35	44	26
25	33	21	32	34	35	40	40	36	39	27	28	37	29	32	35	37	30
5	33	18	30	30	41	36	45	39	34	24	15	29	34	31	36	38	29
31	32	13	28	35	37	44	35	40	34	24	8	18	25	30	51	41	26
36	31	19	26	28	36	44	37	40	29	21	15	30	30	28	36	41	24
26	31	23	22	35	33	36	32	34	38	20	27	32	30	30	30	40	24
12	30	22	24	32	32	39	32	36	32	21	22	27	33	29	32	38	25
14	28	18	24	30	33	33	31	35	24	21	22	16	28	29	37	37	22
38	25	15	23	21	32	35	26	31	28	16	11	22	22	26	30	32	21
39	22	18	20	19	26	23	34	23	25	21	16	20	25	22	23	26	20
28	21	11	14	22	26	28	30	27	22	16	8	19	19	20	26	24	19
9	20	19	14	19	22	23	22	20	19	19	21	21	16	20	23	24	17
27	20	13	17	21	19	25	24	23	21	13	18	17	16	24	21	24	17
42	18	18	16	19	18	22	16	18	20	18	16	19	17	21	17	23	15
17	18	6	10	18	25	23	28	25	19	8	7	16	15	21	21	25	13
15	18	21	11	15	21	22	18	19	18	12	20	13	18	18	22	24	13
29	17	15	14	18	18	18	22	20	20	10	14	15	16	20	17	22	14
21	15	9	12	13	18	19	20	16	15	13	14	19	12	13	15	18	12
35	14	2	6	15	19	25	19	21	16	4	0	9	12	14	22	21	10
41	11	6	10	9	13	12	17	14	10	6	3	9	9	13	11	13	8
32	8	4	3	10	10	13	10	11	9	4	3	8	6	8	11	11	6
37	5	2	4	4	5	9	4	7	4	2	0	1	3	6	8	7	4
For the average theft type	42%	34%	39%	42%	43%	46%	46%	45%	43%	37%	33%	39%	40%	42%	45%	47%	38%

* = A, Professional, Semi-professional and executive; B, Highly skilled; C, Skilled; D, Moderately skilled; E, Semi-skilled; F, Unskilled.

Table A2.2
Percentage of boys who have ever committed certain types of theft at Level 2 or over*. Analysed by characteristics of boys: occupational background of parents; school; age; excitement seeking

Identification no. of type of theft (see p. 72)	Percentage who have done it (Level 2 or over)	Occupational level of boys' father†						Type of school last attended				Age of boy				Boy goes out 'just looking for fun and excitement'	
		A (%)	B (%)	C (%)	D (%)	E (%)	F (%)	Secondary modern (%)	Comprehensive (%)	Grammar (%)	Public (%)	12/13 (%)	14 (%)	15 (%)	16/17 (%)	Yes (%)	No (%)
1	89	83	90	92	87	92	93	91	92	88	83	79	90	93	94	93	87
10	39	45	36	40	35	40	38	41	36	36	48	16	35	47	55	42	37
18	63	56	62	61	66	64	71	66	63	60	58	43	57	69	79	65	61
13	37	22	30	43	40	46	46	45	37	28	18	28	36	40	44	46	31
40	64	57	67	65	64	64	66	66	70	58	57	53	61	66	73	71	59
6	53	37	56	54	54	65	54	60	55	46	35	44	54	53	62	63	46
33	60	41	56	67	65	67	64	67	70	50	29	48	58	63	70	69	54
30	47	46	39	50	45	52	48	49	45	43	51	29	38	53	64	54	42
43	28	18	25	33	30	35	26	30	34	25	14	24	22	29	38	34	24
2	50	33	46	58	50	57	55	55	51	43	33	40	49	50	59	58	43
16	40	24	37	39	45	50	55	50	40	31	15	35	39	38	49	48	35
44	51	42	46	49	55	58	59	59	53	39	36	42	46	55	59	61	43
4	51	43	56	55	49	55	49	55	50	48	43	46	49	56	54	57	47
7	40	28	43	41	43	45	40	42	46	35	29	31	35	42	50	47	35
3	38	26	40	42	39	42	36	45	36	28	30	30	36	39	46	47	32
19	35	34	28	33	40	37	41	36	36	31	35	29	32	37	42	41	31
8	35	44	36	30	34	32	34	36	27	34	49	32	31	37	39	37	33
11	36	28	36	36	35	44	37	39	39	32	26	33	31	39	40	44	30
22	38	24	36	35	44	47	42	44	37	32	23	39	35	36	41	45	33
34	31	20	31	35	29	32	41	36	30	25	16	30	28	35	31	39	25
23	21	18	18	23	22	23	22	22	24	18	17	10	15	22	34	24	19
20	29	18	27	32	24	41	33	31	32	27	16	26	22	29	36	33	26
24	11	2	8	11	11	18	17	14	13	4	3	8	10	10	14	15	8
25	22	13	17	23	23	28	28	24	25	16	20	21	19	21	26	24	20
5	20	11	16	18	26	25	29	26	22	11	8	18	19	18	25	24	17
31	25	9	20	27	29	38	28	32	29	17	7	11	20	23	44	33	20
36	28	15	24	25	34	43	33	37	27	19	9	27	28	26	34	39	22
26	27	18	19	33	31	34	28	31	34	18	26	27	27	28	27	37	21
12	15	11	12	16	14	23	16	19	17	10	10	10	17	16	18	18	14
14	22	8	20	23	27	31	24	29	22	14	7	11	21	22	33	32	16
38	23	12	21	19	28	34	24	29	27	13	8	19	21	25	27	29	19
39	17	12	13	13	22	19	28	18	20	14	10	11	17	18	21	20	15
28	20	11	14	18	25	26	29	25	19	14	8	16	18	19	24	21	18
9	16	14	11	15	18	18	18	16	15	14	16	15	12	17	18	19	13
27	18	10	15	20	18	24	21	22	19	12	14	14	14	24	20	22	15
42	11	10	6	12	12	14	11	12	14	9	8	8	12	13	10	14	9
17	17	6	10	16	23	23	26	23	19	6	7	15	13	19	20	24	12
15	15	16	10	14	17	20	14	17	16	10	16	11	15	15	20	22	11
29	7	4	4	8	10	8	11	10	8	4	0	9	5	9	6	10	5
21	12	6	9	9	14	16	18	13	13	10	10	14	11	11	11	14	10
35	14	2	6	15	19	25	19	21	16	4	0	9	12	14	22	21	10
41	9	3	6	8	12	10	16	12	9	3	4	7	7	10	10	11	7
32	7	3	3	7	9	11	8	9	8	3	3	6	5	7	8	9	5
37	5	1	4	4	5	9	4	7	4	2	0	1	2	6	8	7	3
For the average theft type	30%	22%	28%	31%	32%	36%	34%	34%	32%	25%	22%	24%	28%	32%	36%	36%	26%

*Appendix Tables A2.1—A2.4 are a series in the sense that they involve increasing seriousness of theft as a qualification for including in the count of thefts. See Part One for details of this system and also the following summary of it.

a *Level 1 or over:* Any theft counts irrespective of its value or seriousness. For example: if the boy has stolen from home at some time or other, he qualifies with regard to that type of theft, no matter how small the value of what was taken.

b *Level 2 or over:* The qualifying value is small, being set at 1/6d or over. For example, if the boy has 'stolen from work' at some time, he qualifies with regard to that type of theft only if the value of the biggest thing 'ever taken from work was 1/6d or

over. Similarly with regard to the value of the biggest thing ever stolen 'from a car or lorry or van'. Similarly for each of the other 42 types of theft.

c *Level 3 or over:* The qualifying value is set at 4/6d for each of the 44 classes of theft.

d *Level 4 or over:* The qualifying value is set at £1 for each of the 44 classes of theft.

†A, Professional, Semi-professional and executive; B, Highly skilled; C, Skilled; D, Moderately skilled; E, Semi-skilled; F, Unskilled.

Table A2.3

Percentage of boys who have ever committed certain types of theft at Level 3 or over*. Analysed by characteristics of boys: occupational background of parents; school; age; excitement seeking

Identification no. of type of theft (see p. 72)	Percentage who have done it (Level 3 or over)	Occupational level of boys' father†						Type of school last attended				Age of boy				Boy goes out 'just looking for fun and excitement'	
		A (%)	B (%)	C (%)	D (%)	E (%)	F (%)	Secondary modern (%)	Comprehensive (%)	Grammar (%)	Public (%)	12/13 (%)	14 (%)	15 (%)	16/17 (%)	Yes (%)	No (%)
1	71	55	66	72	76	83	74	76	80	63	51	60	67	76	80	77	67
10	16	14	15	18	12	19	15	17	13	12	26	3	13	18	27	18	14
18	43	41	36	43	49	46	46	44	46	41	42	21	34	51	64	46	42
13	15	8	11	16	18	20	20	19	14	12	6	7	14	19	19	19	13
40	21	17	26	18	22	23	22	23	23	16	24	9	14	29	32	24	19
6	36	22	36	38	38	47	38	43	38	29	24	29	35	35	46	46	30
33	52	31	48	59	55	59	58	58	62	42	24	38	48	56	63	62	45
30	27	29	19	31	25	31	25	27	25	26	29	10	19	33	43	32	24
43	15	11	10	14	15	24	13	18	15	10	10	13	10	14	22	18	12
2	36	24	32	39	36	46	47	43	36	28	28	28	33	38	45	44	31
16	22	8	22	23	25	30	20	30	22	11	9	16	19	23	28	29	17
44	39	34	34	37	44	48	40	47	39	28	32	31	32	43	49	47	34
4	39	28	37	44	39	43	41	43	41	33	27	30	37	40	46	55	34
7	24	18	22	25	25	27	26	25	30	21	18	17	19	25	33	27	21
3	28	21	27	32	26	33	30	35	24	21	22	22	24	30	35	36	23
19	27	26	24	24	29	29	34	29	26	23	27	21	23	29	34	31	25
8	21	29	19	18	22	20	17	21	14	21	30	19	14	22	28	23	20
11	28	21	26	28	27	36	32	30	30	24	22	23	22	29	36	33	24
22	23	15	20	22	28	29	25	28	24	16	15	26	17	22	28	29	20
34	22	13	20	25	21	24	30	26	18	18	11	20	18	25	23	27	18
23	10	10	6	10	11	14	11	11	14	8	8	5	7	11	17	12	9
20	21	12	19	23	16	30	23	22	22	19	15	17	15	20	28	24	18
24	3	1	2	4	3	5	4	4	4	1	2	2	3	4	4	4	2
25	13	4	9	14	14	19	18	16	18	5	8	12	11	14	13	14	12
5	12	7	9	11	15	16	15	15	13	7	4	8	10	13	16	16	9
31	18	5	15	17	22	29	22	24	19	10	5	7	14	16	33	25	13
36	25	14	20	23	29	38	28	34	21	15	9	20	24	23	31	34	19
26	21	13	11	27	22	29	25	24	30	12	14	18	21	23	23	30	15
12	9	9	6	9	9	12	13	12	9	6	8	5	9	10	13	11	8
14	17	4	15	17	21	25	20	23	16	11	4	8	16	16	26	24	12
38	19	10	18	16	22	30	20	25	22	10	6	17	17	19	24	26	15
39	12	8	9	9	17	15	22	14	16	10	4	7	11	13	18	16	10
28	15	6	10	14	21	21	24	20	14	11	4	13	13	15	20	17	14
9	10	10	5	9	11	13	14	11	8	9	11	7	7	13	13	12	8
27	15	8	10	19	16	22	18	19	16	10	11	12	12	20	17	19	13
42	8	8	4	10	9	8	9	8	10	5	6	6	7	10	8	10	7
17	15	5	8	13	20	22	22	20	17	6	7	13	10	17	19	21	10
15	12	13	7	11	12	16	11	13	12	6	14	6	8	14	18	16	8
29	6	2	4	6	7	6	10	8	5	3	0	6	4	8	5	8	4
21	8	5	7	7	9	11	15	9	11	7	9	9	7	8	9	10	7
35	14	2	6	15	19	25	19	21	16	4	0	9	12	14	22	21	10
41	8	2	6	5	11	10	15	11	7	3	3	6	6	9	3	10	6
32	5	2	2	5	7	9	6	7	6	2	2	4	4	5	6	7	4
37	5	1	4	4	5	9	4	7	4	2	0	1	2	6	8	7	3
For the average theft type	21%	14%	17%	21%	22%	26%	24%	24%	22%	15%	14%	15%	17%	22%	27%	25%	17%

*Appendix Tables A2.1–A2.4 are a series in the sense that they involve increasing seriousness of theft as a qualification for including in the count of thefts. See Part One for details of this system and also the following summary of it.

a *Level 1 or over:* Any theft counts irrespective of its value or seriousness. For example: if the boy has stolen from home at some time or other, he qualifies with regard to that type of theft, no matter how small the value of what was taken.

b *Level 2 or over:* The qualifying value is small, being set at 1/6d or over. For example, if the boy has 'stolen from work' at some time, he qualifies with regard to that type of theft only if the value of the biggest thing 'ever taken from work' was 1/6d or

over. Similarly with regard to the value of the biggest thing ever solten 'from a car or lorry or van'. Similarly for each of the other 42 types of theft.

c *Level 3 or over:* The qualifing value is set at 4/6d for each of the 44 classes of theft.

d *Level 4 or over:* The qualifying value is set at £1 for each of the 44 classes of theft.

†A, Professional, Semi-professional and Executive; B, Highly skilled; C, Skilled; D, Moderately skilled; E, Semi-skilled; F, Unskilled.

Table A2.4
Percentage of boys who have ever committed certain types of theft at Level 4 or over*. Analysed by characteristics of boys: occupational background of parents; school; age; excitement seeking

Identification no. of type of theft (see p. 72)	Percentage who have done it (Level 4 or over)	Occupational level of boys' father†						Type of school last attended				Age of boy				Boy goes out 'just looking for fun and excitement'	
		A (%)	B (%)	C (%)	D (%)	E (%)	F (%)	Secondary modern (%)	Comprehensive (%)	Grammar (%)	Public (%)	12/13 (%)	14 (%)	15 (%)	16/17 (%)	Yes (%)	No (%)
1	40	24	34	42	43	52	45	46	45	31	17	29	33	44	53	46	36
10	2	3	1	3	3	3	4	2	2	1	5	0	2	3	4	3	2
18	13	14	8	15	14	12	18	13	15	11	20	6	6	17	22	13	13
13	5	2	3	6	7	4	7	5	6	3	5	2	4	7	6	6	3
40	1	0	0	1	1	2	3	1	1	1	0	0	1	1	1	2	0
6	16	10	11	17	18	21	16	20	16	9	10	9	14	15	22	21	11
33	33	16	26	38	39	41	39	42	37	21	15	18	27	39	48	42	27
30	7	5	7	6	6	8	10	7	9	4	8	1	3	5	16	10	4
43	5	3	6	5	5	8	2	7	6	2	2	4	3	3	9	5	5
2	18	8	15	21	21	25	20	24	18	9	15	10	14	21	26	23	15
16	6	3	7	7	8	5	7	9	4	2	6	4	5	8	8	8	5
44	22	17	16	18	29	26	26	28	23	10	18	16	16	24	29	29	16
4	17	8	13	19	17	21	26	20	18	12	6	11	14	16	25	20	14
7	6	6	4	5	8	7	7	7	6	6	4	3	5	6	10	6	6
3	13	4	14	16	15	15	17	18	11	7	6	8	12	13	20	18	10
19	8	9	7	4	10	8	16	10	7	4	12	6	5	9	12	10	7
8	8	13	6	8	6	9	9	10	6	5	12	7	5	7	14	10	7
11	11	9	10	9	10	16	21	14	11	7	9	6	7	11	20	14	10
22	8	7	4	8	10	9	9	10	6	21	4	7	5	8	11	9	7
34	10	7	9	11	9	13	13	12	8	8	3	8	7	13	11	14	8
23	2	0	0	2	3	3	3	3	2	0	0	1	1	3	2	3	1
20	9	4	8	11	9	10	11	11	9	5	8	5	6	9	14	11	7
24	1	0	0	1	1	0	2	1	0	0	0	0	1	1	1	1	1
25	3	0	0	5	4	6	8	5	5	0	0	2	3	4	5	4	3
5	4	3	4	3	5	7	6	5	4	4	2	3	3	5	6	6	3
31	8	3	6	7	12	14	8	11	9	5	4	3	6	5	18	12	6
36	12	4	9	10	15	20	16	17	9	7	1	7	11	10	20	16	10
26	11	3	8	12	12	16	15	14	14	5	7	7	11	13	11	16	7
12	4	2	3	5	3	5	4	5	3	2	4	1	3	4	6	6	2
14	8	3	6	9	8	11	11	12	7	4	2	3	6	8	14	12	5
38	13	4	10	11	18	18	12	17	15	6	2	8	11	12	18	19	8
39	6	5	4	4	7	8	11	7	7	5	3	4	4	7	9	9	4
28	8	2	4	7	11	11	12	12	6	4	0	6	3	9	12	10	6
9	4	5	2	3	4	5	8	5	2	4	7	2	4	5	6	4	4
27	9	3	5	11	9	15	13	12	10	3	6	6	6	13	11	12	7
42	3	2	1	4	4	2	5	4	3	3	2	1	3	5	4	4	2
17	11	3	5	10	16	16	18	16	13	3	4	8	7	12	17	16	7
15	5	5	3	3	7	7	8	6	7	3	5	3	4	6	9	7	4
29	4	2	4	2	4	5	6	5	3	2	3	4	2	5	3	5	3
21	4	2	3	3	5	4	8	5	4	3	4	4	3	4	5	4	4
35	14	2	6	15	19	23	19	21	15	3	0	8	11	14	21	20	9
41	4	1	2	3	6	6	10	7	3	1	0	2	3	6	6	6	3
32	2	1	1	2	3	4	4	3	3	0	2	2	2	3	2	3	2
37	5	1	4	4	5	9	4	7	4	2	0	1	2	6	8	7	3
For the average theft type	9%‡	5%	7%	9%	11%	12%	12%	12%	9%	6%	6%	6%	7%	10%	14%	12%	7%

‡See Table A2.1

*Appendix Tables A2.1–A2.4 are a series in the sense that they involve increasing seriousness of theft as a qualification for including in the count of thefts. See Part One for details of this system and also the following summary of it.

a *Level 1 or over:* Any theft counts irrespective of its value or seriousness. For example: if the boy has stolen from home at some time or other, he qualifies with regard to that type of theft, no matter how small the value of what was taken.

b *Level 2 or over:* The qualifying value is small, being set at 1/6d or over. For example, if the boy has 'stolen from work' at some time, he qualifies with regard to that type of theft only if the value of the biggest thing 'ever taken from work' was 1/6d or over. Similarly with regard to the value of the biggest thing ever stolen 'from a car or lorry or van'. Similarly for each of the other 42 types of theft.

c *Level 3 or over:* The qualifying value is set at 4/6d for each of the 44 classes of theft.

d *Level 4 or over:* The qualifying value is set at £1 for each of the 44 classes of theft.

†A, Professional, Semi-professional and Executive; B, Highly skilled; C, Skilled; D, Moderately skilled; E, Semi-skilled; F, Unskilled.

91

Table A2.5

Ages at which boys first committed certain types of theft (Level 2 or over)

Identification no. of type of theft	Percentage who committed it at Level 2 or over (%)	Age of first committing this type of theft							Average age at first theft of this kind (years)
		6 or less (%)	7—8 (%)	9—10 (%)	11—12 (%)	13—14 (%)	15—16 (%)	Not known (%)	
1	89	28	23	21	15	6	2	5	8.7
10	39	8	12	23	32	20	4	2	10.7
18	63	9	14	19	34	19	4	1	10.6
13	37	22	20	26	21	9	1	2	9.2
40	64	4	9	19	27	30	10	1	11.6
6	53	11	17	28	25	14	2	3	10.0
33	60	3	5	13	26	35	16	3	12.2
30	47	4	5	10	28	35	14	3	12.2
43	28	4	9	13	28	30	15	1	11.9
2	50	8	10	17	30	24	9	3	11.1
16	40	15	22	23	23	13	3	1	9.7
44	51	13	18	21	23	19	3	3	10.2
4	51	5	9	18	25	33	8	2	11.5
7	40	3	7	19	30	32	7	2	11.6
3	38	7	12	18	30	21	10	2	11.1
19	35	7	12	16	34	25	-5	2	11.0
8	35	17	14	23	25	14	4	3	10.0
11	36	15	17	14	23	22	7	2	10.5
22	38	25	21	23	18	11	1	1	9.1
34	31	8	17	18	24	24	8	1	10.8
23	21	1	2	8	20	41	27	2	13.2
20	29	3	6	15	26	37	10	3	12.0
24	11	2	10	21	20	34	12	2	11.8
25	22	6	10	23	26	22	11	2	11.2
5	20	7	12	20	26	25	9	2	11.1
31	25	0	1	2	13	35	47	2	14.0
36	28	1	3	13	26	36	18	3	12.5
26	27	2	8	16	28	33	12	2	11.9
12	15	6	8	8	22	40	13	3	12.0
14	22	1	4	10	25	43	16	2	12.6
38	23	2	6	10	25	33	22	3	12.6
39	17	0	1	7	26	39	23	3	13.1
28	20	3	7	18	25	31	16	1	11.9
9	16	10	9	13	30	20	17	2	11.4
27	18	1	7	9	23	42	17	1	12.6
42	11	1	0	7	27	45	18	2	13.0
17	17	1	4	21	25	36	13	1	12.1
15	15	3	12	9	34	28	13	1	11.8
29	7	1	8	11	22	35	17	6	12.4
21	12	6	15	16	29	27	6	2	11.0
35	14	2	3	5	21	47	19	4	13.0
41	9	2	0	12	26	40	19	1	12.7
32	7	0	2	5	19	30	44	0	13.7
37	5	0	1	5	3	42	49	1	14.2
Average	30%	6%	9%	15%	25%	29%	14%	2%	11.6

Table A2.6

Number of years between first and most recent theft of
this kind (= duration) at Level 2 or over

Identification no. of type of theft	Percentage who committed it at Level 2 or over	Less than 1 year (%)	Duration in years (= years between first and most recent theft of this kind)								Average duration in years
			1 year (%)	2 years (%)	3 years (%)	4 years (%)	5 years (%)	6–7 years (%)	8+ years (%)	Not known (%)	
1	89	3	4	8	9	11	10	19	31	6	5.4
10	39	7	12	11	14	13	13	16	13	2	4.1
18	63	8	12	11	16	14	12	13	12	1	3.9
13	37	4	8	9	11	9	14	18	24	3	4.9
40	64	13	19	19	13	12	7	9	7	2	3.0
6	53	7	10	15	11	11	13	16	14	3	4.2
33	60	16	26	15	12	8	8	7	5	3	2.6
30	47	16	20	18	13	9	6	8	6	4	2.8
43	28	18	18	18	11	8	7	11	8	2	3.0
2	50	12	17	18	13	12	6	10	9	4	3.2
16	40	9	11	11	13	13	10	15	16	2	4.2
44	51	8	14	11	11	11	12	15	15	3	4.1
4	51	16	21	16	13	8	8	9	6	3	2.9
7	40	15	18	18	14	11	10	7	7	1	3.0
3	38	14	17	14	12	11	9	11	8	3	3.3
19	35	12	15	13	17	12	9	10	10	2	3.4
8	35	11	10	12	10	11	8	15	20	3	4.2
11	36	9	13	13	12	8	7	15	19	4	4.1
22	38	11	16	13	14	13	9	13	9	2	3.5
34	31	14	17	14	10	14	9	13	9	0	3.4
23	21	25	24	20	15	6	5	3	2	0	2.2
20	29	17	23	21	12	10	5	8	3	2	2.5
24	11	15	24	11	13	13	5	12	6	2	3.0
25	22	21	21	8	11	12	10	11	4	2	2.9
5	20	15	15	15	12	13	8	14	5	3	3.4
31	25	39	35	12	7	3	2	0	0	1	1.3
36	28	23	22	30	10	6	3	3	1	2	1.9
26	27	25	26	16	8	8	5	6	5	2	2.3
12	15	22	26	15	13	4	4	4	7	4	2.4
14	22	24	27	16	11	8	8	3	3	1	2.2
38	23	24	32	14	7	6	6	6	2	4	2.1
39	17	29	33	17	8	3	2	2	1	4	1.6
28	20	26	24	15	10	7	5	8	3	1	2.3
9	16	19	20	15	9	6	6	17	5	4	3.0
27	18	27	32	10	8	7	5	6	3	2	2.1
42	11	30	34	18	5	8	5	1	0	0	1.6
17	17	25	30	15	12	7	3	3	5	1	2.2
15	15	20	23	15	11	10	8	8	4	2	2.6
29	7	17	20	14	16	11	9	6	3	4	2.7
21	12	12	14	14	25	12	5	6	9	3	3.2
35	14	23	34	17	8	5	3	1	3	5	1.8
41	9	29	32	10	14	4	3	1	4	4	1.8
32	7	45	31	7	9	2	4	0	0	2	1.2
37	5	46	37	6	4	0	4	2	0	2	1.2
Average	30%	19%	21%	14%	12%	9%	7%	9%	7%	3%	2.9%

Table A2.7
Number of times the different types of theft were committed at Level 1 or over

Identification no. of type of theft	No. of times committed								Average all boys (with ceiling of 20)	Average excluding boys who had *never* done it (with ceiling of 20)
	0	1	2	3–4	5–7	8–10	11–20	20+		
1	70	204	235	484	585	424	519	592	9.50	9.72
10	115	152	164	307	363	312	551	1149	12.23	12.70
18	393	371	265	457	459	325	420	423	7.44	8.51
13	587	234	213	398	318	313	433	617	8.30	10.23
40	847	561	331	379	330	207	225	233	4.67	6.42
6	947	221	197	295	374	256	372	451	6.74	9.69
33	991	743	404	353	243	133	142	104	3.12	4.58
30	1005	545	260	473	266	177	193	194	4.11	6.06
43	1046	687	340	304	252	150	182	152	3.58	5.40
2	1122	509	296	335	337	156	182	176	3.87	6.05
16	1227	226	158	285	255	214	315	433	5.96	9.83
44	1308	259	157	313	319	220	260	277	4.86	8.38
4	1346	665	253	295	229	92	123	110	2.73	4.82
7	1382	411	247	313	266	124	187	183	3.62	6.51
3	1490	587	244	260	241	111	87	93	2.45	4.71
19	1610	354	214	330	224	103	148	130	2.96	6.16
8	1650	347	152	248	239	106	192	179	3.36	7.15
11	1755	295	186	278	219	123	145	112	2.75	6.17
22	1804	328	188	230	217	104	121	121	2.58	6.14
34	1979	357	122	190	116	92	109	118	2.25	6.19
23	2051	417	180	168	94	77	70	56	1.55	4.55
20	2065	448	176	147	100	67	49	61	1.44	4.29
24	2070	373	133	140	115	93	75	114	1.96	5.85
25	2087	337	192	154	121	63	69	90	1.74	5.29
5	2095	352	141	155	128	89	77	76	1.75	5.36
31	2126	281	123	160	146	62	82	133	2.08	6.54
36	2144	387	156	168	112	35	45	66	1.38	4.43
26	2165	484	135	144	62	49	33	41	1.09	3.59
12	2180	303	195	120	97	54	69	95	1.65	5.52
14	2237	194	101	137	122	64	128	130	2.17	7.73
38	2334	348	145	114	65	31	37	39	0.98	3.93
39	2423	329	137	88	64	31	18	23	0.74	3.35
28	2455	315	93	98	56	34	21	41	0.85	4.00
9	2500	297	132	75	63	15	18	13	0.60	3.06
27	2508	329	91	75	39	19	30	22	0.67	3.44
42	2549	330	66	69	32	32	23	12	0.57	3.16
17	2558	228	53	78	76	26	49	45	0.95	5.33
15	2562	221	123	71	46	25	32	33	0.76	4.31
29	2581	325	60	60	46	14	15	12	0.49	2.88
21	2655	218	64	68	47	24	17	20	0.56	3.81
35	2671	169	94	90	36	16	26	11	0.53	3.74
41	2787	152	51	40	31	27	8	17	0.41	3.95
32	2858	106	56	35	32	5	11	10	0.30	3.72
37	2965	96	24	16	6	0	1	5	0.11	2.38

Table A2.8
Number of times the different types of theft were
committed at Level 2 or over

Identification no. of type of theft	No. of times committed								Average all boys (with ceiling of 20)	Average excluding boys who had *never* done it (with ceiling of 20)
	0	1	2	3–4	5–7	8–10	11–20	20+		
1	339	172	198	397	527	408	494	578	9.00	10.10
10	1902	35	25	80	98	127	224	622	5.78	14.87
18	1165	196	170	317	310	259	339	357	5.86	9.36
13	1950	41	51	134	130	157	231	419	4.74	12.70
40	1134	422	272	344	307	193	214	227	4.37	6.88
6	1455	98	78	213	295	212	336	426	5.91	11.10
33	1244	644	352	311	224	110	126	102	2.82	4.69
30	1665	312	188	315	198	140	144	151	3.05	6.55
43	2230	242	131	161	108	78	75	88	1.72	6.05
2	1572	354	217	269	264	118	149	170	3.24	6.54
16	1854	76	65	167	184	162	248	357	4.61	11.39
44	1536	193	105	268	279	212	257	263	4.55	8.98
4	1523	584	222	271	210	82	114	107	2.53	4.96
7	1870	226	160	241	198	98	160	160	2.94	7.35
3	1929	395	178	190	191	81	66	83	1.92	5.05
19	2020	243	141	228	174	93	109	105	2.25	6.40
8	2034	219	102	195	178	83	157	145	2.65	7.65
11	1997	237	146	210	184	104	142	93	2.37	6.60
22	1941	284	154	206	201	104	115	108	2.38	6.31
34	2161	303	100	155	124	83	95	92	1.88	6.14
23	2460	257	112	114	60	48	40	22	0.88	4.18
20	2227	359	149	133	87	64	47	47	1.25	4.39
24	2782	91	21	45	52	49	27	46	0.77	7.20
25	2437	201	131	97	86	42	55	64	1.23	5.66
5	2485	170	90	99	86	55	67	61	1.27	6.32
31	2334	190	103	124	125	54	69	114	1.74	6.95
36	2221	341	144	156	110	34	41	66	1.32	4.59
26	2260	425	127	130	52	48	32	39	1.01	3.70
12	2636	142	108	65	47	20	38	57	0.89	5.82
14	2424	124	86	116	95	52	100	116	1.80	8.14
38	2400	314	131	108	64	30	33	33	0.89	3.90
39	2592	245	98	67	54	24	15	18	0.58	3.47
28	2511	295	77	83	56	32	20	39	0.79	4.08
9	2631	228	113	52	47	15	16	11	0.49	3.16
27	2551	299	81	72	39	19	30	22	0.65	3.60
42	2775	192	42	49	23	17	7	8	0.32	2.98
17	2597	203	53	68	73	25	49	45	0.92	5.56
15	2643	173	113	62	45	22	31	24	0.66	4.35
29	2884	138	28	24	14	7	11	7	0.24	3.21
21	2755	163	49	55	40	23	8	20	0.46	3.98
35	2671	169	94	90	36	16	26	11	0.53	3.74
41	2842	129	34	31	29	27	4	17	0.36	4.15
32	2907	95	34	30	25	4	9	9	0.25	3.75
37	2965	96	24	16	6	0	1	5	0.11	2.38

Table A2.9
Number of times the different types of theft were
committed at Level 3 or over

Identification no. of type of theft	No. of times committed								Average all boys (with ceiling of 20)	Average excluding boys who had *never* done it (with ceiling of 20)
	0	1	2	3–4	5–7	8–10	11–20	20+		
1	905	138	156	295	407	330	386	496	7.32	10.32
10	2623	13	1	37	33	30	70	306	2.51	15.95
18	1765	101	127	189	212	168	261	284	4.35	10.04
13	2644	25	24	51	43	45	68	213	2.00	13.28
40	2453	85	76	112	99	62	102	124	1.88	8.85
6	1977	56	28	118	172	146	236	380	4.54	12.44
33	1507	525	311	266	206	96	114	88	2.48	4.80
30	2277	173	77	183	126	80	79	118	1.94	7.21
43	2656	114	72	80	64	35	41	51	0.93	6.33
2	1980	226	164	203	211	82	104	143	2.49	6.83
16	2435	27	17	67	85	90	154	238	2.81	12.92
44	1893	123	78	174	215	173	209	248	3.83	9.78
4	1916	397	164	225	168	52	101	90	2.04	5.31
7	2376	82	73	150	129	66	124	113	2.02	8.55
3	2238	296	118	147	151	45	46	72	1.45	5.15
19	2266	181	109	153	149	64	94	97	1.86	6.85
8	2459	119	53	109	109	50	101	113	1.78	8.46
11	2247	178	112	156	135	79	121	85	1.94	6.98
22	2388	127	70	127	151	82	84	84	1.71	7.36
34	2440	232	77	83	90	50	71	70	1.34	6.19
23	2796	110	48	61	36	27	24	11	0.47	4.64
20	2476	236	98	100	67	46	46	44	1.03	5.01
24	3020	37	4	7	14	4	10	17	2.20	7.36
25	2721	128	69	52	42	23	41	37	0.73	5.82
5	2745	90	50	54	57	41	42	34	0.78	6.58
31	2555	112	76	76	86	48	61	99	1.41	7.89
36	2341	259	134	140	105	33	35	66	1.22	4.93
26	2454	297	109	112	43	29	32	37	0.86	4.04
12	2825	64	72	35	31	17	28	41	0.62	6.68
14	2585	69	70	72	78	47	94	98	1.53	9.03
38	2514	252	125	86	55	21	28	32	0.77	4.00
39	2730	171	73	47	41	20	13	18	0.47	3.84
28	2636	223	65	63	52	22	19	33	0.65	4.27
9	2804	134	83	27	34	11	14	6	0.33	3.35
27	2638	258	67	65	20	15	29	21	0.56	3.67
42	2866	152	34	37	9	3	6	6	0.21	2.61
17	2657	172	49	62	59	24	48	42	0.85	5.79
15	2750	124	92	54	28	16	25	24	0.46	4.62
29	2939	102	19	22	11	6	9	5	0.19	3.31
21	2853	95	40	47	34	17	7	20	0.39	4.63
35	2671	169	94	90	36	16	26	11	0.53	3.74
41	2881	110	29	22	29	21	4	17	0.32	4.35
32	2959	66	25	24	19	4	8	8	0.20	4.35
37	2965	96	24	16	6	0	1	5	1.13	2.38

Table A2.10
Number of times the different types of theft were committed at Level 4 or over

Identification no. of type of theft	No. of times committed								Average all boys (with ceiling of 20)	Average excluding boys who had *never* done it (with ceiling of 20)
	0	1	2	3–4	5–7	8–10	11–20	20+		
1	1869	76	61	146	220	184	224	333	4.44	11.11
10	3038	0	0	4	4	12	8	47	0.39	16.13
18	2705	17	34	41	60	44	92	120	1.55	11.79
13	2969	7	7	20	13	9	17	71	0.62	13.43
40	3083	0	0	1	6	4	7	12	0.14	14.13
6	2630	11	5	37	70	34	106	220	2.22	14.33
33	2088	294	173	185	135	80	88	70	1.79	5.45
30	2908	43	19	37	16	18	23	49	0.58	8.80
43	2960	34	20	22	23	14	19	21	0.36	7.38
2	2552	96	76	103	90	44	57	95	1.39	7.71
16	2923	1	2	13	16	36	44	78	0.87	14.28
44	2445	52	34	72	119	100	130	161	2.32	10.81
4	2597	168	61	105	85	22	38	37	0.86	5.22
7	2928	19	6	34	42	15	31	38	0.57	9.61
3	2702	125	55	74	65	22	21	49	0.77	5.81
19	2863	45	18	40	39	22	36	50	0.71	8.84
8	2855	48	22	38	48	22	26	54	0.70	8.50
11	2762	49	44	55	64	40	62	37	0.89	7.90
22	2875	40	9	50	49	37	25	28	0.58	7.59
34	2804	125	43	38	37	23	24	19	0.49	4.94
23	3059	16	9	14	3	2	4	6	0.10	5.57
20	2843	81	28	51	39	25	20	26	0.52	5.94
24	3091	6	1	1	9	0	2	3	0.05	7.11
25	3007	19	24	13	10	8	18	14	0.26	7.58
5	2976	27	20	32	22	9	11	16	0.28	6.44
31	2853	44	25	32	41	20	30	68	0.79	9.45
36	2740	109	52	56	68	18	24	46	0.73	6.09
26	2777	125	59	71	27	16	18	20	0.47	4.39
12	3002	16	33	8	12	6	10	26	0.29	8.21
14	2868	29	29	24	27	29	50	57	0.81	10.24
38	2725	125	87	63	36	21	27	29	0.62	4.96
39	2924	79	39	25	18	9	8	11	0.25	4.11
28	2881	97	35	37	23	11	9	20	0.34	4.63
9	2983	53	35	10	13	5	9	5	0.17	4.00
27	2834	124	54	33	16	4	27	21	0.42	4.72
42	3019	44	15	22	4	0	3	6	0.11	3.63
17	2773	110	41	45	49	23	38	34	0.68	6.23
15	2948	47	38	23	20	7	14	16	0.30	5.60
29	3001	65	19	7	6	6	4	5	0.12	3.39
21	2989	42	13	24	27	10	0	8	0.18	4.55
35	2671	169	94	90	36	16	26	11	0.53	3.74
41	2983	53	24	18	15	6	4	10	0.18	4.38
32	3044	20	13	7	11	4	8	6	0.13	6.04
37	2965	96	24	16	6	0	1	5	0.11	2.38

Table A2.11

Quartile distributions of variety and amount scores
according to characteristics of boys (Level 2 or over)

| Characteristics | Quartile scores for L2+ | | | | | | | |
| | Variety | | | | Amount | | | |
	Q1 (%)	Q2 (%)	Q3 (%)	Q4 (%)	Q1 (%)	Q2 (%)	Q3 (%)	Q4 (%)
Occupational level (Belson)								
1 and 2	35.1	35.3	17.2	12.4	27.6	40.0	18.7	13.7
3	26.4	30.2	26.5	16.9	24.9	24.1	31.7	19.3
4	22.6	19.9	32.6	24.9	22.8	24.9	27.9	24.4
5	24.1	22.9	24.4	28.6	27.0	26.0	20.6	26.3
6	20.3	16.1	28.0	35.6	20.4	22.8	25.1	31.7
7	16.1	26.8	30.3	26.8	17.7	31.1	28.3	22.8
Social class (Registrar General)								
I and II	33.2	32.9	18.8	15.1	27.7	34.8	22.8	14.7
III NM	20.2	26.7	29.3	23.8	20.0	26.9	27.4	25.7
III M	23.5	20.3	29.3	26.9	24.4	23.8	25.6	26.2
IV	21.6	24.0	27.0	27.4	23.1	28.1	23.1	25.6
V	19.2	20.0	29.2	31.6	18.8	26.8	28.8	25.6
Age at time of interview								
12/13 yrs	38.0	25.2	20.4	16.4	35.9	32.4	19.7	12.1
14 yrs	26.0	28.3	26.9	18.9	26.3	30.3	14.7	18.7
15 yrs	22.5	22.4	32.6	22.4	19.0	28.8	26.7	25.6
16/17 yrs	14.4	23.0	25.6	36.9	16.5	20.2	28.3	34.9
Born in UK or not								
Yes	24.2	25.1	26.3	24.4	23.4	28.0	25.3	23.3
No	31.1	20.6	27.2	21.0	31.4	23.7	22.2	22.6
Religion								
Church of England	21.8	26.0	28.9	23.2	22.5	28.1	23.4	26.0
Methodist/Presbyterian/Protestant	27.8	17.9	25.9	28.3	24.1	27.8	17.0	31.1
Roman Catholic/Catholic	20.8	27.0	25.0	27.2	22.8	22.4	29.0	25.8
Christian	25.0	12.5	27.3	35.2	21.0	22.2	34.1	22.7
Greek Orthodox	32.5	15.6	42.9	9.1	32.5	33.8	22.1	11.7
Jewish	44.4	33.2	15.9	6.5	33.2	34.6	29.0	3.3
Other	42.1	21.4	20.0	16.4	37.1	35.0	19.3	8.6
Not applicable (no religion)	20.3	25.6	26.1	28.0	21.6	27.4	25.6	25.4
Type of school								
Secondary modern	18.8	19.9	31.1	30.2	19.9	25.3	27.1	27.7
Technical	13.2	22.6	32.1	32.1	20.8	7.5	41.5	30.2
Grammar	31.9	33.0	19.9	15.2	30.2	30.4	22.8	16.6
Public	39.2	29.4	23.5	7.8	28.2	43.1	14.5	14.1
Comprehensive	24.0	24.8	24.0	27.1	22.6	26.4	26.4	24.6
Other	45.9	29.7	5.4	18.9	48.6	13.5	18.9	18.9
Fun and excitement seeking (at present)								
Yes	15.3	20.9	32.2	31.6	14.7	28.3	28.1	28.9
No	31.4	27.3	22.2	19.0	30.6	26.9	23.0	19.4
All boys	24.8	24.7	26.4	24.1	24.1	27.7	25.0	23.3

Table A2.12

Quartile distributions of variety and amount scores according to characteristics of boys (Level 4 or over)

Characteristics	Quartile scores for L4+							
	Variety				Amount			
	Q1 (%)	Q2 (%)	Q3 (%)	Q4 (%)	Q1 (%)	Q2 (%)	Q3 (%)	Q4 (%)
Occupational level (Belson)								
1 and 2	43.8	31.1	16.6	8.5	43.8	20.8	21.6	13.7
3	36.6	33.1	16.9	13.4	34.8	24.9	24.3	16.0
4	28.9	24.0	25.8	21.2	28.5	21.5	27.4	22.6
5	26.8	26.5	21.6	25.1	26.8	24.3	24.3	24.6
6	18.6	27.5	27.5	26.5	18.4	24.2	26.5	30.9
7	21.3	24.0	28.3	26.4	20.9	24.8	28.7	25.6
Social class (Registrar General)								
I and II	42.2	29.7	16.5	11.6	41.4	20.9	22.5	15.1
III NM	30.0	31.6	21.0	17.5	30.0	27.4	24.1	18.6
III M	27.3	24.9	25.5	22.4	26.7	21.7	27.2	24.5
IV	21.8	30.3	23.1	24.7	21.8	26.7	24.3	27.2
V	20.8	25.6	26.0	27.6	20.4	24.8	27.6	27.2
Age at time of interview								
12/13 yrs	44.5	28.0	17.1	10.4	43.3	21.1	24.3	11.4
14 yrs	34.9	29.2	22.5	13.4	34.9	25.6	24.7	14.8
15 yrs	24.3	31.4	24.5	19.8	24.1	25.1	27.7	23.1
16/17 yrs	18.0	23.2	24.9	33.9	17.5	21.5	24.4	36.6
Born in UK or not								
Yes	30.4	27.5	21.8	20.3	29.9	23.2	24.5	22.4
No	24.5	31.1	28.8	15.6	24.5	24.1	33.5	17.9
Religion								
Church of England	30.7	25.5	23.2	20.6	30.1	20.5	25.7	23.7
Methodist/Presbyterian/Protestant	23.1	33.0	22.2	21.7	23.1	32.5	24.5	19.8
Roman Catholic/Catholic	33.4	24.2	21.4	21.0	32.4	17.4	28.0	22.2
Christian	29.5	22.7	29.0	18.8	29.5	20.5	26.7	23.3
Greek Orthodox	23.4	26.0	33.8	16.9	23.4	31.2	27.3	18.2
Jewish	38.3	39.7	19.2	2.8	40.7	32.2	19.6	7.5
Other	37.9	35.7	10.0	16.4	37.9	30.0	16.4	15.7
Not Applicable (No religion)	24.3	29.3	22.1	24.3	23.2	25.3	25.1	26.4
Type of school								
Secondary modern	22.4	24.5	26.9	26.1	22.4	23.7	27.2	26.7
Technical	18.9	22.6	32.1	26.4	18.9	32.1	22.6	26.4
Grammar	44.6	30.8	14.3	10.3	42.6	23.4	20.2	13.8
Public	42.7	33.3	15.7	8.2	44.7	20.0	19.6	15.7
Comprehensive	24.6	30.8	23.3	21.3	24.2	22.4	29.1	24.2
Other	43.2	32.4	5.4	18.9	43.2	18.9	29.7	8.1
Fun and excitement seeking (at present)								
Yes	21.4	23.6	28.7	26.3	21.1	21.8	28.6	28.5
No	35.7	30.8	18.1	15.4	35.1	24.4	23.0	17.6
All boys	29.9	27.8	22.4	19.9	29.5	23.3	25.2	22.0

APPENDIX 2.2 CORRELATION MATRIX
Correlation matrix for the 44 theft types
(Sample size : weighted 3113; unweighted 1425)

Theft type	1	2	3	4	5	6	7	8	9	10	11	12	13	14	15	16	17	18	19	20	21	22
1	1.00	0.18	0.19	0.13	0.12	0.23	0.15	0.07	0.09	0.15	0.20	0.12	0.17	0.13	0.10	0.19	0.10	0.24	0.15	0.14	0.08	0.16
2	0.18	1.00	0.36	0.16	0.30	0.43	0.33	0.15	0.18	0.19	0.28	0.22	0.37	0.29	0.19	0.30	0.23	0.24	0.24	0.31	0.16	0.32
3	0.19	0.36	1.00	0.15	0.25	0.29	0.27	0.08	0.15	0.14	0.25	0.21	0.33	0.25	0.19	0.21	0.21	0.20	0.26	0.28	0.19	0.22
4	0.13	0.16	0.15	1.00	0.14	0.16	0.15	0.10	0.07	0.12	0.12	0.09	0.16	0.16	0.08	0.17	0.11	0.16	0.12	0.17	0.12	0.14
5	0.12	0.30	0.25	0.14	1.00	0.35	0.28	0.07	0.21	0.19	0.19	0.21	0.30	0.28	0.28	0.38	0.26	0.21	0.25	0.24	0.16	0.24
6	0.23	0.43	0.29	0.16	0.35	1.00	0.38	0.17	0.20	0.25	0.32	0.22	0.50	0.33	0.24	0.36	0.24	0.26	0.27	0.34	0.15	0.35
7	0.15	0.33	0.27	0.15	0.28	0.38	1.00	0.11	0.20	0.25	0.25	0.17	0.32	0.25	0.21	0.27	0.22	0.32	0.29	0.27	0.16	0.28
8	0.07	0.15	0.08	0.10	0.07	0.17	0.11	1.00	0.20	0.08	0.19	0.08	0.13	0.11	0.15	0.10	0.04	0.11	0.18	0.08	0.05	0.19
9	0.09	0.18	0.15	0.07	0.21	0.20	0.20	0.20	1.00	0.17	0.27	0.20	0.17	0.17	0.31	0.12	0.20	0.17	0.25	0.21	0.16	0.30
10	0.15	0.19	0.14	0.12	0.19	0.25	0.25	0.08	0.17	1.00	0.19	0.20	0.28	0.23	0.19	0.16	0.21	0.25	0.20	0.20	0.10	0,13
11	0.20	0.28	0.25	0.12	0.19	0.32	0.25	0.19	0.27	0.19	1.00	0.22	0.25	0.24	0.28	0.20	0.21	0.23	0.46	0.24	0.19	0.36
12	0.12	0.22	0.21	0.09	0.21	0.22	0.17	0.08	0.20	0.20	0.22	1.00	0.24	0.18	0.19	0.20	0.20	0.12	0.23	0.18	0.18	0.15
13	0.17	0.37	0.33	0.16	0.30	0.50	0.32	0.13	0.17	0.28	0.25	0.24	1.00	0.35	0.23	0.35	0.28	0.28	0.25	0.31	0.17	0.30
14	0.13	0.29	0.25	0.16	0.28	0.33	0.25	0.11	0.17	0.23	0.24	0.18	0.35	1.00	0.19	0.23	0.32	0.23	0.22	0.27	0.23	0.23
15	0.10	0.19	0.19	0.08	0.28	0.24	0.21	0.15	0.31	0.19	0.28	0.19	0.23	0.19	1.00	0.16	0.24	0.21	0.40	0.20	0.18	0.25
16	0.19	0.30	0.21	0.17	0.38	0.36	0.27	0.10	0.12	0.16	0.20	0.20	0.35	0.23	0.16	1.00	0.25	0.17	0.18	0.27	0.16	0.30
17	0.10	0.23	0.21	0.11	0.26	0.24	0.22	0.04	0.20	0.21	0.21	0.20	0.28	0.32	0.24	0.25	1.00	0.17	0.23	0.24	0.16	0.25
18	0.24	0.24	0.20	0.16	0.21	0.26	0.32	0.11	0.17	0.25	0.23	0.12	0.28	0.23	0.21	0.17	0.17	1.00	0.32	0.20	0.14	0.22
19	0.15	0.24	0.26	0.12	0.25	0.27	0.29	0.18	0.25	0.20	0.46	0.23	0.25	0.22	0.40	0.18	0.23	0.32	1.00	0.21	0.17	0.28
20	0.14	0.31	0.28	0.17	0.24	0.34	0.27	0.08	0.21	0.20	0.24	0.18	0.31	0.27	0.20	0.27	0.24	0.20	0.21	1.00	0.20	0.29
21	0.08	0.16	0.19	0.12	0.16	0.15	0.16	0.15	0.16	0.10	0.19	0.18	0.17	0.17	0.18	0.16	0.16	0.14	0.17	0.20	1.00	0.20
22	0.16	0.32	0.22	0.14	0.24	0.35	0.28	0.19	0.30	0.13	0.36	0.15	0.30	0.23	0.25	0.30	0.25	0.22	0.28	0.29	0.20	1.00
23	0.13	0.23	0.20	0.17	0.26	0.25	0.29	0.08	0.16	0.24	0.22	0.17	0.25	0.24	0.18	0.26	0.25	0.20	0.24	0.24	0.17	0.21
24	0.10	0.22	0.15	0.07	0.22	0.24	0.23	0.04	0.12	0.21	0.13	0.18	0.25	0.22	0.17	0.23	0.26	0.16	0.17	0.21	0.19	0.19
25	0.11	0.17	0.17	0.19	0.21	0.15	0.17	0.04	0.11	0.14-	0.22	0.12	0.23	0.19	0.17	0.16	0.23	0.14	0.16	0.24	0.21	0.19
26	0.14	0.19	0.16	0.20	0.22	0.23	0.16	0.06	0.14	0.15	0.20	0.19	0.23	0.23	0.19	0.24	0.28	0.18	0.19	0.19	0.23	0.20
27	0.14	0.22	0.20	0.20	0.21	0.20	0.25	0.05	0.19	0.20	0.19	0.15	0.26	0.25	0.27	0.21	0.27	0.20	0.19	0.28	0.24	0.22
28	0.15	0.20	0.19	0.16	0.24	0.16	0.13	0.02	0.11	0.14	0.16	0.19	0.22	0.26	0.15	0.21	0.35	0.18	0.16	0.16	0.16	0.17
29	0.09	0.15	0.15	0.08	0.22	0.16	0.18	0.02	0.21	0.15	0.18	0.16	0.21	0.16	0.27	0.17	0.28	0.15	0.22	0.17	0.20	0.19
30	0.18	0.27	0.25	0.08	0.18	0.25	0.27	0.13	0.17	0.30	0.29	0.27	0.29	0.25	0.19	0.19	0.16	0.31	0.32	0.22	0.14	0.19
31	0.15	0.25	0.17	0.17	0.24	0.31	0.34	0.14	0.20	0.22	0.23	0.21	0.30	0.36	0.23	0.26	0.28	0.27	0.23	0.24	0.15	0.21
32	0.04	0.14	0.11	0.06	0.16	0.11	0.17	0.10	0.15	0.09	0.20	0.13	0.12	0.20	0.22	0.13	0.25	0.14	0.21	0.18	0.17	0.16
33	0.25	0.32	0.25	0.18	0.25	0.38	0.33	0.09	0.14	0.23	0.27	0.18	0.35	0.30	0.19	0.29	0.24	0.33	0.26	0.29	0.20	0.28
34	0.13	0.21	0.21	0.19	0.23	0.25	0.20	0.13	0.18	0.11	0.21	0.14	0.26	0.16	0.19	0.34	0.25	0.15	0.22	0.23	0.17	0.26
35	0.12	0.26	0.25	0.12	0.26	0.26	0.21	0.00	0.15	0.20	0.24	0.24	0.28	0.31	0.25	0.25	0.39	0.19	0.23	0.25	0.23	0.24
36	0.18	0.29	0.24	0.20	0.28	0.31	0.30	0.11	0.18	0.21	0.32	0.26	0.29	0.31	0.29	0.30	0.32	0.21	0.29	0.30	0.18	0.32
37	0.08	0.17	0.19	0.08	0.13	0.12	0.19	0.00	0.12	0.14	0.14	0.21	0.17	0.25	0.20	0.13	0.27	0.12	0.12	0.18	0.11	0.15
38	0.12	0.19	0.21	0.15	0.30	0.25	0.24	0.05	0.18	0.16	0.26	0.23	0.25	0.32	0.28	0.24	0.32	0.23	0.23	0.26	0.18	0.32
39	0.13	0.21	0.17	0.12	0.23	0.22	0.21	0.10	0.18	0.20	0.24.	0.22	0.29	0.23	0.28	0.20	0.22	0.19	0.29	0.21	0.25	0.23
40	0.27	0.26	0.28	0.20	0.20	0.30	0.27	0.07	0.10	0.29	0.21	0.15	0.28	0.22	0.13	0.24	0.19	0.25	0.24	0.24	0.15	0.25
41	0.06	0.21	0.16	0.07	0.19	0.18	0.15	0.06	0.09	0.14	0.18	0.14	0.20	0.26	0.17	0.20	0.29	0.14	0.18	0.18	0.17	0.17
42	0.10	0.16	0.18	0.11	0.20	0.18	0.19	0.06	0.13	0.14	0.14	0.15	0.17	0.21	0.19	0.16	0.18	0.13	0.16	0.13	0.15	0.10
43	0.14	0.23	0.20	0.17	0.25	0.24	0.20	0.01	0.10	0.26	0.17	0.13	0.28	0.29	0.14	0.23	0.20	0.20	0.20	0.23	0.17	0.15
44	0.26	0.36	0.24	0.20	0.30	0.44	0.30	0.39	0.30	0.21	0.34	0.20	0.36	0.29	0.31	0.30	0.25	0.27	0.35	0.29	0.19	0.35
Total out of 44	0.34	0.55	0.49	0.34	0.52	0.60	0.54	0.26	0.39	0.44	0.53	0.41	0.60	0.55	0.48	0.52	0.52	0.48	0.53	0.51	0.37	0.53

23	24	25	26	27	28	29	30	31	32	33	34	35	36	37	38	39	40	41	42	43	44	Total out of 44
0.13	0.10	0.11	0.14	0.14	0.15	0.09	0.18	0.15	0.04	0.25	0.13	0.12	0.18	0.08	0.12	0.13	0.27	0.06	0.10	0.14	0.26	0.34
0.23	0.22	0.17	0.19	0.22	0.20	0.15	0.27	0.25	0.14	0.32	0.21	0.26	0.29	0.17	0.19	0.21	0.26	0.21	0.16	0.23	0.36	0.55
0.20	0.15	0.17	0.16	0.20	0.19	0.15	0.25	0.17	0.11	0.25	0.21	0.25	0.24	0.19	0.21	0.17	0.28	0.16	0.18	0.20	0.24	0.49
0.17	0.07	0.19	0.20	0.20	0.16	0.08	0.08	0.17	0.06	0.18	0.19	0.12	0.20	0.08	0.15	0.12	0.20	0.07	0.11	0.17	0.20	0.34
0.26	0.22	0.21	0.22	0.21	0.24	0.22	0.18	0.24	0.16	0.25	0.23	0.26	0.28	0.13	0.30	0.23	0.20	0.19	0.20	0.25	0.30	0.52
0.25	0.24	0.15	0.23	0.20	0.16	0.16	0.25	0.31	0.11	0.38	0.25	0.26	0.31	0.12	0.25	0.22	0.30	0.18	0.18	0.24	0.44	0.60
0.29	0.23	0.17	0.16	0.25	0.13	0.18	0.27	0.34	0.17	0.33	0.20	0.21	0.30	0.19	0.24	0.21	0.27	0.15	0.19	0.20	0.30	0.54
0.08	0.04	0.04	0.06	0.05	0.02	0.02	0.13	0.14	0.10	0.09	0.13	0.00	0.11	0.00	0.05	0.10	0.07	0.06	0.06	0.01	0.39	0.26
0.16	0.12	0.11	0.14	0.19	0.11	0.21	0.17	0.20	0.15	0.14	0.18	0.15	0.18	0.12	0.18	0.18	0.10	0.09	0.13	0.10	0.30	0.39
0.24	0.21	0.14	0.15	0.20	0.14	0.15	0.30	0.22	0.09	0.23	0.11	0.20	0.21	0.14	0.16	0.20	0.29	0.14	0.14	0.26	0.21	0.44
0.22	0.13	0.22	0.20	0.19	0.16	0.18	0.29	0.23	0.20	0.27	0.21	0.24	0.32	0.14	0.26	0.24	0.21	0.18	0.14	0.17	0.34	0.53
0.17	0.18	0.12	0.19	0.15	0.19	0.16	0.27	0.21	0.13	0.18	0.14	0.24	0.26	0.21	0.23	0.22	0.15	0.14	0.15	0.13	0.20	0.41
0.25	0.25	0.23	0.23	0.26	0.22	0.21	0.29	0.30	0.12	0.35	0.26	0.28	0.29	0.17	0.25	0.29	0.28	0.20	0.17	0.28	0.36	0.60
0.24	0.22	0.19	0.23	0.25	0.26	0.16	0.25	0.36	0.20	0.30	0.16	0.31	0.31	0.25	0.32	0.23	0.22	0.26	0.21	0.29	0.29	0.55
0.18	0.17	0.17	0.19	0.27	0.15	0.27	0.19	0.23	0.22	0.19	0.19	0.25	0.29	0.20	0.28	0.28	0.13	0.17	0.19	0.14	0.31	0.48
0.26	0.23	0.16	0.24	0.21	0.21	0.17	0.19	0.26	0.13	0.29	0.34	0.25	0.30	0.13	0.24	0.20	0.24	0.20	0.16	0.23	0.30	0.52
0.25	0.26	0.23	0.28	0.37	0.35	0.28	0.16	0.28	0.25	0.24	0.25	0.39	0.32	0.27	0.32	0.22	0.19	0.29	0.18	0.20	0.25	0.52
0.20	0.16	0.14	0.18	0.20	0.18	0.15	0.31	0.27	0.14	0.33	0.15	0.19	0.21	0.12	0.23	0.19	0.25	0.14	0.13	0.20	0.27	0.48
0.24	0.17	0.16	0.19	0.19	0.16	0.22	0.32	0.23	0.21	0.26	0.22	0.23	0.29	0.12	0.23	0.29	0.24	0.18	0.16	0.20	0.35	0.53
0.24	0.21	0.24	0.19	0.28	0.16	0.17	0.22	0.24	0.18	0.29	0.23	0.25	0.30	0.18	0.26	0.21	0.24	0.18	0.13	0.23	0.29	0.51
0.17	0.19	0.21	0.23	0.24	0.16	0.20	0.14	0.15	0.17	0.20	0.17	0.23	0.18	0.11	0.18	0.25	0.15	0.17	0.15	0.17	0.19	0.37
0.21	0.19	0.19	0.20	0.22	0.17	0.19	0.19	0.21	0.16	0.28	0.26	0.24	0.32	0.15	0.32	0.23	0.25	0.17	0.10	0.15	0.35	0.53
1.00	0.25	0.20	0.22	0.24	0.25	0.16	0.25	0.32	0.13	0.25	0.20	0.22	0.22	0.19	0.26	0.24	0.24	0.23	0.21	0.23	0.26	0.50
0.25	1.00	0.16	0.18	0.24	0.23	0.15	0.17	0.22	0.17	0.21	0.13	0.28	0.22	0.18	0.18	0.18	0.18	0.16	0.21	0.23	0.19	0.41
0.20	0.16	1.00	0.22	0.25	0.30	0.13	0.16	0.18	0.13	0.20	0.24	0.19	0.23	0.14	0.23	0.20	0.16	0.15	0.16	0.20	0.18	0.41
0.22	0.18	0.22	1.00	0.33	0.29	0.17	0.16	0.23	0.17	0.23	0.22	0.23	0.23	0.12	0.30	0.25	0.20	0.15	0.14	0.18	0.25	0.46
0.24	0.24	0.25	0.33	1.00	0.30	0.18	0.17	0.24	0.14	0.23	0.28	0.25	0.29	0.17	0.31	0.20	0.19	0.27	0.18	0.25	0.23	0.50
0.25	0.23	0.30	0.29	0.30	1.00	0.20	0.14	0.28	0.11	0.22	0.18	0.28	0.28	0.19	0.33	0.22	0.18	0.22	0.16	0.21	0.18	0.45
0.16	0.15	0.13	0.17	0.18	0.20	1.00	0.10	0.19	0.15	0.15	0.11	0.30	0.24	0.14	0.24	0.18	0.09	0.28	0.20	0.16	0.23	0.38
0.25	0.17	0.16	0.16	0.17	0.14	0.10	1.00	0.22	0.18	0.25	0.12	0.19	0.22	0.16	0.18	0.18	0.32	0.17	0.11	0.23	0.27	0.49
0.32	0.22	0.18	0.23	0.24	0.28	0.19	0.22	1.00	0.29	0.25	0.19	0.26	0.30	0.18	0.30	0.27	0.20	0.16	0.16	0.25	0.31	0.53
0.13	0.17	0.13	0.17	0.14	0.11	0.15	0.18	0.29	1.00	0.11	0.12	0.16	0.19	0.14	0.21	0.16	0.09	0.17	0.11	0.16	0.19	0.34
0.25	0.21	0.20	0.23	0.23	0.22	0.15	0.25	0.25	0.11	1.00	0.20	0.23	0.33	0.15	0.28	0.23	0.31	0.16	0.16	0.22	0.32	0.55
0.20	0.13	0.24	0.22	0.28	0.18	0.11	0.12	0.19	0.12	0.20	1.00	0.17	0.21	0.09	0.18	0.18	0.18	0.19	0.18	0.14	0.24	0.44
0.22	0.28	0.19	0.23	0.25	0.28	0.30	0.19	0.26	0.16	0.23	0.17	1.00	0.43	0.38	0.32	0.26	0.19	0.33	0.17	0.24	0.27	0.52
0.22	0.22	0.23	0.23	0.29	0.28	0.24	0.22	0.30	0.19	0.33	0.21	0.43	1.00	0.20	0.42	0.30	0.24	0.23	0.22	0.20	0.35	0.58
0.19	0.18	0.14	0.12	0.17	0.19	0.14	0.16	0.18	0.14	0.15	0.09	0.38	0.20	1.00	0.26	0.12	0.11	0.26	0.15	0.15	0.18	0.35
0.26	0.18	0.23	0.30	0.31	0.33	0.24	0.18	0.30	0.21	0.28	0.18	0.32	0.42	0.26	1.00	0.23	0.20	0.23	0.22	0.20	0.28	0.53
0.24	0.18	0.20	0.25	0.20	0.22	0.18	0.18	0.27	0.16	0.23	0.18	0.26	0.30	0.12	0.23	1.00	0.17	0.16	0.18	0.19	0.25	0.47
0.24	0.18	0.16	0.20	0.19	0.18	0.09	0.32	0.20	0.09	0.31	0.18	0.19	0.24	0.11	0.20	0.17	1.00	0.16	0.13	0.25	0.24	0.48
0.23	0.16	0.15	0.15	0.27	0.22	0.28	0.17	0.16	0.17	0.16	0.19	0.33	0.23	0.26	0.23	0.16	0.16	1.00	0.13	0.18	0.24	0.40
0.21	0.21	0.16	0.14	0.18	0.16	0.20	0.11	0.16	0.11	0.16	0.18	0.17	0.22	0.15	0.22	0.18	0.13	0.13	1.00	0.20	0.16	0.36
0.23	0.23	0.20	0.18	0.25	0.21	0.16	0.23	0.25	0.16	0.22	0.14	0.24	0.20	0.15	0.20	0.19	0.25	0.18	0.20	1.00	0.19	0.46
0.26	0.19	0.18	0.25	0.23	0.18	0.23	0.27	0.31	0.19	0.32	0.24	0.27	0.35	0.18	0.28	0.25	0.24	0.24	0.16	0.19	1.00	0.60
0.50	0.41	0.41	0.46	0.50	0.45	0.38	0.49	0.53	0.34	0.55	0.44	0.52	0.58	0.35	0.53	0.47	0.48	0.40	0.36	0.46	0.60	1.00

APPENDIX 2.3 LIST OF THEFT ITEMS

Theft items referred to in report

1   I have kept something I have found

2   I have stolen something just for fun

3   I have taken something just for a dare

4   I have taken junk or scrap without asking for it first

5   I have stolen something from a stall or a barrow

6   I have stolen something from a shop

7   I have stolen a book or a newspaper or a magazine or a comic

8   I have pinched something from my family or relations

9*   I have pinched something when I was in someone else's home

10   I have got away without paying the fare or the proper fare

11   I have taken things belonging to children or teenagers

12*   I have got something by threatening others

13   I have pinched sweets

14   I have stolen cigarettes

15*   I have stolen something from a changing-room or a cloakroom

16   I have stolen fruit or some other kind of food

17*   I have got into a place and stolen

18*   I have stolen something belonging to a school

19   I have stolen something from someone at school

20   I have pinched something when I was on holiday

21   I have stolen from a park or a playground

22   I have stolen toys

23   I have stolen from a cafe

24   I have stolen milk

25   I have stolen coal or wood or paraffin or something else that is used for burning

26   I have stolen from a building site

27   I have stolen by stripping something from a building

28*   I have stolen from a goods yard, or from the yard of a factory, or from the docks, or from a timber-yard

29*   I have stolen a letter or a parcel

30*   I have cheated someone out of money

31*   I have stolen from work

32*   I have stolen from someone at work

33   I have had something that I knew was stolen

34   I have stolen something out of a garden or out of the yard of a house

35*   I have stolen a bike or a motor bike

36*   I have stolen something *from* a bike or a motor bike

37*   I have stolen a car or a lorry or a van

38*   I have stolen something *from* a car or a lorry or a van

39*   I have stolen from a club

40   I have got into some place without paying the money to go in

41*   I have stolen money from a meter

42*   I have stolen something from a telephone box

43*   I have got things out of a slot machine without paying

44*   I have stolen money

*Denotes items rated as 'serious' by a small sample of the London public

8. APPENDIX 2.4 SOME STUDIES BEARING ON UNDETECTED OF SELF REPORTED DELINQUENCY

R. L. Akers, 'Socio-economic status and delinquent behaviour: a retest.' *Journal of Research in Crime and Delinquency*, **1**, 1964, 38–46.

N. Christie, J. Andanaes, *and* S. Skirbekk, 'A study of self-reported crime'. In Karl O. Christiansen, *ed. Scandinavian studies in criminology.* vol. 1. Oslo: Universitets Forlaget; London: Tavistock Publications, 1965, 86–118.

J. P. Clark, *and* E. P. Wenninger, 'Socio-economic class and area as correlates of illegal behaviour among juveniles', *American Sociological Review*, **27**, 1962, 826–834.

J. P. Clark, *and* E. P. Wenninger, 'The attitude of juveniles toward the legal institution'. *Journal of Criminal Law, Criminology and Police Science*, **55**, 1964, 482–489.

R. A. Dentler, *and* J. L. Monroe, 'Social correlates of early adolescent theft', *American Sociological Review*, **26**, 1961, 733–743.

K. Elmhorn, 'Study in self-reported delinquency among school-children in Stockholm', *In* Karl O. Christiansen, (ed.) *Scandinavian studies in criminology*, vol. 1, Oslo: Universitets Forlaget; London: Tavistock Publications, 1965, 117–146.

M. L. Erickson, *and* L. T. Empey, 'Court records, undetected delinquency and decision-making', *Journal of Criminal Law, Criminology and Police Science*, **54**, 456–469.

H. B. Gibson, 'Self-reported delinquency among school-boys and their attitudes to the police', *British Journal of Social and Clinical Psychology*, **6**, 1967, 46–51.

H. B. Gibson, S. Morrison, *and* D. J. West, 'The confession of known offences in response to a self-reported delinquency schedule', *British Journal of Criminology*, **10**, 1970, 277–280.

Martin Gold, 'Undetected delinquent behaviour', *Journal of Research in Crime and Delinquency*, **3**, 1966, 27–46.

R. H. Hardt, *and* G. E. Bodine, Development of Self-Report Instruments in Delinquency Research, Syracuse, New York: Syracuse University, Youth Development Centre, 1965.

S. R. Hathaway, *and* E. D. Monachesi, Analysing and Predicting Juvenile Delinquency with the M.M.P.I. Minneapolis, Minnesota: Minnesota University Press, 1953.

J. A. Kulik, K. B. Stein, *and* T. R. Sarbin, 'Disclosure of Delinquent Behaviour under Conditions of Anonymity and Non-Anonymity', *Journal of Consulting and Clinical Phychology*, **32**, 1968, 506–509.

L. McDonald, Social Class and Delinquency. London: Faber and Faber, 1965.

F. J. Murphy, M. M. Shirley, *and* H. L. Witmer, 'The incidence of hidden delinquency', *American Journal of Orthopsychiatry*, **16**, 1946, 686–696.

F. I. Nye, Family Relationships and Delinquent Behaviour, New York: Wiley, 1958.

F. I. Nye, *and* J. F. Short, *Jr* 'Scaling delinquent behaviour', *American Sociological Review*, **27**, 1957, 326–331.

F. I. Nye, J. F. Short, *Jr and* V. J. Olson, 'Socio-economic status and delinquent behaviour'. *American Journal of Sociology*, **63**, 1958, 381–389.

A. L. Porterfield, Youth in Trouble. Austin, Texas: Leo Potishman Foundation, 1946.

A. J. Reiss, *Jr, and* A. L. Rhodes, 'The distribution of juvenile delinquency in the social class structure', *American Sociological Review*, **26**, 1961, 720–732.

J. F. Scott, 'Two dimensions of delinquent behaviour', *American Sociological Review*, **24**, 1959, 240–243.

J. F. Short, *and* F. I. Nye, 'Reported behaviour as a criterion of delinquent behaviour', *Social Problems*, **5**, 1957, 207–213.

J. F. Short, *and* F. I. Nye, 'The extent of unrecorded juvenile delinquency: tentative conclusion', *Journal of Criminal Law, Criminology and Police Science*, **49**, 1958, 296–302.

W. L. Slocum, *and* Carol L. Stone, 'Family culture patterns and delinquent-type behaviour', *Marriage and Family Living*, **25**, 1963, 202–208.

E. W. Vaz, 'Self-reported juvenile delinquency and socioeconomic status', *Canadian Journal of Corrections*, **8**, 1966, 20–27.

E. W. Vaz, Middle Class Juvenile Delinquency. New York: Harper and Row, 1967.

H. L. Voss, 'Ethnic differentials in delinquency in Honolulu', *Journal of Criminal Law, Criminology and Police Science*, **54**, 1963, 322–327.

J. S. Wallerstein, and C. J. Wyle, 'Our law-abiding law breakers', *Probation*, **25**, 1947, 107–112.

H. D. Willcock, *and* J. Stokes, 'Deterrents and incentives to crime among youths aged 15–21 years: part 2', London: Government Social Survey, 1968. (Individual studies, no. 352).

9. APPENDIX 2.5 SOME EXAMPLES OF ITEMS VALUED BY BOYS AT ABOUT 1/6, 4/6, £1/0/0 AS SHOWN

Stolen goods valued by boys

(a) *at about 1/6:* a packet of biscuits/a can of fruit/a tin of cat's meat/a potato knife/a plate/a shoe brush/ a tin of shoe polish/a box of nibs/a large magic marker/a magnet/a metal can/a tin of Nivea cream/

(b) *at about 4/6:* a tin of sweets/a library book/a small doll's house/a flute from school/a set of darts/a tube of oil paint/a mixing bowl/a metal comb/a dip stick/a carving knife/a tin of anti-freeze/a plastic ball/a golf ball/a compass/a telephone ear piece/

(c) *at about £1/0/0:* a crate of apples/a brace of pheasant/a jumper/an arm rest from a car/a floor mat/a box of ceiling tiles/a lilo/leather gloves/a fencing sword/a rubber dinghy/a pocket lighter/

(d) *at values well in excess of £1/0/0:* an amplifier/a bike/a vanload of bricks/a large quantity of brass/a motor-bike engine/a fox rug/a pair of opera glasses/a paint spray/a case of canned peaches/a new pram/a parachute/a wedding ring (gold)/a portable radio/ miniature respirator apparatus/a car radiator/a scalextric set/a motor scooter/a slot machine/a violin/

Chapter three
Getting caught for stealing

CONTENTS

1 THE COVERAGE OF THIS CHAPTER

In this chapter I have presented a wide range of information broadly related to 'getting caught' for stealing. This information was collected and processed to serve two associated purposes, the more important of which was to investigate a particular composite of hypotheses about causal factors in the development of juvenile stealing. These hypotheses were as follows.

1 Boys take up stealing or continue to steal partly because they think they will not get caught by the police.

2 Boys take up stealing or continue to steal partly because they think *no one* will catch them.

3 Boys steal less as a result of getting caught by the police for stealing.

4 Boys reduce their stealing because they are discouraged by what they feel would be the consequences of getting caught by the police.

5 Boys reduce their stealing because they don't like the idea of getting caught for it by their parents.

The second purpose of the collected data was to provide general background information about each of the factors or conditions hypothesized as causal in character. For example, with respect to boys' confidence about 'getting away with' stealing, it seemed desirable to establish how this confidence varied with the backgrounds and characteristics of the boys concerned. Similarly for boys' fears over what they felt would be the consequences of getting caught. And with regard to actually getting caught, the concern in the investigation was not only with how many and *who* got caught but with *what happened* to boys when they were caught.

2 RESEARCH PROCEDURES|COMMON TO ALL THE HYPOTHESES DEALT WITH IN THE INQUIRY

The gathering of information relevant to the hypotheses about 'getting caught' was done in the context of an inquiry concerned with over thirty other hypotheses. The techniques relating to the inquiry *as a whole* have been summarized in Chapter 1. That summary deals with sampling procedures; with a technique for getting boys to provide reliable information about any stealing they have done; with questioning procedures for classifying boys in terms of the variables hypothesized as causal factors in the different hypotheses (i.e. in terms of the different independent variables); with strategies for investigating the tenability of hypotheses about causal factors and processes. The reader should refer back to the relevant parts of Chapter 1 as necessary in reading statements of findings in the present and subsequent chapters.

3 RESEARCH PROCEDURES APPLYING ONLY TO THE HYPOTHESES DEALT WITH IN THIS CHAPTER

Whereas many aspects of the total research procedure applied generally to the whole range of hypotheses under study, certain parts of it relate only to the hypotheses defined and dealt with in this chapter. These parts tend to be encapsulated in *one* of the sub-questionnaires put to boys in the course of the total interview and this sub-questionnaire is presented in full in the Appendix A.3.1.

Like the other sub-questionnaires, this one was set out in sections, each section beginning with a general description of its purpose, as follows.

1 Present attitudes towards 'being caught up with' by the police and to the consequences of this.

2 When did he first have contact with the police over pinching and how did this affect his stealing thereafter?

3 How often and when has he been involved with the *police* over stealing? What 'effects' does he say this has had on him (i.e., getting involved with the police)?

4 Parental reactions if/when he pinched.

5 What did his parents do or feel when they found out? What would they do next?

6 Have his mates been caught and what effect* does he think this has had on his own pinching?

Whereas most of the questions were fully structured, some were of the open response kind. In some cases, the open response data was for use in gaining insight into a situation or a position or a process. But in others, its purpose was to help the boy think about his position before trying to formulate it through a fully-structured question. For example:

'How much would you care if the police caught up with you for pinching?'
(LET HIM SPEAK OUT)

   PASS HIM THE ANSWER CARD, READ ANSWERS OUT. SAY:
'Which of those do you think would be true?'
   I WOULD NOT CARE/I WOULD CARE/I WOULD CARE VERY MUCH

---

*Where the boys were asked for what they thought were the 'effects' on them of getting caught or of their reactions to getting caught, there was not expectation that the boy would be fully accurate in what he said. Such impressions are taken as nothing more than impressions and are relevant only in the context of testing a complex of expectations (see Chapter 1).

4 METHODS AND FINDINGS RELATING TO THE INVESTIGATION OF HYPOTHESIS 1

The Nature of Hypothesis 1

The first of the hypotheses about 'getting caught' was:

Boys take up stealing or continue to steal partly because they think they won't get caught by the police.

It was the purpose of the inquiry both to investigate this hypothesis and to provide background information about the independent variable defined in it. This independent variable is confidence that 'the police won't catch me if I am engaged in stealing'.

The Distribution of Boys in terms of the Variable Hypothesized as Causal

In this section are presented details about the questions asked: (*a*) as a basis for classifying boys in terms of the variable hypothesized as causal and (*b*) the distribution of boys in terms of that variable.

The questions asked for classifying boys in terms of confidence that they would not be caught by the police

Several questions were asked in an attempt to classify boys by their feelings about the likelihood of getting caught by the police — or their confidence that the police would not catch them — if they were stealing. These questions were as follows.

---

1 'I want you to imagine that you were pinching things — the sort of things you might feel like pinching.'
'Do you think the *police* would catch you?'
   (ENCOURAGE HIM TO SPEAK OUT)

   THEN PASS THE BOY THE FIVE-ITEM CARD, READ EACH ITEM OUT AND SAY:
'Which of those do you think would be true?'
   I AM SURE THEY WOULD NOT CATCH ME/I DON'T THINK THEY WOULD CATCH ME/THEY MIGHT CATCH ME/THERE IS A GOOD CHANCE OF THEIR CATCHING ME/I AM SURE THEY WOULD CATCH ME.
   (CHALLENGE CHOICE AND THEN UNDERLINE IT.)

---

2 'If you *kept on* pinching things, do you think the *police* would catch you?'
   (ENCOURAGE HIM TO SPEAK OUT)

   THEN PASS HIM THE ANSWER CARD AGAIN, READ THEM THROUGH, AND SAY:
'Which of those do you think would be true?'
   I AM SURE THEY WOULD NOT CATCH ME/I DON'T THINK THEY WOULD CATCH ME/THEY MIGHT CATCH ME/THERE IS A GOOD CHANCE OF THEIR CATCHING ME/I AM SURE THEY WOULD CATCH ME.

   (CHALLENGE CHOICE AND THEN UNDERLINE IT.)

Deciding which of the two questions to use in defining the hypothesis

At the time of designing these two questions, it was expected that they would produce two rather different distributions of boys and that one of these distributions would be more suitable for discriminating between boys than the other. It was the latter that was wanted, though there was no telling, at the time of question design, which of the two this would prove to be. The two distributions are given in Table 3.1 below.

On the evidence of Table 3.1, Question 1 was regarded as more likely to discriminate than Question 2 and thereafter was used to identify boys who *qualified* in terms of *Hypothesis 1*.

The two distributions in their own right

As general background information, however, both questions are important in their own right, for they provide evidence about boys' confidence in 'getting away with stealing'. Thus they seem to indicate a fairly realistic view by the boys that the chances of getting caught go up very markedly if one keeps on stealing. On the other hand, we should note that: (*a*) only 6 per cent felt *sure* they would get caught if they did some stealing (without keeping it up); 32 per cent did not think they would get caught for the occasional theft and 6 per cent felt that they would get away with stealing even if they *kept it up*. In terms of social importance, even the 6 per cent figure converts to a very large number of boys.

Confidence (about getting away with stealing) Analysed by Characteristics and Background of Boys

Confidence according to age, social background and other characteristics

'Confidence that the police would not catch them' was analysed by various of the characteristics of the boys in the sample: father's occupational level, boy's age, type

Table 3.1

Confidence about not getting caught by the police†

	Q.1* If I went in for stealing (%)	Q.2* If I kept on stealing (%)
Sure they would not catch me	5	2
Don't think they would catch me	27	4
They might catch me	40	12
There's a good chance they would catch me	22	36
Sure they would catch me	6	46

†Excluding 'don't knows'
*See wording of Questions 1 and 2 above

Table 3.2
Confidence about not being caught by police, analysed
by characteristics of boys (on basis of response to Q.1)

Characteristics of boys	All cases (weighted) n† (3,113)	Level of confidence about not getting caught by police*					
		Sure they would not catch me (%)	Don't think they would catch me (%)	They might catch me (%)	A good chance of catching me (%)	Sure they would catch me (%)	No Information (%)
Age of boy							
12/13 yrs	721	4	23	41	23	8	1
14 yrs	782	6	27	41	22	4	0
15 yrs	754	6	28	41	20	5	0
16/17 yrs	856	6	29	37	22	6	0
Occupational level of boy's father							
Professional, semi-professional and executive	518	8	36	32	22	2	0
Highly skilled and skilled	1,188	5	28	39	22	6	0
Moderately and semi-skilled	1,147	4	23	44	22	7	0
Unskilled	254	8	19	46	23	4	0
No information	6						
School attended now or previously							
Secondary modern	1,464	3	22	43	24	7	1
Comprehensive	549	6	25	41	22	6	0
Grammar	718	7	37	34	19	3	0
Public	257	13	26	35	20	6	0
Other	105						
No information	20						
Nominal religion							
Protestant	1,370	4	26	39	26	5	0
Catholic	500	8	30	38	17	7	0
Other Christian	176	0	35	39	20	6	0
Greek Orthodox	77	0	18	63	14	5	0
Jewish	214	9	25	38	23	5	0
None	621	9	28	40	19	4	0
Other religions	140						
No information	15						
Coloured							
No	2,994	6	27	40	22	5	0
Yes	119	1	29	34	17	17	2
Born in UK							
Yes	2,856	6	27	40	22	5	0
No	257	3	28	40	17	11	1

*As indicated by response to Question 1
†n = no. of cards (weighted up from 1,425 *cases*)

Table 3.3

'Confidence about getting away with it', analysed by
whether boy caught in past

Has the boy ever been involved with the police?	All cases (weighted)	Sure they would not not catch me	Don't think they would catch me	They might catch me	A good chance of catching me	Sure they would catch me	No information
	n 3,113	(%)	(%)	(%)	(%)	(%)	(%)
Yes	415	5	18	52	18	7	0
No	2,687	6	28	38	23	5	0
No information	11						

of school last attended, nominal religion, whether born in the United Kingdom. Details are set out in Table 3.2.

The details in Table 3.2 indicate a tendency for confidence about 'getting away with it' to increase with occupational level of boys' fathers; to be greater amongst boys with public- or grammar-school backgrounds than amongst those with secondary-modern or comprehensive-school background. In general, however, the trends are small and/or irregular.

'Confidence' analysed by whether boy has ever been caught by police

By *contrast* — and perhaps as must be expected — there are substantial differences (in confidence about 'getting away with it') between those who *have* been caught by the police and those who have not. Details are given in Table 3.3.

Thus, *fewer* of those who had ever been involved with the police over stealing felt that they would 'get away with it' (23:34 per cent) and more felt that they *might* get caught (52.38 per cent). What is particularly interesting here is that those who have been involved with the police are no more convinced than other boys that they *would* get caught (25:28 per cent) — only that they *might*. However, upon consideration this may seem reasonable because it turns out that most boys who have been caught by the police manage to get away with it a lot of times *without* being caught*. So they would have good grounds for believing that they *might* get away with it. On the other hand, the overall difference between those who have been caught and those who have not is quite clear: the former are less confident that they would get away with it next time.

'Confidence' analysed by amount of stealing done by boys

Boys' confidence about getting away with stealing was cross-analysed by the amount and variety of the stealing which boys had in fact done and the results are set out in Table 3.4.

The indications of the evidence from Question 1a are somewhat different from the indications of the evidence from Question 1b. Question 1a dealt with 'confidence in getting away with stealing' while Question 1b dealt with 'confidence in getting away with stealing *if one keeps it up*'.

For the situation dealt with in Question 1a, it appears that *both* those who are sure they would *not* get caught and those who are sure they *would* get caught tend to be less involved in stealing than the other respondents. For the situation dealt with in Question 1b, it appears that the small group claiming to be sure they would not get caught tends to be less involved in stealing than others; but that tendency does not show up for the group who felt 'sure they would get caught'.

However one may interpret the detail in Table 3.4, it is important to remain aware that the three groups specifically referred to are all quite small. One should also note most carefully of Table 3.4 that such 'association' as is indicated in it does not necessarily imply a *causal* relationship. It is certainly possible that boys who are, say, 'sure they would not get caught by the police', are different in relevant ways* from those who feel there is 'a good chance of getting caught by the police'. If this is so, it could have a lot to do with such differences as are found in the theft rates of these two sets of boys. It was for the reduction of any such extraneous differences that the matching technique described in Chapter 1 was used.

Investigating Hypothesis 1

A summary of the basic strategy of investigation
The central strategy for investigating Hypothesis 1 (and indeed, any other of the hypotheses to be studied) was to derive from it a series of testable *expectations* and to test these. A description of this strategy has been made in Chapter 1.

*See Chapter 2.

*That is, in terms of variables correlated with 'expectation of getting caught'.

Table 3.4

Confidence about not being caught by police if engaged in stealing (Q.1a)		Index of variety of stealing				Index of amount of stealing			
		Low score quarter			High score quarter	Low score quarter			High score quarter
		Q.1 (%)	Q.2 (%)	Q.3 (%)	Q.4 (%)	Q.1 (%)	Q.2 (%)	Q.3 (%)	Q.4 (%)
Sure I would not get caught	5%	35	31	17	17	32	29	19	20
Don't think I would get caught	27%	18	24	31	27	17	26	29	28
I might get caught	40%	23	24	28	25	22	29	25	24
Good chance of getting caught	22%	26	26	25	23	26	30	24	20
Sure I would get caught	6%	51	20	13	16	53	19	18	10
Confidence about not being caught by police if I kept on stealing (Q.1b)									
Sure I would not get caught	2%	33	31	27	9	29	38	18	15
Don't think I would get caught	4%	29	27	17	27	29	22	20	29
I might get caught	12%	23	21	31	25	24	28	29	19
Good chance of getting caught	36%	20	25	29	26	18	28	27	27
Sure I would get caught	46%	28	25	24	23	28	27	24	21

The expectations derived

The expectations derived in this case were as follows.

Expectation 1 Those boys who think they *will not* get caught by the police for stealing, do more stealing than other boys and this applies even when the latter are closely matched to the former in terms of the correlates of stealing.

Expectation 2 Expectation 1 applies also with respect to each of the forty-four types of thieving studied in this inquiry.

Expectation 3 Those boys who think they will not get caught for stealing tend to continue with relatively serious stealing over a longer period than other boys, and this applies even when the latter are closely matched to the former in terms of the correlates of stealing.

Testing Expectation 1: methods and results

Methods The testing of Expectation 1 involves the application of a special form of empirical matching (see Chapter 1 for details of this method). The purpose of this specialized matching operation is to eliminate certain extraneous differences between the groups of boys being compared, namely those who qualify in terms of the hypotheses (i.e. the 'qualifiers') and those who do not (i.e. the 'controls'). For instance, if age is correlated with amount of stealing (and it is) and if the controls are younger than the qualifiers, then this difference in age will produce a difference between the control group and the qualifying group which has nothing to do with the hypothesis but which could all too easily lead to an impression that one or another of the expectations had been verified.

The first step in the matching process was to separate out boys who *qualified* in terms of the hypothesis (= the qualifying group) and those who *did not* (= the control group). Thus, the qualifiers in the case of Hypothesis 1 were boys who said either that 'they were sure they would not be caught by the police if they were stealing' and those who said that 'they didn't think they would be caught by the police if they were stealing'. There were, in fact, 420 of these boys. The controls, on the other hand, were made up of boys who said either that 'they were sure the police would catch them if they were stealing' or 'there was a good chance that the police would catch them if they were stealing'. There were 421 of these boys.

Figure 3.1
The matching process

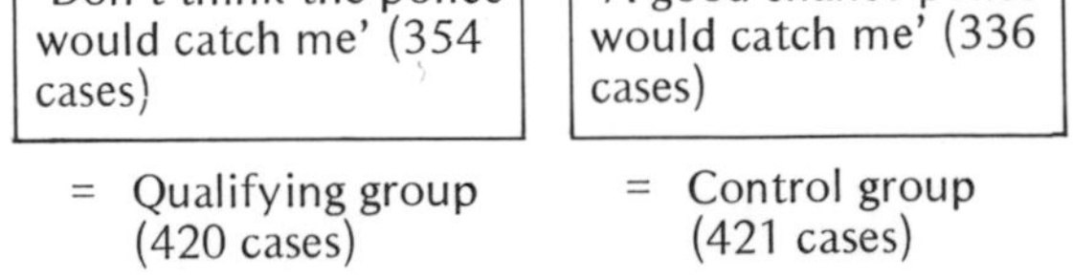

All boys
(1,425, unweighted)

Boys who say:
'Sure I would not be caught' (66 cases)

or

'Don't think the police would catch me' (354 cases)

= Qualifying group
(420 cases)

Boys who say:
'Sure the police would catch me' (85 cases)

or

'A good chance police would catch me' (336 cases)

= Control group
(421 cases)

Figure 3.2

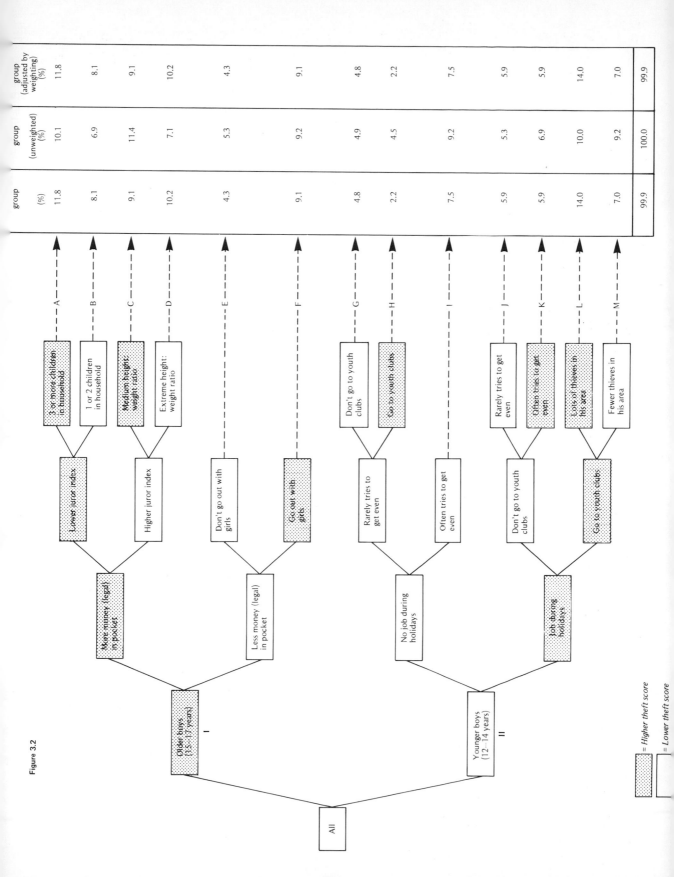

	group (%)	group (unweighted) (%)	group (adjusted by weighting) (%)
A	11.8	10.1	11.8
B	8.1	6.9	8.1
C	9.1	11.4	9.1
D	10.2	7.1	10.2
E	4.3	5.3	4.3
F	9.1	9.2	9.1
G	4.8	4.9	4.8
H	2.2	4.5	2.2
I	7.5	9.2	7.5
J	5.9	5.3	5.9
K	5.9	6.9	5.9
L	14.0	10.0	14.0
M	7.0	9.2	7.0
	99.9	100.0	99.9

= Higher theft score

= Lower theft score

111

In this separation of boys into qualifiers and controls, the intermediate group of boys who said that 'they *might* get caught if they were stealing' have been left out. This is because they are ambiguous as far as the hypothesis is concerned and therefore cannot be regarded as either qualifiers or as controls.

The second step in the matching process was to equate the control group to the qualifiers in terms of a composite of the stable correlates of stealing. This composite of stable correlates has already been shown in Chapter 2 and is repeated on p. 111 along with certain linked information. The method of its derivation has also been detailed in Chapter 1 but for the sake of continuity of presentation, a summary of the main features of the procedure is presented here. A large pool of variables (approximately 200) was assembled and, after the survey, each variable that could reasonably be regarded as stable with respect to the suggested causal factor was correlated with the dependent variable. The one amongst them with the highest correlation was used to split the total sample into two sections, namely sub-groups I and II. Following this, the most powerful predictor of the dependent variable was sought *quite separately in each of the sub-groups* I and II. This led to the separate (further) splitting of I and II. This process was continued as shown in Figure 3.2. The choice of a predictor (for further splitting) was in all cases contingent upon it being a source of difference between the two samples in terms of the dependent variable. In the present case, this splitting was continued to the limit of statistical viability and led to the emergence of sixteen sub-groups the top thirteen of which were regarded as the most appropriate for matching purposes.

In a third step, the qualifying group and the control group were separately split into these thirteen sub-groups on the lines shown in Columns a and b in the right-hand section of Figure 3.2. A simple weighting system was then used to up-weight or down-weight each of the thirteen matching sub-groups of the control group, so that the control group's composition in terms of the matching sub-groups was equal to that of the qualifying group. This is illustrated in Columns a and c in Figure 3.2. This step, too, is described in detail in Chapter 1.

Results (of testing Expectation 1) The results of testing Expectation 1 in the manner just described are shown in Table 3.5 below. It gives the results for both variety* of stealing and amount* of stealing.

For *amount of stealing*, Columns a and b compare the qualifying and control groups *before* any matching had taken place and show that the index of amount is higher for those who think they would NOT get caught than for those who think they WOULD get caught – 106.00:82.50. After the 'matching adjustment', the control group index score became 84.87 (see Column c). Accordingly, we may now say that if the control group was the same as the qualifying group in terms of the variables that make a difference to the amount of stealing being done (i.e. the correlates of stealing), then the qualifying and the control groups would compare as follows with respect to amount of stealing being done.

106.00:84.87

The difference between these two scores is highly significant and hence provides evidence in support of the hypothesis.

Let us be quite clear, however, that this evidence neither proves nor disproves the hypothesis. It simply strengthens it as an hypothesis about a tendency or trend. With regard to *variety* of stealing, the outcome is the same: the evidence strengthens the hypothesis.

Testing Expectation 2.

The matching criteria developed for testing Expectation 1 were next applied separately with respect to each of the forty-four types of theft on which the aggregates (i.e. for variety and amount scores) were based. Thus, for example, a test was made of the expectation that 'getting into a place and stealing' was related to a generalized belief that 'one would not get caught if one stole' – i.e. after matching controls to qualifiers. Matching was done separately for each of the forty-four items. The results are given in Table 3.6.

*See Chapter 2 (pp. 70 to 71) for the derivation of 'variety' and 'amount' indices.

Table 3.5
Differences between qualifiers and controls before and after matching: variety and amount of stealing

Indices of stealing	Average score for qualifiers a	Unadjusted average score for controls b	Adjusted average score for controls c	Differences between qualifiers and adj. controls a–c (P)	Difference a–c as percentage of c
Averaged variety score*	14.10	12.51	12.63	1.47 (0.05)	12
Averaged amount score*	106.00	82.50	84.87	21.13 (0.01)	25

Table 3.6

Differences between qualifiers and controls before and after matching: each of the forty-four types of theft

Types of theft (all at L2+)*	Number and percentage who have done the act at least once at Level 2 or over								Difference a−c as percentage of c
	Unadjusted results for qualifiers a		Unadjusted results for controls b		Adjusted results for controls c		Differences between qualifiers and adj. controls		
	n	(%)	n	(%)	n	(%)	a−c	(P)	
1	383	91.2	378	89.8	376.94	89.7	1.5	0.31	2
2	235	56.0	188	44.7	186.68	44.4	11.6	<0.01	26
3	172	41.0	141	33.5	142.59	34.0	7.0	0.02	21
4	230	54.8	209	49.6	209.57	49.9	4.9	0.08	10
5	99	23.6	83	19.7	84.44	20.1	3.5	0.08	17
6	254	60.5	201	47.7	203.79	48.5	12.0	<0.01	25
7	191	45.5	140	33.3	147.10	35.0	10.5	<0.01	30
8	139	33.1	133	31.6	133.13	31.7	1.4	0.38	4
9	73	17.4	55	13.1	56.85	13.5	3.9	0.10	29
10	186	44.3	149	35.4	154.22	36.7	7.6	0.02	21
11	158	37.6	143	34.0	145.04	34.5	3.1	0.18	9
12	66	15.7	64	15.2	62.05	14.8	0.9	0.34	6
13	182	43.3	144	34.2	144.35	34.4	8.9	<0.01	26
14	100	23.8	101	24.0	102.71	24.4	−0.6	0.42	−3
15	73	17.4	60	14.3	61.16	14.6	2.8	0.21	19
16	184	43.8	171	40.6	168.99	40.2	3.6	0.14	9
17	76	18.1	73	17.3	69.67	16.6	1.5	0.34	9
18	292	69.5	249	59.1	252.01	60.0	9.5	<0.01	16
19	152	36.2	151	35.9	152.67	36.3	−0.1	0.46	—
20	147	35.0	116	27.6	118.00	28.1	6.9	0.01	25
21	45	10.7	61	14.5	58.85	14.0	−3.3	0.08	−24
22	162	38.6	156	37.1	153.00	36.5	2.1	0.16	6
23	112	26.6	78	18.5	81.82	19.5	7.1	<0.01	36
24	54	12.9	46	10.9	47.40	11.3	1.6	0.18	14
25	105	25.0	97	23.0	93.26	22.2	2.8	0.14	13
26	128	30.5	107	25.4	106.57	25.4	5.1	0.04	20
27	79	18.8	78	18.5	78.59	18.7	0.1	0.34	1
28	91	21.7	99	23.5	100.27	23.9	−2.2	0.24	−9
29	34	8.1	23	5.5	23.93	5.7	2.4	0.12	42
30	208	49.5	184	43.7	190.54	45.4	4.1	0.08	9
31	122	29.0	108	25.7	116.82	27.8	1.2	0.38	4
32	31	7.4	21	5.0	21.19	5.0	2.4	0.12	48
33	270	64.3	252	59.9	255.36	60.8	3.5	0.18	6
34	130	31.0	129	30.6	125.30	29.8	1.2	0.38	4
35	65	15.5	57	13.5	56.72	13.5	2.0	0.34	15
36	123	29.3	118	28.0	118.10	28.1	1.2	0.38	4
37	22	5.2	16	3.8	16.48	3.9	1.3	0.24	33
38	100	23.8	77	18.3	79.21	18.9	4.9	0.04	26
39	90	21.4	66	15.7	64.36	15.3	6.1	0.01	40
40	268	63.8	265	62.9	261.98	62.4	1.4	0.27	2
41	35	8.3	32	7.6	30.39	7.2	1.1	0.27	15
42	51	12.1	39	9.3	39.26	9.3	2.8	0.07	30
43	134	31.9	120	28.5	121.31	28.9	3.0	0.16	10
44	233	55.5	200	47.5	203.42	48.4	7.1	0.02	15

*L2+ = When the value of the biggest thing of this sort taken was 4/6 or over

— = Less than 0.5 per cent

Table 3.7

Types of theft for which the expectation:

Tends most to be borne out	Tends least to be borne out
Stealing from someone at work	Getting into a place without paying
Stealing a letter or a parcel	Stealing by keeping something found
Stealing from a club	
Stealing from a cafe	Stealing by stripping from a building
Stealing a car or lorry or van	
Stealing from a telephone box	Stealing from someone at school
	Stealing cigarettes
Stealing a book or newspaper or magazine or comic	Stealing from a goods yard or yard or factory or docks or timber yard
Pinching when in someone else's home	Stealing from a park or playground

Whereas these findings tend generally to strengthen the hypothesis, they suggest that for certain types of theft the hypothesis may not apply, namely the types listed in the right-hand column of Table 3.7.

Testing Expectation 3

The third of the expectations derived from Hypothesis 1 was that: Those boys who think they will not get caught for stealing tend to continue with relatively serious stealing over a longer period of time than do other boys, and this applies even when the latter are closely matched to the former in terms of the correlates of stealing.

It will be remembered that 'serious' stealing was defined in terms of the eighteen acts of theft which a sample of the public had indicated as most serious among the forty-four and that a boy qualified on any one of them if he had committed it at 'Level 3'* or over (see Chapter 2). The reason for specifying *serious* stealing rather than stealing as such was that 'duration' of serious stealing could easily be blurred by the periodic occurrence of some very minor offence (e.g. keeping a small item found).

After matching of the kind already described in this chapter, the following results emerged.

*The qualifying value of such items was set at 4/6d. See further details at foot of Table A2.2 after Chapter 2.

The expectation is thus strongly borne out: appaently a view that one is likely get away with stealing substantially associated with the *continuation* of stealin at a serious level. On balance, the testing of Expectation 3 strengthens Hypothesis 1.

Summing-Up on the Investigation of Hypothesis 1

The tests of Expectations 1 and 3 tend to suppor Hypothesis 1. However, the evidence of the test o Expectation 2 suggests that the hypothesis does no apply for *all* types of theft.

5 METHODS AND FINDINGS RELATING TO THE INVESTIGATION OF HYPOTHESIS 2

The Nature of Hypothesis 2

The second of the hypotheses about getting caught wa

Boys take up stealing or continue to steal partly becaus they think *no one* will catch them.

It was intended in this inquiry both to examine th hypothesis and to provide background informatio about the independent variable defined in it, namel 'confidence on the part of the boy that *no one* will catc him if he engages in stealing'.

The distribution of boys in terms of the variable hypothesized as causal

In this section are presented: (*a*) the question asked as basis for classifying boys in terms of the variabl hypothesized as causal; and, (*b*) the distribution of boy in terms of it.

The question asked as a basis for classifying boys in terms of confidence that no one would catch them for stealing

The following question was asked as a basis fo classifying boys in terms of their confidence that *no one* would catch them if they were engaged in stealing (Se Question 1f in Appendix 3.1.)

Table 3.8

Difference between qualifiers and controls before and after matching: duration of stealing

Theft index	Number of 'serious' types of theft committed at least once			Difference between qualifiers and adj. controls a−c (*P*)	Difference a−c as percentage of c
	Average score for qualifiers **a**	Unadjusted average score for controls **b**	Adjusted average score for controls **c**		
Duration of serious stealing	5.65	3.29	3.75	1.90 (0.01)	51

...asked you about the *police* catching up with you. ...uppose you were pinching things. Do you think *anyone* ...ould catch up with you?

SHOW CARD. RING CHOICE OF ANSWER

...he distribution of boys in terms of the hypo-...hesized causal variable

...he distribution of responses to Question 1f are set out ...n Table 3.9. For comparative purposes the responses to ...uestion 1a, which dealt with the likelihood of the ...olice catching boys, have been included in the same ...able.

...able 3.9

...onfidence about getting away with stealing*

	Likelihood of being caught	
	By 'anyone' Q.1f (%)	By the police Q.1a (%)
...ure they would not catch me	3	5
...on't think they would catch me	11	27
...ight catch me	46	40
...here's a good chance they would catch me	31	22
...ure they would catch me	9	6

*Excluding 'don't knows'

...nvestigating Hypothesis 2

...A summary of the basic strategy of investigation ...As stated under Hypothesis 1, the central strategy for ...nvestigating Hypothesis 2 (and all other of the hypo-...heses to be studied) was to derive from it a series of ...estable expectations and to test these (see also Chapter ...).

...he expectations to be tested ...Three expectations from Hypothesis 2 were derived for ...esting. These were as follows.

...xpectation 1 Boys who think they will not get caught ...y *anyone* (if they are stealing) do more stealing than ...ther boys and this applies even when the latter are ...losely matched to the former in terms of the correlates ...of stealing.

Expectation 2 Expectation 1 also applies with respect to each of the forty-four types of theft studied in the inquiry.

Expectation 3 Boys who think they will not get caught by anyone for stealing keep it up over a longer period than other boys, and this applies even when the latter are closely matched to the former in terms of the correlates of stealing.

Testing Expectation 1: Methods and Findings

Methods Just as for Expectations 1, 2, 3 of Hypothesis 1, the three expectations from Hypothesis 2 called for the close empirical matching of those who did and those who did not qualify in terms of the expectations concerned.

The actual variables in terms of which the matching should be done are of course the same as for Expectations 1, 2 and 3 of Hypothesis 1, namely the *correlates of stealing* as set out on p. 111 of this chapter. Thus, all that remained for the testing of Expectation 1 of Hypothesis 2 was that the boys who did not qualify in terms of that expectation, and those who *did*, should be identified, and that the former be equated to the latter in terms of the composite of matching variables.

Qualifying boys and controls were separated as follows in Figure 3.3.

In this separation of boys, the intermediate group ('someone *might* catch me') was omitted because the position of these boys was considered ambiguous in terms of the expectation.

Figure 3.3
Qualifying boys and controls

All boys
(1,425 unweighted)

Boys who say:
'Sure nobody would catch me (33 cases)
or
'Don't think anyone would catch me'
(153 cases)

= Qualifying group
(186 cases)

Boys who say:
'Sure someone would catch me (133 cases)
or
A good chance someone would catch me'
(419 cases)

= Control group
(552 cases)

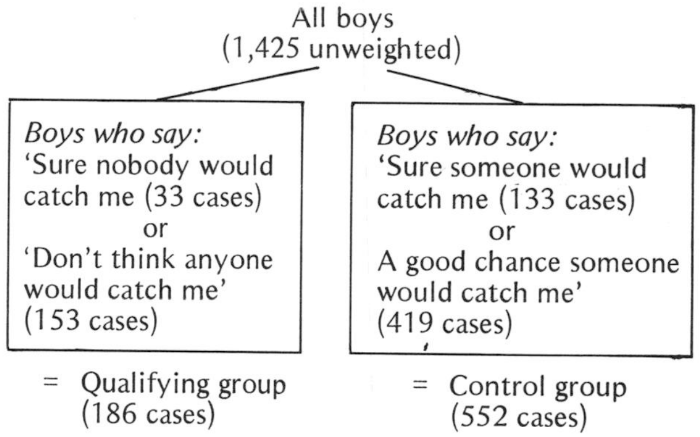

Table 3.10
Matching sub-groups

	A	B	C	D	E	F	G	H	I	J	K	L	M	All
Qualifying group	22	15	17	19	8	17	9	4	14	11	11	26	13	186
Control group	56	38	63	39	29	51	27	25	51	29	38	55	51	552

Table 3.11
Differences between qualifiers and controls before and after matching: variety and amount of stealing

Theft indices	Unadjusted average score for qualifiers a	Unadjusted average score for controls b	Adjusted average score for controls c	Difference between qualifiers and adjusted controls a–c (P)	Difference a–c as percentage of c
Average *variety* score	15.58	12.52	13.12	2.46 (0.01)	19
Average *amount* score	122.29	87.03	93.70	28.59 (0.01)	31

The qualifying group and the control group were then each split into the thirteen sub-groups defined by the matching composite, with results as shown in Table 3.10. Following this, weights were applied to each of the *control* sub-groups sufficient to equate them numerically to the comparable sub-group among the *qualifiers.*

Results (of testing Expectation 1) The results of testing Expectation 1 in the manner described are presented in Table 3.11.

These results support Expectation 1 and hence tend to strengthen the hypothesis.

Testing Expectation 2
The same procedure was used in testing Expectation 2, namely that: Expectation 1 also applies with respect to each of the forty-four types of theft studied in this inquiry. The results are set out in Table 3.12.

The general indications of Table 3.12 are that the expectation holds for most of the types of theft studied but not for all. A listing of the types of theft for which it holds most and least is made in Table 3.13.

Testing Expectation 3
This expectation took the form: Boys who think they will not get caught by anyone for stealing keep it up over a longer period than do other boys, and this applies even when the latter are closely matched to the former in terms of the correlates of stealing. This expectation

was tested in the same manner, and with the same limitations, as was Expectation 3 of Hypothesis 1. The results are set out in Table 3.14 below.

These findings support Expectation 3 and serve to strengthen Hypothesis 2.

Table 3.13
Types of theft for which the expectation:

Tends most to be borne out	Tends least to be borne out
Stealing a letter or parcel	Stealing when in someone else's home
Stealing from a telephone box	
Failing to pay one's fare (or proper fare)	Stealing from a bike or motor bike
Stealing a bike or motor-bike	Taking things belonging to children or teenagers
Stealing from a stall or barrow	Stealing toys
Stealing from a club	Keeping something I have found
Stealing a car or lorry or van	Stealing from a park or playground
Stealing from a building site	Taking junk or scrap without asking for it first
Stealing from a cafe	Cheating someone out of money
	Stealing from my family or relations

Table 3.14
Differences between qualifiers and controls before and after matching: duration of stealing

Theft index	Unadjusted average score for qualifiers a	Unadjusted average score for controls b	Adjusted average score for controls c	Difference between qualifiers and adjusted controls a – c (P)	Difference a–c as percentage of c
Duration of stealing*	4.39	3.43	3.62	0.77 0.01	21

*Serious stealing as defined in terms of the eighteen acts of theft rated as 'more serious' by the public

Table 3.12
Differences between qualifiers and controls before and after matching: each of the forty-four types of theft

| Types of theft (all at L2+)* | Number and percentages who have done the act at least once at Level 2 or over | | | | | | Differences between qualifiers and adj. controls | | Differences a−c as percentage of c |
| | Unadjusted results for qualifiers† a | | Unadjusted results for controls‡ b | | Adjusted results for controls c | | | | |
	n	(%)	n	(%)	n	(%)	a−c	(P)	
1	174	93.5	493	89.3	168.0	90.3	3.2	0.07	4
2	111	59.7	255	46.2	88.6	47.6	12.1	0.01	25
3	80	43.0	202	36.6	72.1	38.8	4.2	0.21	11
4	102	54.8	291	52.7	99.4	53.4	1.4	0.34	3
5	56	30.1	109	19.7	39.3	21.1	9.0	0.02	43
6	125	67.2	273	49.5	96.7	52.0	15.2	<0.01	29
7	95	51.0	194	35.1	70.4	37.8	13.2	0.01	35
8	58	31.1	192	34.8	66.2	35.6	−4.5	(−)0.16	−13
9	31	16.6	75	13.6	28.8	15.5	1.1	0.31	7
10	100	53.8	193	35.0	68.7	36.9	16.9	<0.01	46
11	73	39.2	196	35.5	69.2	37.2	2.0	0.34	5
12	32	17.2	81	14.7	29.0	15.6	1.6	0.38	10
13	92	49.4	200	36.2	72.7	39.1	10.3	0.02	26
14	60	32.2	113	20.5	41.2	22.1	10.1	0.01	46
15	33	17.7	69	12.5	24.7	13.3	4.4	0.08	33
16	91	48.9	226	40.9	79.6	42.8	6.1	0.12	14
17	44	23.6	88	15.9	31.5	16.9	6.7	0.04	40
18	143	76.9	340	61.6	117.3	63.1	13.8	<0.01	22
19	82	44.1	205	37.1	72.0	38.7	5.4	0.16	14
20	73	39.2	155	28.1	54.9	29.5	9.7	0.04	33
21	26	14.0	73	13.2	25.4	13.6	0.4	0.46	3
22	72	38.7	198	35.9	69.2	37.2	1.5	0.34	4
23	52	27.9	103	18.7	38.0	20.4	7.5	0.04	37
24	23	12.4	53	9.6	19.8	10.6	1.8	0.38	17
25	56	30.1	121	21.9	41.9	22.5	7.6	0.07	34
26	67	36.0	136	24.6	48.6	26.1	9.9	0.02	38
27	39	21.0	100	18.1	34.8	18.7	2.3	0.31	12
28	48	25.8	125	22.6	43.5	23.4	2.4	0.24	10
29	23	12.4	28	5.1	10.6	5.7	6.7	0.02	118
30	90	48.4	247	44.7	88.7	47.7	0.7	0.46	2
31	65	34.9	144	26.1	55.2	30.0	4.9	0.16	16
32	14	7.5	37	6.7	13.1	7.0	0.5	0.34	7
33	136	73.1	326	58.9	113.7	61.1	12.0	0.01	20
34	62	33.3	163	29.5	55.4	29.8	3.5	0.27	12
35	41	22.0	79	14.3	28.6	15.4	6.6	0.04	43
36	56	30.1	148	26.8	52.4	28.2	1.9	0.34	7
37	11	5.9	20	3.6	7.9	4.2	1.7	0.18	41
38	46	24.7	101	18.3	35.7	19.2	5.5	0.08	29
39	44	23.6	88	15.9	30.9	16.6	7.0	0.04	42
40	128	68.8	340	61.6	117.3	63.1	5.7	0.12	9
41	19	10.2	41	7.4	15.5	8.3	1.9	0.24	23
42	28	15.0	40	7.2	15.6	8.4	6.6	0.02	79
43	75	40.3	154	27.8	55.0	29.6	10.7	0.02	36
44	108	58.1	260	47.1	92.5	49.7	8.4	0.07	17

*L2+ = when the value of the biggest thing of this sort taken was 4/6d or over.

†Those who qualified in terms of the hypothesis (= sure nobody would catch me + don't think anyone would catch me)

‡Those who did not qualify in terms of the hypothesis (= sure someone would catch me + a good chance that someone would catch me)

Summing-Up on the Investigation of Hypothesis 2

The position of Hypothesis 2 seems to be closely similar to that of Hypothesis 1. Thus, the tests of Expectations 1 and 3 generally support Hypothesis 2. However, the evidence from the test of Expectation 2 suggests that Hypothesis 2 does not apply for *all* types of theft.

6 METHODS AND FINDINGS RELATING TO THE INVESTIGATION OF HYPOTHESIS 3

Nature of the Hypothesis
The third hypothesis about causal factors in stealing was that:

Boys reduce their stealing if they get caught by the police.

It was intended both to investigate this hypothesis and to provide background information about the independent variable defined in it, namely 'getting caught by the police for stealing'.

The Distribution of Boys in Terms of the Variable Hypothesized as Causal
In this section are presented (*a*) the questions asked as a basis for classifying boys as qualifiers or as controls; (*b*) distributions of boys in terms of 'getting caught by the police'; (*c*) characteristics of those who have ever been caught by the police.

The questioning procedure used for classifying boys in terms of the causal hypothesis
A series of questions was asked in order to establish each boy's position in relation to the hypothesis. These questions are set out in context in Appendix 3.1 and in extracted form below. In considering them, however, the

reader should note: (*a*) that at the time of asking, each boy had been through the demanding and revealing procedure used for establishing the nature and extent of any stealing he may have done; (*b*) that a very favourable rapport had been established by this time with most boys; (*c*) that the same conditions of anonymity and of privacy operated here as in the earlier parts of the interview.

The more relevant of the questions asked for classifying boys in terms of the hypothesis were as follows.

Q.2a) 'Have you ever been caught up with for pinching anything?' YES/NO
    IF 'NO' CHECK WITH; 'Never in your life? *Not by anyone at all*?'
    'By Parents? By a shopkeeper? By a store detective? Not even for little things?'
    IF STILL 'NO' GO ON TO Q4.
    IF 'YES' TO (a), ASK AS FOLLOWS:

b) 'How old were you the very first time anyone caught up with you for pinching things?
I mean caught up with by *anyone*.'

    CHECK WITH: 'How can you be sure it was that age?'

c) 'Who caught up with you that first time?'
    IF POLICE MENTIONED, GO TO Q2(e).
    IF *NOT*, CHECK WITH 'Did the police come into it at all?' YES/NO
    IF 'YES', GO TO Q2(e).
    IF STILL 'NO', GO TO Q2(d).

d) Not directly relevant.

e) Not directly relevant.

Table 3.15 The percentage of boys who have been caught for stealing. Based on 3,113 cases, weighted (= 1,425 unweighted)	Frequency of involvement with police		Amount of stealing actually done* by boys			
			Low quartile (= Q.1)	Q.2	Q.3	High quartile (= Q.4)
			(%)	(%)	(%)	(%)
	Caught by police for stealing	13				
	Three or more times 2		2	6	19	73
	Twice 2		4	29	17	50
	Once only 9		8	21	25	46
	Caught for stealing by someone other than the police	37	16	27	31	26
	Never caught by anyone	49	35	30	21	14
	No information	1				
	All	100	24	28	25	23

*Excluding types of theft which had never been committed beyond some trivial level

Q.3a) Q.3a) 'Since then, how often have the police *caught up with you* for pinching?'

IF 'NEVER', ASK: 'Have you done any pinching at all since then?' YES/NO
THEN GO TO Q4.

b) IF HE HAS BEEN INVOLVED WITH THE POLICE SINCE THEN: 'Exactly how many times?'
PRESS FOR A NUMBER, BUT CHALLENGE IT.

Distribution of boys in terms of getting caught by the police

Between them, Questions 2 and 3 provided information about the frequency with which boys had been caught by the police for stealing. Details are given in the left-hand section of Table 3.15.

The dominant finding here is that 13 per cent of London boys in the age range thirteen to sixteen years have at some time been involved with the police over stealing, and that another 37 per cent have been caught for stealing by someone other than the police. It is possible to relate these figures to the amount of stealing done by the boys concerned in the way shown on the right-hand side of Table 3.15. From this evidence it seems that:

1 Boys who have been caught by the police tend quite markedly to be drawn from that section of the boy population most heavily involved in stealing.

2 Those boys who have been caught more often are the ones most heavily involved in stealing.

3 Those boys who have been caught by someone other than the police (37 per cent) are somewhat above average in terms of the extent of their stealing.

Table 3.15 also tells us that 49 per cent of boys have never been caught for stealing *by anyone*. This immediately raises the possibility that they have done nothing to be caught for. However, this is by no means the case, for 14 per cent of these boys are in the top scoring

quarter of the boy population for amount of stealing and 35 per cent of them are in the top half in this respect. In other words, many of these boys are thieves who have 'got away with it'.

The figures in Table 3.15 can be presented another way, namely in terms of the percentage of *heavy* thieves (i.e. those in the top quartile) who have or have not been caught.

Thus: 30 per cent of the boys in the quartile with the top theft rate have never been caught by anyone and only 28 per cent of them have ever been caught by the police. In evaluating this finding, we must keep it in mind that even amongst the boys who *were* caught by the police, the number of thefts they got away with far exceeded the number for which they were caught.

Characteristics and background of those who get caught by the police

Getting caught, analysed by father's occupational level, boy's school, religion, etc.

In Table 3.17, the question of *who* gets caught by the police is taken one step further. This table shows the percentage of those who got caught distributed in terms of the different population sectors. Against each sub-group is shown the quartile distribution by amount of stealing *going on in the sub-group as a whole* so that the percentage of the boys who have been caught by the police can be seen in better perspective. As a further aid in comparing the catching rate in the different population sub-groups, a calculation has been made (for each sub-group) of the ratio of 'percentage caught' to 'an index of amount of stealing actually being done'*.

The indications of Table 3.17 are fairly clear — and striking.

1 There is a lot of variation between sub-groups in the proportion of boys who are caught by the police. Thus only 3 per cent of the sons of the professional, semi-professional and executive class get caught by the police, whereas 23 per cent of the sons of the unskilled get caught by the police. Then again, only 2 per cent of Jewish boys get caught, compared with 20 per cent of Catholic boys; 3 per cent of public-school boys get caught compared with 19 per cent of boys from secondary modern schools.

2 Whereas some of this variability appears to be associated with variability in the *level of thieving* of boys in the different sub-groups, that variability is nowhere near enough to explain the differences in the propor-

Table 3.16
The percentage of heavy thieves who have been caught/ not caught

Degree to which caught	Heavy thieves (%)	(As percentage of total population of boys)
Caught by police three times or more	6	(1.5)
Caught by police twice or more	4	(1.0)
Caught by police once only	18	(4.1)
Caught by someone other than police	42	(9.6)
Never caught by anyone	30	(6.9)
All	100%	(23.1%)

*This index is based on a weighted score across quartile groups. Thus the index for 'sons of the unskilled'

$$= \frac{(18 \times 1) + (31 \times 2) + (28 \times 3) + (23 \times 4)}{100} = 2.56$$

and ratio of percentage caught to 'index of stealing done' =

$$\frac{23.00}{2.56} \fallingdotseq 9.0$$

119

Table 3.17

Relating 'getting caught by police' to backgrounds of boys

Characteristics of boys	Caught by police (%)	Quartile distribution of amount of stealing				Ratio of 'percentage caught' and index of amount of stealing done* (= catching rate)*
		Low score quartile Q.1 (%)	Q.2 (%)	Q.3 (%)	High score quartile Q.4 (%)	
Occupational level of father						
Professional, semi-professional, executive	3	27	40	19	14	1.4
Highly skilled and skilled	10	24	24	30	22	4.0
Moderately and semi-skilled	19	24	24	23	29	7.4
Unskilled	23	18	31	28	23	9.0*
Born in UK						
Yes	13	24	28	25	23	5.3
No	14	32	24	22	22	6.0
Coloured						
No	13	24	28	25	23	5.3
Yes	10	31	23	27	19	4.3
Nominal religion						
Protestant	12	23	28	22	27	4.7
Catholic	20	23	22	29	26	7.7
Other christian	10	21	22	34	23	3.9
Greek orthodox	18	32	34	22	12	8.4
Jewish	2	33	35	29	3	1.0
None	17	22	27	26	25	6.7
School last attended						
Secondary modern	19	20	25	27	28	7.2
Technical	15	21	8	41	30	5.4
Comprehensive	12	23	26	26	25	4.7
Grammar	4	30	30	23	17	1.8
Public	3	28	43	15	14	1.4
Age at interview						
12/13 years	8	36	32	20	12	3.8
14 years	11	26	30	25	19	4.6
15 years	16	19	29	27	25	6.2
16/17 years	17	16	20	29	35	6.0

*The ratio 9.0 shown in Table 3.17 is calculated through 23/2.56 (÷ 8.98). See footnote on p. 119 for derivation of the figure 2.56

tions of those caught by the police. The 'catching rate', which is aimed at balancing out differences in the level of thieving, is disproportionately *high* for: boys whose fathers are in the less-skilled category; Catholic and Greek Orthodox* boys; boys of secondary modern-school background. And by contrast, the 'catching rate' is exceptionally low for boys: whose fathers are in the upper-professional brackets; who are Jewish; who attend grammar schools or public schools.

*The numbers of boys involved is small and hence this finding must be treated with caution

3 It may be of particular interest to many that the data in Table 3.17 do *not* support the view that coloured boys are more likely to be caught for the stealing they do than are white boys. The numbers involved are small but nonetheless are worth noting.

The age of first being caught for stealing

Boys had been asked, amongst other things, for their ages when first caught for stealing: (*a*) by anyone; and, (*b*) by the police. The questions are detailed in Appendix 3.1 and the results are set out in Table 3.18.

From a comparative viewpoint, the only meaningful figures in Table 3.18 are those for the age of twelve and under because it is only these ages that *all* boys in the sample have passed through. Over that particular age range, it is clear that age of first being caught (by at least someone) is rather evenly distributed, with a great many boys being caught quite young.

Age at first, second, third involvement with the police

In Table 3.19 is presented the distribution of boys' ages at the time of first involvement with the police, at the time of second involvement and at the time of third involvement. Just as with the previous table, the age range to be considered in any *comparative* work should be limited to six to twelve years (because these are the only ages that all members of the sample have had in common).

The general indication of this table is that *by the age of twelve*, 7 per cent of the thirteen to sixteen year-old boys had been caught a first time by the police, 1.5 per cent a second time and 0.8 per cent a third time.

Other correlates of 'getting caught'

What happened when the police caught the boy?

Boys who had been involved with the police at some time were asked, with respect to each involvement, what happened to them. Responses were content analysed for the derivation of Tables 3.20 and 3.21.

These two tables indicate amongst other things:

Table 3.18
Ages at which boys are first caught for stealing

| Age at which first caught | First time caught | |
	By anyone (including police) (%)	By police (%)
6 years or less	6	—
7 years	5	—
8 years	5	1
9 years	5	1
10 years	5	1
11 years	5	1
12 years	6	2
13 years	6	2
14 years	4	3
15 years	1	1
16 years	1	—
17 years	—	—
Age not established	1	—
Never caught	49	86
Not known if ever caught	1	1

— = less than 0.5 per cent

1 An increase in the proportion of boys who are sent to Court as the number of their past apprehensions by police increases — though 12 per cent of those apprehended a third time were *not* sent to Court.

Table 3.19
Ages of boys at first, second and third involvements with the police

| Age at time of involvement with police | a First involvement (415 cases*) | | b Second involvement (135 cases*) | | c Third involvement (66 cases*) | |
	n	cn†	n	cn†	n	cn†
6 years or less	14	14	0			
7 years	10	24	0			
8 years	15	39	2	2		
9 years	38	77	2	4	2	2
10 years	35	112	12	16	2	4
11 years	40	152	14	30	6	10
12 years	62	214	17	47	14	24
13 years	72		24		7	
14 years	77		45		24	
15 years	36		11		3	
16 years	14		5		3	
17 years	0		0		0	
No information	2		3		5	

*Weighted sample (i.e. on 3,113 cases weighted up from original 1,425)
†cn = accumulated total

121

Table 3.20
What happened when
caught by police: whether
or not sent to court

What happened?	On first involvement with police (415 cases*) (%)	On second involvement with police (135 cases*) (%)	On third involvement with police (66 cases*) (%)
Summary classification			
Sent to court	48	65	73
Not sent to court	41	15	12
Not clear or no information	11	20	15

*Weighted sample (i.e. on 3,113 cases weighted up from original 1,425)

2 A relatively low incidence of commitment to some form of detention and a relatively high incidence of simply being warned or 'told off'.

3 A high incidence of being fined and/or having to pay back. It must be remembered, of the data and indications (*a*) that they relate to *claims* by the boys and (*b*) that the numbers of real cases are small.

Whether sent to Court, analysed by characteristics of boys
The question of whether boys who are sent to Court (after first involvement with police) was analysed by the

Table 3.21
Boys' report of what happened when caught by police: details of consequences

Detail of what happened (according to boys)	On first, second, third involvement with police (combined) Total (wtd) = 616 (%)
Of those sent to Court	
Discharged/conditionally discharged	20
Fined	16
Had to pay damages/costs	21
Put on probation	17
Sent to attendance centre/detention centre	2
Sent away (place not specified)	2
Sent to approved school/borstal	2
Other consequences	3
Of those not sent to Court	
Nothing	7
He was asked questions	2
He was searched	2
He was warned/told off	19
He was hit	1
Name and address taken	7
Parents informed	4
Taken to police station	3
Had to apologise/pay back	2
Other consequences	3

characteristics of boys. Details for sub-groups are given in Table 3.22 and should be compared with the figure of 48 per cent for *all* boys (see Table 3.20).

Some of the numbers in this table are small and hence any of their indications must be interpreted with much care. In this very tentative context, it may be that the following boys are somewhat less likely to be sent to Court than are other boys: the sons of skilled workers, Protestant boys, boys with a grammar- or public-school background, younger boys. Whereas this may quite possibly reflect a degree of differential treatment of boys, we must not lose sight of the other possibility that the boys concerned tend to commit thefts of a more serious — or a different — kind.

Investigating Hypothesis 3

Basic strategy of investigation
Here again, the central strategy for testing this hypothesis was to derive from it a series of testable expectations and to test these. In the present case we must be particularly careful about the expectations we derive. Thus it would not be reasonable to 'expect' from the hypothesis that boys *who had been caught by the police* would have lower theft scores (i.e. on the grounds that getting caught reduces subsequent stealing). The reason for saying this is that the theft scores involved in this inquiry are based upon a whole lifetime of stealing and not just stealing since the boy concerned was first caught.

The expectations that may be derived
In fact, in the present case the testable expectations do not give us much chance to challenge the hypothesis in the necessarily unambiguous or rigorous manner. The only expectations available to us involve different sorts of testimony by boys, namely the following.

Expectation 1 If boys who have stolen are caught for this by the police, they will tend to claim that getting caught in this way reduced their involvement in stealing.

Expectation 2 If a boy's mates get caught for stealing, he will say that this has led him to do less stealing himself.

Table 3.22
Whether or not sent to Court on first involvement with police, analysed by characteristics of boys

Characteristics	Total involved with police	Percentage of those involved sent to Court	Characteristics	Total involved with police	Percentage of those involved sent to Court
Weighted cases	415	197	Weighted cases	415	197
	(n)	(%)		(n)	(%)
Age at interview			*Coloured*		
12/13 years	58	40	No	403	46
14 years	87	42	Yes	12	(n = 11)*
15 years	122	50			
16/17 years	148	51	*Nominal religion*		
			Protestant	164	38
Occupational level of boy's father			Catholic	98	51
Professional, semi-professional and			Other Christian	17	(n = 10)*
executive	16	(n = 5)*	Greek Orthodox	14	(n = 5)*
Highly skilled/skilled	123	39	Jewish	3	(n = 0)*
Moderately and semi-skilled	217	51	None	106	46
Unskilled	59	54			
No information	6		*School attended*		
			Secondary modern	283	50
Born in UK			Technical	3	(n = 2)*
Yes	379	47	Comprehensive	67	42
No	36	50	Grammar	28	(n = 11)*
			Public	7	(n = 1)*

*Figure in brackets = unweighted number of individuals involved and not a percentage figure: the base is too small for calculation of a percentage

Table 3.23.1
Boys' testimony about the ways they reacted to getting caught by the police. The first instance of getting caught

Has the boy ever been caught by the police? Q.2a, c	(n)	(%)	What does the boy *think* was the effect of the first instance of his getting caught by the police?			
			Made him steal *more* (%)	Made him steal *less* (%)	Made *no* difference (%)	No reply (%)
Never	2,687	86				
Yes	415	13	4	71	22	3
No information or not clear	11	—				

— = less than 0.5 per cent

Table 3.23.2
Subsequent instances of getting caught

Q.3a–e	(n)	What does the boy *think* was the effect of any subsequent instances of his getting caught by the police?			
		Made him steal *more* (%)	Made him steal *less* (%)	Made *no* difference (%)	No reply (%)
Caught by police more than once	135	1	74	21	4

123

Table 3.24

What happened to you when the police caught you? (*all* occasions considered)	Boy says that as a result he:			
	Did *more* (%)	Did *less* (%)	*No difference* (%)	No reply (%)
Sent to Court	3	73	22	2
Not sent to Court	3	71	22	4

Testing either expectation

Clearly the testing of these two expectations does not involve matching of any kind. The evidence available is nothing more than testimony with its obvious weaknesses, though in the present case it is possible to study it in contrasting and challenging situations.

Testing Expectation 1

A series of questions had been asked which served to identify those boys who had at some time been caught by the police for stealing. These boys were then asked what the police did and what differences this made to the amount of stealing they did thereafter (see Questions 2a, 2c and 2e and Questions 3a to e in Appendix 3.1). Details of what the police did and of how the boys felt this affected their subsequent stealing were collected separately for the first instance of getting caught and for subsequent instances of getting caught. The results are given in Tables 3.23.1 and 3.23.2.

The indications of these two tables are as follows.

1 Though there are plenty of individual exceptions to Expectation 1, there is a marked tendency for it to be borne out for the sample as a whole.

2 On the other hand, there is little to suggest that second or third involvements with the police are more effective than the first one in making the boy do less stealing. This raises the question of whether the expected consequence (next time) was in fact as bad as the boy thought it would be. On this point, it is worth noting that *according to the testimony of boys*, whereas they tend *more* to be sent to Court on second and third involvements with the police (see Table 3.20), there is no evidence of a general stepping-up of the seriousness or unpleasantness or constructiveness of what happened to them on subsequent occasions. Nor, incidentally, does 'getting sent to Court' appear to be *more* associated with boys' claims that they did less thereafter. This evidence is, of course, 'according to the claims of boys', but its indications do seem to be worthy of investigation.

3 There were ten responses (from eight boys*) to the effect that getting caught (the first time) made them steal *more*. Whereas this must be regarded as serious at the individual level, it gives little support to a view that is frequently put forward that 'getting caught' is a major

*Unweighted cases.

factor in leading boys to continue stealing: in fact, on this limited evidence, it appears very much more often to work the other way.

Boys' reasons for claims about the effect of getting caught Boys were asked to explain why they answered LESS or MORE or NO DIFFERENCE when asked what they thought was the effect, on their stealing, of what happened when they got caught. Explanations of the response LESS are given in Table 3.25 below.

There is little that is surprising about Table 3.25. It serves simply to support the view that boys are deterred from further theft by the prospect of unfortunate consequences. In general, of course, it is in support of Expectation 1.

Boys who said that getting caught led them to do MORE stealing or that it made NO DIFFERENCE to the amount of stealing they did were also asked to explain that response. The results of a content analysis of these explanations is given in Table 3.26.

Some important indications of Table 3.26 appear to be that 'getting caught' makes little or no difference to subsequent stealing: (*a*) where the boy feels he will not get caught next time; (*b*) where the boy was let off altogether or lightly the last time; and, (*c*) where he does not care what happens.

Table 3.25

Explanation of why he claimed that getting caught by police *reduced* his stealing

	(%)
Boy was worried/frightened/shocked	8
It taught me a lesson	2
Boy did not want to get caught again (no elaboration)	14
The hurt/worry/anger of parents	7
Fear or awareness of consequences next time (no elaboration)	16
Consequences may be *worse* next time	4
Prospect of losing his job	—
Prospect of going to Court	5
Prospect of paying a fine	1
Prospect of probation	4
Prospect of being put away/sent to approved school/ sent to borstal	28
Other reasons	12

— = Less than 0.5 per cent

Table 3.26

Why getting caught made me do more/made no difference to my stealing

Made no difference		(%)
He thinks there is little likelihood of getting caught if he continues stealing/now he knows how to avoid getting caught	14 ⎱	
He thinks it was just an odd chance that he was caught previously	5 ⎰	19
Last time he was caught he got let off	11 ⎱	
He thinks he will be let off again, just as last time	11 ⎰	22
He is undeterred by the sort of punishment he got last time (e.g. nothing, name and address taken, warned, discharged, conditionally discharged) or by threat of punishment		26
He does not care if caught or punished		19
Other reasons, including 'got back into company of mates who were pinching' (2%); 'you can't break a habit like that' (2%)		9
No information		9

Made me do more	n
	(8 boys giving 10 reasons)
It gets into the papers and makes you feel good	1
You can boast to your mates	1
You tell your mates they won't catch me next time	1
I wanted to see if I would get caught again	1
I wanted to get my own back/wanted revenge/they gave me too much and I wanted to get even	3
There were others in there who had done more than I had	1
He learned how to do it from others who were being detained with him	2

The second part of Table 3.26 deals with the views of the few boys who say that getting caught led them to steal *more*. For the few boys concerned (eight boys giving ten replies), the reasons given included: the effects of publicity, boasting to mates, revenge, learning techniques from boys in detention with them. There is by no means enough information here for anything like action, but clearly it would be of great value for those administering 'treatment' of boys caught for stealing to have available to them detailed information of this kind relating to a large number of boys who have been caught and processed in different ways and who have thereafter either continued to steal or increased the level of their stealing.

The relevance of a statement by a boy that he steals less (or more) after getting caught by the police We must of course at all times maintain a scientific scepticism about the meaningfulness of a boy's claim that getting caught led him to steal less or more or that it made no difference. Human testimony — particularly in this delicate area — being what it is, we must be willing to

suspect that an answer LESS may not mean 'less' at all. Similarly for an answer MORE or NO DIFFERENCE. On the other hand, there is some opportunity here to challenge the consistency of such claims with other of the evidence given by boys and this has been done on the pattern indicated in Figure 3.4.

From this evidence it appears that if boys say that their first involvement with the police led them to steal *less* thereafter, they will: (a) also claim a much lower rate of 'being caught again' than will those who answered MORE or NO DIFFERENCE; and (b) be more likely to claim no more stealing at all since the first involvement. This sort of internal consistency of replies is encouraging — though by no means enough to warrant complacency in interpreting claims.

The evidence also brings home the fact that where the boy says he did LESS stealing after getting caught, he does not necessarily mean no more stealing at all. The majority of such boys will in fact do at least *some* more stealing.

Summing up on the testing of Expectation 1 On balance, it seems that Expectation 1 is borne out *as a trend*, though clearly the evidence here presented suggests that:

1 For the many individuals for whom it *is* borne out, 'getting caught' is by no means enough to lead boys to give up stealing altogether.

2 For a sizeable minority of boys, 'getting caught' does not appear to reduce stealing at all.

It seems also to suggest that:

3 Getting caught more than once does not reduce *further* a boy's tendency to steal thereafter.

4 Whether the boy goes to Court or not does not affect his tendency to steal thereafter.

Table 3.27

What boys think happened to mates when caught (weighted base = 2,229)

	(n)	(%)
Discharged/conditionally discharged	29	1
Fined	219	10
Had to pay damages/costs	26	1
Put on probation	572	26
Sent to attendance centre/detention centre	74	3
Sent to remand home	112	5
Sent to approved school	127	6
Sent to borstal	447	20
Sent to prison	151	7
Sent to 'boarding school'	14	1
Put away/sent away	237	11
Was warned/cautioned/told off	83	4
Expelled from school	22	1
Other consequences	141	6
Don't know	53	2

Figure 3.4
Challenging consistency of claims

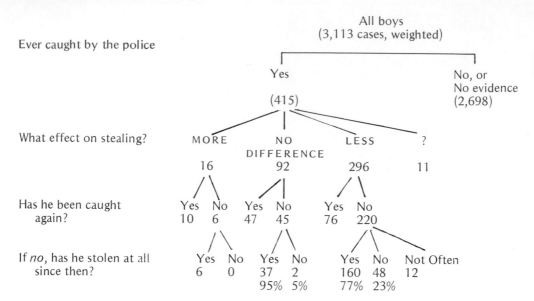

Testing Expectation 2

This expectation has been stated as: 'If a boy's *mates* get caught by the police for stealing, he will say that this has led him to do less stealing himself'. The questions asked in relation to this expectation are set out on the fourth page of the sub-questionnaire about 'getting caught' (Appendix 3.1). Through them, boys were asked if the police had caught any of their mates for stealing, what happened to these mates and how this affected their *own* stealing. They were also asked to *explain* the estimate given of how the apprehension and treatment of mates affected them.

What did the boy say happened to the mates who got caught? Details of boys' impressions on this score are set out in Table 3.27.

The first thing to note about Table 3.27 is that the claims of 'consequence' listed in it are as offered by the boys. In the circumstances it is perhaps not surprising that the majority of these consequences relate to Court processing, the likelihood being that boys hear much more about police apprehensions (of other boys) that lead to Court appearances than about those that do not. Also, we must expect a lot of hearsay and inaccuracy to condition the frequencies set against each category. The upshot of all this is that the details set out in Table 3.27 must be seen only as what the respondent *heard* or *thought* he heard of what happened to apprehended mate(s). In this sense the details are nonetheless informative in that they indicate popular impressions (among boys generally) of what happens when other boys are caught by the police for stealing.

Percentage whose mates have been caught and the claimed effects on themselves The percentage of boys who say their mates have been caught by the police is given in Table 3.28, along with boys' opinions about its effects on their own behaviour.

The number of boys who know of mates being caught (71 per cent) is, of course, much larger than the number

Table 3.28

Have the police caught any of his mates for stealing? (Q.3)	(n)	(%)	What difference did the treatment of his mates (when caught) make to his own behaviour (Q.3b)			
			Stole more (%)	No difference (%)	Stole less (%)	No information (%)
Yes	2,217	71	—	41	58	1
No	887	28				
No information	9	—				

— = less than 0.5 per cent

126

of boys who have themselves been caught by the police (13 per cent). Here, too, however, a majority of those whose mates have been caught reckon that this had led to a reduction in their *own* stealing. This majority (58 per cent) is less than in the case where the respondent himself had been caught (71 per cent as in Table 3.23). Nonetheless, the 58 per cent represents a trend which is in line with Expectation 2.

Interestingly, only one of the many respondents reported doing *more* stealing because of what he heard had happened to mates, indicating perhaps that publicity of this sort may *in general* be more of a deterrent than something to imitate or live up to. Publicity about 'getting off' could of course be another matter entirely.

Another point to note is that the stories heard by boys (about what happened to their mates) appear to have been exaggerated with regard to their more punitive aspects, (compare Tables 3.21 and 3.27). On the present body of evidence, this would appear to be a positive outcome from a preventative viewpoint.

Whether the findings support a case for promoting publicity about boys who are caught for stealing and what happens to him is a complex issue in that the effects of the publicity upon the boy receiving it have to be considered. But the matter is certainly worthy of careful consideration, along with what might be done without naming the boys concerned.

Boys' explanations of why the fate of mates led them to steal less/made no difference to them are set out in Table 3.29.

The details under 'It made NO DIFFERENCE' demonstrate the ways in which boys can exclude themselves from the implications of a situation – e.g.: his mates were doing a different kind of stealing or more serious stealing; his mates were rather stupid or just unlucky to get caught; he did not think about it. Details under 'It made me do LESS stealing' which are explanations of why the boy feels he stole 'less', give support to Expectation 2.

Summing-up of Expectation 2
The evidence collected tends to support Expectation 2. Just as with Expectation 1, there were individuals whose positions contradicted it and for the others the evidence leaves plenty of room for the operation of other causal variables.

There appear to be ways in which the phenomena involved in Expectation 2 could be exploited in a deterrent programme.

Summing-up on the study of Hypothesis 3
The results of testing Expectations 1 and 2 lend support to the hypothesis. At the same time, these results leave plenty of room for the operation of other factors as well.

7 METHODS AND FINDINGS RELATING TO THE INVESTIGATION OF HYPOTHESIS 4

The nature of the hypothesis
The fourth of the hypotheses about 'getting caught' was:

Boys reduce their stealing because they are discouraged by what they feel would be the consequences of getting caught by the police.

It was the purpose of the inquiry both to examine this hypothesis and to provide information about the variable defined in it as causal in character, namely 'whether or not the boy *cares* about the possibility of getting caught by the police'.

The distribution of boys in terms of how much they care about the possibility of getting caught by the police
In this section are presented: (*a*) the questions asked as a basis for classifying boys in terms of the variable hypothesized as causal; and, (*b*) distribution of boys in terms of this variable and its relationship to the various characteristics of the boys.

The questions asked
After boys had expressed their views on the likelihood of their getting caught by the police if they were stealing, they were asked:

Table 3.29
Reasons for claims about effect on his own behaviour

	(%)
'It made NO DIFFERENCE'	
The respondent does not do much pinching	16
He was not pinching at that time/in that period	24
His mates did more pinching than he did/did more serious pinching	8
His mates do a different *kind* of pinching	7
He was not involved in the job they were doing at the time	9
He thought his mates were stupid to get caught/careless	8
It made him more careful	2
It was just bad luck for them that they were caught	1
He did not think it would happen to him	8
He didn't care what happened to the other boys	8
He didn't know the mates very well	3
He wasn't worried or scared about it	4
He didn't think about it/forgot about it	1
He couldn't stop because he would have lost the respect of his mates	2
'It made me do LESS stealing'	
The prospect of getting caught himself	30
Thought it would happen to him	13
Didn't want what his mates got	19
Didn't want the unpleasant consequences of getting caught	31
He became frightened/scared	3
He feared that the mate might split on him/give him away to police	2
He had lost the mates he normally did his stealing with	1

Q.1c 'How much would you care if the police caught up with you for pinching?' (LET HIM SPEAK OUT)
    PASS HIM THE ANSWER CARD' READ ANSWERS OUT SAY:
'Which of these do you think would be true?'
    (I WOULD NOT CARE/I WOULD CARE/I WOULD CARE VERY MUCH)

Following this (and as a basis for testing an expectation based on *testimony*) the boy was asked:

Q.1d 'If the police caught up with you, what do you think would happen to you?'

Q.1e 'You said you (WOULD/WOULD NOT) care if the police caught up with you. Does this attitude make any difference at all to *how much* pinching you do?' YES/NO
    IF 'NO': 'How do you explain that?'
    IF 'YES': 'What sort of difference?'
            'Why does it make that difference?'

Distribution of boys according to responses to Question 1c

The choice of answers to this question was distributed as follows:

Table 3.30

	(%)
I would not care	2
I would care	13
I would care very much	85

This finding alone may indicate something of what lies behind the support already given to the hypothesis that expectation of getting caught is a deterrent with regard to stealing. In other words, the great bulk of boys *would care very much* if the police caught-up with them for stealing.

Reactions to 'getting caught' analysed by characteristics and background of boys

Caring' about getting caught analysed by occupational level, schooling, age

Reactions to the idea of getting caught by the police for stealing were analysed by age, religion, racial characteristics and by occupational level of fathers. Results are set out in Table 3.31.

The outstanding feature of Table 3.31 is the uniformity of attitude toward 'getting caught by the police'. For no sub-group is there any marked departure from the pattern for the sample as a whole (as shown in Table 3.30). In so far as there *are* variations, there is some slight tendency for boys to care more in going up the educational and social scale.

Reaction (to getting caught) related to frequency of actually being caught by the police

In Table 3.32, reaction to 'getting caught' by the police is related to previous involvement with the police, if any.

What Table 3.32 shows is that the greater the past involvement (of the boy) with the police, the less tendency there is for the boy to 'care very much' at the prospect of being caught by them (again). Whereas it may be that boys who have been involved several times

Table 3.31
Reactions to the idea of getting caught by the police analysed by characteristics and background of boys

Characteristics and background	All cases	Reactions to idea of getting caught by police (Q.1c)			
		Would care very much	Would care	Would not care	No information
Weighted cases	3,113	2,643	392	70	8
	(n)	(%)	(%)	(%)	
Age of boy					
12/13 yrs	721	83	15	1	
14 yrs	782	85	12	3	
15 yrs	754	86	11	3	
16/17 yrs	856	86	12	2	
Occupational level of father					
Professional, semi-professional and executive	518	90	9	1	
Highly skilled and skilled	1,188	86	12	2	
Moderately skilled and semi-skilled	1,147	82	14	3	
Unskilled	254	81	16	3	
No information	6				*continued*

Table 3.31 (continued)

Characteristics and background	All cases	Reactions to idea of getting caught by police (Q.1c)			
		Would care very much	Would care	Would not care	No information
Weighted cases	3,113	2,643	392	70	8
	(n)	(%)	(%)	(%)	
School last attended					
Secondary modern	1,464	81	15	3	
Comprehensive	549	88	12	0	
Grammar	718	90	9	1	
Public	257	91	8	1	
Other	105				
No information	20				
Nominal Religion					
Protestant	1,370	87	11	2	
Catholic	500	85	13	2	
Other Christian	176	79	18	3	
Greek Orthodox	77	82	18	0	
Jewish	214	92	8	0	
None	621	80	15	5	
Other religions	140				
No information	15				
Coloured					
No	2,994	84	13	2	
Yes	119	92	3	3	
Born in UK					
Yes	2,856	85	13	2	
No	257	87	10	2	

Table 3.32

Ever involved with the police				Extent of caring		
	(n)	(%)	(%)	Would care very much (%)	Would care (%)	Would not care (%)
Never	2,687		86	86	12	2
Yes	415		13	79	14	7
No information	11		—			
Yes, once only	278	9		83	12	5
Yes, twice	69	2		75	19	6
Yes, three or more times	68	2		69	18	13

with the police start out with a lesser concern about being caught by them, another possibility is that involvement with the police leads boys to be less concerned with becoming involved with them again. The evidence is ambiguous in its implications, but either way it points to an issue of importance.

Reaction to getting caught by the police analysed by total amount of stealing done

Boys' reactions to getting caught (again) by the police (for stealing) were cross-analysed by the extent of their past involvement in stealing.

At the risk of being repetitive, I am stressing here that the existence of a numerical association does not necessarily mean that a causal relationship exists. In the present case it is certainly possible that the positive correlation between 'not caring' and 'amount of thieving

Table 3.33

Reaction to possibility of being caught by the police for stealing	Percentage distribution (%)	Index of variety of stealing				Index of amount of stealing			
		Low-score quartile Q.1 (%)	Q.2 (%)	Q.3 (%)	High-score quartile Q.4 (%)	Low-score quartile Q.1 (%)	Q.2 (%)	Q.3 (%)	High-score quartile Q.4 (%)
Would care very much	85	26	26	27	21	25	28	25	22
Would care	13	22	19	27	32	23	29	21	27
Would not care	2	7	11	10	72	10	11	29	50

done' arises from some other factor, for example from the views of associates, from parental attitudes of some kind. All we may say in the present case is that the boys who say they would not care if the police caught them for stealing tend to be the boys who have done a lot of stealing.

What boys think would happen to them if they were caught by the police

Boys' ideas about what would happen to them if the police caught them for stealing are indicated by the details in Table 3.34. For comparative purposes, other information of a relevant kind is included in this table.

Since 86 per cent of these boys had not been caught by the police (for stealing) we may take it that the great bulk of the replies given to the question were not based upon close or realistic experience of consequences. At the same time, the replies given are important because they represent the *expectations of boys* -- and anyone

Table 3.34

Consequences named	Percentage naming consequence		
	If caught (this question) (3,113 cases) (%)	When actually caught (415 cases) (%)	What happened to mates (2,229 cases) (%)
Discharged/conditionally discharged	3	20	1
Fined	36	16	10
Had to pay damages/costs	3	21	1
Put on probation	50	17	26
Sent to attendance centre/detention centre	4	2	3
Sent to remand home	6	—	5
Sent to approved school	8 ⎫		6 ⎫
Sent to borstal	22 ⎬	2	20 ⎬
Sent to prison	6		7
Sent to boarding school	1	0	1
Put away/sent away	10	2	11
Warned/cautioned/told off	14	19	4
He would be let off/nothing	5	7	0
He would get known to the authorities	8	*	*
He would get a bad name	5	*	*
Parents would be informed	6	4	0
Parents would punish him	4	0	0
Expelled from school	0	0	1
Other consequences	8	5	6
He was asked questions		2	
He was searched		2	
He was hit		1	
Name and address taken		7	
Taken to police station		3	

*Not appropriate as reply, but implied through other responses

concerned with the provision to boys of relevant or strategically-desirable information on this front should know that this is the position from which he must start. The more commonly-expected consequences were: that he would be put on probation; that he would be fined; that he would be sent to borstal; that he would be warned/cautioned/ told off.

Another noteworthy feature of Table 3.34 are the differences between *what boys expect*, what the 13 per cent who had been caught said *did* happen to them, and what boys thought happened to mates who were caught. The nature of these differences is clear from the table and should provide further guide-lines for those interested in the provision of relevant information to boys.

Investigating Hypothesis 4

A summary of the basic strategy of investigation
As with Hypotheses 1, 2 and 3, the research strategy used here was to derive from Hypothesis 4 several testable propositions, referred to in this inquiry as 'expectations'. A negative result in respect of one or more of these would be sufficient to weaken the hypothesis — and a positive result to strengthen it.

The expectations
The following expectations were derived from Hypothesis 4.

Expectation 1 Boys who 'would not care' if they were caught for stealing are more involved in stealing than those who would care very much, and this applies when the latter are matched to the former in terms of the correlates of stealing.

Ordinarily, several more expectations in this series would be set up, one dealing with the forty-four types of theft (considered separately) and another dealing with the duration of stealing. But the smallness of the qualifying group in this case (2 per cent of the sample) militates against the mounting of further checks of a kind that really call for a substantial numerical base. Moreover, in the circumstances, the testing of Expectation 1 must be regarded with some wariness — as a kind of mini-test.

Expectation 2 Boys who say they 'would not care' will tend more than the others to claim that getting caught would *not* reduce the extent of their stealing.

Testing Expectation 1: Method and Findings
The testing of Expectation 1 involved the usual matching operation as indicated below.

Identifying the qualifying and control groups The qualifying and control groups were derived as follows:

Figure 3.5

All boys
(1,425, unweighted)

Boys who say
'Would not care'
(35 cases, unweighted)
= Qualifying group

Boys who say
'Would care very much'
(1,200 cases, unweighted)
= Control group

The 185 who said they 'would care' have been left out of this analysis as involving some degree of ambiguity with respect to the hypothesis, though as will be seen from the statement of findings it was later — and very tentatively — combined with those who said they would not care in order to provide a bigger group who did not qualify in terms of the hypothesis.

Other stages in the matching process The controls were now matched to the qualifiers in terms of the composite of correlates of stealing established for general matching purposes and given on p. 111.

Results of testing Expectation 1 The results of the matching operation are shown in Table 3.35 below. Weighting served to close the gap to some extent between qualifiers and controls, but that gap nonetheless remained wide and highly significant in the statistical sense.

Table 3.35 Differences between qualifiers and controls before and after matching: variety and amount of stealing	Unadjusted average score for qualifiers	Unadjusted average score for controls	Adjusted average score for controls	Differences between qualifiers and adj. controls	Difference a—c as percentage of c
Theft indices	a	b	c	a—c P	of c
Average variety* score	22.40	13.11	15.17	7.23 (0.01)	48
Average amount* score	158.07	92.73	113.02	45.05 (0.01)	40

*See Chapter 2 for method of deriving these indices

Table 3.36
Differences between qualifiers and controls before and after matching: variety and amount of stealing

Theft indices	Unadjusted average score for qualifiers a	Unadjusted average score for controls b	Adjusted average score for controls c	Differences between qualifiers and adj. controls a−c P	Difference a−c as percentage of c
Average variety score	14.09	13.11	12.63	1.46 (0.05)	12
Average amount score	106.00	92.73	84.87	21.13 (0.01)	25

Table 3.37
Relating boys' concern over getting caught to their opinions about the effects upon their stealing

Claimed extent of concern at prospect of getting caught by police		Claimed influence of this attitude upon amount of stealing			
		Makes me do more (%)	Makes no difference (%)	Makes me do less (%)	Don't know (%)
I would not care	2%	4	84	0	12
I would care	13%	0	24	69	7
I would care very much	85%	0	14	78	8
All		0	17	75	8

Table 3.38

Explanation of how getting caught would make him steal LESS	(%)	(%)	Explanation of how getting caught would make NO DIFFERENCE to his stealing	(%)	(%)
He does not want to get caught	33	44	He avoids thinking about getting caught	11	44
He is frightened of getting caught	11		He does not believe he would be caught	15	
He does not want to be 'put away'		9	He does not do much pinching anyway	18	
The hurt or wrong to his parents	11	15	He accepts the risk of getting caught		3
Parental action towards him	4		The consequences don't deter him	7	17
It would give him a bad reputation	13	19	Don't care/not worried	10	
The police would always be after him	2		He no longer steals things		18
He does not want a police record	4		Once you start you can't stop		3
The serious consequences of getting caught specified	11	29			
The consequence would be serious	13				
Don't want a fine or probation	5				

As an extra safeguard against the dangers that go with a sample as small as thirty-five (the size of the qualifying group), the expectation was re-stated with those saying they 'would care' included with those saying that they would not care – in contrast with the control group whose members 'would care very much'. The results of testing these modifications of Expectation 1 are shown in Table 3.36.

Testing Expectation 2 This expectation has been stated as: 'Boys who say they "would not care" will tend more than the others to claim that getting caught would *not* reduce the extent of their stealing'. The test of it involves nothing more than the testimony of boys on this particular point and it must not be over-played in terms of its relevance to the hypothesis. The questions asked in this context were Q.1c, d, e on the first page of the questionnaire in Appendix 3.1.

The results of testing Expectation 2 are set out in Table 3.37. Table 3.37 confirms Expectation 2: boys who say that they would not care if they got caught by the police for stealing also claim that getting caught would make no difference to the extent of their stealing, whereas boys who claimed they would care very much also claim that getting caught would make them steal less.

The evidence relating to Expectation 2 may with advantage be considered in the context of boys' reasons for saying that their stealing would be affected in one way or another if they were caught by the police. These are presented in Table 3.38.

Summing-up on the testing of expectations from Hypothesis 4

The tests of the several expectations lend some degree of support to the hypothesis and must be regarded as strengthening it. At the same time the tests available are by no means crucial and they leave the situation more open than is desirable.

The fact that Hypothesis 4 gains support from the tests conducted may to many be no surprise. In other words, they may deem it obvious that boys who do not want to get caught for stealing will thereby be led to do less stealing. But the implication of such a finding may not be so obvious. It seems to imply that anything that

serves to reduce boys' concern at getting caught by the police will lead to a greater degree of stealing by them.

8 METHODS AND FINDINGS RELATING TO THE INVESTIGATION OF HYPOTHESIS 5

The nature of the hypothesis
The fifth hypothesis identified for study was:

Boys reduce their stealing because they don't like the idea of getting caught for it by their parents.

This section of the chapter deals both with the distribution of boys in terms of reactions to the idea of getting caught by parents (for stealing) and with the testing of various expectations derived from the fifth hypothesis. In addition the chapter presents a range of relevant findings dealing with the extent to which boys have, in fact, been caught by their parents, what the parents did to them and what boys think might be the effect on their parents of learning that their sons have been stealing.

The distribution of boys in terms of their reactions to the idea of getting caught by parents for stealing

The questions asked
A range of questions was asked of each boy about parental reactions to his engaging in stealing and about his *own reactions* to the prospect of his parents finding he was stealing. These questions are all set out on the third page of the sub-questionnaire presented in Appendix 3.1, but the most pertinent of them (in relation to Hypothesis 5) were the following:

Q.1a 'If you did some pinching and your parents found out, *would you care?*' YES/NO

IF 'YES', ASK: 'How much would you care?' SHOW CARD.
CIRCLE CHOICE (NOT/CARE/CARE VERY MUCH)
IF HE OBJECTS THAT THEY *DID* FIND OUT GO TO Q.2.

Table 3.39
Degree to which boy would care if parents found out he was stealing

How much would/did he care	Whether yet caught by parents				
	Yes 1,229 cases* (%)	No 1,868 cases (%)	Not clear 16 cases (%)	All 3,113 cases (*n*)	(%)
Would/did care very much	36	42	0	1,230	40
Would/did care	17	9	0	386	12
Would/did care, but extent of caring unestablished	34	46	0	1,270	41
Would/did not care	12	3	13	216	7
No information	–	–	3	11	–

*Weighted sample
– = less than 0.5 per cent

Table 3.40
Relating caring to stealing done

Reactions to parents finding out (that he was stealing)	All cases†	Index of variety of stealing				Index of amount of stealing			
		Q.1* (%)	Q.2 (%)	Q.3 (%)	Q.4 (%)	Q.1 (%)	Q.2 (%)	Q.3 (%)	Q.4 (%)
Would *not* care/did *not* care	203†	14	25	28	33	17	19	41	23
Would care (to at least some degree)	2,894	25	25	26	24	24	28	24	24
Would care/did care/cared but degree not specified	1,659	24	26	27	23	24	29	25	22
Would care very much	1,235	27	22	26	25	25	28	21	26
All	3,097†	25	25	26	24	24	28	25	23

*Q.1 = Low score quartile, Q.4 = high score quartile
† = Less thirteen cases for whom not clear whether or not yet caught by parents

Table 3.41
Reasons for caring related to whether found out

Reasons given for caring/not caring	Have parents ever found out?	
	Yes 1,868 cases* (n)	No 1,229 cases (n)
For caring (if found out)		
He would be letting his parents down/failing to meet standards taught by parents	337	
Blame or guilt would fall on parents as well as on boy	107	
Public disgrace to family or boy	169	
Parents would not like it/be hurt/worry	192	
Parents would no longer trust him	339	
Parents would not like him/would be ashamed of him/would not speak to him	100	
Parents would think him a thief/a bad boy	182	
Parents would hit or hurt him	129	
Parents would stop his pocket money	49	
Parents would make him leave home	6	
Parents would tell the police	23	
Parents would take some other action against him	274	
He would not want his parents to know	77	
Boy would feel embarrassed/guilty/ashamed	194	
Other reasons	175	
For not caring when/if found out		
He does not care what his parents think	4	14
Parents can't do anything about it	10	—
Make no difference if they knew	7	—
They would not say anything/did not say anything	2	—
They would not *do* anything/did not do anything	7	25
They would/did only tell him off	7	19
They would/did only hit him	3	—
They would not let him down/tell on him/give him a bad name	5	—
They would not care/did not care	4	9
He only stole small/unimportant things	—	49
He was too young/did not understand	—	23
He feels justified in stealing	—	10
He told his parents himself	—	18
The police were not involved	—	3

*Totals exceed 1,868 because some respondents could give more than one reason
— = less than 0.5%

Q.1b 'Have they ever found out?'   YES/NO.
   IF 'YES', GO TO Q.2.

Q.2a 'The last time they found out, did you care?'
   YES/NO.
   IF 'NO', ASK: 'Why?'
   IF 'YES', ASK: 'How much did you care?' SHOW
   CARD.
   CIRCLE   CHOICE   (NOT/CARE/CARE   VERY
   MUCH)

Response distributions
The distribution of responses for these questions is shown in Table 3.39. Approximately 7 per cent of boys denied that they would care if their parents found out they were stealing, and the figure was 3 per cent for those who said they had never been found out by their parents. Amongst the 39 per cent who said their parents *had* in fact found out they were stealing, 12 per cent claimed they did not care (i.e. that their parents had found out).

Degree of concern/caring analysed by characteristics and background of boys
Extent of 'caring' was analysed in terms of the extent of boys' past involvement in stealing (i.e. with regard to both the variety and the amount of it). Details are

presented in Table 3.40. There is some tendency here for those who say they would *not* care (if their parents found out they were stealing) to have committed more thefts than other boys. On the other hand, there is no meaningful difference between those who say they would care and those who say they would care *very much*.

Boys' attitudes and expectations in relation to parents finding out they have been stealing

Reasons given for caring or not caring
Boys who had never been caught stealing by parents were asked would they care if caught by parents. If they said 'No', they were asked why they felt that way. The 'why' question was not put to those who said they *would* care. If the boy *had* been caught, he was asked to explain whatever attitude he had towards getting caught. Details are set out in Table 3.41.

Reasons for caring (if parents found out the boy was stealing) were principally in terms of: hurt to his parents, loss of respect for him by his parents, punishment by parents, embarrassment or guilt on the part of the boy. Reasons for *not* caring were principally in terms of: parents are unlikely to do anything about it, the boy does not care what parents think, the theft concerned was only small.

Table 3.42

| | Have their parents found out? | |
| | Yes 1,229 cases | No 1,868 cases |
Parental action taken/suggested	(*n*)	(*n*)
Informed authorities/would tell police	23	156
Threatened to inform authorities	12	—
Made him repay/would make him repay	64	104
Made him apologise	2	—
Gave him a hiding/would give him a hiding	411	625
Stopped pocket money/would stop or reduce pocket money	119	311
Deprived him of enjoyments/would deprive of enjoyments	68	162
Made him stay in/would make him stay in	194	394
Sent him to bed/would send him to bed	81	—
Gave him a good talking to/would give him a good talking to	412	548
Told him not to do it again/would tell him not to do it again	110	—
Told him he would get into trouble next time	13	—
Nothing/would do nothing	112	112
They were worried/upset/would be annoyed	17	32
Would ignore him	—	80
Would not trust him	—	64
Would throw him out of the house	—	47
Would punish him	—	29
Put him in a home/have him put away	—	72
Make him do extra jobs at home	—	12
Tell other people about it	—	4
Ask him to explain why	—	21

— = less than 0.5 per cent

What would/did parents do to the boy for pinching?

Boys whose parents *had* found out were asked what their parents did to them. Those who had never been 'found out' by parents were asked what they thought their parents *would* do if they did find out. Responses are set out in Table 3.42.

The more recurrent parental actions or expected actions were in terms of the parent: giving the boy a good talking to; giving him a hiding; making the boy stay in; stopping or reducing his pocket money.

Table 3.43

Did parents threaten to do anything next time?

	(n)	(%)
Yes	691	22
No	538	17
Not applicable	1,868	60
No information	16	1
All cases	3,113	100%

Parental threats and whether believed by the boy

An outstanding feature of Table 3.43 is that about half the boys whose parents had found out they were stealing claimed their parents made no threat about doing anything if it happened again. For the other half the more recurrently made threats were in terms of: telling the police, saying he would be put away, hitting him (see Table 3.44).

Whether boy was found out by parents, analysed: by characteristics, by whether parents threatened punishment; by whether boys believed the threat would be carried out

An analysis was made of the kinds of boys who had been found out by parents and who are threatened by them with punishment 'next time'. The results are given in Table 3.45, along with evidence of whether the boys believed the threats made.

There is little in Table 3.45 that is suggestive of any general trend — beyond, perhaps, a tendency for boys in 'frequent-rows' homes to believe less than other boys the parental threats made to them. The general picture is one of broad similarity, from home to home, in terms of parental threats and of boys' reactions to these.

Table 3.44

What parents threatened next time (691 cases)

What did parents threaten?	All cases (n)	Did boy think parents would do it?		
		Yes (n)	No (n)	Don't know (n)
Tell the police	228	111	94	23
Beat him/hit him	139	89	34	16
Cut down pocket money	57	43	9	5
Deprive him of his enjoyments	24	21	–	3
Stop him going out	21	10	6	5
Would make him leave home	35	21	11	3
Told him he would be sent away/put away (presumably by authorities)	161	78	71	12
Would cut off his hands/burn his hands	10	1	8	1
Total references	675	374	233	68

Table 3.45

Parental threats analysed by background

Characteristics of boys	Parents have found out (n)	Did parents threaten?				If 'Yes', does boy believe them?					
		No		Yes		Yes		No		No information	
		(n)	(%)	(n)	(%)	(n)	(%)	(n)	(%)	(n)	(%)
Base	1,229	538	43.8	691	56.2	374	54.1	236	34.1	81	11.7
Age at interview											
12, 13 years	264	111	42.0	153	58.0	96	62.7	42	27.5	15	9.8
14 years	277	123	44.4	154	55.6	77	50.0	60	39.0	17	11.0
15 years	305	140	45.9	165	54.1	103	62.4	37	22.4	25	15.2
16, 17 years	381	164	43.0	217	57.0	96	44.2	97	44.7	24	11.1

continued

Table 3.45 (continued)

Characteristics of boys	Parents have found out (n)	Did parents threaten?				If 'Yes', does boy believe them?				No information	
		No (n)	(%)	Yes (n)	(%)	Yes (n)	(%)	No (n)	(%)	(n)	(%)
Base	1,229	538	43.8	691	56.2	374	54.1	236	34.1	81	11.7
Social class											
I and II	276	142	51.4	134	48.6	85	63.4	40	29.9	9	6.7
II NM	159	94	59.1	65	40.9	38	58.5	20	30.8	7	10.8
III M	491	177	36.0	314	64.0	162	51.6	105	33.4	47	15.0
IV	182	69	37.9	113	62.1	63	55.8	42	37.2	8	7.1
V	119	56	47.1	63	52.9	26	41.3	27	42.8	10	15.9
NI	2	0	*	2	*	0	*	2	*	0	*
Occupational level											
1 and 2	184	106	57.6	78	42.4	53	67.9	16	20.5	9	11.5
3	189	94	49.7	95	50.3	61	64.2	32	33.7	2	2.1
4	235	87	37.0	148	63.0	79	53.4	52	35.1	17	11.5
5	264	101	38.3	163	61.7	78	47.9	64	39.3	21	12.9
6	222	89	40.1	133	59.9	71	53.4	39	29.3	23	17.3
7	133	61	45.9	72	54.1	32	44.4	31	43.1	9	12.5
NI	2	0	*	2	*	0	*	2	*	0	*
Born in UK											
Yes	1,107	481	43.5	626	56.5	334	53.4	218	34.8	74	11.8
No	122	57	46.7	65	53.3	40	61.5	18	27.7	7	10.8
Coloured											
Yes	66	33	50.0	33	50.0	19	57.6	8	24.2	6	18.2
No (assumed not)	1,163	505	43.4	658	56.6	355	54.0	228	34.7	75	11.4
Religion											
Church of England	434	208	47.9	226	52.1	134	59.3	69	30.5	23	10.2
Methodist	23	9	39.1	14	60.9	9	64.3	0	0.0	5	35.7
Presbyterian	0										
Protestant	54	23	42.6	31	57.4	8	25.8	12	38.7	11	35.5
Roman Catholic	182	80	44.0	102	56.0	53	52.0	36	35.3	13	12.7
'Catholic'	37	16	43.2	21	56.8	10	47.6	9	42.9	2	9.5
Christian	77	31	40.3	46	59.7	25	54.3	21	45.7	0	0.0
Greek Orthodox	37	20	54.1	17	45.9	12	70.6	3	17.6	2	11.8
Jewish	52	23	44.2	29	55.8	17	58.6	6	20.7	6	20.7
Other	66	36	54.5	30	45.5	4	13.3	20	66.7	6	20.0
Not applicable	260	89	34.2	171	65.8	99	57.9	59	34.5	13	7.6
NI	7	3	*	4	*	3	*	1	*	0	*
Type of school											
Secondary modern	682	222	32.6	460	67.4	246	53.5	169	36.7	45	9.8
Technical	14	9	*	5	*	1	*	4	*	0	*
Grammar	219	153	69.9	66	30.1	42	63.6	16	24.2	8	12.2
Public	83	41	49.4	42	50.6	26	61.9	7	16.7	9	21.4
Approved	2	2	*	0	*	0	*	0	*	0	*
'Special'	7	4	*	3	*	2	*	1	*	0	*
Comprehensive	202	105	52.0	97	48.0	45	46.4	35	36.1	17	17.5
Other	6	0	*	6	*	4	*	0	*	2	*
NI	14	2	*	12	*	8	*	4	*	0	*

*Not calculated because base too small.

continued

Table 3.45 (continued)

Characteristics of boys	Parents have found out (n)	Did parents threaten?				If 'Yes', does boy believe them?				No information	
		No		Yes		Yes		No			
		(n)	(%)	(n)	(%)	(n)	(%)	(n)	(%)	(n)	(%)
Base	1,229	538	43.8	691	56.2	374	54.1	236	34.1	81	11.7
Rows at home											
Every day	94	48	51.1	46	48.9	17	37.0	19	41.3	10	21.7
Most days	331	125	37.8	206	62.2	114	55.3	72	34.9	20	9.7
About once a week	379	172	45.4	207	54.6	109	52.7	78	37.7	20	9.7
Once a month	184	76	41.3	108	58.7	63	58.3	29	26.9	16	14.8
Hardly ever	217	101	46.5	116	53.5	63	54.3	38	32.8	15	12.9
Never	8	7	*	1	*	1	*	0	*	0	*
NI	15	9	*	6	*	6	*	0	*	0	*
How much time at home											
No time	35	17	48.6	18	51.4	14	77.8	2	11.1	2	11.1
Not much	177	98	55.4	79	44.6	23	29.1	39	49.4	17	21.5
Less than half	218	81	37.2	137	62.8	64	46.7	52	38.0	21	15.3
About half	491	206	42.0	285	58.0	175	61.4	88	30.9	22	7.7
Most of it	261	118	45.2	143	54.8	83	58.0	41	28.7	19	13.3
All of it	32	10	31.3	22	68.8	9	40.9	13	59.1	0	0.0
NI	14	8	*	6	*	5	*	1	*	0	*

*Not calculated because base too small.

Investigating Hypothesis 5

The expectations derived from Hypothesis 5
The following expectations were derived from Hypothesis 5.

Expectation 1 Boys who say they would not care (did not care) about their parents finding out they were stealing are more involved in stealing than other boys and this applies even when the latter are closely matched to the former.

Expectation 2 Boys who are threatened by parents with what will happen to them next time, feel that this threat makes them do less stealing thereafter.

Testing Expectation 1: methods and findings
The testing of Expectation 1 involved the usual matching of controls to qualifiers. These two groups were defined as in Figure 3.6. The results of the test through matching are as shown in Table 3.46. The findings in Table 3.46 generally support Expectation 1 though not to any overwhelming degree.

Testing Expectation 2: methods and findings
Boys were asked if their parents had threatened them with what would happen next time and, if so, how they thought this threat would affect their stealing thereafter. Such claims or testimony must be regarded warily in terms of their implications for Hypothesis 5. Results are shown in Tables 3.47, 3.48 and 3.49.

Table 3.46
Differences between qualifiers and controls before and after matching: variety and amount of stealing

Indices of stealing	Unadjusted average score for qualifiers a	Unadjusted average score for controls b	Adjusted average for controls c	Differences between qualifiers and adj. controls a−c	P	Difference a−c as percentage of c (%)
Average variety score*	17.07	13.26	14.34	2.73	(0.05)	19
Average amount score†	123.00	96.70	105.64	17.36	(0.05)	16

*'Score' out of forty-four, computed as described in Chapter 2
†An index of total amount of stealing computed as described in Chapter 2

Figure 3.6
Division of sample for testing expectations

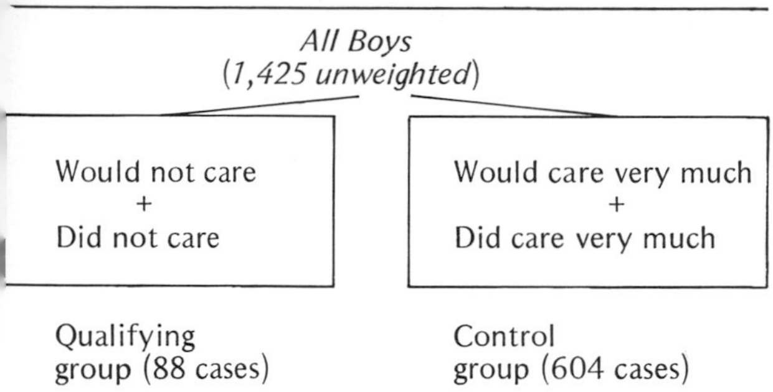

All Boys
(1,425 unweighted)

Would not care + Did not care	Would care very much + Did care very much
Qualifying group (88 cases)	Control group (604 cases)

Table 3.47 relates the occurrence of parental threats and boys' claims about the likely effect of such threats on subsequent stealing. The figures in Table 3.47 tend to support the expectation. In other words, when, in addition to the boy being caught by parents, the parents threaten there will be punishment of some kind if the offence is repeated ... when this happens, boys tend somewhat to do less stealing afterwards (i.e. according to the testimony of boys).

Table 3.48 relates claimed effects of threats to the claimed nature of the threat made. Its evidence does not indicate any appreciable variation in claimed effect as the nature of the threats varied.

Boys also gave reasons for claiming that parental action altered the amount of stealing they were doing (or left it unaltered). The reasons given for 'doing less' (Table 3.49) are fairly predictable, namely the development in the boy of an awareness that further detection would bring punishment or unpleasantness of some kind. What is less predictable is the set of reasons given for claiming that parental threats made *no difference* to subsequent stealing. These reasons were principally:

1 That he doubted that his parents would catch him again, or that he would not tell them next time.

2 That he didn't think they would carry out the threats made.

3 That he was not worried about the sort of threat made.

4 That the threatened punishment was not severe last time.

Table 3.47
Claimed effect (on stealing) of parental threats about what would happen next time

	Boy says parental threats would			
	Make him steal *MORE* (%)	Make him steal *LESS* (%)	Have no effect (%)	No information (%)
Boy *was* threatened	—	70	23	7
Boy was *not* threatened	1	59	31	9

— = Less than 5 per cent

Table 3.48
Was the type of threat made associated with different claims about its effects on subsequent stealing?

		Boy says parental threats would			
Type of action threatened	Number of cases	Make him steal *MORE* (%)	Make him steal *LESS* (%)	Have no effect (%)	No information (%)
Tell the police	228	—	69	24	6
Beat him/hit him	139	2	66	21	11
Cut down pocket money	57 }				
Deprive him of his enjoyment	24 }	0	79	12	9
Stop him going out	21 }				
Make him leave home	35 }				
Told him he would be sent away/put away	161 }	0	73	22	5
Would cut off his hands/ burn his hands	10*				

— = Less than 0.5 per cent
* = base too small for calculation of percentages

Table 3.49
Reasons given for claim that parental threats had one or another kind of effect on subsequent stealing

Reasons given		No. of references (n)
Made me do more		
You get so fed up with them (parents) that you pinch when you feel like it		1
Because I know they wouldn't do anything to me		1
Because I know I can get away with it		1
Because they don't do anything to me		1
Because they didn't seem to care about my money needs		1
Made no difference		
He was not worried/bothered/did not care what parents said or did		40
He didn't think parents would carry out threat	13 ⎫	
He didn't think parents would tell police/probation officer	6 ⎬	20
He didn't think parents would send him away	1 ⎭	
He would not tell his parents again		10
The influence wore off		29
The threatened punishment was not severe/he was let off last time		47
The influence of his mates was stronger		16
Didn't think he would be caught again (by parents)		25
There's nothing much else to do/nothing else of an exciting kind to do		2
He does not do any pinching		17
Made me do less		
It made him come to his senses/think		71
He knew what would happen next time		48
He knew he would be in serious trouble next time		83
He didn't want to get caught again		107
He was worried/scared		18
He didn't want the police brought into it		65
He didn't want to be taken back to the person from whom he stole		4
He didn't want to be sent away/put away		93
He didn't want to be beaten		78
He didn't want his pocket money stopped		24
He didn't want to kept inside of the home		30
He didn't want to lose his enjoyments		10
He didn't want a bad reputation		26
It upset his parents/harmed his parents		67
The thought of his parents knowing about his stealing		12

5 That there is nothing much else to do.

6 That the influence of his mates was stronger.

Summing-up on the testing of Hypothesis 5
The evidence stemming from the testing of expectations gives support to Hypothesis 5 but not in any marked or overwhelming way. Moreover, Expectation 2 is rather indirect in character.

9 SUMMING-UP ON THE INVESTIGATION OF THE FIVE HYPOTHESES

Hypothesis 1

Boys take up stealing or continue to steal partly because they think they won't get caught by the police.

This hypothesis was investigated through the testing of three expectations derived from it and specified as follows.

Expectation 1 Those boys who think they *won't* get caught by the police for stealing, do more stealing than other boys and this applies even when the latter are closely matched to the former in terms of the correlates of stealing.

Expectation 2 Expectation 1 applies also with respect to each of the forty-four types of thieving studied in this inquiry.

Expectation 3 Those boys who think they won't get caught for stealing tend to continue with relatively serious stealing over a longer period than other boys, and this applies even when the latter are closely matched to the former in terms of the correlates of stealing.

The tests of Expectations 1 and 3 generally support Hypothesis 1. However, the evidence of the test of Expectation 2 suggests that the hypothesis does not apply for *all* types of theft. The evidence available in Table 3.7 can be used for the generation of ideas about the *kinds* of theft for which the hypothesis does not apply. One possibility is that these are the less purposive and less serious kinds of theft. But the reader is invited to think independently, using the full array of data in Table 3.6.

Hypothesis 2

Boys take up stealing or continue to steal partly because they think no one will catch them.

This hypothesis was investigated through the testing of three expectations derived from it and specified as follows.

Expectation 1 Boys who think they will not get caught by *anyone* (if they are stealing) do more stealing than other boys and this applies even when the latter are closely matched to the former in terms of the correlates of stealing.

Expectation 2 Expectation 1 also applies with respect to each of the forty-four types of theft studied in this inquiry.

Expectation 3 Boys who think they won't get caught by anyone for stealing keep it up over a longer period than other boys, and this applies even when the latter are closely matched to the former in terms of the correlates of stealing.

The position of Hypothesis 2 seems to be closely similar to that of Hypothesis 1. Thus, the test of Expectations 1 and 3 generally support Hypothesis 2. However, the evidence from the test of Expectation 2 suggests that Hypothesis 2 does not apply for *all* types of theft. Here, too, the reader is advised to study the detail of Table 3.12 as a basis for developing ideas about the kinds of theft for which the hypothesis tends not to apply.

Hypothesis 3

Boys reduce their stealing if they get caught by the police.

This hypothesis was investigated through the testing of two expectations derived from it and specified as follows.

Expectation 1 If boys who have stolen are caught for this by the police, they will tend to claim that getting caught in this way reduced their involvement in stealing.

Expectation 2 If a boy's mates get caught for stealing, he will say that this has led him to do less stealing himself.

The results of testing Expectations 1 and 2 lend support to the hypothesis. At the same time these results leave plenty of room for the operation of other factors as well.

We should note that the investigation of this hypothesis was limited to a study of the claims of boys about the effects, upon their stealing, of getting caught by the police. Though these claims were themselves challenged in various ways and held up against such challenges, testimony in such matters cannot in the present state of knowledge be regarded as anything like fully valid or reliable. On the other hand, the results give no general support to the common suggestion that getting caught leads to increased stealing — though there were a few boys in the sample (8 in 1,425) who claimed that getting caught *did* lead them to an increase in the amount of stealing they were doing.

Hypothesis 4

Boys reduce their stealing because they are discouraged by what they feel would be the consequences of getting caught by the police.

This hypothesis was investigated through the testing of two expectations derived from it and specified as follows.

Expectation 1 Boys who 'would not care' if they were caught for stealing are more involved in stealing than those who would care very much, and this applies when the latter are matched to the former in terms of the correlates of stealing.

Expectation 2 Boys who say they 'would not care' will tend more than the others to claim that getting caught would *not* reduce the extent of their stealing.

The testing of Expectation 1 was weakened by the fact that so few boys fell into the qualifying group (though many failed to endorse the extreme response: 'would care *very much*').

The tests conducted lend some degree of support to the hypothesis and must be regarded as strengthening it. At the same time (a) the tests available are by no means crucial and they leave the situation more open than is desirable; (b) they leave a lot of room for the operation of causal factors additional to that involved in Hypothesis 4.

Hypothesis 5

Boys reduce their stealing because they don't like the idea of getting caught for it by their parents.

This hypothesis was investigated through the testing of expectations derived from it and specified as follows.

Expectation 1 Boys who say they would not care (did not care) about their parents finding out they were stealing are more involved in stealing than other boys, and this applies even when the latter are closely matched to the former.

Expectation 2 Boys who are threatened by parents with what will happen to them next time feel that this threat makes them do less stealing thereafter.

The evidence constituted by these tests of Expectations 1 and 2 give support to Hypothesis 5, though not in any marked or overwhelming way.

10 SOME COMMENTS AND POSSIBLE ACTION

The tenability of all five hypotheses was strengthened by the tests conducted, though more for some than for others. However, for Hypotheses 1 and 2 at least, there is evidence of untenability with respect to *certain kinds* of theft, quite possibly the more petty and the less purposive kind.

In considering this outcome, it must be kept in mind that the independent variable named in an hypothesis (e.g. fear of consequences of getting caught) is put forward only as a *partial* cause of stealing — never as a sole cause.

Having said this, it remains true that the findings presented here strengthen the case for considering that stealing in general tends to be damped down or reduced by:

1 A belief on the part of the boy that he will get caught (by the police or others) if he steals or keeps on stealing.

2 Actually getting caught by the police (for stealing).

3 A fear of the possible consequences if he is caught by the police.

4 The prospect of getting caught (for stealing) by parents.

It may well seem to some that the outcome with respect to 1 and 3 (namely that boys steal less if they think they may get caught or if they fear the consequences of getting caught by the police) is quite obvious. And this may well be so. But the implications of such findings may not be quite so obvious. Thus, they seem to imply that the incidence of theft is likely to be increased by any action or policy that serves either (*a*) to make boys feel that they can get away with stealing; or (*b*) to reduce their fears about the possible consequences of getting caught. Conversely, the results also seem to imply that the incidence of theft is likely to be reduced by action designed to increase boys' fears about the consequences of getting caught and by increasing the degree to which they expect the police to catch them if they engage in stealing. Action designed to produce such beliefs and impressions will call for very careful consideration lest it inadvertently produce side-effects of a damaging kind. But certainly it should be possible, using film and other media, to communicate to young school-children realistic impressions of the adverse consequences of getting caught for stealing including hurt to parent and damage to family relationships. It may be, too, that publicity could with advantage be given to police success in catching young thieves. Let me repeat that the steps taken, whatever they may be, will have to be considered very carefully; and they should be tested in some meaningful way before being taken. But the findings with respect to Hypotheses 1 and 4 point quite strongly to the case for taking action of some kind, with a view to increasing boys' expectation of getting caught if they engage in thieving and to increasing their fears of the consequences of this. And, of course, the case is equally strong for avoiding action and policies likely to produce the opposite effects.

The outcome of investigating Hypothesis 3 calls especially for comment. It is suggested by some criminologists that being caught by the police tends to make boys identify with thieves and thereby to increase the extent of their own involvement in stealing. The evidence of this inquiry does not support that finding, except in a very few cases: the opposite appears to apply. This, of course, is not the same as concluding that a period in a custodial institution or situation will reduce theft level (once the boy is released). The hypothesis relates only to 'getting caught by the police' — an event which, on the evidence here presented, only rarely led to anything more than probation and, in the great majority of cases, to something less (see Table 3.21). It appears that it is 'getting caught' that is the deterrent — provided (see Table 3.26) that the processing thereafter is not of the kind that boys can 'laugh off' or treat lightly.

Here too, then, the findings provide broad pointers to certain classes of action following 'being caught' by the police — probably some form of action that consolidates and augments the off-putting effects or the awakening produced by being caught by the police.

11 APPENDIX 3.1

The sub-questionnaire used
Getting caught by the police

I Q.1 To assess the boy's present attitude towards being caught by the police and to the consequences of this.
Q.2 To find out when he had first contact with the police (over stealing) and to get an indication of the impact of this on future stealing.
Q.3 To get the boy's estimate of how many contacts he had with the police and the impact of these contacts upon his future stealing.

Q.1 Present attitudes towards being caught up with by the police and to the consequences of this

---

SAY:
'I have just been asking you about getting away with pinching things. I want to ask you a bit more about that.'

SAY:
'I want you to imagine that you were pinching things —
the sort of things you might feel like pinching.'

a 'Do you think the *police* would catch you?'
(ENCOURAGE HIM TO SPEAK OUT)
THEN PASS THE BOY THE FIVE-ITEM CARD.
READ EACH ITEM OUT AND SAY:
'Which of those do you think would be true?'
I AM SURE THEY WOULD NOT CATCH ME/I
DON'T THINK THEY WOULD CATCH ME/THEY
MIGHT CATCH ME/THERE IS A GOOD CHANCE
OF THEIR CATCHING ME/I AM SURE THEY
WOULD CATCH ME
(CHALLENGE CHOICE AND UNDERLINE IT)

1b 'If you *kept on* pinching things, do you think the
police would catch you?'
(ENCOURAGE HIM TO SPEAK OUT)
THEN PASS HIM THE ANSWER CARD AGAIN,
READ THEM THROUGH, AND SAY:
'Which of those do you think would be true?'
I AM SURE THEY WOULD NOT CATCH ME/I
DON'T THINK THEY WOULD CATCH ME/THEY
MIGHT CATCH ME/THERE IS A GOOD CHANCE
OF THEIR CATCHING ME/I AM SURE THEY
WOULD CATCH ME.
(CHALLENGE CHOICE AND UNDERLINE IT)

1c 'How much would you care if the police caught-up
with you for pinching?'
(LET HIM SPEAK OUT)
PASS HIM THE ANSWER CARD, READ ANSWERS
OUT, SAY:
'Which of those do you think would be true?'
I WOULD NOT CARE/I WOULD CARE/I WOULD
CARE VERY MUCH

1d 'If the police caught-up with you, what do you think
would happen to you?'
'What else?'

1e 'You said you (WOULD CARE/WOULD NOT) if the
police caught up with you. Does this attitude make any
difference at all to *how much* pinching you do?' YES/
NO
IF 'NO': 'How do you explain that?'
IF 'YES': 'What sort of difference?' 'Why does it
make that difference?'

1f 'I asked you about the *police* catching-up with you.
Suppose you were pinching things. Do you think *anyone*
would catch up with you?'
PASS CARD. RING CHOICE
(NOT/DON'T THINK/MIGHT/COULD/SURE)
IF DIFFERENT FROM 1a, FIND OUT WHY AND
ALSO WHOM HE HAD IN MIND AS CATCHING/
NOT CATCHING

Q.2 When did he first have contact with the police over
pinching and how did he think this affected his stealing
thereafter?

2a 'Have you ever been caught-up with for pinching
anything?' YES/NO
IF 'NO' CHECK WITH: 'Never in you life? *Not by
anyone at all?*'
'By parents? By a shopkeeper? By a store detective?
Not even for little things?'
IF STILL 'NO' GO ON TO Q.4
IF 'YES' TO 2a, ASK AS FOLLOWS:

2b 'How old were you the very first time anyone
caught-up with you for pinching things?' 'I mean
caught-up with by *anyone*.'
CHECK WITH: 'How can you be sure it was that
age?'

2c 'Who caught-up with you that first time?'
IF POLICE MENTIONED, GO TO 2e.
IF *NOT*, CHECK WITH 'Did the police come into it
at all?' YES/NO
IF 'YES' GO TO 2e
IF STILL 'NO', GO TO 2d

2d IF POLICE NOT INVOLVED IN FIRST PINCHING,
SAY: 'How old were you the first time the police *did*
come into it?'
IF THERE *WAS* A FIRST TIME, CHALLENGE
HIM: 'How can you be sure it was at *that* age?'
ENTER AGE IF OK
IF NEVER, ASK: 'What difference did that make to
the amount of pinching you have done?'
SHOW CARD, CIRCLE CHOICE. (MORE/LESS/
NO DIFFERENCE)
'Why was that?'
NOW GO TO Q.4

2e 'Exactly what did the police do, that first time?'
'Did this make any difference at all to the amount of
pinching you did after that?'
SHOW CARD, CIRCLE CHOICE. (MORE/LESS/NO
DIFFERENCE).
IF 'NO' DIFFERENCE: 'Exactly why was that?'
(PROBE)
IF 'MORE' OR 'LESS' SAY: 'Exactly why did it
make that sort of difference?'
(PROBE)

Q.3 How often and when has he been involved with the
police over stealing?
What effects does he say this has had on him (i.e. getting
involved with police).

3a 'Since then, how often have the police *caught up
with you* for pinching?'
IF 'NEVER', ASK: 'Have you done any pinching at
all since then?' YES/NO
THEN GO TO Q.4.

3b IF HE HAS BEEN INVOLVED WITH THE POLICE SINCE THEN: 'Exactly how many times?' PRESS FOR A NUMBER, BUT CHALLENGE IT.

3c 'Tell me what ages you were at those times?' PRESS HARD FOR THIS INFORMATION. CHALLENGE FOR PRECISE ANSWER.

3d 'So the police caught up with you (SAY THE NUMBER) times more after that first time? What did they do to you? Start with the first time (when you were . . . .')
'And the next time, when you were . . . .?'
'And the time after that when you were . . . .?'
(TRACK BACK OVER ALL OCCASIONS)

3e 'What difference has this (REFER TO WHAT HAP-PENED UNDER (d)) made to the amount of pinching you have done?' SHOW CARD, CHAL-LENGE CHOICE' CIRCLE IT.
(MORE/LESS/NO DIFFERENCE)
IF 'NO' DIFFERENCE: 'Exactly why was that?'
IF 'MORE' OR 'LESS': 'Exactly why did it make that sort of difference?'
IF NECESSARY, UNTANGLE WHAT DID WHAT.

II Q.1 Parental reaction *if* he pinched
Q.2 Parental reaction *when* he pinched

Q.1 Parental reaction if/when he pinched

1a 'If you did some pinching and your parents found out, *would you care*?' YES/NO
IF 'YES', ASK: 'How much would you care?' SHOW CARD, CIRCLE CHOICE
(NOT/CARE/CARE VERY MUCH)
IF HE OBJECTS THAT THEY *DID* FIND OUT, GO TO Q.2

1b 'Have they ever found out?' YES/NO
IF 'YES', GO TO Q.2

1c 'You said you would/would not care if they found you out for pinching. Why would you feel like that?'

1d 'Exactly what would they do to you if they found out you had been pinching things?'

1e 'If you were pinching things and your parents found out, how do you think they would feel about it?'

1f 'Would you care if they felt that way?' YES/NO
IF 'NO', ASK: 'Why?'
IF 'YES', ASK: 'How much would you care?' SHOW CARD. CIRCLE CHOICE
(NOT/CARE/CARE VERY MUCH)

NOW GO TO III

Q.2 What did his parents do or feel when they *did* find out?
What would they do next time?

THIS QUESTION IS ONLY FOR THOSE WHOSE PARENTS *HAVE* FOUND OUT. OTHERWISE GO TO III

2a 'The last time they found out, did you care?' YES/NO
IF 'NO', ASK: 'Why?'
IF 'YES', ASK: 'How much did you care?' SHOW CARD. CIRCLE CHOICE
(NOT/CARE/CARE VERY MUCH)

2b 'What did they do to you the last time they found out?'

2c Did they threaten to do anything to you *next time*?' YES/NO
IF 'YES':
(i) 'What did they threaten?'
(ii) 'Do you think they will do that?' YES/NO
IF 'YES': 'Would you care very much if they did?' YES/NO

2d 'So the last time they (REPEAT WHAT THEY DID) and they threatened to (REPEAT THREAT)
'Did that make any difference to the amount of pinching you have done since then?'
SHOW CARD. CIRCLE CHOICE. (MORE/LESS/NO DIFFERENCE)
IF NO DIFFERENCE: 'Why was that?'
IF MORE/LESS: 'Exactly why did it make that difference?'

2e 'When your parents found out about any pinching you were doing, how did they feel about it?'
IF ANSWER INDICATES PARENTS WERE WORRIED OR UPSET, ASK: 'Did you care about their feeling this way?' YES/NO
IF 'YES': 'How much did you care?' SHOW CARD. CIRCLE CHOICE
(NOT/CARE/CARE VERY MUCH)

III Q.1 Have his mates been caught, and what effect does he think this has had on his own pinching?

'Have the police caught up with any of your mates for pinching?' YES/NO

IF 'NO', CHALLENGE
IF 'YES'
i 'What was the worst thing that happened to any of them?'
ii 'Now think of what happened to any of your mates who were caught.' (PAUSE)
'Did this ever make any difference to your own pinching?'
(REPEAT AND EXPLAIN IF NECESSARY)
SHOW CARD. CIRCLE CHOICE. (NO DIFFER-ENCE/MORE/LESS)
iii 'Can you tell me why it has made no difference/why it has made that sort of difference?' PROBE

Chapter four
The desire for fun and excitement

CONTENTS

1 THE COVERAGE OF THIS CHAPTER

In this chapter I have presented a wide range of information broadly related to 'the desire for fun and excitement'. This information was collected and processed to serve two associated purposes, the more important of which was to investigate a particular composite of hypotheses about causal factors in the development of juvenile stealing. These hypotheses were as follows.

1 A desire for a lot of fun and excitement is a contributing factor to the initiation and maintenance of juvenile stealing.

2 Going out looking for fun and excitement is a contributing factor to the initiation and maintenance of juvenile stealing.

The second purpose of the collected data was to provide general background information about each of the factors or conditions hypothesized as causal in character. How, for instance, is 'the desire for fun and excitement' distributed amongst boys and how does it vary with their backgrounds and characteristics? Then again, to what extent *do* boys go out looking for fun and excitement and what sorts of boys do this?

2 THE SPECIAL 'URBAN' CHARACTER OF THE TWO HYPOTHESES

The two hypotheses about which this chapter is concerned were derived from intensive interviews with London boys. These boys were broadly of two kinds: boys in the general population living at home and not known to be especially involved in stealing; boys held in approved schools (and a classifying centre), and with thefts of different kinds entered on their records.

These two sources are consistent with our original intention of studying hypotheses about causal factors operative in *London* — as distinct from, say, some rural setting or some imaginary town where major emphasis was given to the provision of acceptable (and legal) outlets for the fun and excitement-seeking of boys.

The special point about *London* is that many London boys felt that suitable outlets for their particular fun and excitement-seeking were *not* available. This was apparent during the intensive interviewing used to develop hypotheses and it was confirmed by the findings from the subsequent survey, as indicated in Tables 4.6 and 4.27.

3 RESEARCH PROCEDURES COMMON TO ALL THE HYPOTHESES DEALT WITH IN THE INQUIRY

The gathering of information relevant to the hypotheses about 'desire for fun and excitement' was done in the context of an inquiry concerned with over thirty other hypotheses. The techniques relating to the inquiry *as a whole* have been summarized in Chapter 1. That summary deals with sampling procedures; with a technique for getting boys to provide reliable information about any stealing they have done; with questioning procedures for classifying boys in terms of the variables

hypothesized as causal factors in the different hypotheses (i.e. in terms of the different independent variable with strategies for investigating the tenability of hypotheses about causal factors and processes. The read should as necessary refer back to the relevant parts Chapter 1 in reading statements of findings in the present and subsequent chapters.

4 RESEARCH PROCEDURES APPLYING ONLY TO THE HYPOTHESES DEALT WITH IN THIS CHAPTER

Whereas many aspects of research procedure applie generally to the whole range of hypotheses under stud certain parts of it related only to the hypotheses abo 'fun and excitement seeking'. These parts tend to b encapsulated in the sub-questionnaires put to boys in th course of the interview and presented in full in th Appendix 4.1. This questionnaire was made up of sever. sections, each section beginning with a description of i purposes as follows.

1 The extent of the boy's present interest in fun an excitement.

a
b

2 Does he get *enough* fun and excitement? What form does it take? What blocks his getting enough?

a
b
c

3 Was there a time when his wants were different When?

a
b

4 Has he ever gone out just looking for fun and excitement?

a
b
c
d
e

5 His views about pinching for fun and excitement and how much excitement he gets when he *does* pinch?

a
b
c

The questions asked were of two kinds: fully structure and open response. Some of the fully-structured ques tions were used for defining the factors involved in th causal hypotheses and others for developing distribu

ns of relevant behaviour and attitudes. Open-response
estions were used for two purposes: to provide insight
to a position or problem or process; to help each boy
ink about his own position before asking him to
rmulate it through a fully-structured question. For
ample:

ow much fun and excitement would you like to have?'

PROBE TO GET HIM THINKING AND ALSO TO
PROVIDE A CHECK ON HIS LATER CHOICE OF
ANSWER FROM CHOICE CARD.

IF HE ASKS WHAT WE MEAN BY FUN AND
EXCITEMENT, PUSH THE QUESTION BACK AT
HIM (i.e. 'Whatever *you* think of as fun and excite-
ment.')

/hich of these comes nearest to the amount of fun and
:citement you would *like* to have?'
SHOW CARD. READ OUT CHOICES. CIRCLE
CHOICE MADE.
(TERRIFIC/QUITE A LOT/FAIR BIT/SOME/NOT
MUCH/NONE)

METHODS AND FINDINGS RELATING TO
HE INVESTIGATION OF HYPOTHESIS 1

he nature of the hypothesis

ypothesis 1 took the following form:

*desire for a lot of fun and excitement is a contributing
ctor to the initiation and maintenance of juvenile
ealing.*

s stressed in Section 2, this hypothesis must be seen as
elating to London, where legal and acceptable outlets
or fun and excitement seeking do not appear to many
oys to be sufficiently available.
It was one of the purposes of the inquiry to examine
nd challenge this hypothesis through testing a series of
ropositions drawn from it and to develop and present
ackground information related to the main variables
ivolved in the hypothesis.

Table 4.1
Amount of fun and excitement which boys say they
vant

Amount wanted	(n)	Distributions	
		(n)	(%)
A terrific amount of it		463	15
Quite a lot		1,102	36
A fair bit		979	31
Some	511		
Not much	48	562	18
None	3		
No information		7	—
All cases (weighted)		= 3,113	100%

— = Less than 0.5 per cent

The distribution of boys in terms of the
variable hypothesized as a 'causal factor'

The questions asked for classifying boys in terms of the amount of fun and excitement wanted by them

These questions were detailed in Section 4 of this
chapter and the full questionnaire is presented in
Appendix 4.1. In brief, the boy was asked first to say, in
his own words, how much fun and excitement he
wanted and then to choose that expression on a choice
card which came nearest to the amount of fun and
excitement he wanted. The distribution of responses to
this question is set out in Table 4.1.

The form of fun and excitement wanted by boys
It is essential for a proper understanding of this chapter
that we should know what boys had in mind by 'fun and
excitement'. One might, of course, have started with a
set definition of this broad concept, but the whole
approach in this inquiry argued against that being done.
Thus, the hypothesis as originally derived was in terms
of whatever boys happen to mean by this particular
concept. As a concept, it *came from them* in the first
place and at that stage is was quite clear that it was a
broad concept linked to no single activity or type of
activity. It was therefore kept that way, for to tighten-
up the concept would have been to risk changing it.
At the same time, the inquiry produced evidence
about what sorts of things boys did, in fact, have in
mind by it and this evidence, based on the 1,425 boys
interviewed in the survey, is set out in Table 4.2.

The amount of fun and excitement wanted by
London boys analysed by characteristics and
background

Amount wanted, analysed by age, occupational
background, education, religion, etc.
The fun and excitement wants of boys were analysed by
a number of characteristics and background factors as
set out in Table 4.3. Perhaps the most noteworthy thing
about Table 4.3 is the degree to which the desire for fun
and excitement is spread throughout the sampled
population (i.e. London boys aged thirteen to sixteen).
That spread may not be surprising but, clearly, it is of
relevance to the study of the hypothesis.
This wide spread of the desire for fun and excitement
does not rule out some variation in the sub-sections of
the sampled population and these variations have been
identified with an asterisk in Table 4.3. Thus, the desire
for fun and excitement seems to be *greater* amongst
boys:

1 Of secondary-modern or comprehensive-school background.

2 Who have left school.

3 Who have a lot of personal interests or hobbies.

147

Table 4.2
The different forms of fun and excitement secured or
wanted by boys

Form of activity named	Amongst all boys* (3,113 cases, weighted) Percentage securing it this way	Amongst those not getting enough f/e** (1,487 cases, weighted) Percentage wanting it this way
	(%)	(%)
Any direct reference to stealing	4	0.4†
Annoying or cheeking people/making fun of people/cheeking people just to get chased by them	14	2
Destroying property/vandalism	3	1
Fighting or watching fights	7	0.4
Gambling/betting	0.3 ⎫	
Drinking/getting drunk	3 ⎪ 4	0.9
Smoking	0.6 ⎪	
Drugs/stimulants	0.4 ⎭	
Informal or unstructured local activity (e.g. mucking about/going out/going to pubs, cafes, onto streets/Having a joke. . . .)	43	14
Playing about or mucking about at school	6	0.2
Activities at school (not organized)	4	0.4
Sports or games (organized, but type not specified)	9	4
Physically active *sports* which could take place in or near Metropolis (e.g. football/cricket/tennis/judo/volley-ball/bowling/table tennis/athletics)	41	17
Physically-active pastimes that normally take place *outside a Metropolis* (e.g. sailing/canoeing/rock climbing/fishing/water ski-ing/flying/parachuting/riding/camping/hiking)	19	16
Other physically-active pastimes (e.g. cycling/motor bikes/scooters/going out in cars)	25	21
Activities of a more sedentary or indoor kind (e.g. billiards, snooker, cards, monopoly, darts, chess)	9	1
Work on a constructive hobby of some kind (e.g. model-making/tinkering about with motor bike or with gear of some kind/electrical work of some kind/stamp collection)	12	4
Participation in clubs or youth clubs	13	18
Participation in organized movements of some kind (other than clubs) (e.g. scouts/boys' brigade/sea cadets)	6	2
Watching sports or racing	11	3
Going to shows, concerts, plays	2	1
Cinema going	25	7
Television/radio/records	13	0.4
Reading books	4	1
Girls/going out with girls	17	7
Funfairs/circus	11	8
Dancing/parties/going to hear pop groups	21	14
Playing a musical instrument	2	0.3
Going on holiday/to seaside	6	6
Travelling/visiting places/making trips	12	21
Attending classes/evening classes	1	0
Looking after pets	1	0
By working/getting a job	1	0.3

*Responses to Questions 2b and 2c (combined) on p. 170
**Responses to Question 2c on p. 170
†Given to first decimal place where less than 1 per cent.
 Otherwise given to nearest whole number

Table 4.3
Amount of fun and excitement wanted analysed by
characteristics and backgrounds of boys
(3,113 cases, weighted)

Characteristics and background of boys		All cases	Terrific amount	Quite a lot	Fair bit	Some/not much/none
		(n)	(%)	(%)	(%)	(%)
Age of boy						
12/13 yrs		721	15	40	23	22
14 yrs		782	11	38	34	17
15 yrs		754	14	32	35	19
16/17 yrs		856	20	31	33	16
Occupational level of father						
Professional, semi-professional, managerial		518	15	28	33	24
Highly skilled		514	13	40	32	15
Skilled		674	15	29	35	21
Moderately skilled		630	14	40	31	15
Semi-skilled		517	16	38	28	18
Unskilled		254	18	42	27	13
No information		6				
	All	3,113	15%	36%	31%	18%
Type of school attended						
Secondary modern		1,464	16	39	30	15
Comprehensive		549	16	39	28	17
Grammar*		718	8	30	36	26
Public		257	15	26	42	17
Other		105				
No information		20				
Nominal religion						
Protestant*		1,370	8	17	33	42
Catholic*		500	10	19	25	46
Christian (only)		176	14	41	36	9
Jewish		214	15	28	38	19
None		621	17	38	27	18
Other religions		217				
No information		15				
Born in UK?						
Yes		2,856	15	35	32	18
No*		257	13	43	29	14
At full-time school						
Yes		2,402	13	35	32	20
No		711	23	36	29	12
Interest score in Quartiles†						
1st high quartile*		723	18	44	28	9
2nd quartile		647	13	32	35	20
3rd quartile		834	11	38	31	20
4th (low) quartile		892	16	28	32	23
No information		17				

Table 4.3 (continued)

Characteristics and background of boys	All cases	Amount of fun and excitement wanted			
		Terrific amount	Quite a lot	Fair bit	Some/no much/no
	(n)	(%)	(%)	(%)	(%)
How often bored?					
All the time*	45	29	42	16	13
Often*	714	21	39	27	13
Now and then	2,185	13	34	33	20
Never	164	10	39	28	23
No information	5				
Does he get enough fun and excitement?					
Yes	1,622	10	29	35	26
No	1,487	20	43	28	10
No information	4				
How much of his spare time does he want to spend at home?					
No time*	65	49	29	19	3
Not much	406	22	48	19	11
Less than half	531	14	37	36	13
About half	1,352	13	32	37	18
Most	672	9	34	29	28
All*	59	32	20	24	24
No information	28*				
Truancy					
Once a week*	331	25	42	19	14
Once a month*	262	26	42	22	10
Hardly ever	766	16	39	33	12
Never	1,745	11	32	35	22
No information	9				
Has he a girl friend?					
Yes*	1,151	20	36	28	16
No, but goes out with girls*	1,029	14	42	33	11
No, and does not go out with girls	931	10	28	34	28
No information	2				

*Noteworthy variations in 'fun and excitement' seeking
†Number of interests (out of the twenty asked about) endorsed

4 Who are often bored.

5 Who say they do not as yet get enough fun and excitement.

6 Who do not want to spend much of their spare time away from home.

7 Who are more frequently involved in truancy.

8 Who go out with girls.

9 Who say they are Jewish, or are Christian but of no particular denomination.

10 Who say they have no religion.

By contrast, there is very little variation in terms of the occupational level of the father and of the boy's age.

Some of the correlates of fun and excitement seeking may seem to be odd both in their own right and in relation to each other. How, for instance, can both the bored and those with *a lot of different interests* be seekers of a lot of fun and excitement? Presumably bored boys want to escape that condition whilst those with lots of different interests have had their appetite stimulated and so want more. Possibly, even, those with many different interests are somewhat shallowly interested people who are constantly looking out for new diversion. On this line, it is certainly possible to conceive of boys with just a few interests being absorbed by them and are, hence, far from being bored.

desire for fun and excitement analysed by
variety and amount of past stealing

Boys' desire for fun and excitement was analysed in terms of the extent and variety of their past involvement in stealing. Results are set out in Table 4.4 below.

Clearly, there is a high degree of association between, on the one hand, 'extent of desire for fun and excitement' and, on the other, extent or variety of stealing: the greater the desire for fun and excitement, the greater the extent and the variety of involvement in theft.

Having said this, it is essential to point out that 'association' between two variables does not necessarily imply a causal relationship between them. Certainly, it is possible that some other variable lies behind that association. It is for this reason that the investigation of the hypothesis has included the use of high-powered matching techniques of the kind referred to in this chapter (see pp. 153—154), and described in Chapter 1.

Desire for fun and excitement analysed by
whether he gets enough of it

Amount of fun and excitement wanted was analysed by amount of it actually secured. This could be an important variable in the sense that boys who do not get as much fun and excitement as they want may (according to the hypothesis) find it in stealing. For this analysis, boys had been asked: '. . . do you get *enough* fun and excitement?' Results are shown in Table 4.5.

There are several ways of reading Table 4.5. One of them is that boys who do not get enough fun and excitement are the ones who want it most of all — and who are therefore likely (according to the hypothesis) to

find it in stealing. Certainly, such boys have been involved in more stealing than others.

On the other hand, it is also possible that boys who do get enough fun and excitement have thereby reduced their *desire* for it. The uncertainty here is typical of that featuring any purely correlational finding.

Other Apsects of Fun and Excitement Seeking

Whether he gets enough fun and excitement analysed by characteristics and background

The possibly important variable of 'whether he gets enough fun and excitement' was analysed by the characteristics and backgrounds of the boys. Results are given in Tables 4.6 and 4.7. For the full sample, 52 per cent said they got enough fun and excitement and of the others some 98 per cent said that they did get *some* fun and excitement.

The different population sub-groups were remarkably similar in terms of 'getting enough fun and excitement', the only marked variations occurring with the following sub-groups, each of which tended more than average to 'get enough fun and excitement': those not born in the United Kingdom; those involved in *less* stealing than the average boy; Jewish boys.

Investigating Hypothesis 1

The basic strategy of investigation

As with all other hypotheses investigated in this inquiry, the basic strategy of the investigation was to derive from the hypothesis a range of testable propositions and to test these. These propositions are referred to here as 'expectations' (see Chapter I).

Table 4.4
Amount of fun and excitement wanted analysed by
past involvement in theft
(3,113 cases, weighted)

Amount of fun and excitement he says he wants	All cases		Index of amount of stealing				Index of variety of stealing			
			0.1*	0.2	0.3	0.4†	0.1*	0.2	0.3	0.4†
	(n)	(%)	(%)	(%)	(%)	(%)	(%)	(%)	(%)	(%)
A terrific amount	463	15	13	19	30	38	14	17	29	40
Quite a lot	1,102	36	17	31	26	26	20	22	30	28
A fair bit	979	31	27	28	26	19	28	27	28	17
Some Not much } None	562	18	41	27	18	14	37	31	16	16
No information	7	—								
All	3,113	100%	24%	28%	25%	23%	25%	25%	26%	24%

* Lowest scoring quarter
† Highest scoring quarter
— = Less than 0.5 per cent

Table 4.5
Amount of fun and excitement wanted, analysed by 'amount got'

Weighted cases	Do you get enough fun and excitement							
	Yes 1,622 cases (= 52% of sample) (%)				No 1,487 cases (= 48% of sample) (%)			
Amount of fun and excitement wanted								
Terrific amount	10				20			
Quite a lot	29				43			
A fair bit	35				28			
Some/not much/none	26				10			
All	100%				100%			
Theft level (in quartiles)	Q.1 (%)	Q.2 (%)	Q.3 (%)	Q.4 (%)	Q.1 (%)	Q.2 (%)	Q.3 (%)	Q. (%
Index of variety of stealing	30	29	20	21	19	20	32	28
Index of amount of stealing	31	29	20	19	16	26	31	27

Table 4.6
How much fun and excitement do boys get?

	(n)	(%)
Do you get enough (fun and excitement)?		
Yes	1,622	52
No	1,487	48
No information	4	–
All	3,113	100%
If 'No' or 'No information' Do you get any at all?		
Yes	1,468	98
No	17	1
No information	6	–
All	1,491	99%

– = Less than 0.5 per cent

The derivations of the expectations

The following expectations were derived from the hypothesis.

1 Those who want a lot of fun and excitement are more involved in stealing than those who want some lesser amount of fun and excitement.

2 Expectation 1 holds even when those wanting relatively little fun and excitement are closely matched, in terms of the correlates of stealing, to boys who want a lot of fun and excitement.

3 Expectation 2 holds with respect to the length of time that boys have been involved in serious stealing (i.e. the duration of involvement in serious stealing).

4 Expectation 2 holds for each of the forty-four type of theft.

5 Boys will volunteer/admit that they steal in order to get fun and excitement. And the more fun and excitement they want, the more they will tend to volunteer admit that they steal in order to get fun and excitement.

6 Boys will admit that stealing gives them fun and excitement. And the more fun and excitement they want, the more they will tend to admit that stealing gives them fun and excitement.

7 A large number of boys will endorse the statement that they have at some time stolen in order to get fun and excitement.

8 The greater the claimed frequency of stealing in order to get fun and excitement, the greater will be the boy's involvement in stealing.
9 Those who say they do, in fact, get fun and excitement from stealing have done more stealing than other boys.

10, Those who say they do in fact get fun and excitement from stealing will admit a higher frequency (than other boys) of stealing *in order to get* fun and excitement.

Testing Expectation 1

This expectation was that: 'Those who want a lot of fun and excitement are more involved in stealing than those who want some lesser amount'. A test of this expectation is by no means a crucial check on the hypothesis,

Table 4.7
Whether boy gets enough fun and excitement analysed
by various characteristics and background

Characteristics	Weighted cases	Percentage saying 'Yes' 1,622 (= 52%)	Characteristics	Weighted cases	Percentage saying 'Yes' 1,622 (= 52%)
Occupational level of boy's father			*Interest score in Quartiles**		
Professional, semi-professional, higher managerial		57	1st (high) quartile		47
Highly skilled		49	2nd quartile		51
Skilled		53	3rd quartile		55
Moderately skilled		54	4th (low) quartile		56
Semi-skilled		50			
Unskilled		48	*Has he a girl-friend?*		
			Yes		54
Type of school attended			No, but goes out with girls		46
Secondary-modern		47	No, and does not go out with girls		57
Comprehensive		56			
Grammar		55	*Total no. of siblings (excluding himself)*		
Public		57	0		51
			1		51
Nominal religion			2		53
Protestant		50	3		52
Catholic		43	4+		53
Christian (only)		52			
Jewish		63	*Index of variety of stealing*		
None		56	1st (low) quartile		63
			2nd quartile		62
Age at interview			3rd quartile		40
12/13 yrs		56	4th (high) quartile		45
14 yrs		53			
15 yrs		52	*Index of amount of stealing*		
16/17 yrs		49	1st (low) quartile		67
			2nd quartile		55
Born in UK			3rd quartile		42
Yes		51	4th (high) quartile		44
No		64			
At full-time school?					
Yes		54			
No		47			

*Based on twenty areas of interest asked about at interview

but a reversal of it would constitute a serious challenge (to the hypothesis). We do, of course, know already that this expectation is borne out — that there is a marked tendency for variety and amount of stealing to be positively associated with amount of fun and excitement wanted. (See Table 4.4.)

Testing Expectation 2
This expectation was that: 'Expectation 1 holds even when those wanting relatively little fun and excitement are closely matched, in terms of the correlates of stealing, to boys who want a *lot* of fun and excitement'. Matching was in terms of the composite of predictors (correlates) of stealing already developed for the inquiry as a whole. The qualifying and control groups were split as shown in Figure 4.1.

Figure 4.1
Splitting qualifying and control groups

All cases (1,425, unweighted)

Want 'a terrific amount' of fun and excitement (219 cases) plus Want 'quite a lot' of fun and excitement (521 cases)

Want 'some' (226) plus Want 'not much' (22) plus Want 'none' (1)

= Qualifying group (740) = Control group (249)

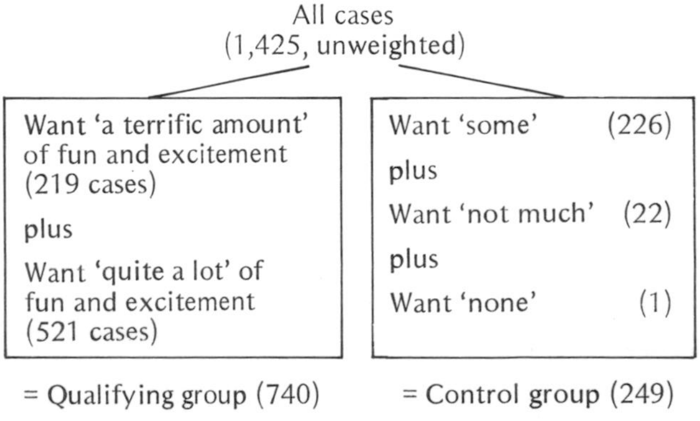

Both the control group and the qualifying group were now split into the thirteen matching sub-groups and the control group composition (in terms of the sub-groups) was equated to the qualifying composition. The results of this process are shown in Table 4.8. Expectation 2 was strongly confirmed and the evidence from its testing strengthens Hypothesis 1.

Testing Expectation 3
The third expectation was that boys who want a lot of fun and excitement will, even after matching, be involved in stealing over a longer period than boys who want relatively little fun and excitement. The results of testing this expectation are also shown in Table 4.8. They support the expectation.

Testing Expectation 4
This expectation is that Expectation 2 applies for each of the forty-four different types of theft studied. The method of testing the expectation was the same as that used in testing Expectation 2. The results were as shown in Table 4.9. In general, the findings of Table 4.9 support the expectation, but the latter is borne out much more strongly for some types of theft than for others.

Expectations 5 and 6
Expectation 5 was that: 'Boys will volunteer/admit that they steal in order to get fun and excitement. And the more fun and excitement they want, the more they will tend to volunteer/admit that they steal in order to get fun and excitement'. Research findings relating to this expectation are set out in Table 4.10, as are the findings related to Expectation 6, which was: 'Boys will admit that stealing *gives* them fun and excitement. And the more fun and excitement they want, the more they will tend to admit that stealing gives them fun and excitement'. The indications of Table 4.10 are as follows.

1 Though only 4 per cent directly volunteered stealing as a means of getting fun and excitement, the proportion so doing increased progressively from 2 to 8 per cent in going from those who want 'no' or 'very little' fun and excitement to those who want 'a terrific amount' of fun and excitement.

2 Over half the boys admitted stealing for fun and excitement at some time or other and the proportion so doing increased as the amount of fun and excitement wanted rose (i.e. 42, 52, 59, 63 per cent).

3 About half the boys admitted that stealing does give them fun and excitement.

Thus, the two expectations (Expectations 5 and 6) tend to be borne out. At the same time, it is obvious that factors additional to fun and excitement seeking are present in the causal situation.

Expectation 7
This expectation was that: 'A large number of boys will endorse the statement that they have at some time stolen in order to get fun and excitement'. Findings are set out in Table 4.11. The expectation is supported by the evidence gathered.

Expectation 8
This expectation was linked to the previous one and was that: 'The greater the claimed frequency of stealing in order to get fun and excitement the greater will be the boy's involvement in stealing'. Findings are given in Table 4.12.

Table 4.12 indicates that a quarter of the boys in the sample admit that 'at least now and then' they steal in order to get fun and excitement. Table 4.12 also links frequency of stealing for fun and excitement to the variety and amount of boys' past stealing and this evidence clearly supports Expectation 8.

Expectation 9
This expectation was that: 'Boys who say they do, in fact, get fun and excitement from stealing, have done more stealing than other boys'. The results of testing the expectation are set out in Table 4.13 and they tend to support the expectation.

Expectation 10
This expectation was that: 'Boys who say they do, in fact, get fun and excitement from stealing, will admit a higher frequency (than other boys) of stealing *in order to get* fun and excitement'. The results of testing this

Table 4.8

Differences between qualifiers and controls before and after matching: variety, amount and duration of stealing

Indices of stealing	Unadjusted average score for qualifiers a	Unadjusted average score for controls b	Adjusted average score for controls c	Differences between qualifiers and adj. controls a–c P	Difference a–c as percentage of c
Averaged indices of variety of stealing	15.55	10.33	12.44	3.11 (0.01)	25
Averaged indices of amount of stealing	106.85	61.46	75.57	31.28 (0.01)	41
Averaged duration of stealing*	4.09	3.03	3.69	0.40 (0.05)	11

*Of the more serious kind†
†See Chapter 1 for definition of 'serious'.

Table 4.9
Differences between qualifiers and controls before and after matching: each of the forty-four types of theft

Types of theft (L2+)	Unadjusted average score for qualifier*		Unadjusted average score for controls+		Adjusted average score for controls		Differences between qualifiers and adj. controls†		Difference a−c as percentage of c
	a		b		c		a−c		
	(n)	(%)	(n)	(%)	(n)	(%)	(%)	P	(%)
1	688	93.1	208	82.9	632.87	85.6	7.5	0.06	9
2	423	57.2	104	41.4	322.07	43.6	13.6	0.00	31
3	343	46.4	75	29.9	265.44	35.9	10.5	0.00	29
4	424	57.4	97	38.6	334.64	45.3	12.1	0.00	27
5	196	26.5	35	13.9	130.73	17.7	8.8	0.00	50
6	465	62.9	102	40.6	369.65	50.0	12.9	0.00	26
7	334	45.2	80	31.9	260.15	35.2	10.0	0.00	28
8	268	36.3	77	30.7	262.12	35.5	0.8	0.26	2
9	136	18.4	29	11.6	98.85	13.4	5.0	0.02	38
10	309	41.8	72	28.7	258.06	34.9	6.9	0.01	20
11	315	42.6	72	28.7	241.96	32.7	9.9	0.00	30
12	137	18.5	29	11.6	125.79	17.0	1.5	0.18	9
13	349	47.2	67	26.7	238.32	32.3	14.9	0.00	46
14	221	29.9	34	13.5	145.54	19.7	10.2	0.00	52
15	148	20.0	20	8.0	83.43	11.3	8.7	0.00	77
16	369	49.9	90	35.9	350.95	47.5	2.4	0.31	5
17	180	24.4	31	12.4	121.64	16.5	7.9	0.00	48
18	508	68.7	136	54.2	435.51	58.9	9.8	0.01	17
19	307	41.5	67	26.7	227.96	30.9	10.6	0.00	35
20	248	33.6	55	21.9	209.86	28.4	5.2	0.02	18
21	115	15.6	24	9.6	102.41	13.9	1.7	0.16	12
22	341	46.1	76	30.3	251.91	34.1	12.0	0.00	35
23	192	26.0	39	15.5	160.46	21.7	4.3	0.05	20
24	116	15.7	18	7.2	75.68	10.2	5.5	0.00	53
25	183	24.8	49	19.5	176.79	23.9	0.9	0.20	4
26	246	33.3	56	22.3	204.35	27.7	5.6	0.02	20
27	175	23.7	30	12.0	108.95	14.7	9.0	0.00	61
28	196	26.5	48	19.1	183.34	24.8	1.7	0.22	7
29	73	9.9	13	5.2	41.25	5.6	4.3	0.00	77
30	379	51.3	94	37.5	345.47	46.8	4.5	0.05	10
31	234	31.7	43	17.1	159.53	21.6	10.1	0.00	47
32	72	9.7	6	2.4	28.02	3.8	5.9	0.00	157
33	524	70.9	133	53.0	456.94	61.8	9.1	0.02	15
34	266	36.0	65	25.9	219.97	29.8	6.2	0.02	21
35	167	22.6	27	10.8	124.44	16.8	5.8	0.00	34
36	279	37.8	47	18.7	210.82	28.5	9.3	0.01	32
37	53	7.2	7	2.8	33.38	4.5	2.7	0.00	59
38	196	26.5	50	19.9	181.43	24.6	1.9	0.22	8
39	166	22.5	30	12.0	118.04	16.0	6.5	0.00	41
40	519	70.2	123	49.0	435.69	59.0	11.2	0.01	19
41	89	12.0	16	6.4	67.40	9.1	2.9	0.13	32
42	111	15.0	18	7.2	82.16	11.1	3.9	0.02	35
43	267	36.1	48	19.1	160.47	21.7	14.4	0.00	66
44	447	60.5	101	40.2	357.59	48.4	12.1	0.00	25

*Qualifying group: boys seeking 'a terrific amount' or 'quite a lot' of fun and excitement
+Control group: boys seeking 'some', 'not much', or 'no' fun and excitement. (Those answering 'a fair bit' (= 432 cases) are excluded from either group)
†Probability that this difference is the result of chance differences between the two samples

Table 4.10
Amount of fun and excitement wanted, analysed by boys' tendency to volunteer/admit that they steal in order to get fun and excitement
3,113 cases, weighted

How much fun and excitement does he want?	All cases		Did he volunteer stealing as a means of getting fun and excitement		Did he admit 'ever stealing for fun and excitement'			When he pinches things, does that give him fun and excitement		
			Yes	No	Yes	No	?	Yes	No	?
	(n)	(%)	(%)	(%)	(%)	(%)	(%)	(%)	(%)	(%)
A terrific amount	463	15	8	92	63	37	0	50	47	3
Quite a lot	1,102	36	4	96	59	40	1	52	46	2
A fair bit	979	31	3	97	52	48	0	48	49	3
Some Not much None }	562	18	2	98	42	57	1	43	51	6
No information	7	–								
All	3,113	100%	4%	96%	55%	45%	–	49%	48%	3%

— = Less than 0.5 per cent

Table 4.11

	(n)	(%)
Boy says he *has* pinched to get fun and excitement	1,705	55
Boy denies doing this	1,403	45
No information	5	–
All	3,113	100
Boy gives 'fun and excitement as his only reason for stealing	223	7

expectation are set out in Table 4.14 and they tend to support the expectation.

Supplementary data relating to Hypothesis 1
Stealing in order to get fun and excitement has been analysed by a number of characteristics of boys and the details are set out in Table 4.15.

The striking feature of the evidence in Table 4.15 is the similarity of involvement (i.e. stealing for fun and excitement) of boys from all sorts of backgrounds. At the same time there are *some* differences, with the following boys being somewhat more involved in this sort of behaviour: boys from secondary-modern and comprehensive schools; older boys; boys with a high degree of involvement in stealing. By contrast, the involvement of sons of those in professional occupations, Jewish boys and of boys doing comparatively little stealing is relatively low.

Table 4.12
Relating frequency of 'pinching for fun and excitement' to variety and amount of past stealing
3,113 cases weighted

Claimed frequency of pinching for fun and excitement	All cases		Quartile distribution of amount of stealing				Quartile distribution of variety of stealing			
			Q.1	Q.2	Q.3	Q.4	Q.1	Q.2	Q.3	Q.4
	(n)	(%)	(%)	(%)	(%)	(%)	(%)	(%)	(%)	(%)
Often/fair bit	239	8	2	16	40	42	3	16	28	53
Now and then	538	17	6	19	34	41	6	16	35	43
Hardly ever	928	30	13	31	29	27	13	24	34	29
Never	1,403	45	41	31	17	11	43	30	18	9
No information	5	–								
All	3,113	100%	24%	28%	25%	23%	25%	25%	26%	24%

— = Less than 0.5 per cent

Table 4.13
Relating to: (a) whether boys get fun and excitement from stealing; and (b) the amount of stealing they have done
3,113 cases, weighted

Does he claim he gets fun and excitement from stealing?	All cases		Index of variety of stealing				Index of amount of stealing			
			0.1	0.2	0.3	0.4	0.1	0.2	0.3	0.4
	(n)	(%)	(%)	(%)	(%)	(%)	(%)	(%)	(%)	(%)
Yes	1,514	49	13	23	29	34	13	22	29	36
No	1,494	48	32	33	22	13	34	28	25	13
Not sure or no information	105	3								
All	3,113	100%	24%	28%	25%	23%	25%	25%	26%	24%

Table 4.14
Relating to: (a) whether they do in fact get fun and excitement out of stealing; and (b) frequency of stealing for fun and excitement
(3,113 cases, weighted)

Does he claim he gets fun and excitement from stealing?	All cases		Claimed frequency of stealing for fun & excitement			
			Often/ fair bit	Now & then	Hardly ever	Never
	(n)	(%)	(%)	(%)	(%)	(%)
Yes	1,514	49	13	29	35	22
No	1,494	48	2	6	25	66
Not sure or no information	105	3				
All	3,113	100%	8%	17%	30%	45%

Studying Hypothesis 1 in reverse

One of the problems to be faced in investigating any causal hypothesis is the possibility, however remote it may seem, that there exists a causal relationship of a reverse order to that hypothesized. In the present case, that possibility would be that: stealing causes the desire for fun and excitement. This particular possibility and what is required for checking it is discussed in Chapter 1. In the present case, the problem was approached through a single challenging type of expectation, namely: 'If stealing is the cause of fun and excitement seeking, we may expect boys to volunteer, under exhaustive probing, that something of this kind has occurred'. In fact, when this was done, only 1 per cent of the boys volunteered 'stealing' as leading to their wanting fun and excitement. Details are given in Table 4.16.

Summing-up on the testing of Hypothesis 1

Whereas the evidence provided by expectation testing *cannot* by its very nature prove or disprove Hypothesis 1, it *can* serve to weaken or strengthen it. In the present case, each expectation was borne out and the total effect of this was to strengthen the hypothesis. The test of a single expectation derived from the hypothesis in reverse showed that the expectation was not borne out to any

appreciable degree and the effect of this is also to strengthen Hypothesis 1. In other words, the evidence provided by the expectation testing renders Hypothesis 1 more tenable.

6 METHODS AND FINDINGS RELATING TO THE INVESTIGATION OF HYPOTHESIS 2

The Nature of the Hypothesis
Hypothesis 2 took the form:

Going out looking for fun and excitement is a contributing factor to the initiation and maintenance of juvenile stealing.

Just as for Hypothesis 1, this hypothesis must be seen as relating to London, where legal and acceptable outlets for fun and excitement seeking do not appear to boys to be sufficiently available.

It was a purpose of the inquiry to examine and challenge this hypothesis through a series of propositions drawn from it and to develop and present background information relevant to the main variables involved in the hypothesis.

Table 4.15
Frequency of stealing for fun and excitement analysed by various characteristics and backgrounds of the boy (3,113 cases, weighted)

Characteristics	Frequency of stealing for fun and excitement			
	Often/ fair bit	Now & then	Hardly ever	Never
Weighted cases	239 cases	538 cases	928 cases	1,403 cases
	(%)	(%)	(%)	(%)
Occupational level of boy's father				
Professional & semi-professional	7	7	27	59
Highly skilled	11	14	31	44
Skilled	4	21	31	43
Moderately skilled	11	19	27	43
Semi-skilled	5	21	32	42
Unskilled	12	22	30	36
All	8	17	30	45
	(%)	(%)	(%)	(%)
Type of school last attended				
Secondary modern	10	20	31	39
Comprehensive	6	19	34	41
Grammar	6	12	29	53
Public	5	9	26	60
Nominal religion				
Protestant	8	17	33	42
Catholic	10	19	25	46
Christian (only)	6	23	29	42
Jewish	0	8	24	68
None	9	20	33	38
Age at interview				
12/13 yrs	7	11	31	50
14 yrs	6	18	29	47
15 yrs	9	16	29	46
16/17 yrs	9	23	30	38
Born in UK				
Yes	8	17	30	45
No	8	16	27	48
Index of variety of stealing				
1st (low) quartile	1	5	15	79
2nd quartile	5	11	30	54
3rd quartile	8	23	39	30
4th (high) quartile	17	31	35	17
Index of amount of stealing				
1st (low) quartile	1	4	17	77
2nd quartile	4	12	33	51
3rd quartile	12	24	34	30
4th (high) quartile	14	30	35	21

Table 4.16
Boys' explanation of how they came to want fun and excitement

Initiating factor named	Weighted cases = 2,640 (%)
Reference to some kind of 'stealing'	1
Always wanted a lot/no particular starter event	19
Boredom	22
Example/influence of mates and other people	20
Television	1
Cinema	1
Excessive homework/work	4
Miscellaneous special experiences (e.g. going to a fair/ camping/going abroad . . .)	13
Going out with girls/getting interested in girls	2
Getting a bike/motorbike/scooter/car	1
Going to parties/dances/clubs	2
Going out more/mixing more	3
Going to work	2
Being at school	3
Having more money	1
Getting older	8

The Distribution of Boys in Terms of the Variable Hypothesized as Causal

The questions asked for classifying boys in terms of tendency to 'go out looking for fun and excitement'

The questions actually asked are given in their full context in Appendix 4.1. They were as follows.

Q.2a 'Some boys go round hoping they'll find something to give them fun and excitement. They go out just looking for fun and excitement (PAUSE). Have you *ever* done that?'   YES/NO . . .
  IF 'NO', CHALLENGE WITH: 'Never in your whole life?'
  IF STILL 'NO', GO TO SECTION III.
  IF 'YES', GO TO Q.2b.

Q.2b 'How old were you when you first started to go out just looking for fun and excitement?' (CHALLENGE THAT IT REALLY WAS FAIRLY AIMLESS LOOKING ROUND FOR IT) . . .

Q.2c 'What did you do that time?'

Q.2d 'Did you keep it up (i.e. DID HE MAKE A HABIT OF GOING OUT LIKE THAT)?'

Q.2e '*These days*, do you go out just looking around for fun and excitement — looking round hoping you'll find some fun and excitement?' YES/NO
  IF 'NO', CHALLENGE. THEN GO TO SECTION III
  IF 'YES', ASK:
'Just how often do you do that these days?'

SHOW CARD (OFTEN/FAIR BIT/NOW AND THEN/HARDLY EVER)
CHALLENGE AND THEN CIRCLE FINAL CHOICE

Distributions relating to the variable hypothesized as causal
The distributions of answers to the above questions are given in Table 4.17.

On this evidence, the majority (72 per cent) have at some time gone out just looking for fun and excitement, a large minority (31 per cent) made a habit of it and about a seventh (14 per cent) of all boys do so now with substantial frequency.

Going out looking for fun and excitement analysed by characteristics and background of boys
The dependent variable in Hypothesis 2 was analysed by a range of characteristics and by background of boys. Results of the analysis are given in Table 4.18. In this table, the dependent variable is split in several ways, designed to indicate the duration and intensity of the behaviour defined as causal.

The indications of Table 4.18 are as follows.

1 First, and most important, 'going out just looking for fun and excitement' is widely distributed across the boy population of London.

2 At the same time, the incidence of it varies with the background of boys. Thus a maintained tendency of this sort is to be found more frequently amoungst: the sons of the less skilled; those with secondary-modern or comprehensive schooling; those who have now left school; those who commit truancy; those who volunteer stealing as a way of getting fun and excitement; those who do a lot of stealing.

Going out looking for fun and excitement, analysed by involvement in stealing
Table 4.19 presents details of an analysis of the hypothesized causal factor by amount of stealing done. These details indicate a high degree of relationship between 'going out just looking for fun and excitement' and 'amount of stealing done'. Obviously this relationship does not prove *causal* association, but to this point we will come in the section of this chapter which deals with the challenging or investigation of Hypothesis 2.

Ages of boys on first occurrence of going out just looking for fun and excitement
Table 4.20 includes two different streams of information: (*a*) it shows the ages of boys on first going out just looking for fun and excitement and indicates that about 3 per cent of the boys in the London population have gone out just looking for fun and excitement by the age of six and that 19 per cent had done so by the age of ten; (*b*) it indicates that boys who started early in this particular practice have a somewhat lower theft rate than those who started at age thirteen or over.

Table 4.17	Questions asked		Responses available	Distribution of Responses		
Proportion who go out just looking for fun and excitement (3,113 cases, weighted)				(*n*)	(%)	
	Q.2a	Have you ever gone out just looking for fun and excitement?	Yes No	2,229 884	72 28	
			All	3,113	100%	
	Q.2b	Did you keep it up? (i.e. make a habit of it)? (Asked only of the 2,229 boys who said they had ever done this).	Yes No No information (Not applicable)	975 973 281	44 44 12	* (31%) (31%) (9%) (28%)
			All	2,229	100%	
	Q.2c	These days, how often do you go out just looking for fun and excitement? (Asked of all the 2,229 boys who ever go out 'just looking for fun and excitement')	Not at all Hardly ever Now and then A fair bit Often Not clear how often (Not applicable)	939 236 605 260 182 7	42 11 27 12 8 —	* (30%) (8%) (20%) (8%) (6%) (28%)
			All	2,229	100%	

— = Less than 0.5 per cent
*Based on the whole sample (3113, weighted)

Investigating Hypothesis 2

The basic strategy of investigation

As with all other hypotheses investigated in this inquiry, the basic research strategy was to derive from the hypothesis as many testable propositions as possible and to test these. These propositions are referred to here as 'expectations'.

The nature of the expectations

The following expectations were derived from Hypothesis 2.

1 Boys who have ever gone out just looking for fun and excitement are more involved in stealing than other boys.

2 Those who have ever gone out looking for fun and excitement and *have kept it up*, are involved in more stealing than others.

3 Those who, these days, frequently go out just looking for fun and excitement have been more involved in stealing than have boys who do this less often or not at all.

4 Boys who have persisted in going out just looking for fun and excitement have been more involved than others in stealing and this applies after close matching.

5 Expectation 4 applies for each of the forty-four types of theft studied.

6 Expectation 4 applies with respect to the duration of stealing.

7 Boys will admit stealing that stems directly from outings when they were 'just looking for fun and excitement'.

Testing Expectations 1 and 2

The results of testing the first two expectations are set out in Table 4.21 below. On the evidence of Table 4.21, Expectations 1 and 2 are borne out.

Testing Expectation 3

Expectation 3 is that: 'boys who, these days, frequently go out looking for fun and excitement have been more involved in stealing than other boys'. The evidence gathered in testing this expectation is given in Table 4.22 and tends to confirm the expectation.

Expectation 4

The special difficulty about Expectations 1 to 3 is that they leave open the possibility that the groups of boys being compared were different from each other in terms of various of the correlates of stealing. We must also face the possibility, as with Hypothesis 1, that it is *stealing* that causes boys to go out 'just looking for fun and excitement' and not vice versa.

Expectation 4 goes some way towards reducing the ambiguity inherent in Expectations 1 to 3: 'boys who have persisted in going out just looking for fun and excitement have been more involved than others in stealing and this applies after close matching. To test this

160

Table 4.18
Characteristics of those who go out just looking for fun
and excitement
(3,113 cases, weighted)

Characteristics Cases (weighted)	All cases 3,113	Has he ever done this? No 884	Yes 2,229	He has done it and kept it up for a time 975	He kept it up and he still does it Sometimes* 403	Frequently† 284
	(n)	(%)	(%)	(%)	(%)	(%)
Occupational level of boy's father						
Professional, semi-professional, executive	518	44	56	24	9	2
Highly skilled	514	27	73	30	15	8
Skilled	674	27	73	26	10	7
Moderately skilled	630	22	78	38	15	12
Semi-skilled	517	23	77	35	15	13
Unskilled	254	29	71	39	16	14
Not known	6					
All	3,113	28%	72%	31%	13%	9%
		(%)	(%)	(%)	(%)	(%)
Type of school attended						
Secondary modern	1,464	19	81	39	16	14
Comprehensive	549	26	74	29	12	6
Grammar	718	40	60	21	9	4
Public	257	48	52	23	10	4
Other	105					
No information	20					
Nominal religion						
Protestant	1,370	26	74	32	13	8
Catholic	500	27	73	31	14	10
Other Christian	176	24	76	31	7	17
Jewish	214	54	46	20	6	3
None	621	25	75	36	14	12
Other religions	217					
No information	15					
Age at interview						
12/13 yrs	721	30	70	29	12	12
14 yrs	782	28	72	33	12	9
15 yrs	754	32	68	27	13	6
16/17 yrs	856	25	75	36	14	9
Born in UK?						
Yes	2,856	28	72	32	12	9
No	257	35	65	30	20	6
Full-time school now?						
Yes	2,402	32	68	28	12	8
No	711	17	83	41	17	13
Interest score in quartiles						
1st (high) quartile	723	20	80	36	16	10
2nd quartile	647	24	76	31	14	9
3rd quartile	834	31	69	30	11	10
4th (low) quartile	892	26	74	28	11	8
No information	17					

Table 4.18 (continued)

| Characteristics | All cases | Has he ever done this? | | He has done it and kept it up for a time | He kept it up and he still does it | |
| | | No | Yes | | Sometimes* | Frequently† |
Cases (weighted)	3,113	884	2,229	975	403	284
	(n)	(%)	(%)	(%)	(%)	(%)
Truancy						
Once a week	331	10	90	50	19	21
Once a month	262	16	84	44	18	10
Hardly ever	766	18	82	36	15	10
Never	1,745	38	62	24	11	6
No information	9					
Has he a girl friend?						
Yes	1,151	26	74	34	14	11
No, but he goes out with girls	1,029	20	80	35	16	9
No, and does not go out with girls	931	41	59	24	9	6
No information	2					
How often does he pinch for fun and excitement?						
Often	56	24	76	49	6	22
Fair bit	183	15	85	55	23	14
Now and then	538	14	86	42	16	14
Hardly ever	928	22	78	34	16	10
Not at all	1,403	40	60	22	9	6
No information	5					
Does he get enough fun and excitement?						
Yes	1,622	37	63	27	10	8
No	1,487	19	81	36	17	11
No information	4					
Does he get any fun and excitement out of pinching?						
Yes	1,514	20	80	41	18	12
No	1,494	35	65	24	9	7
No information	105					
Did he volunteer 'stealing' as a way of getting fun and excitement?						
Yes	125	4	96	42	22	14
No	2,988	29	71	31	13	9
Index of variety of stealing						
1st (low) quartile	771	51	49	16	8	4
2nd quartile	769	34	66	29	13	6
3rd quartile	822	17	83	37	15	11
4th (high) quartile	751	12	88	44	16	15
Index of amount of stealing						
1st (low) quartile	749	49	51	16	7	5
2nd quartile	861	32	68	30	15	7
3rd quartile	779	21	79	34	14	10
4th (high) quartile	724	11	89	47	15	16

*Now and then/hardly ever
†Often/a fair bit

Table 4.19
Going out looking for fun and excitement related to amount of stealing done (3,113 cases, weighted)

| | All cases | | Index of amount of stealing | | | |
| | | | Q.1 | Q.2 | Q.3 | Q.4 |
	(n)	(%)	(%)	(%)	(%)	(%)
No, never went out looking for it	884	28	42	31	18	9
Yes, but did not keep it up	973	31	22	27	26	25
Yes, but not known if kept it up	281	9	17	26	35	21
Yes, and kept it up	975	31	12	26	27	35
— and still does so	687	22	12	28	27	33
— but not now	288	9	10	23	28	39
All	3,113	100%	24	28	25	23

Table 4.20
Ages at which boys first went out just looking for fun and excitement (3,113 cases, weighted)

| Age of first occurrence | All cases 3,113 cases | | Those boys who have kept it up 975 cases | Index of amount of stealing by those who have kept it up | | | |
| | | | | Q.1 | Q.2 | Q.3 | Q.4 |
	(%)	(%)	(%)	(%)	(%)	(%)	(%)
Less than 4 yrs	0.6						
5—6 yrs	2						
7—8 yrs	6	19	28	13	33	23	31
9—10 yrs	10						
11—12 yrs		21	28	16	24	33	27
13—14 yrs	26						
15—16 yrs	6	32	44	9	23	26	42
17 yrs	0						
Never did so		28					

Table 4.21
Going out just looking for fun and excitement analysed by amount and variety of stealing (3,113 cases, weighted)

Has he ever gone out just looking for fun and excitement?	All cases	Index of variety of stealing				Index of amount of stealing			
		Low quartile			High quartile	Low quartile			High quartile
		Q.1	Q.2	Q.3	Q.4	Q.1	Q.2	Q.3	Q.4
		(%)	(%)	(%)	(%)	(%)	(%)	(%)	(%)
No, never	884	45	30	16	10	42	31	18	9
Yes	2,229	17	23	30	30	17	26	28	29
Yes, but did not keep it up	973	21	23	30	26	22	27	26	25
Yes, but not known if he kept it up	281	18	21	32	29	17	26	35	21
Yes and kept it up	975	12	23	31	34	12	26	27	35
— and still does	687	14	22	30	34	12	28	27	33
— but not now	288	10	25	33	33	10	23	28	39
All	3,113*	25	25	26	24	24	28	25	23

*Weighted total

Table 4.22
Relating frequency of going out looking for fun and excitement to variety and amount of stealing
(3,113 cases, weighted)

Claimed frequency of going out looking for fun and excitement (these days)	All cases	Index of variety of stealing				Index of amount of stealing			
		0.1	0.2	0.3	0.4	0.1	0.2	0.3	0.4
		(%)	(%)	(%)	(%)	(%)	(%)	(%)	(%)
All 687 who 'do now'									
Often/a fair bit these days ⎫	284 ⎫	11	17	31	41	12	20	26	41
Now and then these days ⎬ 687	289 ⎬ 687	15	22	33	30	13	33	26	28
Hardly ever these days ⎭	114 ⎭	22	27	30	20	20	34	30	16
All others	2,426	28	26	25	21	27	28	25	20

Figure 4.2
Division of sample for testing expectation 3

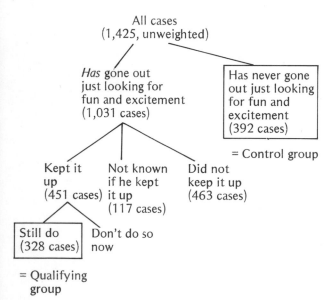

All cases
(1,425, unweighted)

Has gone out just looking for fun and excitement
(1,031 cases)

Has never gone out just looking for fun and excitement
(392 cases)
= Control group

Kept it up
(451 cases)

Not known if he kept it up
(117 cases)

Did not keep it up
(463 cases)

Still do
(328 cases)

Don't do so now

= Qualifying group

expectation, the sample of boys was first split as follows:

The control group, as defined above, was then matched to the qualifying group in terms of the correlates of stealing as defined by the matching composite set out in Chapter 1. The results of applying the matching technique can be seen in the top section of Table 4.23. They strongly support Expectation 4.

Testing Expectation 5

This expectation was similar to Expectation 4 but applied to the forty-four different *types* of theft considered separately. The same splitting of the sample (into qualifying and control groups) was carried out and the same process of matching was applied. The results are set out in the lower part of Table 4.23.

Generally, the results of this test confirm the expectation. But there are clearly some types of theft for which the expectation is borne out much more strongly than for others — and some where it is not borne out at all. Those for which it applies most and least are set out in Table 4.24.

Anything that is said about Table 4.24 must be purely speculative in character. At this level it appears

Table 4.23
Differences between qualifiers and controls before and
after matching: each of the forty-four types of theft

Indices of stealing*	Unadjusted average score for qualifiers a		Unadjusted average score for controls b		Adjusted average score for controls c		Differences between qualifiers and adj. controls a−c	P	Difference a−c as percentage of c
Averaged indices of variety of stealing at L.2+	16.29		9.23		11.09		5.20	(0.01)	47
Averaged indices of amount of stealing at L.2+	120.78		59.45		75.63		45.15	(0.01)	60
Theft types	(n)	(%)	(n)	(%)	(n)	(%)			(%)
1	314	95.7	328	83.7	290.4	88.5	7.2	0.13	8
2	199	60.7	141	36.0	139.1	42.4	18.3	<0.01	43
3	165	50.3	101	25.8	101.0	30.8	19.5	<0.01	63
4	198	60.4	157	40.1	153.6	46.8	13.6	<0.01	29
5	99	30.2	42	10.7	44.7	13.6	16.6	<0.01	122
6	209	63.7	148	37.8	147.3	44.9	18.8	<0.01	42
7	148	45.1	101	25.8	105.1	32.0	13.1	<0.01	41
8	106	32.3	133	33.9	119.4	36.4	−4.1	0.17	−11
9	64	19.5	34	8.7	40.2	12.3	7.2	<0.01	59
10	141	43.0	112	28.6	114.0	34.8	8.2	0.02	24
11	149	45.4	106	27.0	108.8	33.2	12.2	<0.01	37
12	59	18.0	38	9.7	44.8	13.7	4.3	0.09	32
13	158	48.2	98	25.0	102.7	31.3	16.9	<0.01	54
14	119	36.3	46	11.7	54.1	16.5	19.8	<0.01	120
15	71	21.6	25	6.4	26.1	8.0	13.6	<0.01	172
16	174	53.0	113	28.8	112.2	34.2	18.8	<0.01	55
17	93	28.4	34	8.7	41.5	12.7	15.7	<0.01	124
18	220	67.1	209	53.3	197.5	60.2	6.9	0.08	11
19	145	44.2	91	23.2	90.1	27.5	16.7	<0.01	61
20	115	35.1	75	19.1	79.7	24.3	10.8	<0.01	44
21	56	17.1	29	7.4	33.3	10.2	6.9	<0.01	68
22	156	47.6	109	27.8	104.6	31.9	15.7	<0.01	49
23	91	27.7	50	12.8	63.9	19.5	8.2	0.01	42
24	59	18.0	21	5.4	28.8	8.8	9.2	<0.01	105
25	97	29.6	52	13.3	47.5	14.5	15.1	<0.01	104
26	127	38.7	64	16.3	68.7	21.0	17.7	<0.01	85
27	74	22.6	40	10.2	42.3	12.9	9.7	<0.01	75
28	89	27.1	58	14.8	66.7	20.3	6.8	0.01	33
29	36	11.0	14	3.6	17.2	5.2	5.8	<0.01	107
30	181	55.2	132	33.7	128.7	39.2	16.0	<0.01	41
31	117	35.7	66	16.8	81.2	24.8	10.9	<0.01	44
32	28	8.5	14	3.6	17.0	5.2	3.3	0.16	65
33	235	71.7	185	47.2	190.7	58.1	13.6	<0.01	23
34	128	39.0	80	20.4	74.3	22.7	16.3	<0.01	72
35	88	26.8	23	5.9	28.7	8.8	18.0	<0.01	207
36	134	40.9	65	16.6	76.3	23.3	17.6	<0.01	76
37	27	8.2	5	1.3	7.3	2.2	6.0	<0.01	270
38	101	30.8	48	12.2	53.6	16.3	14.5	<0.01	88
39	84	25.6	44	11.2	54.2	16.5	9.1	<0.01	55
40	238	72.6	184	46.9	175.7	53.6	19.0	<0.01	36
41	40	12.2	17	4.3	19.5	5.9	6.3	<0.01	105
42	53	16.2	29	7.4	7.6	2.3	13.9	<0.01	597
43	124	37.8	71	18.1	79.8	24.3	13.5	<0.01	55
44	209	63.7	139	35.5	140.8	42.9	20.8	<0.01	48
Duration of 'serious' thieving at L.2+	4.33		2.72		3.29		1.04	0.01	31.61%

*At Level 2 and above as defined in Chapter 2. See Chapter 2 also for derivation of 'variety' and 'amount' indices
†Probability that this difference is the product of chance differences between the two samples

Table 4.24

Showing the types of theft for which the hypothesis applied most and least

Applied most	Applied least
Stealing from a telephone box	Stealing from family or relations
Taking a car or lorry or van	
Taking a bike or a motor bike	Keeping something found
Stealing from a changing-room or cloakroom	Stealing from school
	Avoiding paying fare/proper fare
Getting into a place and stealing	
Stealing from a stall or barrow	Stealing junk or scrap
Stealing cigarettes	Getting something by threatening others
Stealing a letter or parcel	Stealing from a goods yard, factory yard, etc.
	Getting in without paying

that the types of stealing most associated with 'going out just looking for fun and excitement' are of the more serious kind and may also be of the sort that is more successfully done with the aid of a look-out (or look-outs). Those types least associated with the hypothesis tend (with perhaps two exceptions) to be less serious and of the sort that is committed alone. Still at this highly speculative level, this complex of evidence would fit in with 'going out just looking for fun and excitement' being a group activity and involving some degree of risk taking and challenge.

Testing Expectation 6

This expectation refers to the period of time over which the boy persisted in serious stealing, the expectation being that boys who have persisted in going out just looking for fun and excitement have been committing serious thefts for a longer period than boys who have not gone out just looking for fun and excitement. The same matching techniques as were applied in testing Expectation 4 were re-applied here. The results are shown at the foot of Table 4.23. They support the expectation.

Testing Expectation 7

This expectation was that boys will admit stealing as stemming from outings when they were 'just looking for fun and excitement'. The question put to them was: 'What did you do that first time you went out "just looking for fun and excitement"?' The replies to this question were analysed to detect any direct reference to stealing. The results are given in Table 4.25.

For that first time of going in for this sort of behaviour, the number of boys directly volunteering stealing was 105 (out of the 2,224 who had ever 'gone out just looking for fun and excitement' (=5 per cent). In addition, however, a great many of the volunteered activities can be regarded as dangerous in the sense of taking the boy either to the edge of unlawful behaviour or beyond it.

Table 4.25

Activities named by boys as pursued when first went out just looking for fun and excitement
2,224 cases, weighted

	n	n
Any direct reference to stealing (fully volunteered, no prompting)		105
Annoying/cheeking/making fun of people	239	
Annoying people to get chased by them	67	306
Entering forbidden premises/mucking about in forbidden premises/causing mischief in forbidden premises		153
Destroying property/vandalism		144
Fighting and watching fights		105
Informal or unstructured local activities with or without mates (e.g. playing near the river/stroll through the park/went over the woods/played with other boys/went about town)		1,030
Funfairs/funfair type amusements		51
Went to a cinema		110
Going out with girls/girls		160
Going to parties/dances . . .		79
Participation in physically active sports/games (e.g. football/cricket/tennis/swimming/judo/volley ball/table tennis/athletics/cycling)		358
Participation in organised group activities of any kind (Scouts/Sea Cadets/Boys' Brigade)		3
Attended club/Youth club		82
Travel/going visiting/seaside holiday		256
Went out on motor bike/scooter		34

Summing-Up on the Investigation of Hypothesis 2

The various tests of expectations were all borne out and together they lend support to Hypothesis 2. However, just as with Hypothesis 1, it appears that there are some types of theft for which Hypothesis 2 does not apply, namely certain thefts of a less serious kind that ordinarily tend to be done.

Some other evidence

Certain other classes of evidence which could be of relevance to the matter under study were also collected.

Other 'reasons' for stealing

Boys who claimed they had never stolen for fun and excitement were asked: 'What *are* your main reasons for pinching things?' In addition, boys who said they *had* stolen for fun and excitement were asked: 'Have you got any *other* reasons for pinching? . . . What are they?' The 'reasons' evoked through these questions are set out in Table 4.26.

One important indication of Table 4.26 is that 55 per cent of boys said they had at some time stolen for fun and excitement and that 13 per cent of these claimed that they had *no other* reason for stealing. One must be very wary indeed in one's interpretation of such claims, but it seems reasonable to regard them as giving support to — rather than weakening — the hypotheses. The other entries in Table 4.26 do serve, however, to suggest something of the broader 'causal' context within which fun and excitement seeking appears to operate: lack of

Table 4.26
Reasons for stealing, other than for fun and excitement

Reasons/additional reasons given for stealing	Among those who claim they		All cases
	Never stole for fun & excitement	*Have* stolen for fun & excitement	
Weighted cases	1,403	1,705	3,113
	(%)	(%)	(%)
No reason/no other reason	2	13	8
He *cannot afford* to buy the things he steals	16	18	17
He steals because he *needs* them	20	14	17
He steals because he *wants* them	27	23	25
He steals because he *likes* them	5	2	3
He steals because the things stolen are useful	4	2	3
He steals to make money/save money/get money	7	15	12
He steals because he is jealous of others' possessions	3	3	3
He steals because of example of his mates/influence of mates	6	5	6
He steals to get prestige in the eyes of mates/to prove himself	9	8	9
He steals because he is challenged by mates	6	7	7
He steals for something to do	1	5	3
He steals on impulse	2	1	2
He steals because tempted	2	2	2
He steals because they are only small things/of no value	2	—	1
He steals things that will not be missed/will not harm anyone	3	1	2
He steals for revenge/out of spite/to get own back	4	4	4

Theft level (in quartiles)	Q.1 (%)	Q.2 (%)	Q.3 (%)	Q.4 (%)	Q.1 (%)	Q.2 (%)	Q.3 (%)	Q.4 (%)	
Index† of variety of stealing	43	29	18	9	9	20	34	37	
Index† of amount of stealing	41	31	17	11	9	25	32	34	

*Total of percentages is more than 100 per cent because boys could give more than one reason
†See Part One (Methods) of report
— = Less than 0.5 per cent

financial means for buying what he wants; a feeling of need or want for what was stolen; prestige seeking (in eyes of mates); because dared by mates.

What stops boys from getting as much fun and excitement as they want/need?

Boys who said they did *not* get enough fun and excitement had been asked what they would *like* to do to get enough fun and excitement and, then, why they did not do 'something like that'. That particular question was asked because it seemed likely to provide guides to factors that stand in the way of boys getting enough fun and excitement ... and, hence, of relevance to the reduction of juvenile stealing. The results are set out in Table 4.27.

The blocking factors included in Table 4.27 principally involve: lack of money; lack of time; insufficient facilities or equipment; being kept in by parents; being too young; not enough mates. Of these, lack of money

Table 4.27
'Things' that stop boys from getting as much fun and excitement as they need

Circumstances named as stopping him	Proportion naming it Weighted base = 1,487 (%)
He has not got enough money	35
He has not got sufficient time because of homework/study	10 ⎫ 21
He has not sufficient time for *other* reasons	11 ⎭
He has not got enough mates	11
He is kept in by parents	3 ⎫ 11
Parents would prevent him	8 ⎭
Inadequate facilities/lack of equipment	20 ⎫
Facilities too far away	10 ⎪ 38
Facilities available only occasionally	5 ⎪
He does not know where to get facilities	3 ⎭
He is too young	11
He cannot be bothered	2
He is shy/has inferiority feelings	2

Table 4.28
Explanation of why or how he does/does not get fun and excitement out of such pinching as he does

Ways in which stealing gives him fun and excitement	Percentage saying this		Index of amount of stealing			
Weighted base	1,514		Q.1	Q.2	Q.3	Q.4
	(%)	(%)	(%)	(%)	(%)	(%)
Gets prestige in eyes of mates	9					
Talking or laughing with mates about it	5	25	9	25	30	36
Personal pride/sense of achievement	11					
The risk of getting caught	12					
Breaking-in is exciting	2					
Getting chased	8	29	8	20	33	39
The daring of it/feeling of daring	4					
Knowing you are doing wrong/something forbidden	3					
Outwitting people/getting away with it	22					
The thought or the sight of people when they miss what you took	5	27	16	27	20	37
The feeling he has when admitting it		7	18	24	30	28
All			13	23	29	34

Explanations of how it is that stealing does not give him fun or excitement	Percentage saying this		Index of amount of stealing			
Weighted base	1,494		Q.1	Q.2	Q.3	Q.4
	(%)	(%)	(%)	(%)	(%)	(%)
He thinks it is wrong/feels guilty	19	25	34	35	24	7
He does not like it	6					
He sees nothing funny in it	6	12	33	27	30	10
He sees nothing clever in it/nothing achieved by it	6					
Risk of being caught	19					
Fear or worry about consequences	6	33	21	32	29	18
Nervous/scared	8					
Prefers to get things by working	9					
He steals because he needs/wants/likes things taken (*not* for fun)	14	20	32	32	17	18
Steals for other reasons (*not* for fun)	6					
He would get fun or excitement only by stealing big things	2	4	44	31	13	12
The sorts of things he steals do not give him any excitement	2					
All			32	33	22	13

— = Less than 0.5 per cent

and insufficient facilities were mentioned by 35 and 38 per cent respectively. The second of them, insufficient facilities, may be particularly important in that it seems to be actionable by local authorities or parents or both.

What is it about stealing that gives the boy fun and excitement?

If, as seems to be the case, fun and excitement seeking is causally related to stealing, then it is important to know just what it is about stealing that gives boys fun and excitement. To secure leads in this matter, boys were asked to explain how it was that stealing gave them fun and excitement (i.e. 'How do you explain that?'). Where boys said that stealing did *not* provide fun and excitement, they were similarly asked, 'How do you explain that?' Responses are given in Table 4.28. Table 4.28 also links '*how* stealing gives fun and excitement' with degree of *involvement* in stealing. The indications of Table 4.28 are as follows.

1 Whereas all eleven items in the top half of Table 4.28 seem to be acceptable interpretations of fun and

168

xcitement, they together constitute a fairly broad range f concepts that appear to enter into and that give reater meaning to the 'fun and excitement' variable. hese concepts include: a heightening of relationships ith mates; personal pride at achievement; the provision r risk or tension; the uncertainty of outcome.

The different 'ways' listed in the top half of Table 28 tend to be associated with a generally higher level f theft — though individually there is not much differ-nce between them in this respect: they thus appear to e fairly equally relevant to an understanding of how un and excitement seeking' contributes to the develop-ent of juvenile stealing.

The risk element also features in the reactions of boys ho say they *do not* get fun and excitement from tealing. Presumably, this sort of reaction is, for these oys, so much mixed with unpleasantness for them that hey could not class it as fun and excitement. At the ame time it is worth noting that these boys are onetheless somewhat more involved in stealing than oys giving other explanations for their denial that tealing gave them fun and excitement.

7 SUMMING-UP ON THE INVESTIGATION OF THE TWO HYPOTHESES

n this chapter the results of investigating two hypo-heses concerned with fun and excitement seeking have been presented. They are:

1 A desire for a lot of fun and excitement is a contributing factor to the initiation and maintenance of juvenile stealing.

2 Going out looking for fun and excitement is a contributing factor to the initiation and maintenance of juvenile stealing.

The method of investigating these hypotheses was that of testing a large number of expectations which were derived from the hypotheses — i.e. the testing of propo-sitions which one would expect to be true if the hypotheses were true. There were seventeen such ex-pectations to be tested and they were all verified by the tests made. This outcome was regarded as a sufficient basis for concluding that the two hypotheses had been rendered more tenable by the challenging or investi-gating procedure adopted.

The hypotheses had *not* postulated fun and excite-ment seeking as a *sole* cause of stealing and this feature was also borne out by the tests conducted. In other words, 'fun and excitement seeking' appears to be an important contributing factor operating within a com-plex of other factors. On the evidence presented in this chapter, these include factors such as lack of money for buying what the boy wants; seeking prestige amongst boys already engaged in stealing; a feeling of need or want for what was stolen; being dared by mates already engaged in stealing. Other chapters present additional causal factors of this partial kind.

The operative importance of fun and excitement seeking as a causal factor is emphasized by the wide-spread demand amongst London boys for some form of fun and excitement, by the non-contructive form of behaviour to which this demand frequently leads and by the fact that about half the boys in the sample claimed, that they do not get enough 'fun and excitement'.

8 SOME COMMENTS AND POSSIBLE ACTION

The evidence suggests that fun and excitement seeking is something of a catalyst, moving boys into forms of behaviour conditioned by their wants and circumstances (e.g. lack of money for buying what they want, prestige seeking amongst boys already engaged in stealing).

This outcome in turn suggests that the remedial action required is the development of alternative outlets for fun and excitement seeking. Such outlets should be forms of activity which are both socially acceptable and attractive to boys of the kind already engaged in stealing or 'at risk'. If such outlets can also be made to reduce the needs or conditions that at present seem to attract stealing, they are the more likely to be adopted and maintained.

The identification and development of such alternate outlets for fun and excitement seeking will call for a considerable amount of searching inquiry and for close liaison with both delinquent boys and local authorities. A proposal for such work has been developed and is available for study.

9 APPENDIX 4.1

The Sub-Questionnaire used

Questionnaire used for investigating hypotheses about seeking fun and excitement

I Q.1 The extent of his present interest in fun and excitement

Q.2 The form taken by presenting fun and excitement and what blocks it when the boy is not getting enough

Q.1 Extent of his present interest in fun and excitement

1a 'How much fun and excitement would you like to have?'

PROBE TO GET HIM THINKING AND ALSO TO PROVIDE A CHECK ON HIS LATER CHOICE OF ANSWER FROM CHOICE CARD

IF HE ASKS WHAT WE MEAN BY FUN AND EXCITEMENT, PUSH THE QUESTION BACK AT HIM (i.e. 'What ever *you* think of by fun and excitement.')

1b 'Which of these comes nearest to the amount of fun and excitement you would *like* to have?'

SHOW CARD. READ OUT CHOICES. CIRCLE CHOICE MADE
(TERRIFIC/QUITE A LOT/FAIR BIT/SOME/NOT MUCH/NONE)

Q.2 Does he get enough fun and excitement? The form taken by it. What blocks his getting enough?

2a 'Think carefully about this. Do you get *enough* fun and excitement?'

YES/NO/ABOUT RIGHT ... CHALLENGE. THEN CIRCLE CHOICE
IF 'NO' OR 'NOT SURE', GO TO Q.2c
IF 'YES' OR 'ABOUT RIGHT', ASK Q.2b

2b 'How do you get it?'
(PROBE AND STIMULATE WITH: 'What other ways do you get your fun and excitement?')
'What else?'
NOW GO TO II

2c 'Do you get any fun and excitement at all?'
YES/NO
IF 'YES', ASK: 'How do you get it?' (PROBE WITH: 'Anything else?'
ii 'What are the things you'd like to do so as to have enough fun and excitement?'
'What else?'
iii 'Why don't you do something like that?' (FIND OUT WHAT STOPS HIM)

II Q.1 Was there a time when his wants were different? When?
Q.2 Has he ever gone out just hoping that fun and excitement will turn up?

Q.1 Was there possibly a time when his wants were different? When? IF RESPONDENT WANTS TERRIFIC/LOTS/FAIR BIT OF FUN AND EXCITEMENT, ASK Q1b
IF RESPONDENT WANTS *LESS THAN* 'A FAIR BIT' OF FUN AND EXCITEMENT, ASK Q.1a

1a 'You said you wanted only (GIVE CARD CHOICE) of fun and excitement.
Was there ever a time when you wanted more than that?' YES/NO
IF 'NO', GO TO Q.2
IF 'YES', ASK:

i 'What was it made you want more?'
(GET NATURE OF CHANGE AND REASONS. IF SEVERAL, GET THESE)

ii 'How old were you then?' IF DIFFERENT PERIODS INVOLVED, GET DIFFERENT AGES IF POSSIBLE, IN THE SAME ORDER AS IN (i)

1b 'You said you want (GIVE CARD CHOICE) of fun and excitement. What started you wanting this much fun and excitement?'

IF HE SAYS OR IMPLIES 'ALWAYS', CIRCL THIS AND THEN GO TO Q.2
IF HE HAS SOME EVENT IN MIND, CHALLENG THAT THIS WAS A STARTER EVENT AND THE SAY:
'So what age were you when you started to wan (GIVE CARD CHOICE) or fun and excitement?'
IF NOT ANY STARTER EVENTS, CIRCLE THIS NO STARTER EVENTS

Q.2 Has he ever gone out just looking around for fur and excitement?

2a 'Some boys go round hoping they'll find something to give them fun and excitement. They go out jus looking for fun and excitement (PAUSE). Have you *eve* done that?' YES/NO
IF 'NO', CHALLENGE WITH: 'Never in your whole life?'
IF STILL 'NO', GO TO III
IF 'YES', GO TO Q.2b

2b 'How old were you when you first started to go out just looking for fun and excitement?' (CHALLENGE THAT IT REALLY WAS FAIRLY AIMLESS LOOKING ROUND FOR IT)

2c 'What did you do that time?'
2d 'Did you keep it up (i.e. DID HE MAKE A HABIT OF GOING OUT LIKE THAT)?'

2e '*These days*, do you go out just looking around for fun and excitement — looking round hoping you'll find some fun and excitement?' YES/NO
IF 'NO' CHALLENGE. THEN GO TO III
IF 'YES', ASK:
'Just how often do you do that these days?' SHOW CARD
(OFTEN/FAIR BIT/NOW AND THEN/HARDLY EVER)
CHALLENGE AND THEN CIRCLE FINAL CHOICE

III Q.1 His views about pinching for fun and excitement and how much fun and excitement he gets when he *does* pinch

---

1a 'Lots of boys pinch things so as to get fun and excitement. They pinch mostly to get fun and excitement. Have you ever done that?' YES/NO

IF 'NO', CHALLENGE. THEN SAY:
'What *are* your main reasons for pinching things?'
IF 'YES', CHALLENGE AND ASK:
i 'How often do you pinch mostly for fun and excitement?' SHOW CARD. RING CHOICE
(OFTEN/FAIR BIT/NOW AND THEN/HARDLY EVER)
ii 'Have you got any *other* reasons for pinching?' What are they?

b 'When you do pinch things, do you get any fun and/or excitement out of that?' YES/NO
c 'How do you explain that?'

Chapter five Permissiveness in relation to stealing

CONTENTS

1 THE COVERAGE OF THIS CHAPTER

In this chapter I have presented a wide range of information broadly related to the permissiveness of boys' attitudes towards stealing. This information was collected and processed to serve two associated purposes, the more important of which was to investigate a particular composite of hypotheses about causal factors in the development of juvenile stealing. These hypotheses were as follows.

1 Boys take up stealing and continue to steal partly because they have permissive attitudes towards stealing (Sub-Hypothesis 1a).

2 Boys take up stealing and continue to steal partly because they are without any generalized opposition to stealing (Sub-Hypothesis 1b).

3 Boys take up stealing and continue to steal partly because they are lacking in any sense of remorse in relation to stealing (Hypothesis 2).

4 Boys take up stealing and continue to steal partly because they have received relatively little instruction about *not* stealing (Hypothesis 3).

The second purpose of the collected data was to provide general background information about each of the factors or conditions hypothesized as causal in character. For example, it seemed desirable to establish: (*a*) to what extent boys with different backgrounds differed in terms of the kinds of theft they regard as 'all right'; and, (*b*) the extent to which boys of different backgrounds receive instructions about not stealing.

2 RESEARCH PROCEDURES COMMON TO ALL THE HYPOTHESES DEALT WITH IN THE INQUIRY

The gathering of information relevant to the hypotheses about 'permissiveness in relation to stealing' was done in the context of an inquiry concerned with over thirty other hypotheses. The techniques relating to the inquiry as a whole have been summarized in Chapter 1. That summary deals with sampling procedures; with a technique for getting boys to provide reliable information about any stealing they have done; with questioning procedures for classifying boys in terms of the variables hypothesized as causal factors in the different hypotheses (i.e. in terms of the different independent variables); with strategies for investigating the tenability of hypotheses about causal factors and processes. The reader should as necessary refer back to the relevant parts of Chapter 1 in reading statements of findings in the present and in subsequent chapters.

3 RESEARCH PROCEDURES APPLYING ONLY TO THE HYPOTHESES DEALT WITH IN THIS CHAPTER

Whereas many aspects of research procedure applied generally to the whole range of hypotheses under study,

certain parts of it related only to the four hypotheses listed in this chapter and relating to one or another aspect of 'permissiveness'. These parts tend to be encapsulated in one of the sub-questionnaires put to boys in the course of the total interview and the sub-questionnaire is presented in full in Appendix 5.1.

Like the other sub-questionnaires, this one was designed in sections, each section beginning with general description of its purpose, as follows.

1 His ideas about what is right and wrong in relation to stealing.

2 Further views about stealing, endorsed by respondent as 'agree' or 'disagree'.

3 Boy's training in right/wrong in relation to stealing.

4 Would the boy feel badly about pinching of the kind he rated as wrong?

5 When did the boy first feel this way about stealing and what led to this?

Practically all the questions were of a fully-structured kind, many of them involving card sorting of one kind or another.

4 METHODS AND FINDINGS RELATED TO THE INVESTIGATION OF SUB-HYPOTHESES 1a AND 1b

The nature of Sub-Hypotheses 1a and 1b

The first of the sub-hypotheses to be investigated was:

Boys take up stealing and continue to steal partly because they have permissive attitudes towards stealing.

The second was:

Boys take up stealing and continue to steal partly because they are without any form of generalized opposition to stealing.

The questions asked of boys in terms of the variables hypothesized as causal

In this section are presented details about the questions asked as a basis for classifying boys in terms of the variables hypothesized as causal. There were in fact two series of such questions, identified as Question 1 and Question 2. The Question 1 series related to the investigation of Sub-Hypothesis 1a and the Question 2 series to the investigation of Sub-Hypothesis 1b.

Q.1 His ideas about what is right and wrong in relation to stealing
(Involving a card sorting technique in which boys sort as 'quite all right', 'nothing much wrong with it'. . . . 'very wrong', a sequence of 25 types of theft).

GET BOY'S HELP IN SETTING UP SORTING BAGS*. THESE READ: QUITE ALL RIGHT/ NOTHING MUCH WRONG WITH IT/A BIT WRONG/FAIRLY WRONG/VERY WRONG/CAN'T DECIDE.
SEE THAT THE 'CAN'T DECIDE' BAG IS WELL TO THE RIGHT (AND WELL AWAY FROM THE BAG NEXT TO IT).
TEACH BOY BAGS IF HE IS ILLITERATE.
THEN SAY:
'On these green cards are some things that people might do. There's one on each card. I want you to look at each card in turn and tell me if you think it is all right to do it.' PAUSE. 'If you think it is QUITE ALL RIGHT to do it, you put it in this bag' (POINT). 'If you think there is NOTHING MUCH WRONG WITH IT, you put it here' (POINT). 'A BIT WRONG, here' (POINT). 'FAIRLY WRONG, here' (POINT). 'VERY WRONG, here' (POINT). 'If you just CAN'T DECIDE, you put it over here' (POINT).
'Will you start by reading out for me what's on each of these bags.'
THEN GIVE BOY THE FIRST CARD. (CARD 1).
'Going absolutely by your own opinion, which bag would you put that one in?'
SAY:
'Why that bag?' CORRECT IF HE HAS THE SORTING IDEA WRONG.
SAY:
'Now we'll do the same thing with all the rest. I'll give them to you one at a time.'
'I won't watch where you put them. Please put them exactly where YOU think they go. Don't bother about what ANYONE ELSE thinks. I won't watch.'
PASS CARDS ONE AT A TIME, NOT WATCHING WHERE HE PUTS THEM.
READ OUT ALL (WHITE) REMINDER CARDS

Q.2 Further views about stealing, endorsed by respondents as agree or disagree

---

(Involving a card sorting technique in which boys sort into various bags cards stating different views about stealing, e.g. stealing is wrong, if someone I hated was stealing I would tell on him).

PUT UP THE FOUR YELLOW BAGS†. THESE ARE: AGREE/PARTLY AGREE/DISAGREE/CAN'T DECIDE
'Here are just a few more cards to put into the yellow bags. Here is the first one.'
PASS HIM THE CARD 'SOMETIMES IT IS ALL RIGHT TO PINCH THINGS'. SAY:
'If you AGREE with that, put it in this bag. If you DISAGREE with it, put it in this bag.
If you PARTLY AGREE, put it in this bag. And if you CAN'T DECIDE, put it in this one. O.K.?'

*See Figure 5.1 for presentation of the sorting-bag operation. See facing column for list of statements on cards.
†Similar system to that used in Question 1 and shown in Figure 5.1. See p.174 for list of statements on these cards.

I won't look. But please be very truthful. Put that one in the bag that shows what you personally think.'
PASS THE REST, ONE AT A TIME, BUT WITHOUT WASTING TIME

Question 1, with its twenty-five cards, was intended to yield attitudinal information about a wide range of types of theft. This would be of value in its own right but it was also intended to make possible the derivation of a general index of permissiveness for use in classifying boys in preparation for investigating Hypothesis 1a.
The statements on the twenty-five cards were as follows.

Card 1 Pinching from someone who is rich.

Card 2 Robbing a bank.

Card 3 Doing a hold-up.

Card 4 Breaking into a place and taking things.

Card 5 Taking things from Woolworths.

Card 6 Taking pencils or rubbers from school.

Card 7 Keeping something you found.

Card 8 Buying things you know were pinched.

Card 9 Taking things from where you work.

Card 10 Pinching something quite small.

Card 11 Pinching things from a big company.

Card 12 Pinching things that belong to the government.

Card 13 Taking little things from where you work.

Card 14 Taking someone's car just for a drive.

Card 15 Just helping someone to pinch things.

Card 16 Just keeping a look-out for mates who were pinching.

Card 17 Pinching from a shop.

Card 18 Taking things just left lying around.

Card 19 Pinching from an old lady.

Card 20 Pinching from someone who has plenty of what you took.

Card 21 Pinching from a little kid.

Card 22 Pinching things from home.

Card 23 Pinching things from a friend.

Q.1

Figure 5.1
Sorting cards

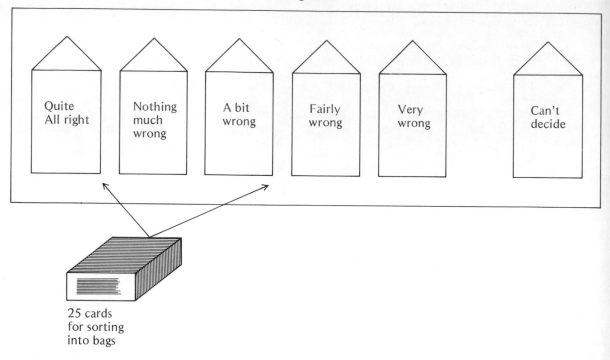

| Quite All right | Nothing much wrong | A bit wrong | Fairly wrong | Very wrong | Can't decide |

25 cards
for sorting
into bags

Card 24 Taking something that is not yours.

Card 25 Pinching anything at all.

Two indices of permissiveness were derived from boys' ratings of these statements:

1 The percentage of statements sorted as 'quite all right'.

2 The weighted average for each statement, where 'quite all right' = 5 and 'very wrong' = 1.

Question 2 was similar in intention to Question 1 and was intended to aid the investigation of Sub-Hypothesis 1b. The statements sorted were more general in character, as indicated below.

Card 1 Sometimes it is all right to steal.

Card 2 If you know someone who is stealing, you should keep it to yourself.

Card 3 If someone I hated was stealing I would tell on him.

Card 4 If you know someone is stealing you should tell on him.

Card 5 Anyone who steals should be punished.

Card 6 Stealing is wrong.

Card 7 We should help the police to catch people wh pinch things.

Responses to these statements were to be reported i their own right but in addition they were to be used t derive two indices:

1 An index of general permissiveness, calculated b weighting as in Footnote*.

2 An index of willingness to help the police, calculate by weighting as in Footnote†.

Response Distributions relating to Permissiveness about Stealing (Sub-Hypothesis 1a)

Response distributions for each of the twenty-five types of theft
Each of the twenty-five types of theft had been rated by boys in terms of how right or wrong they thought it to be. Results are set out in Table 5.1. Table 5.1 indicates:

*For statements 1 and 2: agree = 3/partly agree = 2/disagree = 1/can't decide = 2.
For statements 4-7: agree = 1/partly agree = 2/disagree = 3/can' decide = 2.
Statement 3 is not included in this calculation.
†For statement 2: agree = 3/partly agree = 2/disagree = 1/can't decide = 2.
For statements 3, 4, 7: agree = 1/partly agree = 2/disagree = 3/can't decide = 2.

174

There is a considerable variation in the degree to which different types of theft are regarded as permissible (i.e. 'quite all right' or 'nothing much wrong'), the range being from 48 per cent for 'keeping something you found' to 15 per cent for 'pinching from a big company' to less than 1 per cent for 'pinching from an old lady'.

For only five of the listed acts did the number saying 'very wrong' pass the 75 per cent level. Even for these five, which included 'doing a hold up' and 'robbing a bank', the number saying 'very wrong' did not exceed 93 per cent.

'Pinching from an old lady' was regarded as less permissible than 'robbing a bank'.

Other types of theft for which the distributions are noteworthy are: 'buying things you know were pinched', 'just keeping a look-out for mates who were stealing', 'pinching things from a big company', 'pinching things that belong to the government', 'taking things from where you work'.

5 The averages for all twenty-five items are given at the foot of Table 5.1, from which it might with reservation be said that 12 per cent regarded the average item in the list as 'permissible' and 50 per cent regarded it as 'very wrong'.

Permissivness in different sectors of the boy population of London

Comparisons were made of permissiveness in different sectors of London's boy population. To facilitate such comparisons, the distributions of permissiveness for each theft type was turned into a weighted average where

Table 5.1
Boys' ideas about the rightness or wrongness of certain types of theft

Type of theft*	Ratings of theft as right or wrong						
	Quite all right	Nothing much wrong	A bit wrong	Fairly wrong	Very wrong	Can't decide	No evidence
	(%)	(%)	(%)	(%)	(%)	(%)	(%)
Keeping something you found	19	29	24	17	6	2	2
Taking things just left lying around	8	21	24	27	16	2	2
Taking pencils or rubbers from school	8	21	26	26	17	–	2
Buying things you know were pinched	7	16	24	26	25	1	2
Pinching from someone who has plenty	9	13	14	28	32	3	2
Pinching something quite small	5	14	22	28	29	1	1
Pinching from someone who is rich	7	11	15	20	44	2	2
Just keeping a look-out for mates who are stealing	5	10	19	32	31	1	2
Pinching things from a big company	5	10	12	23	48	1	2
Taking little things from where you work	4	10	17	29	38	1	2
Taking things from Woolworths	4	8	11	27	47	1	1
Pinching things that belong to the government	6	5	10	19	56	2	2
Just helping someone to pinch things	2	7	17	33	38	1	2
Taking someone's car just for a drive	2	6	11	23	55	1	2
Pinching from a shop	3	5	13	25	51	1	2
Taking things from where you work	1	6	12	25	52	2	2
Taking something that is not yours	2	4	13	26	51	3	2
Pinching anything at all	2	4	10	26	50	6	2
Pinching things from home	1	3	9	16	68	2	2
Robbing a bank	1	3	4	7	83	2	2
Breaking into a place and taking things	1	2	5	13	76	1	2
Doing a hold-up	1	1	4	7	84	2	1
Pinching things from a friend	–	1	7	17	72	1	2
Pinching from a little kid	–	–	4	11	83	1	2
Pinching from an old lady	–	–	1	4	93	–	2
Average item	4	8	13	21	50	2	2

*These items are arranged in order according to the proportion answering *either* 'quite all right' or 'nothing much wrong'.
– = Less than 0.5 per cent

'quite all right' =5, 'nothing much wrong with it' =4, 'a bit wrong' =3, 'fairly wrong' =2, 'very wrong' =1, 'can't decide' =3. The results are set out in Tables 5.2 to 5.4.

By occupational level of boys' fathers

Table 5.2 presents evidence about the relative permissiveness in boys drawn from different occupational backgrounds. Whereas this table shows that permissiveness increases as we go down the occupational scale, the extent of this trend is quite small. Figure 5.2 illustrates the direction and the size of it. It is noteworthy that such trend as there is tends to be reversed in going from the semi-skilled to the unskilled.

The general direction of this averaged trend and i smallness, seem to be mirrored in most of the individu types of theft as well. The two exceptions to this ar 'stealing from home' and 'stealing from an old lad (where permissiveness amongst the sons of the profe sional and semi-professional is not less than that among other boys).

By school attended, nominal religion and age

Tables 5.3 and 5.4 compare permissiveness (for each o the twenty-five theft types) in boys according to schoc last attended, nominal religion and age.

Table 5.2
Average right/wrong ratings* of different types of theft analysed by occupational levels of fathers
(3,113 cases, weighted)

Type of theft*	Sample size (weighted)	All cases 3,113	Occupational level of fathers					
			A* 518	B 514	C 674	D 630	E 517	F 254
Keeping something you found		3.33	3.1†	3.3	3.4	3.4	3.5	3.3
Taking things just left lying around		2.72	2.5	2.6	2.8	2.8	3.0	2.7
Taking pencils or rubbers from school		2.70	2.4	2.6	2.7	2.8	2.9	2.8
Buying things you know were pinched		2.50	2.1	2.4	2.7	2.5	2.7	2.6
Pinching from someone who has plenty		2.33	2.0	2.2	2.4	2.4	2.6	2.6
Pinching something quite small		2.34	2.0	2.2	2.4	2.5	2.6	2.6
Pinching from someone who is rich		2.13	1.8	1.9	2.1	2.4	2.4	2.4
Just keeping a look-out for mates who are stealing		2.20	1.9	2.0	2.2	2.2	2.6	2.3
Pinching things from a big company		1.96	1.7	1.8	2.0	2.0	2.3	2.2
Taking little things from where you work		2.08	1.8	2.0	2.1	2.1	2.4	2.1
Taking things from Woolworths		1.90	1.5	1.8	2.0	2.0	2.2	2.0
Pinching things that belong to the government		1.82	1.7	1.9	1.8	1.9	2.0	1.8
Just helping someone to pinch things		1.98	1.6	1.9	2.1	2.0	2.2	2.1
Taking someone's car just for a drive		1.72	1.6	1.6	1.8	1.7	1.8	1.9
Pinching from a shop		1.78	1.5	1.6	1.8	1.8	2.0	2.0
Taking things from where you work		1.74	1.5	1.6	1.8	1.8	2.0	1.8
Taking something that is not yours		1.74	1.6	1.6	1.8	1.8	1.9	1.9
Pinching anything at all		1.75	1.5	1.6	1.8	1.9	1.8	1.9
Pinching things from home		1.47	1.7	1.5	1.5	1.4	1.4	1.5
Robbing a bank		1.28	1.1	1.2	1.3	1.3	1.4	1.4
Breaking into a place and taking things		1.35	1.2	1.2	1.3	1.4	1.6	1.6
Doing a hold-up		1.24	1.1	1.1	1.3	1.3	1.4	1.4
Pinching things from a friend		1.33	1.2	1.3	1.4	1.3	1.4	1.4
Pinching from a little kid		1.19	1.1	1.1	1.2	1.3	1.2	1.3
Pinching from an old lady		1.06	1.1	1.0	1.1	1.0	1.1	1.1
Averages		1.94	1.69	1.80	1.95	1.96	2.10	2.03

*Computed by allotting weights to each rating, as follows
Quite all right 5
Nothing much wrong 4
A bit wrong 3
Fairly wrong 2
Very wrong 1
Score range = 1.0 – 5.0
The higher the score the more 'all right' boy thinks it is

† A — Professional, semi-professional, executive
B — Highly skilled
C — Skilled
D — Moderately skilled
E — Semi-skilled
F — Unskilled

Figure 5.2
Permissiveness related to the occupational level

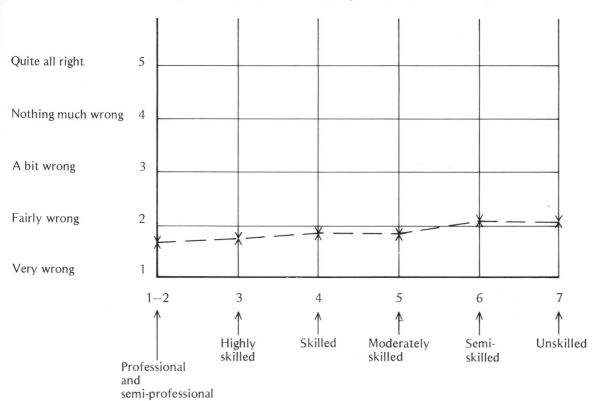

On this evidence, permissiveness: (a) increases in going from those with public-school background, to grammar school, to comprehensive school, to secondary-modern school; (b) increases in going from Jewish to Protestant to Catholic boys and even more in going to boys of *no* religion at all; (c) is little related to the age of boys in the range thirteen to sixteen years. At the level of the individual type of theft, 'pinching things from home' and 'pinching from an old lady' do not appear to conform to the trend for the overall average.

Permissiveness analysed by other characteristics of boys

In Table 5.5, permissiveness is expressed in terms of two different indices, namely percentage of the different types of theft which a boy says it is 'quite all right' to do (= index *a*) and the weighted average of ratings (index *b*). The latter index has already been featured in several tables of this chapter, namely Tables 5.2 to 5.4. The other index, *a*, is an index of the *breadth* or variety of a boy's permissiveness. The two should broadly reflect each other but they do relate to slightly different things.

Tables 5.2 to 5.4 had between them indicated the extent of the relationship of index *b* to each of 'occupational level of fathers', 'school last attended', 'religion' and 'age'. The findings with respect to the index of *variety* of permissiveness (i.e. *a*) are broadly the same,

namely a tendency for variety of permissiveness: to increase as we go down the occupational scale and down the educational scale; to maximize for boys with 'no' religion and to minimize for Jewish boys.

Table 5.5 takes the comparison to further sections of the boy population, with results some of which may be unexpected.

1 On either index, permissiveness is relatively low when boys are exposed to all sources of honesty teaching (i.e. church, school, home). Where there is only one source, permissiveness is at its greatest — indeed, greater than when there is no source at all.

2 Permissiveness is greater when boys have a lot of association with thieves ... and less when there is no association.

3 Permissiveness is greater for boys who want to spend none of their time at home, falls off with each increase in the amount of time boys want to spend at home, but rises for boys who want to spend all of their time at home.

4 Boys who say they are not punished at all by their parents and those who are punished a lot are more permissive than those who are punished to some intermediate degree.

Table 5.3
Average right/wrong ratings*
of different types of theft
analysed by schooling and
religion
(3,113 cases, weighted)

Type of theft*	All cases	School attended				Nominal religion				
	All	Secondary modern	Comprehensive	Grammar	Public	Protestant	Catholic	Other Christian	Jewish	None
Sample size (weighted)	3,113	1,464	549	718	257	1,370	500	176	214	621
Keeping something you found	3.33	3.4	3.4	3.4	3.1	3.2	3.3	3.2	3.1	3.6
Taking things just left lying around	2.72	2.9	2.6	2.6	2.5	2.7	2.8	2.8	2.3	3.0
Taking pencils or rubbers from school	2.70	2.8	2.7	2.6	2.4	2.7	2.7	2.8	2.3	3.0
Buying things you know were pinched	2.50	2.6	2.7	2.4	2.1	2.5	2.5	2.4	1.9	2.8
Pinching from someone who has plenty	2.33	2.5	2.4	2.1	1.8	2.3	2.4	2.3	1.8	2.6
Pinching something quite small	2.34	2.5	2.3	2.2	1.8	2.3	2.6	2.4	1.7	2.5
Pinching from someone who is rich	2.13	2.3	2.2	1.9	1.6	2.0	2.2	2.1	1.6	2.5
Just keeping a look-out for mates who are stealing	2.20	2.3	2.2	2.0	1.8	2.2	2.3	2.3	1.7	2.4
Pinching things from a big company	1.96	2.1	2.1	1.9	1.5	1.9	2.2	1.8	1.4	2.3
Taking little things from where you work	2.08	2.2	2.0	2.1	1.7	2.0	2.2	2.1	1.6	2.3
Taking things from Woolworths	1.90	2.1	2.0	1.8	1.3	1.9	2.0	1.8	1.4	2.2
Pinching things that belong to the government	1.82	1.8	1.9	1.8	1.7	1.7	1.9	1.6	1.6	2.2
Just helping someone to pinch things	1.98	2.1	2.0	1.9	1.5	2.0	2.1	2.0	1.5	2.2
Taking someone's car just for a drive	1.72	1.8	1.7	1.7	1.5	1.7	1.9	1.5	1.6	1.8
Pinching from a shop	1.78	1.9	1.8	1.7	1.3	1.8	1.9	1.7	1.3	2.0
Taking things from where you work	1.74	1.9	1.7	1.7	1.4	1.7	1.7	1.7	1.5	1.9
Taking something that is not yours	1.74	1.9	1.7	1.6	1.5	1.7	1.9	1.6	1.3	2.0
Pinching anything at all	1.75	1.9	1.8	1.6	1.4	1.7	1.8	1.7	1.4	2.0
Pinching things from home	1.47	1.5	1.3	1.6	1.7	1.4	1.5	1.4	1.7	1.5
Robbing a bank	1.28	1.4	1.4	1.2	1.0	1.3	1.4	1.2	1.0	1.4
Breaking into a place and taking things	1.35	1.5	1.4	1.2	1.1	1.3	1.4	1.3	1.1	1.5
Doing a hold-up	1.24	1.3	1.3	1.1	1.0	1.2	1.3	1.2	1.0	1.3
Pinching things from a friend	1.33	1.4	1.3	1.3	1.2	1.3	1.4	1.2	1.3	1.4
Pinching from a little kid	1.19	1.3	1.2	1.1	1.1	1.2	1.3	1.2	1.0	1.2
Pinching from an old lady	1.06	1.1	1.1	1.1	1.1	1.0	1.1	1.1	1.1	1.1
Averages	1.94	2.02	1.93	1.82	1.60	1.87	1.99	1.86	1.57	2.11

*Computed by allotting weights to each rating, as follows

Quite all right	5
Nothing much wrong	4
A bit wrong	3
Fairly wrong	2
Very wrong	1

Score range = 1.0 − 5.0
The higher the score the more 'all right' boy thinks it is

No particular explanation is offered of the several oddities set out above but it may well be that extended consideration of them will suggest an insightful solution. On the other hand the oddities may simply be a function of some of the small sub-samples involved.

Permissiveness and past involvement in stealing
Boys' permissiveness with regard to stealing was analysed by their past involvement in stealing and the results are set out in Tables 5.6 to 5.8. As in previous references to association tables of this kind, it must be emphasized that a numerical association does not necessarily involve *causal* association. In each of Tables 5.6 to 5.8, boys are split into four quartile groups in terms of the extent of their past involvement in stealing — a least-involved quartile (Q.1), a most-involved quartile (Q.4) and two intermediate quartiles (Q.2 and Q.3).

Table 5.6 compares the permissiveness of the four groups of boys with respect to each of the twenty-five types of theft studied. According to Table 5.6 — and perhaps not surprisingly — there is a positive relationship between extent of involvement in stealing and degree of permissiveness towards it. This relationship applies not only to the twenty-four types of theft taken in combination, but to most of them considered separately, the exceptions being: 'pinching things from home', 'pinching from a friend', 'pinching from a little kid', 'pinching from an old lady'.

Table 5.4
Average right/wrong ratings* of different types of theft analysed by boys' ages and by amount of stealing done
(3,113 cases, weighted)

Type of theft	All cases	Age of boy			
		12/13	14	15	16/17
Sample size (weighted)	3,113	721	782	754	856
Keeping something you found	3.33	3.3	3.3	3.4	3.4
Taking things just left lying around	2.72	2.8	2.8	2.7	2.7
Taking pencils or rubbers from school	2.70	2.7	2.6	2.8	2.8
Buying things you know were pinched	2.50	2.4	2.4	2.5	2.7
Pinching from someone who has plenty	2.33	2.4	2.3	2.3	2.3
Pinching something quite small	2.34	2.4	2.4	2.3	2.4
Pinching from someone who is rich	2.13	2.0	2.2	2.2	2.2
Just keeping a look-out for mates who are stealing	2.20	2.2	2.2	2.2	2.1
Pinching things from a big company	1.96	1.8	2.0	2.1	2.0
Taking little things from where you work	2.08	2.0	2.0	2.0	2.2
Taking things from Woolworths	1.90	1.9	1.9	1.9	1.9
Pinching things that belong to the government	1.82	1.6	1.7	1.8	2.1
Just helping someone to pinch things	1.98	2.0	2.0	1.9	2.0
Taking someone's car just for a drive	1.72	1.7	1.7	1.7	1.8
Pinching from a shop	1.78	1.8	1.8	1.7	1.8
Taking things from where you work	1.74	1.7	1.7	1.6	2.0
Taking something that is not yours	1.74	1.8	1.8	1.7	1.8
Pinching anything at all	1.75	1.8	1.7	1.7	1.8
Pinching things from home	1.47	1.6	1.5	1.4	1.4
Robbing a bank	1.28	1.2	1.2	1.3	1.4
Breaking into a place and taking things	1.35	1.3	1.3	1.3	1.4
Doing a hold-up	1.24	1.2	1.2	1.2	1.3
Pinching things from a friend	1.33	1.5	1.4	1.3	1.3
Pinching from a little kid	1.19	1.3	1.3	1.2	1.1
Pinching from an old lady	1.06	1.1	1.1	1.1	1.0
Averages	1.94	1.90	1.90	1.89	1.96

*Computed by allotting weights to each rating as follows:
Quite all right   5
Nothing much wrong   4
A bit wrong   3
Fairly wrong   2
Very wrong   1
Score range = 1.0 − 5.0
The higher the range the more 'all right' boy thinks it is

Table 5.5
Indices of permissiveness analysed by characteristics of boys

a = Percentage of the twenty-five types of theft rated as 'quite' all right'

b = Weighted average of ratings, when 5 = 'quite all right' and 1 = 'very wrong'*

(1,425 cases, unweighted)

Characteristics	a Variety index 4.21	b Overall averag 1.94
Index of instructions about not pinching		
No source	4.75	1.94
One source only	5.19	2.04
Two sources	4.53	1.97
Three sources	2.78	1.81
Association with thieves		
A lot	8.07	2.22
A fair bit	5.34	2.06
Not much	2.46	1.83
None at all	—	—
Spare time spent at home		
None**	9.48	2.28
Not much	6.46	2.15
Less than half	4.10	1.99
About half	3.94	1.93
Most	2.59	1.74
All**	4.83	2.03
Punishment by parents		
A lot**	5.65	1.97
A fair bit	3.84	1.93
A little	3.94	1.93
Some (but amount not specified)	6.40	2.03
None	5.84	2.02
Born in UK?		
Yes	4.09	1.94
No	5.51	1.97

*Calculated weighted average for each of the twenty-five items when:
1 = very wrong
2 = fairly wrong
3 = a bit wrong
4 = nothing much wrong
5 = quite all right
3 = can't decide
**Less than fifty cases
— Insufficient cases for calculation of index

Table 5.6
Average permissiveness scores, item by item, for boys with different degrees of past involvement in stealing
(3,113 cases, weighted)

Types of theft	Amount of stealing done			
	0.1 749 cases	0.2 861 cases	0.3 779 cases	0.4 724 case
Keeping something you found	3.0	3.1	3.5	3.8
Taking things just left lying around	2.3	2.5	2.9	3.2
Taking pencils or rubbers from school	2.2	2.4	2.9	3.3
Buying things you know were pinched	2.0	2.2	2.7	3.1
Pinching from someone who has plenty	1.8	2.0	2.4	3.2
Pinching something quite small	2.0	2.1	2.4	3.0
Pinching from someone who is rich	1.6	1.8	2.3	2.8

continued

Table 5.6 (continued)

Types of theft	Amount of stealing done			
	Q.1	Q.2	Q.3	Q.4
	749 cases	861 cases	779 cases	724 cases
Just keeping a look-out for mates who are stealing	1.7	2.0	2.4	2.8
Pinching things from a big company	1.5	1.7	2.0	2.8
Taking little things from where you work	1.7	1.9	2.2	2.6
Taking things from Woolworths	1.4	1.7	2.0	2.6
Pinching things that belong to the government	1.4	1.6	2.0	2.4
Just helping someone to pinch things	1.6	1.7	2.2	2.6
Taking someone's car just for a drive	1.4	1.6	1.8	2.1
Pinching from a shop	1.3	1.5	1.9	2.4
Taking things from where you work	1.4	1.6	1.9	2.2
Taking something that is not yours	1.4	1.5	1.8	2.3
Pinching anything at all	1.5	1.5	1.8	2.3
Pinching things from home	1.5	1.5	1.5	1.4
Robbing a bank	1.1	1.1	1.3	1.7
Breaking into a place and taking things	1.1	1.2	1.3	1.8
Doing a hold-up	1.1	1.1	1.2	1.6
Pinching things from a friend	1.3	1.3	1.4	1.3
Pinching from a little kid	1.2	1.2	1.2	1.2
Pinching from an old lady	1.1	1.0	1.1	1.0
Averages	1.58	1.71	2.00	2.38

*Q.1 = low score quartile; Q.4 = top score quartile

Table 5.7
Permissiveness related to
variety and amount of
stealing
3,113 cases, weighted

Permissiveness score (based on weighted average of all 25 ratings)*	All cases	Indices of variety of stealing				Indices of amount of stealing			
		Low-score Quartile Q.1	Q.2	Q.3	High-score Quartile Q.4	Low-score quartile Q.1	Q.2	Q.3	High-score quartile Q.4
No. of cases (weighted)	3,113	771	769	882	751	749	861	779	724
	(%)	(%)	(%)	(%)	(%)	(%)	(%)	(%)	(%)
Higher score*	28.4	8.4	13.0	31.9	46.8	8.2	15.4	30.6	45.8
Intermediate score	35.2	23.0	29.7	28.4	18.9	23.5	35.1	22.4	19.0
Lower score	35.1	39.7	28.6	20.3	11.3	37.7	29.7	23.1	9.5
No information	1.3								
All	100.0								

*Higher score: weighted mean of all twenty-five ratings = 2.3 or more
Intermediate score: weighted mean of all twenty-five ratings = 1.6 − 2.2
Lower score: weighted mean of all twenty-five ratings = 1.5 or less

Table 5.8
Two different indices of permissiveness related to amount and variety of stealing (3113 cases weighted)

Permissiveness indices	All cases	Index of variety of stealing				Index of amount of stealing			
		Q.1†	Q.2	Q.3	Q.4	Q.1	Q.2	Q.3	Q.4
No. of Cases (Weighted)	3,113	771	769	882	751	749	861	779	724
a Permissiveness expressed as per cent of theft types rated as 'quite all right'	4.21	1.1	1.5	4.5	10.0	1.0	1.7	3.8	10.4
b Permissiveness expressed as the mean of attitude ratings on a 5-point scale*	1.94	1.6	1.7	2.0	2.4	1.6	1.7	2.0	2.4

*A five-point scale where: quite all right = 5, nothing much wrong = 4, a bit wrong = 3, fairly wrong = 2, very wrong = 1, can't decide = 3
†Where Q.1 is the quartile least involved in stealing and Q.4 the quartile most involved in stealing

Table 5.7 compares the theft involvements of boys with high, low and intermediate indices of permissiveness. Its factual content overlaps that of Table 5.6 but also goes beyond it in that theft involvement is expressed both as variety of past stealing and amount of past stealing. The association between permissiveness and stealing is, on this evidence, a substantial one.

Table 5.8 compares the theft involvement of boys with different degrees of permissiveness, where permissiveness is expressed directly in terms of indices a and b.

Table 5.8 confirms the evidence of Table 5.7, namely that permissiveness is substantially correlated with the extent and variety of past involvement in stealing.

Response distributions relating to generalized attitude towards law-support

The detail of this section of the report relates to the second part of Hypothesis 1, namely Sub-Hypothesis 1b which took the following form:

Table 5.10
Extent of agreement with statements about stealing, expressed as weighted means and analysed by characteristics of boys
(3,113 cases, weighted)

Statements put to boys	All cases	Occupational level					
		Professional/ semi-prof.	Highly skilled	Skilled	Moderately skilled	Semi-skilled	Unskilled
Cases (weighted)	3,113	518	514	674	630	517	254
†Stealing is wrong	1.19**	1.1	1.2**	1.2	1.2	1.3	1.3
†Anyone who steals should be punished	1.47	1.4	1.5	1.5	1.5	1.4	1.5
†We should help the police to catch people who pinch things	1.68	1.5	1.7	1.7	1.7	1.8	1.7
*If you know someone who is stealing, you should keep it to yourself	2.14	1.9	2.1	2.2	2.2	2.4	2.2
†If someone I hated was pinching, I would tell on him	2.20	2.1	2.2	2.2	2.3	2.2	2.2
†If you know someone is stealing, you should tell on him	2.26	2.0	2.3	2.3	2.3	2.4	2.3
*Sometimes it is all right to steal	1.67	1.5	1.6	1.7	1.7	1.8	1.8
Average items	1.80	1.64	1.80	1.83	1.84	1.90	1.86

*Score range = 1.0—3.0: the *higher* the score the more boy agrees with the statement
**These figures are weighted averages for the sample or the sub-sample concerned. Thus for statement 1, agree = 1, partly agree = 2, disagree = 3, can't decide = 2. Hence an average rating of 1.19 is between agree and partly agree but is much nearer to agree. And for this item, a high average figure indicates a tendency towards non-support of the law, while a low figure

Table 5.9

Boys' general views about stealing and about reporting thefts to the police

Statements put to boys	Extent of agreement or disagreement with statements				
	Agree	Partially agree	Disagree	Can't decide	No evidence
	(%)	(%)	(%)	(%)	(%)
1 Stealing is wrong*	82	12	4	1	1
2 Sometimes it is all right to steal	16	33	46	4	2
3 Anyone who steals should be punished	59	28	10	2	2
4 We should help the police to catch people who pinch things	44	35	16	4	2
5 If you know someone is stealing, you should tell on him	19	25	48	5	2
6 If someone I hated was pinching, I would tell on him	22	22	45	9	2
7 If you know someone who is stealing, you should keep it to yourself	37	34	20	7	1

*For statements 1, 3 to 6, the following weights are linked to the ratings: agree = 1, partly agree = 2, disagree = 3, can't decide = 2

For statements 2 and 7, the following weights are linked to the ratings: agree = 3, partly agree = 2, disagree = 1, can't decide = 2

Boys take up stealing and continue to steal partly because they are without any generalized opposition to stealing.

The variable central to this hypothesis is sometimes referred to hereunder as 'support or non-support' for the law.

Response distributions for each of the seven generalized attitude items

The distributions of responses in the card-sorting procedure involved in Q.2 were as set out in Table 5.9. There are several challenging features to Table 5.9.

School attended				Religion					Age			
Secondary modern	Compre- hensive	Grammar	Public	Protestant	Catholic	Other Christian	Jewish	None	12/ 13	14	15	16/ 17
1,464	549	718	257	1,370	500	176	214	621	721	782	754	856
1.2	1.2	1.2	1.1	1.2	1.2	1.2	1.2	1.3	1.2	1.2	1.1	1.2
1.5	1.5	1.4	1.5	1.5	1.5	1.7	1.4	1.5	1.4	1.5	1.5	1.5
1.8	1.7	1.6	1.4	1.6	1.7	1.8	1.4	1.8	1.6	1.6	1.8	1.7
2.2	2.2	2.0	2.1	2.1	2.2	2.2	1.9	2.2	2.0	2.2	2.2	2.2
2.2	2.3	2.2	2.2	2.2	2.4	2.0	2.0	2.2	2.0	2.3	2.3	2.2
2.3	2.4	2.1	2.1	2.3	2.3	2.2	2.1	2.3	2.2	2.3	2.3	2.3
1.7	1.7	1.6	1.5	1.7	1.7	1.7	1.4	1.8	1.6	1.7	1.6	1.7
1.84	1.84	1.71	1.70	1.74	1.86	1.83	1.63	1.87	1.71	1.83	1.83	1.83

indicates a tendency towards support of the law. In some of the other statements, namely those marked with an asterisk, an opposite weighting system is used but the outcome of the final figure is the same: a high average indicates a tendency towards non-support of the law and vice versa

†Score range = 1.0–3.0: the *lower* the score the more boy agrees with the statement

1 Relatively few disagreed with the statement that 'stealing is wrong' but only 46 per cent appear to have taken the view that it is *always* wrong to steal. In other words, it appears that many of the boys interviewed felt *both* that stealing is wrong and that there were operational exceptions. This of course is fully in line with the findings so far reported; and it indicates that boy-morality in this matter is by no means subject to easy generalizations.

2 In line with the position described above, only 59 per cent would agree that anyone who steals should be punished, and less (44 per cent) that 'we should help the police catch those who pinch things'.

3 The foregoing rather tentative position about the morality of stealing and about the case for apprehending and punishing thieves shows its fuller form in the mere 19 per cent who agreed that they *should tell* on anyone they knew to be stealing. When one adds the condition that the thief is someone hated by the respondent, the 19 per cent lifts to only 22 per cent evidence of the firmness of the attitude that one should not tell.

Anyone seeking to develop in boys a hole-proof resistance to stealing in any form and a willingness to report thieving whenever they come across it, will need to keep in mind both the reluctance of many boys to condemn stealing outright and their widespread reluctance to report people known to be stealing.

Table 5.11
Relating 'non-support' for the law to past involvement in stealing

	Index of amount			
	0.1	0.2	0.3	0.4
Statements put to boys				
Cases (weighted)	749	861	779	724
†Stealing is wrong	1.1	1.1	1.2	1.3
†Anyone who steals should be punished	1.3	1.4	1.6	1.6
†We should help the police to catch people who pinch things	1.4	1.6	1.7	2.1
*If you know someone who is stealing, you should keep it to yourself	1.9	2.0	2.3	2.4
†If someone I hated was pinching, I would tell on him	2.1	2.2	2.3	2.3
†If you know someone is stealing, you should tell on him	2.0	2.2	2.4	2.5
*Sometimes it is all right to steal	1.4	1.6	1.7	2.0
Average items	1.60	1.73	1.89	2.03

*Score range = 1.0–3.0: the *higher* the score the more boy agrees with the statement
†Score range = 1.0–3.0: the *lower* the score the more boy agrees with the statement

Response distribution according to characteristics of boys
Responses to the generalized statements about stealing were analysed by various characteristics of boys: father occupation, school last attended, religion, age. Results are given in Table 5.10.

In Table 5.10, the numerical values are all weighted averages and the larger the average, the less the boy's tendency to be supportive of the law with respect to stealing.

There is some evidence of 'tendency to support the law' (in the sense defined in this context) to decrease as one goes down the occupational and the educational scales. Such trends or differences are small, however, and the outstanding indication of Table 5.10 is that the level of boys' support of the law is of the same general order in the different occupational, educational, age and religious sectors.

Response distribution according to past involvement in stealing
Table 5.11 shows the extent of variation in 'law support' according to the extent of boys' past involvement in stealing. The greater the boys' past involvement in stealing, the less is his 'law supportiveness'.

Response distributions according to other factors
In Table 5.12, the analysis of 'law-supportiveness' is taken further. For brevity of expression, the measure of 'support' had been reduced to an index consisting of the mean of the ratings of all the individual statements, just as in Table 5.10 (see Footnote** to that table for weighting system used).

One indication of the evidence in Table 5.12 is that 'law supportiveness': is greater as the number of sources of instruction (not to steal) increases; is greater as the proportion of a boy's time spent at home increases; is less as the amount of the boy's association with thieves increases. Amount of punishment by parents seems little related to 'law supportiveness' except for cases where there is *no* punishment — for whom 'law supportiveness' is at a slightly higher level. Boys born outside the United Kingdom appear to be more supportive of law than boys born in the United Kingdom.

Investigating Sub-Hypothesis 1a
Just as in previous chapters, the central strategy for investigating this sub-hypothesis was to derive from it expectations and to test these. See Chapter 1 for details of this approach. The expectations in this case were as follows.

Expectation 1 Boys who are permissive in their attitudes towards stealing do more stealing than other boys and this applies even when the latter are closely matched to the former in terms of the correlates of stealing.

Table 5.12

Index* of belief that action should be taken against thieves, analysed by several background factors

Background factor	Index of 'law supportiveness'**
Claimed source of instruction about not stealing (maximum of 3 sources)	
No source	1.84
One source only	1.81
Two sources	1.78
Three sources	1.68
Association with thieves	
A lot	1.96
A fair bit	1.85
Not much	1.71
Not at all	1.42
Amount of spare time spent at home	
None	2.03
Not much	1.91
Less than half	1.84
About half	1.73
Most	1.64
All	1.69
No information	–
Punishment by parents	
A lot	1.76
A fair bit	1.77
A little	1.75
('Some' but amount not stated)	1.85
None	1.67
Born in UK?	
Yes	1.77
No	1.67

*The index is calculated as detailed in the footnote to Table 5.10
**The smaller the index, the greater the law-supportiveness

Expectation 2 Boys who are more permissive in attitude towards stealing will tend to continue with relatively serious stealing over a longer period of time than other boys and this applies even when the latter are closely matched to the former in terms of the correlates of stealing.

Testing Expectation 1

The method used was the matching technique which was described in Chapter 1 and applied in Chapters 2, 3 and 4. The total sample was broken into three groups according to degree of permissiveness. Degree of permissiveness was calculated through respondent ratings of how right or wrong they regarded each of the twenty-five acts. Each of these acts could, it will be remembered, be rated as 'quite all right' or 'nothing much wrong with it' or 'a bit wrong' or 'fairly wrong' or 'very wrong' or 'can't decide'. These ratings were given weights of 5, 4, 3, 2, 1, 3 respectively and these weights were now used to calculate a weighted mean for each boy, based on all of his twenty-five ratings. This weighted mean was his 'permissiveness' score and the three-way split of the total sample in terms of this score took the form shown in figure 5.3.

Within the rationale of 'testing by matching' shown in Figure 5.3, Group 3 was called the qualifying group and Group 1 the control group. Group 2 was left out of the matching procedure so that the qualifying and control groups might be considered unambiguous in terms of the hypothesis. Group 1 was now matched to Group 3 in terms of the composite of correlates of stealing as defined in Chapter 1. Results are set out in the top two rows of Table 5.13.

On this evidence the control on the qualifying groups are markedly different even after close matching in terms of the correlates of stealing. Expectation 1 is thus strongly verified.

Testing Expectation 2

The same procedure was used in testing Expectation 2, with results as shown in the bottom row of Table 5.13. Expectation 2 is substantially verified.

Table 5.13

Differences between qualifiers and controls before and after matching: variety, amount and duration of stealing

Indices of stealing	Unadjusted average score for qualifiers a	Unadjusted average score for controls b	Adjusted average score for controls c	Differences between qualifiers and adj. controls a–c P	Difference a–c as percentage of c
Averaged variety score	19.13	9.47	10.86	8.27 (0.01)	76
Averaged amount score	146.15	59.58	71.91	74.24 (0.01)	103
Duration of stealing	5.03	2.94	3.38	1.65 (0.01)	49

Figure 5.3
Division of sample

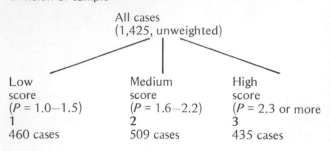

All cases
(1,425, unweighted)

Low score ($P = 1.0-1.5$) 1 460 cases	Medium score ($P = 1.6-2.2$) 2 509 cases	High score ($P = 2.3$ or more 3 435 cases

Summing-up on the expectation tests

Each of the expectations was borne out, thereby strengthening Sub-Hypothesis 1a that: 'Boys take up stealing and continue to steal partly because they have permissive attitudes towards stealing'.

Investigating Sub-Hypothesis 1b

It will be recalled that Sub-Hypothesis 1b was:

Boys take up stealing and continue to steal partly because they are without any form of generalized opposition to stealing.

This sub-hypothesis was not investigated separately principally because of heavy demand on computing facilities and also because it seemed too similar to Sub-Hypothesis 1a to warrant the analysis it called for.

5 METHODS AND FINDINGS RELATED TO THE INVESTIGATION OF HYPOTHESES 2 & 3

The Nature of Hypotheses 2 and 3

These two hypotheses were as follows:

Boys take up stealing and continue to steal partly because they are lacking in any sense of remorse in relation to stealing (Hypothesis 2).

Boys take up stealing and continue to steal partly because they have received relatively little instruction about not stealing (Hypothesis 3).

The Questions Asked of Boys in Terms of the Variables Hypothesized as Causal

The two sets of questions asked in relation to Hypotheses 2 and 3 were as set out below under I and II.

I *Concerning potential for remorse*

Q.4 Would he feel badly about pinching of the kind he rated as wrong?

> NOW TAKE A SECOND PACK OF GREEN CARDS AND PREPARE TO HAVE BOY SORT THEM INTO THE *GREEN AND PURPLE BAGS.*

PUT UP THESE BAGS WITH 'WOULD NOT FEEL SORRY' ON LEFT AND 'WOULD FEEL VERY SORRY' ON RIGHT.
SAY:

'This time I want you to pretend that you had done whatever is on the card. *Just pretend you have done it.*
'This first one is "Pinching from someone who is rich." Just supposing you had done *that*, how would you feel about it? *Just put it in the bag that shows how you would feel about it.*'
'I won't look where you put it ... But *please* be absolutely straight with me.'
'If you think you'd NOT feel sorry, put it *there*' (POINT TO THAT BAG). 'If you think you'd feel a BIT sorry put it *there*' (POINT).'*Here* if you'd feel FAIRLY SORRY and *here* if you'd feel VERY SORRY. Just put it in the bag that shows how you would *really* feel.'
'I won't watch where you put them. *Start with the one gave you.*'

> NOW PASS REST ONE AT A TIME. EACH FOURTH OR FIFTH CARD, REMIND HIM TO PUT IT IN THE BAG THAT SHOWS HOW HE WOULD *REALLY* FEEL.
> TAKE DOWN BAGS AND PUT TO ONE SIDE *WITH CONTENTS IN.*

Q.5 When did he first feel this way about stealing, and what led to this?

SAY:

5a 'Now we have been finding out how you feel these days about pinching things. I want to ask you a few more things about that.'
'How old were you when you first started to feel *the way you do these days* about pinching things?'
> (CLARIFY IF NECESSARY THAT YOU MEAN *WHATEVER* HIS OPINIONS OR FEELINGS ACTUALLY ARE).
> EXCLUDE ANY CHANGE *WE* HAVE PRODUCED. CHALLENGE HIS CHOICE OF AGE AND THEN ENTER AGE ...

5b 'Exactly what started you feeling the way you do these days about pinching?' (PROBE HARD) 'What else made you feel the way you do these days about pinching things?'

The cards selected in this operation were the same twenty-five as were involved in the 'Permissiveness' sorting (see p. 173 for a full list of the twenty-five acts concerned).
The point of Q.5b in this section of questions was to find out if the respondent denied that it was stealing itself that led to, or contributed to his potential for, feeling remorse about stealing. More will be said about this in the statement on 'Investigating Hypotheses 2 and 3' (p. 197).

2.3 His training in right/wrong in relation to pinching.

a 'Did anyone ever try to teach you about *not
inching*?'   YES/NO
WHETHER 'YES' OR 'NO', CHECK AS FOLLOWS
in b, c, d.

b 'What about at home?'   YES/NO/
IF 'YES':

'At home, who tried to teach you about not pinching?'
i 'How much of the teaching did you get at home?'
SHOW CARD. (A LITTLE/A LOT/IN BETWEEN)

3c 'What about at school?'   YES/NO/
IF 'YES':
i 'At school, who tried to teach you about not
pinching?'
ii 'How much of this teaching did you get at school?'
SHOW CARD. (A LITTLE/A LOT/IN BETWEEN)

3d 'What about at church/chapel/synagogue?'
YES/NO/
IF 'YES':
i 'At . . ., who tried to teach you about not pinching?'
ii 'How *much* of this teaching did you get at . . .?'
SHOW CARD. (A LITTLE/A LOT/IN BETWEEN)

Table 5.14
Potential remorse or
regret for each of
twenty-five acts of
theft
(1,425 cases, unweighted)

Ratings of extent of remorse if he did the act
concerned

Type of theft*	Not sorry	Bit sorry	Fairly sorry	Very sorry	Can't decide or no evidence
	(%)	(%)	(%)	(%)	(%)
Keeping something you found	55	24	11	4	6
Taking pencils or rubbers from school	45	29	16	8	3
Taking things just left lying around	38	29	19	11	4
Pinching from someone who is rich	36	26	19	15	4
Buying things you know were pinched	36	26	21	14	4
Pinching from someone who has plenty	33	25	22	16	4
Pinching something quite small	30	34	20	13	3
Taking things from Woolworths	29	25	24	19	3
Just keeping a lookout for mates who are stealing	27	28	26	17	3
Pinching things from a big company	27	21	22	27	3
Pinching things that belong to the government	23	18	21	35	3
Just helping someone to pinch things	21	30	25	22	2
Taking little things from where you work	21	27	26	24	3
Robbing a bank	18	14	17	49	3
Pinching from a shop	17	25	28	28	2
Taking someone's car just for a drive	16	20	27	35	2
Taking something that is not yours	15	24	30	28	2
Taking things from where you work	14	23	25	35	3
Pinching anything at all	14	25	30	28	3
Doing a hold-up	13	14	20	52	2
Breaking into a place and taking things	11	20	23	44	2
Pinching things from home	4	11	16	68	2
Pinching things from a friend	2	10	22	64	2
Pinching from a little kid	2	7	15	74	2
Pinching from an old lady	2	2	5	89	2
Average items	22	22	21	33	3

*These items are arranged in order according to the proportion
answering 'not sorry'
— = Less than 0.5 per cent

Response Distributions Relating to Potential for Remorse over Stealing

Response distributions for each of the twenty-five acts asked about

Each of the twenty-five acts of theft had been rated by boys in terms of the degree to which they would be sorry if they had committed it, namely:

I would feel *very* sorry about it ⎫
I would feel *fairly* sorry about it ⎬ If I had done this
I would feel *a bit* sorry about it ⎪
I would *not* feel sorry about it ⎭
I can't decide

Table 5.14 presents the distribution of responses for each of the twenty-five acts.

The indications of Table 5.14 are similar to those of Table 5.1.

1 There is considerable variation in the degree to which different types of theft evoke an expression of regret. Thus, while 55 per cent said they would *not* feel sorry about keeping something found, 23 per cent would not feel sorry at 'pinching things belonging to the government' and only 2 per cent felt they would take this view over 'pinching from an old lady'.

Table 5.15

Potential remorse or regret for each of twenty-five acts of theft, analysed by occupational level of father and age of boy*

(3,113 cases, weighted)

Type of theft	All	Occupational level of fathers						Age of boy			
		A	B	C	D	E	F	12/ 13	14	15	16/ 17
Maximum cases (weighted)	3,113	518	514	674	630	517	254	721	782	754	856
Keeping something you found	3.21	3.2	3.3	3.2	3.2	3.1	3.3	3.1	3.2	3.3	3.3
Taking pencils or rubbers from school	3.05	3.0	3.1	3.0	3.1	3.1	3.1	2.8	3.1	3.1	3.2
Taking things just left lying around	2.87	3.0	2.8	2.8	2.9	2.9	2.9	2.8	3.0	2.9	2.8
Pinching from someone who is rich	2.74	2.5	2.7	2.7	2.9	2.8	2.9	2.5	2.8	2.8	2.9
Buying things you know were pinched	2.75	2.6	2.8	2.8	2.8	2.8	2.8	2.6	2.8	2.8	2.9
Pinching from someone who has plenty	2.69	2.7	2.6	2.7	2.8	2.7	2.8	2.5	2.7	2.8	2.8
Pinching something quite small	2.76	2.6	2.7	2.7	2.9	2.8	2.9	2.6	2.9	2.8	2.8
Taking things from Woolworths	2.59	2.6	2.6	2.5	2.7	2.6	2.6	2.4	2.7	2.6	2.7
Just keeping a look-out for mates who are stealing	2.60	2.4	2.5	2.6	2.7	2.7	2.7	2.5	2.7	2.6	2.6
Pinching things from a big company	2.42	2.3	2.3	2.4	2.4	2.5	2.6	2.2	2.4	2.4	2.6
Pinching things that belong to the government	2.24	2.3	2.2	2.2	2.3	2.3	2.3	2.0	2.2	2.2	2.6
Just helping someone to pinch things	2.43	2.3	2.4	2.4	2.5	2.5	2.5	2.3	2.6	2.5	2.4
Taking little things from where you work	2.39	2.4	2.3	2.3	2.5	2.5	2.6	2.3	2.4	2.3	2.5
Robbing a bank	1.95	1.9	1.8	2.0	2.0	2.0	2.0	1.8	1.9	1.9	2.2
Pinching from a shop	2.27	2.2	2.2	2.3	2.4	2.3	2.3	2.2	2.4	2.3	2.3
Taking someone's car just for a drive	2.13	2.2	2.2	2.1	2.1	2.2	2.1	2.0	2.2	2.1	2.2
Taking something that is not yours	2.21	2.1	2.1	2.2	2.3	2.4	2.1	2.1	2.2	2.2	2.3
Taking things from where you work	2.12	2.1	2.0	2.1	2.2	2.3	2.2	2.0	2.1	2.1	2.3
Pinching anything at all	2.19	2.1	2.0	2.1	2.2	2.4	2.3	2.1	2.3	2.2	2.3
Doing a hold-up	1.84	1.7	1.7	1.9	1.9	1.9	1.9	1.7	1.9	1.8	2.0
Breaking into a place and taking things	1.93	1.8	1.9	1.9	2.0	2.0	2.1	1.8	2.0	1.9	2.0
Pinching things from home	1.47	1.7	1.5	1.5	1.4	1.4	1.5	1.5	1.5	1.4	1.4
Pinching things from a friend	1.47	1.4	1.4	1.5	1.5	1.6	1.4	1.6	1.5	1.4	1.4
Pinching from a little kid	1.34	1.3	1.3	1.3	1.4	1.4	1.5	1.4	1.4	1.3	1.3
Pinching from an old lady	1.13	1.2	1.2	1.1	1.1	1.1	1.1	1.1	1.2	1.1	1.1
Average items	2.27	2.22	2.22	2.25	2.33	2.33	2.34	2.16	2.32	2.27	2.36

*Computed by allotting weights to each rating as follows:

Not sorry	4
Bit sorry	3
Fairly sorry	2
Very sorry	1

A = Professional, semi-professional, executive
B = Highly skilled
C = Skilled
D = Moderately skilled
E = Semi-skilled
F = Unskilled

2 With the exception of 'pinching from an old lady', not more than 75 per cent would feel 'very sorry' about any of the acts in the list and only 52 per cent said they would feel 'very sorry' over 'doing a hold-up'.

3 Other noteworthy results are as follows:

a In this imaginary scene, 'pinching things from home' is a matter for greater potential remorse than 'doing a hold-up'.

b Thirty-six per cent said they would *not* be sorry over buying things they knew were pinched.

c The apparent monetary dimensions of the different acts appear to be out of step with the level of potential remorse put against them.

Potential remorse related to the characteristics of boys: occupational level, age, schooling, religion

Comparisons were made of the potential remorse in various sectors of the population, i.e. in terms of occupational level, type of school last attended, age, and nominal religion. The results are presented in Tables 5.15 and 5.16. The indications of Tables 5.15 and 5.16 are as follows.

1 For the average boy in the sample, and for the average act in the list of twenty-five, remorse level was between 'fairly sorry' and 'a bit sorry' but nearer the former.

Table 5.16
Potential remorse or regret for each of twenty-five acts of theft, analysed by last school attended and by nominal religion*
(3,113 cases, weighted)

Type of theft	All	School attended				Nominal religion				
		Secondary modern	Compre-hensive	Grammar	Public	Protestant	Catholic	Other Christian	Jewish	None
Maximum cases (weighted)	3,113	1,466	549	718	255	1,370	500	176	214	621
Keeping something you found	3.21	3.2	3.1	3.3	3.1	3.2	3.2	3.2	3.2	2.9
Taking pencils or rubbers from school	3.05	3.1	3.0	3.2	3.0	3.1	3.1	2.8	3.0	3.2
Taking things just left lying around	2.87	2.9	2.7	3.0	2.8	2.8	2.8	2.8	3.0	3.1
Pinching from someone who is rich	2.74	2.9	2.6	2.7	2.4	2.7	2.7	2.7	2.6	3.0
Buying things you know were pinched	2.75	2.8	2.8	2.8	2.5	2.8	2.8	2.8	2.5	2.9
Pinching from someone who has plenty	2.69	2.8	2.6	2.6	2.6	2.7	2.7	2.5	2.5	2.9
Pinching something quite small	2.76	2.8	2.6	2.9	2.5	2.7	2.8	2.8	2.7	3.0
Taking things from Woolworths	2.59	2.6	2.5	2.6	2.5	2.6	2.6	2.4	2.5	2.9
Just keeping a lookout for mates who are stealing	2.60	2.7	2.6	2.5	2.3	2.6	2.7	2.6	2.4	2.7
Pinching things from a big company	2.42	2.5	2.3	2.4	2.3	2.4	2.5	2.2	2.2	2.7
Pinching things that belong to the government	2.24	2.2	2.2	2.3	2.4	2.2	2.3	2.0	2.1	2.5
Just helping someone to pinch things	2.43	2.5	2.4	2.4	2.2	2.5	2.5	2.3	2.2	2.6
Taking little things from where you work	2.39	2.4	2.2	2.6	2.3	2.4	2.3	2.0	2.1	2.5
Robbing a bank	1.95	2.0	1.9	1.9	1.6	1.9	1.9	1.9	2.0	1.5
Pinching from a shop	2.27	2.4	2.3	2.2	2.1	2.3	2.3	2.1	2.1	2.5
Taking someone's car just for a drive	2.13	2.1	2.1	2.3	2.1	2.1	2.2	2.0	2.4	2.2
Taking something that is not yours	2.21	2.3	2.1	2.2	2.0	2.2	2.1	2.0	2.0	2.5
Taking things from where you work	2.12	2.2	2.0	2.2	2.0	2.1	2.2	2.0	2.2	2.2
Pinching anything at all	2.19	2.3	2.1	2.2	1.8	2.1	2.2	2.0	2.1	2.5
Doing a hold-up	1.84	1.9	1.8	1.7	1.6	1.8	1.9	1.7	1.9	2.0
Breaking into a place and taking things	1.93	2.1	1.9	1.9	1.6	1.9	2.0	1.9	1.8	2.1
Pinching things from home	1.47	1.4	1.3	1.6	1.6	1.4	1.5	1.3	1.5	1.5
Pinching things from a friend	1.47	1.6	1.3	1.5	1.3	1.4	1.4	1.5	1.4	1.5
Pinching from a little kid	1.34	1.4	1.3	1.4	1.2	1.3	1.4	1.3	1.5	1.4
Pinching from an old lady	1.13	1.1	1.0	1.2	1.2	1.1	1.1	1.0	1.3	1.2
Average item	2.27	2.33	2.19	2.30	2.12	2.25	2.29	2.15	2.21	2.40

*Computed by allotting weights to each rating as follows:

Not sorry	4
Bit sorry	3
Fairly sorry	2
Very sorry	1

2 There is relatively little variation in remorse level between occupational sub-groups, the greatest variation between groups (in fact the top and the bottom occupational groups) being only 0.14 in a range of 1.00 to 4.00. This similarity in rating level applies not only to the average gradings for all twenty-five acts but tends also to apply for each of the acts in its own right.

3 Younger boys (twelve to thirteen years) endorse more 'remorseful' answers than do older boys, the other age-groups tending to be much the same. This tends also to be the case to a substantial degree for all the twenty-five items considered separately.

4 For school last attended, there is some variation by type of school but it is small and irregular. In addition, boys claiming no nominal religion express less remorse than other boys, but here again the difference is not of a major order.

Response distributions according to other factors

In Table 5.17, expression of remorse is analysed by several other factors. The indications of Table 5.18 are: that 'remorse' increases when boys are subject to 'teaching' from all three sources, namely home, school, church; that 'remorse' is inversely related to the amount of time spent in association with thieves, being least when association is greatest; that it is directly related to proportion of spare time spent at home; that it is greater for boys born outside of the United Kingdom; that it is greater for boys who say they receive 'a lot' of punishment from parents.

Remorse related to past involvement in stealing

In Table 5.18 evidence is given about the association between degree of past involvement in stealing and level of claimed remorse. For all twenty-five acts considered together, there is a steady reduction in the claimed 'degree of remorse' in going from those who do least stealing to those who do most. This also applied to a substantial degree to the twenty-five acts considered separately. The exceptions include: 'pinching from an old lady', 'pinching things from home', where there is virtually no relationship to amount of stealing done.

Response distributions relating to source of instruction against stealing

The questions asked about sources of instruction against stealing are set out on p. 188 and in Appendix 5.1.

Tables 5.19 to 5.21 present the distribution of responses for all 1,425 boys (weighted to 3,113). Amongst other things, these distributions indicate:

1 The church (or chapel or synagogue) gets much less mention than either home or school as a source of instruction about not stealing — a finding presumably conditioned by many boys being non-attenders at church.

2 Seven per cent deny all three sources as providing them with any instruction 'not to steal', but 28 per cent claimed all three as sources.

3 For each source, a substantial minority claimed getting a lot of this sort of instruction (26, 19 and 15 per cent from home, school and church respectively).

For the information relating to teaching at home, there is also evidence about *who* it was who provided such teaching as was given. Table 5.22 presents this evidence.

Claimed sources of teaching analysed by characteristics of boys

Table 5.23 presents evidence about the relationship of 'number of sources' claimed and certain characteristics of boys. For occupational level, last school attended and past involvement in stealing, the evidence does not

Table 5.17
Potential remorse analysed by several background factors

Background factor	Weighted mean of ratings for all twenty-five acts*
Claimed sources of instruction about not stealing (maximum = 3 sources)	
No source	2.43
One source only	2.45
Two sources	2.37
Three sources	2.17
Association with thieves	
A lot	2.58
A fair bit	2.47
Not much	2.28
None at all	2.17
Spare time spent at home	
None	2.52
Not much	2.51
Less than half	2.40
About half	2.35
Most	2.14
All	2.21
Punishment by parents	
A lot	2.14
A fair bit	2.33
A little	2.38
None	2.37
Born in UK?	
Yes	2.42
No	2.00

*Weighted mean rating for all twenty-five acts, where 1 = very sorry, 2 = fairly sorry, 3 = a bit sorry, 4 = not sorry. *Hence the higher the mean rating the less the remorse*

Table 5.18
Average* of sorry/not sorry ratings analysed by past involvement in stealing

Types of theft	All cases	Amount of stealing done			
		Q.1	Q.2	Q.3	Q.4
Cases (weighted)	3,113	749	861	779	724
Keeping something you found	3.21	3.0	3.2	3.3	3.4
Taking things just left lying around	3.05	2.7	3.0	3.2	3.4
Taking pencils or rubbers from school	2.87	2.7	2.8	2.9	3.1
Buying things you know were pinched	2.74	2.3	2.6	2.8	3.3
Pinching from someone who has plenty	2.75	2.4	2.7	2.9	3.1
Pinching something quite small	2.69	2.3	2.6	2.7	3.1
Pinching from someone who is rich	2.76	2.4	2.7	2.9	3.1
Just keeping a look-out for mates who are stealing	2.59	2.1	2.5	2.8	3.1
Pinching things from a big company	2.60	2.2	2.5	2.7	3.1
Taking little things from where you work	2.42	2.0	2.3	2.5	2.9
Taking things from Woolworths	2.24	1.9	2.1	2.4	2.6
Pinching things that belong to the government	2.43	2.0	2.4	2.5	2.9
Just helping someone to pinch things	2.39	2.1	2.4	2.5	2.7
Taking someone's car just for a drive	1.95	1.6	1.8	2.1	2.3
Pinching from a shop	2.27	1.8	2.2	2.3	2.8
Taking things from where you work	2.13	1.9	2.2	2.2	2.3
Taking something that is not yours	2.21	1.7	2.1	2.3	2.7
Pinching anything at all	2.12	1.7	2.1	2.3	2.4
Pinching things from home	2.19	1.8	2.1	2.3	2.6
Robbing a bank	1.84	1.5	1.8	1.9	2.2
Breaking into a place and taking things	1.93	1.6	1.8	1.9	2.4
Doing a hold-up	1.47	1.5	1.5	1.5	1.4
Pinching things from a friend	1.47	1.4	1.5	1.5	1.5
Pinching from a little kid	1.34	1.3	1.4	1.4	1.4
Pinching from an old lady	1.13	1.1	1.2	1.2	1.1
Average items	2.23	1.96	2.02	2.36	2.60

*Computed by allotting weights to each rating as follows:
Not sorry   4
Bit sorry   3
Fairly sorry   2
Very sorry   1
Can't decide 2
Q.1 = bottom quartile in terms of amount of stealing
Q.4 = top quartile in terms of amount of stealing
Qs2, 3 = intermediate quartile in terms of stealing

Table 5.19
Claims of boys about receiving instructions 'not to steal' (3,113 cases, weighted)

	Yes (%)	No (%)	No information (%)
Did anyone ever try to teach respondent about not stealing?	83.2	15.5	1.3
Someone at home	80.1	18.5	1.4
Someone at school	68.0	30.7	1.3
Someone at church	39.9	58.5	1.6

Table 5.20
Number of different sources of teaching claimed (3,113 cases, weighted)

	(%)
All three sources claimed	27.6
Two sources claimed	40.9
One (only) source claimed	22.6
All three denied	7.1
No information	1.7
All	99.9

Table 5.21
Claims about nature and extent of teaching 'not to steal' received by boy

Source of teaching	None at all (%)	Not known (%)	At least some (%)	Amount claimed			
				A lot (%)	A little (%)	In-between (%)	Not known (%)
At home	18.5	1.4	80.1	26.3	19.8	33.6	0.4
At school	30.7	1.3	68.0	18.5	29.3	19.8	0.4
At church	58.5	1.6	39.9	15.4	14.0	10.0	0.5

Table 5.22
Persons named as providing teaching at home (against stealing)

	Percentage of boys so claiming
Father	11.1
Mother	13.7
Both parents	52.8
Grandparent(s)	1.2
Brother(s) or sister(s)	3.4
The family/others in the family	1.3
Other relatives	1.3
Others	0.1

Table 5.23
Index of instruction about not stealing, analysed by characteristics of boys and by past involvement in stealing
(3,113 cases, weighted)

Characteristics of boys	No. of claimed sources of instruction (out of 3)				
	3	2	1	0	No Information
Cases (weighted)	860	1,273	704	222	54
Occupational level of father					
Professional, semi-professional & executive	34.7	32.4	23.4	8.3	
Highly skilled	28.4	40.9	22.6	5.3	
Skilled	26.1	40.7	25.2	7.1	
Moderately skilled	23.3	47.8	20.8	6.1	
Semi-skilled	27.1	42.4	20.7	8.1	
Unskilled	28.0	39.4	21.3	9.4	
School last attended					
Public	32.2	32.5	23.1	10.6	
Grammar	30.5	38.9	26.5	3.5	
Comprehensive	26.4	42.1	20.9	7.3	
Secondary modern	25.5	43.5	20.7	8.5	
Nominal religion					
Protestant	27.4	42.8	22.1	6.9	
Catholic	49.4	34.2	9.8	4.6	
Other Christian	21.0	46.6	21.0	8.0	
Jewish	24.3	27.1	39.7	7.5	
None	10.3	45.1	32.0	9.5	

Table 5.23 (continued)
Index of instruction about not stealing, analysed by characteristics of boys and by past involvement in stealing (3,113 cases, weighted)

		No. of claimed sources of instruction (out of 3)				
Characteristics of boys		3	2	1	0	No Information
	Cases (weighted)	860	1,273	704	222	54
Past involvement in stealing: Variety of stealing						
Low-involvement quartile —	Q.1	28.5	42.2	19.6	9.1	
Intermediate quartiles —	Q.2	36.0	31.5	23.4	5.6	
Intermediate quartiles —	Q.3	24.0	41.4	25.3	8.0	
High-involvement quartiles —	Q.4	22.0	48.8	22.0	5.7	
Past involvement in stealing: Amount of stealing						
Low-involvement quartile —	Q.1	29.4	40.2	22.2	7.6	
Intermediate quartiles —	Q.2	30.5	35.2	23.1	8.7	
Intermediate quartiles —	Q.3	26.6	40.6	23.2	6.8	
High-involvement quartiles —	Q.4	23.5	48.7	21.8	5.1	

Table 5.24
Amount of home instruction against stealing analysed by characteristics of boys and past involvement in stealing (3,113 cases, weighted)

		Amount of home instruction claimed				
Characteristics of boys	All cases (wtd)	None	A little	In-between	A lot	No information
Sample size (weighted)	3,113	575	617	1,046	820	55
	(*n*)	(%)	(%)	(%)	(%)	
Occupational level of fathers						
Professional, semi-professional, executive	518	18.0	23.4	33.6	23.0	
Highly skilled	514	17.5	18.6	38.5	22.1	
Skilled	674	17.6	22.5	31.5	27.7	
Moderately skilled	630	18.3	17.8	32.4	29.8	
Semi-skilled	517	20.7	18.4	32.9	26.5	
Unskilled	254	20.1	15.7	33.5	29.1	
No information	6					
Nominal religion						
Protestant	1,370	18.2	19.8	34.6	26.2	
Catholic	500	16.4	22.0	37.0	22.6	
Other Christian	176	21.6	14.8	38.6	18.7	
Jewish	214	21.5	25.2	28.0	23.8	
None	621	20.0	19.0	33.0	25.8	
Other religions	217					
No information	15					
Frequency of rows at home						
Every day	196	19.9	27.0	26.1	26.1	
Most days	800	18.9	23.2	32.9	23.4	
Once a week	917	19.8	19.1	34.8	25.0	
Once a month	516	15.1	20.2	42.0	21.4	
Hardly ever Never	642	17.4	14.9	30.0	36.4	
No information	42					

193

Table 5.24 (continued)

Characteristics of boys	All cases (wtd)	Amount of home instruction claimed				
		None	A little	In-between	A lot	No information
Sample size (weighted)	3,113	575	617	1,046	820	55
Number of siblings						
0	408	17.2	17.4	28.5	35.1	
1	986	15.4	26.4	32.1	25.0	
2	714	19.3	16.4	41.5	21.1	
3	451	21.6	14.6	34.9	28.4	
4–5	352	19.9	23.1	31.2	23.6	
6 or more	161	24.2	9.9	28.0	38.0	
No information	41					
Index* of parental control (0–3)* at age of ten years						
0	589	24.0	25.2	32.0	17.5	
1	1,350	19.0	20.0	35.0	24.2	
2	815	13.4	17.3	36.0	32.2	
3	270	15.2	15.2	25.2	42.7	
Amount of punishment handed out by parents at age of ten years						
A lot	74	15.8	22.4	19.7	42.0	
A fair bit	1,105	16.5	15.3	40.4	26.3	
A little bit	1,553	20.4	20.9	35.1	23.0	
None	147	25.9	26.6	23.7	22.2	
No information	234					
Does the boy come from a broken home?						
Yes	359	19.8	20.1	32.9	25.6	
No	2,735	18.3	19.6	33.6	26.4	
No information	19					
Index** of stealing: variety						
First quartile	771	18.4	17.3	31.3	31.9	
Second quartile	769	17.9	18.7	34.5	26.0	
Third quartile	822	20.4	23.1	33.1	21.8	
Fourth quartile	751	16.9	20.0	35.7	26.0	
Index** of stealing: amount						
First quartile	749	19.4	17.2	28.8	33.9	
Second quartile	861	17.2	20.2	33.0	26.2	
Third quartile	779	21.2	21.1	33.6	22.1	
Fourth quartile	724	16.2	20.7	39.2	23.2	

*Total = 3 (i.e. when boys say parents *did* exercise much
control over how much of his spare time he spent out of the
house + had a lot of say over *where* he spent spare time + had
a lot of say over whom he got around with
**First quartile = lowest theft quartile of boys; 4th quartile =
highest theft quartile of boys

support a conclusion of substantial relationship with number of sources of instruction. Table 5.23 does indicate, however, that Catholic boys tend more than other boys to get their instruction from all three sources.

Table 5.24 presents an analysis of the claimed amount of 'instruction against stealing' received by boys at *home*. The analysis is in terms of occupational level of father, nominal religion, claimed frequency of rows at home, number of boy's siblings, pervasiveness of parental control over the boy, amount of parental punishment handed out, whether from a broken home, past involvement in stealing. The indications of Table 5.24 are as follows.

1 Neither occupational level nor religion appear to be related to any appreciable degree to receipt of instruction at home. Similarly for the number of boy's siblings.

2 Similarly, boys from broken homes do not differ, in respect of home instruction, from other boys.

3 Homes in which there are rarely or never rows, provide somewhat more instruction against stealing than those in which there are *a lot* of rows.

4 Extent of parental control at age ten years is substantially related to the amount of home instruction (against stealing) provided.Similarly for the extent of punishment received at that age.

5 There is only a minor tendency for amount of home instruction to be related to variety and amount of stealing.

Table 5.25 presents an analysis of the claimed extent of

Table 5.25
Amount of instruction not to steal, received at church (chapel or synagogue), analysed by background of boys and past involvement in stealing
(3,113 cases, weighted)

Characteristics of boys		All cases (wtd)	Amount of *church* instruction				
			None	A little	In-between	A lot	No information
	Cases (weighted)	3,113	1,821	446	311	481	54
		(*n*)	(%)	(%)	(%)	(%)	
Nominal religion							
Protestant		1,370	58.0	15.6	9.5	16.1	
Catholic		500	34.4	19.8	16.0	28.6	
Other Christian		176	55.4	21.5	14.2	5.1	
Jewish		214	65.0	10.2	9.8	13.6	
None		621	81.0	6.6	3.2	5.5	
Other religions		217					
No information		15					
Church (or chapel or synagogue attendance)							
Never		1,012	80.8	7.7	2.8	7.1	
Hardly ever		774	60.3	14.0	10.2	13.4	
Once a month		356	38.4	24.6	16.2	19.1	
Once a week		791	32.3	20.0	17.9	28.9	
No information		180					
Index of stealing: variety							
First quartile		771	57.1	19.1	12.8	10.4	
Second quartile		769	47.6	18.9	12.5	18.1	
Third quartile		822	61.7	12.4	8.3	16.4	
Fourth quartile		751	67.7	11.6	6.4	12.3	
Index of stealing: amount							
First quartile		749	55.7	18.6	12.9	12.1	
Second quartile		861	55.4	16.1	10.8	15.7	
Third quartile		779	58.4	13.6	7.8	17.2	
Fourth quartile		724	65.2	13.4	8.3	11.9	

church instruction received by boys. Analysis is in terms of nominal religion, frequency of church attendance, variety and extent of past involvement in stealing.

The indications of Table 5.25 are as follows.

1 Catholic boys make greatest claim to having received church instruction against stealing.

2 Frequency of attendance at church, chapel or synagogue is substantially related to the claimed amount of instruction by church (chapel or synagogue) against stealing.

3 Past involvement in stealing is related to only a minor degree to church instruction against stealing. Table 5.26 presents an analysis of the claimed extent of school instruction against stealing. This analysis is in terms of type of school attended, relationships with teachers and past involvement in stealing. The main indication of Table 5.26 is that: slightly more school instruction

against stealing is claimed by: boys with comprehensive or secondary-modern school background; boys who say they get on well with teachers.

Summing-up on the analysis of stealing by characteristics of boys

Claimed amount of instruction against stealing was not substantially related to any of the characteristics in terms of which it was analysed. At the same time it is worth noting that: (*a*) Catholic boys claim a greater number of different sources of instruction (against stealing) than do other boys; (*b*) there is more *home* instruction against stealing in homes where there are rarely any rows and in those where boys are subject to a lot of parental control; (*c*) there is more *church* instruction against stealing given to boys who frequently attend church or chapel or synagogue and more to Catholic boys; (*d*) there is slightly more *school* instruction against stealing for boys in comprehensive and secondary-

Table 5.26

Amount of school instruction not to steal analysed by characteristics of boys and past involvement in stealing (3,113 cases, weighted)

Characteristics of boys		Amount of *school* instruction					
		All cases	None	A little	In-between	A lot	No information
	Cases (weighted)	3,113	959	912	617	576	49
		(*n*)	(%)	(%)	(%)	(%)	
Type of school last attended							
Secondary modern		1,464	29.9	28.3	20.9	20.9	
Comprehensive		549	26.8	28.6	18.2	23.5	
Grammar		718	33.2	32.1	16.6	17.5	
Public		257	34.5	28.3	24.6	12.5	
Other		105					
No information		20					
Relationship with teachers							
Got on well		1,287	26.6	27.3	23.1	20.8	
Average		1,481	35.0	28.9	17.6	17.3	
Not very well		235	25.5	41.2	17.8	14.1	
Badly		110	32.7	31.7	14.5	16.4	
Index of stealing: variety							
First quartile		771	33.5	25.9	22.0	18.0	
Second quartile		769	30.0	28.3	19.8	18.3	
Third quartile		822	34.1	29.6	18.4	17.2	
Fourth quartile		751	25.3	33.4	19.2	20.6	
Index of stealing: amount							
First quartile		749	32.7	27.1	23.8	15.8	
Second quartile		861	35.5	27.4	17.4	17.4	
Third quartile		779	27.9	29.8	20.4	19.4	
Fourth quartile		724	26.4	33.3	18.0	21.7	

modern schools and for boys who get on well with their teachers.

Investigating Hypotheses 2 and 3
Just as in previous chapters, the central strategy for investigating this hypothesis was to derive from it testable expectations and to test these. See Chapter 1 for details of this approach.

Concerning Hypothesis 2
It will be recalled that Hypothesis 2 was:

Boys take up stealing and continue to steal partly because they are lacking in any sense of remorse in relation to stealing.

From this hypothesis the following expectations were derived.

Expectation 1 Boys who express considerable regret over a series of hypothetical thefts (e.g. doing a hold-up, keeping something found) have done less stealing than boys who express little or no regret and this applies when the latter group has been closely matched to the former in terms of the correlates of stealing.

Expectation 2 Boys who express considerable regret over a series of hypothetical thefts (e.g. doing a hold-up, keeping something found) will tend to continue with relatively serious stealing over a longer period of time than boys who express little or no regret, and this applies even when the latter are closely matched to the former in terms of the correlates of stealing.

Testing Expectations 1 and 2 of Hypothesis 2
The method used for testing these two expectations was the matching technique described in Chapter 1. The total sample was broken into three groups according to stated level of regret. Lack of regret was calculated, for each boy, through his response to the question of how sorry he would feel if he had done the types of theft indicated in the twenty-five statements listed earlier in this chapter (e.g. robbing a bank, stealing from an old lady). A weighting system was used, namely:

Not sorry   = 1
A bit sorry   = 2
Fairly sorry = 3
Very sorry   = 4
Can't decide = 2.5

For each boy, an average over the whole twenty-five acts was calculated. This weighted average was the boy's 'remorse' score. The whole sample was then split, as in Figure 5.4 in terms of remorse score.

Within the rationale of 'testing through matching', Group 1 was called the qualifying group and Group 3 the control group. Group 2 was left out of the matching process so that the qualifying and the control groups would be fairly unambiguous in terms of the hypothesis. Group 3 was now matched to Group 1 in terms of the correlates of stealing. These correlates and the method of their application are set out in Chapter 1. The results of the matching process are set out in Table 5.27 and they clearly indicate that Expectation 1 is borne out.

The test of Expectation 2 was conducted in much the same way, using the same splits of the total sample. Just as in the testing of the 'duration expectation' in the context of other hypotheses, 'serious' stealing was defined in terms of the eighteen acts of theft which a sample of adults had rated as the more serious among the forty-four. Boys qualified on specific acts only if they had committed that act of theft at Level 3 or over*. On the basis of this double criterion, a calculation was made of the period of years over which the boy had been engaged in one or another of the eighteen serious acts (at Level 3 or over). This period was the measure of 'duration' used.

The control group, as defined in Figure 5.4, was matched to the qualifying group in terms of the correlates of stealing, with results as set out in the last row of Table 5.27. Expectation 2 was strongly borne out.

Concerning Hypothesis 3
This hypothesis was:

Boys take up stealing and continue to steal partly because they have received relatively little instruction about not stealing.

For this hypothesis, several expectations were drawn, as follows.

*The qualifying value of such items was set at 4/6d (old money). See details at foot of Table A2.2.

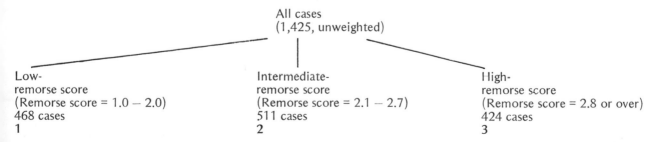

Figure 5.4
Sample division in terms of remorse score

All cases
(1,425, unweighted)

| Low-remorse score (Remorse score = 1.0 − 2.0) 468 cases 1 | Intermediate-remorse score (Remorse score = 2.1 − 2.7) 511 cases 2 | High-remorse score (Remorse score = 2.8 or over) 424 cases 3 |

Table 5.27

Differences between qualifiers and controls before and after matching: variety, amount and duration of stealing

Indices of stealing	Unadjusted average score for qualifying group (424 cases) a	Unadjusted average score for control group (468 cases) b	Adjusted average score for control group c	Differences between qualifiers and adj. controls a–c P	Difference a–c as percentage of c
Variety of stealing	17.79	9.56	10.92	6.87 (0.01)	63
Amount of stealing	135.32	59.41	71.89	63.43 (0.01)	88
Duration of 'serious' stealing*	4.93	2.61	3.38	1.55 (0.01)	46

*The period of years over which serious stealing is continued. For details of the calculation of a duration score based on serious stealing, see hereunder text concerning the test of Expectation 2 and the way in which it was conducted

Expectation 1 Boys who say they have received instruction against stealing from one or none of school, home, church, have been more involved in stealing than boys who claim they have received instruction against stealing from two or three of those sources, and this applies after close matching of the latter to the former group in terms of correlates of stealing.

Expectation 2 Expectation 1 applies with respect to each of the forty-four acts of theft studied.

Expectation 3 Expectation 1 applies with respect to duration of serious stealing.

Testing Expectations 1 to 3 of Hypothesis 3
The methods used to test Expectations 1 to 3 were closely similar to those used in testing expectations derived from Hypothesis 2. The sample of boys was split into two groups, according to the number of sources of instruction claimed. Group 1 was called the qualifying group and Group 2 the control group. Group 2 was now matched to Group 1 in terms of the correlates of stealing, with the results set out in Tables 5.28 and 5.29. Neither of the two expectations dealt with in Table 5.28 (i.e. Expectations 1 and 3) was borne out.

The results of testing Expectation 2 are given in Table 5.29. The expectation is not borne out, except for several of the forty-four theft items.

Summing-up on Hypotheses 2 and 3
The evidence presented supports Hypothesis 2 but *not* Hypothesis 3.

Miscellaneous information relating to the tenability of Hypotheses 1 to 3
Several questions were asked as a basis for further challenging the hypotheses being investigated. These questions were as follows.

Q.5 When did he first feel this way about stealing and what led to this?

SAY:
5a Now we have been finding out how you feel these days about pinching things. I want to ask you a few more things about that.
How old were you when you first started to feel *the way you do these days* about pinching things? (CLARIFY IF NECESSARY THAT YOU MEAN *WHATEVER* HIS

Figure 5.5
Division of sample for testing expectations 1, 2, 3

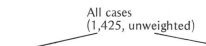

All cases
(1,425, unweighted)

Instruction received from none or one of home, school, church
424 cases
1

Instruction received from two or three of home, school, church
973 cases
2

Table 5.28 Differences between qualifiers and controls before and after matching: variety, amount and duration of stealing	Indices of stealing	Unadjusted average score for qualifying group (424 cases) a	Unadjusted average score for control group (973 cases) b	Adjusted average score for control group c	Differences between qualifiers and adj. controls a−c *P*	Difference a−c as percentage of c
	Variety of stealing	13.6	13.6	13.2	0.4 NS	3
	Amount of stealing	88.2	92.4	88.8	−0.6 NS	−1
	Duration of stealing	3.6	3.7	3.6	0 NS	0

OPINIONS OR FEELINGS ACTUALLY ARE). EX-CLUDE ANY CHANGE *WE* HAVE PRODUCED. CHALLENGE HIS CHOICE OF AGE AND THEN ENTER AGE.

5b 'Exactly what started you feeling the way you do these days about pinching?'
  (PROBE HARD)
'*What else* made you feel the way you do these days about pinching things?'

Question 5a was designed only as a lead-up to Question 5b. Moreover, the purpose of Question 5b was to assess the degree to which boys volunteered stealing itself as a cause of their feeling permissive towards stealing or of some lack of remorsefulness over theft. If, in fact, boys did volunteer stealing in this way, then a tendency for those attitudes to be associated with a high theft level leaves open the possibility that permissiveness (or lack of remorse) was a *result* of theft activity and not a cause of it. The nature and the frequency of the responses given can be seen in Table 5.30.
  Table 5.30 provides little to support the suggestion that a permissive attitude springs out of involvement in stealing and hence tends to leave Hypotheses 1 and 2 unweakened.
  However, the detail of Table 5.30 may well be of value to those aiming to reduce permissiveness and to increase potential remorsefulness.

6 SUMMING-UP ON THE INVESTIGATION OF SUB-HYPOTHESES 1a, 1b, AND HYPOTHESES 2 AND 3

The evidence from the inquiry appears to strenghten Sub-Hypothesis 1a and Hypothesis 2, namely that:

Boys take up stealing and continue to steal partly because they have permissive attitudes towards stealing (Sub-Hypothesis 1a).

Boys take up stealing and continue to steal partly because they are lacking in any sense of remorse in relation to stealing (Hypothesis 2).

On the other hand, Hypothesis 3 is not supported by the evidence and must be regarded as weakened by it. This hypothesis was:

Boys take up stealing and continue to steal partly because they have received relatively little instruction about not stealing.

Sub-Hypothesis 1b was not subject to expectation testing. At the same time its close similarity to Sub-Hypothesis 1a should be noted. It was:

Boys take up stealing and continue to steal partly because they are without any generalized opposition to stealing.

7 SOME COMMENTS AND POSSIBLE ACTION

1 Sub-Hypothesis 1a, dealing with permissiveness towards stealing, was rendered more tenable by the investigation made of it. Furthermore, the evidence indicated that this factor is a fairly potent one in relation to juvenile stealing. Though the degree of permissiveness varies with the occupational, educational and religious backgrounds and with other characteristics of boys, the similarities between sub-groups (in terms of permissiveness) tend to be greater than the differences.
  On the other hand, there is a great deal of difference in permissiveness in going from one type of theft to another — differences which tend to be common to all the sub-groups of boys investigated. Thus 'keeping something you found' is subject to a high degree of permissiveness, whereas 'pinching from an old lady' is virtually taboo.
  These being the findings, the reduction of permissiveness towards many types of stealing is clearly a target for remedial action and a broad line of such action has been suggested under Recommendations.
  In this same general context, it is particularly noteworthy that law supportiveness in terms of reporting people known to be stealing is generally weak. Here,

Table 5.29
Differences between qualifiers and controls before and after matching: each of the forty-four types of theft

Theft types at Level 2 or over	Unadjusted average score for qualifying* group (424 cases) a		Unadjusted average score for control* group (973 cases) b		Adjusted average score for control group c		Differences between qualifiers and adj. controls		Difference a−c as percentage of c
	(n)	(%)	(n)	(%)	(n)	(%)	a−c	P	(%)
1	380	89.6	888	91.3	385.65	90.8	−1.2	NS†	−1
2	239	56.4	481	49.4	204.66	48.2	8.2	(0.05)	17
3	166	39.2	387	39.8	165.24	39.0	0.2		−
4	221	52.1	516	53.0	224.84	53.0	−0.9		−2
5	108	25.5	205	21.1	86.03	20.3	5.2	0.05	26
6	247	58.3	530	54.5	225.75	53.2	5.1		9
7	177	41.7	392	40.3	166.36	39.2	2.5		6
8	146	34.4	320	32.9	137.41	32.4	2.0		6
9	59	13.9	157	16.1	67.41	15.9	−2.0		−12
10	166	39.2	385	39.6	161.36	38.0	1.2		3
11	151	35.6	373	38.3	160.73	37.9	−2.3		−6
12	62	14.6	153	15.7	63.65	15.0	−0.4		−3
13	163	38.4	383	39.4	161.83	38.1	0.3		1
14	100	23.6	225	23.1	92.98	21.9	1.7		8
15	67	15.8	154	15.8	64.49	15.2	0.6		4
16	189	44.6	425	43.7	182.42	43.0	1.6		4
17	84	19.8	178	18.3	73.94	17.4	2.4		14
18	282	66.5	616	63.3	261.39	61.6	4.9	0.05	8
19	137	32.3	374	38.4	158.16	37.3	−5.0	0.05	−13
20	119	28.1	304	31.2	130.64	30.8	−2.7		−9
21	45	10.6	134	13.8	55.56	13.1	−2.5		−19
22	164	38.7	379	39.0	160.71	37.9	0.8		2
23	92	21.7	218	22.4	89.91	21.2	0.5		2
24	61	14.4	114	11.7	46.69	11.0	3.4		31
25	87	20.5	238	24.5	101.53	23.9	−3.4		−14
26	126	29.7	268	27.5	114.47	27.0	2.7		10
27	78	18.4	190	19.5	81.69	19.2	−0.8		−5
28	104	24.5	213	21.9	91.64	21.6	2.9		13
29	30	7.1	71	7.3	30.03	7.1	0.0		0
30	187	44.1	456	46.9	192.78	45.4	−1.3		−3
31	120	28.3	267	27.4	109.02	25.7	2.6		10
32	28	6.6	72	7.4	28.76	6.8	−0.2		−3
33	267	63.0	619	63.6	264.77	62.4	0.6		1
34	119	28.1	318	32.7	137.44	32.4	−4.3	0.05	−13
35	76	17.9	160	16.4	63.81	15.0	2.9		19
36	137	32.3	282	29.0	118.89	28.0	4.3	0.05	15
37	21	5.0	44	4.5	17.02	4.0	1.0		23
38	93	21.9	228	23.4	96.22	22.7	−0.8		−3
39	84	19.8	181	18.6	76.43	18.0	1.8		10
40	266	62.7	634	65.2	270.90	63.8	−1.1		−2
41	36	8.5	90	9.2	35.99	8.5	0.0		0
42	46	10.8	113	11.6	49.99	11.8	−1.0		−8
43	133	31.4	285	29.3	118.45	27.9	3.5		12
44	216	50.9	511	52.5	215.32	50.7	0.2		−

*Qualifying group: boys who have received instruction about not stealing either from *one* of home, school or church, or from *none* of these

*Control group: boys who have received instruction about not stealing from either *two* or *three* of home, school or church

†NS = not significant at 0.05 level. If no entry, assume NS at level 0.05
− = less than 0.5 per cent

Table 5.30
Factors or circumstances named by boys as
'affecting' attitudes towards stealing

	Percentage volunteering a specific factor
a) *Apparently inhibiting factors*	
Parents' influence (mother's and father's)	15
Being taught at school	7
Religion/religious instruction	4
Experience of being caught	6
Fear of getting caught and/or consequences (unspecified) of getting caught	16
Fear of being put away in a home/in borstal/prison	5
Fear of police	—
Knowing/seeing those who had been caught, punished	18
Personal experience of being robbed	5
Knowing people who had been robbed, realization of how it feels to be robbed/wouldn't like it to happen to him/feeling sorry for people who have been robbed	21
Boy separated from mates on leaving school/don't see mates so much	2
Boy has more sense now, has grown up, matured, can make up his own mind	16
No gain from stealing/not worth it	8
Boy does not need to steal, e.g. now at work, has enough money	5
Fear of not getting a job/holding a job	3
Boy found other interests/other hobbies to occupy his mind	1
Boy realized that it would disgrace/dishonour the family — get family into trouble/would be a worry to parents/would hurt parents	4
Fear of being expelled from school/wanting to continue studies at school	1
Stealing would give him a bad name/a record	2
Fear of specified consequences, e.g. going to Court, being put on probation	—
Scout law/loyalty to scouts (authority to sea cadets)	—
(b) *Not clear whether inhibiting or encouraging*	
Influence of friends, girl friend	13
Influence of other people (specified or unspecified)	4
Influence of papers/films/television	12
(c) *Factors which appear to encourage stealing*	
It's easy to get away with/finding out you don't get caught	1
Boy gained from stealing (materially) therefore continued	—
Boy found fun and excitement in stealing	—
Boy gave up because fed up with stealing	1

too, there is a strong case for remedial action, principally in the form of school training for the young. (See Recommendations.)

2 Hypothesis 2 dealt with an 'absence of remorse or regret concerning thefts of different kinds'. This factor is similar to the permissiveness factor in Hypothesis 1, without being the same. Here, too, the evidence collected increased quite markedly the tenability of the hypothesis. Remedial action is desirable and should start with programmes of training for children in school — not as indoctrination, just as part of generalized school training in 'living together'. (See Recommendations.)

3 Hypothesis 3, dealing with instruction against stealing received through school, the church and the home, was not supported by the evidence. In attempting to interpret this finding it is most important that it should not be seen to prove that training against stealing *cannot* be effective. The evidence simply means that the kinds and amount of training against stealing *actually being administered* by school, church and home are not at present causally differentiating with respect to the amount of stealing being done. What might happen with a vigorous and purposive programme of training could well be quite another matter. (See Recommendations.)

APPENDIX 5.1
The Sub-Questionnaire used on the boys:
Ideas about it being right or wrong to steal

I Q.1 His ideas about what is right and what is wrong in relation to stealing.
Q.2 Further views.
Q.3 Training in right and wrong in relation to stealing.
Q.4 Would he feel badly about pinching things?
Q.5 When did he first feel as he does about stealing?
Q.6 Do his views affect the amount of his stealing and vice versa?
Q.7 Did stealing produce or affect his views about stealing being right or wrong?

Q.1 His ideas about what is right and wrong in relation to stealing. (GREEN CARDS)

GET BOY'S HELP IN SETTING UP THE BAGS. THESE READ: QUITE ALL RIGHT/NOTHING MUCH WRONG WITH IT/A BIT WRONG/FAIRLY WRONG/VERY WRONG/CAN'T DECIDE. SEE THAT THE *'CAN'T DECIDE'* BAG IS WELL TO THE RIGHT (A BIT AWAY FROM THE ONE NEXT TO IT). TEACH BOY BAGS IF ILLITERATE.

THEN SAY:

'On these green cards are some things that people might do. There's one on each card. I want you to look at each card in turn and tell me if you think it is all right to do it.' (PAUSE). 'If you think it is QUITE ALL RIGHT to do it, you put it in *this* bag. If you think there is NOTHING MUCH WRONG WITH IT, you put it *here*. A BIT WRONG, here. FAIRLY WRONG, *here*. VERY WRONG, *here*. If you just CAN'T DECIDE, you put it over *here*.'
'Will you start by reading out for me what's on each of these bags.'
THEN GIVE BOY THE FIRST CARD. (CARD 1).

'Going absolutely by your own opinion, which bag would you put *that* one in?'

SAY:

'Why *that* bag?' CORRECT IF HE HAS THE SORTING IDEA WRONG

SAY:

'Now we'll do the same thing with all the rest. I'll give them to you one at a time'.
'*I won't watch where you put them. Please put them exactly where YOU think they go.*
Don't bother about what ANYONE ELSE thinks. I won't watch.'

PASS CARDS ONE AT A TIME, NOT WATCHING

WHERE HE PUTS THEM. READ OUT ALL (WHITE) REMINDER CARDS

Q.2 Further views about stealing, endorsed as 'Agree' o 'Disagree' (Orange cards)

PUT UP THE FOUR YELLOW BAGS. THESE ARE AGREE/PARTLY AGREE/DISAGREE/CAN'T DECIDE.

'Here are just a few more cards to put into the *yellow* bags. Here is the first one'.

PASS HIM THE CARD 'SOMETIMES IT IS ALL RIGHT TO PINCH THINGS'. SAY:

'If you AGREE with that, put it in *this* bag. If you DISAGREE with it, put it in this bag. If you PARTLY AGREE, put it in *this* bag. And if you CAN'T DECIDE, put it in *this* one. O.K?'
'*I won't look. But please be very truthful. Put that one in the bag* that shows what *you personally* think.'

PASS THE REST, ONE AT A TIME, BUT WITHOUT WASTING TIME

Q.3 His training in right/wrong in relation to stealing

3a 'Did anyone ever try to teach you about *not pinching*?' YES/NO
WHETHER 'YES' OR 'NO', CHECK AS FOLLOWS in b, c, d.

3b 'What about at home?' YES/NO
IF 'YES':
i 'At home, who tried to teach you about not pinching?'
ii 'How much of this teaching did you get at home?'
SHOW CARD.
(A LITTLE/A LOT/IN BETWEEN)

3c 'What about at school?' YES/NO
IF 'YES':
i 'At school, who tried to teach you about not pinching?'
ii 'How much of this teaching did you get at school?'
SHOW CARD.
(A LITTLE/A LOT/IN BETWEEN)

3d 'What about at church/chapel/synagogue?' YES/NO/
IF 'YES':
i 'At ...., who tried to teach you about not pinching?'
ii 'How *much* of this teaching did you get at ...?
SHOW CARD.
(A LITTLE/A LOT/IN BETWEEN)

Q.4 Would he feel badly about pinching of the kind he rated as wrong?

NOW TAKE A SECOND PACK OF GREEN CARDS

AND PREPARE TO HAVE BOY SORT THEM INTO
THE *GREEN AND PURPLE BAGS*.
PUT UP THESE BAGS WITH 'WOULD NOT FEEL
SORRY' ON LEFT AND 'WOULD FEEL VERY
SORRY' ON RIGHT.
  SAY:
This time I want you to pretend that you had done
whatever is on the card. *Just pretend you have done it*.'
This first one is 'Pinching from someone who is
rich.' Just supposing you had done that how would you
feel about it? *Just put it in the bag that shows how you
would feel about it*.'
'I won't look where you put it ... But *please* be
absolutely straight with me.'
'If you think you'd NOT feel sorry, put it *there*' (POINT
TO THAT BAG). 'If you think you'd feel A BIT sorry,
put it *there*' (POINT). '*Here* if you'd feel' FAIRLY
SORRY 'and *here* if you'd feel' VERY SORRY. 'Just put
it in the bag that shows how you would *really* feel.'
'I won't watch where you put them. *Start with the one I
gave you*.'

> NOW PASS REST ONE AT A TIME. EACH
> FOURTH OR FIFTH CARD, REMIND HIM TO PUT
> IT IN THE BAG THAT SHOWS HOW HE WOULD
> REALLY FEEL
> TAKE DOWN BAGS AND PUT TO ONE SIDE *WITH
> CONTENTS IN*

Q.5 When did he first feel this way about stealing and
what led to this?

  SAY:
5a 'Now we have been finding out how you feel these
days about pinching things. I want to ask you a few
more things about that.'
'How old were you when you first started to feel *the
way you do these days* about pinching things?'
(CLARIFY IF NECESSARY THAT YOU MEAN
WHATEVER HIS OPINIONS OR FEELINGS
ACTUALLY ARE). EXCLUDE ANY CHANGE *WE*
HAVE PRODUCED. CHALLENGE HIS CHOICE OF
AGE AND THEN ENTER AGE ...

5b 'Exactly what started you feeling the way you do
these days about pinching?' (PROBE HARD)
'*What else* made you feel the way you do these days
about pinching things?

APPENDIX 5.2.1

Code to theft numbers.

The different classes of theft†

1 Pinching from someone who is rich

2 Robbing a bank.

3 Doing a hold-up.

4 Breaking into a place and taking things.

5 Taking things from Woolworths.

6 Taking pencils or rubbers from school.

7 Keeping something you found.

8 Buying things you know were pinched.

9 Taking things from where you work.

10 Pinching something quite small.

11 Pinching things from a big company.

12 Pinching things that belong to the government.

13 Taking little things from where you work.

14 Taking someone's car just for a drive.

15 Just helping someone to pinch things.

16 Just keeping a look-out for mates who were pinching.

17 Pinching from a shop.

18 Taking things just left lying around.

19 Pinching from an old lady.

20 Pinching from someone who has plenty of what you took.

21 Pinching from a little kid.

22 Pinching things from home.

23 Pinching things from a friend.

24 Taking something that is not yours.

25 Pinching anything at all.

†These twenty-five classes of theft do not constitute the web of
stimuli used for measuring the extent and nature of boys'
stealing.

APPENDIX 5.2.2 Correlation Matrix based on 'right-wrong' ratings

Table A2.1
Correlation Matrix† based on 'right-wrong' responses to twenty-five classes of theft and upon a numerical base ranging from 1,390 to 1,425 cases

*Class of theft	1	2	3	4	5	6	7	8	9	10	11	12
1	1.00	–	–	–	–	–	–	–	–	–	–	–
2	0.46	1.00	–	–	–	–	–	–	–	–	–	–
3	0.41	0.76	1.00	–	–	–	–	–	–	–	–	–
4	0.49	0.61	0.62	1.00	–	–	–	–	–	–	–	–
5	0.61	0.50	0.47	0.57	1.00	–	–	–	–	–	–	–
6	0.53	0.34	0.29	0.43	0.64	1.00	–	–	–	–	–	–
7	0.44	0.29	0.25	0.33	0.46	0.57	1.00	–	–	–	–	–
8	0.43	0.35	0.32	0.43	0.51	0.48	0.52	1.00	–	–	–	–
9	0.42	0.38	0.34	0.41	0.51	0.48	0.36	0.44	1.00	–	–	–
10	0.54	0.34	0.33	0.46	0.64	0.60	0.47	0.48	0.52	1.00	–	–
11	0.67	0.53	0.44	0.50	0.62	0.53	0.44	0.47	0.52	0.58	1.00	–
12	0.50	0.49	0.40	0.46	0.50	0.45	0.38	0.43	0.47	0.41	0.63	1.00
13	0.43	0.33	0.30	0.39	0.51	0.54	0.39	0.40	0.68	0.62	0.55	0.47
14	0.37	0.39	0.36	0.47	0.40	0.32	0.28	0.33	0.32	0.36	0.39	0.34
15	0.52	0.45	0.42	0.55	0.60	0.50	0.42	0.52	0.46	0.56	0.53	0.44
16	0.49	0.37	0.36	0.48	0.59	0.49	0.42	0.49	0.44	0.54	0.48	0.41
17	0.56	0.46	0.45	0.58	0.73	0.57	0.44	0.49	0.51	0.65	0.58	0.48
18	0.47	0.27	0.26	0.37	0.52	0.53	0.51	0.44	0.42	0.56	0.48	0.39
19	0.07	0.08	0.09	0.15	0.08	0.08	0.07	0.08	0.10	0.09	0.06	0.04
20	0.70	0.43	0.38	0.48	0.62	0.53	0.45	0.47	0.46	0.59	0.65	0.52
21	0.15	0.06	0.12	0.15	0.20	0.21	0.15	0.11	0.21	0.30	0.13	0.11
22	0.11	0.04	0.05	0.11	0.11	0.14	0.18	0.13	0.23	0.21	0.14	0.10
23	0.21	0.12	0.15	0.19	0.23	0.22	0.17	0.15	0.23	0.32	0.19	0.11
24	0.52	0.45	0.42	0.56	0.62	0.51	0.41	0.50	0.49	0.58	0.56	0.51
25	0.47	0.42	0.37	0.50	0.56	0.46	0.41	0.45	0.44	0.53	0.50	0.43
All classes of theft	0.74	0.61	0.56	0.69	0.81	0.73	0.63	0.66	0.68	0.78	0.77	0.67

*See list on p. 203. These twenty-five classes of theft do not constitute the 'web of stimuli' used in measuring the nature and extent of boys' stealing
†The correlation indices shown in Table A2.1 were calculated by using the BMDO3D program called 'Correlation With Item Deletion'. This program was developed at the Health Sciences Facility at U.C.L.A. (University of California, Los Angeles). It provides correlation coefficients among all data used for every case where information exists for the two variables being correlated. The coefficient developed is roughly analogous to Pearson's correlation coefficient 'r'.

13	14	15	16	17	18	19	20	21	22	23	24	25
—	—	—	—	—	—	—	—	—	—	—	—	—
—	—	—	—	—	—	—	—	—	—	—	—	—
—	—	—	—	—	—	—	—	—	—	—	—	—
—	—	—	—	—	—	—	—	—	—	—	—	—
—	—	—	—	—	—	—	—	—	—	—	—	—
—	—	—	—	—	—	—	—	—	—	—	—	—
—	—	—	—	—	—	—	—	—	—	—	—	—
—	—	—	—	—	—	—	—	—	—	—	—	—
—	—	—	—	—	—	—	—	—	—	—	—	—
—	—	—	—	—	—	—	—	—	—	—	—	—
—	—	—	—	—	—	—	—	—	—	—	—	—
—	—	—	—	—	—	—	—	—	—	—	—	—
1.00	—	—	—	—	—	—	—	—	—	—	—	—
0.33	1.00	—	—	—	—	—	—	—	—	—	—	—
0.49	0.48	1.00	—	—	—	—	—	—	—	—	—	—
0.49	0.44	0.77	1.00	—	—	—	—	—	—	—	—	—
0.55	0.41	0.64	0.61	1.00	—	—	—	—	—	—	—	—
0.47	0.37	0.53	0.53	0.55	1.00	—	—	—	—	—	—	—
0.07	0.12	0.11	0.09	0.14	0.76	1.00	—	—	—	—	—	—
0.51	0.41	0.55	0.52	0.59	0.54	0.10	1.00	—	—	—	—	—
0.23	0.16	0.25	0.26	0.25	0.21	0.23	0.22	1.00	—	—	—	—
0.25	0.17	0.17	0.17	0.14	0.20	0.15	0.13	0.23	1.00	—	—	—
0.27	0.20	0.27	0.27	0.26	0.26	0.18	0.22	0.39	0.41	1.00	—	—
0.51	0.38	0.59	0.55	0.65	0.50	0.12	0.56	0.26	0.16	0.29	1.00	—
0.48	0.34	0.51	0.52	0.58	0.43	0.12	0.52	0.20	0.15	0.22	0.61	1.00
0.71	0.56	0.77	0.74	0.80	0.69	0.16	0.77	0.32	0.28	0.37	0.76	0.70

APPENDIX 5.2.3 Correlation matrix based on 'sorry-not sorry' ratings

Table A2.2
Correlation matrix† based upon 'sorry-not sorry'
responses to twenty-five classes of theft and upon a
numerical base ranging from 1,390 to 1,425 cases

*Class of theft	1	2	3	4	5	6	7	8	9	10	11	12
1	1.00	–	–	–	–	–	–	–	–	–	–	–
2	0.53	1.00	–	–	–	–	–	–	–	–	–	–
3	0.47	0.83	1.00	–	–	–	–	–	–	–	–	–
4	0.50	0.66	0.69	1.00	–	–	–	–	–	–	–	–
5	0.63	0.56	0.52	0.61	1.00	–	–	–	–	–	–	–
6	0.53	0.37	0.34	0.40	0.63	1.00	–	–	–	–	–	–
7	0.41	0.27	0.25	0.26	0.41	0.52	1.00	–	–	–	–	–
8	0.45	0.39	0.35	0.39	0.51	0.49	0.46	1.00	–	–	–	–
9	0.44	0.43	0.43	0.46	0.51	0.42	0.29	0.43	1.00	–	–	–
10	0.58	0.41	0.39	0.48	0.61	0.56	0.40	0.45	0.52	1.00	–	–
11	0.64	0.58	0.53	0.53	0.61	0.46	0.33	0.47	0.53	0.56	1.00	–
12	0.52	0.56	0.51	0.48	0.54	0.43	0.27	0.42	0.48	0.47	0.70	1.00
13	0.46	0.37	0.37	0.44	0.51	0.47	0.30	0.40	0.72	0.59	0.52	0.48
14	0.35	0.42	0.45	0.46	0.41	0.33	0.26	0.36	0.34	0.36	0.40	0.38
15	0.53	0.45	0.47	0.53	0.60	0.47	0.38	0.54	0.44	0.55	0.53	0.47
16	0.49	0.42	0.44	0.50	0.58	0.45	0.37	0.53	0.41	0.52	0.49	0.40
17	0.55	0.54	0.52	0.58	0.66	0.50	0.34	0.47	0.49	0.57	0.61	0.52
18	0.43	0.32	0.33	0.37	0.48	0.45	0.45	0.40	0.34	0.49	0.43	0.35
19	0.10	0.19	0.25	0.25	0.14	0.09	0.05	0.08	0.24	0.12	0.14	0.16
20	0.68	0.50	0.46	0.50	0.60	0.47	0.37	0.46	0.42	0.57	0.65	0.51
21	0.15	0.15	0.20	0.23	0.20	0.15	0.11	0.10	0.26	0.24	0.17	0.14
22	0.12	0.08	0.13	0.14	0.12	0.14	0.16	0.08	0.22	0.18	0.13	0.13
23	0.17	0.15	0.21	0.23	0.19	0.16	0.13	0.10	0.26	0.24	0.16	0.16
24	0.54	0.53	0.53	0.57	0.62	0.47	0.34	0.48	0.50	0.54	0.58	0.53
25	0.52	0.49	0.51	0.56	0.60	0.43	0.32	0.47	0.49	0.53	0.57	0.51
All classes of theft	0.74	0.71	0.70	0.74	0.80	0.67	0.51	0.64	0.68	0.74	0.77	0.70

*See list on p.203. These twenty-five classes of theft do not
constitute the 'web of stimuli' used in measuring the nature and
extent of boys' stealing
†ditto p. 204

3	14	15	16	17	18	19	20	21	22	23	24	25
—	—	—	—	—	—	—	—	—	—	—	—	—
—	—	—	—	—	—	—	—	—	—	—	—	—
—	—	—	—	—	—	—	—	—	—	—	—	—
—	—	—	—	—	—	—	—	—	—	—	—	—
—	—	—	—	—	—	—	—	—	—	—	—	—
—	—	—	—	—	—	—	—	—	—	—	—	—
—	—	—	—	—	—	—	—	—	—	—	—	—
—	—	—	—	—	—	—	—	—	—	—	—	—
—	—	—	—	—	—	—	—	—	—	—	—	—
—	—	—	—	—	—	—	—	—	—	—	—	—
—	—	—	—	—	—	—	—	—	—	—	—	—
1.00	—	—	—	—	—	—	—	—	—	—	—	—
0.38	1.00	—	—	—	—	—	—	—	—	—	—	—
0.47	0.48	1.00	—	—	—	—	—	—	—	—	—	—
0.44	0.42	0.81	1.00	—	—	—	—	—	—	—	—	—
0.51	0.41	0.63	0.60	1.00	—	—	—	—	—	—	—	—
0.42	0.32	0.48	0.49	0.48	1.00	—	—	—	—	—	—	—
0.17	0.15	0.14	0.14	0.19	0.07	1.00	—	—	—	—	—	—
0.47	0.41	0.53	0.52	0.58	0.48	0.09	1.00	—	—	—	—	—
0.22	0.16	0.21	0.22	0.21	0.16	0.41	0.19	1.00	—	—	—	—
0.24	0.18	0.15	0.14	0.09	0.18	0.25	0.13	0.32	1.00	—	—	—
0.27	0.19	0.24	0.24	0.24	0.20	0.32	0.17	0.43	0.46	1.00	—	—
0.50	0.45	0.59	0.57	0.66	0.44	0.19	0.56	0.24	0.16	0.29	1.00	—
0.49	0.41	0.60	0.55	0.63	0.43	0.19	0.54	0.25	0.15	0.26	0.70	1.00
0.69	0.59	0.76	0.73	0.78	0.62	0.28	0.74	0.34	0.28	0.36	0.78	0.75

Chapter six
Association
with thieves

CONTENTS

1 THE COVERAGE OF THIS CHAPTER

In this chapter I have presented a wide range of information broadly related to 'association with boys who steal'. This information was collected and processed to serve two associated purposes, the more important of which was to investigate a particular hypothesis about causal factors in the development of juvenile stealing. This hypothesis was: 'Association of a boy with thieves increases his own involvement in stealing'.

The second purpose of the collected data was to provide general background information about the factor hypothesized above as causal in character. How, for instance, is 'association with thieves' distributed amongst boys and how is it related to their backgrounds and characteristics? How much stealing do those associates do? When did boys in the sample first associate with thieves and for how long was the association maintained?

2 RESEARCH PROCEDURES COMMON TO ALL THE HYPOTHESES DEALT WITH IN THE INQUIRY

The gathering of information relevant to the hypothesis about association with thieves was done in the context of an inquiry concerned with over thirty other hypotheses. The techniques relating to the inquiry *as a whole* have been summarized in Chapter 1. That summary deals with sampling procedures; with a technique for getting boys to provide reliable information about any stealing they have done; with questioning procedures for classifying boys in terms of the variables hypothesized as causal factors in the different hypotheses (i.e. in terms of the different independent variables); with strategies for investigating the tenability of hypotheses about causal factors and processes. The reader should as necessary refer to the relevant parts of Chapter 1 in reading statements of findings in the present and subsequent chapters.

3 RESEARCH PROCEDURES APPLYING ONLY TO THE HYPOTHESIS DEALT WITH IN THIS CHAPTER

Whereas many aspects of research procedure applied generally to the whole range of hypotheses under study, certain parts of it related only to the hypothesis defined in this chapter. These parts tend to be encapsulated in one of the sub-questionnaires put to boys in the course of the total interview and this sub-questionnaire is presented in full in Appendix 6.1.

Like all the other sub-questionnaires, this one was designed in sections, each section beginning with a general description of its purposes, as follows.

I The purpose of this section is to get the boy's areas of residence, how long he lived at each residence, the degree to which he sees the place where he lived as a thief area. The purpose of this section is also to help prepare for the questioning procedures in Sections II to V.

II Q.1 Has boy *ever* mixed with 'pinchers'?
Q.2 What was his age of greatest association with

'pinchers'? Was it ever great? Were the 'pinchers' the doing a lot of pinching?

III At time of greatest association with 'pinchers', ho many 'pinchers' were known (to boy) locally and n locally; how many 'non-pinchers' were known to bc locally and non-locally?

IV Q.1 Age of *first* association with 'pinchers'?
Q.2 How many were there at that stage and what w the extent of their pinching?

V Association at present (with 'pinchers')

VI His views about the effects of association wit 'pinchers': first and later.

VII Why did he start getting round with boys wh pinched?

Questions under Section I were asked partly to prepar the boy and the interviewer for later questioning ir Sections II to V. Practically all questions were of the structured kind. The few others were concerned with extracting from boys their reasons for certain of the answers previously given: e.g. 'Why did it start then?' ... 'Can you tell me why it was that you *never* go around with *any* boys who pinched things?'

4 METHODS AND FINDINGS RELATED TO THE INVESTIGATION OF THE HYPOTHESIS

The Nature of the Hypothesis

The hypothesis dealt with in this chapter took the following general form:

Association of a boy with thieves increases his ow involvement in stealing.

There are, however, different kinds and degrees o association with thieves and these are specified in the following sub-hypotheses of the main hypothesis.

1 There is a positive causal relationship between the proportion of a boy's associates who steal and his own involvement in stealing.

2 There is a positive causal relationship between the amount of stealing being done by a boy's associates and his own involvement in stealing.

3 There is a positive causal relationship between the duration in years of a boy's association with thieves and his own involvement in stealing.

4 There is a negative causal relationship between a boy's age on first association with thieves and his own involvement in stealing.

The Questions Asked to Assess the Nature and Extent of Boys' Association with Thieves

Various questions were asked to determine each boy's position in relation to the different kinds of association with thieves that are defined in the different sub-hypotheses. These questions, which are set out in this section, are given in their full context in Appendix 6.1.

The questions relating to the amount of stealing being done by the boy's associates

This measure was linked to the period at which the boy said he had *greatest association with thieves*. Obviously this is not the same as some average based on the boy's whole life, but it does have the advantage of being relevant and fairly measurable.

Various questions were asked, primarily to lead the thoughts of the boys up to the period of this greatest association with thieves, the sequence of these being as follows.

Had he ever known boys who stole?

Had he ever got around with any of these boys himself?

Was there a time when he got around with them quite a lot?

Where was he living then?

What was his age at that time?

Only after this was he asked for information about the degree to which his mates of that time (i.e. the time of his greatest association with thieves) were involved in stealing:

Q.2c 'At that time, how much pinching were those boys doing?'
PASS CARD, READ OUT. ENCOURAGE CHOICE.
CHALLENGE IT
(A LOT/A FAIR BIT/NOT MUCH/NONE AT ALL)

The questions relating to the age at which boy first associated with thieves

Subsequently, the boy was questioned as follows:

Q.1a 'Now in just the same way I want you to think back to the time you *first* started to get around with any boys who pinched things. *The time when you FIRST started to get around with any boys at all who pinched things.*'
Where were you living then?'
CHECK GRID ENTRIES TO SEE IF A PREVIOUS AREA LIVED IN HAD HIGHER PROPORTION OF THIEVES. IF SO, CHALLENGE WITH THIS INFORMATION BY ASKING HIM HOW HE DIDN'T GET STARTED WHEN HE LIVED IN *THAT* AREA

Q.1b WHEN AREA ESTABLISHED, REMIND HIM OF HIS AGE *ON GOING THERE AND ON LEAVING.*

ASK IF THESE ARE CORRECT THEN ASK, *SLOWLY:*
'Exactly what age were you when you started to get round with those boys who pinched?' How old when you first got round with boys who pinched?'
CHALLENGE:
'Why didn't you start earlier?'
'What makes you think it was then?'
THEN ENTER 'STARTING' AGE

Duration of association with thieves
Later in the questionnaire boys were asked (after being reminded of age on *first* associating with thieves):

'For how many years did you get round with them?'

Proportion of boy's associates who were thieves
This matter was also linked to the period of the boy's *greatest* association with thieves. The following question was asked to ascertain the proportion of the boy's associates who were thieves at that time.

Q.IIIa 'So it was when you were aged . . ., that you got around *most* with boys who pinched things.'
SAY SLOWLY
'Exactly how many were there of these boys you got round with when you were (GIVE AGE) — I mean the ones who were pinching things?'

c 'You said that at the age of . . . you were getting round with . . . boys who pinched things. Is that right? At that time, did you get around with any boys at all who were *NOT* pinching things? When you were . . . years old, did you get round with any boys who were *NOT* pinching things?' YES/NO
IF 'NO', CHALLENGE. *IF STILL 'NO', GO TO SECTION IV*
IF 'YES', ASK:
'Exactly *how many* of these boys did you get round with?'
CHALLENGE THAT:
(i) HE REALLY MEANS *NON*-PINCHERS

(ii) HE *MEANS* THE NUMBER GIVEN
ENTER FINAL NUMBER

The two numbers derived through IIIa and c were then used to calculate the proportion of each boy's associates (at the time of *greatest* thief association) who were thieves.

The distribution of boys in terms of the variables named in the sub-hypotheses and in terms also of the characteristics featured in other of the questions asked
In addition to the variables directly involved in the sub-hypotheses, there were others about which information was gathered as general background to the study of thief association. The latter are included in the following set of distribution tables (Tables 6.1, 6.2, 6.4 to 6.7 and figure 6.1).

Table 6.1
The number of homes in which boys have lived
(= an index of 'area mobility')
(3,113 cases, weighted)

	(n)	(%)
Only the one at present lived in	757	24
1 other	1,315	42
2 others	638	21
3 others	252	8
4 or more others	149	5
Not known how many others	2	—

Table 6.2
Boys' estimates of how many of the local boys are
engaged in stealing (i.e. in district in which he lives now)
[= a pointer to density of his surrounding of thieves]
(3,113 cases, weighted)

	(n)	(%)
All boys in area thought to be stealing	128	4
3/4	589	19
1/2	901	29
1/4	663	21
1/8	755	24
Less than 1/2	67	2
No information	10	—

— = Less than 0.5 per cent

Table 6.3
Age of first and maximum association with thieves
(3,113 cases, weighted)

Age	When first associated		Of maximum association	
	(n)	(%)	(n)	(%)
Never	334	11	334	11
6 or less	384	12	49	2
7	324	10	82	3
8	357	11	121	4
9	315	10	164	5
10	324	10	255	8
11	408	13	381	12
12	318	10	525	17
13 or over*	340	11	1,186	38
No information	9	—	16	1

*Not taken further because a quarter of sample aged only
thirteen or less, a half aged fourteen or less, three-quarters aged
fifteen or less
— = Less than 0.5 per cent

Various aspects of thief association analysed by various characteristics of boys

In this sub-section is presented evidence of the ways
which the variables hypothesized as causal are distributed amongst the sampled population. These variable
hypothesized as causal were, it will be remembered:

1 Association with thieves, expressed as 'proportion o
the boy's associates who were involved in stealing' (se
Table 6.6).

2 The involvement of the associates in stealing (se
Table 6.7).

3 Age at which boys began associating with thieves (se
Table 6.3).

4 Duration of the boy's association with thieves (se
Table 6.4).

Table 6.4
Duration of association with thieves
(3,113 cases, weighted)

Duration claimed	(n)	(%)
Never	334	11
Did not continue	331	11
1–2 yrs	622	20
3–5 yrs	975	31
6 or more years	730	23
No information	121	4

Table 6.5
At time of greatest association with thieves how many
thief-associates did the boy have?
(3,113 cases, weighted)

Number claimed	Living locally n	All cases n
No period of association	334	334
0	235	0
1	284	125
2	335	279
3	370	366
4	278	342
5	285	272
6–10	618	829
11–20	265	421
21–30	55	77
31–40	12	19
41–50	7	16
51 or over	12	26
No information	23	7
Average number of associates per boy (excluding no information)	5.38	7.38

Table 6.6
What proportion of boys'
associates were thieves?
(3,113 cases, weighted)

At time of greatest association	(n)	(%)	At present* (= time of interview)	(n)	(%)
Nil, because no thief associates	334	11	Nil, because no thief associates	1,288	41
1–20%	421	14	1–50%	1,133	36
21–40%	698	22			
41–60%	564	18	51–99%	438	14
61–80%	602	19			
81–100%	482	15	100%	163	5
Not known	12	–	No information	91	3

– = Less than 0.5 per cent

*The proportions used in this part of the table were decided upon to meet the requirements of certain aspects of hypothesis testing

Figure 6.1
Proportion of boys who said they did at some time get around
with thieves: (a) 'at all': (b) 'quite a lot'
(shown in segmentation form)

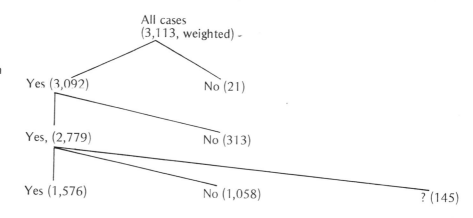

Was the respondent ever known
any boys who steal? II Q.1a

Was the respondent ever
'got around' with boys
who steal? (II Q.1b)

Was there ever a time when
the respondent 'got around'
with these 'quite a lot'?

All cases (3,113, weighted)

Yes (3,092) — No (21)

Yes, (2,779) — No (313)

Yes (1,576) — No (1,058) — ? (145)

Table 6.7
How much stealing were
the boys' associates doing?
(3,113 cases, weighted)

Degree to which associates were said to be stealing	At time of greatest association		At present (i.e. at time of interview)	
	(n)	(%)	(n)	(%)
Nil, because no thief associates	334	11	1,288	41
Not much	1,078	35	1,029	33
A fair bit	1,240	40	468	15
A lot	288	9	122	4
Not known	173	6	206	7

Extent of association with thieves analysed by various characteristics of boys

Extent of association is expressed as 'proportion of boy's associates who were thieves' (at time of greatest association) and this index was analysed by each of: occupational level of boy's father; type of school attended; boy's position in class; frequency of truancy; whether or not he ever went out just looking for fun an excitement; age on first associating with thieves; vig lance of parents in relation to the boy; the opportuni the boy has for stealing; his own permissiveness towar stealing; his expectation of getting caught if stealing; h attitude towards school-work (i.e. likes or dislikes it); h interests; the frequency with which he becomes bore The results of these analyses are set out in Table 6.8.

Table 6.8
Relating association with thieves to characteristics and background of boys
(3,113 cases, weighted)

Characteristics of boys Cases (weighted)	All cases 3,113	At time of greatest association with thieves Percentage of friends who were thieves						
		0 334	1–20 421	21–40 698	41–60 564	61–80 602	81–100 482	N 1:
	(n)	(%)	(%)	(%)	(%)	(%)	(%)	(%
Occupational level of boy's father								
Professional, semi-professional, managerial	518	21	22	21	19	14	3	0
Highly skilled	514	10	17	23	15	21	15	0
Skilled	674	10	10	27	16	20	16	1
Moderately skilled	630	9	12	19	21	19	21	0
Semi-skilled	517	7	10	22	21	22	19	—
Unskilled	254	7	10	21	17	21	23	1
No information	6							
Type of school attended								
Secondary-modern	1,464	9	18	23	19	21	20	1
Comprehensive	549	8	12	22	18	22	18	0
Grammar	718	15	21	23	18	16	7	0
Public	257	18	28	22	13	17	2	0
Other	105							
No information	20							
Position in class								
Top sector in class	762	9	9	23	18	19	22	—
Next sector in class	692	7	11	22	19	23	18	0
Next sector in class	383	9	7	21	20	22	22	—
Bottom sector in class	94	10	4	16	25	19	26	0
No information	1,182							
Did he ever play truant?								
Yes, once a week	331	2	6	13	16	26	36	1
Yes, once a month	262	3	7	16	15	32	27	—
Yes, but hardly ever	766	4	12	25	18	20	21	—
(Yes, not known how often)	3							
No	1,745	16	17	24	19	16	7	—
No information	6							
Ever gone out just looking for fun and excitement?								
Yes	2,229	6	12	24	17	22	18	—
No	884	23	17	19	21	12	8	—
Age at first association with thieves								
6 yrs or less	384	0	9	14	17	22	37	1
7–8 yrs	681	0	13	25	17	27	17	1
9–10 yrs	639	0	12	26	24	23	15	0
11–12 yrs	726	0	21	26	23	19	11	0
13 or over	340	0	21	33	17	15	14	0
Never associated	334	100	0	0	0	0	0	0
No information	9							

Table 6.8 (continued)

Characteristics of boys Cases (weighted)	All cases 3,113	At time of greatest association with thieves Percentage of friends who were thieves						
		0 334	1–20 421	21–40 698	41–60 564	61–80 602	81–100 482	NI 12
	(n)	(%)	(%)	(%)	(%)	(%)	(%)	(%)
Vigilance of parents								
Score 0	589	5	11	20	22	20	20	2
1	1,350	10	14	25	16	21	15	–
2	815	12	15	22	19	15	17	–
3	270	24	13	20	18	17	8	0
No information	89							
Ease of/or opportunity for stealing								
A lot of places to steal from	237	2	18	16	11	19	32	1
A fair number	828	6	14	22	19	24	16	–
A few	1,775	13	13	24	18	18	14	–
None	178	22	13	22	20	13	9	1
No information	95							
Permissiveness towards stealing								
Group 1 – high score	885	3	7	18	16	30	26	–
Group 2 – intermediate	1,096	10	16	23	21	17	13	–
Group 3 – low score	1,093	18	17	26	17	12	10	–
No information	39							
Would police catch you if you were stealing?								
Sure they would not	172	12	22	11	14	27	13	1
Don't think they would	832	7	13	22	16	21	21	0
They might catch me	1,243	9	13	23	21	18	16	–
A good chance they would	684	15	13	23	19	18	11	1
I'm sure they would	174	21	14	30	13	17	6	0
No information	8							
Does he like school work?								
Dislikes it very much	81	2	5	22	14	20	37	0
Dislikes it	597	6	14	17	16	25	21	1
Likes it	2,117	11	12	24	20	19	14	–
Likes it very much	312	17	27	25	13	9	9	–
No information	6							
Interest score quartiles								
Top score quartile	723	9	13	25	18	19	14	–
Next quartile	647	13	13	23	17	19	15	1
Next quartile	834	11	12	20	20	22	13	1
Bottom score quartile	892	10	16	20	18	18	19	–
No information	8							
Ever bored or fed-up?								
Yes, all the time	45	11	2	40	11	24	11	0
Yes, often	714	7	17	23	15	19	18	0
Yes, now and then	2,185	11	13	22	19	19	15	1
Yes, but frequency not given	4							
No	164	19	10	22	20	20	9	0
No information	1							

*Score 3 for boys where parents: decided how much of his spare time he could spend out of the home; decided where he would spend his spare time; decided which boys he would get round with. Score 0 where parents decided none of these things. See extended index of vigilance in Chapter 8

– = Less than 0.5 per cent

The evidence of Table 6.8 is that the tendency of the boys to associate with thieves does, at the period of its greatest incidence, vary markedly with the characteristics and background of the boy. Thus boys who associate most with thieves will tend to be those: whose fathers are in less-skilled jobs; who come from secondary-modern or comprehensive schools; who play truant; who go out just looking for fun and excitement; who started to mix with thieves early in their lives; whose parents are less vigilant in the sense that they do not control boys in relation to the friends they have and where they spend their spare time; who know a lot of places from which it is easy to steal; who are permissiv in their attitudes towards stealing; who feel the polic are unlikely to catch them if they go in for stealing; wh dislike school. On the other hand, the tendency of boy to have thief associates does *not* go along with thing like: claimed position in class; extent to which boys sa they have lots of interests; the degree to which they ge bored or fed-up.

One implication of this finding is that 'tendency t associate with thieves' is a sensitive variable in that i moves quite a lot with the characteristics of boys.

Table 6.9
Amount of stealing being done by associates analysed by respondents' characteristics

Characteristics	All cases 3,113	At time of respondents' maximum association with thieves, amount of stealing being done by respondents' associates (3,113 cases weighted)				
		Never associated 334	Not much stealing 1,078	Fair bit of stealing 1,240	Lot of stealing 288	No information 173
	(n)	(%)	(%)	(%)	(%)	(%)
Occupational level of father						
Professional, semi-professional, executive	518	21	44	28	6	1
Highly skilled	514	10	38	43	7	3
Skilled	674	10	34	41	8	7
Moderately skilled	630	9	32	44	9	7
Semi-skilled	517	6	30	42	12	10
Unskilled	254	7	28	41	20	4
No information	6					
Type of school attended						
Secondary-modern	1,464	9	30	44	12	6
Comprehensive	549	8	32	44	9	7
Grammar	718	15	43	31	5	7
Public	257	18	43	30	9	0
Other	105					
No information	20					
Position in class						
1st sector†	762	9	29	44	10	8
2nd sector	692	7	35	44	9	5
3rd sector	383	9	26	46	10	9
4th sector	94	10	18	41	18	13
No information	1,182	15	42	33	7	3
Ever played truant?						
Yes, once a week	331	2	21	51	19	8
Yes, once a month	262	3	25	50	14	8
Yes, hardly ever	766	4	32	49	10	5
Yes, no information how often	3					
All 'Yes'	1,362	3	28	50	13	6
All 'No'	1,745	16	40	32	7	5
No information	6					
Ever gone out just looking for fun and excitement?						
Yes	2,229	6	33	45	11	6
No	884	23	40	26	6	5
No information	0					

†1st sector = top group, based on class position data

Table 6.9 (continued)

Characteristics	All cases 3,113	At time of respondents' maximum association with thieves, amount of stealing being done by respondents' associates				
		Never associated 334	Not much stealing 1,078	Fair bit of stealing 1,240	Lot of stealing 288	No information 173
	(n)	(%)	(%)	(%)	(%)	(%)
Age on first association with thieves						
0–6 yrs	384	0	26	49	15	10
7–8 yrs	681	0	34	49	9	8
9–10 yrs	639	0	41	45	9	5
11–12 yrs	726	0	42	42	11	5
13 or over*	340	0	50	37	10	4
Never associated	334	100	0	0	0	0
No information	9					
Vigilance of parents						
Index 0	589	5	32	47	11	5
1	1,350	10	37	40	9	4
2	815	12	35	37	9	8
3	270	24	29	36	6	5
No information	89					
No. of places he can steal from						
A lot	237	2	25	36	25	11
A fair number	828	6	31	46	11	6
A few	1,775	13	36	40	6	5
None	178	22	49	19	9	1
No idea	81	19	37	25	12	7
No information	14					
Permissiveness						
High score	885	3	28	50	13	6
Intermediate score	1,096	10	35	40	10	6
Low score	1,093	18	40	32	5	5
No information	39					
Would the police catch him?						
Sure not	172	12	26	40	16	5
Don't think so	832	7	34	43	10	6
Might	1,243	9	36	40	9	6
Good chance	684	15	37	36	6	6
Sure would	174	21	29	35	14	1
No information	8	–	-–	–	–	–
Would the police catch him if he kept on stealing?						
Sure not	45	16	33	20	27	4
Don't think so	125	10	34	25	24	8
Might	362	7	38	35	11	9
Good chance	1,131	8	34	47	7	4
Sure would	1,437	14	34	38	9	6
No information	13					

*Not taken further because a quarter of sample aged only thirteen or less, half aged only fourteen or less, three-quarters aged fifteen or less

Table 6.9 (continued)

Characteristics	All cases 3,113	At time of respondents' maximum association with thieves, amount of stealing being done by respondents' associates				
		Never associated 334	Not much stealing 1,078	Fair bit of stealing 1,240	Lot of stealing 288	No information 173
	(n)	(%)	(%)	(%)	(%)	(%)
Attitudes towards schoolwork						
Dislike very much	81	3	26	38	22	11
Dislike	597	6	33	42	11	8
Like	2,117	12	37	40	7	4
Like very much	312	17	30	31	14	7
No information	6					
Interest score						
Top score quartile	723	10	32	40	12	6
Next quartile	647	13	32	39	7	9
Next quartile	834	11	35	38	11	4
Bottom score quartile	892	10	38	42	7	4
No information	8					
Frequency of being bored						
Yes	2,948	10	35	40	9	6
All the time	45	11	18	47	20	4
Often	714	7	34	42	14	4
Now and then	2,185	11	35	39	8	6
Frequency not given	4					
No	164	20	37	32	11	—
No information	1					

— = Less than 0.5 per cent

The amount of stealing being done by boy's associates, analysed by his own characteristics

The amount of stealing being done by boy's associates was regarded as one aspect of 'association with thieves' — in the sense that it helped define to what degree the associates *were* thieves (in the eyes of the respondent).

In Table 6.9 details are given of the ways in which the amount of stealing by associates varied with the background of respondents. The background variables analysed in this way were: occupational level of the boy's father; type of school last attended by the boy; position in class; whether he ever played truant and to what extent; whether he goes out 'just looking for fun and excitement'; age at first association with thieves; vigilance of parents; opportunity to steal; permissiveness towards stealing; confidence that the police would not catch him for stealing; reactions to school work; number of interests; frequency of being bored.

The principal indications of Table 6.9 are that boys who tend to have the more active thieves as associates tend to be: the sons of the less skilled; those with secondary-modern or comprehensive-school backgrounds; those who play truant; those who go out looking for fun and excitement; those who started to associate with thieves quite early; those whose parents exercise less control over them (than do other parents); those who know of a lot of places they might steal from; those with a high level of permissiveness in relation to stealing; those who have disliked school.

Table 6.10
Age at which boy first 'got around' with thieves,
analysed by respondents' characteristics
(3,113 cases, weighted)

Characteristics and background Cases (weighted)	All cases 3,113	Age at which boy first got round with thieves					
		6 or less 384	7–8 681	9–10 639	11–12 726	13+ 349	Never associated. 334
	(n)	(%)	(%)	(%)	(%)	(%)	(%)
Occupational level of father							
Professional, semi-professional, executive	518	7	19	22	16	15	21
Highly skilled	514	12	21	18	29	11	10
Skilled	674	13	20	23	24	10	10
Moderately skilled	630	15	23	21	20	12	9
Semi-skilled	517	14	24	19	28	9	7
Unskilled	254	15	25	20	24	9	7
No information	6						
Type of school last attended							
Comprehensive	549	14	20	27	24	8	8
Secondary-modern	1,464	14	22	21	23	12	9
Grammar	718	10	22	18	26	9	15
Public	257	7	24	16	11	23	18
Other	105						
No information	20						
Vigilance of parents							
Index 0	589	17	26	25	19	8	5
1	1,350	11	23	18	26	12	10
2	815	12	18	22	25	12	12
3	270	8	13	18	24	13	24
No information	89						
Age at maximum association with thieves							
Never	334	0	0	0	0	0	100
8 or less	252	47	53	0	0	0	0
9–10	419	16	45	39	0	0	0
11–12	906	10	20	27	43	0	0
13 or over†	1,186	10	16	18	27	29	0
No information	16						
Does he associate now?							
Never	334	0	0	0	0	0	100
Yes	954	13	22	21	29	16	0
No	1,734	15	26	25	25	10	0
No information	91						

*Not calculated because mixed group or because meaningless
†These were grouped because the over-thirteen year olds cannot
qualify for a later age of maximum association

continued

Table 6.10 (continued)

Characteristics and background Cases (weighted)	All cases 3,113	Age at which boy first got round with thieves					
		6 or less 384	7–8 681	9–10 639	11–12 726	13+ 349	Never associated 334
	(n)	(%)	(%)	(%)	(%)	(%)	(%)
Percentage of associates who were thieves at time of maximum association							
Over 60%	1,084	21	28	22	20	9	0
60% or less/never associated	2,017	7	19	20	26	13	16
No information	12						
Duration of association							
Never associated	334	0	0	0	0	0	100
Less than 1 yr	331	4	11	14	39	32	0
1–2 yrs	622	4	11	19	38	28	0
3–5 yrs	975	5	23	33	32	7	0
6+ yrs	730	38	43	17	3	–	0
No information	121	15	30	22	27	7	0

The age at which boys started to associate with thieves, analysed by characteristics of boys

The 'age at which boys first got round with thieves' has been hypothesized as a causal factor in the development of stealing by the boys themselves. In Table 6.10, this factor has been analysed by a wide range of characteristics.

The principal indications of Table 6.10 are that those who started to get round with thieves at quite an early age tend to be: the sons of the less skilled; those whose parents are less prone to exercise control over their sons; those who *maximized* their association with thieves at a relatively early age; those who were themselves thieves.

Also, those who have never associated with thieves tend to be: the sons of the professional and the semi-professional sectors; those with public- or grammar-school backgrounds; those whose parents are the more prone to control their sons.

Duration of association with thieves, analysed by characteristics

This variable was analysed in terms of age of first association with thieves. Results are shown in Table 6.11. Duration of association with thieves is greater for boys who began their association at an early age.

Investigating the Hypothesis

A summary of the basic strategy of investigation
As with all the other hypotheses dealt with in this volume, the central strategy for investigating the 'association' hypothesis was to derive from it a series of testable expectations and to test these. A lengthy statement about this strategy was made in Chapter 1.

The expectations to be tested
The basic hypothesis was, it will be recalled:

Association of a boy with thieves increases his own involvement in stealing.

It will also be recalled that four sub-hypotheses had been developed from the basic one. Whereas it would be quite possible to derive separate expectations for each of the four and test each set separately, the similarity of the four sub-hypotheses makes it unrealistic to do this and so, on this occasion, expectations were derived from all the sub-hypotheses, twelve expectations in all, and these have been tested in sequence without reference at the time to which sub-hypothesis they specifically refer to.

The twelve derived expectations are set out below:

Expectation 1 The greater the proportion of a boy's associates who steal, the more likely is he himself to steal.

Expectation 2 As for Expectation 1, even after empirical matching.

Expectation 3 The less the involvement of a boy's associates in stealing, the less likely is he himself to be involved in stealing.

Expectation 4 As for Expectation 3, even after empirical matching.

Expectation 5 The earlier a boy starts to associate with thieves, the more likely is he, himself, to be involved in stealing.

Expectation 6 As for Expectation 5, even after empirical matching.

Expectation 7 The longer the period of a boy's association with thieves, the more likely is he himself to be involved in stealing.

Expectation 8 As for Expectation 7, even after empirical matching.

For each of Expectations 1 to 8, the tests conducted relate to both variety and amount of stealing. For Expectation 6, they relate also to the duration of serious stealing by boys and to each of the forty-four types of theft involved in assessing total amount of thieving.

Expectation 9 Boys will claim that when they started to associate with thieves, their own stealing started or increased.

Expectation 10 Boys will claim that a *continued* association with thieves will lead to an increase in their own stealing; a discontinuation of association with thieves will lead to a reduction in their own stealing.

Expectation 11 Boys will claim that after a protracted association with thieves, discontinuing the association will lead to less stealing.

Expectation 12 Boys will tend to deny that they initially chose thief associates just because they themselves were stealing.

Expectation 12 is concerned with the possibility that the 'association' hypothesis might be true in reverse.

Testing Expectations 1 to 12: a general statement about methods

In the testing of Expectations 1, 3, 5 and 7, it was necessary only to relate the independent and the dependent variables, noting the extent of association between them. The testing of Expectations 2, 4, 6 and 8 called for the empirical matching of a control to a qualifying group. the qualifying group being made up in each case of the boys who qualified in terms of the expectation — as illustrated in Figures 6.2 to 6.5. The matching criteria were in each case those defined in the matching composite set out in Chapter 1.

For Expectations 9 to 12, the testing procedure consisted primarily of an examination of the testimony of the boys. Details are given in the context of the expectation testing itself.

Testing Expectation 1

The results of testing Expectation 1 are set out in Table 6.12 below. They are given in terms both of variety of stealing and the amount of it. The results clearly support the expectation.

Table 6.11
Duration of association with thieves analysed by age of first association
3,113 cases, weighted

Age of first association with thieves	All cases	Duration of association with thieves						
		Nil	0–1 yrs	2 yrs	3–4 yrs	5–8 yrs	9 or more yrs	NI
	(n)	(%)	(%)	(%)	(%)	(%)	(%)	(%)
6 yrs or less	384	0	5	4	6	39	40	5
7–8 yrs	681	0	10	5	18	52	9	6
9–10 yrs	639	0	12	14	40	29	—	5
11–12 yrs	726	0	25	24	38	8	—	5
13 or over	340	0	50	28	19	0	0	3
Never	334	100	0	0	0	0	0	0
No information	9							

— = Less than 0.5 per cent

221

Figure 6.2
Proportion of associates stealing at time of greatest
association with thieves

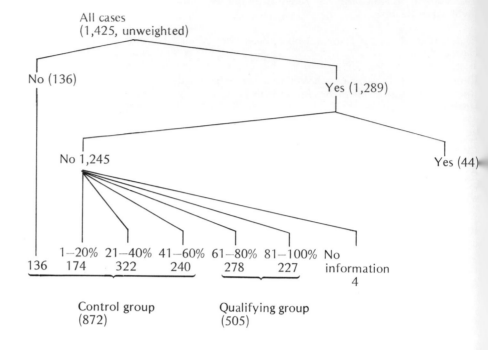

Has the boy *ever*
associated with thieves?

No (136)

Yes (1,289)

Did he choose thief
associates *because*
he himself was
already stealing?

No 1,245

Yes (44)

At period of maximum
association with
thieves, what *proportion*
of his associates were
thieves?

	1–20%	21–40%	41–60%	61–80%	81–100%	No
136	174	322	240	278	227	information 4

Control group
(872)

Qualifying group
(505)

Figure 6.3
Amount of stealing by associates at time of
greatest association with thieves

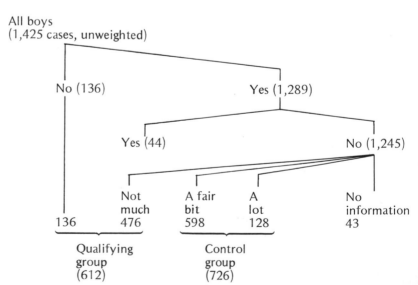

Has he *ever* associated
with thieves?

No (136)

Yes (1,289)

Did he choose thief-
associates because he himself
was stealing already?

Yes (44)

No (1,245)

At time of greatest association
with thieves, how much stealing
were these associates doing?

	Not much	A fair bit	A lot	No information
136	476	598	128	43

Qualifying
group
(612)

Control
group
(726)

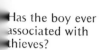

Figure 6.4
Age of first associating with thieves

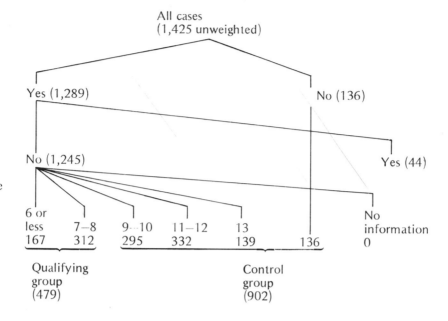

All cases
(1,425 unweighted)

Has the boy ever associated with thieves?

Yes (1,289)   No (136)

Did he select thief associates because he himself was already stealing?

No (1,245)   Yes (44)

At what age did the boy first associate with thieves?

6 or less	7–8	9–10	11–12	13		No information
167	312	295	332	139	136	0

Qualifying group (479)   Control group (902)

Figure 6.5
Duration of association with thieves

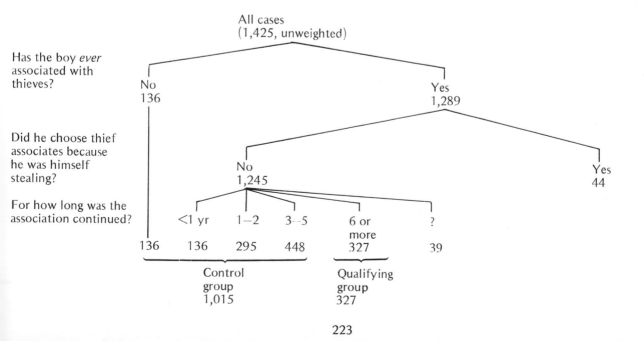

All cases
(1,425, unweighted)

Has the boy *ever* associated with thieves?

No 136   Yes 1,289

Did he choose thief associates because he was himself stealing?

No 1,245   Yes 44

For how long was the association continued?

	<1 yr	1–2	3–5	6 or more	?
136	136	295	448	327	39

Control group 1,015   Qualifying group 327

Table 6.12
Proportion of respondents' associates who are thieves,
analysed by variety and amount of stealing being done
by respondents
(3,113 cases, weighted)

Percentage of associates who were 'thieves' at time of maximum association with thieves	All cases	Index of variety of stealing				Index of amount of stealing			
		Low score quartile Q.1	Q.2	Q.3	Top score quartile Q.4	Low score quartile Q.1	Q.2	Q.3	Top score quartil† Q.4
	(n)	(%)	(%)	(%)	(%)	(%)	(%)	(%)	(%)
No association at all*	334	69	24	7	0	63	27	0	0
1–20	421	41	31	21	7	37	34	18	11
21–40	698	22	34	28	16	23	35	25	17
41–60	564	21	26	30	23	22	33	23	22
61–80	602	11	20	28	41	11	19	35	35
81–100	482	6	11	35	48	6	17	32	45
No information	12								

*That is, boys who never associated with thieves
†Not strictly quartiles because breaks in distributions came at
other than quartile points

Expectation 2 (using unweighted sample, 1,425 cases)

The testing of Expectation 2 called for the identification
of qualifying and control groups as Figure 6.2. The use of
'period of maximum association' was aimed at securing
both a memorable unit of information and a period of
seemingly special relevance. It is not, of course, the only
aspect of association that was studied (see Expectations
3 to 8).

After this splitting and identifying process, the
control group was matched to the qualifying group in
terms of the correlates of stealing. Matching was done
quite separately for a test of the expectation in terms of
variety of stealing and a test in terms of amount of
stealing. Results are set out in Table 6.13.

The test results shown in Table 6.13 verify Expectation 2, the residual difference between the qualifying
group and the reconstituted control group being large
and highly significant.

Testing Expectations 3 and 4

Expectations 3 and 4 were as follows.

Expectation 3 The less the involvement of a boy's
associates in stealing, the less likely is he himself to be
involved in stealing.

Expectation 4 As for Expectation 3, even after empirical
matching.

The results of testing Expectation 3 are set out in
Table 6.14 and serve to verify it.

In testing *Expectation 4*, using the unweighted
sample of 1,425 cases, the following splitting system
illustrated in Figure 6.3 was employed to identify qualifying and control groups. After this splitting and
identifying process, the control group was matched to the
qualifying group in terms of the correlates of stealing,
with the results shown in Table 6.15. Matching was done
quite separately for a test in terms of variety of stealing
and a test in terms of amount of stealing.

Table 6.13
Differences between qualifiers and controls before and
after matching: variety and amount of stealing

Indices of stealing	Qualifying group average unadjusted a (505 cases)	Control group average unadjusted b (872 cases)	Control group average adjusted c	Differences between qualifiers and adj. controls a–c P	Difference a–c as percentage of c
Variety index	18.17	10.93	12.23	5.94 (<0.01)	49
Amount index	128.86	69.72	82.19	46.67 (<0.01)	57

Table 6.14
Relationship between the involvement in boys' stealing and the extent of theft activity of their associates
(3,113 cases weighted)

Amount of stealing claimed as being done by thief-associates at time of maximum association with thieves	All cases (w'td)	Index of variety of stealing				Index of amount of stealing			
		Low score quartile Q.1	Q.2	Q.3	High score quartile Q.4	Low score quartile Q.1	Q.2	Q.3	High score quartile Q.4
	(n)	(%)	(%)	(%)	(%)	(%)	(%)	(%)	(%)
No association with thieves	334	69	24	7	0	63	27	10	0
Not much	1,078	27	33	25	15	27	36	23	14
A fair bit	1,240	14	23	31	32	13	24	29	34
A lot	288	12	10	31	47	16	16	26	42
No information	173								

Table 6.15
Differences between qualifiers and controls before and after matching: variety and amount of stealing

Indices of stealing	Qualifying group average unadjusted a (612 cases)	Control group average unadjusted b (728 cases)	Control group average adjusted c	Differences between qualifiers and adj. controls a−c P	Difference a−c as percentage of c
Variety index	10.0	16.4	14.9	−4.9 (<0.01)	−33
Amount index	60.6	117.8	102.7	−42.1 (<0.01)	−41

Table 6.16
Relationship between involvement in boys' stealing and age of first association with thieves
(3,113 cases, weighted)

Age at which boy claimed he first associated with thieves	All cases	Index of variety of stealing				Index of amount of stealing			
		Low-score quartile Q.1	Q.2	Q.3	High-score quartile Q.4	Low-score quartile Q.1	Q.2	Q.3	Low-score quartile Q.4
	(n)	(%)	(%)	(%)	(%)	(%)	(%)	(%)	(%)
At 6 or less	384	12	19	34	35	16	19	29	36
At 7–8	681	15	25	31	29	15	27	28	30
At 9–10	639	17	26	29	28	15	35	28	22
At 11–12	726	28	25	26	21	29	25	24	22
At 13 or over	340	25	26	23	26	20	33	25	22
Never associated with thieves	334	69	24	7	0	63	27	10	0
No information	9								

The test results presented in Table 6.15 verify Expectation 4, the residual difference between the qualifying and the reconstructed control groups being large and highly significant in the statistical sense.

Testing Expectations 5 and 6
These two expectations concern the age at which boys first began to associate with thieves, namely:

Expectation 5 The earlier a boy starts to associate with thieves, the more likely is he, himself, to be involved in stealing.

Expectation 6 As for Expectation 5, even after empirical matching and with special reference to:

a) Variety and amount of stealing.

b) Duration of serious stealing.

c) The forty-four different types of theft on which the total theft score was based.

The findings with respect to Expectation 5 are as set out in Table 6.16. This evidence supports Expectation 5, though clearly the relationship is not a strongly direct one.

In testing Expectation 6, using the unweighted sample of 1,425 cases, the respondents were sub-divided on the system shown in Figure 6.4. The control group was then matched to the qualifying group in terms of the correlates of stealing, with results as shown in Tables 6.17 and 6.18.

The findings in Table 6.17 support Sub-Expectations 6a and 6b. The results of testing Sub-Expectations 6c are set out in Table 6.18. The evidence in Table 6.18 supports Sub-Expectation 6c. All the residual differences in the right-hand column are positive and many of them are large. At the same time, a clear feature of the findings is that there is marked variation, in going from one class of theft to another, in the degree to which the expectation is borne out.

As with other data of this kind, a comparison has been made of the classes of theft for which the expectation is the more markedly borne out with those for which it is least borne out (see Table 6.19). If anything is to be said about this table, it must be at the level of mere speculation. At that level, it may be that boys who started to associate with thieves at an early age tend thereby to have stolen items widely differing in terms of the ages at which such items might reasonably be expected to be stolen (e.g. 'toys' and 'things from parks or playgrounds' at the one extreme and 'vehicles' at the other). On the other hand, the two columns in Table 6.19 do not seem to differ in terms of anything suggesting 'solitary' versus 'group' stealing.

More might be said of Table 6.19 but, at the non-speculative level, its main indication is that the expectation is differently borne out for different types of theft.

Expectations 7 and 8
Expectations 7 and 8 deal with the duration of association with thieves, as follows:

Expectation 7 The longer the period of a boy's association with thieves, the more likely is he himself to be involved in stealing.

Expectation 8 As for Expectation 7 after empirical matching.

Table 6.17
Differences between qualifiers and controls before and after matching: variety, amount and duration of stealing

Indices of stealing	Qualifying group average unadjusted a (479 cases)	Control group average unadjusted b (902 cases)	Control group average adjusted c	Differences between qualifiers and adj. controls a−c (P)	Difference a−c as percentage of c
Variety index	15.7	12.4	13.1	2.6 <0.05	20
Amount index	113.6	79.4	86.4	27.2 <0.01	32
Duration of serious stealing*	4.6	3.2	3.4	1.2	35

*Based on the eighteen more 'serious' types of theft (see Chapter 1) where the value of the item stolen was in excess of 4/6d (at time of study)

Table 6.18
Differences between qualifiers and controls before and after matching: each of the forty-four types of theft

Theft type** at L2†	Unadjusted results for qualifiers* a (479 cases)		Unadjusted results for controls b (914 cases)		Adjusted results for controls c		Differences between qualifiers and adj. controls a–c	Difference a–c as percentage of c
	(n)	(%)	(n)	(%)	(n)	(%)		
1	448	93.5	820	89.7	431.40	90.4	3.1	3
2	273	57.0	439	48.0	236.74	49.6	7.4	15
3	212	44.3	332	36.3	117.28	37.2	7.1	19
4	277	57.8	464	50.8	256.27	53.7	4.1	8
5	132	27.6	179	19.6	100.16	21.0	6.6	32
6	309	64.5	462	50.5	252.15	52.9	11.6	22
7	229	47.8	337	36.9	183.48	38.5	9.3	24
8	166	34.7	300	32.8	159.19	33.4	1.3	4
9	91	19.0	122	13.3	65.37	13.7	5.3	39
10	214	44.7	339	37.1	186.02	39.0	5.7	15
11	220	45.9	307	33.6	167.10	35.0	10.9	31
12	90	18.8	126	13.8	74.17	15.5	3.3	21
13	228	47.6	312	34.1	172.58	36.2	11.4	31
14	132	27.6	190	20.8	108.83	22.8	4.8	21
15	88	18.4	133	14.6	74.96	15.7	2.7	17
16	255	53.2	351	38.4	188.02	39.4	13.8	35
17	105	21.9	156	17.1	91.67	19.2	2.7	14
18	334	69.7	564	61.7	302.05	63.3	6.4	10
19	225	47.0	287	31.4	160.32	33.6	13.4	40
20	174	36.3	247	27.0	134.65	28.2	8.1	29
21	81	16.9	97	10.6	57.65	12.1	4.8	40
22	242	50.5	295	32.3	163.28	34.2	16.3	48
23	119	24.8	189	20.7	106.84	22.4	2.4	11
24	76	15.9	94	10.3	53.39	11.2	4.7	42
25	126	26.3	196	21.4	108.84	22.8	3.5	15
26	168	35.1	228	24.9	128.22	26.9	8.2	30
27	118	24.6	154	16.8	87.47	18.3	6.3	34
28	129	26.9	188	20.6	104.83	22.0	4.9	22
29	45	9.4	58	6.3	35.26	7.4	2.0	27
30	245	51.1	397	43.4	214.28	44.9	6.2	14
31	146	30.5	236	25.8	136.11	28.5	2.0	7
32	46	9.6	57	6.2	33.92	7.1	2.5	35
33	333	69.5	559	61.2	301.97	63.3	6.2	10
34	182	38.0	254	27.8	139.63	29.3	8.7	30
35	106	22.1	126	13.8	77.21	16.2	5.9	36
36	166	34.7	250	27.4	138.35	29.0	5.7	20
37	30	6.3	36	3.9	21.72	4.6	1.7	37
38	148	30.9	173	18.9	99.01	20.8	10.1	49
39	107	22.3	152	16.6	86.40	18.1	4.2	23
40	354	73.9	545	59.6	298.50	62.6	11.3	18
41	51	10.6	75	8.2	46.13	9.7	0.9	9
42	60	12.5	96	10.5	52.67	11.0	1.5	14
43	162	33.8	251	27.5	138.76	29.1	4.7	16
44	296	61.8	428	46.8	239.42	50.2	11.6	23

*Qualifying group: boys who began associating with thieves at age eight or less††
**Thefts exclusive of acts involving items of only trivial value. See Chapter 1 for details. See Appendix 1.2 for identity of the forty-four types of theft

†Control group: boys who began associating with thieves at nine or older.†† Also, boys who never associated with thieves
††Excluding any boys who claimed that they chose thief-associates because they themselves were already stealing

Testing Expectation 8

The results of testing Expectation 7 are as set out in Table 6.20 below. On the evidence in Table 6.20, Expectation 7 is clearly and strongly borne out.

Testing Expectation 8 (using 1,425 cases, unweighted)

The testing of Expectation 8, involving the empirical matching of a control group to a qualifying group, called first for the identification of those two groups. Figure 6.5 shows the way in which the identification of control and qualifying groups was done.

The control group was next matched to the qualifying group in terms of the composite of correlates of stealing, with results as shown in Table 6.21. The results support Expectation 8.

Testing Expectation 9

The testing of Expectation 9 involved methods quite different from those employed in dealing with Expectations 1 to 8, namely examination of the testimony of boys. The limitations of this class of evidence have already been stressed. Its use here is simply as an element of evidence within a fairly large composite of evidence gathered in various ways (see the testing of the other expectations).

Expectation 9 was that: 'Boys will claim that when they started to associate with thieves their own stealing started or increased'. Boys had been asked for details of what happened to such stealing as they may have been doing when they first started to get round with boys who were stealing. The wording of the questions asked is given in II Q.1a, 1b; II Q.1b(i); VI Q.1a; VI Q.2a. These

Table 6.19
Types of theft for which the expectation:

Tends most to be borne out	Tends least to be borne out
I have stolen something *from* a car or lorry or van I have stolen toys I have stolen milk I have stolen from a park or a playground I have stolen something from someone at school I have pinched something when I was in someone else's home I have stolen a car or lorry or van	I have kept something I have found I have pinched something from my family or relations I have stolen from work I have taken junk or scrap without asking for it first I have stolen money from a motor I have stolen something belonging to a school I have had something I knew was stolen I have stolen from a cafe

Table 6.20
Relationship between respondents' involvement in stealing and the duration of respondents' association with thieves
(3,113 cases, weighted)

Claimed duration of association with thieves	All cases (w'td)	Index of variety of stealing				Index of amount of stealing			
		Low-score quartile Q.1	Q.2	Q.3	High-score quartile Q.4	Low-score quartile Q.1	Q.2	Q.3	High-score quartile Q.4
	(*n*)	(%)	(%)	(%)	(%)	(%)	(%)	(%)	(%)
Has never associated	334	69	24	7	0	63	27	10	0
Less than 1 yr	331	41	28	21	10	40	37	11	12
1–2 yrs	622	28	32	27	14	28	32	24	16
3–5 yrs	975	19	28	25	28	17	29	29	25
6 or more yrs	730	6	17	35	42	8	18	30	44
No information*	121								

*The large number of 'no information' cases arises out of a change in the wording of a question shortly after the start of field work, leading to the discarding of these cases from this particular analysis. The figure 121 is, of course, a weighted-up figure

Table 6.21 Differences between qualifiers and controls before and after matching: variety and amount of stealing	Theft index	Qualifying group average unadjusted a (327 cases)	Control group average unadjusted b (1,015 cases)	Control group average adjusted c	Differences between qualifiers and adj. controls a–c	Difference a–c as percentage of c
	Variety index	18.5	11.9	13.5	5.0	37
	Amount index	139.7	76.0	96.0	43.7	46

are given in full in Appendix 6.1. On the basis of these questions, the response data were split up as in Figure 6.6.

This testimony quite strongly supports the expectation, namely that following the commencement of association with thieves, there was a tendency for those already stealing to do *more* stealing and for those not previously stealing to *start* stealing.

However, several questions arise from the evidence in Figure 6.6.

A) For boys who have never associated with thieves, *what* led them to take up such stealing as they did do (if any?). And what was it that stood in the way of these boys associating with thieves? Boy's responses to both questions are given in Table 6.22.

Perhaps not surprisingly, this evidence: (*a*) supports the common belief that association with thieves may be staved-off by a boy having companions who *do not* steal and by the development of a hostile attitude towards stealing and thieves; and, (*b*) suggests a range of *other* causal factors (in relation to stealing) for these boys, namely emulating thieves known to them (without being their associates), being 'dared' to steal, a desire for 'things', a desire to try it out, impulse.

B) Another question raised by the detail of Figure 6.6 is: since these 1,149 boys were stealing *before* they started to go round with thieves, what *did* get them started in stealing? The question asked in this case was VI Q.1, as set out in Appendix 6.1. The explanations given by boys are set out in Table 6.23. These reasons are broadly

Figure 6.6
Claimed effects of starting to get around with thieves

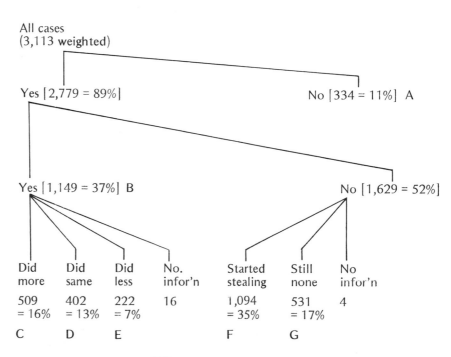

Table 6.22

Why some boys never 'got round' with thieves and what led these boys to commit such thefts as they did carry out

*Why did they never get round with thieves?** (334 cases)		*What, then, did get them started in stealing †* (excluding any who have never stolen) (334 cases, less those who have ever stolen)	
He has his own friends who don't steal	91	He wanted to copy mates/be like them (*but did not actually go round with them*)	42
He chooses friends who don't steal	12	To show off/be big	5
He has no friends/few friends	19	He was dared/challenged/threatened	16
He doesn't know any thieves	26	He wanted things/fancied things	32
He doesn't like thieves	127	He wanted lots of money	30
Thieves are bullies/'show offs'	35	He needed something	52
He kept away from them	6	For spite/to get own back	6
He was forbidden to mix with them	13	Jealous of others' possessions	3
He dislikes stealing	39	To try it out/see if it was easy	21
He doesn't want to get into trouble	26	As a practical joke	10
He might be blamed for what *they* did	12	On impulse	35
		Could not be bothered to pay	2

*See II Q.1b(i) in Appendix 6.1
†See II Q.1b(ii) in Appendix 6.1

Table 6.24

Why he did more	(*n*)	*Why no difference*	(*n*)	*Why he did less*	(*n*)
To gain prestige/show off/look big/show he wasn't scared	66	Frightened/worried about getting caught/about getting into trouble/didn't want to take any risks	86	*Relevant answers* Deterred by other boys getting caught/getting into trouble	51
To be accepted as one of the group	173	Deterred by mates being caught	13	Chances of being caught greater when there are a lot of boys involved	21
Because he was taunted/challenged by associates	48	Counter-influenced by parents/family members	19	The other boys pinched to excess/pinched things that were too valuable	13
Because he was dared by associates	35	He thought stealing was wrong	21	He didn't like what the others stole	3
Because he was bullied/threatened by associates	11	He saw no point in stealing more than before	60	The more there were in it, the less for each	5
He was encouraged by mates (no reference to pressure by them)	47	He did not join in when they were pinching things	37	Seeing other boys pinching made him see it as unfair/wrong	24
He was encouraged by mates getting away with it	33	He did not join in when they were stealing excessively/big things	10		
He was more confident because of mates' experiences	5	He did not associate much or for long with them	42	*At least partly irrelevant answers* He did not always go pinching with them	15
He just copied/followed example of mates	71	He thought they were stupid/looked down on them/disliked them	37	He didn't take an active part in it	19
He thinks it is easier/safer to pinch in a group	37	They didn't do much pinching	36	He was afraid of getting caught	27
More opportunity in a group	33	He associated with non-thieves, too	7	Deterred by having been caught/nearly caught	12
Had more courage in a group	22	He was not influenced by them	26	Parents advised against going pinching	11
He learned techniques from mates	7			He began to cut down on association with thieves/to associate with non-thieves	17
He was tempted by seeing what mates got away with	15			He realized stealing was wrong as he grew older	23
				He tried to reform his friends/self	13
				He had more pocket money/less need to pinch	10
				Not interested in pinching/had other interests	26

Table 6.23

'Things' that started them stealing
(asked of 1,149* boys who were stealing before starting to associate with thieves)

Volunteered Explanations	(n)
He wanted to keep up with mates (i.e. regarding their possessions and activities)	59
He copied the stealing of others (not associates whose stealing he knew of/had heard about	172
He was dared, challenged, to steal/threatened if he did not	45
To show off/be big	27
He wanted things but had insufficient money/could not afford things	216
He needed something/wanted to use it	151
He wanted it/liked it	245
Greed for others' property	12
Out of spite/revenge/to get his own back	23
To try it out/see if it was easy	23
Because stealing is easy	50
He just found things lying around	60
For fun/as a joke	64
He was bored/had nothing to do	10
On impulse	134
Could not be bothered paying for it	29

*Within weighted sample of 3,113 cases

similar to those given by the boys whose responses are reported in the right-hand column of Table 6.22. The more recurrent of them are: copying the stealing of others; keeping up with others; a desire for property or 'things'; because it was easy; for fun or a joke; on impulse. The full set of reasons in the table should be carefully studied. Some of them have a strong 'other boys' element in them even though the boys concerned were not at that stage *getting round* with thieves.

C,D,E The 1,149 boys who said they were already stealing before they began to get round with thieves were asked what happened to the level of their stealing thereafter — and answered as shown in Figure 6.7. They were then asked *why* their theft level was affected in this way, with results as shown in Figure 6.24.

Figure 6.7
Level of stealing after getting around with thieves

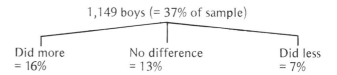

1,149 boys (= 37% of sample)

Did more = 16%   No difference = 13%   Did less = 7%

The 'reasons' set out in Table 6.24 support the following tentative conclusions.

1 Association with thieves *facilitates theft* through: prestige seeking and a desire for acceptance by thief-associates; being taunted or threatened by the other boys; being generally encouraged by them or by the evidence of their getting away with it; feeling safer when stealing in a group; copying thief associates.

2 At a minority level, association with thieves can *discourage* theft through: awareness of other boys in the

Table 6.25

Reasons for starting or not starting to steal following association with thieves

Reasons for starting (1,094 cases)		Reasons for not starting (531 cases)	
He stole to be one of the group/to avoid being left out	370	Because some of his mates were caught	25
He copied mates/followed their example	205	Boy scared/deterred by thought of getting into trouble with parents	47
They actively encouraged him to steal	109	Boy deterred by thought of getting into trouble with others (i.e. persons other than or additional to parents)	163
He was encouraged/made more confident because mates got away with stealing	80	Didn't want to give family or himself a bad name	8
Mates made it look easy	18	Lack of courage by boy	32
They showed him things they had stolen	48	He thought stealing wrong	89
They had stolen things he would like to have	18	Brought up not to steal	61
He learned the methods from other boys	21	He didn't want to pinch	68
He was dared/taunted/challenged	267	Parents disapproved/stopped him associating with thieves	22
He was bullied/threatened	43	He saw no point in stealing	91
To gain prestige in eyes of mates/to show off/to prove he was not a coward	145	He was never asked by mates to join in the pinching	21
Just for a laugh/a game/fun	113	He didn't associate much or for long	102
		Mates did not do much stealing	58
		He thought his thief associates stupid/disliked them	36
		He also mixed with non-thieves	15

group getting caught or getting into trouble; belief that there is a greater chance of getting caught when a lot of boys are involved; the spectacle of others stealing making it seem wrong.

3 For some boys, thief association seems to make no difference to their thieving, namely where: the boy is fearful of being caught; the boy sees no point in stealing even more than formerly; he does not join in with them when they actually steal; he thinks these particular boys are stupid or he dislikes them; his association with them is not intense or of long duration; the thief associates are not doing a lot of pinching.

According to F and G of Figure 6.6, some 1,629 boys were not doing any stealing before they started to associate with thieves. Thereafter, 1,094 of them started to steal and 531 did not. Each group 'explained' why it was that they behaved in this way after starting to associate with thieves. Reasons are presented in Table 6.25.

Reasons given for stealing following association with thieves were principally: to be one of the group; copying or following the example of mates; being encouraged by his associates; being taunted or 'dared' by his associates; to gain prestige in the eyes of his mates.

The reasons offered for *not* stealing following association with thieves could be of special importance. They were principally: fear of getting into trouble; his association was not intense or prolonged; he thought or had been taught that stealing was wrong; he saw no point in stealing; his thief associates were not in fact doing a lot of stealing.

Summing-up on 'explanations' and 'reasons'
Hereunder, I have brought together the apparent indications of the explanations offered by boys for being in one or another of the situations A to F as defined in Figure 6.6.

1 Association of a boy with thieves tends to promote thieving by that boy, the more recurrently-given explanations for this being that:

a He wanted to be accepted by the boys in his group.
b He wanted to look big in the eyes of his mates in the group or to show he wasn't scared.
c He was threatened or bullied or challenged or dared.
d He copied them.
e He was encouraged by them.
f He was encouraged by noting the experiences of his mates in relation to stealing (e.g. by their getting away with it, by seeking what they got away with, by the success of mates making it look easy, by their stealing things he would like to have himself).
g For a laugh, as part of a game, for fun (presumably in relation to his thief associates).
h He had more courage or felt safer when stealing as a member of a group.
i He found it easier to steal as a member of a group/was aware of more opportunities to steal.
j He learned new methods from mates.

2 Association of boys with thieves may, for a small minority of them, have reduced the level of their stealing, principally because:

a The boys concerned were deterred by their knowledge of others in the group getting caught/getting into trouble.
b Seeing others steal made them see stealing as unfair/wrong.
c The chances of getting caught seemed greater when a lot of boys were involved.
d The thief-associates stole to excess or stole things that were too valuable (thereby causing some boys to draw back).

3 Association of a boy with thieves will not necessarily have started him stealing, because:

a His association happened to be marginal (e.g. the association was brief, the thief associates did very little stealing, the boy's parents stopped the association.
b He was never asked to join in.
c He did not want to get into trouble with his parents or with anyone else.
d He was brought up not to steal or thought stealing wrong or didn't want to steal.
e He saw no point in stealing.
f He thought his thief associates stupid or disliked them.
g He lacked the courage to steal.
h He worried because some of his mates were caught.
i He also mixed with *non*-thieves.

4 Some boys -- a small minority -- don't associate with thieves, principally because:

a They have as friends boys who don't steal.
b These boys don't know or like boys who are thieving or don't want to mix with them.
c They have been forbidden to mix with thieves.
d They dislike stealing.
e They don't want to get into trouble or to be blamed for what other boys (i.e. thieves) did.

Testing Expectation 10
This expectation was that: 'Boys will claim that a *continued* association with thieves will lead to an increase in their own stealing; a discontinuation of association with thieves will lead to a reduction in their own stealing'. Here, too, the evidence used in testing the expectation was primarily the testimony of boys as offered through VI Q.2a (see Appendix 6.1). Boys had been asked if they continued to get round with thieves (after a first period of association) and, if they *did* so continue, how this affected the amount of thieving they were doing, and why. On the basis of this form of questioning, the response data were split-up as in Figure 6.7.

This evidence supports Expectation 10, namely, that there is a tendency for boys who *discontinue* getting around with thieves to do less stealing thereafter; that

Figure 6.7
Respondent segmentation leading to what happened to stealing when original association with thieves was broken

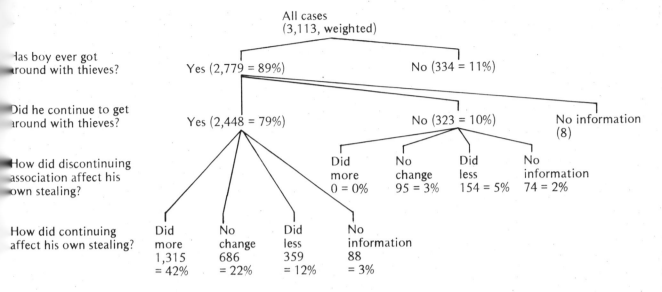

for those who *continue* that association, there is a tendency to do more stealing thereafter.

Boys were asked to explain their answers to various of the questions that led to the segmentation shown in Figure 6.7, namely:

1 Their reasons for ceasing to get round with thieves (**VI** Q.2a(i))(see Table 6.26).

2 Why they did less stealing after ceasing to associate with thieves (**VI** Q.2a(iii)(see Table 6.27).

Table 6.26
Why did some boys cease going around with thieves?
(323 cases, weighted)

Reasons given (**VIQ.2a(i)**)	(*n*)
He got fed-up with them/had a row with them/didn't like them/no longer respected them	47
He thought stealing was wrong/thought it was stupid or no point in it/. . .	36
His mates got into trouble for stealing/got caught	19
He thought of mates caught/he would be implicated too	6
Deterred by prospect of being caught himself	24
Deterred by having been caught himself/in trouble himself	11
Parents stopped him from associating with thieves	23
He found new friends who did not pinch	29
He no longer went to the same school	37
He no longer lived in the same area	38
He found new interests	10
The group stopped stealing	11

3 Why ceasing association made no difference to the extent of their stealing (**VI** Q.2a(iii))(see Table 6.28).

4 Why they did *more* stealing as they continued their association with thieves (**VI** Q.2a(ii))(see Table 6.29).

Table 6.27
Why, after ceasing to associate with thieves, did some boys steal less?
(154 cases, weighted)

'Reasons' directly related to loss of thief associates (**VIQ.2a(iii)**)	(*n*)
No longer any need to gain prestige/show off/show he wasn't scared	22
No longer chased, threatened, forced to steal	7
Now he mixed with *non*-thieves	26
He didn't find fun or excitement in stealing alone	11
Too nervous to pinch alone	8
He was aware that mates who stole got caught/got into trouble	22
He was afraid of getting into trouble himself (primarily on basis of mates getting into trouble)	31

'Reasons' probably not relating to discontinuance of association with thieves (**VIQ.2a(iii)**)	
Boy now thinks stealing is wrong/has come to his senses/does not like it	36
Boy deterred or prevented by parents from pinching	7
Less opportunity to steal (for reasons other than loss of thief associates — e.g. no time, found other interests)	15

233

Table 6.28
Why, after ceasing to associate with thieves, did some boys' stealing level remain unchanged?
(95 cases, weighted)

Reasons given (VI Q.2a(iii))	(n)
Boy had not been influenced by his association with thieves	6
He had been under the influence of non-thieves	6
He had not done much pinching when with them anyhow/had never pinched during association with thieves	66

Table 6.29
Why did some boys do more stealing as their association with thieves continued?
(1,315 cases, weighted)

Reasons given (VI Q.2a(ii))	(n)
He was actively encouraged by mates (but no mention of bullying)	92
He was dared by mates	76
He was taunted/challenged by mates	131
He was bullied or threatened by mates	26
He stole more to be one of the group/to avoid being left out	295
To gain prestige/show off/look big/show he wasn't a coward	119
He copied mates/followed example of mates	273
Because he got away with it when with mates	87
Mates made it look easy	34
More scope when pinching with mates	26
He feels safer when stealing with mates	22
Mates had stolen things which boys wanted/showed him such things	63
Mates were getting older and so wanted more money or better things to steal	20
Stealing was the sole activity of his mates	15
He learned the techniques of stealing from mates	29

Table 6.30
Why did some boys do less stealing as their association with thieves continued?
(359 cases, weighted)

Reasons given (VI Q.2a(ii))	(n)
Deterred by other boys in group being caught/getting into trouble	9:
Deterred by being almost caught	1:
Afraid of getting caught	5:
The whole group stopped stealing	:
He started to get round with boys who did not steal/had less to do with thieves	3:
He got other interests	14
The other boys went on to pinch bigger things/more things and boy was deterred	10
He realized stealing was wrong as he got older/realized it was wrong or unfair/he looked down on thieves	14
He felt that it was not worth doing/no sense in it/he disliked the idea of it	44
He had no need to steal now	41
Other boys did the pinching for him	16

Table 6.31
Why did some boys break a protracted association with thieves?
(1,527 cases, weighted)

Reasons given (VI Q.2b(i))	(n)
He got fed-up with thieves/had a row or fight with them/didn't like them	229
Group split-up	27
Parents disapproved and stopped the association	108
He moved out of the district/mates moved out of the district	221
He changed school/mates changed school	227
He made or found new friends who did not steal	183
They were going too far/pinching to excess	67
He was worried or scared by prospect of getting caught/getting into trouble	138
His mates got caught/got into trouble	93
He himself got caught/got into trouble	101
He came to his senses/saw it was wrong or serious	144
He grew out of it	27
He could not be bothered going out with them/going out with them so much	6
He got interested in other things/got a girl friend	149

5 Why they did *less* stealing as they continued to associate with thieves (VI Q.2a(ii))(see Table 6.30).

The reasons given are set out in the tables indicated. In broad terms, they repeat the evidence presented in Tables 6.22 to 6.25 and summarized on p. 232. Because of this, fresh comment is not entered under Tables 6.26 and 6.30.

Testing Expectation 11
This expectation took the form: 'Boys will claim that after a protracted association with thieves, discontinuing the association will lead to less stealing'. Here too, boys were asked to say what they believed had happened to the level of such stealing as they were doing when they broke an enduring association with boys who were stealing. The questions asked are presented in Appendix 6.1 and allowed the following segmentation of respondents shown in figure 6.8.

The evidence presented in Figure 6.8 confirms Expectation 11. Boys were also asked to say: (a) what caused such break or breaks in their association; and, (b) why the break led to their doing less or more stealing. Their 'reasons' are given in Tables 6.31 and

Figure 6.8

Respondent segmentation leading to what happened to stealing when protracted association with thieves was broken

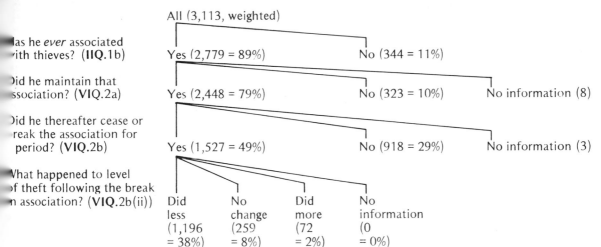

Has he *ever* associated with thieves? (**IIQ.1b**)
All (3,113, weighted)
Yes (2,779 = 89%) · No (344 = 11%)

Did he maintain that association? (**VIQ.2a**)
Yes (2,448 = 79%) · No (323 = 10%) · No information (8)

Did he thereafter cease or break the association for period? (**VIQ.2b**)
Yes (1,527 = 49%) · No (918 = 29%) · No information (3)

What happened to level of theft following the break in association? (**VIQ.2b(ii)**)
Did less (1,196 = 38%) · No change (259 = 8%) · Did more (72 = 2%) · No information (0 = 0%)

6.32. The details in Table 6.31 are closely similar to those in Table 6.26 whilst those in Table 6.32 closely resemble the reasons given in Table 6.27.

Table 6.32

Why did some boys do less stealing when they broke a protracted association with thieves?
(1,196 cases, weighted)

'Reasons' directly related to his loss of thief associates (**VIQ.2b(iii)**)	(*n*)
No longer necessary to gain prestige/show off/look big/ show he wasn't scared	87
No longer dared/threatened	39
He now associated with non-thieves	232
Association with thieves had ceased	312
No fun or excitement in pinching by himself	8
Too nervous or scared to pinch alone	35
He needs mates to help him carry it through (e.g. somebody to keep watch, advice of mates)	22
He does not like to pinch alone	69
He was aware of thief associates getting caught/getting into trouble	74
He was scared or worried about getting caught (presumably on basis of mates getting caught or into trouble)	124

'Reasons' probably not relating to break in association with thieves	
He now thinks stealing is wrong/does not like stealing/ has no need to steal/has come to his senses	313
Less opportunity to steal for reasons other than break of association (e.g. no time, too much work)	142

Testing Expectation 12

This expectation was of a special kind in that it was meant to probe the possibility that the reverse of the hypothesis applied, namely that: 'Thieving causes association with thieves'. The test or probe applied was by no means extensive or exhaustive. The expectation embodying this test was as follows: 'Boys will tend to deny that they initially chose thief associates just because they themselves were stealing'. The questions asked were **VII** Q.a and **VII** Q.b which took the following forms.

Table 6.33

Reasons volunteered for getting around with boys who were thieves
(2,778 cases, weighted)

Reasons given	(*n*)
Because they pinched/he himself liked pinching	51
He wanted to be in a gang	27
They were tough/he wanted to be tough too/he wanted to be big too	114
They were friendly/easy to get on with/nice	631
They were fun/lively/a laugh	364
They had the same interests (other than pinching) as the boy himself (respondent)	308
They were *his* type/his own age	98
Because they would help you out	141
They went to the same school as the boy	722
They were older than he was	22
He looked up to them/respected them	62
Mates forced/dared/encouraged him to join them	64
There was no one else to go round with/didn't know anyone else	477

Q.a 'You have mixed with boys who pinched things. Exactly why did you mix with these particular boys?'

Q.b 'Did you ever choose them *just because* they were pinching things?'
    IF 'YES': 'Can you tell my why?'

Table 6.34
Did boys choose thieves as associates just because they were pinching things?
(3,113 cases, weighted)

	(n)	(%)
Yes	108	3
No	2,489	80
Don't know	171	5
Has never associated with thieves	345	11

For the unweighted sample of 1,425 boys, there were forty-four respondents who answered 'Yes'

The results of this questioning procedure are given in Tables 6.33 and 6.34. Open-response material cannot be regarded as giving evidence of all that there is to be told, but the present evidence gives only minor support to the *reverse hypothesis.*

Table 6.35
Choosing thief associates just because they were thieves: further reasons
(108 cases, weighted)

Reasons given (**VII Q.b**)	(n)
Because he wanted to steal	7
They got what they wanted through stealing/he wanted to get things/easier to pinch with more boys	32
They know how/what to pinch/they showed him how to pinch	6
They were adventurous/active/go ahead/exciting going with them	18
They were tough/big/he could feel big associating with them	35
They could be trusted/would not let you down	14
He was bored	7

A more direct probe in relation to the reverse hypothesis
VII Q.b is direct and structured: 'Did you ever choos[e] them *just because* they were pinching things?' — whe[re] 'them' refers to the previous question's central referren[t] namely 'boys who have pinched things'. Responses ar[e] given in Table 6.34. Boys who answered 'yes' to tha[t] question were asked to explain that answer. Replies ar[e] given in Table 6.35.

From Table 6.35 it seems that by no means all of th[e] 3 per cent (see Table 6.34) who said 'Yes' (i.e. 'I chos[e] them *just because* they were pinching things') did in fac[t] choose their thief associates *because* the latter wer[e] thieves. But even the full 3 per cent is a very low figur[e] and does little to support the reverse hypothesis.

As one would expect, boys who claimed they chos[e] thief associates just *because* the latter were stealing wer[e] found to have been much more heavily involved i[n] stealing than other boys, as shown in Table 6.36.

5 SUMMING-UP ON THE INVESTIGATION OF THE HYPOTHESIS
1a The numerous tests of expectations made in thi[s] chapter serve to support and hence to make more tenable Sub-Hypotheses 1 to 4, namely:
(i) There is a positive causal relationship between the proportion of a boy's associates who steal and his own involvement in stealing.
(ii) There is a positive causal relationship between the amount of stealing being done by a boy's associates and his own involvement in stealing.
(iii) There is a positive causal relationship between the duration in years of a boy's association with thieves and his own involvement in stealing.
(iv) There is a negative causal relationship between a boy's age on first association with thieves and his own involvement in stealing.

b The tests of the various expectations also support and make more tenable the more general hypothesis:

Association of a boy with thieves increases his own involvement in stealing.

c The evidence gives little support to the hypothesis in reverse, namely that it was the boy's stealing that led him to choose thief associates rather than vice versa —

Table 6.36
Theft level of those who deliberately chose thieves as associates
(108 cases, weighted)

		Index of variety of stealing				Index of amount of stealing			
Did you ever choose them just because they were stealing?		Low-theft quartile Q.1	Q.2	Q.3	High-theft quartile Q.4	Low-theft quartile Q.1	Q.2	Q.3	High-theft quartile Q.4
	(n)	(%)	(%)	(%)	(%)	(%)	(%)	(%)	(%)
Yes	108	4	5	37	54	4	26	20	50
No	2,489	20	27	28	26	20	28	27	25

ough something like 3 per cent of boys appear to have
one this.

a Early association with thieves is, perhaps under-
andably, associated with a longer duration of serious
ealing.

Early association with thieves is related more to the
ommitting of some types of theft than to others,
hough there is no simple pattern to the differences.

3 There is little doubt *in the minds of most boys* about
he effects on them of association with thieves. Thus,
hey tend strongly to believe that:
a Initial association leads them to take-up stealing or to
increase such stealing as they were doing.
b Continued association leads them to continue or to
increase their stealing.
c Reduced association or discontinuation of association
eads to a reduction or cessation of their own stealing.

4 Boys explained their positions with regard to association with thieves and their engagement in stealing, some
of the more recurrent claims and explanations being as
follows.
a Association of a boy with thieves has tended to
promote thieving by such a boy, the more recurrently
given 'reasons' for this being:
(i) He wanted to be accepted by the boys in his group.
(ii) He wanted to look big in the eyes of his mates in the
group or to show he wasn't scared.
(iii) He was threatened or bullied or challenged or
dared.
(iv) He copied them.
(v) He was encouraged by them.
(vi) He was encouraged by noting the experiences of his
mates in relation to stealing (e.g. by their getting away
with it, by saying what they got away with, by the
success of mates making it look easy, by their stealing
things he would like to have himself).

b Association of boys with thieves may, for a small
minority of them, reduce the level of their stealing
because:
(i) The boys concerned were deterred by their knowledge of others in their group getting caught/getting into
trouble.
(ii) Seeing others steal made them see stealing as
unfair/wrong.

c Association of a boy with thieves will not necessarily
have started him stealing, because:
(i) His association happened to be marginal (e.g. the
association was brief, the thief associates did very little
stealing, the boy's parents stopped the association).
(ii) He was never asked to join in.
(iii) He did not want to get into trouble with his parents
or with anyone else.
(iv) He was brought-up not to steal or thought stealing
wrong or didn't want to steal.
(v) He saw no point in stealing.

d Some boys — a small minority — don't associate with
thieves, principally because:
(i) They have as friends boys who don't steal.
(ii) These boys don't know or like boys who are
thieving or don't want to mix with them.

5 Boys who 'got round with thieves' gave their reasons
for this. The more recurrently given reasons were:
a They were friendly, easy to get on with, were fun,
were good for a laugh, were lively.
b They had his own sort of interests (other than
stealing); they were his type.
c They went to the same school as he did.
d He had no one else to go around with/he didn't know
anyone else.
e They were tough/he wanted to be tough or big too.

6 Reasons for breaking association with thieves were
principally that:

a He got fed-up with these boys/had a row with them.
b He changed school or mates changed school.
c He moved out of the district or mates moved out of
the district.
d He found new friends who did not steal.
e He 'came to his senses'/saw it was wrong or serious.
f He was worried over prospect of getting caught/getting
into trouble.
g His mates got caught/got into trouble.
h He got caught himself/he got into trouble.
i Parents disapproved/stopped the association.
j He got interested in other things/he got a girl friend.

6 SOME COMMENTS AND POSSIBLE ACTION
For the great majority of readers, it will come as no
surprise that the work reported in this chapter strongly
supports the hypothesis that a boy's association with
thieves does in general increase the extent of his own
thieving. At the same time, the present evidence is
important because: it strengthens the existing evidence
about the 'association' phenomenon; it presents 'association with thieves' as an important causal factor contributing to the development of stealing: it provides some
insights into the mechanics of this aspect of the causal
process.
    That third outcome of the inquiry, namely the
provision of insight into the ways in which association
with thieves relates to stealing, is worth exploring for
possible leads to remedial and preventive action.
1 In the first place, it is especially noteworthy that
stealing through association with thieves appears to be
catalysed by the following circumstances: a desire by
boys to be accepted by and to shine in the eyes of their
associates; encouragement provided by the evidence of
mates' success in stealing; pressures to steal and
challenges to steal provided by mates; copying thief
associates. If this is so, then the potency of 'association'
as a causal factor should be reduced: if boys had or
could use other ways of 'shining' in the eyes of mates
and of getting themselves accepted; if the thief associates
had success symbols *other than* their prowess in stealing

or in securing property; if the thief associates got away with stealing less often than they do. Though these are rather big 'IF's, they are not necessarily impossible to achieve. Whereas new goals are not easily inspired on a mass basis, it is nonetheless true that alternative goals and new success symbols do from time to time capture the emotive and intellectual drives of large sections of the youth population — witness the interest and activity centred around soccer, popular music, motor cycles, hair styles, trendy clothes. Whatever one may say about these particular surges and goals, their occurrence points to the possibility of developing or activating culturally constructive drives, goals and success symbols provided that the necessary research, training and promotional facilities are made available. *Research* is needed to investigate the wants and the needs that the new activities and goals would have to satisfy. *Training* is needed where or if the new goal or activity calls for the development of skills. *Promotion* especially through the mass media, is needed where it is necessary that the new activities be presented in a realistic and practical way to large populations of boys.

Well funded, imaginative promotional efforts through the mass media have in the past been used with apparent success in both the cultural and the commercial contexts, so that bringing them to bear in a responsible and constructive way upon the development of goals and drives in boys may not be all that impossible. But it is essential that any such programme of youth development be closely geared to properly elicited information about their wants and needs and that such a project be protected against manipulative abuses.

2 Another feature of the evidence presented in this chapter is that a small minority of boys claimed a *reduction* in their stealing as a result of mixing with thieves. They explained this in terms of: the evidence thereby available to them of mates getting caught; seeing others steal made stealing appear unfair or wrong. The intensive interviewing of boys in this category may well be revealing in its provision of detailed information of an actionable kind about the deterrent or off-putting elements involved. Perhaps more might then be made of such off-putting factors.

3 Whereas there is a marked tendency for boys who mix with thieves to start stealing or to increase the amount of their stealing, some boys who have had thief associates deny this sort of effect. In some cases this appears to have been because the association with thieves was marginal or brief or because the boy concerned was never asked to join in. But in other cases it appears to have been because the boy had been 'brought up not to steal' and/or did not want to get into trouble with his parents or others. Probably, though one cannot be sure, this situation reflects the protective efficiency of specific training against stealing and of some sort of warning input. The intensive interviewing of such boys and their parents could well be rewarding in terms of guidance thereby provided for preventive action modelled on, or developed from, whatever it is that gives such boys protection against the powerful effects of association with thieves.

4 Another general guide to action exists in the overa evidence that the greater the association of a boy wi thieves, the greater is the likelihood that he will thereb be led into stealing. At the more specific level, th danger of a boy taking up stealing increases with: th proportion of his associates who are thieves; the amou of stealing being done by his associates; the length of h association with them; his association with them at a early age. This set of evidence strongly points to th necessity to reduce to a minor level the extent of a boy association with thieves, especially at an early ag However, in many districts of London, the achievemen of this outcome could well call for a degree of vigilanc on the part of parents and others that is unusual. would doubtless require that parents take or provid opportunities to meet their sons' friends, preferably i the boys' own homes, with a view to discouragin associations that they feel to be undesirable. An awar ness of the reputation and the character of boys living the district could be of considerable help here. Paren may in addition encourage or even initiate association (for the boy) of a kind that they believe to be safe. In a likelihood, the parents of a boy may have to help in th provision of interesting things for the boy and his friend to do at home.

To sketch out this sort of parental vigilance is not t suggest that it exists on any large scale — or that majority of parents and boys would be willing to carry through even if the need for it could be broadl communicated. Nonetheless, a concerted and imagina tive effort at achieving such communication, aided b the mass media, could well produce useful results wit caring parents who do not yet appreciate the danger inherent in their son's uncontrolled association wit other boys.

Obviously of course parents can do relatively littl about their sons' impromptu associations *at school*, an it seems highly desirable that a teacher's special know ledge of associations developing at school should b brought to bear on the situation in a constructiv way — including the breaking up of developing linkage of an undesirable kind and discussion with parents Teacher-parent associations might well contribute ver usefully to such liaison and co-ordinated action. Loca police officers, with their special awareness of boy associations and of juvenile stealing in their area, may o occasions be well positioned to discourage certai associations and to alert parents to developing danger for their sons. Social workers likewise have much to offer in helping parents be selective in relation to assessments of local boys.

The evidence of this inquiry is that association with thieves is a fairly potent contributing factor in the development of juvenile stealing. Though there are doubtless ways in which its potency can be reduced, the sheer extent of stealing and of association with thieves, as indicated in this inquiry, has to be carefully noted. The existence of this situation and the potency of the association factor present a problem which only concentrated effort on the part of parents, teachers, social workers, the mass media, the police and other social agencies is, in this present age, likely to solve.

APPENDIX 6.1

ne Sub-Questionnaire used:
ssociation with Thieves

THROUGHOUT THIS SECTION, PROBE AND
CHALLENGE AS NECESSARY. DON'T ACCEPT
SLIP-SHOD ANSWERING. AT THE SAME TIME,
KEEP MOVING AND DON'T WASTE TIME.
INTRODUCTION TO BOY. SAY:

he next few questions are about the boys you get
ound with. (PAUSE). I DON'T WANT TO KNOW
IEIR NAMES. I *won't* be asking for any details about
em. (PAUSE). I won't be asking who they are or
nere they live. Is that alright?'   (PROBE IF NOT)

The purpose of this section is to get the boy's areas of
residence, how long he lived at each residence, the
degree to which he sees the place where he lived as a
thief area. The purpose of this section is also to help
in the questioning procedure in Sections II-V.

.1a 'Exactly how old were you when you moved into
ne house where you live now?'
ENTER ANSWER IN COL. (2) BELOW.

b 'As far as you know, how many of the boys in your
istrict pinch things?'
PASS CARD AND SAY:
ook at these words carefully.'
READ THEM OUT, STARTING AT 'ALL OF
THEM' AND POINTING TO EACH IN TURN.
Vhich of them comes nearest to the number of boys in
our district who pinch things? Think hard before you
noose.'
CHALLENGE CHOICE WITH: 'Why did you choose
hat one?'
IF HE STICKS TO THAT ONE, RING IT IN THE
GRID

many of the boys who lived in *that* district pinched
things?'
PASS CARD, AND SAY:
'Look at these words very carefully.'
READ THEM OUT, STARTING WITH 'ALL OF
THEM' AND POINTING TO EACH.

'Which comes nearest to the number of boys in that
district who pinched things? Think hard before you
choose.'
CHALLENGE CHOICE WITH: 'Why did you choose
that one?'
IF HE STICKS TO THAT ONE, RING IT IN THE
GRID.

Q.3 SAME AS FOR QUESTION 2 FOR THE HOUSE
BEFORE THAT. KEEP GOING BACK TILL YOU
CAN GO NO FURTHER.
IF THE BOY WAS *FIVE OR UNDER* WHEN HE
MOVED OUT OF A HOUSE, DO NOT GET INFOR-
MATION ABOUT NUMBER OF BOYS WHO WERE
PINCHING IN THAT DISTRICT.

II Q.1 Has boy *ever* mixed with pinchers?
Q.2 What was his age of greatest association with
pinchers? Was it ever great? Were the pinchers then
doing a lot of pinching?

Q.1 Has he ever got around with pinchers?

1a 'Listen carefully to this one. As you know, lots of
boys pinch things (PAUSE). Have you *ever* known any
boys who pinch things?'   YES/NO?
IF 'NO', CHALLENGE WITH: 'Not in your *whole*
life? Not even with boys who did hardly any?'
IF STILL 'NO', GO TO *NEXT HYPOTHESIS*

1b 'Have you *ever* got around with any of those boys
yourself?' YES/NO.   IF 'YES', GO TO Q.2

Area lived in (1)	Age first there (2)	How many boys in district were pinching? (3)
Present		ALL / ¾ / ½ / ¼ / ⅛ / FEW / NONE
		ALL / ¾ / ½ / ¼ / ⅛ / FEW / NONE
		ALL / ¾ / ½ / ¼ / ⅛ / FEW / NONE
		ALL / ¾ / ½ / ¼ / ⅛ / FEW / NONE
		ALL / ¾ / ½ / ¼ / ⅛ / FEW / NONE

Q.2a 'Where did you live before that?' GET SUBURB.
ENTER IN COL. (1).
2b 'Exactly how old were you when you went to live in
hat house?' ENTER IN COL. (2).
2c 'Now think about when you lived in...' (SAY THE
UBURB NAMED IN 2(a)). 'As far as you know, how

If 'NO', CHALLENGE WITH: 'I mean any time in
your whole life. Perhaps just for a little time?'
CLARIFY THAT YOU DON'T MEAN BOY WAS
ALSO PINCHING
IF STILL 'NO', ASK:
(i) 'Can you tell me how it was that you *never* got round

with *any* boys who pinched things?' (PROBE)
(ii) (ASK ONLY IF BOY HAS DONE *SOME* PINCH-ING)
'What would you say got you started in pinching?' (PROBE)
NOW GO TO NEXT HYPOTHESIS

Q.2 'What was his age at time of greatest association with pinchers? Was the association ever great? Were the pinchers doing a lot of it?'

2a 'Was there *ever* a time when you got round with those boys *quite a lot?* I mean boys who pinched things?' YES/NO

2b 'I want you to think back to the age when you did this most of all — most often — more often than at any other age. Think about those times, for me, will you?'
NOW BUILD HIS MEMORY AS FOLLOWS: 'Where were you living then?'
CHECK GRID ENTRIES FOR ANY AREA WITH A HIGHER PROPORTION OF BOYS WHO WERE PINCHING.
IF THERE *IS* ONE SUCH AREA, CHALLENGE WITH: 'What about when you were living at (NAME THE AREA)?'
AFTER THIS, ASK:
'So what age were you when you got round most of all with those boys — boys who pinch things?'
CHALLENGE THAT HE MEANS *MOST* AND THAT *THIS WAS* THE AGE

2c 'At that time, how much pinching were those boys doing?'
PASS CARD. READ OUT. ENCOURAGE CHOICE. CHALLENGE IT
(A LOT/A FAIR BIT/NOT MUCH/NONE AT ALL)

III At time of greatest association with pinchers, how many pinchers were known (to boy) locally and not locally; how many 'non-pinchers' were known to boy locally and non-locally.

(KEEP REASONABLE BALANCE IN PROBING. DON'T JUST GO ON AND ON, FOR WE DON'T HAVE TIME FOR THIS. PROBE AS INDICATED, BUT MAKE IT VERY MUCH TO THE POINT AND MAINTAIN SPEED)

1a 'So it was when you were aged ... that you got around *most* with boys who pinched things?'
SAY SLOWLY:
'Exactly how many were there of these boys you got around with when you were (AGE) — I mean the ones who were pinching things?'
CHALLENGE NUMBER TO SEE THAT:
(i) HE REALLY MEANS 'PINCHERS';
(ii) HE IS COUNTING THEM ALL, EVEN IF NOT LOCAL;
(iii) HE MEANS THAT THE TIME WHEN HE GOT ROUND WITH THEM *MOST*
ENTER FINAL NUMBER

1b 'And exactly how many of these boys lived in you own district?'
CHALLENGE THAT:
(i) HE IS TALKING ABOUT PINCHERS;
(ii) HE IS TALKING OF THE TIME WHEN HE GO ROUND WITH 'PINCHERS' *MOST OF ALL*:
(iii) HE REALLY MEANS THE NUMBER HE GAVE
ENTER FINAL NUMBER

1c 'You said that at the age of ... you were gettin round with ... boys who pinched things. Is that right 'At that time, did you get round with any boys at a who were *NOT* pinching things? When you were .. years old, did you get round with any boys who wer *NOT* pinching things?' YES/NO
IF 'NO', CHALLENGE. *IF STILL 'NO' GO TC SECTION* IV
IF 'YES', ASK:
'Exactly *how many* of these boys did you get rounc with?'
CHALLENGE THAT:
(i) HE REALLY MEANS NON-PINCHERS;
(ii) HE MEANS THE NUMBER GIVEN.
ENTER FINAL NUMBER

1d 'You said that when you were ... years old, you got round with ... boys who were *NOT* pinching.'
Exactly how many of these lived *in your own district?*'
CHALLENGE THAT:
(i) HE IS TALKING ABOUT NON-PINCHERS;
(ii) HE IS TALKING ABOUT THEIR LIVING IN HIS OWN DISTRICT.
ENTER FINAL NUMBER

IV Q.1 Age of *first* association with pinchers?
Q.2 How many were there at that stage and what was the extent of their pinching?

Q.1 What was his age on *first* association with pinchers

1a 'Now in just the same way, I want you to think back to the time you *FIRST* started to get round with any boys who pinched things. *The time when you FIRST started to get round with any boys at all who pinched things.*'
'*Where were you living then?*'
CHECK GRID ENTRIES TO SEE IF A PREVIOUS AREA LIVED IN HAD HIGHER PROPORTION OF THIEVES. IF SO, CHALLENGE WITH THIS INFORMATION BY ASKING HOW HE DIDN'T GET STARTED WHEN HE LIVED IN *THAT* AREA

1b WHEN AREA ESTABLISHED, REMIND HIM OF HIS AGE *ON GOING THERE AND ON LEAVING.* ASK IF THESE ARE CORRECT. THEN ASK, *SLOWLY*
'Exactly what age were you when you started to get round with those boys who pinched? How old when you first got round with boys who pinched?'
CHALLENGE: e.g. 'Why didn't you start earlier? What makes you think it was then?'

THEN ENTER 'STARTING' AGE
IF THIS AGE WAS SAME AS FOR MAXIMUM ASSOCIATION OR WITHIN 12 MONTHS OF IT, *GO TO SECTION* **V**.

Q.2 How many pinchers known locally and not locally? How many non-pinchers known locally and not locally?

2a 'So it was when you were . . . that you *first* got round with boys who were pinching things? . . . Is that right?'
   SAY SLOWLY
Exactly how many were there of these boys that you got round with then?'
   CHALLENGE:
(i) THAT HE IS STILL REFERRING TO PINCHERS;
(ii) THAT HE IS COUNTING THEM *ALL*, EVEN IF NOT LOCAL. ENTER FINAL NUMBER

2b 'At that time, how much pinching were these boys doing?'

   PASS CARD. READ OUT. CHALLENGE CHOICE. THEN RING IT.
   (A LOT/A FAIR BIT/NOT MUCH/NONE AT ALL)

2c 'Exactly how many of those (GIVE NUMBER) boys lived *in your own district?*'
   CHALLENGE THAT:
(i) HE *IS* THINKING OF 'PINCHERS' HE *FIRST* GOT ROUND WITH.
(ii) HE *IS* THINKING OF HIS OWN DISTRICT. ENTER FINAL NUMBER

2d 'You said that when you were . . . years old, you *first* got round with boys who pinched things. Is that right?'
   SAY SLOWLY
'At that time, were you getting round with any boys who were *NOT* pinching things?' YES/NO
   IF 'NO', CHALLENGE: IF STILL 'NO', *GO TO SECTION* **V**.
   IF 'YES', *SAY SLOWLY*: 'Exactly how many were there of *these* boys?'
   CHALLENGE THE NUMBER GIVEN;
(i) TO SEE HE *IS* TALKING ABOUT BOYS WHO *DIDN'T* PINCH;
(ii) TO SEE HE IS TALKING ABOUT WHEN HE WAS . . . YEARS OLD.
(iii) TO SEE THAT THE NUMBER GIVEN IS FAIRLY FIRM/MEANINGFUL.
   ENTER FINAL NUMBER

2e 'So when you were . . . years old, you were getting round with . . . boys who were NOT pinching things. Exactly how many of these boys lived in your own district?'
   CHALLENGE THAT:
(i) HE *IS* THINKING OF HIS OWN DISTRICT AND OF *NON*-PINCHERS.
(ii) THAT HE *MEANS* THE NUMBER GIVEN. ENTER FINAL NUMBER

V Association at present (with pinchers.)

1a 'These days, how many boys do you get round with who are pinching things?'
   IF NONE, CHALLENGE. IF STILL NONE, *GO TO SECTION* **VI**
   CHALLENGE:
(i) THAT HE *IS* THINKING OF PINCHERS
(ii) THAT HE IS THINKING OF *ALL* AREAS
   ENTER FINAL NUMBER

1b 'How much pinching do these boys do?'
   PASS CARD. READ OUT. CHALLENGE CHOICE. THEN ENTER IT
   (A LOT/A FAIR BIT/NOT MUCH/NONE AT ALL).

1c 'How many of these boys live in your own district?'
   CHALLENGE AND ENTER FINAL NUMBER
1d 'And these days, how many boys do you get round with who are *NOT* pinching?'
   CHALLENGE AND ENTER FINAL NUMBER
   IF NONE, GO TO VI
1e 'How many of these live locally?'
   CHALLENGE TO SEE HE *IS* THINKING OF *NON*-PINCHERS AND OF *LOCAL* BOYS.
   ENTER FINAL NUMBER

VI His views about the effects of association with 'pinchers': first and later.

Q.1 Effects at time of first association.

'You told me that when you were . . . years old, you first started to get around with boys who pinched things. Were you doing any pinching before that?' YES/NO
   IF 'YES', ASK:

(i) 'Well, then, how did you get started on pinching?'
(ii) 'And *after* you started to get round with these boys, what happened to the amount of pinching you were doing?'
   SHOW CARD, CIRCLE CHOICE: (STAYED THE SAME/I DID LESS/I DID MORE/I STARTED)
(iii) 'Why did it get more/less/stay the same/start then?' (CHALLENGE ANY EXPLANATION IN TERMS OF MATES)
   IF 'NO', ASK:
(i) 'After you started to get round with these boys, what happened as far as pinching was concerned?' STARTED/STILL NONE.

(ii) 'Why did it/didn't it start then?'

   (PROBE ANY EXPLANATION IN TERMS OF MATES)

Q.2 Effects of later association.

2a 'When you were (GIVE AGE OF FIRST ASSOCIATION) you *first* got round with boys who pinched things. (PAUSE). Since then have you got round with any boys who pinched things?' YES/NO

IF 'NO" CHALLENGE. IF STILL 'NO', ASK:
(i) 'Why did you stop?'
(ii) 'When you stopped getting round with those boys, what happened to the amount of pinching you were doing?' MORE/LESS/SAME
(iii) 'Why was that?'
    NOW GO TO **VII**.
    IF 'YES', ASK:
(i) 'For how many years did you get round with them?'
(ii) 'Exactly what difference has this made to the amount of pinching you have done *yourself*?'
    SHOW CARD. RING CHOICE (NO DIFFERENCE/ LESS/MORE/DON'T KNOW).
    IF MORE OR LESS, ASK: 'How has it done that?'

2b 'Were there any times at all when you stopped getting round with boys who pinched things?' YES/NO

IF 'NO', CHALLENGE AND THEN GO TO **VII**
IF 'YES',
(i) 'Why did you stop?'
(ii) 'When you stopped getting round with those boys, what happened to the amount of pinching you were doing?'
(iii) 'Why was that?'

VII Why did he start getting round with boys who pinched?

1a 'You have mixed with boys who have pinched things Exactly why did you mix with those particular boys?'

1b 'Did you ever choose them *just because* they were pinching things?' YES/NO?
    IF 'YES': Can you tell me why?

242

Chapter seven
Home
conditions

CONTENTS

1 THE COVERAGE OF THIS CHAPTER

In this chapter I have presented a wide range of information broadly related to home conditions. This information was collected and processed to serve two associated purposes, the more important of which was to investigate a particular composite of hypotheses about causal factors in the development of juvenile stealing. These hypotheses were as follows.

1 Boys who do not like being at home are thereby made more likely to engage in stealing.

2 Boys who prefer to spend little or none of their spare time at home are thereby made more likely to steal.

3 If a boy feels there is little or nothing interesting to do at home, he is thereby made more likely to steal.

4 If there are frequently rows in his family, a boy is thereby made more likely to steal.

The second purpose of the collected data was to provide general background information about each of the factors or conditions hypothesized as causal in character. For example, with respect to attitude towards being at home, it seemed desirable to establish the distribution of boys' attitudes and how these varied with the background and characteristics of boys. Similarly, with regard to boys' views about how much of their spare time they wanted to spend at home, the degree to which they felt that there were interesting things to do at home and the frequency of rows in the family.

2 RESEARCH PROCEDURES COMMON TO ALL THE HYPOTHESES DEALT WITH IN THE INQUIRY

The gathering of information relevant to the hypotheses about 'home conditions' was done in the context of an inquiry concerned with over thirty other hypotheses. The techniques relating to the inquiry *as a whole* have been summarized in Chapter 1. That summary deals: with sampling procedures; with a technique for getting boys to provide reliable information about any stealing they have done; with questioning procedures for classifying boys in terms of the variables hypothesized as causal in the different hypotheses (i.e. in terms of the different independent variables); with strategies for investigating the tenability of hypotheses about causal factors and processes. The reader should as necessary refer to the relevant parts of Chapter 1 in reading statements of findings in the present and subsequent chapters.

3 RESEARCH PROCEDURES APPLYING ONLY TO THE HYPOTHESES DEALT WITH IN THIS CHAPTER

Whereas many aspects of research procedure applied generally to the whole range of hypotheses under study, certain parts of it related only to the four hypotheses about home conditions. These 'parts' tend to be encapsulated in one of the sub-questionnaires put to boys in the course of the interview and presented in full in the Appendix 7.1.

This questionnaire was designed in sections, each section beginning with a general description of its purpose as follows.

1 Does he like being at home?
Does he want to spend spare time there?

2 Is home a place where he can do things of interest to him?

3 Are there rows? Is he in them? Is home a happy place or not?

4 What are his relationships with others in the family, particularly his parents? Will he bring his friends home? Is home attractive to him?

5 When did he feel differently about being at home and why?

6 His *impressions** about the effects (on his theft behaviour) of such changes as have occurred in the way he feels about being at home.

7 His *impressions** about the effects of his present attitude towards being at home.

Whereas most of the questions were fully structured, some were of the open-response kind. In some cases the open-response question was for use in gaining insight into a situation or a position or a process. But in other cases such questions were asked in order to help boys formulate their positions in response to a fairly structured question yet to be asked. An example of such a procedure is given in the next section of this chapter.

4 METHODS AND FINDINGS RELATING TO THE INVESTIGATION OF HYPOTHESIS 1

The nature of Hypothesis 1

The first of the hypotheses about 'home conditions' was:

Boys who do not like being at home are thereby rendered more likely to engage in stealing.

It was a purpose of the inquiry both to examine this hypothesis and to provide background information about the independent variable defined in it. This independent variable is 'attitude towards being at home' defined in terms of liking/disliking.

The distribution of boys in terms of the variable defined as causal

In this section are presented: (*a*) details about the questions asked as a basis for classifying boys in terms of the independent variable; and (*b*) the distribution of boys in terms of that variable.

*Where boys were asked what they thought were the effects on them of how they felt about being at home, there was no assumption that the boy would be accurate in what he said. Such impressions were taken as nothing more than impressions.

he questions asked

everal questions were asked in order to assess the
egree to which the respondent 'liked being at home'.
he first two were asked primarily to set the respondent
ninking in realistic terms about how he actually felt
ver 'being at home'. The third involved the use of a
ting scale. These three questions are set out below.

.1 FIRST OF ALL, PREPARE THE BOY FOR
THIS SECTION. SAY:

Now I want to ask you about how things are at home.
f course it's absolutely private — just between the two
f us.'

TAKE FURTHER STEPS AS NECESSARY TO
PREPARE THE BOY FOR THESE QUESTIONS.

'What are the things you *like* about being at home?'
'What are the things that you *don't like* about being at
ome?'

ENCOURAGE WITH: 'Most boys find that there's
omething that they don't like at home.'

IF HE GIVES YOU NOTHING, TRY: 'Not a *single*
hing?'

'Now I want you to read all the things on this card.
(PASS CARD) 'Read them all aloud for me please.'

Table 7.1

Distribution of responses to Question 1c
(3,113 cases, weighted)

	(%)
Dislike it very much	1
Dislike it	4
In between like and dislike	—
Like it	33
Like it very much	44
Like it tremendously	18
No information	—

— = Less than 0.5 per cent

THEN SAY:
'Now here is the question. Think carefully about it
before you answer. Which of those (POINT) is nearest to
the way *you* feel about being at home?' (REPEAT).
DISLIKE IT VERY MUCH/DISLIKE IT/IN
BETWEEN LIKE AND DISLIKE/LIKE IT/LIKE IT
VERY MUCH/LIKE IT TREMENDOUSLY

Distribution of responses to Question 1C

For the sample as a whole, the distribution of responses
to Question 1c are set out in Table 7.1.

ble 7.2

pects of being at home
at boys like/dislike
13 cases (weighted)

Things liked	(n)	Things disliked	(n)
Being with the family/the company of the family/being with specific members of the family	1,406	Parents row/argue/too many rows	266
The happy or friendly atmosphere of the family/the family is nice to him	769	Does not get on with father/ disapproves of father's behaviour	49
It is restful/relaxed/peaceful	238	He objects to brothers or sisters/ quarrels with them/does not get on with them	407
The home is comfortable	368	Dislikes behaviour of relatives/ lodgers/visitors	60
Parents can be relied upon/family gives him sense of security/home is a place to go	730	Parents scold/nag/punish him	433
Parents look after his physical needs/ give him all he wants	550	His parents do not like the same things as he does/do not agree with him/do not understand him	30
Food/home cooking	251	He dislikes being told what to do	645
Can watch television/play records/ listen to the radio	571	Not free to come and go as please	374
Other activities he can pursue at home (e.g. hobbies, study, indoor games, homework, pets)	467	He wants to be independent	33
Can get himself something to eat	11	His parents treat him as a child	17
Can have friends in	78	He dislikes housework/chores/ shopping	350
Has his own room/own bed to sleep in	228	Home is overcrowded/no privacy	116
He has privacy	68	Too much noise/parents talk too much	19
Freedom to do what he wants there	396	Nothing to do/boring/too quiet at home	448
Allowed to come and go as he pleases	73	Dislikes appearance of house/dislikes district/dislikes neighbours	84
He is provided with money by family	54	Dislikes television	55
He can talk freely with his parents/ discuss his problems with parents	199	Parents fuss about him/worry about him/pamper him	32
He likes everything about the home	8	He does not like being alone in the house	38
He likes his neighbourhood	64	He prefers to go out	197

Table 7.1 indicates a very considerable tendency for boys to like being at home, with 44 per cent saying that they like it 'very much' and 18 per cent liking it 'tremendously'.

The responses to the two preliminary questions (Questions 1a and 1b) are also worthy of study and are shown in Table 7.2.

Boys also rated home life in terms of how happy a home they considered theirs to be. They had been asked:

Q.3c Which of these would you say is true of your home?

PASS CARD. CIRCLE CHOICE

A VERY UNHAPPY PLACE FOR ME

A FAIRLY UNHAPPY PLACE FOR ME

A BIT UNHAPPY FOR ME

JUST A BIT HAPPY FOR ME

A FAIRLY HAPPY PLACE FOR ME

A VERY HAPPY PLACE FOR ME

IN BETWEEN HAPPY AND UNHAPPY

What is it that makes it a happy/unhappy place for you?

The distribution of responses to Question 3c were as follows:

Table 7.3
Distribution of responses to Question 3c (3,113 cases weighted)

	(%)
A very happy place for me	47
A fairly happy place for me	34
Just a bit happy for me	5
In-between happy and unhappy	11
A bit unhappy for me	3
A fairly unhappy place for me	–
A very unhappy place for me	–
No information	–

– = Less than 0.5 per cent

The detail in Table 7.3 is closely in line with that in Table 7.1, the great majority of boys regarding their homes as either very happy or fairly happy places.

In Table 7.4 are set out the reasons given by boys for regarding their homes as happy/unhappy.

The more frequently-given reasons for regarding home as a happy place (for the boy concerned) were: that the family members get on well together, are nice to him and are nice to be with; that he is free to do as he likes at home; that there are many activities he can pursue at home (e.g. hobbies, indoor games, having pets, study); that his family has few or no rows; that his family can be relied on, gives him security and friendly help; that his home is a comfortable and restful place to be in.

On the negative side, very few boys rated home as even 'a bit unhappy'. For these few, the principal reasons given were: the occurrence of rows with and between family members; he dislikes being told what to do.

Table 7.4

Reasons given for rating home as happy/unhappy (3,113 cases, weighted)

Reasons for regarding home as happy place for him	(n)
He gets on well with his father/loves father	12
He gets on well with his mother/loves mother	13!
He gets on well with parents	41!
He gets on well with brothers/sisters	29!
The family gets on well together/friendly atmosphere in family/family nice to boy/boy likes being with the family	1,12!
Family has no rows/few rows	55!
Parents do not scold or nag	3!
He is free to do as he wants/no restrictions	51!
He can come and go as he pleases	9!
Parents can be relied on/give boy feeling of security/give him advice/give him friendly help	38!
Parents understand him/take an interest in him	7!
Parents look after his physical comforts/give him what he wants	32!
Food/home cooking	2!
Watching television/playing records/radio/tape recorder	18!
A convenience/somewhere to go to/somewhere to eat	1!
Other activities he can pursue at home (e.g. hobbies, study, homework, indoor games, pets, plenty to do, never bored)	432
His own room/privacy/he likes being home	148
A bed to sleep in	27
He can invite friends home	123
Its his own home/its comfortable/restful/a good place to be/relaxing/at ease there/can sit around there	387
People there you can talk to/have discussion with	84
Can go out as a family	50
He likes the neighbourhood/district	16

Reasons for regarding home as an unhappy place to be	(n)
Parents row/argue/do not get on together	9
He rows with father/does not get on with father	33
He rows with mother/does not get on with mother	16
He quarrels with/objects to brothers or sisters	6
Rows in the family/always angry	20
Rows in which he is involved	27
He dislikes being told what to do/cannot do what he wants	33
Cannot come and go as he pleases	9
He prefers to go out	6
He is not understood by family/is the odd one out/has different views from them	9
He is not adequately provided for (and so has to steal)	1
He dislikes household chores/shopping	5
Nothing to do/no one to play with/boring/too quiet	14
Dislikes the house/lack of amenities in house or district	2
No privacy/not enough room for boy to be by himself	3
He misses his father	1
He is sometimes happy/sometimes unhappy	345

246

'Liking/disliking being at home' analysed by characteristics and backgrounds of boys

The independent variable was analysed in terms of various aspects of boys' backgrounds and characteristics: father's occupational level; boy's age at time of interview; whether he has a room to himself; nominal religion; whether he goes out 'just looking for fun/ excitement'; how much of his spare time he would like to spend at home; the degree to which he has personal interests; frequency of family rows; rated happiness of home. Details are set out in Table 7.5.

Table 7.5
Attitude towards being at home analysed by characteristics of boys
(3,113 cases, weighted)

Characteristics Cases weighted	All cases 3,113		Attitude towards being at home			
			Dislike very much/dislike 152	Like 1,016	Like very much/ like tremendously 1,920	No information or between\like and dislike 25
	(n)	(%)	(%)	(%)	(%)	(%)
Occupational level of father						
Professional, semi-professional, managerial	518	17	0	39	61	0
Highly skilled	514	17	6	31	62	1
Skilled	674	22	7	29	63	1
Moderately skilled	630	20	4	36	59	1
Semi-skilled	517	17	8	31	60	—
Unskilled	254	8	2	28	70	—
No information	6	—				
Age at interview						
12 or 13 yrs	721	23	1	24	74	1
14 yrs	782	25	5	26	68	1
15 yrs	754	24	5	39	55	1
16 or 17 yrs	856	27	7	41	52	—
Religion						
Protestant	1,370	44	5	31	64	0
Catholic	500	16	5	27	67	1
Christian (only)	176	6	—	36	59	5
Jewish	214	7	1	35	64	—
None	621	20	6	37	56	1
Other religions	217	7				
No information	15	—				
A room to yourself?						
Yes	1,886	61	6	34	60	—
No	1,208	39	3	32	65	—
No information	19	1				
Persisted in going out 'just looking for fun and excitement'?						
Yes	975	31	8	35	57	—
No	1,857	60	2	31	66	1
Not clear if persisted	281	9				
Amount of spare time he would like to spend at home						
None	65	2	55	34	11	—
Not much	406	13	15	49	35	1
Less than half	531	17	6	46	48	—
About half	1,352	43	2	31	67	—
Most	672	22	1	17	82	—
All	59	2	0	12	88	—
No information	28	1				

Table 7.5 (continued)

Characteristics	All cases 3,113		Attitude towards being at home			
Cases weighted			Dislike very much/dislike 152	Like 1,016	Like very much/ like tremendously 1,920	No information or between like and dislike 25
	(n)	(%)	(%)	(%)	(%)	(%)
How many interesting things can he do at home?						
None	216	7	22	37	39	2
A few	619	20	7	47	46	–
A fair number	710	23	1	28	71	–
A lot	342	11	–	13	87	–
Yes (but number not given)	1,207	39	4	33	61	2
No information	19	1				
Frequency of family rows						
Every day	196	6	10	40	50	–
Most days	800	26	9	38	53	–
Once a week	919	30	4	36	60	–
Once a month	514	17	3	30	67	–
Hardly ever	617	20	1	20	79	–
Never	25	1	4	40	56	–
No information	42	1				
How often is he in family rows himself?						
Every day	80	3	19	47	34	–
Most days	569	18	9	44	47	–
Once a week	930	30	5	36	59	–
Once a month	543	17	4	31	65	–
Hardly ever	891	29	2	23	75	–
Never	76	2	1	26	73	–
No information	24	1				
Is it a happy/unhappy home?						
Unhappy (very/fairly/a little)	95	3	40	54	6	–
In between happy and unhappy	351	11	8	45	46	1
Just a bit happy	149	5	26	58	16	–
Fairly happy	1,051	34	3	50	46	1
Very happy	1,449	47	1	13	86	–
No information	18	1				

– = Less than 0.5 per cent

The reading of Table 7.5 must be done with an awareness that the great majority of boys say they like being at home — with only 5 per cent claiming they dislike it. The principal indication of Table 7.5 is that the boys who say they do not like being at home tend to be: the older boys; those who feel there is little or nothing of an interesting kind to be done at home; those who say there are very frequent rows at home and that they themselves are very frequently involved in family rows. Perhaps predictably, these are also the boys who say that they have at some time persisted in going out just looking for fun and excitement, who do not like spending any of their spare time at home, who regard home as an unhappy place for them.

Investigating Hypothesis 1

The basic strategy of investigation
The central strategy for investigating Hypothesis 1 (and indeed any of the other hypotheses to be studied) was to derive from it a series of testable *expectations* and to test these. A summary of this strategy appears in Chapter 1. The expectations derived from Hypothesis 1 are set out below.

The derivation of the expectations
Hypothesis 1 was:

Boys who do not like being at home are thereby made more likely to engage in stealing.

Attitude towards being at home	All cases		Quartile distribution of variety of stealing				Quartile distribution of amount of stealing			
			Q.1	Q.2	Q.3	Q.4	Q.1	Q.2	Q.3	Q.4
	(n)	(%)	(%)	(%)	(%)	(%)	(%)	(%)	(%)	(%)
Dislike very much/ dislike	152	5	6	14	34	46	5	12	41	42
Like	1,016	33	20	25	28	27	18	30	28	24
Like very much/ like tremendously	1,920	62	29	25	25	21	29	28	22	21
Between like and dislike or no information	25	1								

Table 7.6
Relating attitude towards being at home to amount and variety of stealing
(3,113 cases weighted)

The following expectations were derived from the hypothesis.

1 Boys who do not like being at home and who have long felt this way will have done more stealing than other boys.

2 Expectation 1 applies even when those who like being at home are closely matched, in terms of the correlates of stealing, to those who *do not* like being at home.

3 Boys will tend to *claim* that a 'dislike of being at home' leads them to do more stealing; that a 'liking of being at home' reduces the amount of stealing they do.

4 Boys will tend to claim that when they changed from liking to disliking with respect to 'being at home', their stealing increased; and vice versa.

Testing Expectation 1

This expectation was that: 'Boys who do not like being at home and who have long felt this way will have done more stealing than other boys'.

A test of this expectation is by no means a crucial check of the hypothesis, but a rejection of it would constitute a serious challenge (to the hypothesis). The results of the test are shown in Table 7.6. They support the expectation.

Testing Expectation 2 (using unweighted sample, 1,425 cases)

Expectation 2 was that: Expectation 1 applies even when those who like being at home are closely matched, in terms of the correlates of stealing, to those who do not like being at home.

Matching was in terms of the composite of correlates (of stealing) already developed for the inquiry as a whole. The qualifying and control groups were identified as follows:

Figure 7.1
Qualifying and control groups

All boys (unweighted)

Boys who dislike being at home (= 61)
plus
Boys who dislike it very much (= 7)

Qualifying group (= 68)

Boys who like being at home (= 436)
plus
boys who like it very much (= 636)
plus
Boys who like it tremendously (= 272)

Control group (= 1,344)

Both the control group and the qualifying group were now split into the thirteen matching sub-groups and the control composition (in terms of the thirteen sub-groups) was equated to the qualifying composition. The results of this process are shown in Table 7.7.

On the above evidence, Expectation 2 was strongly borne out.

Testing Expectation 3

This expectation was: that 'Boys will tend to claim that "a dislike of being at home" leads them to do more stealing; that a "liking of being at home" reduces the amount of stealing they do'. The following questions were asked in order to test this double statement See Appendix 7.1 for full questionnaire.

II Q.3a 'At *present*, you LIKE/DON'T LIKE being at home.' (SAY WHICHEVER HE CHOSE IN ANSWER TO I, Q.1c). 'Exactly what difference does this make to *where* you spend your spare time?'

Table 7.7
Differences between qualifiers and controls before and after matching: variety and amount of stealing

Indices of stealing	Unadjusted average score for qualifiers a (68 cases)	Unadjusted average score for controls b (1,344 cases)	Adjusted average score for controls c	Differences between qualifiers and adj. controls a−c P	Difference a−c as percentage of c
Averaged indices of *variety* of stealing	18.3	13.3	14.7	3.6 0.01	24
Averaged indices of *amount* of stealing	127.8	89.2	102.1	25.7 0.01	25

Q.3b 'Exactly what difference does it make to the amount of pinching you do?'
SHOW CARD. CIRCLE CHOICE.

It is not hard to imagine that these two questions would be somewhat undiscriminating for many boys, namely those for whom there is no prolonged contrast (in terms of attitude towards being home) against which to make a comparison. But nonetheless it was thought that the two questions would together provide an additional pointer to the tenability of Hypothesis 1.

The responses to these two questions are presented in Tables 7.8 and 7.9.

The data in Table 7.9 give some degree of support to the expectation.

Testing Expectation 4
The fourth expectation was that: 'Boys will tend to claim that, when they changed from liking to disliking with respect to being at home, their stealing increased; and vice versa'. A series of questions was asked in order to collect the information necessary for testing Expectation 4. These questions were as follows:

II Q.1b (IF BOY SAYS THERE WAS EVER A TIME WHEN HIS ATTITUDE TOWARDS BEING AT HOME WAS DIFFERENT FROM WHAT IT IS NOW, ASK:)

(i) 'Exactly when was that?' GET HIS AGE AT START OF THIS PERIOD. ENTER IN GRID

(ii) 'How long did that last?' ENTER DURATION IN GRID

(iii) 'What caused/was the reason for that change?' ENTER REASON IN GRID

II Q.1c *NOW TRY FOR ANY OTHER PERIOD WHEN HE FELT DIFFERENTLY FROM AT PRESENT (ABOUT BEING AT HOME). GET THE SAME DETAILS AND ENTER IN GRID.*

NOTE CAREFULLY *YOU SHOULD AVOID A CLUTTER OF VERY SHORT PERIODS OF DIFFERENCE.* WHAT IS WANTED MOST OF ALL

IS DATA ABOUT ANY ENDURING PERIOD O CHANGE. IF BOY REFERS TO SOME GENER ALITY SUCH AS 'WEEKENDS', 'ODD DAYS', ETC ENTER THIS AS A CATEGORY ACROSS COLS (1 AND (2) AND GET REASON(S).

(PRESENT STATE = DVM/D/L/LVM/LT (in answe to I Q.1c)

Age at start of change (1)	Duration of diff. (2)	(3)
		1a Reason for difference 2b(i) Effect on where time spent: NO DIFF/ 2b(ii) Effect on pinching: NO DIFF/LESS, MORE/STARTED ME
		1a Reasons: 2b(i) Effect on where: NO DIFF/ 2b(ii) Effect on pinching: NO DIFF/LESS, MORE/STARTED ME/
		1a Reasons: 2b(i) Effect on where: NO DIFF/ 2b(ii) Effect on pinching: NO DIFF/LESS, MORE/STARTED ME/
		1a Reasons: 2b(i) Effect on where: NO DIFF/ 2b(ii) Effect on pinching: NO DIFF/LESS, MORE/STARTED ME/
		1a Reasons: 2b(i) Effect on where: NO DIFF/ 2b(ii) Effect on pinching: NO DIFF/LESS/ MORE/STARTED ME
		1a Reasons: 2b(i) Effect on where: NO DIFF/ 2b(ii) Effect on pinching: NO DIFF/LESS/ MORE/STARTED ME/

Q.2 Effects of changes
ASK 2a and 2b FOR EACH DIFFERENCE ENTERED IN GRID

a 'Now you changed from . . . to . . . when you were
~~g~~ed . . .' 'Exactly what difference did this make to
~~w~~here you spent your spare time then?'

   ENTER RESPONSE IN GRID

~~2~~b 'And as far as pinching was concerned, what differ-
~~e~~nce did it make?'

   SHOW CARD. CIRCLE CHOICE IN GRID

   The yield of responses to this set of questions is set
~~o~~ut in Tables 7.10 to 7.12 below.

The main indications of these tables, taken in relation
to other of the collected data, appear to be as follows.

1 The great majority of boys (94 per cent) had claimed
that they liked being at home and somewhat more than
half of these (58 per cent) claimed that they had never
disliked being at home (see Table 7.10). Of the small
proportion who said they disliked being at home (5 per
cent), somewhat less than half (40 per cent) had claimed

Table 7.8
Claimed (i.e. volunteered)
effect of liking/disliking
home upon where he
spends his spare time
(3.113 cases, weighted)

Likes being at home (2,936 cases, weighted)	(n)*	Dislikes being at home (152 cases, weighted)	(n)*
No effect	860	No effect	14
Little effect	711	Spends more of his time in his	
Spends more time at home	934	own room	3
Feels free to be at home or out		Gets out more/gets away from	
as he pleases	204	family	93
Spends time at places his		Spends his time at sport/youth	
parents will approve of	52	clubs/with girls/with other	
Helps him avoid going round		people/on other things	65
with rough/tough people	24	He gets out with his parents	1
Other replies	192	He steals/pinches	3

*Totals exceed base figure because some boys gave more than
one reply

Table 7.9
Claimed effect of liking/
disliking home upon level
of theft

How boy feels about being at home	All	Claims it caused him				
		to steal *More*	to steal *Less*	to *Start*	No difference	No information
	(n)	(%)	(%)	(%)	(%)	(%)
Likes being at home	2,936	—	43	—	50	6
Dislikes being at home	152	4	11	1	63	21

— = Less than 0.5 per cent

Table 7.10
Has the respondent's like/
dislike of being at home
ever been otherwise?*
(3,113 cases weighted)

Feeling now	All cases*	Has he ever felt differently?		
		Yes	No	All
	(n)	(%)	(%)	(%)
Likes it	2,936	42	58	100
Dislikes it	152	60	40	100

*Less the 'in-between' and 'no information' cases

Table 7.11
Claimed effect of change
upon time spent at home
(3,113 cases, weighted)

Feeling about being at home	All cases	Claims change caused a change in time spent at home			
		Yes	No	No information	All
	(n)	(%)	(%)	(%)	(%)
Dislike now but once *liked*	92	59	26	15	100
Like now but once disliked	1,249	54	39	7	100
No change	1,772				

Table 7.12
Claimed effect on stealing of change in attitude towards being at home (3.113 cases, weighted)

At some time or other he changed attitude as below	All cases	Claims the change in attitude towards being at home caused him:				
		to *start stealing*	to steal *more*	to steal *less*	No difference	No information
	(*n*)	(%)	(%)	(%)	(%)	(%)
Dislike now but at some time *liked*	92	3	7	14	55	21
Like now but at some time *disliked*	1,249	3	7	9	75	6
No change	1,772					

that they had always disliked it there. In other words, enduring dislike of being at home is the condition of about one boy in fifty (i.e. 2 per cent), and enduring 'liking' is the condition of about 55 per cent.*

2 The remaining 43 per cent claimed that there had been times in their lives when their feelings were different from what they are now and there was some tendency for these boys to claim that this change altered the amount of time they spent at home (see Table 7.11).

3 The next element of evidence has to be considered with care and wariness, because the question as asked seems, on review, to be ambiguous: 'And as far as pinching is concerned, what difference did it make?' The difficulty is that though 'it' actually refers to a change from dislike to like or vice versa, the complexity of the questioning and the vagueness of the word 'it' throws some doubt upon what *direction* of *change* the boy had in mind. An examination of the questionnaire will make this point fairly clear. Nonetheless the evidence in Table 7.12 is in line with part of Expectation 4 (i.e. that boys will tend to report a change in theft level) but is out of line with the other part of it (i.e. concerning the direction of the claimed change). Taking the evidence of Table 7.12 at face value, the following processes are indicated.

a A period of dislike in the life of a boy who now *likes* being at home seems to have initiated theft or to have increased it for about 10 per cent of such boys, to have reduced it for about the same proportion** and to have left theft level unchanged for most of the rest of these boys.

b A period of *like* in the life of a boy who now dislikes home similarly seems to promote or increase theft for about as many boys as have their thieving reduced by it. The proportion of *these* boys experiencing 'no change' in theft level may well be less than the 75 per cent making this claim amongst those with an interim period of *dislike* (see a above), though the large number of 'no information' cases leave the situation uncertain.

* = 58 per cent of 94 per cent
**For example, as when the boy is in trouble at home over stealing and is thereby led to reduce the extent of his stealing.

Though these particular indications (i.e. a and b above) may arise solely from confusion in response, they are presented here because they *are* findings and because it is not impossible that they 'hint at' some important process of change. For what it is worth, this 'hint' is that a change in theft level (either way) is more likely to occur when boys who *dislike* being at home pass through a period of *liking* it (i.e. more likely than for boys experiencing the opposite process).

Summing up on the testing of the expectations drawn from Hypothesis 1
The testing of Expectations 1, 2 and 3 renders Hypothesis 1 more tenable. On the other hand, the uncertain evidence gathered in attempting to test Expectation 4 does not support the hypothesis. Having noted this, it is important to be aware that the evidence concerned does not so much conflict with the hypothesis as call for sophisticated speculation about the dynamics or mechanics connected with it. Thus — accepting the evidence from the testing of Expectation 4 at face value — it may well be that in referring to a boy's 'liking or disliking being at home' as a factor in the development or non-development of juvenile stealing, we ought really to be talking about the more enduring or persisting or usual state of that attitude. Perhaps, too, we should be hypothesizing about the nature of the influence on some boys of temporary variations away from their more common or usual attitudinal state.

5 METHODS AND FINDINGS RELATING TO THE INVESTIGATION OF HYPOTHESIS 2

The nature of the hypothesis
Hypothesis 2 took the form:

Boys who prefer to spend little or none of their spare time at home are thereby made more likely to steal.

It was the intention in this inquiry both to investigate this hypothesis and to provide background information about the independent variable defined in it, namely 'preference for spending little or no time at home'.

The distribution of boys in terms of the variable defined as causal

The question asked as a basis for classifying boys in terms of how much time they wish to spend at home

Question IQ.1d was asked as a means of classifying boys in terms of the independent variable in the hypothesis. A related question, IQ.1e, was asked with a view to extending awareness of the nature of that variable.

I Q.1d 'How much of your spare time would you like to spend at home?'
AFTER HIS REPLY' PASS THE CARD AND SAY:

'Which of these comes nearest to the amount of spare time you would like to spend at home?'
SHOW CARD
[NO TIME/NOT MUCH/LESS THAN HALF/ABOUT HALF/MOST OF IT/ALL OF IT]
RING THE ONE CHOSEN

I Q.1e 'And if you had to spend most of your spare time at home, how would you feel about that?'
SHOW CARD
[DISLIKE IT VERY MUCH/DISLIKE IT/LIKE IT/ LIKE IT VERY MUCH/LIKE IT TREMEND-OUSLY]
RING THE ONE CHOSEN

Distribution of responses

The distributions of responses to Questions 1d and 1e are set out in Tables 7.13 and 7.14.

Data already presented in this chapter had indicated that the great majority of boys regarded home as a happy place and one that they liked to be in. The findings presented in Tables 7.13 and 7.14 do not suggest, however, that the majority of boys want to spend most of their spare time there. Rather, they suggest: (a) a slight tendency for boys to want to spend their time *out* of the house; and (b) a substantial rejection of the idea of spending *most* of their spare time at home.

Amount of spare time boy wants to spend at home analysed by characteristics and background of boys

The independent variable in Hypothesis 2 was analysed by a range of characteristics and by aspects of the background of the boys. Results are given in Table 7.15.

The main indications of Table 7.15 are as follows:

1 The proportion of time that boys want to spend at home has very little relationship to:

a Occupational level.
b Nominal religion.

2 The proportion of time boys want to spend at home is appreciably related to:

a Age of boy (older boys want to spend less time at home).

b Tendency to go out looking for fun and excitement (those who *do not* do this want to spend *more* time at home).

c Having a room of one's own (those who *do not* have a room of their own want to spend somewhat *more* time at home — perhaps a surprising result).

Table 7.13		(*n*)	(%)
Amount of spare time boy wants to spend at home (3,113 cases, weighted)	No time	65	2
	Not much of his spare time	406	13
	Less than half his spare time	531	17
	About half his spare time	1,352	43
	Most of it	672	22
	All of it	59	2
	No information	28	1

Table 7.14		(*n*)	(%)
How boy would feel if he had to spend most of his spare time at home (3,113 cases, weighted)	Dislike it very much	337	11
	Dislike it	1,572	50
	Like it	859	28
	Like it very much	257	8
	Like it tremendously	62	2
	No information	26	1

Table 7.15
Proportion of spare time boy wants to spend at home
analysed by characteristics and background of boys
(3,113 cases, weighted)

Characteristics Cases (weighted)	All cases 3,113		Proportion of the spare time he wants to spend at home				
			Not much/ none 471	Less than half 531	About half 1,352	Most/ all 731	No information 28
	(n)	(%)	(%)	(%)	(%)	(%)	(%)
Occupational level of father							
Professional, semi-professional, managerial	518	17	13	14	49	24	0
Highly skilled	514	17	14	23	41	20	1
Skilled	674	22	15	16	43	25	1
Moderately skilled	630	20	17	15	41	26	1
Semi-skilled	517	17	16	17	47	19	1
Unskilled	254	8	14	19	39	28	0
No information	6	—					
Age at interview							
12 or 13 yrs	721	23	8	17	41	32	2
14 yrs	782	25	12	13	48	27	—
15 yrs	754	24	20	17	43	19	1
16 or 17 yrs	856	27	20	21	42	16	1
Religion							
Protestant	1,370	44	16	14	46	23	1
Catholic	500	16	18	22	39	20	1
Christian	176	6	10	21	44	22	3
Jewish	214	7	16	17	50	17	0
Other religions	217	7					
None	621	20	15	16	42	26	—
No information	15	—					
Persisted in going out 'just looking for fun and excitement'							
Yes	975	31	21	19	42	17	1
No	1,857	60	11	16	45	28	1
Not clear if persisted	281	9					
Has he a room to himself?							
Yes	1,886	61	16	18	45	20	—
No	1,208	39	14	16	41	29	—
No information	19	1					
How many interesting things can he do at home?							
None	216	7	41	22	25	7	5
A few	619	20	25	26	37	12	—
A fair number	710	23	8	17	48	27	—
A lot	342	11	4	11	39	46	0
Yes, but no information about how many	1,207	39	13	14	48	24	1
No information	19	1					

Table 7.15 (continued)

Characteristics Cases (weighted)	All cases 3,113		Proportion of the spare time he wants to spend at home				
			Not much/ none 471	Less than half 531	About half 1,352	Most/ all 731	No information 28
	(n)	(%)	(%)	(%)	(%)	(%)	(%)
How often are there family rows?							
Every day	196	6	26	25	33	14	3
Most days	800	26	20	21	44	16	0
Once a week	919	30	15	18	42	24	1
Once a month	514	17	13	17	43	26	0
Hardly ever	617	20	8	9	50	33	0
Never	25	1					
No information	42	1					
How often is boy himself involved *in family rows?*							
Every day	80	3	32	19	34	9	6
Most days	569	18	24	20	44	12	0
Once a week	930	30	16	20	42	21	1
Once a month	543	17	9	20	49	22	0
Hardly ever	891	29	10	13	44	33	—
Never	76	2	21	7	27	45	0
No information	24	1					
Is this a happy/unhappy home?							
Very unhappy/fairly unhappy/a bit unhappy	95	3	51	15	28	2	4
In between happy and unhappy	351	11	19	18	40	22	1
Just a bit happy	149	5	36	24	34	6	0
Fairly happy	1,051	34	18	23	41	18	—
Very happy	1,449	47	8	12	49	31	—
No information	18	1					

— = Less than 0.5 per cent

d Having interesting things that one can do at home (those who claim a lot of interesting things to do at home tend to want to spend *more* time at home).

e Having family rows (the more frequently these occur, the less the boy wants to spend his time at home).

f Being involved in family rows himself (the more frequently this occurs, the less the boy wants to spend his time *at home*).

g Whether the home is a happy one (the more unhappy it is the more the boy wants to spend his time away from home).

There is a peculiarity to the distribution referred to in g in that boys who say their home is 'between happy and unhappy' present an anomaly in the table. The same thing is evident in Table 7.5. It is as if this rating was being interpreted as equivalent to 'fairly happy'. On the other hand this particular outcome may not represent a misinterpretation of the rating item but some

phenomenon that is related to the special intermediate position of this rating unit (i.e. 'between happy and unhappy').

The other oddity in Table 7.15 is that boys with a room of their own are somewhat *more* disposed to want to spend their spare time *away* from home. This contrasts with a finding presented in Table 7.5, namely that boys with rooms of their own tend to 'like being at home' slightly more than do boys without rooms of their own. At the purely speculative level it may be that having a room of one's own is sufficiently lonely and 'shut in' to make boys want to escape from it — in spite of it tending to make them like home more.

Investigating Hypothesis 2

The basic strategy of investigation
As with all other hypotheses in this inquiry, the basic research strategy was to derive from the hypothesis as many testable propositions as possible and to test these. The propositions are referred to here as 'expectations'.

The nature of the expectations

The following expectations were derived from Hypothesis 2.

1 Boys who want to spend a lot of their spare time at home are less involved in stealing than boys who want to spend less time at home. This applies both to the *amount* and to the *variety* of their stealing.

2 Expectation 1 applies even when these two groups are closely matched. Expectation 2 applies also to both the amount and the variety of stealing.

3 Expectation 2 applies to the duration of serious stealing by boys (i.e. how long they carry it on for).

4 Expectation 2 applies generally to the forty-four 'types' of theft studied.

Testing Expectation 1

This expectation was that: 'Boys who want to spend a lot of their spare time at home are less involved in stealing than boys who want to spend less of their spare time at home. This applies both to the amount and to the variety of their stealing'. Testing this expectation involved a simple comparison of the theft levels of boys who want to spend different amounts of their spare time at home. Details of this comparison are shown in Table 7.16.

This evidence confirms Expectation 1.

Testing Expectation 2 (using unweighted sample, 1,425 cases)

The expectation in this case was that Expectation 1 would still apply when boys who want to spend a lot of spare time at home are closely matched to those who want to spend little or none of their spare time at home.

Matching was in terms of the empirically-derived composite of correlates of stealing already developed for the inquiry as a whole and described in Chapter 1 of this report. The qualifying and control groups were split out as follows. (Figure 7.2)

Figure 7.2
Splitting of qualifying and control groups

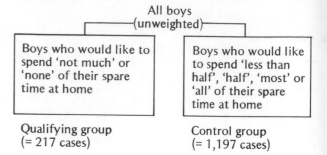

Each of the control and the qualifying groups was now split into the thirteen matching sub-groups which earlier work had indicated as appropriate for empirical matching. In terms of the matching composite, the constitution of the control group was equated to that of the qualifying group. The results of this process are shown in Table 7.17.

The data in Table 7.17 confirm the test of Expectation 2.

Testing Expectation 3 (using unweighted sample, 1,425 cases)

This expectation was that Expectation 2 applies also to the *duration* of boys' more serious stealing. Duration score was calculated for each boy with respect to those classes of theft which the public had, in an earlier small inquiry, judged to be the more serious among the forty-four types of theft covered in the theft study. 'Duration' was simply the number of years over which the boy had engaged in this class of stealing even if only sporadically.*

*See Chapter 1 for a fuller definition of the terms, 'duration' and 'serious stealing'.

Table 7.16
Relating desire to spend time at home to amount and variety of stealing
(3,113 cases, weighted)

Proportion of his spare time he wants to spend at home	All cases		Quartile distribution of variety of stealing				Quartile distribution of amount of stealing			
	(n)	(%)	0.1 (%)	0.2 (%)	0.3 (%)	0.4 (%)	0.1 (%)	0.2 (%)	0.3 (%)	0.4 (%)
No time/not much	471	15	12	20	31	37	7	26	30	37
Less than half his spare time	531	17	17	29	28	26	20	23	30	27
About half his spare time	1,352	43	28	23	26	23	25	29	23	23
Most or all of his spare time	731	23	33	28	23	16	36	30	22	12
No information	28	1								

Table 7.17 Differences between qualifiers and controls before and after matching: variety, amount and duration of stealing	Indices of stealing	Unadjusted average score for qualifiers a 217 cases	Unadjusted average score for controls b 1,197 cases	Adjusted average score for controls c	Differences between qualifiers and adj. controls a−c P	Difference a−c as percentage of c
	Averaged index of variety of stealing	17.2	12.9	14.2	3.0 (0.01)	21
	Averaged index of amount of stealing	126.1	84.6	98.3	27.8 (0.01)	28
	Duration of 'serious' stealing at level 3+*	4.5	3.6	4.3	0.2 (NS)	5

*Level 3+ refers to the theft of articles valued at 4/6d or above (pre-decimalization)

The control group as already defined was matched to the qualifying group in the manner already described as necessary in this class of operation. The results are shown in the last row of Table 7.17. They do not confirm Expectation 3 and hence reduce the tenability of Hypothesis 2 from this point of view i.e. with regard to 'a desire to spend less time at home' being a causal factor in extending *the duration* of a boy's involvement in serious stealing.

Testing Expectation 4 (using unweighted sample, 1,425 cases)

This expectation was that Expectation 2 applies generally to the forty-four 'types' of theft studied. To test this expectation, each of the forty-four classes of theft was investigated separately. For each of them, the control group was matched to the qualifying group in terms of the composite of empirically-derived predictors of thieving (see Chapter 1 for details). The results of this matching operation are set out in Table 7.18.

The results of this test confirm Expectation 4. But clearly there are some classes of theft for which the expectation is borne out much more strongly than for others. Those for which it applies most and least are set out in Table 7.19 below.

Noteworthy about this table is that the types of theft which most strongly line up with Expectation 4:

1 Are of a relatively serious nature.

2 Include five that have to do with vehicles.

Summing-up on the testing of expectations from Hypothesis 2

Expectations 1 and 2 were confirmed. In other words, boys who tend to want to spend their spare time away from home are more involved in stealing than other boys

and this applies even after matching in terms of the correlates of stealing. Expectation 4 was also confirmed, though there was evidence suggesting that it applies somewhat more for thefts that are somewhat more serious in character and for vehicle-linked thefts.

Expectation 3 was not confirmed, namely the expectation that a desire to spend relatively little time at home is associated with a greater *duration* of involvement in stealing.

6 METHODS AND FINDINGS RELATING TO THE INVESTIGATION OF HYPOTHESIS 3

The nature of the hypothesis
Hypothesis 3 took the following form:

If a boy feels there is little or nothing interesting to do at home he is thereby made more likely to steal.

It was one of the aims of the overall inquiry to examine and challenge this hypothesis through a series of propositions derived from it and to develop and present background information related to the independent variable involved in the hypothesis.

The distribution of boys in terms of the variable hypothesized as a causal factor

The question asked as a basis for classifying boys in terms of whether they think there is anything interesting they can do at home

The question asked of boys as a basis for classifying them in terms of the independent variable is set out below along with two related questions.

257

Table 7.18
Differences between qualifiers and controls* before and after matching: each of the forty-four types of theft

Theft type† at Level 2+	Unadjusted average score for qualifiers a (216 cases)		Unadjusted Average Score for Controls b (1,197 cases)		Adjusted Average Score for Controls c		Differences between Qualifiers and Adj. Controls a−c	Difference a−c as percentage of c
	(n)	(%)	(n)	(%)	(n)	(%)	(a−c)	(%)
1	211	97.7	1,071	89.5	201.19	92.0	5.7	6
2	124	57.4	602	50.3	118.53	54.2	3.2	6
3	114	52.8	446	37.3	90.50	41.4	11.4	28
4	126	58.3	622	52.0	118.17	54.0	4.3	8
5	65	30.1	250	20.9	50.98	23.3	6.8	29
6	144	66.7	638	53.3	125.56	57.4	9.3	16
7	103	47.7	469	39.2	94.73	43.3	4.4	10
8	77	35.6	395	33.0	73.76	33.7	1.9	6
9	48	22.2	169	14.1	35.30	16.1	6.1	38
10	125	57.9	431	36.0	93.77	42.9	15.0	35
11	102	47.2	428	35.8	86.90	39.7	7.5	19
12	46	21.3	174	14.5	35.66	16.3	5.0	31
13	112	51.9	441	36.8	88.29	40.4	11.5	29
14	79	36.6	251	21.0	56.29	25.7	10.9	42
15	48	22.2	175	14.6	35.01	16.0	6.2	39
16	122	56.5	494	41.3	98.98	45.3	11.2	25
17	73	33.8	192	16.0	38.30	17.5	16.3	93
18	156	72.2	755	63.1	152.31	69.6	2.6	4
19	90	41.7	429	35.8	86.01	39.3	2.4	6
20	84	38.9	343	28.7	72.43	33.1	5.8	18
21	36	16.7	145	12.1	26.88	12.3	4.4	36
22	90	41.7	459	38.3	85.56	39.1	2.6	7
23	70	32.4	246	20.6	58.18	26.6	5.8	22
24	36	16.7	140	11.7	29.22	13.4	3.3	25
25	63	29.2	266	22.2	51.97	23.8	5.4	23
26	76	35.2	323	27.0	62.07	28.4	6.8	24
27	57	26.4	218	18.2	45.96	21.0	5.4	26
28	60	27.8	264	22.1	55.11	25.2	2.6	10
29	23	10.6	80	6.7	16.42	7.5	3.1	41
30	123	56.9	529	44.2	110.60	50.6	6.3	12
31	87	40.3	300	25.1	70.46	32.2	8.1	25
32	19	8.8	82	6.9	16.42	7.5	1.3	17
33	160	74.1	740	61.8	147.59	67.5	6.6	10
34	89	41.2	353	29.5	66.73	30.5	10.7	35
35	64	29.6	175	14.6	37.32	17.1	12.5	73
36	95	44.0	330	27.6	66.50	30.4	13.6	45
37	24	11.1	42	3.5	10.30	4.7	6.4	136
38	75	34.7	252	21.1	51.92	23.7	11.0	46
39	55	25.5	212	17.7	44.49	20.3	5.2	26
40	166	76.9	746	62.3	145.08	66.3	10.6	16
41	30	13.9	98	8.2	20.66	9.4	4.5	48
42	32	14.8	127	10.6	24.58	11.2	3.6	32
43	82	38.0	342	28.6	71.69	32.8	5.2	16
44	143	66.2	593	49.5	116.68	53.4	12.8	24

*Qualifying group: boys who would like to spend 'not much' or 'no' time at home

Control group: boys who would like to spend 'less than half', 'about half', 'most' or 'all' their time at home

Excluded: Twelve cases giving 'no information'
†Thefts exclusive of acts involving items of only trivial value. See Chapter 1 for details. See Appendix to Chapter 1 for identity of the forty-four types of theft

Q.2a 'Is there anything *interesting* you can do in your own home — anything you like doing?' YES/NO ... IF YES, ask 'How many things?'
    SHOW CARD [A FEW/A FAIR NUMBER/A LOT]
    IF 'YES': 'What would that be?' PROMPT WITH: 'Anything else?'
    IF 'NO': 'Why is that?'

Q.2b 'Have you got a room all to yourself at home?' YES/NO

Q.2c 'How many people sleep in the same room as you do?'

IF HE SAYS HE HAS A ROOM ALL TO HIMSELF BUT *ALSO* THAT HE SHARES HIS BEDROOM, *CHALLENGE* AND SOLVE THE APPARENT CONTRADICTION

The responses to these questions are set out in Tables 7.20 to 7.24.

Table 7.19
Showing the classes of theft for which the expectation was borne out most and least

Applied most	Applied least
I have stolen a car or lorry or van	I have stolen something belonging to a school
I have got into a place and stolen	I have pinched something from my family or relations
I have stolen a bike or motorbike	I have stolen something just for fun
I have stolen money from a meter	I have stolen something from someone at school
I have stolen something from a car or lorry or van	I have kept something I have found
I have stolen something from a bike or motor bike	I have taken junk or scrap without asking for it first
I have stolen cigarettes	I have stolen a book or newspaper or magazine or comic
I have stolen a letter or a parcel	I have got things out of a slot machine without paying
I have stolen something from a changing-room or a cloakroom	I have got into some place without paying the money to go in
I have pinched something while I was in someone else's home	I have stolen something from a shop

Table 7.20
Is there anything interesting the boy can do at home?
(3,113 cases, weighted)

Response	(n)	(%)	(n)	(%)
Yes, a lot of things	342	11 ⎫		
Yes, a fair number of things	710	23 ⎬ 2,878	2,878	92
Yes, a few things	619	20		
Yes (but number not given)	1,207	39 ⎭		
Nothing interesting to do	216		216	7
No information	19		19	1

Table 7.21
The types of interesting things that boys can do at home
(3,113 cases, weighted)

Interest/Activity named	(n)
Hobbies of an active or constructive kind	
Musical instruments (e.g. guitar)	225
Making models	359
Painting/drawing/designing/sculpture	409
Mending bikes/bikes	106
Playing about with/mending electrical or mechanical or scientific apparatus	248
Carpentry/woodwork	120
Writing (all forms)	78
Making things (generally)	67
Technical hobbies (e.g. astronomy, photography)	71
Maintenance of fishing tackle	26
Collecting things (e.g. stamps, coins)	261
Other hobbies (e.g. model railways)	75

Table 7.21 (continued)

Interest/Activity named	(n)
Games	
Playing cards, chess, draughts, dominoes, monopoly	593
Table tennis, billiards, snooker, darts	338
Listening to records, radio, tape recorder	885
Playing with model cars, railway models, trains	183
Puzzles, crosswords, competitions	33
Playing games (unspecified)	413
Sports	
Guns/shooting	44
Karate/Judo/weight lifting/boxing	24
Spectator Activities	
Watching television	1,279
Housework	
Doing things round the house/helping in the garden	543
Cooking meals (and eating)	107
Social	
Talking to/being with members of the family	143
Phoning friends/having friends round (including girl friends)	126
Parties	21
Other	
Sleeping/resting/thinking/relaxing	132
Mucking about/fighting/making a nuisance of oneself	23
Reading/studying/homework	1,207
Playing with pets/looking after pets	218

Relatively few boys say there is *nothing* interesting to do at home (7 per cent) though there are many who find only 'a few' interesting things to do at home.

The boys who said there *were* interesting things to do at home were asked what these were. Their responses are set out in Table 7.21. The list of these is a long one and relatively few of its items are of an obviously anti-social kind.

The boys who claim that interesting things could *not* be done in their homes were asked to say why this was. Their replies follow in Table 7.22.

Perhaps the most interesting of the above 'reasons' is the claim that the family watches television too much, presumably leaving the boy to find his interests either in the viewing-room or alone elsewhere in the house or out of the house. Another interesting 'reason' is the aloneness of some boys within the house.

Following this question, each boy was asked two further questions. One was about whether he had a room all to himself at home (Question 2b); and the other dealt with how many people slept in the same room as he did. These two questions were asked because they seemed to bear on the degree to which the boy would be free to pursue individual types of hobbies or interests where there was lack of space or a distracting situation or lack of facilities — as when the boy has no room of his own (e.g. when he shares it with a younger brother). The

Table 7.22
Why little or nothing of interest could be done in some boys' homes
3,113 cases, weighted

	(n)
Boy is an only child/no siblings of his age	12
No mates to associate with/lacks other company/boy is lonely	13
Home overcrowded/too small/noisy	8
Family watches television all the time/boy fed up with television	46
Boy not allowed to do as he pleases/has to help parents/cannot make a mess	13
Boy prefers to go out/prefers playing sport	41
He finds nothing to do at home/bored with things/fed up	93

information derived from Questions 2b and 2c is presented in Tables 7.23 and 7.24.

The numbers saying 'no other' (i.e. 1,884) strengthens the evidence in Table 7.23, namely that 1,886 'have a room to themselves'. It is noteworthy both that sixteen of the boys (on the weighted base of 3,113) say they have between four and seven others sleeping in the same room with them, 6 per cent have two or three others, 32 per cent one other and that 61 per cent claim that no other person sleeps in the same room with them.

Investigating Hypothesis 3
Hypothesis 3 was:

If a boy feels there is little or nothing interesting to do at home, he is thereby made more likely to steal.

The basic strategy of investigation
As with all other hypotheses investigated in this inquiry, the basic strategy of investigation was to derive from the hypothesis as many as possible testable propositions and to test these. These propositions are referred to here as 'expectations'. Details of the method and the rationale of this testing system are given in Chapter 1.

Table 7.23		(n)	(%)
Has the boy got a room to himself? (3,113 cases, weighted)	Yes	1,886	61
	No	1,208	39
	No information	19	1

Table 7.24		(n)	(%)
How many sleep in the same room with the boy? (3,113 cases, weighted)	Respondent only	1,884	61
	One other	989	32
	2 others	170	5
	3 others	31	1
	4–6 others	13	–
	7 or more	3	–
	No information	23	1

– = Less than 0.5 per cent

The nature of the expectations
The following expectations were derived from the hypothesis.

1 Boys who claim there is 'nothing' interesting to do at home or 'very few' or 'only a few' interesting things to do at home (qualifiers) will have engaged in more stealing than boys who claim there is some greater number of interesting things to do at home (controls).

2 Expectation 1 applies even after the controls have been closely matched to the qualifiers in terms of the correlates of stealing.

3 Expectation 2 applies also to the *duration* of the boys' more serious stealing.

4 Expectation 2 applies with respect to the forty-four different types of theft studied.

Testing Expectation 1
This expectation, detailed above, was tested by comparing the 'theft scores' of boys claiming differently about the number of interesting things they can do at home. Table 7.25 presents the comparative data.

The information in Table 7.25 confirms Expectation 1. In other words, the more interesting things the boy can do at home (according to him), the less the amount of his stealing. The fourth line in Table 7.25 may seem to contradict this, but it represents a 'Yes' response where 'number' was not given. It does, in fact, correspond fairly closely to the average of all the 'Yes' rows and contrasts sharply with the 'nothing' row.

Testing Expectation 2 (using unweighted sample, 1,425 cases)
This expectation, detailed above, was tested through the matching operation used on a similar type of expectation related to Hypothesis 1. Thus the sample was first split as into control and qualifying groups as in Figure 7.3.

Following this, the control group was matched to the qualifying group in terms of the empirically-established correlates of stealing (as described in principle in

Table 7.25 Relating numbers of interesting things to do at home to amount and variety of stealing (3,113 cases, weighted)	Claimed number of interesting things he can do at home	All cases		Index of variety of stealing				Index of amount of stealing			
				0.1	0.2	0.3	0.4	0.1	0.2	0.3	0.4
		(n)	(%)	(%)	(%)	(%)	(%)	(%)	(%)	(%)	(%)
	Yes, a lot of things	342	11	32	25	28	15	33	31	18	18
	Yes, a fair number	710	23	26	28	22	24	25	32	20	23
	Yes, a few	619	20	18	17	32	34	16	19	34	31
	Yes (but number not given)	1,207	39	28	28	25	19	28	31	24	17
	Nothing interesting to do	216	7	10	18	33	39	11	14	32	43
	No information	19	1								

Figure 7.3
Division of sample for testing expectations

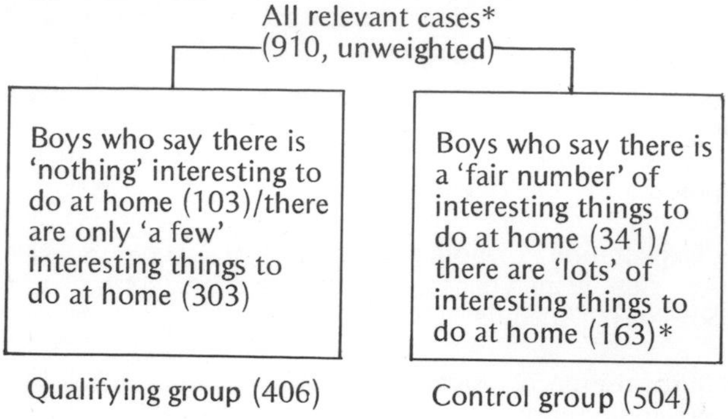

All relevant cases*
(910, unweighted)

Boys who say there is 'nothing' interesting to do at home (103)/there are only 'a few' interesting things to do at home (303)	Boys who say there is a 'fair number' of interesting things to do at home (341)/ there are 'lots' of interesting things to do at home (163)*
Qualifying group (406)	Control group (504)

*Those saying 'Yes' but not giving number of interesting things, were excluded. These were all boys who had been interviewed with a form of the questionnaire that did not ask for this sort of information but which was later amended to its final form as shown in Appendix 7.1. It was, of course, desirable to include such boys, but the nature of the above split made it impossible to decide which of the remaining 515 cases should go into the qualifying group and which into the control group.

Chapter 1). The results of the matching process are shown in Table 7.26.

The evidence in Table 7.26 confirms Expectation 2, though only at the 0.05 level of significance.

Testing Expectation 3 (using unweighted sample, 1,425 cases)

On the evidence of Table 7.26, Expectation 3 was not borne out. In other words, boys who say there is little or nothing of an interesting kind to do at home are not appreciably different from other boys in terms of the span of years over which their serious stealing is spread.

Testing Expectation 4 (using unweighted sample, 1,425 cases)

This expectation was that: Expectation 2 applies with respect to the forty-four different 'types' of theft studied. The method of testing this expectation was the same as for Expectation 4 with regard to Hypothesis 2. In other words, the control group was matched to the qualifying group in terms of the composite of matching variables used for matching purposes throughout this inquiry and following this the qualifying and modified control scores for each of the forty-four types of theft were compared. The basic statistic involved in this analysis relates to whether or not the boy ever committed the class of theft concerned (i.e. at Level 2 or over). The results follow in Table 7.27.

The details in Table 7.27 tend to confirm the expectation, though not for all the forty-four types of theft. In Table 7.28 are set out, on the left, the types of theft for which the expectation is most strongly borne out, while on the right are the types of theft for which the expectation tends *not* to be borne out.

Summing up on Hypothesis 3

Expectations 1 and 2 were borne out. In other words, boys who feel there is little or nothing interesting to do at home are more involved in stealing than are other boys and this applies even after close matching. Expectation 4 tends also to be borne out. Thus, boys who feel there is little of interest to do at home were more likely to have committed the individual types of theft amongst the forty-four than boys who felt there was rather more of interest to do at home. However, there were some exceptions to this outcome and there was quite a lot of variation, in going from one type of theft to another, in the degree to which the expectation was borne out.

Expectation 3 was *not* borne out. In other words, tendency to feel that there are/are not interesting things to do at home is not much related, even after matching, to the number of years over which boys extend their stealing.

The implication of these tests is that living in a home where there are interesting things to do tends to reduce the variety and amount of a boy's stealing and this applies to most, though not all, types of stealing. But living in a home where there are interesting things to do is not related to the period of years over which boys tend to commit serious thefts.

Table 7.26
Differences between qualifiers and controls before and after matching: variety, amount and duration of stealing

Indices of stealing	Unadjusted average score for qualifiers a (406 cases)	Unadjusted average score for controls b (504 cases)	Adjusted average score for controls c	Differences between qualifiers and adj. controls a−c P	Difference a−c as percentage of c
Averaged variety score	16.0	12.6	14.0	2.0 (0.05)†	14
Averaged amount score	114.2	83.7	99.0	15.2 (0.05)†	15
Duration of stealing	4.4	3.6	4.2	0.2 (NS)*	5

*Not significant at the 0.05 level
†Significant at 0.05 or better but not at the 0.01 level

Table 7.27
Differences between qualifiers and controls before and after matching: each of the forty-four types of theft (1,425 cases, unweighted)

Theft type at† 12+	Unadjusted average score for qualifiers* a (406 cases)		Unadjusted average score for controls* b (504 cases)		Adjusted average score for controls* c		Differences between qualifiers and adj. controls a−c	Difference a−c as percentage of c
	(n)	(%)	(n)	(%)	(n)	(%)		
1	383	94.3	455	90.3	373.38	92.1	2.2	2
2	253	62.3	244	48.4	214.97	53.0	9.3	18
3	200	49.3	189	37.5	168.77	41.6	7.7	19
4	228	56.2	256	50.8	212.89	52.5	3.7	7
5	119	29.3	111	22.0	99.01	24.4	4.9	20
6	264	65.0	258	51.2	228.42	56.3	8.7	15
7	185	45.6	192	38.1	176.44	43.5	2.1	5
8	154	37.9	173	34.3	138.23	34.1	3.8	11
9	79	19.5	76	15.1	72.98	18.0	1.5	8
10	200	49.3	183	36.3	178.59	44.0	5.3	12
11	178	43.8	188	37.3	165.18	40.7	3.1	8
12	77	19.0	69	13.7	62.90	15.5	3.5	23
13	189	46.6	168	33.3	152.66	37.6	9.0	24
14	132	32.5	90	17.9	93.48	23.0	9.5	41
15	72	17.7	81	16.1	72.84	18.0	−0.3	−2
16	209	51.5	200	39.7	182.11	44.9	6.6	15
17	106	26.1	74	14.7	72.65	17.9	8.2	46
18	296	72.9	314	62.3	276.31	68.1	4.8	7
19	173	42.6	185	36.7	164.20	40.5	2.1	5
20	139	34.2	122	24.2	117.34	28.9	5.3	18
21	62	15.3	68	13.5	57.83	14.3	1.0	7
22	168	41.4	203	40.3	175.06	43.2	−1.8	−4
23	121	29.8	95	18.8	103.68	25.6	4.2	16
24	65	16.0	45	8.9	43.19	10.6	5.4	51
25	105	25.9	110	21.8	97.88	24.1	1.8	7
26	128	31.5	139	27.6	125.46	30.9	0.6	2
27	101	24.9	87	17.3	84.34	20.8	4.1	20
28	106	26.1	107	21.2	95.16	23.5	2.6	11
29	41	10.1	32	6.3	33.08	8.2	1.9	23
30	219	53.9	227	45.0	204.23	50.4	3.5	7
31	150	36.9	108	21.4	110.14	27.2	9.7	36
32	31	7.6	37	7.3	32.74	8.1	−0.5	−6
33	299	73.6	297	58.9	264.23	65.1	8.5	13
34	139	34.2	140	27.8	113.70	28.0	6.2	22
35	94	23.2	69	13.7	70.83	17.5	5.7	33
36	152	37.4	125	24.8	117.43	29.0	8.4	29
37	33	8.1	13	2.6	15.68	3.9	4.2	108
38	113	27.8	113	22.4	108.35	26.7	1.1	4
39	107	26.4	80	15.9	73.87	18.2	8.2	45
40	303	74.6	315	62.5	266.69	65.7	8.9	14
41	55	13.5	37	7.3	36.51	9.0	4.5	50
42	48	11.8	44	8.7	43.25	10.7	1.1	10
43	145	35.7	130	25.8	118.88	29.3	6.4	22
44	250	61.6	246	48.8	220.35	54.3	7.3	13

*Qualifying group: boys who have nothing, or only a few things, to interest them at home
Control group: boys who say they have 'a fair number' or 'a lot' of interesting things at home
Rejects: 515 cases (question not asked on early version of questionnaire) were rejected from the original 1,425, leaving 910
†Thefts exclusive of acts involving items of only trivial value. See Chapter 1 for details. See Appendix 1.2 for identity of forty-four types of theft.

Table 7.28
Types of theft more and less associated with having interesting things to do at home

High level of association	Low level of association
I have stolen a car or lorry or van	I have stolen from someone at work
I have stolen milk	I have stolen toys
I have stolen money from a meter	I have stolen something from a changing-room or a cloakroom
I have got into a place and stolen	I have kept something I have found
I have stolen from a club	I have stolen from a building site
I have stolen cigarettes	I have stolen something *from* a car or lorry or van
I have stolen from work	I have stolen a book or newspaper or magazine or comic
I have stolen a bike or motor bike	I have stolen something from someone at school
	I have cheated someone out of money

7 METHODS AND FINDINGS RELATING TO THE INVESTIGATION OF HYPOTHESIS 4

The Nature of Hypothesis 4
Hypothesis 4 took the form:

If there are frequently rows in his family, a boy is thereby made more likely to steal.

It was the intention in this inquiry to examine and challenge this hypothesis through testing a series of expectations derived from it and to develop and present background information relating to the variable hypothesized as causal.

The distribution of boys in terms of the variable hypothesized as causal and in terms of broadly similar variables

The questions asked
The question asked of boys as a basis for assessing to what extent their families had rows is given below along with certain related questions. The full questionnaire is set out in Appendix 7.1. The classifying question was asked only after the boys had been taken through a number of preparatory questions which were asked partly to provide additional information and partly to set the boys thinking realistically about the key (classifying) question, namely I Question 3b.

3a 'Most families have quite a lot of rows. That's what *we* find.'
(i) 'In *your* family — when there are rows, who are they between?' . . . Who else?
(ii) 'How often are *you* in the rows yourself? You might be *having* the row, or you might just be mixed up in *someone else's row.* Either way, how often are you in rows at home?'
  SHOW CARD. CIRCLE CHOICE

EVERY DAY/MOST/ABOUT ONCE A WEEK/ONCE A MONTH/HARDLY EVER/NEVER
(iii)   IF HE IS *EVER* IN ROWS, ASK:
'Who do you usually have rows with in the family?'
'Who else?'

3b 'Now thinking of the whole family, how often are there rows in your family at home?'
  PASS CARD STRAIGHT AWAY. SAY:
'Please choose your answers from these. Be very truthful about it, because we must have correct information.' -
  CIRCLE CHOICE:
EVERY DAY/MOST/ONCE A WEEK/ONCE A MONTH/HARDLY EVER/NEVER

Response distributions
The distributions of responses to these questions are given in Tables 7.29 to 7.33. On this evidence, a

Table 7.29
Frequency of rows in the boy's family (3,113 cases, weighted)

	(*n*)	(%)	
Every day	196	6	
Most days	800	26	62%
Once a week	919	30	
Once a month	514	17	
Hardly ever	617	20	38%
Never	25	1	
No information	42		1%

majority of boys' families (62 per cent) are involved in rows at least once a week and 38 per cent once a month or less. Six per cent claimed family rows every day and 1 per cent said they never had family rows.

Through Question 3a(i) boys were asked: 'In your family — when there are rows, who are they between?' Responses were distributed as in Table 7.30. The frequency of the involvement of different members of the family is better seen through Table 7.31. Obviously, the figures in Table 7.31 cannot be expected to sum to

Table 7.30
Persons involved in the
family rows
(3,113 cases, weighted)

	(n)	(%)
Between mother and father (including step parent)	1,516	49
Between mother and brother(s)/sister(s)	411	13
Between father and brother(s)/sister(s)	378	12
Between parents and brother(s)/sister(s)	57	2
Between parents and children	35	1
Between boy and parents	215	7
Between boy and mother	682	22
Between boy and father	614	20
Between boy and sister(s)	698	22
Between boy and brother(s)	634	20
Between boy and others in family	51	2
Between boy and other relations	99	3
Between brother(s)/between sister(s)/ between brother(s) and sister(s)	343	11
Between parent(s) and grandparent(s)	77	2
Between aunt(s) and uncle(s)	19	1
Between grandparents	8	—
Between other relations	60	2
Between everyone in the family	255	8

— = Less than 0.5 per cent

Table 7.31
Reference to specific
persons involved in the
family rows
(3,113 cases, weighted)

	(n)	(%)
Between the parents	1,516	49
Between parent(s) and brother(s)/sister(s)	881	28
Between parent(s) and boy	1,511	49
Between parent(s) and grandparent(s)	77	2
Between boy and parent(s)	1,511	49
Between boy and sibling(s)	1,332	43
Between boy and others	150	5
Between siblings other than boy	343	11
Between everyone	255	8
Between others	87	3

3,113, because of multiple references by individual boys; and obviously, too, there is much duplication between the first two sets in Table 7.31. Noteworthy features of these two tables are:

1 A high frequency of reference to the two parents being the protagonists.

2 A high frequency of claimed involvement of one or both parents in the family rows.

3 A high frequency of claimed involvement of the respondent himself in the family rows.

4 A relatively low frequency of claimed involvement of grandparent(s) in the family rows.

The last of these features is interesting in view of what is frequently said of the role of parents-in-law, particularly the mother-in-law, in family disagreements.

Another question put to the boy concerned the *frequency* of his *own* involvement in family rows.

Response distributions are set out in Table 7.32. As must be expected: (*a*) the distribution here is similar to that for family rows generally; and, (*b*) the boy is less often involved than there are family rows (i.e. he is not in *all* of them). Nonetheless, involvement of the boy in family rows seems to be considerable and this is in line with the evidence in Tables 7.30 and 7.31.

Following this question (i.e. Question 3a(ii), boys were asked to say *who* they usually rowed with in the family. Responses were as in Table 7.33.

Table 7.32
Frequency of family rows
in which the boy himself
is involved
(3,113 cases, weighted)

	(n)	(%)	
Every day	80	3	
Most days	569	18	51%
Once a week	930	30	
Once a month	543	17	
Hardly ever	891	29	48%
Never	76	2	
No information	24		1%

Table 7.33
Family member(s) with
whom the boy usually
rows
3,113 cases, weighted

	(n)	(%)
Father	1,257	40
Mother	1,461	47
Brother(s)	1,117	36
Sister(s)	1,068	34
Grandmother/grandfather/grandparents	66	2
Other relations	79	3
Everybody/all of them	67	2

Table 7.34
Frequency of family rows analysed by characteristics and
background of boys
(3,113 cases, weighted)

Characteristics Cases (weighted)	All cases 3,113		*Claimed* frequency of family rows					
			Every day 196	Most days 800	Once a week 919	Once a month 514	Hardly ever/ never 642	No information 42
	(n)	(%)	(%)	(%)	(%)	(%)	(%)	(%)
Occupational level of father								
Professional, semi-professional, managerial	518	17	3	30	35	12	19	1
Highly skilled	514	17	7	28	30	16	17	1
Skilled	674	22	9	23	25	18	23	2
Moderately skilled	630	20	4	21	32	17	25	2
Semi-skilled	517	17	6	28	26	20	19	1
Unskilled	254	8	9	27	28	18	17	1
No information	6	—						
Age of boy at interviews								
12 or 13 yrs	721	23	7	19	30	18	24	2
14 yrs	782	25	6	28	27	17	23	—
15 yrs	754	24	9	28	29	14	18	2
16 or 17 yrs	856	27	4	27	31	18	19	2
Nominal religion								
Protestant	1,370	44	6	20	29	21	22	1
Catholic	500	16	5	32	30	13	18	1
Christian (no denomination claimed)	176	6	10	23	22	20	22	4
Jewish	214	7	7	33	32	8	21	0
None	621	20	6	31	33	12	17	1
Others	217	7						
No information	15	—						
How boys feel about being at home								
Dislike it very much/dislike it	152	5	13	47	23	11	6	0
Between like and dislike	25	1	—	—	—	—	—	—
Like it	1,016	33	8	30	33	15	13	2
Like it very much/tremendously	1,920	62	5	22	29	18	26	1

Table 7.34 (continued)

Characteristics Cases (weighted)	All cases 3,113		Claimed frequency of family rows					
			Every day 196	Most days 800	Once a week 919	Once a month 514	Hardly ever/ never 642	No information 42
	(n)	(%)	(%)	(%)	(%)	(%)	(%)	(%)
How happy/unhappy is the home?								
Very unhappy/fairly unhappy/ a bit unhappy	95	3	14	34	43	1	5	3
In between happy and unhappy	351	11	11	35	24	18	12	—
Just a bit happy	149	5	12	52	23	7	4	1
Fairly happy	1,051	34	6	26	36	18	15	—
Very happy	1,449	47	5	20	27	17	30	1
No information	18	1						
Persisted in going out 'just looking for fun and excitement'								
Yes	975	31	8	29	26	19	18	—
No	1,857	60	5	24	32	15	23	2
Not clear if persisted	281	9						
Do his parents control what he does?								
Yes	1,582	51	7	27	29	14	22	1
No	1,494	48	6	24	30	20	20	1
No information	37	1						
Do his parents punish him?								
Yes	1,629	52	7	27	31	17	18	1
No	1,453	47	6	25	28	17	23	1
No information	31	1						
How often is he in rows himself?								
Every day	80	3	78	14	0	0	0	8
Most days	569	18	15	78	4	1	3	0
Once a week	930	30	3	30	60	3	3	—
Once a month	543	17	1	8	35	50	6	—
Hardly ever	891	29	2	5	14	23	57	—
Never	76	2	0	0	13	5	68	13
No information	24	1						

— = Less than 0.5 per cent

These data are broadly in line with the responses to Question 3a(i). They indicate that boys 'row': *most* with one or the other or both parents; infrequently with grandparent(s) (2 per cent referred to such rows).

Frequency of family rows analysed by characteristics and background of boys

The variable named as causal in character in Hypothesis 3 was analysed by different characteristics and aspects of background of boys. Results are shown in Table 7.34. On the evidence of Table 7.34, boys who live in homes where there are relatively few rows:

1 Tend to be drawn somewhat more from those whose nominal religion is Protestant.

2 Tend to be those who like being at home.

3 Tend to be those who regard home as a happy place.

4 Tend to be those who are themselves infrequently involved in family rows.

In addition:

1 There is only a slight tendency for boys from homes where there are frequent rows to be engaged in 'going out just looking for fun and excitement'.

2 There is only minor relationship between the frequency of rows in the home and:
  a Occupational level of father.
  b Age of boy.
  c Whether his parents control his movements or punish him.

267

Investigating Hypothesis 4

Hypothesis 4 was that:

If there are frequently rows in his family, a boy is thereby made more likely to steal.

The basic strategy of investigation

As with all other hypotheses investigated in this inquiry, the main strategy was to derive from the hypothesis as many testable propositions as possible and to test these. These propositions are referred to here as expectations. Details of this form of methodology are given in Chapter 1.

The expectations derived

The following expectations were derived from the hypothesis.

1 Boys who claim there are frequent rows in the family (qualifiers) are more likely to have been engaged in stealing than other boys (controls).

2 Expectation 1 applies even when the controls are closely matched to the qualifiers in terms of the correlates of stealing.

3 Expectation 2 applies for the forty-four different types of theft involved in the inquiry.

Testing Expectation 1

This expectation, detailed above, was tested by comparing the theft scores of boys claiming different frequencies of family rows. Table 7.35 presents the comparison. This evidence tends to support Expectation 1.

Testing Expectation 2 (using unweighted sample, 1,425 cases)

This expectation was tested through the matching operation used on the parallel expectation from Hypothesis 1. Thus, the sample was first split as in Figure 7.4 and the controls were then matched to the qualifiers in terms of the correlates of stealing.

The control group was next matched to the qualifying group with the results shown in Table 7.36.

Figure 7.4
Division of sample for testing expectation 2.

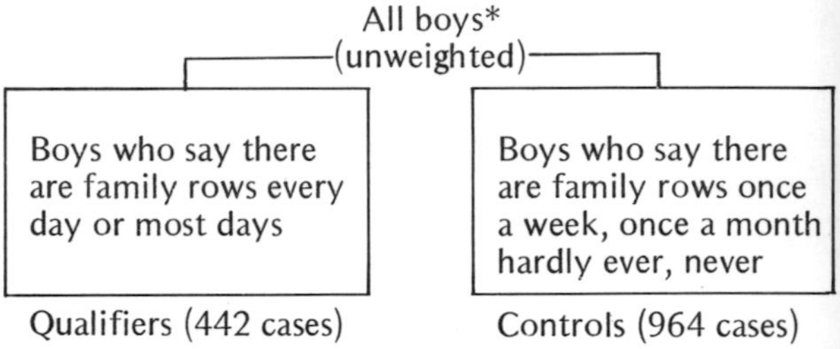

All boys* (unweighted)

Boys who say there are family rows every day or most days	Boys who say there are family rows once a week, once a month hardly ever, never
Qualifiers (442 cases)	Controls (964 cases)

*Boys in intermediate positions were excluded as being in somewhat ambiguous positions with regard to the hypothesis

Table 7.35
Relating frequency of family rows to amount and variety of stealing (3,113 cases, weighted)

Claimed frequency of family rows	All cases		Index of variety of stealing				Index of amount of stealing			
			0.1	0.2	0.3	0.4	0.1	0.2	0.3	0.4
	(n)	(%)	(%)	(%)	(%)	(%)	(%)	(%)	(%)	(%)
Every day	196	6	16	13	31	40	16	21	25	38
Most days	800	26	18	27	29	26	18	28	31	24
Once a week	919	30	25	28	28	20	24	28	26	21
Once a month	514	17	25	22	28	25	22	33	22	23
Hardly ever	617	20	36	23	19	23	36	24	18	22
Never	25	1								
No information	42	1								

Table 7.36
Differences between qualifiers and controls before and after matching: variety and amount of stealing

Indices of stealing	Unadjusted average score for qualifiers a (442 cases)	Unadjusted average score for controls b (964 cases)	Adjusted average score for controls c	Differences between qualifiers and adj. controls a–c	P	Difference a–c as percentage of c
Index of variety of stealing	15.1	12.9	13.2	1.9	(0.05)	14
Index of amount of stealing	103.9	85.0	89.4	14.5	(0.05)	16

Table 7.37
Differences between qualifiers and controls before and after matching: each of the forty-four types of theft

Theft types at† L2+	Unadjusted average score for qualifiers* a (442 cases)		Unadjusted average score for controls* b (964 cases)		Adjusted average score for controls c		Differences between qualifiers and adj. controls a−c	Difference a−c as percentage of c
	(n)	(%)	(n)	(%)	(n)	(%)	(a−c)	(%)
1	410	92.8	864	89.8	400.41	90.3	2.5	3
2	252	57.0	466	48.4	218.59	49.3	7.7	16
3	194	43.9	362	37.6	170.26	38.4	5.5	14
4	248	56.1	496	51.6	233.65	52.7	3.4	6
5	120	27.1	192	20.0	92.56	20.9	6.2	30
6	276	62.4	501	52.1	235.78	53.2	9.2	17
7	197	44.6	373	38.8	176.28	39.8	4.8	12
8	172	38.9	300	31.2	139.25	31.4	7.5	24
9	76	17.2	140	14.6	65.40	14.8	2.4	16
10	195	44.1	356	37.0	172.18	38.8	5.3	14
11	188	42.5	342	35.6	162.88	36.7	5.8	16
12	81	18.3	136	14.1	65.91	14.9	3.4	23
13	207	46.8	338	35.1	159.46	36.0	10.8	30
14	114	25.8	213	22.1	103.38	23.3	2.5	11
15	76	17.2	148	15.4	71.70	16.2	1.0	6
16	207	46.8	403	41.9	190.11	42.9	3.9	9
17	98	22.2	165	17.2	80.18	18.1	4.1	23
18	308	69.7	596	62.0	280.88	63.4	6.3	10
19	180	40.7	338	35.1	161.03	36.3	4.4	12
20	149	33.7	274	28.5	128.96	29.1	4.6	16
21	68	15.4	113	11.7	51.72	11.7	3.7	32
22	206	46.6	340	35.3	159.07	35.9	10.7	30
23	103	23.3	211	21.9	101.24	22.8	0.5	2
24	67	15.2	107	11.1	51.94	11.7	3.5	30
25	106	24.0	223	23.2	104.23	23.5	0.5	2
26	146	33.0	251	26.1	119.10	26.9	6.1	23
27	90	20.4	179	18.6	85.34	19.3	1.1	6
28	111	25.1	211	21.9	101.47	22.9	2.2	10
29	43	9.7	60	6.2	28.86	6.5	3.2	49
30	242	54.8	406	42.2	194.40	43.9	10.9	25
31	148	33.5	238	24.7	115.98	26.2	7.3	28
32	38	8.6	64	6.7	29.57	6.7	1.9	28
33	301	68.1	594	61.7	279.96	63.2	4.9	8
34	139	31.4	301	31.3	140.12	31.6	−0.2	−1
35	84	19.0	150	15.6	75.69	17.1	1.9	11
36	155	35.1	266	27.7	128.13	28.9	6.2	21
37	22	5.0	45	4.7	21.96	5.0	0.0	0
38	130	29.4	195	20.3	93.90	21.2	8.2	39
39	92	20.8	172	17.9	82.50	18.6	2.2	12
40	303	68.6	603	62.7	283.84	64.0	4.6	7
41	43	9.7	82	8.5	42.91	9.7	0.0	0
42	53	12.0	105	10.9	48.47	10.9	1.1	10
43	144	32.6	276	28.7	130.05	29.3	3.3	11
44	269	60.9	465	48.3	222.12	50.1	10.8	22

*Qualifying group: Boys who say that there are family rows 'every day' or 'most days'

*Control group: Boys who say there are rows 'once a week', once a month', 'hardly ever', or 'never'.

Excluded: Twenty cases where insufficient information was available

†Thefts exclusive of acts involving items of only trivial value. See Chapter 1 for details. See Appendix 2.1 for the identity of the forty-four acts

On this evidence, Expectation 2 is borne out, though not in any very marked way.

Testing Expectation 3 (using unweighted sample, 1,425 cases)

This expectation was that Expectation 2 applies with respect to the forty-four different types of theft involved in the inquiry. The method of testing it was through matching controls to qualifiers with a view to seeing if, for each class of theft, there was a residual difference between these groups in terms of the percentage of boys who had committed the act concerned. Results are set out in Table 7.37.

On the evidence of Table 7.37, Expectation 3 was borne out. The evidence suggests, however, that Hypothesis 4 is more tenable for some classes of theft than for others, as indicated in Table 7.38.

Short of fairly unrestrained speculation, it is difficult to point to any consistent difference(s) between these two columns and its seems safer at this point to conclude simply that Expectation 4 is borne out less for some kinds of theft than for others. The reader is invited to make [warily] something more of the detail in Table 7.38.

8 THE DISTRIBUTION OF RESPONSES TO A WIDE VARIETY OF STATEMENTS ABOUT CONDITIONS AT HOME

In one part of the questioning procedure, boys were asked to sort as TRUE or FALSE a set of thirty-three statements about conditions or happenings at home. For example:

1 I have always got on well with my father.

2 I have often had rows with my mother.

3 All my brothers and sisters like me.

4 There would be a row if I brought my friends home.

5 My home is too crowded.

The thirty-three statements were to be sorted by boys into 'sorting bags'. There were four such bags, labelled respectively TRUE, PARTLY TRUE, NOT TRUE, QUERY. The instruction to the boys, as to how to sort the printed statements, were as set out below.

Table 7.38 The types of theft for which the hypothesis applied most and least	Applied most	Applied least
	I have stolen a letter or a parcel I have stolen something *from* a car, lorry or van I have stolen from a park or playground I have pinched sweets I have stolen something from a stall or barrow I have stolen toys I have stolen milk I have stolen from someone at work I have stolen from work	I have stolen something out of a garden or backyard of a home I have stolen money from a meter I have stolen a car or lorry or van I have stolen coal or wood or paraffin or something else that is used for heating I have stolen from a cafe I have kept something I found I have stolen by stripping something from a building I have stolen something from a changing-room or cloakroom I have taken junk or scrap without asking first

Summing-up on the investigation of Hypothesis 4

Expectations 1 and 2 are borne out. In other words, boys whose families have frequent rows are more likely to be involved in stealing than other boys and this applies both to the variety and the amount of stealing they do. It continues to apply when the boys in 'rowing' and 'less rowing' homes are closely matched in terms of the correlates of stealing. These findings apply to a wide range of types of theft but more for some than for others.

It thus appears that the tests conducted tend to support Hypothesis 4, though not for *all* the forty-four types of theft investigated.

Q.4 What are his relationships with others in the family, particularly his parents? Will he bring his friends home? Is home attractive to him?

IN DEALING WITH ILLITERATES, REMEMBER TO TEACH THEM THE NAMES OF THE BAGS AND TO CHECK THAT THEY KNOW THEM.
TAKE BOY TO THE UPRIGHT SORTING BOARD, SAY:

'On these blue cards are some things that different boys have said about how it is at home. I want you to look at each card in turn and tell me if it is true or not as far as you are concerned. If it is *not true* for you, put it in *this*

270

ag. If it is *true for you*, put it in *this* bag. If it is only
artly true, put it in *this* one. If you just can't make up
our mind, put it in *this* one.'
Vill you start by reading out for me what's on each of
nese bags.'

   THEN GIVE THE BOY THE FIRST CARD TO
   LOOK AT (CARD 1)
Which bag do you think that card should go in?
Why that bag?'

   CORRECT IF WRONG. THEN GIVE HIM THE
   REST, ONE AT A TIME, READING OUT ALL
   REMINDERS. SAY:
 won't watch where you put them. Please be very

honest about this. Put them exactly where they should
go. *I won't watch where.*'
   PASS CARDS ONE AT A TIME, NOT WATCHING
   WHERE HE PUTS THEM.
   THE WHITE CARDS ARE REMINDERS, TO BE
   READ OUT *BY YOU* TO THE BOY, AND THEN
   RETAINED BY YOU.

   IF A CARD PROVES TO BE *NOT APPLICABLE*
   FOR A BOY, MARK IT N/A AND SAY WHY. THEN
   PUT IT IN AN N/A BAG HELD BY YOU (ALONE).

The purpose of this sorting system was to provide

Table 7.39
Distributions of responses to statements about
conditions at home
(3,113 cases, weighted)

Statements rated	Boys' choice of reply					
	True	Partly true	Not true	Cannot decide	Not applicable	No evidence
	(%)	(%)	(%)	(%)	(%)	(%)
1 I have been told off by one of my parents	93.4	4.3	0.6	0.1	0	1.5
2 I have always got on well with my father	53.9	31.5	9.4	0.9	2.7	1.4
3 I have always got on well with my mother	63.1	27.7	7.0	0.7	0.3	1.2
4 I have often had rows with my brother	29.7	18.3	11.2	0.9	38.3	1.4
5 I have often had rows with my sister	33.6	15.1	12.1	0.7	36.6	1.9
6 I have always got on well with all my brothers and sisters	27.4	30.9	14.9	0.8	24.4	1.6
7 I have often had rows with my mother	21.2	32.0	43.9	1.3	0.4	1.3
8 I have often had rows with my father	22.2	29.1	43.1	1.2	2.8	1.6
9 My father loves me	75.3	8.4	2.5	8.7	3.7	1.4
10 My mother loves me	85.5	6.0	1.0	5.7	0.4	1.5
11 I love my father	76.5	13.4	2.8	2.4	3.4	1.4
12 I love my mother	86.4	9.0	1.2	2.0	0.3	1.1
13 All my brothers and sisters like me	52.2	15.8	3.1	3.7	23.9	1.3
14 I like all my brothers and sisters	58.6	12.8	2.5	0.9	23.7	1.4
15 I respect my father	77.4	11.4	4.1	2.1	3.5	1.5
16 I respect my mother	85.3	9.3	1.7	1.9	0.4	1.4
17 My parents ask me to bring my friends home	40.2	35.1	21.2	2.1	0.1	1.3
18 My home is the sort of place I would bring my friends to	68.2	20.6	7.5	2.5	0	1.2
19 There would be a row if I brought friends home	4.6	8.5	82.9	2.7	0	1.3
20 We always help each other in my family	55.2	37.4	5.1	1.0	0	1.3
21 My parents always look after me well	91.8	5.7	0.6	0.4	0.1	1.3
22 I like to meet my family again at the end of the day	76.4	16.9	2.6	2.6	0.2	1.3
23 I like to get away from my family	12.3	32.0	51.6	2.8	0	1.3
24 I always like being with my family	46.1	36.2	13.9	1.9	0	1.8
25 I like to get home at the end of a day	80.4	14.1	3.0	0.6	0.2	1.8
26 I used to get sent into the street to play	7.7	14.3	75.3	1.3	0	1.4
27 I get picked-on too much at home	10.9	22.5	63.1	2.1	0	1.4
28 I get too many jobs to do at home	5.4	17.8	73.8	1.6	0	1.3
29 I enjoy being at home	68.0	25.2	4.4	0.7	0	1.7
30 I like to get out of the house quite a lot	38.3	42.6	16.3	1.1	0.3	1.4
3' I keep out of my house as much as I can	7.0	12.0	78.5	0.8	0	1.6
32 I get most of my fun away from home	30.4	39.3	26.4	2.4	0	1.5
33 My parents give me most things I ask for	44.7	41.9	9.4	2.2	0.1	1.7

general background to the investigation of Hypotheses 1 to 4. This background information could be related to 'home conditions' for the sample as a whole and to home conditions for different sections of the sample. It can be noted that some of the sorted statements are similar to those involved in one or another of the four hypotheses. Others are different.

The distribution of 'home conditions'

In Table 7.39 are presented all thirty-three statements about home conditions. Against each of these is the proportion of boys in the sample who claimed it was true, partly true or not true for them personally.

Within this table, the reader may wish to note that:

1 About 15 per cent of the boys either denied or found only partly true the statement 'I respect my father'; the figure was 11 per cent for mothers.

2 Twenty-one per cent denied that their parents asked them to bring their friends home.

3 Twelve per cent said it was true that they liked to get away from the family.

4 Eight per cent agreed that they used to be sent into the street to play and a further 14 per cent said this was true to some extent.

5 Thirty per cent agreed that they got most of their fun away from home.

Beyond this, however, the reader is invited to study Table 7.39 for his own surprises or for confirmation of what he already feels he knows.

In this context, the reader will find a considerable degree of consistency between the indications of Table 7.39 and those of other tables in the chapter, starting with Tables 7.1 and 7.3. Table 7.39 should, of course, be read comparatively as well as in absolute terms.

The distribution of responses analysed by characteristics and background of boys

Home conditions were analysed by the characteristics and backgrounds of the boys. For simplicity of presentation, the reactions of boys to specific statements have been expressed in the form of averages. This involved allocating a weight to each of the four classes of answer available to boys, as follows.

True	= 3
Partly true	= 2
Not true	= 1
Cannot decide	= 2

Thus, the higher an average, the more it indicates agreement with the statement. Table 7.40 compares the responses of boys differing in terms of social background, age, religion, attitudes towards being at home, amount of stealing done and several other factors.

The main indications of Table 7.40 seem to be as follows.

1 One of the outstanding features of Table 7.40 is the stability of responses across *some* of the population sectors and the variability of response across *others*. Thus, there is very little variation in boys' responses to the thirty-three statements as we go from boys whose fathers are in the top occupational sector to those whose fathers are in the bottom occupational sector. Similarly, there is very little difference in going from one religion to another. By contrast and as is to be expected, there are many differences in relation to the thirty-three statements as we go from boys in happy homes to boys in less happy homes, from boys who like being at home to those who do not, from boys who want to spend a lot of time at home and those who want to spend relatively little time there.

2 Boys who *rate their homes as unhappy places* tend more than others to:

a Deny they get on well with father.

b Deny their home is the sort of place they can bring friends to.

c Agree they like to get away from the family.

d Deny they like to be *with* the family.

e Agree they get picked on too much at home.

f Deny they enjoy being at home.

g Agree they keep out of the house as much as they can.

h Agree they get most of their fun away from home.

On the other hand, many of the attitude statements got much the same degree of acceptance/rejection by boys from happy as distinct from unhappy homes.

The listed items may therefore be regarded as the more discriminating with regard to whether a boy will rate his home as a happy or unhappy place to be.

3 The pattern is broadly similar (to 2 above), but with some differences, for boys who claim they *dislike being at home* and for boys who would *prefer to spend relatively little time at home.*

4 In terms of occupational level, the only substantial differences occur with respect to the statement 'I used to get sent into the street to play' this is *least*-frequently endorsed by boys whose fathers are in the professional, semi-professional and managerial groups and most often endorsed by the sons of the unskilled. If we accumulate the weighted averages for the cohesive statements we find no evidence of overall trend in going from one occupational extreme to the other.

Table 7.40

Conditions at home analysed by characteristics of boys
(3,113 cases, weighted)

Statements rated	All Cases	Indices of agreement† Occupational level* 1/2	3	4	5	6	7	Age 12/13	14	15	16/17	Religion Protestant	Catholic	Christian (only)	Jewish	None
1 I have been told off by one of my parents	2.9	3.0	3.0	2.9	3.0	3.0	2.9	2.9	3.0	2.9	3.0	2.9	2.9	2.9	3.0	2.9
2 I have always got on well with my father	2.5	2.4	2.5	2.5	2.4	2.4	2.4	2.5	2.5	2.4	2.4	2.5	2.4	2.4	2.5	2.4
3 I have always got on well with my mother	2.6	2.5	2.5	2.6	2.6	2.6	2.7	2.6	2.7	2.5	2.5	2.6	2.6	2.5	2.5	2.5
4 I have often had rows with my brother	2.3	2.3	2.3	2.3	2.3	2.4	2.2	2.4	2.4	2.2	2.2	2.3	2.3	2.4	2.3	2.4
5 I have often had rows with my sister	2.3	2.3	2.4	2.4	2.3	2.3	2.4	2.5	2.4	2.4	2.2	2.4	2.4	2.3	2.3	2.4
6 I have always got on well with all my brothers and sisters	2.2	2.0	2.2	2.3	2.2	2.2	2.2	2.2	2.2	2.0	2.2	2.2	2.0	2.3	2.2	2.1
7 I have often had rows with my mother	1.8	1.7	1.9	1.7	1.8	1.9	1.8	1.7	1.8	1.8	1.7	1.7	1.7	1.9	1.8	1.8
8 I have often had rows with my father	1.8	1.8	1.8	1.7	1.7	1.9	1.9	1.7	1.8	1.8	1.8	1.8	1.8	1.9	1.8	1.8
9 My father loves me	2.8	2.8	2.8	2.8	2.7	2.7	2.7	2.8	2.8	2.7	2.7	2.8	2.8	2.7	2.9	2.7
10 My mother loves me	2.9	2.9	2.9	2.9	2.8	2.9	2.8	2.9	2.9	2.9	2.8	2.9	2.9	2.9	2.9	2.8
11 I love my father	2.8	2.8	2.8	2.8	2.8	2.8	2.7	2.9	2.8	2.7	2.7	2.8	2.8	2.8	2.8	2.7
12 I love my mother	2.9	2.9	2.8	2.9	2.8	2.9	2.9	3.0	2.8	2.8	2.8	2.9	2.9	2.9	2.8	2.8
13 All my brothers and sisters like me	2.7	2.7	2.7	2.7	2.6	2.6	2.6	2.6	2.7	2.6	2.7	2.7	2.7	2.8	2.7	2.6
14 I like all my brothers and sisters	2.7	2.8	2.8	2.8	2.7	2.7	2.8	2.7	2.7	2.7	2.8	2.8	2.7	2.9	2.7	2.7
15 I respect my father	2.8	2.8	2.8	2.8	2.8	2.7	2.7	2.8	2.8	2.7	2.7	2.8	2.8	2.7	2.7	2.7
16 I respect my mother	2.9	2.8	2.8	2.9	2.8	2.8	2.9	2.9	2.9	2.8	2.8	2.9	2.9	2.9	2.8	2.8
17 My parents ask me to bring my friends home	2.2	2.4	2.2	2.2	2.1	2.1	2.1	2.0	2.1	2.2	2.4	2.2	2.1	2.1	2.5	2.1
18 My home is the sort of place I would bring my friends to	2.6	2.6	2.6	2.6	2.6	2.6	2.6	2.7	2.6	2.6	2.6	2.7	2.6	2.6	2.6	2.5
19 There would be a row if I brought friends home	1.2	1.2	1.2	1.2	1.2	1.2	1.3	1.3	1.2	1.2	1.2	1.2	1.2	1.2	1.2	1.3
20 We always help each other in my family	2.5	2.4	2.5	2.5	2.5	2.5	2.5	2.5	2.5	2.5	2.5	2.6	2.3	2.6	2.4	2.5
21 My parents always look after me well	2.9	2.9	2.9	2.9	2.9	2.9	3.0	3.0	2.9	2.9	2.9	2.9	2.9	2.9	2.9	2.9
22 I like to meet my family again at the end of the day	2.8	2.7	2.7	2.7	2.8	2.8	2.8	2.9	2.8	2.7	2.6	2.8	2.8	2.8	2.8	2.7
23 I like to get away from my family	1.6	1.6	1.7	1.6	1.5	1.6	1.6	1.5	1.5	1.6	1.7	1.6	1.5	1.5	1.6	1.6
24 I always like being with my family	2.3	2.2	2.3	2.4	2.4	2.4	2.5	2.5	2.4	2.2	2.2	2.3	2.4	2.2	2.3	2.3
25 I like to get home at the end of a day	2.8	2.7	2.8	2.8	2.8	2.3	2.9	2.9	2.8	2.7	2.7	2.8	2.8	2.8	2.8	2.7
26 I used to get sent into the street to play	1.3	1.1	1.3	1.3	1.4	1.4	1.5	1.3	1.3	1.3	1.3	1.3	1.4	1.3	1.1	1.3
27 I get picked-on too much at home	1.5	1.4	1.5	1.5	1.4	1.4	1.5	1.4	1.5	1.5	1.4	1.4	1.5	1.4	1.6	1.5
28 I get too many jobs to do at home	1.3	1.3	1.3	1.2	1.3	1.4	1.5	1.4	1.3	1.3	1.3	1.3	1.4	1.3	1.2	1.3
29 I enjoy being at home	2.6	2.7	2.6	2.6	2.6	2.6	2.7	2.8	2.7	2.6	2.5	2.7	2.6	2.6	2.7	2.6
30 I like to get out of the house quite a lot	2.2	2.3	2.3	2.2	2.2	2.2	2.2	2.1	2.2	2.3	2.3	2.2	2.2	2.3	2.3	2.2
31 I keep out of my house as much as I can	1.3	1.1	1.3	1.3	1.3	1.3	1.3	1.2	1.2	1.3	1.4	1.3	1.3	1.2	1.2	1.4
32 I get most of my fun away from home	2.0	1.9	2.1	2.1	2.0	2.1	2.1	1.9	2.0	2.1	2.2	2.0	2.2	2.0	1.9	2.1
33 My parents give me most things I ask for	2.4	2.3	2.3	2.4	2.4	2.4	2.3	2.4	2.4	2.4	2.3	2.4	2.3	2.2	2.4	2.4

*1/2 = professional, semi-professional, managerial; 3 = highly skilled; 4 = skilled; 5 = moderately skilled; 6 = semi-skilled; 7 = unskilled

†Weighted mean based on True = 3, partly true = 2, not true = 1, cannot decide = 2

Table 7.40 (continued)

Statements rated	All	Go out looking for fun and excitement		How happy is the home?			Amount of stealing by quartiles				Dislike being at home	Like being at home	Prefer to spend little time at home	Prefer to spend a lot of time at home	Frequent rows at home	Infrequent rows at home
		Yes	No	Unhappy	Between happy and unhappy	Happy	Q.1*	Q.2	Q.3	Q.4						
1 I have been told off by one of my parents	2.9	3.0	2.9	3.0	2.9	2.9	2.9	3.0	2.9	2.9	2.9	2.9	3.0	2.9	3.0	2.
2 I have always got on well with my father	2.5	2.4	2.5	1.8	2.2	2.5	2.6	2.5	2.4	2.4	2.0	2.5	2.2	2.5	2.3	2.
3 I have always got on well with my mother	2.6	2.5	2.6	2.1	2.4	2.6	2.7	2.6	2.5	2.5	2.0	2.6	2.3	2.6	2.4	2.
4 I have often had rows with my brother	2.3	2.3	2.3	2.3	2.4	2.3	2.2	2.3	2.4	2.3	2.1	2.3	2.3	2.3	2.4	2.
5 I have often had rows with my sister	2.3	2.4	2.3	2.3	2.4	2.3	2.3	2.4	2.4	2.3	2.3	2.4	2.3	2.4	2.5	2.
6 I have always got on well with all my brothers and sisters	2.2	2.2	2.2	2.0	2.0	2.2	2.3	2.2	2.0	2.2	1.8	2.2	1.9	2.2	2.0	2.
7 I have often had rows with my mother	1.8	1.9	1.7	2.3	2.0	1.7	1.7	1.7	1.9	1.9	2.1	1.8	1.9	1.7	2.0	1.
8 I have often had rows with my father	1.8	1.9	1.7	2.3	2.1	1.7	1.7	1.8	1.8	1.9	2.1	1.8	1.9	1.8	2.0	1.
9 My father loves me	2.8	2.8	2.8	2.5	2.6	2.8	2.8	2.8	2.7	2.8	2.6	2.8	2.7	2.8	2.7	2.8
10 My mother loves me	2.9	2.8	2.9	2.6	2.8	2.9	2.9	2.9	2.8	2.9	2.6	2.9	2.7	2.9	2.8	2.9
11 I love my father	2.8	2.7	2.8	2.3	2.7	2.8	2.9	2.8	2.7	2.7	2.5	2.8	2.7	2.8	2.7	2.9
12 I love my mother	2.9	2.8	2.9	2.6	2.8	2.9	2.9	2.9	2.8	2.8	2.5	2.9	2.7	2.9	2.8	2.9
13 All my brothers and sisters like me	2.7	2.7	2.7	2.6	2.5	2.7	2.7	2.6	2.7	2.7	2.5	2.7	2.6	2.7	2.5	2.
14 I like all my brothers and sisters	2.7	2.7	2.8	2.6	2.6	2.8	2.8	2.7	2.7	2.8	2.5	2.8	2.7	2.8	2.6	2.
15 I respect my father	2.8	2.7	2.8	2.2	2.7	2.8	2.9	2.8	2.7	2.7	2.4	2.8	2.6	2.8	2.7	2.
16 I respect my mother	2.9	2.8	2.9	2.5	2.9	2.9	2.9	2.9	2.8	2.8	2.6	2.9	2.7	2.9	2.8	2.
17 My parents ask me to bring my friends home	2.2	2.2	2.2	1.9	2.0	2.2	2.2	2.1	2.2	2.2	2.2	2.2	2.1	2.2	2.1	2.
18 My home is the sort of place I would bring my friends to	2.6	2.6	2.6	1.8	2.5	2.7	2.7	2.6	2.6	2.6	2.0	2.6	2.4	2.7	2.5	2.7
19 There would be a row if I brought friends home	1.2	1.2	1.2	1.7	1.3	1.2	1.2	1.2	1.2	1.2	1.5	1.2	1.3	1.2	1.3	1.2
20 We always help each other in my family	2.5	2.5	2.5	2.1	2.4	2.5	2.6	2.5	2.5	2.4	2.1	2.5	2.2	2.6	2.3	2.6
21 My parents always look after me well	2.9	2.9	2.9	2.6	2.9	2.9	3.0	2.9	2.9	2.9	2.6	2.9	2.8	3.0	2.9	2.9
22 I like to meet my family again at the end of the day	2.8	2.7	2.8	2.2	2.7	2.8	2.8	2.8	2.6	2.7	2.2	2.8	2.5	2.8	2.6	2.8
23 I like to get away from my family	1.6	1.6	1.6	2.3	1.7	1.6	1.4	1.6	1.7	1.7	2.4	1.6	2.0	1.5	1.8	1.5
24 I always like being with my family	2.3	2.3	2.4	1.6	2.2	2.4	2.5	2.4	2.2	2.2	1.6	2.4	1.9	2.4	2.1	2.4
25 I like to get home at the end of a day	2.8	2.8	2.8	2.5	2.7	2.8	2.9	2.8	2.8	2.7	2.2	2.8	2.5	2.8	2.7	2.8
26 I used to get sent into the street to play	1.3	1.4	1.3	1.2	1.4	1.3	1.2	1.3	1.3	1.4	1.4	1.3	1.4	1.3	1.3	1.3
27 I get picked-on too much at home	1.5	1.5	1.4	2.3	1.7	1.4	1.4	1.4	1.5	1.5	2.3	1.4	1.7	1.4	1.7	1.3
28 I get too many jobs to do at home	1.3	1.3	1.3	1.7	1.4	1.3	1.3	1.2	1.4	1.3	1.5	1.3	1.3	1.3	1.4	1.3
29 I enjoy being at home	2.6	2.6	2.7	1.9	2.5	2.7	2.8	2.7	2.5	2.6	1.7	2.7	2.2	2.7	2.5	2.7
30 I like to get out of the house quite a lot	2.2	2.4	2.1	2.7	2.4	2.2	2.0	2.2	2.4	2.3	2.8	2.2	2.6	2.1	2.4	2.1
31 I keep out of my house as much as I can	1.3	1.3	1.2	2.1	1.4	1.2	1.2	1.2	1.4	1.4	2.2	1.2	1.7	1.2	1.4	1.2
32 I get most of my fun away from home	2.0	2.2	1.9	2.7	2.2	2.0	1.8	2.0	2.2	2.2	2.8	2.0	2.6	1.9	2.2	2.0
33 My parents give me most things I ask for	2.4	2.4	2.4	2.0	2.4	2.4	2.4	2.4	2.3	2.3	2.1	2.4	2.2	2.4	2.3	2.4

*Q.1 = low level of theft; Q = high level of theft

† Weighted mean based on true = 3, partly true = 2, not true = 1, cannot decide = 2

In terms of religious denomination, the only substantial variation occurs in relation to the statement: 'My parents ask me to bring my friends home'. This statement is endorsed more frequently by Jewish boys. When all twenty of the 'cohesive' statements are accumulated, the total for the 'no religion' group is lower than for any of the religious groups, indicating a lesser degree of cohesiveness in the families of the 'no religion' boys.

In terms of age, substantial variation is limited to six statements, namely:

a 'I have often had rows with my sister': younger boys endorse it more often than older boys.

b 'My parents ask me to bring friends home': younger boys endorse it less often than older boys.

c 'I like to meet my family again at the end of the day': younger boys endorse it more often than older boys.

d 'I always like being with my family': younger boys endorse it more often than older boys.

e 'I enjoy being at home': younger boys endorse it more often than older boys.

f 'I get most of my fun away from home': younger boys endorse it less often than older boys.

In general, younger boys tended more than older boys to endorse statements indicating family unity.

In terms of involvement in stealing, the only *substantial* difference occurs with respect to the following items:

a 'I like to get away from my family': thieves endorse this item more often.

b 'I always like being with my family': thieves endorse this less often.

c 'I get most of my fun away from home': thieves endorse this more often.

d 'I like to get out of the house quite a lot': thieves endorse this more often.

There is in addition an overall tendency for boys who engage in a lot of stealing to endorse less than other boys the statements indicating family unity.

9 SUMMING-UP ON THE INVESTIGATION OF THE HYPOTHESES

The tenability of the four hypotheses
The four hypotheses being investigated were as follows.

1 Boys who do not like being at home are thereby made more likely to engage in stealing.

2 Boys who prefer to spend little or none of their spare time at home are thereby made more likely to steal.

3 If a boy feels there is little or nothing interesting to do at home he is thereby made more likely to steal.

4 If there are frequently rows in his family, a boy is thereby made more likely to steal.

In *general* terms, the tests of the various expectations derived from the four hypotheses tend to render each of the hypotheses more tenable. At the same time, this outcome must be qualified in certain ways.

1 For Hypotheses 2 and 3, the presence of the hypothesized causal factor was not associated with the duration of the boy's stealing; no check on this class of association was made with respect to Hypotheses 1 and 4. What the findings for Hypotheses 2 and 3 seem to imply is that whereas boys who are not very keen on their homes or on being there will as a consequence be more prone to engage in stealing, and will tend to do so for a period, the time for which they keep it up has a duration that is not influenced by the degree of their dissatisfaction with home. (See comments in next sub-section.)

2 For three of the hypotheses (i.e. 2, 3, 4 as listed above) expectations had been developed to the effect that, after matching, the control group would have the lower 'score' for *each* of the forty-four acts of theft on which the total score for theft was based. This expectation is meant to provide a check on the generality of the hypothesis with which it was associated. For each of the three hypotheses concerned, the expectation *tended* to be borne out but: (*a*) there was a lot of variation in the degree to which it held for specific acts; and, (*b*) there were a few instances in which it was not borne out at all. In other words, Hypotheses 2, 3 and 4 seem to apply less for some kinds of theft than for others. The evidence does not provide a clear indication of the special character of these particular classes or kinds of theft.

Though Hypothesis 1 was not checked in this way, it seems likely that it, too, will have this particular limitation to its applicability.

The distribution of the hypothesized causal factors
As part of the hypothesis investigation operation, boys had been asked to rate home and home life in terms of a wide range of issues: how much they liked or disliked being at home, whether they thought it a happy or unhappy place for them, how much of their spare time they preferred to spend there, to what extent they felt that there were interesting things for them to do at home, the frequency of rows there and who they were between. In addition each boy rated over thirty state-

275

ments about conditions at home, saying of each whether it was true or not true for him. Some of the seemingly more noteworthy findings stemming from this rating operation were as follows.

1 The great majority of boys claimed that they liked being at home and that home is a fairly or very happy place for them. The more frequently-given reasons for regarding home as a happy place were: that the family members got on well together, were nice to him and were nice to be with; that he was free to do as he liked at home; that there were many activities he could pursue at home; that his family had few or no rows; that his family could be relied on, gave him security and friendly help; that his home was a comfortable and restful place to be in. On the negative side, the principal reasons for regarding home as an unhappy place were: the (very frequent) occurrence of rows with one or another member of the family; being told what to do (all the time).

2 The majority of boys (62 per cent) claimed that there were rows in the family at least once a week, about half the sample said that they themselves were in family rows at least once a week and 21 per cent of them that they were in family rows on most days. These rows were fairly-evenly spread between the parents and the boy's siblings. Grandparents living in the home appear to have been involved only very infrequently in the rows.

3 Relatively few boys (7 per cent) said there was nothing interesting for them to do at home, but there was an additional 20 per cent who claimed that there were only 'a few' interesting things to do at home. A fairly small minority claimed 'a lot' of interesting things to do at home. Principal reasons offered for there being relatively little to do at home were: the boy was an 'only child'; he was lonely or lacked friends; the house was overcrowded or too small; the family watched television all the time; he was not allowed to do as he wanted there. Sixty per cent of the boys claimed that they had a room of their own, 38 per cent that they had to sleep in the same room as one or more others.

4 Boys who said that they were unhappy at home or did not much like being there, tended somewhat to be: the older boys; those who felt there was little or nothing to do at home; those who said there were very frequent rows at home and who were frequently involved in those rows themselves; those who tended to go out just looking for fun and excitement. The sons of the occupationally unskilled tended somewhat more than the others to like being at home, though there was relatively little difference between the other occupational sectors in this regard.

10 SOME COMMENTS AND POSSIBLE ACTION

Perhaps the most important of the findings reported in

this chapter is that the great majority of boys rega their homes as at least 'fairly' happy places for them a as places they like to be in. This does not mean that th majority of boys' homes are places of comfort or financial security or of blissful relationships. It simp means that from the standpoint of their own values a experiences and backgrounds they regard their homes at least fairly happy and they like being there.

On the other hand, there is a small minority that rat home as an unhappy or an unpleasant place to be – a these boys are involved in much more stealing than a other boys. Moreover, that association appears to k moderately causal in character. Accordingly, it seen important to understand as well as possible just what is that makes home a happy or an unhappy place fc boys. The detail in this chapter provides very usefu guide-lines in this respect, such that the constructiv reader could develop from it a picture of what boy themselves regard as the home they want to be in, as th things they would regard as interesting to do there an of the family relationships and roles that they eithe want or could not stand.

Just how a miserable or unhappy home produce thieving in boys is still very much a matter fc speculation. However, it is particularly noteworthy (a) that boys from such homes tend more than others t want to spend time away from home; and, (b) tha association with thieves (see Chapter 6) is a fairly poten factor in the initiation and maintenance of stealing Hence, it may well be that the mechanism of initiatio in this situation is that boys from miserable homes ge out of such homes as much as possible and are thereb made more likely to mix with local boys. If those loca boys happen to be stealing, then the escapee from th miserable home will be in special danger. It is nc suggested for a moment that this process is the only on that may be in operation for such boys, but it worth considering as one of several possible processes.

That there is anything that can be done to rende unpleasant homes less unpleasant, is by no mean assured. This chapter provides a lot of information abou what makes a home unpleasant to be in, what sorts o things boys find interesting to do at home, and so or But the transformation of the miserable home is no something that is likely to be in the hands of th would-be transformer. It will probably be more effectiv to try to provide 'safe' activities or conditions for boy who temporarily escape from miserable homes. To d this sort of thing does, however, raise not only th problem of reliably identifying boys in the danger grou but also the need to discover or to devise outsid activities or conditions of an effective kind. To b effective, such activities or conditions would have bot to be acceptable to the boys concerned and potent ir keeping them out of the company of local thieves.

One particular limitation of this part of the inquiry i that the sample used did not include boys who hac 'cleared out' of home already (without returning) Maybe this group is rather small, but its absence from the sample seems likely to have led to some degree o understatement here of the importance of home con ditions in the development of juvenile stealing.

1 APPENDIX 7.1

The Sub-Questionnaire used

Atmosphere at home

The following questions are aimed at finding out if the boy wants to spend his spare time at home, if home is a place where he can do things of interest to him, and if there is a happy atmosphere there.

Q.1 Does he like being at home/Does he want to spend spare time there?

FIRST OF ALL, PREPARE THE BOY FOR THIS SECTION, SAY:
'Now I want to ask you about how things are at home. Of course it's absolutely private — just between the two of us.'
TAKE FURTHER STEPS AS NECESSARY TO PREPARE THE BOY FOR THESE QUESTIONS

1a 'What are the things you *like* about being at home?'

1b 'What are the things that you *don't like* about being at home?'
(ENCOURAGE WITH: 'Most boys find that there's *something* that they don't like at home.')

IF HE GIVES YOU NOTHING, TRY: 'Not a *single* thing?'

1c 'Now I want you to read all the things on this card. (PASS CARD) Read them all aloud for me please.'

THEN SAY:
'Now here is the question. Think carefully about it before you answer. Which of those (POINT) is nearest to the way *you* feel about being at home.' (REPEAT)
DVM/D/L/LVM/LT/BET (RING THE ONE CHOSEN)

1d 'How much of your spare time would you like to spend at home?'

AFTER HIS REPLY, PASS THE CARD AND SAY:
'Which of these comes nearest to the amount of your spare time you would like to spend at home?'
NO TIME/NOT MUCH/LESS THAN ½/ABOUT ½/MOST OF IT/ALL OF IT (RING THE ONE CHOSEN).

1e 'And if you had to spend most of your spare time at home, how would you feel about that?'

SHOW CARD AND RING CHOICE DVM/D/L/LVM/LT

Q.2 Is home a place where he can do things of interest to him?

2a 'Is there anything *interesting* you can do in your own home — anything you like doing?'

YES/NO. IF YES, ask 'How many things?' FEW/FAIR NUMBER/LOT

IF 'YES'; 'What would that be?' PROMPT WITH: 'Anything else?'
IF 'NO'; 'WHY IS THAT?'

2b 'Have you got a room all to yourself at home?'
YES/NO

2c 'How many other people sleep in the same room as you do?'
IF HE SAYS HE HAS A ROOM ALL TO HIMSELF BUT *ALSO* THAT HE SHARES HIS BEDROOM, *CHALLENGE* AND SOLVE THE APPARENT CONTRADICTION

Q.3 Are there rows? Is he in them? Is home a happy place or not?

3a 'Most families have quite a lot of rows. That's what *we* find.'
(i) 'In *your* family — when there are rows, who are they between?' . . . 'who else'
(ii) 'How often are you in the rows yourself? You might be *having* the row, or you might just be mixed-up in *someone else's* row. Either way, how often are you in rows at home?' SHOW CARD. CIRCLE CHOICE

(EVERY DAY/MOST/ABOUT ONCE A WEEK/ ONCE A MONTH/HARDLY EVER/NEVER).

(iii) IF HE IS *EVER* IN ROWS, ASK:
'Who do *you* usually have rows with in the family?'
'Who else?'
3b 'Now thinking of the whole family, how often are there rows in your family at home?'
PASS CARD STRAIGHT AWAY. SAY:
'Please choose your answer from these. Be very truthful about it, because we must have correct information.'
CIRCLE CHOICE:
EVERY DAY/MOST/ONCE A WEEK/ONCE A MONTH/HARDLY EVER/NEVER

3c 'Which of these would you say is true of *your* home?' PASS CARD. CIRCLE CHOICE
A VERY UNHAPPY PLACE for me/A FAIRLY UNHAPPY PLACE for me/A BIT UNHAPPY for me/JUST A BIT HAPPY for me/A FAIRLY HAPPY PLACE for me/A VERY HAPPY PLACE for me/IN-BETWEEN HAPPY AND UNHAPPY
'What is it that makes it a happy/unhappy place for you?' (PROBE AND ENCOURAGE)

Q.4 What are his relationships with others in the family, particularly his parents? Will he bring his friends home? Is home attractive to him?

IN DEALING WITH ILLITERATES, REMEMBER TO TEACH THEM THE NAMES OF THE BAGS AND TO CHECK THAT THEY KNOW THEM.
TAKE BOY TO THE UPRIGHT SORTING BOARD. SAY:

'On these blue cards are some things that different boys have said about how it is at home.* I want you to look at each card in turn and tell me it it is true or not as far as you are concerned. If it is *not true* for you, put it in *this bag.* If it is *true for you*, put it in *this* bag. If it is only *partly true*, put it in *this* one. If you just can't make up your mind, put it in *this* one.'
'Will you start by reading out for me what's on each of these bags?'

THEN GIVE THE BOY THE FIRST CARD TO LOOK AT (CARD 1)

'Which bag do you think that card should go in?'
'Why that bag?'

CORRECT IF WRONG. THEN GIVE HIM THE REST, ONE AT A TIME, READING OUT ALL REMINDERS. SAY:

'*I won't watch where you put them.* Please be very honest about this. Put them exactly where they should go. *I won't watch where.*'

PASS CARDS ONE AT A TIME, NOT WATCHING WHERE HE PUTS THEM. THE WHITE CARDS ARE REMINDERS, TO BE READ OUT *BY YOU* TO THE BOY, AND THEN RETAINED BY YOU. IF A CARD PROVES TO BE NOT APPLICABLE FOR BOY, MARK IT N/A AND SAY WHY. THEN PUT IT IN A N/A BAG HELD BY YOU (ALONE).

II Q.1 To find out if things were different at anytime and, if so, *when* they were different and the reason(s) for the change.

*'Home' is where he lives now.

Q.2 Effects of changes and of present status, wi special reference to pinching.

Q.1 *When* did he feel differently about being at hon and *why*?

1a REMIND YOURSELF OF HIS ANSWER TO I Q.1 THEN SAY:

'You told me that you (DVM/D/L/LVM/LT) being home. Think very carefully about this for me (PAUSE Was there ever a time when you (DID NOT LIKE LIKED) being at home?'

(GIVE OPPOSITE TO HIS PRESENT STATE) YES/NO

IF 'NO' CHALLENGE (e.g. 'Not even for a sho time?')

IF STILL 'NO', GO TO Q.3

1b IF 'YES' ASK:

(i) 'Exactly when was that?' GET HIS AGE AT STAR OF THIS PERIOD. ENTER IN GRID

(ii) 'How long did that last?' ENTER DURATION IN GRID

(iii) 'What caused/was the reason for that change? ENTER REASON IN GRID

1c *NOW TRY FOR ANY OTHER PERIOD WHEN HE FELT DIFFERENTLY FROM AT PRESENT (ABOUT BEING AT HOME). GET THE SAME DETAILS AND ENTER IN GRID*

Age at Start of change (1)	Duration of diff. (2)		
		1a	Reason for difference
		2b(i)	Effect on where time spent: NO DIFF/
		2b(ii)	Effect on pinching: NO DIFF/LESS/MORE/STARTED ME
		1a	Reasons:
		2b(i)	Effect on where: NO DIFF/
		2b(ii)	Effect on pinching: NO DIFF/LESS/MORE/STARTED ME
		1a	Reasons:
		2b(i)	Effect on where: NO DIFF/
		2b(ii)	Effect on pinching: NO DIFF/LESS/MORE/STARTED ME
		1a	Reasons:
		2b(i)	Effect on where: NO DIFF/
		2b(ii)	Effect on pinching: NO DIFF/LESS/MORE/STARTED ME
		1a	Reasons:
		2b(i)	Effect on where: NO DIFF/
		2b(ii)	Effect on pinching: NO DIFF/LESS/MORE/STARTED ME
		1a	Reasons:
		2b(i)	Effect on where: NO DIFF/
		2b(ii)	Effect on pinching: NO DIFF/LESS/MORE/STARTED ME

NOTE CAREFULLY *YOU SHOULD AVOID A CLUTTER OF VERY SHORT PERIODS OF DIFFERENCE'.* WHAT IS WANTED MOST OF ALL IS DATA ABOUT ANY ENDURING PERIOD OF CHANGE. IF BOY REFERS TO SOME GENERALITY SUCH AS 'WEEKENDS', 'ODD DAYS' ETC., ENTER THIS AS A CATEGORY ACROSS COLS (1) & (2), AND GIVE REASONS.
(PRESENT STATE = DVM/D/L/LVM/LT)

Q.2 Effects of changes

ASK 2a & 2b FOR EACH DIFFERENCE ENTERED IN GRID

2a 'Now you changed from ... to ... when you were aged ...'
'Exactly what difference did this make to *where* you spent your spare time then?'
ENTER RESPONSE IN GRID

2b 'And as far as pinching was concerned, what difference did it make?'
SHOW CARD. CIRCLE CHOICE IN GRID

Q.3 Effects of present state

3a 'At present, you LIKE/DON'T LIKE being at home. (SAY WHICH EVER HE CHOSE IN ANSWER TO I Q.1c. Exactly what difference does this make to *where* you spend your spare time?'

3b 'Exactly what difference does it make to the amount of pinching you do?'
SHOW CARD, CIRCLE CHOICE
(NO DIFF/LESS/MORE/STARTED ME OFF)

Chapter eight
Parental control and punishment of boys

CONTENTS

1 THE COVERAGE OF THIS CHAPTER

In this chapter I have presented a wide range of information broadly related to 'parental control and punishment' of boys. This information was collected and processed to serve two associated purposes, the more important of which was to investigate a particular composite of hypotheses about causal factors in the development of juvenile stealing. These hypotheses were as follows.

Concerning Parental Control

1 If the 'going out' of a child is not controlled by parents, the child is thereby made more likely to steal.

2 If a child is not controlled by parents with respect to *where* he spends his spare time, the child is thereby made more likely to steal.

3 If a child's choice of associates is not controlled by parents, the child is thereby made more likely to steal.

Concerning punishment by parents

1 If a boy is not punished by parents for misbehaviour, he is thereby made more likely to steal.

2 If the punishment a boy gets from parents is erratic or inconsistent, he is thereby made more likely to steal.

The second purpose of the collected data was to provide general background information about each of the factors or conditions hypothesized as causal in character. For example, with respect to parental control over boys' 'going out', it seemed desirable to establish how this varied with the background and the characteristics of the boys concerned; similarly, with respect to boys' choice of associates, where boys spend their spare time, the use of punishment and the consistency of punishment.

2 RESEARCH PROCEDURES COMMON TO ALL THE HYPOTHESES DEALT WITH IN THE INQUIRY

The gathering of information relevant to the hypotheses about 'parental control and discipline' was done in the context of an inquiry concerned with over thirty other hypotheses. The techniques relating to the inquiry *as a whole* have been summarized in Chapter 1. That summary deals with: sampling procedures; a technique for getting boys to provide reliable information about any stealing they have done; questioning procedures for classifying boys in terms of the variables featured in the different hypotheses (i.e. in terms of the different independent variables); strategies for investigating the tenability of hypotheses about causal factors and processes. The reader should as necessary refer back to the relevant parts of Chapter 1 in reading statements of findings in the present and subsequent chapters.

3 RESEARCH PROCEDURES APPLYING ONLY TO THE HYPOTHESES DEALT WITH IN THIS CHAPTER

Whereas many aspects of research procedure applied generally to the whole range of hypotheses under study, certain parts of it related only to our five hypotheses about 'parental control and punishment'. These parts tend to be encapsulated in the sub-questionnaires put to boys in the course of the interview and presented in full in the Appendix 8.1.

The questionnaire was made up of several sections, each section beginning with a description of its purposes as follows.

1 To get the boy thinking back to when he was ten years old

2 To get boy's opinions about the extent of parental control exercised over him

3 To get his ideas about the punishment he received, how much of it he got, its fairness or unfairness

4 Does he think his parents' control and discipline in relation to himself stopped him from pinching? Did they start controlling him because he was pinching?

The questions asked were of two kinds: fully structured and open response. Some of the latter kind were meant solely to set the boy thinking about when he was ten years old, and others to prepare him for fully-structured questions, each with its choice of responses.

4 METHODS AND FINDINGS RELATING TO THE INVESTIGATION OF HYPOTHESES 1 to 3

The nature of these hypotheses
Hypotheses 1 to 3 took the following forms.

If the 'going out' of a child is not controlled by parents, the child is thereby made more likely to steal (Hypothesis 1).

If a child is not controlled by parents with respect to where he spends his spare time, the child is thereby made more likely to steal (Hypothesis 2).

If a child's choice of associates is not controlled by parents, the child is thereby made more likely to steal (Hypothesis 3).

The distribution of boys in terms of the variables hypothesized as 'causal factors'

The questions asked
The questions asked as a basis for classifying boys in terms of the 'causal factors' were introduced by a verbal sequence asking the boy to think back to when he was 10 years old – an age at which it is thought that the

parentally-controlled boy could be expected still to be 'in harness', but not so far back as to rule out meaningful recall. This section was as follows.

Q.1 SAY:
'I want you to think back to the time when you were ten years old. Where were you living then?' (IF THAT IS HIS PRESENT ADDRESS, *DO NOT ASK FOR IT*. JUST TELL HIM TO THINK OF IT). (PAUSE FOR REPLY)
'Can you remember anything special that happened when you were ten years old?' (LET HIM RECALL BUT DO NOT RECORD).
   TO HELP HIM, PROBE ON BIRTHS IN FAMILY, HOLIDAYS, ANYTHING SPECIAL DONE BY OTHERS IN FAMILY, ANYTHING SPECIAL OF A PERSONAL KIND.

'Now keep on thinking of the time when you were ten and answer these questions for me.'

It would be unrealistic to think that this process of questioning made possible detailed and accurate recall of the boy's circumstances at precisely the age of ten. But it was expected to contribute quite substantially to the meaningful recall of what the circumstances were when the boy was 'younger' — which was really all that was wanted.

Table 8.1
Concerning control over spare-time activities spent out of house at age of ten years
(3,113 cases, weighted)

	(*n*)	(%)
Did he spend much of his spare time out of the house?		
Yes	1,739	56
No	1,348	43
No information	26	1
Did he have to ask his parents first?		
Yes	2,278	73
No	790	25
No information	45	1
Did parents have much control over where he spent his spare time?		
A lot	1,016	33
A fair bit	1,309	42
A little	628	20
None	133	4
No information	27	1
Did his parents have much say over which boys he got round with?		
A lot	538	17
A fair bit	982	32
A little	1,059	34
None	506	16
No information	28	1

After this orientation process, the boy was asked questions designed to allow his classification in terms of the several variables relevant to 'parental control' and dealing respectively with:

1 Whether at the age of ten he had to ask his parents for permission to spend his spare time away from the home.

2 Whether at the age of ten his parents decided *where* he would spend his spare time.

3 Whether at the age of ten his parents had much say over which boys he *associated with*.

The first two were dealt with in several steps, the sequence for 1 being as follows (Question 2a):

(i) 'When you were ten, did you spend much of your spare time out of the house — in the street, at a club, at friends — anywhere at all out of your own house?' YES/NO
(ii) 'When you *did* go out of the house, did you have to ask your parents first?'   YES/NO. CHALLENGE WITH: 'was this when you were ten?'
(iii) 'So when you were ten, *who* decided how much time you could spend out of the house? (I mean you, or your mother, or your father — or who?)'   (PROBE)

The questions asked in relation to 2 and 3 above were in broadly similar form and are set out in full in Appendix 8.1. In addition, and as general background to the issue of 'control', boys were asked (Question 3b):

'These days, do they try to control what you do in your spare time?'   YES/NO
   If 'YES': 'In what way?'
   If 'NO': 'Why is that?'

The Main Findings
The detail of responses to the questions just referred to are set out in Tables 8.1 and 8.2.

PARENTAL CONTROL ANALYSED BY CHARACTERISTICS AND BACKGROUND OF BOYS
Boys' statements about the control parents exercise over them were analysed by a wide range of characteristics of boys and by background variables. Details are given in Table 8.3. The main indications of the data in Table 8.3 are as follows (for boys at the age of ten).

1 Parental permission to go out tended to be required more amongst Jewish boys and boys who deny having got about with thieves. Otherwise there is little in the way of systematic variation in going from one to another sector of the boy population.

2 Parental control over *where* boys spend their spare time appears to be somewhat greater amongst boys born outside the United Kingdom and amongst boys who say they do not get round with thieves. Otherwise there is

Table 8.2
Concerning attempts by parents to control him now
(3,113 cases, weighted)

Do they try to control him now?	(n)	(%)
Yes	1,582	51
No	1,494	48
No information	37	1

If 'Yes', in what ways do they try to control him now?		
Tell him/suggest to him what to do/ where to go	271	9
Stop him/are opposed to his going to certain places/stop him going out at all	515	17
They want to know what he is doing/ where he is going/who he is going with	251	8
He has to be in by a certain time/ parents stop him from staying out late	346	11
Advise him who to associate with/stop him associating with certain boys	288	9
Tell him not to go to clubs, etc.	52	2
Tell him to stop hanging around in street/getting into trouble or fights	47	2
Stop him going to the cinema	27	1
Stop him from pursuing his hobbies, sports, etc.	52	2
Stop him from smoking, drinking	23	1
Discourage him from stealing	8	—
Stop him spending too much money	26	1
Make him study/do homework	105	3
Tell him to stop hanging round the house/ tell him to go out/go to clubs	48	2
Encourage him to go to sports/do hobbies	40	1
Give him chores/jobs to do	35	1
Advise him on his appearance	14	—

If 'No', why don't they try to control the boy?		
They think no control needed/ he can look after himself	534	17
He does nothing to warrant control	183	6
He can be trusted	139	4
They know where he is/what he is doing/ who he is with/agree with what he is doing	205	7
Leave him to do what he wants/treat him as an independent person	296	10
Do not know what he does in spare time/ do not often see one another	51	1
Parents do not care or mind what he does	111	4
He does not go out very much	37	1

little difference except for several very small sub-sample groups.

3 Parental control over choice of associates appears to be somewhat greater amongst boys born outside the United Kingdom and boys who say they do not get round with thieves.

4 An interesting feature of the findings is the way in which parental control varies within broken homes. For the small number of boys who had lost their mother, the control exercised was relatively low; with both parents gone, the level of control (i.e. exercised by guardians) appears to rise substantially. The latter finding may, of course, be due to sampling error associated with the very small number of cases involved. Nonetheless the contrast is worth noting.

Investigating Hypotheses 1 to 3

The basic strategy of investigation
As with all the other hypotheses, the central strategy for investigation was to derive a series of testable expectations from each hypothesis and to test them. Because the three hypotheses involved here are so similar in character, they are being dealt with as one for the derivation of the expectations. Details of the expectation system are given in Chapter 1 of this report.

The derivation of expectations
The following expectations were derived from the three hypotheses.

Expectation 1 Boys whose parents have tended not to control 'going out' in spare time are more likely to have engaged in stealing than are other boys. This expectation refers to both variety and amount of stealing.

Expectation 2 Expectation 1 applies even when those who are subject to a lot of control are matched (in terms of the correlates of stealing) to those subject to little control.

Expectation 3 Expectation 2 applies with respect to duration of serious stealing.

Expectation 4 Boys whose parents have tended not to control where they went in their spare time are more likely to have engaged in stealing than are other boys. This expectation refers both to variety and to amount of stealing.

Expectation 5 Expectation 4 applies even when those who are subject to a lot of control over where spare time is spent are matched (in terms of the correlates of stealing) to those subject to little control of this kind.

Expectation 6 Expectation 5 applies with respect to duration of serious stealing.

Expectation 7 Boys whose parents have tended not to control *which* boys their sons associate with in spare time are more likely to have engaged in stealing than are other boys. This applies to both variety and amount of stealing.

Expectation 8 Expectation 7 applies even after boys subject to a lot of parental control over choice of associates are matched (in terms of the correlates of stealing) to those subject to little control of this kind.

Table 8.3
Parental control analysed by characteristics and
background of boy
(3,113 cases, weighted)

Characteristics and background of boys	All cases 3,113	Permission to go out in spare time					How much parental control over where he spends his spare time					How much parental control over which boys he associates with				
		Lot of time but no permission	Not much time but no permission	Lot of time and permission	Not much time and permission	No information	A lot	A fair bit	A little	None	No information	A lot	A fair bit	A little	None	No information
	(n)	(%)	(%)	(%)	(%)	(%)	(%)	(%)	(%)	(%)	(%)	(%)	(%)	(%)	(%)	(%)
Occupational background of father																
Professional, managerial	518	11	12	36	39	1	35	44	18	3	0	18	27	37	18	0
highly skilled	514	12	7	35	43	3	34	42	18	5	1	18	34	31	16	1
Skilled	674	16	9	39	35	—	36	40	19	5	—	17	34	29	19	1
Moderately skilled	630	18	10	41	29	2	25	44	26	3	1	18	27	42	12	1
Semi-skilled	517	20	9	46	25	1	34	42	18	4	1	15	36	32	17	1
Unskilled	254	26	7	35	29	3	32	37	23	7	2	19	30	33	15	3
No information	6															
School attendance																
Secondary modern	1,464	17	7	44	31	1	30	44	20	5	1	17	36	30	16	1
Comprehensive	549	20	12	36	30	2	34	38	21	5	1	19	32	32	16	1
Grammar	718	16	9	34	40	2	36	41	19	4	—	17	25	44	15	0
Public	257	9	15	32	42	2	35	42	22	2	0	14	28	32	26	0
Other	105															
No information	20															
Religion																
Protestant	1,370	18	10	38	33	1	32	41	21	4	1	16	31	36	15	1
Roman Catholic	500	14	8	42	33	3	39	42	14	3	1	20	36	27	15	2
Christian (only)	176	15	6	40	35	3	23	60	13	0	4	16	38	31	11	4
Jewish	214	5	7	25	60	2	36	45	13	7	0	18	22	43ʹ	17	0
None	621	19	12	41	27	—	29	41	25	5	—	14	29	35	22	—
Other religions	217															
No information	15															
Born UK?																
Yes	2,856	17	9	38	35	1	32	43	20	4	1	16	32	35	16	1
No	257	12	11	49	26	2	41	31	19	7	2	33	27	23	15	2
Ever get round with thieves																
Yes, a lot	1,576	17	9	38	34	2	28	43	24	4	1	15	33	38	13	1
Yes, but not a lot*	1,058	17	10	42	29	1	34	42	19	5	—	16	30	35	19	—
No	334	8	6	33	51	1	43	41	14	0	2	30	36	24	8	1

*Excluding 49 cases who said 'yes' but did not say 'how much'.

continued

Table 8.3 (continued)

Characteristics and background of boys	All cases 3,113	Permission to go out in spare time					How much parental control over where he spends his spare time					How much parental control over which boys he associates with				
		Lot of time but no permission	Not much time but no permission	Lot of time and permission	Not much time and permission	No information	A lot	A fair bit	A little	None	No information	A lot	A fair bit	A little	None	No information
	(n)	(%)	(%)	(%)	(%)	(%)	(%)	(%)	(%)	(%)	(%)	(%)	(%)	(%)	(%)	(%
Number of siblings																
0	408	16	11	36	35	1	41	32	20	6	—	20	39	30	11	—
1	986	14	8	39	38	1	33	46	18	3	—	13	33	36	18	—
2	714	14	9	44	32	—	30	43	23	4	—	17	26	41	16	—
3	451	20	9	38	31	2	32	43	22	3	—	19	34	31	15	1
4	230	28	9	35	28	—	30	41	21	8	—	22	27	26	24	—
5	122	13	11	44	32	0	26	50	18	6	0	14	43	31	12	0
6+	161	21	11	28	37	3	37	36	20	7	0	27	19	32	22	0
No information	41															
Broken home																
No breakdown	2,754	16	9	40	34	1	33	42	20	4	1	17	32	34	16	1
Father gone	246	22	5	36	33	3	33	40	20	5	2	19	31	27	22	2
Mother gone	76	32	5	30	33	0	16	46	37	1	0	9	26	50	13	1
Both parents gone	32	10	3	31	56	0	41	47	6	3	3	56	19	22	0	3
No information	5															
Mother's Job																
Full-time	885	15	10	40	35	—	33	41	21	5	0	18	33	36	13	0
Part-time	1,010	20	10	39	29	2	27	48	19	5	1	12	34	37	16	1
Shift-work*	50	28	8	42	22	0	36	44	16	4	0	16	8	50	26	0
Housewife only	1,121	15	8	38	38	1	38	37	21	3	—	22	28	31	18	—
Two or more jobs†	71	14	7	42	35	1	17	58	14	10	1	11	41	31	15	1
Does boy like being at home?																
Dislike	152	13	9	44	32	2	38	37	19	4	2	13	34	26	25	2
Like	1,016	16	8	39	36	—	30	42	21	6	—	16	29	34	20	1
Like very much	1,920	17	10	39	33	1	34	43	20	3	—	18	33	35	14	—
Between like and dislike	25†															
Rows at home																
Every day	196	27	2	34	37	1	27	47	23	3	1	18	35	24	23	1
Most days	800	18	10	39	32	1	35	37	21	6	—	17	28	36	19	—
Once a week	919	15	8	39	36	2	33	43	21	3	—	18	31	36	15	—
Once a month	514	15	11	41	33	—	29	45	22	3	0	12	34	37	17	1
Hardly ever/never	642	13	9	41	35	1	35	44	15	5	1	21	36	30	13	—
No information	42															

*These have also been included in the full-time/part-time categories

† = Base too small for calculation of percentages
— = Less than 0.5 per cent

continued

Table 8.3 (continued)

Characteristics and background of boys	All cases 3,113	Permission to go out in spare time					How much parental control over where he spends his spare time					How much parental control over which boys he associates with				
		Lot of time but no permission	Not much time but no permission	Lot of time and permission	Not much time and permission	No information	A lot	A fair bit	A little	None	No information	A lot	A fair bit	A little	None	No information
	(n)	(%)	(%)	(%)	(%)	(%)	(%)	(%)	(%)	(%)	(%)	(%)	(%)	(%)	(%)	(%)
Has boy ever gone out looking for fun and excitement?																
Yes	2,229	17	10	41	31	1	32	43	21	4	1	16	33	35	15	1
No	884	14	8	35	41	2	36	40	19	5	1	20	27	32	21	—
Is home a happy place for the boy?																
Unhappy	95	26	6	25	38	4	26	44	21	4	4	24	35	24	13	4
In-between happy and unhappy	351	19	11	40	29	1	30	43	24	3	—	15	35	29	21	—
Just a bit happy	149	8	3	55	33	1	38	44	7	11	1	21	25	35	17	2
Fairly happy	1,051	16	6	39	38	1	33	42	20	4	0	15	32	36	16	—
Very happy	1,449	16	11	39	33	1	33	42	21	4	—	17	31	35	15	—
No information	18															

Expectation 9 Expectation 8 also applies with respect to duration of serious stealing.

Expectation 10 Boys whose parents tend to exercise control over them in terms of going out in spare time, where they go, with whom they go ... tend less than other boys to have engaged in stealing.

Expectation 11 Expectation 10 applies even after those subject to relatively little control of the kinds listed have been matched (in terms of the correlates of stealing) to those subject to more control.

Testing Expectation 1

This expectation was that: 'Boys whose parents have tended not to control 'going out' in spare time are more likely to have engaged in stealing than are other boys. This expectation refers to both variety and amount of stealing'. Table 8.4 presents the results of this 'test by comparison'.

The evidence in Table 8.4 gives very little support to Expectation 1. On the other hand, it gives somewhat *more* support to a view that boys who spend a lot of their spare time away from home are more involved in

stealing than those who spend relatively little of their time away from home.

Testing Expectation 2 (using unweighted sample, 1,425 cases)

To test Expectation 2, the sample was divided as shown in Figure 8.1. The controls were matched to the qualifiers in terms of the correlates of stealing in the manner used in all such operations in this inquiry, with

Figure 8.1
Division of sample for testing expectation 2

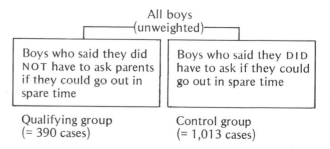

All boys
(unweighted)

Boys who said they did NOT have to ask parents if they could go out in spare time	Boys who said they DID have to ask if they could go out in spare time
Qualifying group (= 390 cases)	Control group (= 1,013 cases)

Table 8.4
Relating variety and amount of stealing to parental control over boys 'going out in spare time' (3,113 cases, weighted)

Parental control over boys 'going out in spare time'	All cases		Quartile distribution of variety of stealing				Quartile distribution of amount of stealing			
			Q.1	Q.2	Q.3	Q.4	Q.1	Q.2	Q.3	Q.4
	(n)	(%)	(%)	(%)	(%)	(%)	(%)	(%)	(%)	(%)
With permission	2,276	73	25	26	25	23	25	28	26	21
Spends a lot of time away from home	1,220	39	22	25	25	28	22	28	25	26
Spends a little time away from home	1,056	34	28	28	26	18	28	28	27	17
Without permission	789	25	24	19	30	27	22	27	23	29
Spends a lot of time away from home	510	16	23	19	30	28	20	27	22	32
Spends a little time away from home	279	9	28	19	29	25	25	26	24	25

Table 8.5
Differences between qualifiers and controls before and after matching: variety, amount and duration of stealing

Indices of stealing	Unadjusted average score for qualifiers a (390 cases)	Unadjusted average score for controls b (1,015 cases)	Adjusted average score for controls c	Differences between qualifiers and adj. controls a−c	Difference a−c as percentage c
Averaged index of variety of stealing	14.8	13.1	13.6	1.2 (NS)	9
Averaged index of amount of stealing	102.5	86.6	90.7	11.8 (0.05)	13
Averaged duration of stealing	4.1	3.5	3.6	0.5 (0.05)	14

NS = Not significant at the 0.5 level

Table 8.6
Relating variety and amount of stealing to parental control over where their boys spend spare time (3,113 cases, weighted)

Parental control over where boy spent spare time	All cases (weighted)		Quartile distribution of variety of stealing				Quartile distribution of amount of stealing			
			Q.1	Q.2	Q.3	Q.4	Q.1	Q.2	Q.3	Q.4
	(n)	(%)	(%)	(%)	(%)	(%)	(%)	(%)	(%)	(%)
A lot	1,016	33	28	23	25	24	27	24	25	24
A fair bit	1,309	42	22	28	25	25	21	30	26	23
A little	628	20	26	20	32	22	27	29	21	24
None	133	4	17	30	23	29	18	28	33	21
No information	27	1								

Figure 8.2
Division of sample for testing Expectation 5

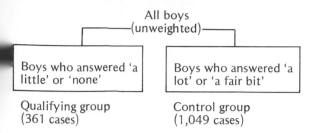

the results shown in Table 8.5. The evidence in Table 8.5 tends to support Expectation 2 but not to any substantial degree.

Testing Expectation 3 (using unweighted sample, 1,425 cases)
Expectation 3 also tends to be supported by the evidence in Table 8.5, but not to any substantial degree.

Testing Expectation 4
This expectation was that: 'Boys whose parents have tended not to control where they went in their spare time are more likely to have engaged in stealing than are other boys. This expectation refers both to variety and to amount of stealing'. Table 8.6 presents the results of this 'test by comparison'. There is a slight trend in Table 8.6 such as to give some small degree of support to Expectation 4.

Testing Expectation 5 (using unweighted sample, 1,425 boys).
Expectation 5 was that Expectation 4 applied even after close matching of the boys whose parents tended to control where they spent their spare time ... to the boys whose parents tended not to exercise this sort of control.

To test this expectation, the sample was first split as shown in Figure 8.2. The controls were matched to the qualifiers in terms of the correlates of stealing in the manner employed in all such operations in this inquiry, with the results shown in Table 8.7. The evidence in Table 8.7 gives but little support to Expectation 5.

Table 8.7
Differences between qualifiers and controls before and after matching: variety, amount and duration of stealing

Indices of stealing	Unadjusted average score for qualifiers a	Unadjusted average score for controls b	Adjusted average score for controls c	Differences between qualifiers and adj. controls a–c P	Difference a–c as percentage of c
Averaged index of variety of stealing	14.1	13.4	13.3	0.8 (NS)	6
Averaged index of amount of stealing	92.2	90.6	88.9	3.3 (NS)	4
Averaged duration of stealing	3.8	3.7	3.6	0.2 (NS)	6

NS = Not significant in the 0.05 level

Table 8.8
Relating variety and amount of stealing to parental control over who the boy 'gets around' with (3,113 cases, weighted)

Control exercised by parents over boy's choice of associates	All cases		Quartile distribution of variety of stealing				Quartile distribution of amount of stealing			
	(n)	(%)	Q.1 (%)	Q.2 (%)	Q.3 (%)	Q.4 (%)	Q.1 (%)	Q.2 (%)	Q.3 (%)	Q.4 (%)
A lot	538	17	29	22	25	24	29	21	25	25
A fair bit	982	32	22	24	31	23	22	28	27	23
A little	1,059	34	27	24	25	25	25	28	24	24
None	506	16	23	29	24	25	22	34	23	21
No information	28	1								

Testing Expectation 6 (using unweighted sample, 1,425 cases)

This expectation was that Expectation 5 applies also to the *duration* of serious stealing. The evidence in Table 8.7 gives but little support to this expectation.

Testing Expectation 7

This expectation was that: 'Boys whose parents have tended not to control *which* boys their sons associate with in spare time are more likely to have engaged in stealing than are other boys. This applies to both variety and amount of stealing'. Table 8.8 presents the results of this 'test by comparison'. The evidence in Table 8.8 gives little or no support to the expectation.

Testing Expectation 8 (using unweighted sample, 1,425 cases)

This expectation was that Expectation 7 applies even after boys subject to a lot of control (over choice of associates) are matched, in terms of the correlates of stealing, to boys who are subject to little control. Table 8.9 presents differences between these control and qualifying groups before and after matching. On this evidence, Expectation 8 is *not* borne out; similarly for Expectation 9.

Testing Expectation 10

This expectation was that: 'Boys whose parents tend to exercise control over them in terms of going out in spare time, where they go, with whom they go . . . tend less than other boys to have engaged in stealing'.

The testing of this expectation required that a single index of 'control' be derived from the evidence about the three aspects of control referred to in the statement of the expectation (i.e. control over going out in spare time, over where the boy went in his spare time and over whom he associated with in his spare time). Where a boy claimed that no control was exercised over him with respect to any of these three, he was given a score of zero. If he claimed control over going out, a 'lot' of

control over where he went and a 'lot' of control over whom he went out with, he was given a parental control rating of seven. Other ratings fall in-between according to the amount of control claimed with respect to 'where' and 'with whom'.

The results of testing Expectation 10 are set out in Table 8.10. There is some degree of support for the expectation at the upper extreme of parental control (i.e. 'a great deal' versus any lesser amount), but over the total range of the control index, the expectation gets but little support from the evidence. *The indication may be, however, that it is only at the level of unrelenting control, that parents are able to keep their sons out of such theft opportunities as exist in boys' environments.* In this respect, it must be noted that the number of boys in this extreme category was small (118 cases before weighting). This fact bears in an obvious way upon the statistical meaningfulness of the findings. It also means that 'unrelenting' control over the boy may be a fairly unusual phenomenon and, hence, of less practical importance than some more widespread prevention conditions. But as a factor it must be noted and further research might with advantage be focused on it.

Testing Expectation 11

Computer operator oversight led to the last of the eleven expectations remaining untested.

Summing up on the investigation of Hypotheses 1, 2 and 3

Hypothesis 1 gets a limited amount of support from the evidence gathered; Hypothesis 2 but little support. Hypothesis 3 is not supported by the evidence. There are grounds for setting-up an alternative hypothesis that where parents exercise control on a widespread and consistent basis — as distinct from one or other of the bases specified in Hypotheses 1, 2 and 3 — some prevention of thieving may be achieved.

Table 8.9 Differences between qualifiers and controls before and after matching: variety, amount and duration of stealing	Theft indices	Unadjusted average score for qualifiers a (718 cases)	Unadjusted average score for controls b (690 cases)	Adjusted average score for controls c	Differences between qualifiers and adj. controls a−c P	Difference a−c as percentage of c
	Index of variety of stealing	13.5	13.7	13.5	0.0 (NS)	0
	Index of amount of stealing	89.1	92.5	91.0	−1.9 (NS)	−2
	Duration of serious stealing	13.8	3.6	3.5	0.3 (NS)	9

NS = Not significant at the 0.5 level

Table 8.10
Relating variety and
amount of stealing to
an index of parental control
(3,113 cases, weighted)

Index of parental vigilance	All cases (weighted)		Quartile distribution of variety of stealing				Quartile distribution of amount of stealing			
			Q.1	Q.2	Q.3	Q.4	Q.1	Q.2	Q.3	Q.4
	(n)	(%)	(%)	(%)	(%)	(%)	(%)	(%)	(%)	(%)
0–2	436	14	22	32	20	25	24	23	28	25
3	536	17	24	28	27	21	26	24	27	24
4	638	20	24	29	22	24	22	29	25	25
5	673	22	21	26	28	25	22	24	28	26
6	503	16	21	29	29	21	25	24	28	23
7	274	9	39	18	21	23	37	22	20	21
No information	53	2								

5 METHODS AND FINDINGS RELATING TO THE INVESTIGATION OF HYPOTHESES 4 AND 5

Hypotheses 4 and 5 took the following forms:

If a child is not punished by parents for misbehaviour, he is thereby made more likely to steal.

and,

If the punishment a child gets from parents is erratic or inconsistent he is thereby made more likely to steal.

The distribution of boys in terms of the variables hypothesized as causal

The questions asked
The questions asked followed on from questions about parental control over the boys as detailed in Section 4 of this chapter and in Appendix 8.1. Thus, through Question 1 the boy had already been helped to think back to when he was ten or less. In Question 3, he was asked:
'Looking back to when you were younger than ten, did your parents punish you if you misbehaved?'

 YES/NO/?
 IF HE CANNOT BE SURE, SAY: 'Do you *think* they did?' YES/NO/?

Boys who said 'No' were asked to say *why* that was.

Boys who said 'Yes' were asked: (a) 'Did they ever let you off when you deserved punishment?' YES/NO/?; and (b) 'The punishment they gave you – do you think it was *ever* unfair?' YES/NO/? They were next asked to say *what sort* of punishment their parents gave them, how much they got of it and who administered it.

Questions about present-day punishment were also asked and boys were finally requested to say what they thought was the effect on them of their parents' punishment of them and control over them.

The main findings
The distributions of replies to the questions asked are given in Table 8.11. Some of the main indications of

Table 8.11 are as follows: (a) non-punishment of boys under ten appears to be relatively infrequent; (b) the majority of them (74 per cent) regard what was done to them as fair or just; (c) of those who received punish-

Table 8.11
Concerning punishment both before and after the boy was aged ten
(3,113 cases, weighted)

	(n)	(%)
Before age ten		
Did (he say) his parents punished him if he misbehaved?		
Yes	2,943	94
No	147	5
No information	23	1
Did they ever let him off when he deserved punishment?		
Yes	1,756	56
No	1,178	38
No information	32	1
Not applicable	147	5
Was his punishment ever unfair?		
Yes	647	21
No	2,292	74
No information	27	1
Not applicable	147	5
How much punishment did they give him?		
A lot	74	2
A fair bit	1,105	36
A little	1,553	50
No information	234	8
Not applicable	147	5
These days, do they punish him for misbehaviour?		
(see later for distribution by present age)		
Yes	1,629	52
No	1,453	47
No information	31	1

Table 8.12
Various details relating to punishment of the boy before he was aged ten
(3,113 cases, weighted)

What sorts of punishment did his parents give him (before age ten)?	(n)	(%)
Parents reasoned with him/talked to him	6	—
He was told off/parents complained at him	383	12
He was threatened/warned	23	1
Sent to his room/sent to bed early	912	29
He was kept in/not allowed out with his friends	1,024	33
Pocket money was stopped/cut down	583	19
Denied some meals	163	5
Generally restricted/deprived of privileges (other than those specified above)	326	11
He was made to do chores	32	1
He was made to study	23	1
He was made to pay for damage done	3	—
Physically punished with an object (belt/strap/cane)	290	9
He was smacked/slapped/hit round head	941	30
He was hit (object not specified)/given hiding/beaten	1,122	36
Other physical punishment	14	—

Who did the punishing (before boy was ten)?		
Both parents	1,865	60
Mainly mother or stepmother	463	15
Mainly father or stepfather	567	18
Grandparents	34	1
Uncle/aunt	13	—
Brother/sister	49	2
Other relatives	2	—

— = Less than 0.5 per cent

ment, relatively few (2 per cent) claimed that they got a lot of it; (*d*) about half the boys claimed that (as under-tens) their parents sometimes let them off from punishments they deserved.

In Table 8.12 are set out boys' statements about the kinds of punishments they received (when under ten). The principal forms of punishment listed in Table 8.12 are: physical punishment; being kept at home and away from his friends; being sent to his room; having pocket money stopped or reduced; other forms of reduction or loss of privileges; being told off or 'complained at'. The fact that less than half of one per cent claimed that their parents 'reasoned with them or talked to them' may mean no more than that many boys did not regard this as punishment. This could also apply to the relatively small number claiming that their parents 'threatened or warned'. After all, the question asked was in terms of 'the punishments they gave you'. It is noteworthy that mothers and fathers are named almost equally as the administrators of punishment — though it is still possible that mothers and fathers tended to administer different kinds of punishment.

Table 8.13 relates to the punishment of boys 'these days', i.e. of boys aged mainly from thirteen to sixteen.

According to these boys, about half of them still receive punishment for misbehaviour. For those not punished, the main reasons appear to be that: he does not much misbehave or get into trouble these days; he is now regarded as being responsible for his own behaviour; he is too old or too big to be punished; these days they just tell

Table 8.13
Various details relating to punishment of boys (these days)
(3,113 cases, weighted)

These days, is he punished?	(n)	(%)
Yes	1,629	52
No	1,453	47
No information	31	1

If 'no', why is that? (1,453 cases, weighted)	(n)	(%)
He does not much misbehave/get into trouble	510	16
He is old enough now to be responsible for own actions/to look after himself/to know better	328	11
He has independence (of) parents	22	1
Parents trust him	19	1
He is too big now/too old to be punished	207	7
He is physically bigger than parents/as big as parents	92	3
He would hit parents back	28	1
They are getting too old to punish him	10	—
They tell him off but no other punishment	183	6
They explain/talk it over with him/reason with him	54	2
They do not bother/don't think it worthwhile	40	1
They do not believe in punishing him	31	1
They do not find out	102	3
He is out of the house most of the time	54	2

How is he punished (these days)?	(n)	(%)
Parents reason with him	52	2
Complained at/moaned at	355	11
Threatened/warned	51	2
Parents do not speak to him	6	—
Denied some meals	17	1
Kept in/not allowed to go out	606	20
Sent to room early/bed early	141	5
Pocket money stopped/cut down	371	12
Not allowed to smoke	10	—
Stopped from going to school	7	—
Generally restricted (other than above)	294	9
Made to do chores	27	1
Made to study	8	—
Made to pay for damages	7	—
Physically punished with *object*	82	3
Smacked, slapped, hit round head, thumped	149	5
Hit (means unspecified)	381	12
Some other form of physical punishment	9	—

— = Less than 0.5 per cent

Table 8.14
Punishments (under ten years) analysed by
characteristics and backgrounds of boys
(3,113 cases, weighted)

Characteristics and background of boy	All cases	Consistency of punishment when under ten years						Frequency of being punished				
		Let off/** Sometimes unfair†	Not let off/ Sometimes unfair	Let off/ Punishment fair	Not let off/ Punishment fair	Not punished	Insufficient information	A lot	A fair bit	A little	Not punished	Insufficient information
Cases (weighted)	3,113	363	282	1,393	893	147	35	74	1,105	1,553	145	236
	(n)	(%)	(%)	(%)	(%)	(%)	(%)	(%)	(%)	(%)	(%)	(%)
Occupational level of father												
Professional, semi-professional, managerial	518	13	15	36	30	6	—	1	27	65	7	1
Highly skilled	514	15	6	43	29	6	1	2	40	46	4	7
Skilled	674	10	8	46	31	4	—	2	35	50	4	9
Moderately skilled	630	11	8	46	29	4	2	2	38	47	4	8
Semi-skilled	517	11	9	48	25	4	1	4	31	48	4	12
Unskilled	254	9	7	50	26	4	4	2	47	39	4	9
No information	6											
School attended												
Secondary modern	1,464	13	9	47	26	3	1	3	41	46	3	8
Comprehensive	549	10	7	42	34	6	2	4	32	46	6	13
Grammar	718	11	8	48	28	4	1	1	37	52	4	7
Public	257	7	19	29	38	8	0	2	17	71	8	2
Other	105											
No information	20											
Religion												
Protestant	1,370	8	7	49	29	4	1	2	35	50	5	8
Roman Catholic	500	17	10	44	26	2	1	2	39	45	2	12
Christian	176	16	11	46	17	5	4	1	38	51	5	6
Jewish	214	14	8	33	37	7	1	2	32	55	5	6
None	621	11	10	44	27	8	1	2	32	53	8	5
Other religions	217											
No information	15											
Place of birth												
UK	2,856	11	8	47	28	5	1	2	35	51	5	7
Outside UK	257	18	19	21	34	6	3	4	41	38	6	11
Number of siblings												
0	408	7	9	51	24	7	1	3	32	52	7	6
1	986	12	7	45	30	5	1	2	30	55	4	9
2	714	13	9	44	28	5	—	3	38	50	4	4
3	451	10	10	43	31	4	1	2	34	52	4	8
4	230	10	16	43	26	5	—	—	53	30	7	9
5	122	15	1	47	34	3	1	3	40	48	2	7
6+	161	17	11	39	29	3	1					
No information	41											

continued

Table 8.14 (continued)

Characteristics and background of boy	All cases	Consistency of punishment when under ten years						Frequency of being punished				
		Let off/** Sometimes unfair†	Not let off/ Sometimes unfair	Let off/ Punishment fair	Not let off/ Punishment fair	Not punished	Insufficient information	A lot	A fair bit	A little	Not punished	Insufficient information
Cases (weighted)	3,113	363	282	1,393	893	147	35	74	1,105	1,553	145	236
	(n)	(%)	(%)	(%)	(%)	(%)	(%)	(%)	(%)	(%)	(%)	(%)
Broken home?												
No breakdown	2,754	12	9	46	28	5	1	Analysis not made				
Father gone	246	9	17	30	29	14	0					
Mother gone	76	12	9	36	37	4	2					
Both parents gone	32	3	13	47	34	0	3					
No information	5											
Mother's job												
Full-time	885	14	7	41	34	4	1	Analysis not made				
Part-time	1,010	12	9	45	27	6	1					
Shift	50	10	12	54	18	6	0					
Housewife only	1,121	10	8	48	28	5	1					
Two or more jobs	71	11	21	39	27	0	1					
Rows at home												
Every day	196	4	8	52	31	5	1	3	37	48	3	9
Most days	800	14	15	38	27	5	–	3	41	47	5	5
Once a week	919	14	9	45	28	4	1	2	34	51	4	9
Once a month	514	13	5	51	25	5	–	2	36	51	5	7
Hardly ever/never	642	7	6	47	34	5	–	3	31	55	5	6
No information	42											
Like living at home?												
Dislike it	152	17	15	32	24	10	2	9	36	26	10	19
Like it	1,016	12	15	41	26	5	1	3	34	47	5	11
Like it very much	1,920	11	6	48	31	4	–	2	36	54	4	4
Between like and dislike	25*											
Happy home?												
Unhappy	95	25	26	22	12	11	4	14	21	41	11	14
Between unhappy and happy	351	14	20	40	24	1	1	3	42	48	1	5
Just a bit happy	149	22	17	43	12	5	1	1	45	35	9	10
Fairly happy	1,051	11	9	48	28	3	1	3	35	52	3	7
Very happy	1,449	10	5	46	33	6	–	1	35	51	6	7
No information	18											

* = Base too small for calculation of percentages
**Sometimes let off when he deserved punishment
†Sometimes a punishment given him was unfair
– = Less than 0.5 per cent

him off; they do not find out (about his misbehaviour). The forms taken by punishment 'these days' appear to be broadly of the same kind as those administered to the under-tens, though at a lower level of frequency: being kept at home; being physically punished; having pocket money or other privileges stopped: being 'complained at'; being sent to room or bed early.

Punishment analysed by characteristics and background of boys

Certain of boys' statements about the punishment parents gave them when under ten were analysed by various characteristics and background factors. Details are given in Table 8.14.

The main indications of the data in Table 8.14 appear to be as follows.

1 In terms of consistency of punishment:

a Boys with public-school backgrounds are subject to somewhat more consistent punishment than other boys.

b Boys born outside the United Kingdom are peculiarly positioned in regard to punishment by parents. Thus, they are more likely than other boys to receive punishment which is inconsistent and regarded by them as unfair. Oddly enough, they also tend to have amongst them a greater proportion of boys whose parents are fairly consistent in their administration of punishment.

c Boys whose homes are featured by either 'daily rows' or virtually no rows, are less subject to inconsistent punishment than are other boys.

d Inconsistent punishment is slightly more common amongst boys who dislike being at home than amongst other boys. Similarly, for boys who rate the home as unhappy.

2 In terms of frequency of receiving punishment, there is evidence of some degree of *difference* between certain population sectors. Thus, it tends to be slightly more frequent amongst: boys whose fathers are in unskilled jobs; boys born outside the United Kingdom. Punishment tends to be *less* frequent amongst boys with public-school background. Boys who dislike being at home and those who rate home as unhappy are over-represented both in terms of receiving a lot of punishment for misbehaviour and in terms of receiving no punishment at all.

3 The overall picture, however, is one of relatively small relationship between the various characteristics studied and amount of punishment received. This seems to suggest that frequency of punishment and its degree of consistency (or inconsistency) are fairly evenly distributed through the London population of boys.

Investigating Hypotheses 4 and 5

The basic strategy of investigation

As with all the other hypotheses dealt with in this inquiry, the basic strategy of investigation was to develop from the hypotheses a number of expectations and to test these.

The expectations

The expectations developed for testing were as follows, with Expectations 1 and 2 relating to Hypothesis 4, Expectations 3 and 4 relating to Hypothesis 5 and Expectation 5 relating to *both* hypotheses.

Expectation 1 Boys who say they are *not* punished by their parents for misbehaviour will have committed more thefts than other boys.

Expectation 2 Expectation 1 applies even after the close and empirical matching of boys who are punished by parents to those who are not punished by parents for their misdemeanours.

Expectation 3 Boys who get erratic or inconsistent punishment from their parents commit more thefts than other boys.

Expectation 4 Expectation 3 applies even after those whose punishment is consistent are matched, in terms of the correlates of stealing, to those whose punishment is *inconsistent.*

Expectation 5 (being a challenge to the *reverse* hypothesis, namely that it is the occurrence of stealing that leads to the imposition of control and punishment). Boys will deny that it was *stealing* by them that led to the imposition of controls and punishments by parents.

Testing Expectation 1

This expectation was that: 'Boys who say they are *not* punished by their parents for misbehaviour will have committed more thefts than other boys'. Table 8.15 presents the results of testing this expectation. On this evidence, Expectation 1 is *not* borne out. In fact, its opposite seems to apply.

Testing Expectation 2 (using unweighted sample, 1,425 boys)

This expectation was that: 'Expectation 1 applies even after the close and empirical matching of boys who are punished by parents to those who are not punished by parents for|their|misdemeanours'. To test Expectation 2, the sample was split as shown in Figure 8.3.

Figure 8.3

Division of sample for testing Expectation 1

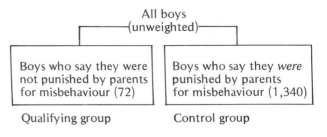

All boys
(unweighted)

Boys who say they were not punished by parents for misbehaviour (72)	Boys who say they *were* punished by parents for misbehaviour (1,340)
Qualifying group	Control group

295

Table 8.15
Relating variety and amount of stealing to whether parents punished boy (3,113 cases, weighted)

Was he punished for misbehaviour when under ten?	All cases	Quartile distribution of variety of stealing				Quartile distribution of amount of stealing			
		Q.1	Q.2	Q.3	Q.4	Q.1	Q.2	Q.3	Q.4
	(n)	(%)	(%)	(%)	(%)	(%)	(%)	(%)	(%)
Yes	2,943	24	25	27	24	23	28	26	23
No	147	45	17	17	21	40	25	15	20
No information	23								

Table 8.16
Differences between qualifiers and controls before and after matching: variety and amount of stealing

Indices of stealing	Unadjusted average score for qualifiers a (72 cases)	Unadjusted average score for controls b (1,340 cases)	Adjusted average score for controls c	Differences between qualifiers and adj. controls a−c	Difference a−c as percentage of c
Index of variety of stealing	10.8	13.7	12.3	−1.5	−12
Index of amount of stealing	65.8	92.4	79.3	−13.5	−17

Table 8.17
Relating variety and amount of stealing to indices of inconsistency and unfairness (3,113 cases, weighted)

Class of response	All cases	Quartile distribution of variety of stealing				Quartile distribution of amount of stealing			
		Q.1	Q.2	Q.3	Q.4	Q.1	Q.2	Q.3	Q.4
	(n)	(%)	(%)	(%)	(%)	(%)	(%)	(%)	(%)
Was boy let off when he deserved punishment?									
Yes	1,756	24	26	27	24	23	29	25	24
No	1,178	24	24	28	24	24	26	27	22
Was he punished unfairly?									
Yes	647	21	24	32	23	19	27	34	20
No	2,292	25	25	26	25	24	28	23	24
Not normally punished	147	45	17	17	21	40	25	15	20

Table 8.18
Differences between qualifiers and controls before and after matching: variety, amount and duration of stealing

Indices of stealing	Unadjusted average scores for qualifiers a	Unadjusted average scores for controls b	Adjusted average score for controls c	Differences between qualifiers and adj. controls a−c P		Difference a−c as percentage of c
Index of variety of stealing	14.0	13.2	13.4	0.6	(NS)	4
Index of amount of stealing	94.0	87.8	88.6	5.4	(NS)	6
Duration of serious stealing (in years)	3.9 yrs	3.7 yrs	3.7 yrs	0.2	(NS)	5

NS = Not significant at the 5 per cent level

The controls were now matched to the qualifiers in terms of the correlates of stealing as detailed in Chapter 1. The results are shown in Table 8.16.

The evidence in Table 8.16 does not support the expectation—in fact, it would support an expectation opposite in character to Expectation 2.

Testing Expectation 3

This expectation was that: 'Boys who get erratic or inconsistent punishment from their parents commit more thefts than other boys'. Inconsistent punishment was evidenced in two ways: (a) through boys being let off when they 'deserved punishment'; (b) through being punished when, in the boy's view, he did not deserve it.

The following table presents evidence in respect of each class of evidence.

The evidence in Table 8.17 does not support the expectation in either of its forms.

For special comparison, a line from Table 8.15 has been included at the foot of Table 8.17. It indicates that the position for boys who are normally free of punishment is substantially different (with regard to stealing) from that of boys who, though normally punished for misbehaviour, are at times let off punishment.

Testing Expectation 4 (using unweighted sample, 1,425 cases)

This expectation was that: 'Expectation 3 applies even after those whose punishment is consistent are matched, in terms of the correlates of stealing, to those whose punishment is *inconsistent*'. For the testing of this expectation, boys were separated into qualifying and control groups as shown in Figure 8.4. All case numbers in it are *un*weighted.

Figure 8.4
Split sample for Expectation 4

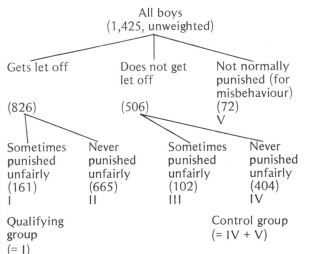

Group I was identified as the qualifying group (in that it included the boys for whom punishment was inconsistent and unfair), while Groups IV and V were

identified as together making up the control group. Matching was conducted in the manner usual in this inquiry. Results are set out in Table 8.18.

The evidence in Table 8.18 does not support expectation.

Testing Expectation 5

This expectation was formulated as a challenge to the possibility that the original hypotheses were true *in reverse*, i.e. that it was *stealing* which led to the imposition of parental control on a boy and to the nature of the punishment imposed.

The boy was asked (Question 4b):

'The sort of control they kept over you ... the sort of punishment they gave you ... were these just *because* they knew you were pinching?' YES?/NO?

The responses to this question were as follows:

Table 8.19

	(n)	(%)
Yes	284	9
No	2,509	81
No information	320	10

This evidence suggests that Hypotheses 1 to 5 may be true in reverse for a small proportion of the boys but not for the great majority.

Summing-up on the investigation of Hypotheses 4 and 5

In general, neither hypothesis is supported by the evidence. Indeed, there is something in the evidence to suggest that boys who are not punished by their parents for their misbehaviour are thereby led to commit less stealing. Expectation 5 was concerned with the possibility that stealing by boys led to greater control over them (and more punishment of them) rather than the other way round as originally hypothesized. The evidence suggests that this may be so for a small minority of boys but not for the great majority.

These findings are fully summarized and evaluated in Sections 6 and 7 of this chapter.

6 SUMMING-UP ON THE INVESTIGATION OF HYPOTHESES 1 TO 5

Concerning parental control

1 Hypotheses 1 to 3 all concern the influence upon stealing of parental control. Between them they postulate that the boys are more likely to steal if parents have not controlled them in terms of (a) 'going out', (b) where they spend their spare time, (c) whom they have as associates when going out.

2 About three-quarters of the boys in the sample claimed that, when aged about ten, they had to ask their parents if they could go out. About the same proportion claimed that their parents exercised at least 'a fair bit' of control over where they went in their spare time. And about half of them said their parents had a least 'a fair bit' of say over which boys they got around with. If we grade boys in terms of the proportion of them who are subject to substantial control on *all three* of the above aspects of control, no more than 9 per cent qualify in those terms.

3a There is a limited degree of support for the hypothesis that boys who have to ask parents if they can go out are thereby less involved in stealing than other boys and that the likelihood of their keeping it up at a serious level for a long period is also less. But the evidence does not suggest that this factor is anything like a strong causal discriminant.

b There was little in the evidence to support the hypothesis that boys are less involved in stealing if their parents exercise control over *where* they spend their spare time. See Section 7 for an interpretative comment on this finding.

c The evidence gathered does not support the hypothesis that parental control (as actually exercised) over boys' choice of associates when out reduces theft level. See Section 7 for comment.

d There are grounds in the evidence for setting-up an alternative hypothesis to the effect that where parents exercise control on a widespread and consistent basis — as distinct from one or another of the bases specified in Hypotheses 1 to 3 — some prevention of thieving may be achieved.

4 Control over whether boys go out in their spare time and over where and with whom they go, is much the same in going from one to another section of the boy population of London. Against that background there is nonetheless a slight tendency for control of one or another kind to be greater for boys born outside the United Kingdom, for Jewish boys and for those who say they do not associate with thieves.

Concerning Punishment

1 Two 'punishment' hypotheses were investigated: (*a*) that if a boy is not punished by parents for his misbehaviour, he is thereby made more likely to steal; (*b*) that if the punishment a boy gets is frequently erratic or inconsistent, he is thereby made more likely to steal.

2 The evidence collected about the administration of punishment to boys indicates: that non-punishment of boys under ten (for misbehaviour) is relatively infrequent; that a majority (74 per cent) of the boys questioned regarded the punishments they received as fair; that of those who received punishment, relatively few (2 per cent) claimed they got 'a lot' of punishment that about half the boys claimed that (as under-ten their parents sometimes let them off punishments the deserved.

3 Similarities between various sub-groups of boys wer greater than the dissimilarities with regard to punishment received and the consistency of such punishment Some of the sub-groups more often involved in som degree of difference tended to be: boys with public school backgrounds (more consistent and less frequent) boys born outside the United Kingdom (more ofte punished); boys who rate their homes as relativel unhappy places or who dislike being there (less consis tent).

4 In general, neither hypothesis is supported by th evidence. Indeed, there is something in the evidence t suggest that boys who are not punished by their parent for their misbehaviour are thereby led to commit les stealing. Expectation 5 was concerned with the possibility that stealing by boys led to greater control over them (and more punishment of them) rather than the other way round as originally hypothesized. The evidence suggests that this may be true for a smal minority but not for the great majority.

7 SOME COMMENTS AND POSSIBLE ACTION

The outcome of the investigation of hypotheses about parental control may to some seem strange — in that it indicates that parental control has not been functioning to any appreciable degree to reduce stealing by boys. However, what one must keep in mind in considering this finding is that 'parental control' as referred to here means parental control as it actually occurs — lax or rigorous or diplomatic or crude, or whatever else it may be. The term does not necessarily mean that form or system of parental control that would be most effective in preventing or reducing juvenile stealing. Whatever such a system would have to be, it seems likely that it would be rather more than what many parents intuitively, or emotionally or erratically do. The sheer limits of parental control over their boys must also be recognized. Thus, parents would have virtually to keep their boys at home if they were to prevent them from mixing with undesirable boys — some of their classmates, for instance. And what proportion of parents would really be able to exercise full control over *where* their boys went once they were out of the home?

The outcome of the investigation of the 'punishment' hypotheses may also seem strange. But several things have to be kept in mind in appraising that outcome. In the first place, it is possible that there was some misinterpretation of the question: 'Looking back to when you were younger than ten, did your parents punish you if you misbehaved?' Thus, it seems possible that this question was interpreted by some boys as ending with the words: '. . . did your parents punish you?' The loss of a qualifying clause at the end of a sentence is one of the more common types of question misinterpretation. In such an eventuality, boys who do not much

isbehave may well have said 'No' instead of saying the
question did not much apply. This in turn could help to
explain the finding that boys who said 'No' to Question
a were less involved in stealing than other boys.

Having said this, it may still be the case that the
finding concerned is genuine. Thus, it could be that
parents who do not punish their children by hitting or
depriving or 'complaining at' them may instead have
taken some other action, not excluding discussing and
talking round the misbehaviour concerned. And that
other action may perhaps be such as to strengthen the
parents' control over their boys. Without further
evidence, this matter is not likely to be resolved. But in
the meantime the finding must remain challenging in
character.

The action most called for by the present findings
seems to be a re-shaping of the hypotheses dealing with
parental control and punishment and the extensive
gathering of evidence with which to challenge the revised
hypotheses. At the same time, and perhaps in the
context of modifying the present hypotheses, it should
be very useful to try to postulate systems and techniques
of parental control which seem likely both to be
acceptable to boys and to be effective in guarding boys
against involvement in stealing. Both boys and parents
would need to be involved in such postulation and much
challenging of an empirical kind would have to follow.

8 APPENDIX 8.1

The sub-questionnaire used

The purpose of this section is to find out if the boy's
parents controlled his movements and his choice of
friends (when he was still quite young) and whether or
not they punished him for misbehaviour and how.

Q.1 To get boy thinking back to when he was ten years
old

SAY:
I want you to think back to the time when you were ten
years old. Where were you living then? (IF THAT IS HIS
PRESENT ADDRESS, *DO NOT ASK FOR IT.* JUST
TELL HIM TO THINK OF IT.) (PAUSE FOR REPLY)
Can you remember anything special that happened
when you were ten years old? (LET HIM RECALL BUT
DO NOT RECORD).
   TO HELP HIM, PROBE ON BIRTHS IN FAMILY,
   HOLIDAYS, ANYTHING SPECIAL DONE BY
   OTHERS IN FAMILY, ANYTHING SPECIAL OF A
   PERSONAL KIND.
Now keep on thinking of the time when you were ten
and answer these questions for me.

Q.2 To get boy's opinions about the extent of parental
control exercised over him

2a When you were ten, did you spend much of your
spare time out of the house — in the street, at a club, at
friends — anywhere at all out of your own house?
   YES/NO

When you *did* go out of the house, did you have to ask
your parents first? YES/NO ... CHALLENGE WITH:
Was this when you were ten?
So when you were ten, *who* decided how much time you
could spend out of the house? (I mean you, or your
mother or your father — or who?) (PROBE)

2b And when you were ten, did your parents have much
say over *where* you would spend your spare time? A
LOT/A FAIR BIT/A LITTLE/NONE
So when you were ten, who decided where you would
spend your spare time? I mean you, or your mother, or
your father — or who?) (PROBE)

2c And when you were ten, did your parents have much
say over *which* boys you got around with in your spare
time?
   SHOW CARD. CHALLENGE CHOICE AND THEN
   RING IT. A LOT/A FAIR BIT/A LITTLE/NONE

Q.3 To get boy's ideas about the punishment he
received: how much; its fairness or unfairness.

3a Looking back to when you were younger than ten,
did your parents punish you if you misbehaved?
YES/NO? ... (IF HE CANNOT BE SURE, SAY: Do
you *think* they did? YES/NO)
   IF 'NO': Why was that?

   IF 'YES':
(i) Did they ever let you off when you deserved
punishment? YES/NO
(ii) The punishment they gave you — do you think that
it was *ever* unfair? YES/NO
   IF 'NO': Why do you say that?
   IF 'YES': How was it unfair?
(iii) What sort of punishment did your parents give you?
(iv) *How much* punishment did they give you?
   SHOW CARD. CIRCLE CHOICE. A LOT/A FAIR
   BIT/A LITTLE
(v) Who did the punishing? Anyone else?

3b *These days*, do they punish you for misbehaviour of
any kind? YES/NO
   IF 'YES': How?
   IF 'NO': Why is that?
These days, do they try to control what you do in your
spare time? YES/NO
   IF 'YES': In what way?
   IF 'NO': Why is that?

Q.4 Does he think their control and discipline stopped
him pinching?
Did they start controlling him *because* he was pinching?

4a You said that when you were ten, your parents
(REPEAT TO HIM THE EXTENT OF PARENTS'
CONTROL AND DISCIPLINE). Is this right? (GET
IT RIGHT IF YOU WERE WRONG).
   THEN SAY:
What sort of difference do you think that has made to
the amount of pinching you have done? (PROBE AND
CHALLENGE)

4b IF BOY PINCHES AND IF PARENTS CONTROL/
   DISCIPLINE HIM, SAY:
The sort of control they kept over you ... the sort of
punishment they gave you ... were these just *because*
they knew you were pinching? YES/NO

Chapter nine
Separation from parents and related factors

CONTENTS

1 THE COVERAGE OF THIS CHAPTER

In this chapter I have presented a wide range of information broadly related to 'separation from parents'. This information was collected and processed to serve two related purposes, the more important of which was to investigate a particular composite of hypotheses about causal factors in the development of juvenile stealing. These were as follows.

1 *Concerning temporary separation from parents.*

a Boys who underwent substantial separation from mother up to the age of five years are thereby made more likely to steal.

b Ditto a but in the age range six to thirteen years.

c–d Ditto a, b but with respect to fathers.

e Boys who underwent separation from both parents at some time during their first thirteen years are thereby made more likely to steal.

2 *Concerning working mothers and shift-working fathers.*

a Boys who, when smaller, frequently got home before mother were thereby made more likely to steal.

b Boys whose mothers have been in paid employment at some time are thereby made more likely to steal.

c Boys whose fathers are on shift-work are thereby made more likely to steal.

3 *Concerning presence of grandparents* Boys who have grandparents living in their homes with them are thereby made less likely to steal.

4 *Concerning broken homes* Boys whose homes are permanently broken in some way are thereby made more likely to steal.

The second purpose of the collected data was to provide general background information about each of the factors or conditions hypothesized as causal in character. For example, the degree to which mothers went out to a job and how this varied with social class; the frequency of separation of boys from mothers or fathers or both and how this varied from one social sector to another; the percentage of homes that were broken, the form this took and how this varied with the background of the boy.

A warning

A decision to investigate the hypothesis concerning very early (e.g. under five) separation from mother or father obviously calls for the extraction of separation information from the *parents* – whereas the present inquiry was, for various reasons, to be limited to interviews with boys only. In the circumstances, one might have by-passed altogether the hypotheses relating to separation from parents when the boy was under five years. However, since questions about family matters were being asked of boys for other purposes, it seemed worthwhile to secure boys' impressions about early separation whilst 'at it' and to use this information with great wariness as a marginally useful challenge to the hypotheses about early separation.

Within the logic of the Hypothetico-Deductive Method, this is a legitimate procedure – provided that it is made clear from the outset that the challenging evidence in this case *is weak* and providing that the manner of deriving that evidence is clearly stated.

2 RESEARCH PROCEDURES COMMON TO ALL THE HYPOTHESES DEALT WITH IN THE INQUIRY

The gathering of information relevant to the hypotheses about 'separation' and related factors was done in the context of an inquiry concerned with over thirty other hypotheses. The techniques relating to the inquiry *as a whole* have been summarized in Chapter 1. That summary deals with: the sampling procedures; a technique for getting boys to provide reliable information about any stealing they may have done; questioning procedures for classifying boys in terms of the variables hypothesized as causal factors in the different hypotheses (i.e. in terms of the different independent variables); strategies for investigating the tenability of hypotheses about causal factors and processes. The reader should as necessary refer to the relevant parts of Chapter 1 in reading statements of findings in the present and subsequent chapters.

3 RESEARCH PROCEDURES APPLYING ONLY TO THE HYPOTHESES DEALT WITH IN THIS CHAPTER

Whereas many aspects of research procedure apply generally to the whole range of hypotheses under study, certain parts of it relate only to the hypotheses dealt with in this chapter. These 'parts' tend to be encapsulated in two of the sub-questionnaires put to boys in the course of the interview and presented in full in Appendix 9.1.

The first sub-questionnaire

The first of these sub-questionnaires concerned *separation of the boy from his mother or his father*. Its questions were in three sections, introduced as follows.

I *Concerning the boy and his mother/mother substitute.* The object of this part of the exercise is to find out: for what periods the mother (or her substitute) has been in the home; when and for how long she has been away from home; where she was during her absence from the home; where the boy was during her absence from the home and *who* was looking after him then.

Q.1 (Dealing with the boy whose real mother lives with him)

Q.2 (Dealing with the boy who has a stepmother or some other substitute mother)

II *Concerning the at-homeness of the boy.* Not only must we find out if the mother or mother substitute (M/S.) has left the boy for any period, but we must find out if the boy himself has left the home (for any time) in those periods when the mother or M.S. is in fact there.

III *Concerning the at-homeness of the father and the custody of the boy.* Finally we need to know if the boy's father (F/S.) was away from home for any extended period and, for any such occasion: the length of the absence and the reason for it; who was looking after the boy during his absence (this could in some cases include a temporary father substitute). In some cases the record will be about the boy's real father and in other cases about a father substitute. All entries must be made on the second age-line.

All entries were made on a master sheet on the column system shown below, one column relating to the mother and boy and the other to the father and boy.

The second sub-questionnaire
The second sub-questionnaire dealt with family composition, jobs of mother (if any) and of father, boy's jobs (if any). Its different sections were introduced by instructions of the kind common to this inquiry. In this case they were as follows.

I To establish who else is living in the boy's home as part of his immediate family and the whereabouts of members who are not there now.

Q.1 Enter details of mother and father

Q.2 Recording all siblings and 'others' living at home.

Q.3 Recording all members of the family who no longer live at home.

II To get job details of mother, father and boy. Find out if the mother is generally out when the boy comes home.

Q.1 Father's job(s)

Q.2 Mother's job(s)

Q.3 Boy's job(s)

4 METHODS AND FINDINGS RELATED TO THE INVESTIGATION OF SUB-HYPOTHESES 1a to 1e.

The nature of the hypotheses
These five sub-hypotheses all dealt with the effects on the boy's theft activities of separation from his mother and/or father. They are listed on page 304.

MOTHER (M/S) AND BOY

Events affecting at-homeness of mother or substitute	X here	Boy's age then	X here	Whereabouts and custody of boy during mother's (M/S's) absences from home
Her whereabouts during absences and duration of absences				His own absences from home and his custody during these absences
		17		
		16		
		15		
		14		
		13		
		12		
		11		
		↓		

FATHER (F/S) AND BOY

Events affecting at-homeness of father or substitute	X here	Boy's age then	X here	Whereabouts and custody of boy during father's (F/S's) absences from home
His whereabouts during absences and duration of absences				His own absences from home and his custody during these absences
		17		
		16		
		15		
		14		
		13		
		12		
		11		
		↓		

Boys who underwent substantial separation from mother up to the age of five are thereby made more likely to steal (Sub-Hypotheses 1a).

Boys who underwent substantial separation from mother in the age range of six to thirteen are thereby made more likely to steal (Sub-Hypotheses 1b).

Boys who underwent substantial separation from father up to the age of five or in the age range six to thirteen years, are thereby made more likely to steal (Sub-Hypotheses 1c).

Boys who underwent separation from both parents at some time during their first thirteen years are thereby made more likely to steal (Sub-Hypotheses 1d).

The nature of the questions asked to assess the nature and extent of separation from mother/father.

The general form of these questions has already been indicated in Section 3 and their detail will be found in Appendix 9.1. It seems to be sufficient at this point simply to detail the classes of information which these questions were meant to provide:

1 Duration of any separation from mother, both up to the age of five and within the age range of six to thirteen.

2 Duration of any separation from father, both up to the age of five and within the age range of six to thirteen.

3 Duration of any separation from both parents (at once) at some time during the boy's first thirteen years.

It is most important that the difficulties inherent in getting these particular classes of information from boys be recognized

Whereas boys will probably have an awareness, of a sort of parental absences from the age of six or seven onwards, their awareness of such absences when they (i.e. the boys) were under four or five would almost certainly have its basis in what they had heard from other members of the family. In the circumstances, we must treat this class of evidence *most* warily, regarding it as providing no more than a pointer for the boys who claimed parental absence(s) during their first five years and treating non-claims to that effect as possibly instances of 'no information'. Had the total inquiry been focused on the 'separation' hypotheses, evidence would most certainly have been collected in a different way. This was not the case, but it seemed desirable nonetheless to take advantage of an opportunity to administer some degree of challenge to the early-separation hypothesis rather than ignoring it altogether.

The distribution of boys in terms of the variables named in the sub-hypotheses as causal in character

Incidence of separations of different durations

In Table 9.1 are details about incidence of separation of boys from parents, with breakdown by the period in which the separation occurred and by whether it was separation from mother or father or both. In no case was the period of separation for less than a month.

The indications of Table 9.1 are principally as follows.

1 A small proportion of boys (12 per cent) claimed separation from mother for a month or more during their first five years.

Table 9.1
Showing claimed incidence of separation of boy from parents at different periods in life

Whether separated and nature of any separation	Boy's age when separated (as claimed by boy)					
	1–5 yrs		6–13 yrs		1–13 yrs	
	From mother (%)	From father (%)	From mother (%)	From father (%)	Either parent (%)	Both at once (%)
Boy claims*:						
No separation	88	84	59	57	42	75
At least some separation	12	16	41	43	58	25
For 1–3 months	6	5	23	21	14	
For 3+–6 months	2	3	6	7	18	
For over 6 months	4	8	12	15	26	
Period of separation was made up of:						
A single occasion	10	12	25	17		
Two or more occasions	2	4	16	26		

*Claims by boys about early separation (i.e. under five) must be regarded very warily indeed

304

The claimed incidence of separation from mother is much higher (41 per cent) during the next eight years (between ages of six and thirteen), with 12 per cent being separated (according to claims by boys) from mother for over six months.

Twenty-five per cent claimed separation from *both* parents (for a month or more) up to the age of thirteen.

Reasons for separation, where the boy was during it, who looked after him during it
Boys who claimed separation(s) of a month or more were asked for reasons for it, what they were doing during it and who looked after them in that period. Their claims are given in Tables 9.2 and 9.3.
A noteworthy feature of Table 9.2 is the preponderance of hospitalization (of boy or parent) as a reason for the separation. In Table 9.3 the outstanding feature seems to be that (according to the boy) in over half the separations the boy spent the period away from home.

Separation analysed by characteristics and background of the boys
In this section is presented evidence about the ways in which 'separation' varies with the characteristics and background of the boys. Several different aspects of separation are dealt with:

1 Separation in the first five years of the boy's life (with all the limitations of the evidence available).

2 Separation in the period between the sixth and the thirteenth year of the boy's life.

3 Separation at any time up to the age of thirteen.

4 All of the above for mother and father separately.

The results of these analyses are shown in Table 9.4.
The main indications of Table 9.4 are as follows:

1 There is a *slight* tendency (according to the boys) for separation to occur less often:

a In homes that boys describe as very happy.

b In homes where rows are less frequent.

c In homes where boys claim bonds of affection between them and their parents.

Table 9.2
Reasons given for absence of parent(s) or of boy* (3,113 cases, weighted)

Reasons for separation	During separation in his first 13 years	
	From mother	From father
	(%)	(%)
Mother/father was:		
In hospital/convalescing	21	12
In the services	0	2
Working away/at sea	0	8
Abroad/came to England	2	4
Living with another man/woman	—	—
Away for a time	—	1
With relatives	2	1
On holiday	1	1
In prison	—	—
Boy was:		
In hospital/convalescing	15	15
In a home	2	2
Under some form of detention	—	—
On holiday	8	8
With relatives	7	7
At a boarding school	5	5

*Totals include more than one reason from some boys
— = Less than 0.5 per cent

Table 9.3
Where boy was during period of separation from parent(s) and who looked after him during that period* (3,113 cases, weighted)

	During separation in first five years of his life†		During separation during 6–13 year.	
Where and Who	From mother	From father	From mother	From father
	(%)	(%)	(%)	(%)
Where did the boy spend the period of separation?				
At home	4	9	18	28
At boarding school	0	0	5	4
Away from home but not at a boarding school	8	8	26	25
Partly home/partly away	—	0	—	—
Unclear/ambiguous	—	—	—	—
No information	—	—	—	—
Who looked after him during the separation?				
Those at his boarding school	—	0	5	4
A relative	4	3	14	10
Non-relatives	1	—	4	2
Some unspecified person	6	6	17	16
Other parent	1	8	12	20
No information	—	—	—	—

*In some cases the boy stayed at more than one place in the period of separation
†Boy's claims for this early period must be treated with great wariness
— = Less than 0.5 per cent

Table 9.4
Separation relating to age of occurence and to characteristics and background of boys
(3,113 cases, weighted)

Characteristics, background and reactions	All cases	Claimed separated in first 5 years from				Claimed separated between 6th & 13th years from				Claimed separated at some time up to age of 13 years from					
		Mother		Father		Mother		Father		Mother		Father		Both	
	(n)	Yes (%)	No (%)	Yes (%)	No (%)	Yes (%)	No (%)	Yes (%)	No (%)	Yes (%)	No (%)	Yes (%)	No (%)	Yes (%)	No (%)
Occupational level of father															
Professional, semi-professional, executive	518	16	17	20	16	18	16	20	15					17	17
Highly skilled	514	11	17	12	17	18	15	15	18					16	16
Skilled	674	25	21	21	22	19	24	20	23					21	22
Moderately skilled	630	21	20	20	20	22	19	22	19	Not analysed				22	20
Semi-skilled	517	16	17	19	16	15	18	16	18					15	17
Unskilled	254	11	8	8	8	9	8	8	9					8	8
No information	6														
Happy/unhappy home															
Unhappy	95	3	3	4	3	4	2	4	3					4	3
Between happy and unhappy	351	19	10	12	11	14	10	13	10					14	11
Just a bit happy	149	7	5	6	5	5	4	6	4					7	4
Fairly happy	1,051	33	34	37	33	35	34	35	33	Not analysed				33	34
Very happy	1,449	38	48	41	48	42	50	43	50					42	48
No information	18														
Amount of time he wants to spend at home															
Little or none	471	18	15	16	15	17	14	15	16					17	15
More than that	2,614	81	85	83	85	83	85	85	84	Not analysed				83	85
No information	28														
Like/dislike being at home															
Dislike	152	6	5	5	5	6	4	5	5					8	4
Like	2,936	94	95	95	95	93	96	94	95	Not analysed				92	96
In between like and dislike	25														
Rows in family															
Very frequent	996	41	31	36	31	36	30	35	30					32	32
Less frequent	2,075	59	68	64	67	63	69	64	69	Not analysed				67	67
No information	42														
My mother loves me															
True	2,661									83	89				
Partly true	186									8	4				
Can't decide	177	Not analysed								6	5	Not analysed			
False	30									1	1				
No information	59														
I love my mother															
True	2,689									84	89				
Partly true	280									11	8				
Can't decide	63	Not analysed								3	2	Not analysed			
False	38									1	1				
No information	43														

Table 9.4 (continued)

Characteristics, background and reactions	All cases (n)	Claimed separated in first 5 years from				Claimed separated between 6th & 13th years from				Claimed separated at some time up to age of 13 years from					
		Mother		Father		Mother		Father		Mother		Father		Both	
		Yes (%)	No (%)	Yes (%)	No (%)	Yes (%)	No (%)	Yes (%)	No (%)	Yes (%)	No (%)	Yes (%)	No (%)	Yes (%)	No (%)
father loves me															
true	2,345											74	77		
partly true	261									Not		9	8		
can't decide	272	Not analysed								analysed		9	8		
false	78											3	2		
no information	157														
love my father															
true	2,381											76	79		
partly true	418									Not		14	13		
can't decide	78	Not analysed								analysed		2	3		
false	87											3	3		
no information	149														

2 There is no regular association between occupational level of boy's father and the claimed occurrence of separations.

3 The above findings are not appreciably different for (claimed) separation from *mother* and (claimed) separation from *father*.

An analysis was also made of the way in which the (claimed) duration of separation varied with background factors and the results are set out in Table 9.5.

The main indications of Table 9.5 appear to be as follows:

1 Claimed separations tend slightly to be shorter in homes that boys rate as very happy.

2 The claimed length of separation varies but little with:

a The frequency of rows in the family.

b The amount of time the boy likes to spend at home.

c The occupational level of father.

The slight variation in claimed separation with respect to the happiness or otherwise of the home cannot in the present state of knowledge be interpreted unambiguously. Thus, it *may* mean that the home has become unhappy for the boy because of the separation, though it could equally well mean that separations tend more to occur in homes that were unhappy in any case. The possibility of confusion in boys over separation claims must also be noted.

Investigating the hypothesis and its sub-hypotheses

Investigating procedure
As with all the other hypotheses in this inquiry, the basic research strategy was to derive from the hypothesis as many as possible testable propositions and to test these. The propositions are referred to here as 'expectations'. The procedure is described in full in Chapter 1 of this report.

The expectations derived in this case were of two broad kinds.

1 Boys who claim separation in any of the forms detailed in the sub-hypotheses will have been involved in more stealing than other boys.

2 The foregoing expectation will still apply even when the latter boys are closely matched to the former in terms of the correlates of stealing.

Testing expectations of the first kind
The test in these cases was simply one of association and clearly the results of any such test are ambiguous. Nonetheless an absence of association would reduce the tenability of the sub-hypotheses concerned. The results of this test, relating to all five sub-expectations, are set out in Table 9.6. The expectation relating to 'separation from

307

Table 9.5
Frequency of claimed
separation from either
parent, related to
characteristics and
background of boys
(3,113 cases, weighted)

Characteristics	All cases (n)	Duration of separation			
		Nil or under 1 month (%)	1–3 months (%)	3–6 months (%)	6 month or more (%)
Occupational level of father					
Professional, semi-professional, executive	518	16	16	17	19
Highly skilled	514	17	17	18	15
Skilled	674	24	22	20	18
Moderately skilled	630	18	22	21	23
Semi-skilled	517	18	16	15	17
Unskilled	254	8	8	8	9
No information	6				
Happy/unhappy home					
Unhappy	95	3	1	2	6
Between happy and unhappy	351	10	10	10	15
Just a bit happy	149	4	3	6	6
Fairly happy	1,051	32	36	38	32
Very happy	1,449	51	49	44	41
No information	18				
Amount of time he wants to spend at home					
Little or none	471	16	11	14	17
More than that	2,614	83	89	86	82
No information	28				
Like/dislike being at home					
Dislike	152	5	2	4	8
Like	2,936	95	97	96	94
In between like and dislike	25				
Rows in family					
Very frequent	996	29	34	34	35
Less frequent	2,075	70	66	65	64
No information	42				

mother when aged under five years' gets some degree of support from the evidence in Table 9.6. For the others, the support is only marginal.

Testing expectations of the second kind (Using unweighted sample, 1,425 cases)

To test the five expectations in the second class of expectation, the sample was split two ways on the following system, the point of split depending on the expectation concerned, as shown in Figure 9.1.

Those claiming separation were classed as the qualifying group and those denying it as the control group. The controls were then matched to the qualifiers in terms of the correlates of stealing as defined in Chapter 1, with the results set out in Table 9.7.

The evidence in Table 9.7 gives but little support to four of the five sub-hypotheses. The only post-matching difference that reaches the 5 per cent level of statistical

Figure 9.1
Division of sample

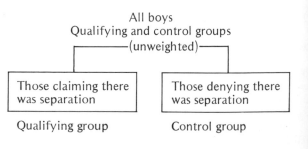

significance is that relating to the amount of stealing by boys who (claim they) have been separated from mother in the first five years of life. Even here, the difference is relatively small.

308

ble 9.6
lationship between
imed separation from
rents and the nature
d extent of boys'
aling
113 cases, weighted)

Nature of claimed† separation	All* cases	Quartile distribution of variety of stealing				Quartile distribution of amount of stealing			
		Q.1	Q.2	Q.3	Q.4	Q.1	Q.2	Q.3	Q.4
	(n)	(%)	(%)	(%)	(%)	(%)	(%)	(%)	(%)
From mother in first 5 yrs									
Yes	364	20	23	33	24	19	25	27	29
No	2,734	25	25	26	24	25	28	25	23
From mother when between 6 and 13									
Yes	1,271	22	24	29	25	22	28	24	26
No	1,827	27	25	25	24	25	28	26	21
From father in first 5 yrs									
Yes	492	24	21	27	28	21	28	25	27
No	2,606	25	25	26	23	25	28	25	23
From father when between 6 and 13									
Yes	1,335	23	25	27	26	23	27	25	25
No	1,763	27	24	27	23	25	29	25	22
From both parents at same time up to age 13									
Yes	765	20	24	32	25	23	25	26	26
No	2,330	26	25	25	24	25	29	25	22

*There were small but variable numbers of 'No information' cases
†See warnings about separation claims, pp. 302, 304

ble 9.7
fferences between
alifiers and controls
fore and after
tching: variety and
ount of stealing

Indices of stealing	Unadjusted average score for qualifiers a	Unadjusted average score for controls b	Adjusted average score for controls c	Differences between qualifiers and adj. controls a−c	Difference a−c as percentage of c
Concerning separation from mother in first 5 years (cases)	(164)	(1,254)			
Variety scores	14.9	13.4	14.0	0.9‡	6
Amount scores	112.3	92.7	99.1	13.2§	13
Concerning separation from mother between ages 6 & 13 ** (cases)	(563)	(855)			
Variety scores	14.2	13.2	13.4	0.8‡	6
Amount scores	100.0	91.6	93.4	6.6‡	7

Table 9.7

Differences between qualifiers and controls before and after matching: variety and amount of stealing

Indices of stealing	Unadjusted average score for qualifiers a	Unadjusted average score for controls b	Adjusted average score for controls c	Differences between qualifiers and adj. controls a−c	Differen a−c as percenta of c
Concerning separation from father in first 5 years† (cases)	(230)	(1,188)			
Variety scores	14.7	13.3	13.8	0.9‡	7
Amount scores	104.9	93.0	98.0	6.9‡	7
Concerning separation from father between ages 6 & 13†† (cases)	(590)	(828)			
Variety scores	14.2	13.1	13.2	1.0‡	8
Amount scores	99.9	91.4	92.1	7.8‡	8
Concerning separation from both parents during first 13 years††† (cases)	(342)	(1,076)			
Variety scores	14.2	13.4	13.7	0.5‡	4
Amount scores	99.3	93.5	96.5	2.8‡	3

*Qualifiers = boys claiming they had been separated from mother for a month or more during the first five years of their lives
**Qualifiers = as above for the period between sixth and thirteenth year of life
†Qualifiers = as for footnote * above but for fathers
††Qualifiers = as for footnote ** above but for fathers
†††Qualifiers = boys claiming they had at some time up to the age of thirteen years been separated from *both* parents for at least a month
‡ Not significant at the 0.05 level
§ Significant at the 0.05 level

Summing up on the investigation of Hypotheses 1a to 1e

The evidence presented in this chapter provides only very marginal support for the hypotheses in general, the one partial exception being Hypothesis 1a, namely that:

Boys who underwent substantial separation from mother up to the age of five years are thereby made more likely to steal.

The status of these findings is very much conditioned by the accuracy of the claims of boys that they have or have not been separated from mother/father in the periods concerned. The investigation of the hypotheses relating to separation under five is thus very much at risk. Indeed, all that should be said of the present findings is that Hypothesis 1a accomodates the evidence brought to bear on it more (with respect to *amount* of

stealing) than do the other separation hypotheses. In the circumstances, it appears that Hypothesis 1a v rendered marginally more tenable (with regard amount of stealing) by the evidence, but that furth investigation, based upon 'separation' evidence collec in its own right (and using the Hypothetico-Deduct Method), is now called for.

5 METHODS AND FINDINGS RELATED TO THE INVESTIGATION OF SUB-HYPOTHES 2a TO 2c

The Nature of the Hypotheses

These hypotheses all relate to the effects on stealing the employment status of boys' parents. They are follows.

Boys who, when smaller, frequently got home before mother were thereby made more likely to steal (Sub-Hypothesis 2a).

Boys whose mothers have been in paid employment at some time are thereby made more likely to steal (Sub-Hypothesis 2b).

Boys whose fathers are on shift-work are thereby made more likely to steal (Sub-Hypothesis 2c).

The nature of the questions asked to measure the 'causal' variables in the five sub-hypotheses

The questions asked as a basis for investigating the different sub-hypotheses are given in full in the second sub-questionnaire in Appendix 9.1. Taken out of context they were as follows.

1 Father's* job

(a) DETERMINE WHICH OF THE FOLLOWING APPLY TO THE BOY'S FATHER* AND RING *ALL* THAT APPLY:
FULL TIME JOB/PART-TIME JOB/SHIFT WORK/2 OR MORE JOBS/OUT OF WORK/RETIRED

(b) IF IN JOB/JOBS, ASK:
'Exactly *what* is his job?' GET A PROPER DESCRIPTION OF IT. IF 2 JOBS, GET THIS FOR EACH
NOW GO TO Q.2
IF NOT NOW IN A JOB, ASK:
'Exactly what was his *last* job?' GET PROPER DESCRIPTION OF IT

2 Mother's* job

(a) DETERMINE WHICH OF THE FOLLOWING APPLY TO THE BOY'S MOTHER* AT PRESENT AND RING ALL THAT APPLY.
IN FULL TIME JOB/IN PART TIME JOB/ON SHIFT WORK/2 OR MORE JOBS/HOUSEWIFE ONLY
    IF IN A JOB, ASK:
(i) 'What time(s) does she actually leave for work?'
(ii) 'What time(s) does she usually get home from work?'
(iii) Any other details that do not fit (i) and (ii)

IF HOUSEWIFE ONLY, ASK: 'Has she *ever* gone out to a job? YES/NO/DON'T KNOW
IF 'NO' OR 'DON'T KNOW', GO TO Q3.

(b) 'How old were you when your mother first went out to a job?'
CHALLENGE AGE GIVEN

'Father' (in *this* context) = 'man of the house'
'Mother' (in *this* context) = 'woman of the house'

(d) FIND OUT WHEN SHE HAD A JOB(S), RELATING JOB DURATION TO BOY'S AGE.

1st job . . . yrs. to . . . yrs. 2nd job . . . yrs. to . . . yrs.
3rd job . . . yrs. to . . . yrs.
4th job . . . yrs. to . . . yrs. 5th job . . . yrs. to . . . yrs.
6th job . . . yrs. to . . . yrs.

Table 9.8
Details relating to occupational backgrounds of mother and boy
(3,113 cases, weighted)

	(n)	(%)
Has mother ever gone out to a job?		
Yes	2,481	80
No	632	20
Is she in job now?		
Not in job	1,121	36
In a job	1,908	61
No information	104	3
Full-time or part-time?		
Full-time	885	29
Part-time	1,010	32
Unclear	13	—
How old was boy when his mother first went out to a job?		
During his first 5 years	969	31
6–8 years	458	15
9–12 years	645	21
Later	298	10
Never	632	20
No information	111	4
When he was under 12 years, were there times when he got home before his mother?		
No	2,069	66
Yes	1,008	32
No information	36	1
How often did this happen?		
All the time	309	10
Often	280	9
Now and then	272	9
Hardly ever	121	4
No information	26	1
What is father's job status?		
Full-time	2,849	92
Part-time	103	3
Unemployed	24	1
Retired	35	1
Shift-work	290	9
Two or more jobs	140	4
No information or not applicable	102	3

Table 9.9

Claims about where boy went when he got home before mother

(1,008 cases, weighted)

	(% on 1,008)	(% on 3,113)
He went indoors and was looked after by an adult	13	4
He went indoors (no reference to being with an adult)	62	20
He waited outside (e.g. on doorstep, in garden)	6*	2*
He went to home of grandparent, neighbour, friend	28	9
He went to see a friend	3*	1*
He played some sport (e.g. cricket, football)	9*	3*
He played some game with mates	8*	3*
He went round the streets or hung around (with or without mates)	7*	2*
He went to the park (with or without mates)	5*	2*
He went to the shops	1*	–*
He went to the cinema	2*	1*

*'Suspect' activities (i.e. suspect in the sense that they might provide opportunity for mischief).

(e) 'When you were smaller, were there times when yc got home *before* she did?'
   YES/NO/DON'T KNOW
   IF 'YES':
(i) 'How often did that happen?' SHOW CARE CIRCLE CHOICE.
   (ALL THE TIME/OFTEN/NOW AND THEN HARDLY EVER)
(ii) 'What ages were you when this happened – whe *you* got home *before* she did?' GET RANGE OI RANGES
(iii) 'Where did you go when that happened?' GE¯ *ALL* PLACES

The details of responses in terms of the variables involved directly or indirectly in the sub-hypotheses as causal in character

These principally involve the working status of th mother now and in the past, how long she has bee going out to work, how often the boy got home befor her when he was smaller, the present working status o the father. Details are given in Table 9.8. Noteworth indications of Table 9.8 include the following.

Table 9.10

Relating employment record of mother to a range of background variables

(3,113 cases, weighted)

Characteristics	All cases	Was mother ever in a job?		For how long was mother in a job?								
		No	Yes	Under 6 mnths	1 yr	2 yrs	3–4 yrs	5–6 yrs	7–10 yrs	11+ yrs	Always	N
Cases (weighted)	3,113	632	2,481	89	293	266	386	336	470	414	40	18
	(n)	(%)	(%)	(%)	(%)	(%)	(%)	(%)	(%)	(%)	(%)	
Type of school attended												
Secondary modern	1,464	36	50	48	44	44	46	47	56	54	52	
Comprehensive	549	12	19	12	17	22	16	21	17	19	23	
Grammar	718	29	22	16	25	22	27	23	22	19	13	
Public	257	19	6	17	7	8	7	5	1	6	13	
Other	105	4	3	7	7	6	4	4	4	2	0	
No information	20											
Ever played truant?												
No	1,745	68	53	61	59	63	57	50	52	42	63	
Yes	1,362	32	47	39	41	36	43	50	49	57	38	
No information	6	–	–									
Frequency												
Once a week	331	6	12	9	3	9	11	9	12	18	13	
Once a month	262	6	9	9	6	6	8	13	12	10	13	
Hardly ever	766	20	26	21	32	20	24	28	24	29	13	
Not clear	3	–	–									

Table 9.10 (continued)

Characteristics Cases (weighted)	All cases 3,113 (n)	Was mother ever in a job?		For how long was mother in a job?								
		No 632 (%)	Yes 2,481 (%)	Under 6 mnths 89 (%)	1 yr 293 (%)	2 yrs 266 (%)	3–4 yrs 386 (%)	5–6 yrs 336 (%)	7–10 yrs 470 (%)	11+ yrs 414 (%)	Always 40	NI 187
Parental vigilance score												
0	47	1	2	2	2	1	3	1	2	1	0	
1–2	389	13	13	12	9	13	10	17	7	17	20	
3–4	1,174	37	38	45	35	30	45	40	42	35	38	
5–6	1,176	35	36	24	46	41	38	37	41	35	43	
7	274	13	8	8	8	11	4	5	8	12	0	
No information	53	1	2	9	–	5	–	–	–	1	0	
I used to be sent into the street to play												
True	239	8	8	8	9	8	6	9	6	7	3	
Partly true	446	11	15	17	24	15	16	15	12	12	10	
Not true	2,343	79	74	72	67	74	77	74	79	78	88	
Other or no information	85	2	3	3	0	3	1	2	3	3	0	
I get too many jobs to do at home												
True	168	4	6	3	6	4	7	3	8	3	20	
Partly true	554	17	18	12	23	18	18	19	17	16	3	
Not true	2,298	77	73	81	72	74	72	76	70	80	78	
Other or no information	93	2	3	4	0	2	3	2	5	1	0	
I get most of my fun away from home												
True	947	27	31	42	21	32	32	26	31	41	33	
Partly true	1,223	40	39	29	45	37	43	49	37	36	35	
Not true	821	30	25	30	30	28	23	23	27	20	33	
Other or no information	122	3	5	4	4	3	3	2	5	3	0	
My parents always look after me well												
True	2,859	94	91	94	88	93	91	93	93	92	100	
Partly true	177	3	6	2	10	5	8	6	4	7	0	
Not true	20	0	1	2	0	0	–	1	2	1	0	
Other or no information	57	3	2	2	2	2	1	0	1	0	0	
I like to get home at the end of the day												
True	2,503	82	80	89	73	78	81	85	86	78	85	
Partly true	439	12	15	9	23	13	14	14	10	18	10	
Not true	92	5	2	1	2	8	3	2	1	1	5	
Other or no information	79	1	3	1	2	1	2	0	3	3	0	

— = Less than 0.5 per cent

1 The relatively small number of mothers who are said never to have gone out to work (20 per cent).

2 The fact that 19 per cent of the boys claimed that when they were smaller (i.e. less than twelve) they often got home before mother (10 per cent said 'all the time').

Boys were also asked where they went on the occasions when they got home before mother. Their replies are set out in Table 9.9. The evidence in Table 9.9 suggests that there might be quite considerable scope for mischievious activity in terms of *where* boys go when waiting for mother to come home. Suspect activities are marked with an asterisk — i.e. suspect in terms of the scope they may provide for mischief.

Employment details analysed by background and characteristics of boys

In this section of the chapter is presented evidence of the ways in which the variables hypothesized as 'causal' are distributed amongst the sampled population. These variables relate, it will be remembered:

1 To whether mother was in a job when the boy was smaller.

2 To whether the boy often got home before the working mother.

3 To whether the father was on shift-work.

Details of the analysis are presented in Tables 9.10 and 9.11. The main indications of Table 9.10 appear to be as follows.

1 There is evidence of a positive association between the mother being in employment, and:

    a The boy having gone to a secondary-modern or comprehensive school.
    b The boy having played truant.

2 There is a very slight negative association between mother being in employment and the exercise of a lot of parental control upon the boy.

3 Mothers who have been working for a long period tend *slightly* more than others to have their sons at secondary-modern schools; to have sons who are more involved in truancy.

Table 9.11 presents further cross-analysis evidence, featuring (*a*) getting home ahead of mother and (*b*) shift-work by father. The details in the first three sections of Table 9.11 are linked to the situation in which the mother gets home before the boy. There are no *major* trends in this part of the table. To the extent that there are any trends at all, they appear to be as follows.

1 Boys who get home ahead of mother tend:

    a To be drawn somewhat more from secondary-modern school backgrounds and somewhat less from public schools.
    b To have engaged in slightly more truancy.

    Beyond that, there are only slight to negligible differences between the views and characteristics of boys who tend to get home before mother and of those who do not.

2 Current paid employment of mother tends slightly to go along with: secondary-modern or comprehensive

school attendance by the boy; a greater degree of truancy by the boy.

The details in the last section of Table 9.11 deal with shift-work by father. Here, too, there are no major trends. To the extent that there are any trends at all, they appear to be as follows: current shift-work by father — possibly suggesting shift-work in the past — tends very *slightly* to go along with the boy being at comprehensive school, with being sent into the street to play and with a greater degree of parental vigilance.

Investigating Hypotheses 2a to 2c

Investigating procedures
As with all the other hypotheses dealt with in this inquiry, the central strategy for investigating the 'employment' hypotheses was to derive from them a series of testable expectations and to test these. A summary of this strategy is presented in Chapter 1.

    Two expectations were generated from each of the three sub-hypotheses.

1 Boys who say that when smaller they frequently got home ahead of mother (the qualifying group in terms of the hypothesis) will have engaged in more stealing than other boys (the control group in terms of the hypothesis).

2 As for Expectation 1, even after the control group has been matched to the qualifying group in terms of the correlates of stealing.

3 Boys who say that mother has *never* been in a paid job (qualifiers) are less likely than other boys (controls) to have engaged in stealing.

4 As for Expectation 3, even after the controls have been matched to the qualifiers in terms of the correlates of stealing.

5 Boys whose fathers have been on shift-work (qualifiers) are more likely to have been engaged in stealing than are other boys (controls).

6 Expectation 5 applies even after the controls have been matched to the qualifiers in terms of the correlates of stealing.

Testing Expectations 1, 3 and 5
This was simply a test by association and clearly its results are ambiguous. Nonetheless, an absence of association would tend to reduce the tenability of the sub-hypothesis concerned. The results of all three tests are given in Table 9.12. Expectation 3 is supported by the evidence; Expectations 1 and 5 get very little support.

Testing Expectations 2, 4 and 6 (using unweighted sample, 1,425 cases)
To test these expectations, the sample was in each case

Table 9.11
Relating 'getting home ahead of mother' to a range of background variables; and relating whether father currently does shift-work to background of boys (3,113 cases, weighted)

Characteristics	All cases	'When under 12' did boy get home before mother?		How often did this happen?				Is mother at present in a job?			Is father at present on shift-work?	
		No	Yes	All the time	Often	Now and then	Hardly ever	Full-time	Part-time	No	Yes	No
Cases (weighted)	3,113	2,069	1,008	309	280	272	121	885	1,010	1,121	290	2,786
	(n)	(%)	(%)	(%)	(%)	(%)	(%)	(%)	(%)	(%)	(%)	(%)
Type of school attended												
Secondary modern	1,464	44	53	51	52	54	61	48	50	42	47	47
Comprehensive	549	18	17	19	19	14	11	20	19	14	24	17
Grammar	718	24	22	24	24	19	17	23	22	26	22	24
Public	257	10	5	3	4	10	7	5	5	13	2	9
Other	105	4	3	3	1	3	4	4	4	5	5	3
No information	20											
Ever played truant?												
No	1,745	58	52	54	43	54	63	53	53	62	59	56
Yes	1,362	42	47	44	57	46	37	46	47	38	41	44
No information	6	–	1	2	–	–	–	1	–	–	–	–
Frequency												
Once a week	331	10	11	12	14	9	5	9	13	9	9	11
Once a month	262	8	9	5	11	14	7	9	10	6	8	8
Hardly ever	766	23	27	27	32	23	25	28	24	23	25	25
Not clear	3	–	–	0	0	–	0	–	–	–	0	–
Parental vigilance												
0	47	2	2	2	4	0	0	2	1	2	1	2
1–2	389	13	12	10	14	8	18	11	14	13	11	13
3–4	1,174	38	38	39	35	40	39	38	42	34	37	36
5–6	1,176	38	39	37	43	39	33	40	37	38	44	37
7	274	9	9	6	5	11	10	9	4	12	7	9
No information	53	1	2	2	1	1	0	–	2	–	–	1
I used to be sent into the street to play												
True	239	8	8	8	9	6	7	Not analysed			5	8
Partly true	446	14	15	15	15	19	11				22	14
Not true	2,343	76	74	74	74	74	81				70	76
Other or no information	85	2	3	3	2	1	1				3	2
I get too many jobs to do at home												
True	168	5	7	8	9	4	3	7	4	5	Not analysed	
Partly true	554	17	19	17	18	22	26	16	17	19		
Not true	2,298	76	70	69	71	71	68	75	74	74		
Other or no information	93	2	4	6	2	3	3	2	4	2		

Table 9.11 (continued)

Characteristics	All cases	'When under 12' did boy get home before mother?		How often did this happen?				Is mother at present in a job?			Is father at present on shift-work?	
		No	Yes	All the time	Often	Now and then	Hardly ever	Full-time	Part-time	No	Yes	No
Cases (weighted)	3,113	2,069	1,008	309	280	272	121	885	1,010	1,121	290	2,786
	(n)	(%)	(%)	(%)	(%)	(%)	(%)	(%)	(%)	(%)	(%)	(%)
I get most of my fun away from home												
True	947	31	29	29	32	30	22	31	33	28	29	31
Partly true	1,223	38	42	38	45	38	55	42	37	41	37	40
Not true	821	27	26	29	20	26	22	24	27	29	29	26
Other/no information	122	3	3	4	3	6	1	3	3	2	5	3
My parents always look after me well												
True	2,859	93	91	93	93	87	96	93	91	94	91	93
Partly true	177	5	6	5	6	11	3	6	7	4	5	6
Not true	20	–	1	1	2	–	1	1	1	–	2	–
Other or no information	57	2	2	1	0	2	0	–	1	2	2	1
I like to get home at the end of the day												
True	2,503	80	83	82	80	83	89	85	78	79	77	81
Partly true	439	15	13	15	15	11	7	12	17	14	14	14
Not true	92	3	3	1	3	4	2	2	2	5	4	3
Other or no information	79	2	1	2	2	2	2	1	3	2	5	2
I enjoy being at home												
True	2,117	Not analysed		Not analysed				71	67	68	61	69
Partly true	786							26	26	23	31	27
Not true	137							3	4	6	5	4
Other or no information	73							0	3	3	3	0

– = Less than 0.5 per cent

split two ways, into qualifying and control groups as shown in Figure 9.2.

For each expectation test, the controls were then matched to the qualifying group in terms of the matching composite presented in Chapter 1.

The evidence in Table 9.13 supports Expectation 4, namely that less stealing is done by boys whose mothers have never been in a job than by boys whose mothers have been in a job — a relationship that holds even after close matching of the two groups. The other post-matching differences are small and are not statistically significant.

Summing up on the investigation of Sub-Hypotheses 2a to 2c

On the evidence presented in this chapter, Sub-Hypothesis 2b is strengthened. Sub-Hypothesis 2a gets only minor — and not statistically significant — support from the collected evidence. Sub-Hypothesis 2c gets no support at all from the evidence.

6 METHODS AND FINDINGS RELATED TO THE INVESTIGATION OF HYPOTHESES 3 AND 4

The nature of the hypotheses

These hypotheses dealt with family composition and particularly with broken homes. They were:

Boys who have grandparents living in their home with them are thereby made less likely to steal (Hypothesis 3).

Boys whose homes are permanently broken in some way are thereby made more likely to steal (Hypothesis 4).

Figure 9.2
Division of sample for testing
Expectations 2, 4 and 6

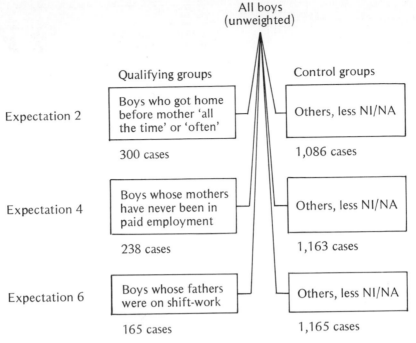

Table 9.12
Relationship between
employment status and
the nature and extent of
boys' stealing
(3,113 cases, weighted)

Nature of employment of parents	All cases	Quartile distribution of variety of stealing				Quartile distribution of amount of stealing			
		Q.1	Q.2	Q.3	Q.4	Q.1	Q.2	Q.3	Q.4
	(n)	(%)	(%)	(%)	(%)	(%)	(%)	(%)	(%)
Expectation 1: boy got home before mother when smaller (i.e. less than 12)									
Yes	1,008	22	30	26	22	22	23	28	27
No	2,069	25	27	24	24	26	25	26	23
Expectation 3: Has mother ever been in paid employment?									
No	632	28	34	23	15	31	28	24	18
Yes	2,481	23	26	25	25	23	24	27	26
Yes for under 6 months	89	36	26	11	27	35	29	18	18
Yes for 1 yr	293	28	26	25	21	26	31	24	19
Yes for 2 yrs	266	19	27	33	21	23	26	29	22
Yes for 3–4 yrs	386	25	19	29	28	26	20	28	27
Yes for 5–6 yrs	336	23	31	23	24	24	24	28	23
Yes for 7–10 yrs	470	24	24	27	25	19	22	30	30
Yes for 11 yrs	414	19	25	24	33	22	20	30	28
Always	40								
Mother is in a job now									
Yes, full-time	885	23	28	26	23	21	25	31	23
Yes, part-time	1,010	24	25	27	25	25	24	26	26
No	1,121	27	30	23	21	28	25	24	23
Expectation 5: Father has been on shift-work									
Yes	290	22	31	22	25	23	22	30	25
No	2,786	24	28	25	23	25	25	26	24

Table 9.13
Differences between qualifiers and controls before and after matching: variety and amount of stealing

Indices of stealing	Unadjusted average score for qualifiers a	Unadjusted average score for controls b	Adjusted average score for controls c	Differences between qualifiers and adj. controls a−c P	Difference a−c as percentage of c
*Concerning getting home before mother (cases)***	(300)	(1,086)			
Variety score	14.1	13.4	13.3	0.8 (NS)	6
Amount score	97.5	94.3	92.3	5.2 (NS)	6
Concerning mother never being in a job (cases)†	(238)	(1,163)			
Variety score	11.4	14.0	13.3	−1.9 (0.05)	−14
Amount score	71.5	100.1	93.0	−21.5* (0.05)	−23
Concerning father being on shift-work (cases)††	(165)	(1,165)			
Variety score	13.3	13.5	13.7	−0.4 (NS)	−3
Amount score	89.7	95.3	96.5	−6.8 (NS)	−7

*Significant at the 0.5 level
**Qualifiers = boys who got home before mother 'all the time' or 'often' when under twelve
†Qualifiers = boys whose mothers had never been in paid employment
††Qualifiers = boys whose fathers were on shift-work

Hypothesis 4 was later re-stated in two more specific forms as follows.

A boy whose father or mother or both was/were missing when he was thirteen is thereby made more likely to have engaged in stealing (Sub-Hypothesis 4a).

and,

A boy whose home has been 'broken' at some time in his first thirteen years is thereby made more likely to engage in stealing (Sub-Hypothesis 4b).

The nature of the questions asked to determine whether the home was 'broken' and if grandparents were present

In a sub-questionnaire called 'family data' the boy was asked a series of questions about both mother and father designed to reveal:

1 Whether either parent was missing from home and if so how old was the boy when the mother/father left.

2 If either parent was missing, had the place of the missing parent been taken by a substitute parent and, if so, how old was the boy at that time?

A home was regarded as having *been* 'broken' at some time if at least one of the parents had gone missing, irrespective of whether or not a substitute parent had moved in later on.

In another sub-questionnaire ('family composition and history') questions were asked to determine the number, sex and age of all siblings and of all other persons living in the home (see Appendix 9.1).

The distribution of boys in terms of variables named in the sub-hypotheses or otherwise relevant to those sub-hypotheses

In Table 9.14 is presented information about (a) the proportion of homes that have been broken during the first thirteen years of the boy's life and associated details; and, (b) the number of homes that were broken/still broken at the boy's age of thirteen years. For the latter distinction, the presence of a substitute parent was

Table 9.14

Table 9.14
Percentage of homes that have been broken and the circumstances of the break
(3,113 cases, weighted)

a Percentage ever broken (up to age of 13 yrs)*

Did the home become broken at any time in the boy's first 13 yrs?	(n)	(%)
Yes	359	12
No	2,735	88
No information	19	1

To whom was the break due?		
Mother only	76	2
Father only	246	8
Both parents	32	1
No information	5	–

Reason for mother's disappearance?		
Death	38	1
Divorce/separation	15	–
Ran away/deserted	22	1
Permanently in institution of some kind (e.g. hospital, prison)	4	–
Other or no information	29	1

Reason for father's disappearance?		
Death	37	1
Divorce/separation	107	3
Ran away/deserted	47	2
Permanently in institution of some kind (e.g. hospital, prison)	60	2
Other or no information	27	1

Was mother replaced by a stable substitute?		
Yes	91	3
No	17	1
No information	0	0

Was father replaced by a stable substitute?		
Yes	159	5
No	117	4
No information	2	–

b Percentage in broken state when boy was aged 13 yrs†

Was the home in a broken state when the boy was aged 13?‡	(n)	(%)
Yes	147	5
No	2,951	95
No information	15	–

*Age thirteen was selected because the age range for boys in the total sample was, with a few exceptions, thirteen to sixteen years. Age thirteen thus marked a point which was or had been common to almost all the boys in the sample
†The difference between the a and b figures for the incidence of broken homes is simply that the a figure deals with whether or not there has *ever* been a break (which might of course have been 'mended' at some later time) whereas the b figure relates to the situation at a single point in time
‡The presence of a stable substitute parent is regarded as 'mending' the home
– = Less than 0.5 per cent

regarded as 'mending' the break. The main indications of Table 9.14 appear to be as follows.

1 Something like 12 per cent of the homes were broken by the enduring departure of one or both parents during the boy's first thirteen years and approximately 5 per cent were in a broken state at the time boys were aged thirteen.

2 Breaks were due more to father's disappearance than to mother's, the reasons for disappearance of either parent being principally: divorce or separation; death; desertion; a parent permanently in some form of institution (e.g. hospital, prison).

3 A greater proportion of the missing mothers than of the missing fathers are replaced by stable substitutes.

Evidence about the number of siblings in the home and about the presence in the home of persons other than the parents is given in Table 9.15. Table 9.16 shows the distribution of household density. These two tables indicate:

1 That about 13 per cent of the boys in this sample had no siblings at all.

Table 9.15
Presence in the home of other family members
(3,113 cases, weighted)

Siblings present in home	(n)	(%)
0	408	13
1	986	32
2	714	23
3–4	681	22
5–6	199	6
7+	84	3
No information	41	1

Others in home, excepting parents		
Grandparents	226	7
Other relations	237	8
Lodgers other than relations	187	6
No information	38	1

Table 9.16
Crowdedness index
(where index equals people/rooms)
(3,113 cases, weighted)

	(n)	(%)
0.50 or less	236	8
0.51–0.75	707	23
0.76–1.00	1,097	35
1.01–1.25	340	11
1.26–1.50	369	12
1.51–1.99	150	5
2.00+	185	6
No information	29	1

2 That there were grandparent(s) in at least 7 per cent of homes, other relations in 8 per cent of them and lodgers in about 6 per cent of them.

3 With respect to crowdedness, 8 per cent of boys cam from relatively uncrowded homes (i.e. at least tw rooms per person) compared with 6 per cent from

Table 9.17
Aspects of family composition analysed by background of boys (3,113 cases, weighted)

Characteristics	All cases	Whether home in broken state at age of 13		Whether home ever broken		Whether grandparent(s living in the home	
		Yes	No	Yes	No	Yes	No
Cases (weighted)	3,113	147	2,951	359	2,735	226	2,887
		(%)	(%)	(%)	(%)	(%)	(%)
Last school attended							
Secondary modern	1,464	47	51	46	54	38	47
Comprehensive	549	17	21	17	19	10	18
Grammar	718	24	16	24	17	28	23
Public	257	8	5	9	5	13	8
Other	217						
No information	6						
Ever played truant?							
No	1,745	44	57	43	58	71	55
Yes	1,368	56	43	57	42	29	45
Frequency							
Once a week	331	12	11	12	11	5	11
Once a month	262	7	8	11	8	3	9
Hardly ever	766	37	24	34	23	21	25
Not clear	9	0	–	–	–	–	–
Parental vigilance index							
0	47	2	1	3	1	3	1
1–2	389	13	14	13	13	14	13
3–4	1,174	38	35	35	38	44	37
5–6	1,176	38	38	38	38	31	39
7	274	9	9	9	9	7	9
No information	53	1	3	2	1	2	1
I like to get home at the end of the day							
True	2,503	86	81	Not analysed		89	80
Partly true	439	11	14			8	15
Not true	92	1	3			3	3
Other or no information	79	1	2			1	2
I enjoy being at home							
True	2,117	Not analysed		66	69	75	68
Partly true	786			25	26	19	26
Not true	137			8	4	4	5
Other or no information	73			2	2	2	2
I get picked on too much at home							
True	338	8	11	Not analysed		Not analysed	
Partly true	700	16	23				
Not true	1,965	71	63				
Other or no information	110	4	3				

— = Less than 0.5 per cent

320

homes where there were at least two persons per room. The modal situation involved between three and four persons per four rooms (i.e. 35 per cent of the homes were of this kind).

Family composition analysed by a range of characteristics and by background of boys

The variables named as causal in Hypotheses 3 and 4 were analysed by a variety of background factors that seemed relevant to those 'causal' variables. Details are presented in Table 9.17.

The main indications of Table 9.17 are as follows.

1 Truancy occurs more among boys from currently or previously broken homes than amongst other boys. It occurs much less in homes where at least one grandparent is present.

2 Parental control, as estimated by the boys themselves, is much the same in broken homes as in non-broken homes, but is somewhat less in homes where grandparents are present.

3 The evidence as it bears on 'home atmosphere' does not suggest that home is especially unpleasant for boys with a broken-home background.

4 Broken-home background is more common amongst those from grammar schools and public schools than amongst boys from secondary-modern and comprehensive schools.

Investigating Hypothesis 3, Sub-Hypotheses 4a and 4b

From these, five expectations were derived*.

Expectation 1 Boys whose homes were in a broken state when they were aged thirteen, will have engaged in more stealing than other boys.

Expectation 2 Expectation 1 applies even after the matching of the two groups of boys in terms of the correlates of stealing.

Expectation 3 Boys whose homes were broken at some time in their first thirteen years will have engaged in more stealing than other boys.

Expectation 4 Expectation 2 applies even after matching the two groups of boys in terms of the correlates of stealing.

Expectation 5 Boys who have grandparents living in the home are less likely to have been engaged in stealing.

Testing Expectations 1, 3 and 5

The testing of Expectations 1, 3 and 5 was done through simple association analysis and the results are set out in Table 9.18. The evidence in Table 9.18 supports

*A sixth expectation had, in fact, been formulated, namely: Expectation 5 applies even after matching the two groups of boys in terms of the correlates of stealing. Computer service failures and then a shortage of computer time left this expectation untested.

Table 9.18
Relationship between aspects of family composition and the extent and nature of stealing
(3,113 cases, weighted)

Conditions postulated in the expectations	All cases	Quartile distribution of variety of stealing				Quartile distribution of amount of stealing			
		Q.1	Q.2	Q.3	Q.4	Q.1	Q.2	Q.3	Q.4
	(n)	(%)	(%)	(%)	(%)	(%)	(%)	(%)	(%)
Expectation 1. Home was in a broken state when he was 13 yrs old									
Yes	147	18	25	31	27	21	33	20	26
No	2,951	25	25	26	24	24	27	25	23
*Expectation 3. Home was broken at some time during his first 13 yrs**									
Yes	359	18	23	30	30	19	28	25	28
No	2,735	26	25	26	23	25	28	25	23
Expectation 5. Grandparent(s) in the home									
Yes	226	39	27	16	18	32	29	26	12
No	2,887	24	25	27	25	23	28	25	24

*A home is regarded as being in a 'broken state' when one or more of the parents has disappeared and where there is no permanent substitute for the person who has gone. A home is regarded as *having been* broken at some time if one or both of the parents disappeared, even though a substitute parent has come in at some later time

Figure 9.3
Division of sample for testing
Expectations 2 and 4

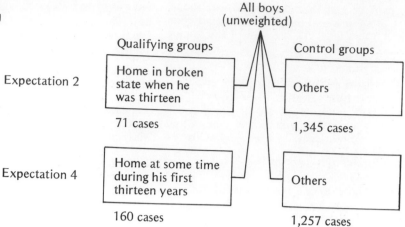

Expectations 1 and 3 to a moderate degree and Expectation 5 rather more.

Testing Expectations 2 and 4 (using unweighted sample, 1,425 cases)

These two expectations were that Expectations 1 and 3 respectively will still apply when the boys from non-broken homes are matched to the other boys in terms of the correlates of stealing. For each test, the total sample was broken into qualifying and control groups, on the pattern shown in Figure 9.3.

In each case, the control group was now matched to the qualifying group in terms of the correlates of stealing (on the system detailed in Chapter 1). The results of the matching process are set out in Table 9.19.

For neither Expectation 2 nor Expectation 4 is the difference in the right-hand column statistically significant at the 0.05 level or anything like it. In other words, the matching process has eliminated much of the difference between qualifying and control groups that showed up in Table 9.18.

Summing-up on Hypothesis 3, Sub-Hypotheses 4a and 4b

The evidence presented in Section 4 of this report is mixed in its indications. Thus, it tends marginally to

Table 9.19
Differences between qualifiers and controls before and after matching: variety and amount of stealing

Theft indices	Unadjusted average score for qualifiers a	Unadjusted average score for controls b	Adjusted average score for controls c	Differences between qualifiers and adj. controls a−c P	Difference a−c as percentage of c
Expectation 2. Concerning home in broken state at his 13th year*					
Index of variety	14.3	13.5	13.9	0.4 (NS)	3
Index of amount	97.8	94.8	98.7	−0.5 (NS)	−1
Expectation 4. Concerning home in broken state during his first 13 years†					
Index of variety	15.0	13.4	14.0	1.0 (NS)	7
Index of amount	104.8	93.6	100.4	0.4 (NS)	4

*Qualifying group = boys whose homes were in a broken state when they were aged thirteen
†Qualifying group = boys whose homes had ever been broken in the period up to their thirteenth year
NS = Not significant at the 0.05 level or better

support Expectation 1 but not Expectation 2. Of these two classes of evidence, that bearing on Expectation 2 is the more meaningful because it has involved the elimination of at least some of the misleading differences between the two groups featured in the Expectation 1 evidence. In the circumstances it must be concluded that Sub-Hypothesis 4a is not supported by the evidence presented in this chapter.

The position is closely similar with respect to Sub-Hypothesis 4b — it is not supported by this evidence.

With regard to Hypothesis 3, the evidence in Table 9.19 tends to be supportive — though in this case we do not have a test by *matching*.

7 SUMMING-UP ON THE INVESTIGATION OF HYPOTHESES 1 to 4

Sub-Hypotheses 1a to 1e concerning separation from parents

The five sub-hypotheses in this group were to the effect that separation from one or the other parent or from both of them for an extended period contributes to the development of stealing by boys: (*a*) from mother up to the age of five; (*b*) from mother in the age range six to thirteen; (*c*) from father up to the age of five; (*d*) from father in the age range six to thirteen; (*e*) from both parents at once up to the age of thirteen.

Some 12 per cent of the boys claimed (presumably mainly from family talk) that they had been separated from their mothers for a month or more during their first five years and 41 per cent claimed separation during the next eight years. The pattern of claims regarding fathers was broadly similar but at a somewhat higher level of incidence. Separation from both parents for a month or more up to the age of thirteen was claimed by 25 per cent of the boys. The chapter stresses the need for wariness in interpreting boy's claims about each separation or early non-separation from parents.

Sub-Hypothesis 1a was rendered marginally more tenable (with regard to amount of stealing) by the evidence. But further investigation, based upon 'separation' evidence collected from the most informed source or sources, and using the Hypothetico—Deductive Method, is now called for.

Sub-Hypotheses 2a to 2c concerning working status of parents

The three sub-hypotheses in this group postulated a causal link between the development of juvenile stealing and certain job situations: (*a*) the situation in which boys frequently get home ahead of mother; (*b*) the situation in which mother has never gone out to work; (*c*) the situation in which father did shift-work.

Eighty per cent of boys claimed their mothers had at some time gone out to work; 36 per cent that mother is in a job 'now' (i.e. at the time of the interview); 19 per cent claimed that they frequently got home before mother when they were under twelve, and 9 per cent that father did shift-work.

The evidence gives but little support to the view that there is a causal link between juvenile stealing and boys frequently getting home ahead of mother and it gives no support at all to the view that fathers' involvement in shift-work increases the level of boys' stealing. On the other hand, the evidence strengthens Sub-Hypothesis 2b, namely that boys will steal less if their mothers have not gone out to work at all (i.e. during the boy's lifetime). In interpreting these findings, it is important to remain aware that the information about parental working situations came from the boys.

Hypothesis 3, concerning the presence of grandparents in the home

The hypothesis in this case was that the presence of a grandparent in a home tends to operate against the development of stealing by boys in that home. Grandparents were present in 7 per cent of the sampled homes. Boys from such homes tended more to have gone to grammar or public school, to have truanted less than others, to have been subject to less *parental* control, to like (somewhat more than others) to get home at the end of the day. The (computer) analysis of the evidence brought to bear on this hypothesis was incomplete, though what there was of it gave some support to the hypothesis.

Sub-Hypotheses 4a and 4b, concerning broken homes

These two sub-hypotheses postulated a causal link between stealing; and, (*a*) the presence of a broken-home situation at a given point in a boy's life (in this case at age thirteen); (*b*) the existence of a broken home any time up to the age of thirteen.

According to the boys in this sample, 12 per cent of their homes were 'broken' at some time during their first thirteen years and 5 per cent were in that state when they reached the age of thirteen. According to the boys concerned, the breaks were due more to the father disappearing than to the disappearance of the mother, and causes of breaks as claimed by boys were principally: divorce or separation; death; desertion; in an institution (e.g. hospital, prison). A greater proportion of the missing mothers than of the missing fathers were replaced by stable substitutes.

Broken homes were somewhat more common amongst boys with grammar- or public-school background than for other boys. Boys from broken homes did not appear to regard their homes as less pleasant than did other boys. They are more involved in truancy than other boys.

The evidence regarding the tenability of these two sub-hypotheses is mixed. Thus, there were differences between the qualifying and the control groups before matching, but these differences tended to disappear when matching was applied. In this circumstance, it must be concluded that the evidence does not support either sub-hypothesis.

8 SOME COMMENTS AND POSSIBLE ACTION

1 One feature of this chapter that calls especially for

comment is the element of support provided by the evidence for the hypothesis that early separation of boys from mothers is causally linked with thieving. This of course ties in with findings by Bowlby[1]. At the same time the degree to which the hypothesis is supported by the evidence is not great *and* a warning has already been issued to the effect that the evidence itself is by no means methodologically safe*.

On the latter point, what has to be noted is that boys who claim separation from mother at an early age (in the first five years in this case) are almost certain to be reporting what others in the family have told them and, because of this, their testimony may well be in error. Furthermore, it is quite possible that many boys who did *not* claim early separation from mother may in fact have been separated in this way but without having been told about it or without otherwise being able to recall it.

What is needed now is a repeat operation using the same strategy of investigation but with evidence of maternal separation collected directly from the parents (the mother in particular). The evidence collected from the parents should be made to include: (*a*) very early separation from either parent; (*b*) very early separation from both parents at once; (*c*) later separation (i.e. between the ages of six and thirteen) from either or both parents. Probing techniques should be used in gathering this information.

This suggestion does not negate or render useless the present finding. The present finding has made the separation hypothesis marginally more tenable without 'proving it'. The proposed step would constitute a further and more rigorous challenge of the hypothesis.

2 Another noteworthy outcome of the investigation reported in this chapter is the way in which the evidence gave support to the hypothesis that a boy is less likely to engage in stealing if his mother has not gone out to work at all (i.e. during boyhood). The evidence also suggests that the shorter the period of such employment, the less likely it is that the boy will engage in stealing (see Table 9.12).

[1] See Bowlby, J. (1946). Forty-four juvenile thieves: their character and home life. Bailliere, Tindall & Cox, London.

*See pp. 302, 303, 304, 310, 323.

This finding has obvious implications of an important kind — though it must be noted that boys could be wrong about the working status of mother during their very early years. If in these two circumstances it is thought desirable to administer further challenges to the hypothesis, then such a check should include close questioning of the mother herself about her job history. In doing this, information should also be collected from her about the period of the boy's life during which she worked, the time she got home from work in different phases of her working life, the arrangements made for looking after the boy in the event of his getting home ahead of her, the presence in the home of anyone to deputize for her in looking after the boy, her philosophy relating to mothers going out to work, her reasons for going out to work. The hypothesis-checking strategy should follow that developed for the present study as should the technique for securing information about the extent of boys' involvement in stealing.

One may wonder why the hypothesis about the effects of boys frequently getting home before mother did not get much support from the evidence — whereas the 'never work' hypothesis got statistically significant support. One possible explanation may be that mothers who frequently got home after the boy did not necessarily do so because of employment. They may, for example, have been shopping, visiting friends, playing afternoon bingo. Also, much may depend upon the arrangements made for looking after boys if mother is late home. Conceivably — and this, too, is merely speculation — mothers who work may have attitudes about raising children which are different from those of mothers who do not go out to work.

3 The 'broken home' hypotheses were not supported by the evidence — a finding that may be surprising to some. What has to be remembered here, however, is that this inquiry was based on boys generally and not simply upon those who had gone through Court proceedings. If in the past boys who were thus processed tended to be from the more impoverished social sector, especially if from broken homes, it would be all too easy for a belief to develop that a broken home is causally linked with stealing — a belief which on present evidence appears to be relatively untenable.

APPENDIX 9.1

The Sub-Questionnaire Used: Family Data

Separations: Instructions to Interviewers

Concerning the boy and his mother/mother substitute The object of this part of the exercise is to find out: for what periods the mother (or her substitute) has been in the home; when and for how long she has been away from the home; where she was during her absence from the home; where the boy was during her absence from the home and *who* was looking after him then.

Example 1 *In most cases* you will find that the boy's real mother is living at home with him at present and that this has been so for all or most of his life. For this simple case, the following set of questions may well be sufficient.

'Is your mother living?'   YES/NO [IF 'NO', PROCEED GENTLY AS IN Q.2]

　　IF 'YES':
'Is she living at home?'   YES/NO

　　IF 'YES' PUT A CROSS (X) AT BOY'S PRESENT AGE (IN THE AGE-COLUMN, AT LEFT) AND SAY:
'And has she been there all your life?'   YES/NO

　　IF 'YES', PUT A CROSS (X) AT AGE 0 (IN LEFT-HAND COLUMN)
'Has she ever been away at all *for a month or more*?'   YES/NO

　　IF 'NO', CHECK WITH:
'In hospital?'
'Looking after a relation?'

　　IF 'YES', FIND OUT FOR WHAT PERIOD IN THE BOY'S LIFE AND MARK ITS DURATION IN THE AGE-COLUMN (AT LEFT). FIND OUT (FOR EACH ABSENCE) WHY SHE WAS AWAY, WHERE THE BOY WAS IN THAT PERIOD, WHO LOOKED AFTER HIM. ENTER THESE DETAILS IN RIGHT-HAND COLUMN.

　　NOW BRACKET IN THE PERIODS WHEN THE MOTHER *WAS* AT HOME AND MARK THEM M/H (AS SHOWN IN DIAGRAM).

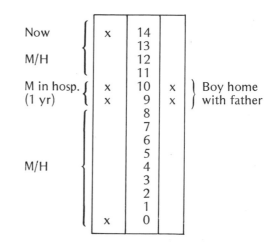

Example 2 *Not all the cases will be as simple as the foregoing one*, but for all of them the information sought is of the same kind, namely the periods when mother was away and who looked after the boy then and where he stayed. Here is another case, this one involving a stepmother.

'Is you mother living?'   YES/NO (CHECK THAT BOY IS REFERRING TO REAL MOTHER)

　　IF 'NO'
'Do you mind if I ask you how old you were when your mother died?'
　　ENTER A CROSS IN AGE-COLUMN AT THIS AGE AND WRITE 'MOTHER DIED'.

'Since then, who looked after you?'
　　IF STEPMOTHER, ASK:
'How old were you when she came to live in your home?'

'Between the time when your mother died and the time when you stepmother came, where were you?'

'Who looked after you then?'
　　BRACKET THE TWO CROSSES AND ENTER THESE DETAILS IN THE RIGHT-HAND COLUMN
(e.g. 'Boy at home with father').

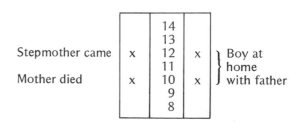

NOW FIND OUT, FOR THE PERIOD *AFTER* STEPMOTHER CAME, IF SHE HAS BEEN LIVING IN THE BOY'S HOME ALL THE TIME OR IF THERE HAVE BEEN PERIODS WHEN SHE WAS AWAY. IN SUCH CASES, ENTER (AGAINST THE APPROPRIATE PART OF THE AGE-COLUMN) WHERE SHE WAS AND FOR HOW LONG, WHERE THE BOY WAS AND WHO LOOKED AFTER THE BOY IN HER ABSENCE (ENTRIES FOR STEP-MOTHER ON LEFT AND BOY ON RIGHT).

Now stepmother at home {

x	14
	13
x	12

NOW WORK *BACK* FROM THE TIME WHEN THE BOY'S MOTHER DIED. MARK THE PERIODS SHE WAS CONTINUOUSLY AT HOME, AND, IF AWAY FOR ANY LENGTHY PERIOD, LOCATE THIS PERIOD AND MARK AGAINST IT: WHERE SHE WAS AND FOR HOW LONG; WHERE THE BOY WAS AND WHO LOOKED AFTER HIM.

Mother died	x	10	x	} Boy at home
Mother to hosp.	x	9	x	} with father
		8		
		7		
		6		
		5		
Mother at home {		4		
		3		
		2		
		1		
		0		

Example 3 *In all cases*, you will have quite a lot of probing and checking to do, but you must always start with the boy's mother, using the opening question: 'Is your mother living?' All your entries must be made on the special age-line chart provided.

II *Concerning the at-homeness of the boy.* Not only must we find out if the mother or mother substitute (MS) has left the boy for any period, but we must find out if the boy himself has left the home (for any time) in those periods when the mother or M/S is in fact there.

In most cases you will find that the boy has not been away much (except for holidays) and it may well be that the following questions will be sufficient in quite a lot of cases. All entries are made in the right-hand age-column used in I above.

'Have you yourself been away from home for any lengthy time?' YES/NO

IF 'YES', FIND OUT TERMINAL AGES AND MARK IN THE AGE-COLUMN (USING X'S) AS SHOWN TO THE RIGHT. AGAINST EACH INTERVAL, WRITE IN WHERE THE BOY WAS, HOW LONG THE ABSENCE WAS AND WHETHER MOTHER OR FATHER WAS WITH HIM. CHECK WITH:

'Were there any other times you were away from home for a month or more?' . . . 'In hospital? . . . At a camp? . . . Some other place?'
  ENTER DETAILS

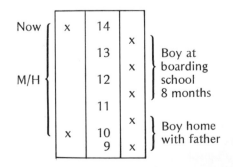

Now {
x	14	
		x
	13	x
	12	x
	11	
	10	x
x	10	
	9	x

M/H {

Boy at boarding school 8 months

Boy home with father

Concerning the at-homeness of the father and the custody of the boy. Finally we need to know if the boy's father (F/S) was away from home for any extended period and, for any such occasion: the length of the absence and the reason for it; who was looking after the boy during his absence (this could in some cases include a temporary father substitute). In some cases the record will be about the boy's real father and in other cases about a father substitute. All entries must be made on the second age-column system.

Proceed here just as you did in **I**. There is no case for repeating a procedure similar to **II** because this inform- ation is independent of whether we are asking about the mother or the father.

Now

	x	14		
		13		
		12		
Father away	x	11	x	Boy at school 8
at ... (1 yr)	x	10	x	months. Rest of
		9		time at home with
		8		mother only
		7		
		6		

Separations: Record Sheet

MOTHER (M/S) AND BOY

Events affecting at-homeness of mother or substitute.

Whereabouts and custody of boy during mother's (M/S's) absences from home.

Her whereabouts during absences and duration of absences.

His own absences from home and custody during these absences.

FATHER (F/S) AND BOY

Events affecting at-homeness of father or substitute.

Whereabouts and custody of boy during father's (F/S's) absences from home.

His whereabouts during absences and duration of absences.

His own absences from home and his custody during these absences.

x here

	x here		x here			x here		x here
		17					17	
		16					16	
		15					15	
		14					14	
		13					13	
		12					12	
		11					11	
		10					10	
		9					9	
		8					8	
		7					7	
		6					6	
		5					5	
		4					4	
		3					3	
		2					2	
		1					1	
		0					0	

THE QUESTIONNAIRE

Family composition and history

I To establish who else is living in the boy's home as part of his immediate family and the whereabouts of members who are not there now.

All entries are to be fitted into the table set out below.

Member of family		Age	Relationship to boy	Other information
Mother or M substitute			Real/Step/Other (say what)	
Father or F substitute			Real/Step/Other (say what)	
Brothers or Sisters	1			
	2			
	3			
	4			
	5			
	6			
Others at/in home				

Q.1 ENTER (LATER) DETAILS OF MOTHER AND FATHER, USING THE B/FAMILY DATA

Q.2 Recording all siblings and others living at home (others includes foster parents and step-siblings).

TELL BOY:
'I want to ask you a few things about your brothers or sisters, *but I don't want to know their names.* I don't want to know their names.'

2a) 'Have you got any brothers or sisters living at home* with you?'   YES/NO

IF 'NO', GO TO Q.2b

IF 'YES', (i.e. respondent *has* got siblings), ASK:
'How many sisters live with you at home?' (SEE THAT

HE IS INCLUDING ANY STEPSISTERS)
'What are their ages?' STRESS: "*I don't want to know their names, just their ages*' ..../..../..../..../..../..../....
ENTER THESE AGES BETWEEN OBLIQUES. 'Are any of them step-sisters?' PUT S/S UNDER AGE IF STEPSISTER.
'And how many brothers live with you at home?' (SEE THAT HE IS INCLUDING ANY STEP-BROTHERS)
'What are their ages?' ..../..../..../..../..../..../.... (STRESS:
'*I don't want to know their names, just their ages*'
ENTER THESE BETWEEN OBLIQUES.
'Are any of them step-brothers?' PUT S/B UNDER AGE IF STEPBROTHER.

2b) 'Now is there anyone *else* who lives in your home with you?'   YES/NO
IF 'NO', CHALLENGE WITH: 'Who else is there?' 'Is that everyone?'
IF 'YES', ASK: 'Who are they?' ENTER IN GRID RELATIONSHIP TO BOY FOR EACH OF THESE.
ALSO APPROX. AGE

*'Home' = place where you live now

328

.3 Recording all members of the family who no longer
~e at home*.

Do any of your brothers and sisters live away from
~ome*?' YES/NO

IF 'YES', ASK:
What are their ages?' ..../..../..../..../..../ 'Any more?'
./..../....

ENTER THESE AGES *AND UNDER THEM THE
RELATIONSHIP OF THE SIBLING TO THE BOY*
(i.e. brother, step-brother, sister, step-sister). FOR
EACH ASK:
) 'Where is he/she now?' ENTER DETAILS IN GRID
BELOW
i) 'What is he/she doing now?' ENTER DETAILS IN
GRID BELOW
*PURSUE ANY INDICATION THAT SIBLING IS IN
A PENAL INSTITUTION*

a) DETERMINE WHICH OF THE FOLLOWING
APPLIES TO THE BOY'S MOTHER* AT PRESENT
AND RING ALL THAT APPLY.
(IN FULL-TIME JOB/IN PART-TIME JOB/ON
SHIFT-WORK/TWO OR MORE JOBS/HOUSEWIFE
ONLY)

2b) *IF IN A JOB ASK:*
(i) 'What time(s) does she usually leave for work?'
(ii) 'What time(s) does she usually get home from
work?'
(iii) Any other details that do not fit (i) and (ii)

IF HOUSEWIFE ONLY, ASK: 'Has she *ever* gone out
to a job?' YES/NO/DON'T KNOW
IF 'NO' OR 'DON'T KNOW', GO TO Q.3

2c) 'How old were you when your mother first went out
to a job?'

ge	Brother or sister	Where is he/she now?	What is he/she doing now?
	B/SB/S/SS		
	B/SB/S/SS		
	B/SB/S/SS		
	B/SB/S/SS		
	B/SB/S/SS		
	B/SB/S/SS		

I To get job details of mother, father and boy. To find
out if the mother is generally out when the boy
comes home.

Q.1 Father's* job(s)

a) DETERMINE WHICH OF THE FOLLOWING
APPLY TO THE BOY'S FATHER* AND RING *ALL*
THAT APPLY (FULL-TIME JOB/PART-TIME JOB/
SHIFT-WORK/TWO OR MORE JOBS/OUT OF
WORK/RETIRED)

b) IF IN JOB, ASK:
'Exactly *what* is his job?' GET A PROPER DESCRIP-
TION OF IT. IF TWO JOBS, GET THIS FOR EACH
NOW GO TO Q.2 IF NOT NOW IN JOB. ASK:
'Exactly what was his *last* job? GET PROPER DESCRIP-
TION OF IT

Q.2 Mother's* job(s)

*'Home' = place where boy lives now
*'Father' (in *this* context) = 'man of the house'
*'Mother' (in *this* context) = 'woman of the house'

CHALLENGE AGE GIVEN
2d) FIND OUT WHEN SHE HAD A JOB(S), RELATING
JOB DURATION TO BOY'S AGE.
1st job: . . . yrs to . . . yrs 2nd job: . . . yrs to . . . yrs
3rd job: . . . yrs to . . . yrs 4th job: . . . yrs to . . . yrs
5th job: . . . yrs to . . . yrs 6th job: . . . yrs to . . . yrs

2e) 'When you were smaller, were there times when you
got home *before* she did?'
YES/NO/DON'T KNOW
IF 'YES':
(i) 'How often did that happen?' SHOW CARD.
CIRCLE CHOICE
(ALL THE TIME/OFTEN/NOW AND THEN/
HARDLY EVER)
(ii) 'What ages were you when this happened — when
you got home *before* she did?'
GET RANGE OR RANGES
(iii) 'Where did you go when that happened?' (GET *ALL*
PLACES)

Q.3 Boy's job(s)

3a FIND OUT WHICH OF FOLLOWING APPLY TO
BOY AT PRESENT. CIRCLE *ALL* THAT APPLY.

(STILL AT SCHOOL/IN FULL-TIME JOB/IN PART-TIME JOB/ON SHIFT-WORK/OUT OF WORK)

IF STILL AT SCHOOL, GO TO NEXT HYPO-THESIS

IF 'OUT OF WORK', ASK: 'Exactly what was your last full-time job?'

THEN GO TO Q.3b

IF IN 'FULL-TIME JOB', ASK: 'Exactly what is your job?'

THEN GO TO Q.3b

IF IN 'PART-TIME JOB' *ONLY*, ASK: 'Exactly what is this job?'

THEN GO TO Q.3b

3b 'How old were you when you got your first full-tir job?'

3c 'When you first left school, how long was it befc you got a full-time job?'
...weeks/months/years

3d 'How many full-time jobs have you had since leavi school (counting the one you have got now)?'

3e 'Have you ever been out of work since leavi school?'   YES/NO

IF 'YES', ASK: 'How many times?'
'How long (for each)?'

330

Chapter ten
Interests, spare time, and television viewing

CONTENTS

1 THE COVERAGE OF THIS CHAPTER

In this chapter I have presented a wide range of information broadly related to 'interests', 'spare time' and 'television viewing'. This information was collected and processed to serve two associated purposes, the more important of which was to investigate a particular composite of hypotheses about causal factors in the development of juvenile stealing. These hypotheses were as follows.

1 A paucity of (legal) interests facilitates the onset and continuance of stealing. For the purposes of this hypothesis, 'interest' is defined in terms of: (a) its passive form (i.e. a 'feeling of interest'); and, (b) its active form (i.e. 'activity associated with the interest').

2 Boys who watch a lot of television are thereby made more likely to engage in stealing.

3 Boys who do not know what to do with their 'spare time' are thereby led to do more stealing.

4 Boys who get bored and fed-up during their spare time are thereby led to do more stealing.

The second purpose of the collected data was to provide background information about each of the factors or conditions hypothesized as causal in character. For example, with respect to boys' interests, it seemed desirable to establish the distribution amongst boys of a fairly wide range of interests and to find out how this distribution varied with the backgrounds and characteristics of the boys.

2 RESEARCH PROCEDURES COMMON TO ALL THE HYPOTHESES DEALT WITH IN THE INQUIRY

The gathering of information relevant to the hypotheses listed in Section I was done in the context of an inquiry concerned with over thirty other hypotheses. The techniques relating to the inquiry *as a whole* have been summarized in Chapter 1. That summary deals with: sampling procedures; a technique for getting boys to provide reliable information about any stealing they have done; questioning procedures for classifying boys in terms of the variables featured in the different hypotheses (i.e. in terms of the different independent variables); strategies for investigating the tenability of hypotheses about causal factors and processes. The reader should as necessary refer back to the relevant parts of Chapter 1 in reading statements of findings in the present and subsequent chapters.

3 RESEARCH PROCEDURES APPLYING ONLY TO THE HYPOTHESES DEALT WITH IN THIS CHAPTER

Whereas many aspects of the research procedure applied generally to the whole range of hypotheses under study, certain parts of it related only to the four hypotheses featured in this chapter. These parts are contained in several of the sub-questionnaires used in the inquiry and presented below in summary form. Each is set out in fu in Appendix 10.1.

The 'Interests' Questionnaire

Boys were taken through the following procedure ar questions.

1 Each boy was handed thirty-one cards, each wit some single interest presented on it. The cards we received one at a time and the boy sorted them int boxes labelled either INTERESTED or NOT INTEF ESTED.

2 After this, the boy took all the cards in th INTERESTED box and sorted these into a new set c containers to indicate how often he did anything acti about those interests. The containers in this case we paper bags each with a frequency label printed in larg letters on it.

These two sorting procedures produced: (a) evidence c at least a *feeling* of interest in the matter concerne and, (b) evidence of activity level in relation to th interest.

The Questions relating to television viewing

Watching television was one of the interests in the list c thirty-one and respondents were asked both if they wer interested in watching television *and* how often the watched it.

The questions about use of spare time and abou boredom

Boys were asked:

1 If they ever felt they did not know what to do wit their spare time and, if so, how often.

2 What they did when they felt like this.

3 Did they ever wish there were more places in which t spend their spare time? If so, how often they felt lik this.

4 Did they get bored or fed-up with things? If so, ho often?

5 Several other related questions.

4 METHODS AND FINDINGS RELATED TO THE INVESTIGATION OF HYPOTHESIS 1

The Nature of the Hypothesis

Hypothesis 1 took the following form:

A paucity of (legal) interests facilitates the onset anc continuance of stealing.

For the purposes of this hypothesis, interest is defined ir terms of: (a) its passive form (i.e. 'a feeling' of interest) nd, (b) its active form (i.e. 'activity associated with the interest'). It was our intention to examine and challenge his hypothesis through testing a series of expectations drawn from it and to present background information relating to the independent variable featured in the hypothesis — in this case 'a paucity of (legal) interests'.

Distribution of Boys in Terms of the Variable Hypothesized as a Causal Factor

The questions asked

These have already been referred to in Section 3 and are given in full in Appendix 10.1. The aim of the questions was to provide two sorts of information about how boys are positioned in relation to each of thirty-one

kinds of interests or hobbies: (a) how many of the boys did or did not *feel* interested in them; (b) how often did boys *do* anything about such interests or hobbies? It is not suggested that the thirty-one types of interest/hobby dealt with here do by any means cover *all* the interests/hobbies of boys. They do, however, provide a sufficiently large and varied basis for discriminating between boys in terms of their degree of involvement in spare time interests/hobbies.

Because the response distributions relating to the thirty-one interests/hobbies dealt with appear to be of value in their own right, they have been presented in full in Table 10.1. However, the main use made of the response data was for the development of two indices of involvement: an index of the number of the boy's (legal) interests (D); an index of the degree to which boys are *actively* involved in the pursuit of (legal) interests (E).

Table 10.1
Distribution of responses to questions about twenty-eight interests

Type of interest	Interested?		Frequency of activity on the part of those interested in the 'items'						
	No	Yes	Most days	A few times a week	Once a week	Once a month	Hardly ever	Never	No information
	(%)	(%)	(%)	(%)	(%)	(%)	(%)	(%)	(%)
1 Watching television	14	86	69	15	1	—	—	—	1
2 A hobby of some kind	10	90	26	23	24	9	6	1	1
3 Going to the cinema	21	79	1	4	31	34	9	—	—
4 Gardening	82	18	1	2	4	4	5	1	1
5 Welfare work of some kind	44	56	1	3	7	12	24	8	1
6 Going to see people on the stage	59	41	—	1	3	11	23	2	1
7 Gymnastics	41	59	7	17	20	5	7	3	—
8 Camping	42	58	—	—	2	9	40	6	1
9 Reading	29	71	34	21	8	3	4	—	1
10 Playing games such as darts, draughts	22	78	14	20	21	15	7	—	1
11 Lectures or discussions	61	39	1	3	7	10	14	3	1
12 Art of some kind	52	48	7	8	15	8	8	2	1
13 Music	25	75	47	15	8	2	2	1	—
14 Getting the latest fashions in clothes	47	53	2	2	8	30	10	1	—
15 Going to see places	20	80	1	3	13	36	26	1	—
16 Looking after a pet	42	58	31	7	2	1	8	8	1
17 Going to a fun fair	44	56	—	1	1	11	41	1	1
18 Dancing	60	40	2	5	12	9	9	2	1
19 Going out with a girl	25	75	10	16	14	13	17	4	1
20 Riding a motor bike or motor scooter	44	56	8	4	4	3	13	24	1
21 Getting around with my mates	15	85	37	26	15	4	2	1	—
22 A sport of some kind	12	88	26	25	26	6	4	1	—
23 Having a bit of a wild time	42	58	8	10	12	13	13	1	1
24 An indoor game of some kind	34	66	11	17	21	9	6	1	1
25 Going to church or chapel	68	32	1	3	16	5	4	1	1
26 Going to evening classes to learn	48	52	1	5	9	3	10	23	1
27 Getting into fights with other boys	81	19	2	2	3	5	5	1	1
28 Reading or hearing about new discoveries in science	41	59	6	8	14	15	13	2	1

— = Less than 0.5 per cent

Table 10.2

For each of the twenty-eight types of interest, relating
ages of boys to: *feeling* of interest; interest-linked activity
(3,113 cases, weighted)

Type of interest	Percentage claiming interest	Ages of those *feeling* an interest				Percentage claiming frequent activity*	Ages of those *actively* interested			
		12/13	14	15	16/17		12/13	14	15	16/17
		(%)	(%)	(%)	(%)		(%)	(%)	(%)	(%)
1 Watching television	86	25	27	23	25	84	25	27	23	25
2 A hobby of some kind	90	24	26	24	26	49	24	27	25	24
3 Going to the cinema	79	22	26	24	28	5	16	23	27	34
4 Gardening	18	31	24	25	20	3	39	17	18	24
5 Welfare work of some kind	56	28	25	22	25	4	54	18	15	13
6 Going to see people on the stage	41	19	22	26	33	1	20	13	31	36
7 Gymnastics	59	28	25	23	24	24	36	29	19	16
8 Camping	58	25	25	24	26	1	35	13	35	17
9 Reading	71	19	27	26	29	55	25	23	23	29
10 Playing games such as darts, draughts	78	24	26	25	25	34	25	25	25	25
11 Lectures or discussions	39	19	24	23	34	4	17	26	21	36
12 Art of some kind	48	25	27	23	25	15	25	30	20	25
13 Music	75	19	23	26	31	62	16	23	28	33
14 Getting the latest fashion in clothes	53	19	26	27	28	4	14	22	40	24
15 Going to see places	80	24	25	23	27	4	25	24	24	27
16 Looking after a pet	58	31	28	20	21	38	30	31	20	19
17 Going to a fun fair	56	27	27	22	23	1	25	20	37	18
18 Dancing	40	12	20	31	37	7	10	15	26	49
19 Going out with a girl	75	15	25	28	32	26	10	17	26	46
20 Riding a motor bike or motor scooter	56	20	25	26	29	12	9	11	19	61
21 Getting around with my mates	85	22	25	24	28	63	21	25	26	28
22 A sport of some kind	88	24	25	24	27	51	27	28	25	21
23 Having a bit of a wild time	58	20	24	24	32	18	20	22	21	37
24 An indoor game of some kind	66	26	27	22	24	28	28	27	21	24
25 Going to church, chapel or synagogue	32	25	27	24	24	4	27	23	33	17
26 Going to evening classes to learn	52	24	22	23	31	6	15	21	28	36
27 Getting into fights with other boys	19	22	24	26	28	4	23	29	19	29
28 Reading or learning about new discoveries in science	59	24	25	24	27	14	27	21	24	28

*That is, claiming action 'most days' or 'a few times a week'

Indices *D* and *E* figured centrally in the investigation of the hypothesis.

For several of the items in the 'interests' list, extra questions were asked. These items were: doing homework; doing odd jobs about the home; doing odd jobs he got paid for. For each of these, boys were asked to say how many hours a week they spent doing them. Results are shown in Table 10.3.

Response Distributions in relation to the thirty-one types of interest

In Table 10.1 are the responses of boys to questions about the first twenty-eight of the interests (i.e. exclusive of the three referred to in the previous paragraph). Some noteworthy features of Table 10.1 are:

1 The relatively high frequency of reported interest in things like welfare work of some kind; gymnastics; reading; going to evening classes; lectures and discussions.

2 The low level of *activity* compared with the level of *felt* interest for certain of the items in the list: namely welfare work of some kind; going to see people on the stage; camping; going to see places; going to evening classes; reading or learning about new discoveries in science.

Table 10.3

Time spent on homework and on odd jobs

Time he claims he spends on the task	Type of Activity		
	Homework	Odd jobs at home	Odd jobs that are paid for
	(%)	(%)	(%)
No time at all	22	4	23
Less than one hour	6	13	22
1–3 hrs	12	32	16
4–5 hrs	15	22	15
6–8 hrs	16	16	9
9–15 hrs	20	9	9
15+ hrs	6	2	2
No information	3	2	4

The relevance of that second point is that such interests may present opportunity for the *active* involvement of boys in particular areas of interest, though obviously the manner of achieving this would call for much care and skill. See also Sections 7 and 8 on this point.

Interests related to the ages of boys

An analysis was made of the ages of boys: (*a*) professing to have a specific interest; and, (*b*) frequently doing something active about specific interests (i.e. more than once a week). Details are shown in Table 10.2.

There is nothing that is particularly controversial about the trends in Table 10.2. Thus, the interests in the left-hand column below tend to have a greater following among younger boys, and those on the right a greater following among older boys. At the same time there is more similarity than dissimilarity between the interests of boys of different ages in the range of thirteen to sixteen years.

A greater following among younger boys	A greater following among older boys
Gardening	Going to the cinema
Welfare work of some kind	Going to see people on the stage
Gymnastics	Lectures or discussions
Camping	Music
Looking after a pet	Getting the latest fashions in clothes
	Dancing
	Going out with a girl
	Riding a motor bike or motor scooter
	Having a bit of a wild time
	Going to evening classes to learn

Time spent on homework and on odd jobs at home and elsewhere

Claims about time spent doing homework and on odd jobs are presented in Table 10.3. It seems worth noting, of Table 10.3, that about one boy in six says he does less than an hour a week on odd jobs about the home and that about a half of all the boys interviewed put in no more than three hours per week in this way.

Calculating an index of number of interests (D)

The hypothesis to be investigated was concerned with a global concept of interests, the best measure of which seemed to be some form of aggregate interest score. This aggregate was developed for each boy in the following way: (*a*) Items 1, 21, 23, 27, 29, 30, 31 were eliminated from the total list of interests because they did not qualify as what might be considered an interest in a strict sense or as 'legal' in character; (*b*) a count was made of the total number of the remaining items in which the boy said he was 'not interested' ($= X$); (*c*) the latter total was divided by the number of items in the list of twenty-four which the boy had rated (i.e. as either 'not interested' or 'interested') ($= A$). The resulting fraction ($= X/A$) was regarded as a negative *index* of the boy's spare-time interests. On the basis of this index, boys could be divided into four 'quartile' groups, ranging from high to low as shown in Table 10.4.

Calculating an index of amount of interest-related activity by boys

The second part of the hypothesis dealt with the level of activity associated with boys' legal interests and for the investigation of this aspect of the hypothesis, a positive *index* of 'activity' was derived: (*a*) items 1, 21, 23, 27, 29, 30, 31 were eliminated from the count; (*b*) a count was made of the number of items for which the claimed activity level was either 'most days' or 'a few times a week' (Y) and this was divided by the number of statements for which an activity rating or a 'not interested' rating had been made (A). The resulting fraction (Y/A) was called E and was regarded as a positive *index* of the boy's active interest level in relation to his spare-time interests. On the basis of this index, boys could be divided into four groups, ranging from high to low, as shown in Table 10.5.

The distribution of interest scores (D and E) by characteristics of boys

The interest indices or scores, D and E, were analysed by various characteristics of the boys: occupational level of the boy's father; type of school last attended; amount of fun and excitement sought by the boy; whether boy ever goes out just looking for fun and excitement; whether he ever gets bored or fed-up. The results of the analysis are presented in Table 10.6.

In Table 10.6 the main focus of variability appears to be desire for fun and excitement: boys who want a lot of fun and excitement tend to be drawn in more than due proportion from those who claim to have a lot of interests and from those who claim a relatively high level of interest-associated activity. But there is no evidence of a trend for: occupational level of father, type of

Table 10.4
(3,113 cases, weighted)

Range of X/A percentage scores	No. of cases	Percentage of all cases	
	(f)	(%)	
0–30	723	23.2	= High interest quartile
31–41	647	20.8	
42–48	834	26.8	
49 and over	892	28.7	= Low interest quartile
No information	17	0.5	

Table 10.5
(3,113 cases, weighted)

Range of Y/A percentage scores	No. of cases	Percentage of all cases	
	(f)		
0–13	1,046	33.6	= Low activity level
14–17	543	17.4	
18–22	597	19.2	
23 and over	919	29.5	= High activity level
No information	8	0.3	

Table 10.6
Relating indices of interest and characteristics of boys (3,113 cases, weighted)

Characteristics and background of boys	All cases 3,113		Index of no. of things the boy feels interested in (= index D)				Index of activity level associated with the boy's interests (= index E)			
Cases (weighted)			Q.1* 723	Q.2 647	Q.3 834	Q.4 892	Q.1† 1,046	Q.2 543	Q.3 597	Q.4 919
	(n)	(%)	(%)	(%)	(%)	(%)	(%)	(%)	(%)	(%)
Father's occupational level										
Professional, semi-professional, managerial	518	17	18	17	17	15	12	22	22	15
Highly skilled	514	17	17	18	16	16	17	15	20	15
Skilled	674	22	21	21	22	23	23	21	17	23
Moderately skilled	630	20	20	18	19	23	22	19	17	21
Semi-skilled	517	17	15	18	18	16	18	15	15	17
Unskilled	254	8	9	8	9	7	7	8	9	9
No information	6	–								
Type of school										
Secondary modern	1,464	47	51	47	45	47	47	46	43	51
Comprehensive	549	18	19	14	19	18	20	16	15	18
Grammar	718	23	15	26	26	24	25	23	29	17
Public	257	8	10	10	7	8	6	11	11	8
Other	105	3								
No information	20	1								
Amount of fun and excitement wanted										
Terrific amount	463	15	18	13	11	16	12	14	16	18
Quite a lot	1,102	35	44	32	38	28	33	38	33	39
Fair bit	979	31	28	35	31	32	35	26	34	29
Some	511	16	9	17	19	20	19	20	17	11
Not much	48	2	–	3	1	3	2	2	–	2
None	3	–								
No information	7	–								
Ever go out just looking for fun and excitement?										
Yes	2,229	72	78	71	71	66	70	70	76	72
No	884	28	22	28	28	33	30	30	24	28
How often does he get bored or fed-up?										
All the time/often	759	24	27	22	26	22	25	25	22	24
Now and then/never	2,349	75	73	78	74	78	75	75	78	76
No information	5	–								

*Q.1 relates to boys from the highest of the four levels of interest   – = Less than 0.5 per cent
†Q.1 relates to boys from the lowest of the four levels of interest

Table 10.7
Relating interest-
involvement to variety and
amount of stealing
(3,113 cases, weighted)

Degree of interest-involvement	All cases		Quartile distribution of variety of stealing				Quartile distribution of amount of stealing			
			Q.1	Q.2	Q.3	Q.4	Q.1	Q.2	Q.3	Q.4
	(n)	(%)	(%)	(%)	(%)	(%)	(%)	(%)	(%)	(%)
D index*										
Q.1	723	23	21	26	27	26	22	26	25	27
Q.2	647	21	29	24	25	22	24	32	26	18
Q.3	834	27	24	24	26	26	27	25	25	24
Q.4	892	29	26	24	28	22	23	28	24	25
No information	17	1								
E index*										
Q.1	1,046	34	26	24	27	23	26	27	26	21
Q.2	543	17	31	25	24	20	25	36	20	19
Q.3	597	19	21	24	29	26	21	26	27	26
Q.4	919	30	22	26	26	27	23	25	25	27
No information	8	—								

*Question 4 for *D* index = low/Question 4 for *E* index = high
— = Less than 0.5 per cent

school attended, whether or not the boy gets fed-up or bored.

Such results may at first seem to be at variance with common experience. In fact, other evidence* strongly indicates that whereas certain interests and the activity level associated with them are strongly and positively correlated with the characteristics of boys, others are negatively related and some not related at all. To this point I will return in a later section.

Investigating Hypothesis 1

The basic strategy for investigating the hypothesis

The central strategy for investigating this hypothesis (and all the others dealt with in this inquiry) was to derive from it a series of testable propositions (called here 'expectations') and to test these (see Chapter 1). The expectations derived for testing were as follows.

Sub-Expectations 1a and 1b Boys with low interest scores will have higher theft scores than boys with high interest scores. This applies both for interests at the passive level (*D* index) and interests at the active level (*E* index).

Sub-Expectations 2a and 2b Sub-Expectations 1a and 1b apply even when the low-interest group (controls) are closely matched to the high-interest group (qualifiers) in terms of the correlates of stealing.

Expectation 3 Boys whose interest level as reflected in the *D* and *E* indices is low, will have been involved in serious stealing over a longer period of time than other

*See later section of this chapter

boys, and this applies even after close matching of the control and the qualifying groups.

Testing Sub-Expectations 1a and 1b

A comparison was made of the theft involvement of boys with different degrees of interest involvement, as indicated by the *D* and *E* indices. Details of the comparison are given in Table 10.7. On the evidence of this table, Sub-Expectations 1a and 1b are not borne out.

Testing Sub-Expectation 2a (using unweighted sample, 1,425 cases)

The testing of Expectation 2a (relating to the *D* index) involved the matching of a control group and a qualifying group in terms of the correlates of stealing. The qualifying group consisted of boys with interest in relatively few of the items in the interest list, while the control group consisted of the remainder.

Table 10.8 compares the *D* scores of the qualifying and the control groups before and after matching. It shows that Sub-Expectation 2a was not borne out.

Testing Sub-Expectation 2b (using unweighted sample, 1,425 cases)

The testing of Sub-Expectation 2b involved a closely-similar process, with the results shown in Table 10.9. Sub-Expectation 2b is *not* borne out on the evidence presented in Table 10.9.

Testing Expectation 3 (using unweighted sample, 1,425 cases)

Expectation 3 concerned the *duration* of serious stealing. The evidence in Tables 10.8 and 10.9 make it clear that the duration of serious stealing is not

Table 10.8
Differences between qualifiers and controls before and after matching: variety, amount and duration of stealing

Indices of stealing	Unadjusted average score for qualifiers a (417 cases)	Unadjusted average score for controls b (1,002 cases)	Adjusted average score for controls c	Differences between qualifiers and adj. controls a−c P	Difference a−c as percentage of c
Index of variety of stealing	13.7	13.6	13.3	0.4 NS	3
Index of amount of stealing	93.2	90.9	89.1	4.1 NS	5
Duration of serious stealing	3.8 yrs	3.7 yrs	3.6 yrs	0.2 NS	6

*In this table, qualifiers were persons whose D score was 50 per cent or over (i.e. lower interest level), while controls were persons with D scores under 50 per cent (i.e. higher interest level)

Table 10.9
Differences between qualifiers and controls before and after matching: variety, amount and duration of stealing

Indices of stealing	Unadjusted average score for qualifiers* a (484 cases)	Unadjusted average score for controls* b (935 cases)	Adjusted average score for controls c	Differences between qualifiers and adj. controls a−c P	Difference a−c as percentage of c
Index of variety of stealing	13.1	13.9	13.5	−0.4 NS	−3
Index of amount of stealing	84.8	94.9	91.7	−6.9 NS	−8
Duration of stealing	3.6 yrs	3.8 yrs	3.7 yrs	−0.1 NS	−3

*Qualifiers were boys whose activity scores were in the range 0 to 13 per cent (= lower activity score), while controls were those with activity scores of 14 per cent or over

significantly associated with either the number of boys' interests or the extent of their interest-linked activities.

Summing-up on the investigation of Hypothesis 2

The evidence developed through the testing of Expectations 1 to 3 markedly reduces the tenability of Hypothesis 1. In other words, having a large number of interests does not necessarily mean that a boy will steal less and this applies whether these activities are passive or active in character.

An alternative view of 'interests' as a factor in the causal sequence

It still remains possible that *some* interests are associated with stealing and *some* associated with non-stealing. The analyses presented in Table 10.10 confirm this, for there are many differences between interests in terms of the theft level of the boys holding them. In other words, some interests are positively associated with stealing whilst others are negatively associated with stealing. Some of the main contrasts in this respect are set out in Table 10.11 below.

Another noteworthy feature of Table 10.10 is that the size of the numerical association between having a given interest and being involved in stealing varies quite a lot in going from the passive to the active form of the interest.

Having drawn attention to these correlational data, it is most important to stress that they are no more than correlational and that one cannot know, at this stage, what would happen if rigorous matching were introduced into the comparisons. In the meantime, however,

338

Table 10.10
Relating involvement in stealing to claimed feeling of
interest in a range of items and claimed activity linked
to interests
(3,113 cases, weighted)

Type of interest	Feeling of interest					Interest-linked activity				
	Claims he was interested or not interested	Quartile distribution of amount of stealing				Claimed frequency of activity	Quartile distribution of amount of stealing			
		Q.1 749 (%)	Q.2 861 (%)	Q.3 779 (%)	Q.4 724 (%)		Q.1 749 (%)	Q.2 861 (%)	Q.3 779 (%)	Q.4 724 (%)
1 Watching television	Not int'd	15	24	31	29	Infreq'nt	19	25	29	27
	Int'd	26	28	24	22	Frequent	25	28	24	23
2 Hobby of some kind	Not int'd	14	24	32	31	Infreq'nt	22	28	24	26
	Int'd	25	28	24	23	Frequent	26	28	25	21
3 Going to the cinema	Not int'd	30	29	20	21	Infreq'nt	24	28	25	22
	Int'd	23	27	26	24	Frequent	19	16	24	41
4 Gardening	Not int'd	23	28	24	25	Infreq'nt	23	28	25	24
	Int'd	29	27	29	15	Frequent	41	19	27	13
5 Welfare work of some kind	Not int'd	18	29	26	27	Infreq'nt	24	28	25	23
	Int'd	29	26	25	21	Frequent	32	22	23	23
6 Going to see people on the stage	Not int'd	26	26	24	24	Infreq'nt	24	28	25	23
	Int'd	22	29	26	23	Frequent	15	21	18	46
7 Gymnastics	Not int'd	23	30	27	21	Infreq'nt	23	27	26	24
	Int'd	25	26	24	25	Frequent	27	29	22	22
8 Camping	Not int'd	27	30	25	19	Infreq'nt	24	28	25	23
	Int'd	22	26	26	27	Frequent	44	9	17	30
9 Reading	Not int'd	15	22	30	32	Infreq'nt	20	25	27	28
	Int'd	28	30	23	20	Frequent	27	30	23	20
10 Playing games like darts, draughts	Not int'd	23	26	24	26	Infreq'nt	25	29	25	21
	Int'd	24	28	25	22	Frequent	22	25	26	27
11 Lectures or discussions	Not int'd	22	27	28	24	Infreq'nt	24	28	25	23
	Int'd	28	29	21	22	Frequent	31	22	27	20
12 Art of some kind	Not int'd	20	28	27	22	Infreq'nt	23	28	26	23
	Int'd	26	27	23	24	Frequent	26	25	22	27
13 Music	Not int'd	30	29	22	19	Infreq'nt	27	29	26	18
	Int'd	22	27	26	25	Frequent	22	27	24	27
14 Getting latest fashions in clothes	Not int'd	34	28	22	16	Infreq'nt	24	28	25	23
	Int'd	15	27	28	30	Frequent	15	21	26	39
15 Going to see places	Not int'd	18	26	24	32	Infreq'nt	24	28	25	22
	Int'd	26	28	25	21	Frequent	16	16	20	49
16 Looking after a pet	Not int'd	21	29	24	26	Infreq'nt	23	28	25	24
	Int'd	26	27	25	21	Frequent	26	27	25	22
17 Going to a funfair	Not int'd	27	28	25	20	Infreq'nt	24	28	25	23
	Int'd	21	28	25	26	Frequent	8	14	43	35
18 Dancing	Not int'd	29	28	24	19	Infreq'nt	25	28	25	22
	Int'd	15	27	27	31	Frequent	11	18	26	45
19 Going out with a girl	Not int'd	41	27	19	12	Infreq'nt	29	30	23	18
	Int'd	18	28	27	27	Frequent	9	20	31	40
20 Riding a motor bike or motor scooter	Not int'd	31	33	22	15	Infreq'nt	26	29	24	21
	Int'd	18	24	28	30	Frequent	9	15	33	42

continued

Table 10.10 (continued)

	Feeling of interest					Interest-linked activity				
	Claims he was interested or not interested	Quartile distribution of amount of stealing					Quartile distribution of amount of stealing			
Type of interest		Q.1 749 (%)	Q.2 861 (%)	Q.3 779 (%)	Q.4 724 (%)	Claimed frequency of activity	Q.1 749 (%)	Q.2 861 (%)	Q.3 779 (%)	Q.4 724 (%)
21 Getting around with my mates	Not int'd	41	32	16	11	Infreq'nt	37	31	21	12
	Int'd	21	27	27	25	Frequent	17	26	27	30
22 A sport of some kind	Not int'd	27	26	20	27	Infreq'nt	25	24	28	23
	Int'd	24	28	26	23	Frequent	23	31	23	23
23 Having a bit of a wild time	Not int'd	37	33	19	11	Infreq'nt	28	31	24	18
	Int'd	14	24	29	33	Frequent	7	14	31	48
24 Indoor games of some kind	Not int'd	21	26	26	27	Infreq'nt	24	28	24	24
	Int'd	26	29	24	21	Frequent	24	27	27	21
25 Going to church or chapel or synagogue	Not int'd	20	27	25	28	Infreq'nt	24	28	24	24
	Int'd	33	29	25	14	Frequent	32	24	36	8
26 Going to evening classes to learn	Not int'd	22	25	27	25	Infreq'nt	23	28	25	24
	Int'd	26	30	23	22	Frequent	36	17	25	22
27 Getting into fights with other boys	Not int'd	26	30	25	19	Infreq'nt	24	29	25	22
	Int'd	12	19	24	45	Frequent	16	7	19	58
28 Reading or hearing about new discoveries in science	Not int'd	20	24	27	29	Infreq'nt	23	28	25	24
	Int'd	27	31	24	19	Frequent	31	28	22	19

the correlational data seem to be sufficient to support the formulation of an *hypothesis* that stealing is causally related to boys' involvement in *certain kinds of interests*, rather than to interest level generally.

5 METHODS AND FINDINGS RELATED TO THE INVESTIGATION OF HYPOTHESIS 2

The Nature of Hypothesis 2
Hypothesis 2 concerns the influence of watching television upon the incidence of stealing by boys and was:

Boys who watch a lot of television are thereby made more likely to engage in stealing.

It was intended that the inquiry should examine this hypothesis and provide background information about television viewing.

The Distribution of Boys in terms of the Variable Hypothesized as Causal
In this section are presented: (*a*) the questions asked as a basis for classifying boys in terms of the variable hypothesized as causal; and, (*b*) the distribution of boys in terms of it.

Table 10.11
Interests correlated with stealing

Positive association at both passive* and active level†	Negative association at both passive and active level
Going to the cinema Getting the latest fashion in clothes Dancing Going out with a girl Riding a motor bike or motor scooter Getting around with mates Having a bit of a wild time Getting into fights with other boys	Watching television‡ Gardening Welfare work of some kind Reading Lectures or discussions Going to church or chapel or synagogue Reading or hearing about new discoveries in science

*D index
†E index
‡This table is about correlations and not necessarily causal relationships

the questions asked as a basis for classifying boys in terms of television viewing

It must be made clear at the outset that information about watching television was collected only incidentally, i.e. in the course of collecting information for another purpose. So whereas opportunity has been taken to use the television information for examining Hypothesis 2, that particular information is less precise and less relevant to the hypothesis than would have been the case if it had been collected solely for checking that hypothesis. Indeed, what is ideally needed is a lengthy questioning process involving the use of a large sample of programmes, carefully-designed questions to ascertain the degree to which the respondent watches the different programmes in the sample, a set of visuals to aid the respondent in his recall processes. That would be far beyond what was (or could be) done in the present case. Nonetheless, the evidence actually gathered is sufficient to differentiate between heavier and lighter viewers and it is only at this level that the hypothesis is being investigated in the present instance.

In the course of gathering information about the involvement of boys in a range of interests, boys sorted the item 'watching television' as INTERESTED IN IT or NOT INTERESTED IN IT. Thereafter, boys who said they *were* interested in it were asked to indicate how often they watched television by choosing the appropriate frequency from: MOST DAYS/A FEW TIMES A WEEK/ONCE A WEEK/ONCE A MONTH/HARDLY EVER/NEVER.

Distribution of responses

Table 10.12 shows a distribution of responses to these questions. The category 'not interested in watching television' is *not* the same as 'never watch television'. But it may safely be taken as involving viewing at less than the top level of 'watch television most days'. See p. 344 for assumption that it involves viewing at a level less than 'most days'.

Table 10.12
Interest in and activity associated with 'watching television'
(3,113 cases, weighted)

Ratings	Frequency (n)	(%)	
Watch television most days	2,133	69	
Watch television a few days a week	452	15	
Watch television once a week	37	1	85%
Watch television once a month	9	—	
Watch television hardly ever	14	—	
Never watch television	5	—	
Not interested in watching television	448		14%
No information	15	—	

— = Less than 0.5 per cent

Watching television, analysed by characteristics and background of boys

Watching television was analysed by: (a) interest in cinema going, in 'getting around with mates', in 'having a bit of a wild time', in 'getting into fights'; (b) age, occupational level of father, type of school attended, amount of homework done, time spent in doing odd jobs, total score for 'level' of interests. Details are given in Table 10.13.

There is markedly little relationship between 'interest in watching television' and most of the variables involved in Table 10.13. This applies whether we think of 'watching television' as something that a boy says he is 'interested in doing' or as actual viewing behaviour. The exceptions are 'age' (with younger boys doing more viewing than older boys) and, to some degree, 'having a bit of a wild time' (with boys who spend a lot of time doing this viewing less than other boys).

Table 10.13
Frequency of watching television analysed by characteristics and other interests of boys
(3,113 cases, weighted)

Characteristics of boys		Interest by frequency of watching							
	All cases	Not interested	Never	Hardly ever	Once a month	Once a week	Few times a week	Most days	NI
	(n)	(%)	(%)	(%)	(%)	(%)	(%)	(%)	(%)
Occupation of father									
Professional, semi-professional, managerial	518	13	0	1	2	2	17	65	0
Highly skilled	514	22	0	1	0	1	15	60	—
Skilled	674	14	0	0	0	1	16	69	—
Moderately skilled	630	12	0	—	0	1	14	72	1
Semi-skilled	517	13	0	0	0	1	13	72	1
Unskilled	254	10	2	1	—	1	8	76	1
No information	6								

continued

Table 10.13 (continued)

Characteristics of boys	All cases	Interest by frequency of watching							
		Not interested	Never	Hardly ever	Once a month	Once a week	Few times a week	Most days	NI
	(n)	(%)	(%)	(%)	(%)	(%)	(%)	(%)	(%)
Age									
12 + 13 yrs	721	7	0	1	0	1	11	80	—
14 yrs	782	9	1	0	1	1	11	77	1
15 yrs	754	18	0	1	0	2	14	66	—
16 + 17 yrs	856	23	0	1	0	2	21	54	1
Type of school									
Secondary modern	1,464	14	0	—	—	1	15	70	1
Comprehensive	549	18	1	1	0	1	13	66	1
Grammar	718	14	0	1	1	2	16	67	—
Public	257	17	0	—	2	2	10	68	0
Other	105								
No information	20								
Going to the cinema									
Not interested	637	19	0	—	1	1	16	63	0
Never go	8	25	0	0	0	0	0	75	0
Hardly ever go	277	12	0	—	—	2	12	74	0
Once a month	1,058	11	1	—	0	2	12	75	0
Once a week	961	17	0	1	—	1	16	64	1
Few times a week	125	13	0	0	0	2	23	62	0
Most days	36	6	0	0	0	0	14	81	0
No information	9								
Getting around with mates									
Not interested	455	23	0	—	0	1	12	64	0
Never do so	17	6	0	0	0	0	0	94	0
Hardly ever do so	67	5	0	0	0	0	15	81	0
Once a month	130	8	4	0	3	0	32	53	0
Once a week	465	14	0	—	0	3	11	72	—
Few times a week	808	11	0	1	1	1	16	71	—
Most days	1,158	15	0	1	0	1	15	68	—
No information	13								
Having a bit of a wild time									
Not interested	1,310	11	—	—	—	2	13	73	0
Never do so	24	0	0	0	0	0	21	79	0
Hardly ever do so	389	8	0	—	0	—	15	77	0
Once a month	406	21	0	2	1	1	16	59	0
Once a week	388	18	0	0	1	1	13	68	—
A few times a week	318	19	0	—	0	1	16	64	0
Most days	259	24	0	0.	0	—	19	55	2
No information	19								
Getting into fights with other boys									
Not interested	2,532	14	—	1	—	1	15	69	0
Never do so	18	33	0	0	0	0	0	67	0
Hardly ever do so	163	18	0	0	0	0	7	75	0
Once a month	144	21	0	0	0	0	20	59	0
Once a week	82	13	0	0	0	1	14	70	1
A few times a week	80	26	0	1	0	3	10	60	0
Most days	61	15	0	0	0	2	3	80	0
No information	33								

Table 10.13 (continued)

Characteristics of boys	All cases	Interest by frequency of **watching**							
		Not interested	Never	Hardly ever	Once a month	Once a week	Few times a week	Most days	NI
	(n)	(%)	(%)	(%)	(%)	(%)	(%)	(%)	(%)

Score D in quartiles

$$\left(= \frac{\text{Total items 'not interested'}}{\text{Total items rated}} \right)$$

Q.1 = Many interests	723	14	0	2	0	1	15	67	1
Q.2 =	647	14	0	–	1	3	11	72	0
Q.3 =	834	14	1	0	1	1	15	69	0
Q.4 = few interests	892	15	0	0	0	–	16	68	0
No information	17								

— = Less than 0.5 per cent

Investigating Hypothesis 2

Research Strategy
As in the investigation of all the other hypotheses, testable propositions were derived from Hypothesis 2. These propositions were in the form of expectations — in the sense that one might *expect* them to be true if the hypothesis were true. There were four of these expectations, as follows.

Expectation 1 Boys who watch a lot of television will be more involved in stealing than boys who watch little television.

Expectation 2 Expectation 1 is true even when the heavier and the lighter viewers are closely matched in terms of the correlates of stealing.

Expectation 3 Boys who watch a lot of television are likely to have been involved in serious stealing over a longer period of years than boys who watch relatively little television and this is so even after close matching of the heavier and the lighter viewing groups.

Expectation 4 Expectation 2 applies with respect to the forty-four different types of theft in terms of which the overall level of boys' stealing was calculated.

Testing Expectation 1
A comparison was made of the theft involvement of boys who watched a lot of television and those who watched relatively little of it. This comparison is shown in Table 10.14.

The evidence in Table 10.14 is complex in its indications. Thus boys who are interested in watching television and who watch it 'most days' are somewhat *less* involved in stealing than boys generally and those who are not interested in watching television are *more*

involved in stealing than other boys. These two results, accounting for over 80 per cent of the boys, give no support to Expectation 1. On the other hand, there is a small section of boys who say they are *interested in watching television but see relatively little of it*, and *these* boys are *markedly less* involved in stealing than other boys. This evidence is suspect in that it is based on relatively few cases; nonetheless it must be noted.

Testing Expectations 2 and 3 (using unweighted sample, 1,425 cases)
Expectation 2 was that Expectation 1 applies even when the controls are closely matched to the qualifiers in terms of the correlates of stealing.

Table 10.14
Comparing the theft levels of heavier and lighter viewers (3,113 cases, weighted)

Amount of viewing claimed	All cases	Index of amount of stealing			
		Q.1*	Q.2	Q.3	Q.4
	(n)	(%)	(%)	(%)	(%)
Watch it most days	2,133	26	29	24	21
Watch it a few times a week	452	22	26	24	28
Watch it once a week	37	42	32	15	11
Watch it once a month	9				
Watch it hardly ever	14				
Never watch it	5				
Not interested in it	448	15	24	31	29
No information	15				

*Q.1 = Lightest quartile and Q.4 = heaviest quartile in terms of amount of thieving

Expectation 3 was that boys who watch a lot of television will have been engaged in serious stealing over a longer period than boys who watch less television, and that this applies even when the control group is closely matched with the qualifying group in terms of the correlates of stealing.

To test these two expectations, the total sample of boys was split as shown in Figure 10.1.

The control group was matched to the qualifying group in terms of the composite of correlates of stealing which had been applied in all the matching operations in this inquiry. The results of this matching operation are shown in Table 10.15.

The evidence in Table 10.15 does *not* support either Expectation 2 or Expectation 3. Whereas *before matching* there were differences of appreciable sizes

Figure 10.1
Division of sample for testing Expectations 2 and 3.

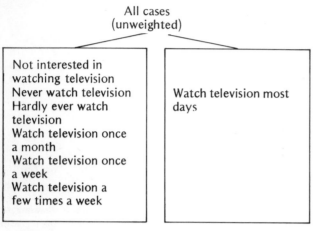

All cases
(unweighted)

Not interested in watching television
Never watch television
Hardly ever watch television
Watch television once a month
Watch television once a week
Watch television a few times a week

Watch television most days

Control group
(= 415 cases, unweighted)

Qualifying group
(= 1,000 cases, unweighted)

Table 10.15
Differences between qualifiers and controls before and after matching: variety, amount and duration of stealing

Indices of stealing	Unadjusted average score of qualifiers a (1,000 cases)	Unadjusted average score of controls b (415 cases)	Adjusted average score for controls c	Differences between qualifiers and adj. controls a--c	Difference a–c as percentage of c %
Average variety score	13.25	14.54	13.29	−0.04*	−
Average amount score	87.24	101.25	90.06	−2.82*	−3
Average duration of stealing	3.48 years	4.25 years	3.63 years	−0.15*	−4

*Not significant at the 0.05 level
− = Less than 0.5 per cent

344

Table 10.16

Differences between qualifiers and controls before and after matching: each of the forty-four types of theft

Theft type at L.2†	Unadjusted average score for qualifiers a (1,000 cases)		Unadjusted average score for controls b (415 cases)		Adjusted average score for controls c		Differences between qualifiers and adj. controls a–c	Difference a–c as percentage of c
	(n)	(%)	(n)	(%)	(n)	(%)		(%)
1	908	90.9	377	90.6	883.96	88.6	2.3	3
2	505	50.6	225	54.1	507.07	50.8	−0.2	–
3	378	37.8	183	44.0	426.47	42.7	−4.9	−11
4	526	52.7	222	53.4	532.98	53.4	−0.7	−1
5	220	22.0	99	23.8	219.39	22.0	0.0	0
6	550	55.1	235	56.5	531.33	53.2	1.9	4
7	403	40.3	173	41.6	374.63	37.5	2.8	7
8	339	33.9	137	32.9	330.75	33.1	0.8	2
9	150	15.0	69	16.6	143.72	14.4	0.6	4
10	336	33.6	222	53.4	449.68	45.1	−11.5†	−25
11	369	36.9	166	39.9	366.26	36.7	0.2	1
12	139	13.9	83	20.0	186.52	18.7	−4.8†	−26
13	394	39.4	160	38.5	344.94	34.6	4.8	14
14	211	21.1	122	29.3	246.91	24.7	−3.6	−15
15	164	16.4	64	15.4	135.90	13.6	2.8†	21
16	434	43.4	186	44.7	402.55	40.3	3.1	8
17	180	18.0	88	21.2	187.50	18.8	−0.8	−4
18	619	62.0	293	70.4	648.15	64.9	−2.9	−4
19	364	36.4	157	37.7	345.67	34.6	1.8	5
20	293	29.3	136	32.7	307.57	30.8	−1.5	−5
21	138	13.8	46	11.1	111.70	11.2	2.6†	23
22	397	39.7	155	37.3	363.53	36.4	3.3	9
23	195	19.5	122	29.3	221.96	22.2	−2.7	−12
24	122	12.2	55	13.2	111.55	11.2	1.0	9
25	229	22.9	101	24.3	255.05	25.6	−2.7	−11
26	283	28.3	118	28.4	269.81	27.0	1.3	5
27	185	18.5	91	21.9	194.74	19.5	−1.0	−5
28	232	23.2	95	22.8	194.73	19.5	3.7†	19
29	72	7.2	33	7.9	75.32	7.5	−0.3	−4
30	436	43.6	219	52.6	455.83	45.7	−2.1	−5
31	252	25.2	137	32.9	244.95	24.5	0.7	3
32	80	8.0	24	5.8	53.54	5.4	2.6†	48
33	623	62.4	279	67.1	627.05	62.8	−0.4	−1
34	322	32.2	123	29.6	287.52	28.8	3.4	12
35	158	15.8	84	20.2	161.84	16.2	−0.4	−2
36	286	28.6	144	34.6	302.35	30.3	−1.7	−6
37	34	3.4	35	8.4	59.59	6.0	−2.6†	−43
38	224	22.4	106	25.5	216.62	21.7	0.7	3
39	194	19.4	75	18.0	161.25	16.2	3.2†	20
40	620	62.1	294	70.7	654.11	65.5	−3.4	−5
41	86	8.6	44	10.6	100.45	10.1	−1.5	−15
42	111	11.1	50	12.0	111.99	11.2	−0.1	−1
43	294	29.4	131	31.5	255.34	25.6	3.8	15
44	523	52.4	220	52.9	479.12	48.0	4.4	9

* =Qualifying group (1,000 cases): boys who watch television 'most days'
Control group (415 cases): boys who watch television less frequently than 'most days'
†=Significant at the 0.05 level or better
– = Less than 0.5 per cent

between the theft levels of the control and the qualifying groups, these differences almost disappeared after the matching of the controls to the qualifiers.

Testing Expectation 4 (using unweighted sample, 1,425 cases)

Expectation 4 was that Expectation 2 would apply with respect to the forty-four different types of theft in terms of which the overall level of boys' stealing was calculated.

The control group was matched to the qualifying group in terms of the correlates of stealing. Table 10.16 compares, before and after matching, the percentages who said they had ever committed the different types of theft listed on the left-hand side of the table. See Chapter 1 for identity of theft numbers.

On the evidence of Table 10.16, Expectation 4 is borne out at the 5 per cent level for only five of the listed acts of theft and is rejected at that level for three of them. Other of the residual differences do nonetheless approach the 5 per cent significance level and so it seems worth while to compare the more sharply differentiated items. This is done in Table 10.17.

Table 10.17

Types of theft which tend to be positively and negatively 'affected' by viewing behaviour

Thefts for which an increase is suggested	Thefts for which a reduction is suggested
I have stolen something from a changing-room or a cloakroom	I have got away without paying the fare or the proper fare
I have stolen from a park or a playground	I have got something by threatening others
I have stolen from a goods yard or from the yard of a factory or from the docks or from a timber yard	I have stolen cigarettes
	I have stolen a car or a lorry or a van
I have stolen from someone at work	I have stolen money from a meter
I have stolen from a club	

The writer sees no clear distinction between the thefts on the left and those on the right of Table 10.17. The reader is invited to speculate about what that distinction might be. But in the meantime all that may be said with reasonable surety is that the test of Expectation 4 was supported for very few of the listed acts of theft, was negated for at least as many, and was in general not borne out.

Summing-up on the investigation of Hypothesis 2

The evidence does not support Hypothesis 2 in any general way. At the same time, the evidence warrants the postulation of a substitute hypothesis to the effect that watching a lot of television contributes to the occurrence of a limited number of particular types of stealing (these types yet to be precisely formulated).

6 METHODS AND FINDINGS RELATED TO THE INVESTIGATION OF HYPOTHESES 3 AND 4

The Nature of Hypotheses 3 and 4

These hypotheses were:

Boys who do not know what to do with their spare time are thereby led to do more stealing (Hypothesis 3).

and

Boys who say they get bored and fed-up during their spare time are thereby led to do more stealing (Hypothesis 4).

The distribution of boys in terms of the variables hypothesized as causal

In this section are presented: (a) the questions asked as a basis for classifying boys in terms of the variables hypothesized as causal; and, (b) the distributions of boys in terms of these variables.

The Questions asked

The questions asked were as follows.

---

a 'Do you ever feel you *don't* know what to do with your spare time?'   YES/NO

    IF 'NO', CHALLENGE
    IF 'YES',
'How often do you feel like this?'   (SHOW CARD)
    ALL THE TIME/OFTEN/NOW AND THEN/NEVER

'What do you do when you feel like this?'   (PROBE ALL YOU CAN USING 'WHAT ELSE')

'Do you go out with your mates when you feel like this?'   YES/NO

    IF 'YES', SAY: 'Would you say "OFTEN" or JUST "NOW AND THEN"?'
    CIRCLE CHOICE. THEN ASK:
'What do you do when you feel like that and go out with your mates?'
    (SEE THAT HE IS TALKING ABOUT WHAT HE DOES WHEN IN COMPANY OF MATES)

b 'Do you ever wish there were more places to go to in your spare time?'   YES/NO

    IF 'NO', CHALLENGE
    IF 'YES',
'How often do you wish there were more places to go to in your spare time?'   ALL THE TIME/OFTEN/NOW AND THEN/NEVER.

c 'Do you ever get bored or fed-up with things?'   YES/NO

    IF 'NO', CHALLENGE
    IF 'YES':

ALL THE TIME/OFTEN/NOW AND THEN/NEVER

Distribution of responses

Table 10.18 presents the results from the structured questions which were asked, the open-response findings being set out in later tables. There are several noteworthy features of Table 10.18.

Table 10.18
Distribution in terms of key variables
(3,113 cases, weighted)

	(*n*)	(%)
Frequency of feeling that they do not know what to do with their spare time		
Not at all/never	677	22
Yes, now and then	2,109	68
Yes, often	297	10
Yes, all the time	28	1
No information	2	–
Frequency of wishing there were more places to go to in spare time		
Not at all/never	729	23
Yes, now and then	1,053	34
Yes, often	974	31
Yes, all the time	356	11
No information	1	–
Frequency of getting bored or fed-up		
Not at all/never	164	5
Yes, now and then	2,185	70
Yes, often	714	23
Yes, all the time	45	1
No information	5	–
Does he go out with mates when he does not know what to do with his spare time?		
Yes	1,742	56
No	1,360	44
No information	11	–

– = Less than 0.5 per cent

1 The first is the relatively small number of boys who reported being bored 'all the time' — about 1 per cent. Nonetheless, boredom appears to be a recurrent condition for quite a lot of boys, with 24 per cent saying they are 'often' (or more frequently) bored.

2 Whereas 24 per cent are 'often' (or more frequently) bored, only 11 per cent report that they often do not know what to do with their spare time. Presumably the others find something to do in spite of — or perhaps because of — being bored. Against this figure of 11 per cent, there were 42 per cent who said they often wished there were more places to go to in their spare time. This information clearly suggests scope for the development and provision of interest outlets for boys.

3 The proportion who said they go out with their mates when they do not know what to do with their spare time is very high — 56 per cent. What matters, of course, in the context of this inquiry, is what they *do* when out with their mates. Table 10.19 presents boys' own statements on this particular score.

Table 10.19
What boys do when they feel they do not know what to do with their spare time and go out with their mates
(1,742 cases, weighted)

What boys say they do:	(*n*)	(%)
Any direct reference to stealing (including getting into cinema/joy riding/evading bus fares)	37	2
Annoying/cheeking/making fun of people (*except* where boy is annoying etc. his own mates)	91	5
Destroying property/vandalism	37	2
Fighting or watching fights	68	4
Trespassing/going to places where they should not be (e.g. building sites)	23	1
Informal or unstructured local activities with mates (e.g. mucking about/larking around/going out/ going to pubs, cafes, park, streets, etc./having a joke/playing around/playing games other than sports)	982	56
Girls/going out with girls/mucking about with girls	162	9
Physically active sports specified (e.g. football/ cricket/tennis/judo/volley ball/bowling/table tennis/athletics	693	40
Hobbies or sports which would normally take place outside London in the countryside (e.g. sailing/canoeing/rock climbing/fishing/water skiing/flying/parachuting/riding)	63	4
Camping or hiking	11	1
Cycling/going out on bikes	296	17
Go out on/in a motor vehicle (i.e. motorbike/ scooter/car)	54	3
Sports or games of a more sedentary indoor nature (e.g. billiards/snooker/cards/monopoly/darts/chess)	174	10
Sports/games, unspecified	57	3
Any mention of clubs/youth clubs	152	9
Watching sports or racing	65	4
Cinema	495	28
Television/radio/listening to records	93	5
Go out to visit places/making trips (e.g. to seaside)	112	6
Go dancing	99	6
Play instruments	24	1
Pursue hobbies	41	2
Funfair, circus, arcades	32	2
Places of interest	29	2
Go for a ride/drive (unspecified)	9	1
Play with pets	14	1
Do some jobs/something useful	28	1
Eating	7	–

There is relatively little volunteered reference to 'stealing' in Table 10.19, though there are many references to activities of a mischievous or unconstructive kind.

Considerable aimlessness also shows up with respect to boys' claimed 'activities when they do not know what to do with their spare time' — irrespective of whether they go out with their mates when feeling this way. Details are given in Table 10.20.

Another noteworthy feature of Table 10.20 is the much higher frequency of reference to *reading* by boys who feel at a loose end 'now and then' as distinct from 'often'. This may mean that boys who have frequently to 'fill in' have not developed reading as a 'fill-in' activity; or it could equally well mean that boys who have already developed a heavy reading habit have less time to fill-in — and that this is the natural thing for them to do when they *do* have unfilled time.

Table 10.20
What boys do when they feel they do not know what to do with their spare time
(2,434 cases, weighted)

Types of activity	All who say they feel they do not know $n = 2,434$		Boys who say they feel they do not know what to do	
			All the time or often $n = 325$	Now and then $n = 2,109$
	(n)	(%)	(%)	(%)
Making a nuisance of himself/getting in people's way/annoying people	55	2	6	2
Going to sleep/to bed	203	8	8	8
Doing nothing (e.g. sitting around, standing about and feeling sorry for himself/window gazing)	403	17	14	17
Informal or unstructured activities with or without mates (e.g. walking around/going to see mates/going out with mates/going out/going to park, pubs, cafes, streets, etc./having a joke/playing around/playing games other than sports)	976	40	41	40
Any volunteered mention of stealing	5	–	–	–
Fighting/watching fights	13	1	1	1
Doing some job/doing something useful (e.g. clearing out his room/collecting brother from school/home housework/errands)	360	15	11	15
Passive indoor entertainment (e.g. radio/television gramophone/tape recorder	1,076	44	39	45
Cinema	202	8	8	8
Physically active sports, specified (e.g. football/cricket/tennis/judo/volley ball/bowling/table tennis/athletics	337	14	15	14
Sports or games of a more sedentary or indoor nature (cards/chess/billiards/darts)	213	9	14	8
Sports or games (unspecified)	40	2	0	2
Watching sports or racing	27	1	0	1
Pursuing hobbies (e.g. stamps/making models/mending bikes/cleaning fishing gear)	474	19	16	20
Reading books/magazines/newspapers/comics	977	40	26	42
Go out on bike/cycling	208	9	5	9
Go out on/in a motor vehicle (e.g. motorbike/scooter/car	37	2	1	2
Playing instruments	129	5	7	5
Playing with pets	77	3	3	3
Any mention of clubs/youth clubs	51	2	5	2
Visit places of interests (e.g. museums, art galleries)	43	2	2	2
Any mention of girls	29	1	1	1
Has a mood or depression	8	–	1	–

— = Less than 0.5 per cent

Table 10.21
Not knowing what to do in spare time analysed by characteristics and backgrounds of boys (3,113 cases, weighted)

Characteristics and background of boys	All cases	Frequency of feeling he does not know what to do with his spare time			
		All the time or often	Now and then	Never	No information
	(n)	(%)	(%)	(%)	(%)
Occupational level of fathers					
Professional, semi-professional, managerial	518	6	69	25	—
Highly skilled	514	4	70	26	—
Skilled	674	11	71	18	0
Moderately skilled	630	13	62	25	0
Semi-skilled	517	11	73	15	0
Unskilled	254	21	57	22	0
No information	6				
Age of boy at interview					
12/13 yrs	721	11	72	16	0
14 yrs	782	9	74	17	—
15 yrs	754	9	68	23	—
16/17 yrs	856	12	58	30	0
Type of school last attended					
Secondary modern	1,464	12	66	22	0
Comprehensive	549	12	66	22	0
Grammar	718	7	71	22	—
Public	257	12	70	17	0
Other	105				
No information	20				
Was school work liked?					
Disliked very much	81	17	56	27	0
Disliked	597	12	66	22	0
Liked	2,117	10	69	20	—
Liked very much	312	9	62	29	0
No information	6				
Is he attending school now?					
Yes	2,402	9	71	19	—
No	711	14	57	29	—
How often did he play truant?					
Once a week	331	16	65	21	0
Once a month	262	7	61	32	0
Hardly ever	766	14	66	20	0
Never	1,745	9	70	21	—
No information	9				
How much of his spare time does he like to spend at home?					
None	65	12	63	25	0
Not much	406	10	59	31	0
Less than half	531	11	68	21	—
About half	1,352	10	70	21	0
Most of it	672	11	70	19	0
All of it	59	17	61	22	0
No information	28				
Does he get enough fun and excitement?					
Yes	1,622	6	66	27	0
No	1,487	14	70	16	—
No information	4				

Table 10.21 (continued)

Characteristics and background of boys	All cases	Frequency of feeling he does not know what to do with his spare time			
		All the time or often	Now and then	Never	No information
	(n)	(%)	(%)	(%)	(%)
How much fun and excitement does he want?					
A terrific amount	463	13	59	27	0
Quite a lot	1,102	14	64	22	0
A fair bit	979	8	73	19	—
Some	511	5	75	20	0
Not much	48	10	55	35	0
None	3				
No information	7				
Girl friend?					
Has a girl friend	1,151	10	61	29	0
Goes out with girls	1,029	10	70	19	—
Does not go out with girls	930	12	72	17	0
No information	3				

— = Less than 0.5 per cent

'Causal' variables analysed by the characteristics and backgrounds of boys

Not knowing what to do with his spare time
Responses to the questions about 'not knowing what to do with one's spare time' were analysed by various of the boys' characteristics and by features of their backgrounds. Details are presented in Table 10.21.

Table 10.21 suggests that the tendency to feel 'at a loose end' about how to spend one's spare time is somewhat greater for:

1 The sons of the less skilled.

2 The younger boys.

3 Those still at school.

4 Those who say they do not get enough fun and excitement.

5 Those who do not have a girl friend.

On the other hand there appears to be no relationship at all between 'frequency of feeling at a loose end' and variables such as: type of school (last) attended; whether he likes school work; frequency of playing truant; how much of his spare time he likes to spend at home.

Frequency of wishing there were more places to go, analysed by characteristics and background of boys
Responses to the question about wishing there were more places to go to in spare time were analysed by the

characteristics and background of boys. Details are presented in Table 10.22.

Perhaps predictably, boys who frequently wish there were more places to spend their spare time tend somewhat to be drawn from:

1 The lower occupational sectors.

2 Those with secondary-modern or comprehensive-school background.

3 Those who play truant more often.

4 Those who say they want a lot of fun and excitement.

5 Those who have a girl friend.

6 Those who often do not know what to do with their spare time.

What is probably less expected is the positive association between number of interests held and frequency of wishing there were more places to go to.

Frequency of feeling bored or fed-up analysed by characteristics and background of boys
Response to questions about frequency of feeling bored or fed-up were analysed by various of the boys' characteristics and by features of their background. Details are presented in Table 10.23.

On the evidence of Table 10.23, a higher frequency of feeling 'bored or fed-up' tends to occur amongst:

1 Those who say they dislike(d) school work.

Table 10.22
Frequency of wishing there were more places to go to, analysed by characteristics and backgrounds of boys (3,113 cases, weighted)

Characteristics and background of boys	All cases	How often does he wish there were more places he could go to?				
		All the time	Often	Now and then	Never	No information
	(n)	(%)	(%)	(%)	(%)	(%)
Occupational level of fathers						
Professional, semi-professional and executive	518	6	25	35	33	0
Highly skilled	514	9	25	41	25	0
Skilled	674	11	32	37	21	0
Moderately skilled	630	11	38	28	23	0
Semi-skilled	517	19	30	31	20	0
Unskilled	254	13	41	30	16	—
No information	6					
Last school attended						
Secondary modern	1,464	14	35	32	19	—
Comprehensive	549	12	35	32	21	0
Grammar	718	7	20	42	31	0
Public	257	9	28	29	34	0
Other	105					
No information	20					
Age of boy at interview						
12/13 yrs	721	14	34	33	19	—
14 yrs	782	9	34	37	20	—
15 yrs	754	13	27	34	27	—
16/17 yrs	856	10	30	31	28	—
Was school work liked?						
Disliked very much	81	24	28	30	19	0
Disliked	597	18	25	38	20	0
Liked	2,117	10	33	33	24	—
Liked very much	312	9	32	34	26	0
No information	6					
Is he attending school now?						
Yes	2,402	10	32	35	22	0
No	711	15	29	29	27	—
How often does he play truant?						
Once a week or more	331	18	38	25	18	0
Once a month	262	19	29	33	21	—
Hardly ever	766	14	34	31	20	0
Never	1,745	7	29	37	26	0
No information	9					
How much of his spare time does he like to spend at home?						
None	65	28	17	22	34	0
Not much	406	19	31	31	20	0
Less than half	531	12	31	38	19	—
About half	1,352	11	32	33	24	0
Most of it	672	6	31	36	27	0
All of it	59	25	27	25	22	0
No information	28					

Table 10.22 (continued)

Characteristics and background of boys	All cases (n)	How often does he wish there were more places he could go to?				
		All the time (%)	Often (%)	Now and then (%)	Never (%)	No information (%)
Does he get enough fun and excitement?						
Yes	1,622	8	25	36	32	—
No	1,487	15	39	32	15	0
No information	4					
How much fun and excitement does he want?						
A terrific amount	463	19	29	29	23	0
Quite a lot	1,102	14	38	31	17	0
A fair bit	979	7	30	35	28	0
Some	511	7	24	42	27	—
Not much	48 ⎫	10	21	42	27	0
None	3 ⎬					
No information	7 ⎭					
Has he a girl friend?						
Has a girl friend	1,151	16	31	33	21	0
Goes out with girls	1,029	9	34	32	25	0
Does not go out with girls	930	9	28	38	25	0
How often does he not know what to do with his spare time?						
All the time/often	325	27	36	20	17	0
Now and then	2,109	11	36	34	20	0
Never	677	7	15	39	39	0
Interest score, in four 'near quartiles'						
Sector 1 (high)	723	16	36	29	19	0
Sector 2	647	13	31	36	20	0
Sector 3	834	9	34	35	23	0
Sector 4 (low)	892	9	25	36	30	—

— = Less than 0.5 per cent

2 Those who say that they want a lot of fun and excitement and those who say they do not get enough of it.

3 Those who say they frequently do not know what to do with their spare time.

4 Those who say they frequently wish there were more places to go to.

By contrast, there is very little relationship between frequency of feeling bored or fed-up and:

1 Occupational level of father.

2 The boy's age.

3 Whether he is still at school.

4 Whether he has a girl friend.

5 The number of his interests.

A particularly important feature of Table 10.23 is its clarification of the relationship between 'frequency of feeling bored or fed-up' and frequency of 'not knowing what to do with spare time', these being the independent variables in Hypotheses 4 and 3 respectively. That part of Table 10.23 clearly indicates that, in spite of a considerable amount of relationship between the two of them, there is nonetheless a lot of non-overlap between them. This makes it reasonable to go on regarding them as relatively separate variables and for investigating *both*

Table 10.23
Frequency of feeling
bored or fed-up analysed
by characteristics and
backgrounds of boys
(3,113 cases, weighted)

Characteristics and background of boys	All cases (n)	How often does he feel bored or fed-up?			
		All the time/ often (%)	Now and then (%)	Never (%)	No information (%)
Occupational level of fathers					
Professional, semi-professional and executive	518	26	69	5	0
Highly skilled	514	27	69	4	0
Skilled	674	25	70	5	0
Moderately skilled	630	26	68	5	—
Semi-skilled	517	18	77	5	0
Unskilled	254	20	67	12	
No information	6				
Last school attended					
Secondary modern	1,464	28	67	5	0
Comprehensive	549	17	78	5	0
Grammar	718	23	73	4	1
Public	257	26	69	6	0
Other	105				
No information	20				
Age at interview					
12/13 yrs	721	25	69	6	—
14 yrs	782	22	74	5	0
15 yrs	754	28	68	4	—
16/17 yrs	856	24	70	7	0
Was school liked?					
Disliked very much	81	42	56	3	0
Disliked	597	30	66	4	0
Liked	2,117	23	72	5	—
Liked very much	312	16	73	11	0
No information	6				
Is he still at school?					
Yes	2,402	24	71	5	—
No	711	25	69	6	—
How often does/did he play truant?					
Once a week or more	331	23	73	4	0
Once a month	262	37	58	4	0
Hardly ever	766	24	72	4	0
Never	1,745	23	71	6	—
No information	9				
How much of his spare time does he like to spend at home?					
None	65	33	62	3	0
Not much	406	26	69	5	0
Less than half	531	21	75	4	0
About half	1,352	26	69	5	0
Most of it	672	23	72	6	0
All of it	59	24	48	29	0
No information	28				

Table 10.23 (continued)

Characteristics and background of boys	All cases	How often does he feel bored or fed-up?			
		All the time/ often	Now and then	Never	No information
	(n)	(%)	(%)	(%)	(%)
How much fun and excitement does he want?					
A terrific amount	463	35	62	4	0
Quite a lot	1,102	27	67	6	0
A fair bit	979	20	74	5	1
Some	511	18	76	6	0
Not much	48 ⎫	17	73	10	0
None	3 ⎬				
No information	7 ⎭				
Does he get enough fun and excitement?					
Yes	1,622	19	74	8	—
No	1,487	31	66	3	—
No information	4				
Has he a girl friend?					
Has one	1,151	24	72	4	0
Goes out with girls	1,029	27	68	5	0
Does not go out with girls	930	22	70	7	—
No information	3				
How often does he not know what to do with his spare time?					
All the time/often	325	40	54	6	1
Now and then	2,109	25	72	3	0
Never	677	16	72	12	—
No information	2				
How often did he wish there were more places to go to?					
All the time	356	39	58	3	—
Often	974	26	71	3	0
Now and then	1,053	26	68	6	0
Never	729	13	78	9	—
No information	1				
Interest score, in four 'near quartiles'					
Sector 1 (high)	723	27	68	5	0
Sector 2	647	22	73	5	0
Sector 3	834	26	70	4	0
Sector 4 (low)	892	22	70	7	1
No information	8				

— = Less than 0.5 per cent

Hypotheses 3 and 4 rather than just one of them or some combination of the two.

Investigating Hypotheses 3 and 4
The two hypotheses to be investigated were:

Boys who do not know what to do with their 'spare time' are thereby led to do more stealing (Hypothesis 3).

and

Boys who say they get bored and fed-up during their spare time are thereby led to do more stealing (Hypothesis 4).

Strategy of investigation
The following expectations were derived from the two hypotheses and were then tested.

Expectation 1 Boys who say they frequently feel they do not know what to do with their spare time will have been involved in more stealing than boys who feel this way less often.

Expectation 2 Expectation 1 applies even when the two samples of boys concerned are closely matched in terms of the correlates of stealing.

Expectation 3 Expectation 2 applies with respect to the duration of serious stealing.

Expectation 4 Expectation 2 applies for the forty-four different types of theft studied.

Expectation 5 Boys who frequently get bored or fed-up will have been involved in more stealing than boys who feel this way less often.

Expectation 6 Expectation 5 applies even when the two samples of boys are closely matched in terms of the correlates of stealing.

Testing Expectation 1
Table 10.24 presents a comparison of the theft involvement of boys who say they often feel they do not know what to do with their spare time and boys who say they feel that way less often. On this evidence, Expectation 1 is borne out but not to any major degree.

Testing Expectation 2 (using unweighted sample, 1,425 cases)
This test involved the close matching of a control group and a qualifying group, where the qualifying group were those who frequently felt they did not know what to do with their spare time and the controls were the rest of the boys in the sample. For the reasons given in Chapter 1, this analysis was based on the unweighted sample. The split into qualifying and control groups was as shown in Figure 10.2.

The control group was matched to the qualifying group in terms of the correlates of stealing as already established in Chapter 1 and as used in all other matching operations in this inquiry. The results are shown in Table 10.25. The evidence of Table 10.25 supports Expectation 2 but not to any marked degree.

Figure 10.2
Division of sample for testing Expectations 2–4

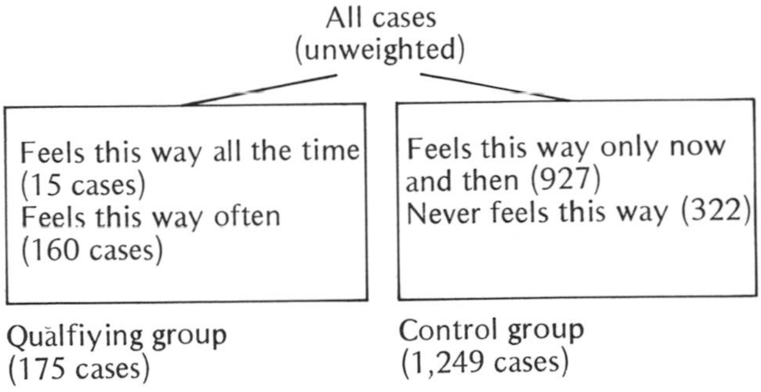

All cases
(unweighted)

Feels this way all the time (15 cases) Feels this way often (160 cases)	Feels this way only now and then (927) Never feels this way (322)
Qualifiying group (175 cases)	Control group (1,249 cases)

Table 10.24
Comparing the theft levels of boys in terms of frequency of feeling they do not know what to do with their spare time (3,113 cases, weighted)

Frequency of feeling he does not know what to do with his spare time	(n)	(%)	Index of variety of stealing				Index of amount of stealing			
			0.1 (%)	0.2 (%)	0.3 (%)	0.4 (%)	0.1 (%)	0.2 (%)	0.3 (%)	0.4 (%)
All the time } Often	325	10	16	23	29	33	19	24	27	29
Now and then	2,109	68	25	25	27	23	23	29	25	23
Never	677	22	28	24	24	24	28	25	25	23
No information	2	–								

— = Less than 0.5 per cent

355

Table 10.25
Differences between
qualifiers and controls
before and after matching:
variety, amount and
duration of stealing

Theft indices	Unadjusted average score for qualifiers a (175 cases)	Unadjusted average score for controls b (1,249 cases)	Adjusted average score for controls c	Differences between qualifiers and adj. controls a—c	Difference a—c as percentage of c
Average variety score	15.7	13.3	13.5	2.2*	16
Average amount score	104.1	89.7	91.0	13.1*	14
Duration of serious stealing in years	4.3	3.6	3.6	0.7*	19

* = Significant at the 0.05 level

Figure 10.3
Division of sample for testing Expectation 6

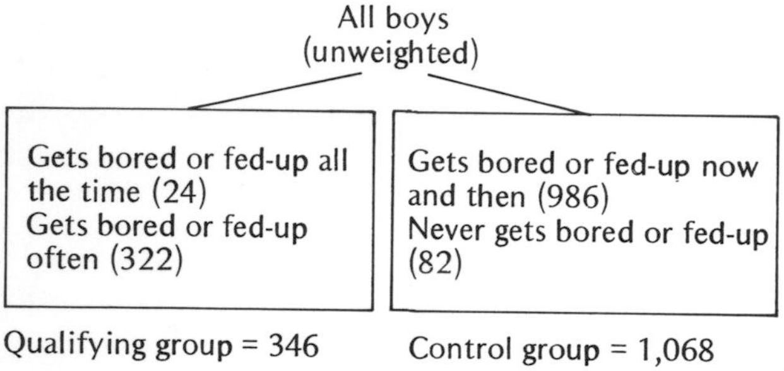

All boys
(unweighted)

Gets bored or fed-up all
the time (24)
Gets bored or fed-up
often (322)

Gets bored or fed-up now
and then (986)
Never gets bored or fed-up
(82)

Qualifying group = 346   Control group = 1,068

Testing Expectation 3 (using unweighted sample, 1,425 cases)
This concerns the duration in years of serious stealing. The evidence supports the expectation, though not to any marked degree (see Table 10.25).

Testing Expectation 4 (using unweighted sample, 1,425 cases)
This concerns the forty-four types of theft on the basis of which the total theft scores were calculated. The pre- and post-matching figures are shown in Table 10.26.

The evidence in Table 10.26 tends to support the expectation, with thirteen of the theft types showing residual differences of a size significant at the 5 per cent level or better. On the other hand, there are some items in the list of forty-four for which the expectation is not borne out, namely those on the right-hand side of Table 10.27, which may be contrasted with those on the left-hand side.

One can only speculate at the nature of the difference between the items on the left and those on the right of Table 10.27. One such speculation is that those on the left are more in line with somewhat aimless behaviour than are those on the right – an interpretation that makes some sense in relation to the hypothesis.

Testing Expectation 5
This expectation was that boys who frequently get bored or fed-up have been involved in more stealing than other boys. Results of the comparison are set out in Table 10.28. On the evidence of Table 10.28, Expectation 5 is borne out.

Testing Expectation 6 (using unweighted sample, 1,425 cases)
The sample was split as shown in Figure 10.3 to yield a qualifying and a control group. The control group was then matched to the qualifying group with the results set out in Table 10.29. The evidence in Table 10.29 gives moderate support to Expectation 6.

Summing-up on the testing of Hypotheses 3 and 4
Hypotheses 3 and 4 each tends to be strengthened by the evidence presented through the testing of expectations. Whereas the variable hypothesized as causal in Hypothesis 3 appears to have that character for theft considered generally, there are particular classes of theft for which there does not appear to be any causal association. (Because of the similarity of the independent variables in Hypotheses 3 and 4, it remains a possibility that the same limitation applies to the variable 'getting bored or fed-up'.)

7 SUMMING-UP ON THE INVESTIGATION OF HYPOTHESES 1 to 4
Hypothesis 1, concerning 'number of interests'
Hypothesis 1 postulated that 'a paucity of (legal) interests facilitates the onset and continuance of stealing'. For the purposes of this hypothesis, 'interest' is defined in terms of (a) its passive form (i.e. a *feeling* of interest) and (b) its active form (i.e. activity associated with an interest).

The evidence brought to bear on this hypothesis reduces its tenability. At the same time, some of the evidence gathered appears to constitute a case for

Table 10.26
Differences between
qualifiers and controls
before and after matching:
each of the forty-four
types of theft

Theft types at Level L2 or over*	Number and percentage who have done the act at least once at Level 2 or over*						
	Unadjusted averages for qualifiers a (175 cases)		Unadjusted averages for controls b (1,249 cases)		Adjusted averages for controls c		Differences between qualifiers and adj. controls a−c	Difference a−c as percentage of c
	(n)	(%)	(n)	(%)	(n)	(%)		(%)
1	160	91.4	1,129	90.8	157.96	91.0	0.4	−
2	105	60.0	626	50.3	88.45	51.0	9.0†	18
3	72	41.1	490	39.4	68.53	39.5	1.6	4
4	91	52.0	662	53.2	92.82	53.5	−1.5	−3
5	52	29.7	268	21.5	38.38	22.1	7.6	34
6	103	58.9	686	55.1	96.89	55.8	3.1	6
7	82	46.9	495	39.8	69.65	40.1	6.8	17
8	73	41.7	404	32.5	56.54	32.6	9.1†	28
9	31	17.7	188	15.1	27.01	15.6	2.1	13
10	69	39.4	490	39.4	70.50	40.6	−1.2	−3
11	77	44.0	457	36.7	64.74	37.3	6.7	18
12	37	21.1	185	14.9	26.81	15.4	5.7	37
13	89	50.9	467	37.5	67.02	38.6	12.3†	32
14	47	26.9	286	23.0	40.85	23.5	3.4	14
15	40	22.9	186	15.0	26.84	15.5	7.4†	48
16	84	48.0	539	43.3	75.37	43.4	4.6	11
17	50	28.6	218	17.5	30.48	17.6	11.0†	63
18	120	68.6	793	63.7	111.83	64.4	4.2	7
19	80	45.7	440	35.4	62.27	35.9	9.8†	27
20	55	31.4	376	30.2	52.68	30.3	1.1	4
21	36	20.6	148	11.9	21.43	12.3	8.3†	67
22	78	44.6	475	38.2	66.89	38.5	6.1†	16
23	41	23.4	276	22.2	39.62	22.8	0.6	3
24	31	17.7	147	11.8	20.90	12.0	5.7	48
25	55	31.4	276	22.2	39.03	22.5	8.9†	40
26	61	34.9	343	27.6	48.63	28.0	6.9	25
27	44	25.1	233	18.7	32.01	18.4	6.7†	36
28	44	25.1	282	22.7	40.02	23.1	2.0	9
29	16	9.1	90	7.2	13.63	7.9	1.2	15
30	86	49.1	569	45.7	80.48	46.4	2.7	6
31	50	28.6	341	27.4	49.03	28.2	0.4	1
32	20	11.4	84	6.8	12.44	7.2	4.2	58
33	123	70.3	782	62.9	110.66	63.8	6.5	10
34	61	34.9	385	30.9	53.59	30.9	4.0	13
35	42	24.0	200	16.1	28.98	16.7	7.3†	44
36	75	42.9	354	28.5	49.47	28.5	14.4†	51
37	10	5.7	59	4.7	8.66	5.0	0.7	14
38	48	27.4	282	22.7	39.93	23.0	4.4	19
39	41	23.4	228	18.3	32.07	18.5	4.9	26
40	112	64.0	805	64.7	113.65	65.5	−1.5	−2
41	23	13.1	108	8.7	15.83	9.1	4.0	,44
42	30	17.1	132	10.6	18.31	10.5	6.6†	63
43	55	31.4	372	29.9	51.68	29.8	1.6	5
44	107	61.1	636	51.1	89.39	51.5	9.6†	19

* = Thefts exclusive of items of very small value. See Chapter 1
for details
† = Significant at the 5 per cent level or better
− = Less than 0.5 per cent

Table 10.27

Items strongly supporting the expectation	Items not supporting the expectation
I have stolen from a park or playground I have got into a place and stolen I have stolen from a telephone box I have stolen from someone at work I have stolen something *from* a bike or a motor bike I have stolen milk I have stolen something from a changing-room or cloakroom	I have got away without paying the fare or proper fare I have taken junk or scrap without asking for it first I have got into some place without paying the money to go in I have kept something I have found I have stolen from work I have stolen from a café I have stolen something just for a dare I have pinched something while I was on a holiday

formulating a substitute hypothesis to the effect that the existence in a boy of a strongly-held and actively-pursued interest (of a legal kind) reduces the likelihood of the boy becoming involved in stealing.

Hypothesis 2, concerning 'watching television'
Hypothesis 2 postulated that:

Boys who watch a lot of television are thereby made more likely to engage in stealing.

The evidence does not support this hypothesis in any general way. At the same time the evidence warrants the postulation of a substitute hypothesis that watching a lot of television contributes to the occurrence of a limited number of particular *types* of stealing.

Hypotheses 3 and 4, concerning 'spare time' and 'boredom'
Hypotheses 3 and 4 were to the effect that stealing by boys is increased where the boys concerned: (*a*) do not know what to do with their spare time; (*b*) frequently get bored or fed-up during their spare time. Each hypothesis is rendered more tenable by the evidence examined.

In evaluating the social relevance of this finding, the following distributions of the variables postulated as causal should be noted.

Table 10.28
Comparing the scores of boys who differ in the frequency with which they get bored or fed-up (3,113 cases, weighted)

Frequency of getting bored or fed-up			Index of variety of stealing				Index of amount of stealing			
			Q.1	Q.2	Q.3	Q.4	Q.1	Q.2	Q.3	Q.4
	(*n*)	(%)	(%)	(%)	(%)	(%)	(%)	(%)	(%)	(%)
All the time	45	1 ⎫	20	20	31	29	18	26	31	24
Often	714	23 ⎬								
Now and then	2,185	70 ⎭	25	26	25	24	25	28	23	24
Not at all/never	164	5	43	31	19	7	46	29	15	9
No information	5	—								

— = Less than 0.5 per cent

Table 10.29
Differences between qualifiers and controls before and after matching: variety and amount of stealing

Theft indices	Unadjusted average score for qualifiers a (346 cases)	Unadjusted average score for controls b (1,068 cases)	Adjusted average score for controls c	Differences between qualifiers and adj. controls a–c	Difference a–c as percentage of c
Averaged variety score	15.1	13.1	13.2	1.9*	14
Averaged amount score	104.9	86.9	86.9	18.0*	21

*Significant at 0.05 level

1 Being 'bored or fed-up' appears to be a recurrent condition for many boys, with 24 per cent saying that they are often or more frequently bored.

2 Eleven per cent of boys reported that they often do not know what to do with their spare time and 42 per cent that they often wished that there were more places to go to in their spare time.

3 Over half (56 per cent) of the boys claimed that they went out with their mates when they did not know what to do with their spare time. An examination of their claimed activities on those occasions (p. 347) indicates that such activity is not infrequently unstructured and relatively aimless and that on occasions it is socially disruptive.

The tendency to get bored or fed-up is fairly similar in going from one to another social sector. The desire for more places to go to in spare time is somewhat more common amongst the sons of the occupationally less skilled and those with secondary-modern or comprehensive-school backgrounds.

8 SOME COMMENTS AND POSSIBLE ACTION

1a The limitations of the evidence relating to boys' interests and to the extent of their watching television have been pointed out, as has the fact that the 'exposure to television' information was gathered only incidentally. The need to collect such information afresh has also been stated. Nonetheless, the information actually used in the present investigation of Hypotheses 1 and 2 is regarded by the writer as sufficient to provide meaningful challenges to their tenability.

b With regard to both hypotheses, the results of the investigation provide grounds for re-formulating them in certain ways. One such re-formulation is that 'the existence in a boy of a very strong interest in some one issue — his special interest, as it were — works against his becoming involved in stealing'. This does not, of course, preclude a wider *background* range of interests. Another re-formulation that seems warranted by the evidence is that a lot of exposure to television will work against the boys concerned becoming involved in certain kinds of stealing (these kinds yet to be adequately formulated).

2 The extent to which boys get bored or fed-up in their spare time, and the extent to which they wish there were more things to do in their spare time, are especially noteworthy, particularly when viewed in relation to the evidence about 'fun and excitement seeking' presented in Chapter 4. This evidence indicated both that boys were 'short' of fun and excitement outlets and that their search for fun and excitement was in present circumstances leading them into theft operations. The evidence from the testing of Hypotheses 3 and 4 appears to call for a greater number of available and acceptable 'things

to do'. Apparently this does *not* mean simply developing in boys a *wider range of interests* (see the results of investigating Hypothesis 1). Rather, it seems to mean providing more outlets in the form of escape from their present environments, presumably including the provision of (legal) outlets for fun and excitement needs.

9 APPENDIX 10.1

The Sub-Questionnaire used

Interests

I Initial sorting of cards to eliminate non-interests

PASS BOY 'READING TEST' CARD AND ASK HIM TO READ IT OUT ALOUD FOR YOU.

IF HE CANNOT READ, YOU WILL HAVE TO READ ALL CARDS FOR HIM.

IF HE CAN READ, SAY:
'So first of all I want to find out what sort of things you are interested in these days. What you are interested in. There is a special way of doing this'.
'Let's start by putting this thing up'.

PUT UP THE SORTING SCREEN AND GET HIM TO HELP YOU INSERT THE 'INTERESTED' AND 'NOT INTERESTED' SORTING SIGNS.

PASS HIM THE FIRST CARD (= WATCHING TELEVISION). SAY:
'Will you read this one out aloud for me please.'

SAY:
'If you *are* interested in WATCHING TELEVISION, put the card in *this* box.'
(POINT TO THE *'INTERESTED'* BOX).

'If you are *not* interested in WATCHING TELEVISION, put it in *this* box.'
(POINT TO THE 'NOT INTERESTED' BOX).

SEE THAT HE SORTS IT INTO ONE BOX OR THE OTHER. THEN SAY:
'Now we'll do the next. You sort that one into the proper box and I will go round here and pass the cards to you one at a time. They will come through this slot. (POINT)

GO BEHIND THE BOARD AND PASS THE CARDS THROUGH THE SLOT ONE AT A TIME KEEPING THEM MOVING REASONABLY FAST.

READ OUT YELLOW REMINDERS AS YOU COME TO THEM.

AT THE END OF THE SORTING PROCESS, PUT RUBBER BAND ROUND THE 'INTERESTED'

CARDS AND 'INTERESTED' LABEL. PUT RUBBER BAND ROUND THE *NOT* CARDS AND THE *NOT* LABEL. PUT EACH PACK TO ONE SIDE. ABOVE ALL, LET HIM GET THE IMPRESSION THAT THIS IS THE END OF ANYTHING THAT IS GOING TO BE ASKED ABOUT THE CARDS PUT INTO EITHER OF THE TWO BOXES.

II Sorting cards to indicate frequency of active pursuit of an interest

---

TAKE UP THE 'I AM INTERESTED' PACK OF CARDS.
ADD THE THREE PINK EXTRAS (PLUS WHITE INSTRUCTION CARDS) TO BACK OF PACK. SAY:
'Now I want to ask you some more about your interests. This time I want to know how often you *do* anything about your interests.'
'There's a special way of doing this.' (GO TO UPRIGHT SORTING BOARD). 'We put the cards into these bags'. (POINT TO THE BAGS WHICH WILL AT THIS STAGE BE LYING ON THE TABLE).

PICK UP THE *NEVER* BAG.
'If you *never* do anything about an interest, you put the card in *this bag.*'

HANG IT UP ON THE *LEFT*-HAND SIDE OF THE BOARD ON THE PEG THAT WILL BE THERE READY FOR IT.
'If you do something about your interest *MOST DAYS,* you put it in *this* one.'

HANG IT UP AT THE EXTREME RIGHT-HAND SIDE OF THE BOARD ON THE PEG WHICH WILL BE THERE FOR IT.
'Now where do I put these others?'

POINT TO THE OTHERS WHICH WILL BE LYING FACE UP (PRINT SHOWING) ON THE SORTING TABLE. GET THEM IN POSITION WITH THE HELP OF THE BOY. SEE THAT HE TAKES PART IN SUCH A WAY THAT HE CAN UNDERSTAND THAT THE TOTAL SET OF BAGS CONSTITUTE A GRADIENT AND SO THAT HE SEES WHAT IS WRITTEN ON EACH ONE OF THEM.
'Now let's take the first of your interests.'

HOLD ONTO CARD AND SAY:
'How often do you actually do anything about *that* one?'

GET HIS ANSWER. CHALLENGE OR PROBE. THEN SAY:
'So which bag do you put it in?'

SEE THAT HE GETS IT RIGHT (i.e. THAT THE BAG HE CHOOSES IS IN LINE WITH HIS STATEMENT ABOUT HOW OFTEN HE DOES ANYTHING ABOUT HIS INTEREST).
'Now let's do the next one the same way. Look at what's

on the card.' HOLD ONTO IT AND SAY: 'Think of how often you do anything about it these days.' (PAUSE). 'How often would that be?' Now find the bag that is nearest to how often you do it. What bag is that?
(PAUSE AND CHALLENGE IF OBVIOUSLY IN ERROR.) 'Put it in *that* bag then.' (PASS HIM THE CARD)

SAY:
'Now let's do the others in the same way. *But please take them carefully.*'

PASS THE REST OF THE CARDS, ONE AT A TIME, AND KEEP THE PACE FAIRLY FAST.

AFTER EACH FOURTH CARD, SAY (ALTERNATIVELY):
'Make sure it's going into the proper bag.' 'Take it carefully.'

TAKE DOWN THE BAGS AT THE END OF THE SORT.

TAKE OUT THE LAST THREE CARDS (CORNERS ON) TO BE SORTED, MARKING BAG TITLES ON BACK, AND THEN ASK BOY THE QUESTION ON BACK OF EACH. IGNORE IF IN 'NEVER' BAG.

LEAVE *ALL OTHER CARDS IN BAGS* FOR LATER PROCESSING.

III Boredom. Facilities in the district

NOW GO BACK TO THE INTERVIEW TABLE AND DEAL WITH THE FOLLOWING QUESTIONS.

1a 'Do you ever feel you *don't* know what to do with your spare time?' YES/NO

IF 'NO', CHALLENGE.
IF 'YES':
'How often do you feel like this?' (SHOW CARD) ALL THE TIME/OFTEN/NOW AND THEN/NEVER

'What do you do when you feel like this?' (PROBE ALL YOU CAN USING "WHAT ELSE")
'Do you go out with your mates when you feel like this?' YES/NO

IF 'YES', SAY: 'Would you say OFTEN or JUST NOW AND THEN?'
CIRCLE CHOICE. THEN ASK:
'What do you do when you feel like that and go out with your mates?' (SEE THAT HE IS TALKING ABOUT WHAT HE DOES WHEN IN COMPANY OF MATES)

1b 'Do you ever wish there were more places to go to in your spare time?' YES/NO
IF 'NO', CHALLENGE.
IF 'YES',
'How often do you wish there were more places to go to in your spare time?'

ALL THE TIME/OFTEN/NOW AND THEN/NEVER.

1c 'Do you ever get bored or fed-up with things?'
YES/NO

   IF 'NO', CHALLENGE.
   IF 'YES':
'How often do you get bored or fed up with things?'
   (SHOW CARD)

ALL THE TIME/OFTEN/NOW AND THEN/NEVER
1d 'When you start doing something, do you usually want to do it *all at once* or *in bits* and pieces?' ALL AT ONCE/BITS AND PIECES. (SHOW CARD) (PRESS FOR THE USUAL SITUATION. IF HE STILL SAYS IT ALL DEPENDS, GET THIS DOWN AND ALSO HIS STATEMENTS AS TO HOW IT VARIES FROM SITUATION TO SITUATION)

Chapter eleven
Wants exceed legal means

CONTENTS

1 THE COVERAGE OF THIS CHAPTER

In this chapter I have presented a range of information broadly related to boys' wants in relation to their legal means. This information was collected and processed to serve two associated purposes, the more important of which was to investigate an hypothesis about a causal factor in the development of juvenile stealing. This hypothesis was as follows.

When a boy's wants exceed his legal means, he will tend to make up the difference by stealing.

The second purpose of the collected data was to provide general background information about the factor hypothesized as causal in character. For example: how much pocket money do boys get?; on what do boys spend their pocket money?; what are the things they want but cannot afford from their pocket money?; what regular payments are boys committed to?; do they borrow money?; how do the above vary with the characteristics of boys?

2 RESEARCH PROCEDURES COMMON TO ALL THE HYPOTHESES DEALT WITH IN THE INQUIRY

The gathering of information related to the hypothesis about 'having wants that exceed one's means' was done in the context of an inquiry concerned with over thirty other hypotheses. The techniques relating to the inquiry as a whole have been summarized in Chapter 1. That summary deals with sampling procedures; with a technique for getting boys to provide reliable information about any stealing they have done; with questioning procedures for classifying boys in terms of the variables hypothesized as causal in the different hypotheses (i.e. in terms of the different independent variables); with strategies for investigating the tenability of hypotheses about causal factors and processes. The reader should as necessary refer to the relevant parts of Chapter 1 in reading statements of findings in the present and subsequent chapters.

3 RESEARCH PROCEDURES APPLYING ONLY TO THE HYPOTHESIS DEALT WITH IN THIS CHAPTER

Whereas many aspects of research procedure applied generally to the whole range of hypotheses under study in this series, certain parts of it related only to the hypothesis about 'wants exceeding means'. These 'parts' tend to be encapsulated in one of the sub-questionnaires put to boys in the course of the interview and this sub-questionnaire is presented in full in Appendix 11.1.

The questionnaire was designed in sections, each section beginning with a general description of its purpose or purposes as follows.

I	1 His lawful allowance

2 How he spends his lawful allowance and what it leaves him wanting

II	1 How does he pay for/get what he wants but canno afford?

2 Do his excessive wants grow out of his stealing?

3 Did he have wants beyond his means when he wa smaller?

Some of the questions were fully structured and other were of the open-response kind. The open-response questions were in some cases designed to allow the boy to reveal certain key ideas or facts without these being suggested to the boy (e.g. that he *stole* to get things he could not afford). Others were intended only to provide general background of a qualitative kind to the 'money behaviour' of boys (e.g. what he spends his pocket money on).

4 METHODS AND FINDINGS RELATING TO THE INVESTIGATION OF THE HYPOTHESIS

The nature of the hypothesis

The hypothesis under investigation was:

When a boy's wants exceed his legal means, he will tend to make up the difference by stealing.

It was the purpose of this inquiry both to examine this hypothesis and to provide background information about the independent variable defined in it. This independent variable is 'having wants that exceed one's legal means'.

The distribution of boys in terms of the variable defined as causal

In this section are presented: (*a*) details about the questions asked as bases for classifying boys in terms of the independent variable; and (*b*) the distribution of boys in terms of that variable.

The questions asked and the responses

A series of questions was asked to help the boy concentrate upon how much legal money he received each week and he was then asked if this was enough to meet his various needs. The questioning procedure was as set out below.

I	Q1 His lawful allowance

1a 'Do you earn any money by working?' YES/NO

IF 'NO' CHALLENGE WITH: '*ANY KIND OF WORK*'

IF HE HAS A JOB, ASK: 'How much a week do you get from this job?' 'How much of that do you keep for your own pocket?'

IF HE WORKS IRREGULARLY, FIND OUT: WORK PERIODS
THE AMOUNT EARNED THEN
THE AMOUNT KEPT FOR POCKET

1b (Apart from that) 'Are you given any pocket money each week?' YES/NO

IF 'YES', 'How much?' (TELL HIM THAT THIS DOES NOT INCLUDE MONEY FOR FARES, OR FOR SCHOOL DINNERS OR THE LIKE)

1c 'You've told me that you get pocket money (and money from working)' (PAUSE) 'Now what other money do you get?'

PROBE AND PROMPT FOR ANY OTHER MONEY FROM ANY SOURCE: THIS INCLUDES SPORADIC EARNINGS, ETC.
GET AMOUNTS AND SOURCES. IF IRREGULAR OR SPORADIC, GIVE DETAILS. WORK HARD ON THIS QUESTION.
IF HE STARTS MENTIONING STOLEN MONEY, TELL HIM YOU MEAN MONEY HE GOT LEGALLY.
IF HE REPORTS LEGAL MONEY UNDER 1c, ASK:
'Exactly how much of that do you keep for yourself — for your own pocket?'

1d ADD UP WHAT HE GETS A WEEK. SAY:
'So, adding it all up, how much money would you say you had for your own pocket each week?'

CHECK AGAINST YOUR OWN ADDITION AND CHALLENGE IF MUCH DIFFERENT. PUT YOUR OWN ADDITION IN BRACKETS, AFTER HIS ADDITION — IF THE TWO ARE CLOSELY SIMILAR.

I Q2 How he spends his lawful allowance and what it leaves him wanting

2a 'Is that enough pocket money or do you need more?'
SHOW CARD, READ OUT, CIRCLE CHOICE (MORE THAN ENOUGH/ABOUT RIGHT/NEED A BIT MORE/NEED MUCH MORE)
IF POCKET MONEY SAID TO BE 'ABOUT RIGHT' OR 'MORE THAN ENOUGH' CHALLENGE WITH: 'You mean that your pocket money of (SAY THE AMOUNT PER WEEK) is enough for — the things you want — that it doesn't leave you wanting things?'

2b 'What do you spend your pocket money on?' (REMIND HIM OF ITS AMOUNT) 'What else?' . . . 'What else?'

2c 'What are the things it is not enough for? I mean the things you definitely want but can't buy with your pocket money?' (PROMPT AND RE-PROMPT WITH STATEMENTS SUCH AS: 'Anything more?' 'What about when you go out?' 'Cigarettes?' 'Sweets?' 'What else?' 'What else?')
IF THERE IS NOTHING HE WANTS UNDER 2c GO TO II, Q.3

Various other questions were asked but I 2a, in combination with II 3 (see below) were the key ones in defining the hypothesized causal factor. II 3 follows.

'When you were younger, did you want a lot of things you could not afford?' YES/NO

For the sample as a whole, the distribution of boys in terms of responses to I 2a was as follows:

Table 11.1.1
Is his pocket money sufficient to meet his wants?
(3,113 cases, weighted)

	(n)	(%)
More than enough	414	13
About right/enough	1,653	53
Need a bit more	810	26
Need much more	210	7
No information	26	1

Closely related to this 'variable' are two others, namely: (a) the boy's confirmation that there is 'nothing' he now wants that his 'pocket money' won't get him: (b) whether boy had 'wants exceeding means' when he was small. Replies to these questions are set out in Table 11.1.2.

Table 11.1.2
(3,113 cases, weighted)

(i) Is there anything he can't afford on his present pocket money?	(n)	(%)
No	775	25
Yes	2,189	70
No information	149	5

(ii) When he was smaller, did his wants exceed what his pocket money would cover?		
Yes	1,862	60
No	1,177	38
No information	74	2

Several features of Tables 11.1.1 and 11.1.2 call for comment.

1 Table 11.1.1 and 11.1.2 may seem to present contradictory information in that 66 per cent of the boys claim that their pocket money is enough to meet their needs and yet 70 per cent claim that there is something they really want but cannot afford on their pocket money. However, it appears that the 66 per cent tend to be referring to regular needs in a general way whereas the 70 per cent (who must include many of the 66 per cent) tend to be referring to special wants (as distinct from ordinary regular needs, e.g. clothes, a bike or motor bike, special equipment for hobbies, a tape recorder; see Table 10.5). Both items of information are important and relevant, namely that 66 per cent of boys appear to regard their pocket money as sufficient for their normal needs but that only 25 per cent deny that there is anything they really want that is beyond being bought out of their pocket money.

2 In terms of the hypothesis, the second system of responses (see Table 11.1.2) is the more relevant one.

3 As might be expected, the percentage with special needs that go beyond what can be secured from pocket money was much smaller when the boys were younger.

A particular combination of variables seemed especially appropriate for the investigation of the hypothesis, namely a combination sufficient to identify two main groups of boys: (a) boys who at the time of the interview felt their pocket money was *not* sufficient to buy them all the things they definitely wanted and who claimed this was also the case when they were younger; and (b) boys who at the time of the interview felt their pocket money *was* sufficient in that same sense and who claimed this was also the case when they were younger. The numerical features of these groups and of the residue are presented in Table 11.1.3.

Table 11.1.3
(3,113 cases, weighted)

	(n)	(%)
(i) Boys who now and previously felt that their pocket money was sufficient for the things they wanted	538	17
(ii) Boys who now and previously felt that their pocket money was insufficient for the things they wanted	749	24
(iii) Those who fall into neither Group (i) nor Group (ii)	1,826	59

Distribution of boys in terms of data closely related to 'causal-type' variables
Certain of the questions asked were meant for use in testing the various 'expectations' derived for the investigation of the hypothesis and will be referred to in that context. Others were meant to provide general background information and this is set out in this section.

How much money?
In working towards getting the boys to provide the responses set out in Tables 11.1.1 to 11.1.3 it was necessary to take them through a series of questions about their earnings and/or pocket money. Responses to these questions are set out in Table 11.2. The reader must keep in mind, however, that the sums referred to relate to the late 1960s and that they are best understood when made the bases of *comparisons* between boys from different social sectors.

For the purposes of the comparisons and analyses to be made, the data in the bottom row of Table 11.2 were grouped into four sectors, as nearly equally as possible in terms of the numbers of boys included in them. These are the four sectors shown in Table 11.3. Reference will be made to them in the context of testing expectations.

Table 11.2
Sources and amounts of money which boy has 'for pocket'
(3,113 cases, weighted)

Source of money for pocket	Not applicable or nil	Up to 5/-	5/1– 10/-	10/1– 15/-	15/1– £1	£1+– £2	£2+– £5	£5+– £10	£10†	No information
	(%)	(%)	(%)	(%)	(%)	(%)	(%)	(%)	(%)	(%)
Weekly earnings from paid job (even if employment irregular)	42	4	6	6	5	10	8	16	2	1
Amount from weekly earnings kept for own pocket	42	11	8	5	5	10	14	3	–	2
Money given as pocket money (apart from any earned in paid job)	35	23	27	6	4	3	1	0	0	1
Legal money retained from sources other than above	22	49	11	5	2	4	1	0	0	7
Total amount for own pocket	1	10	22	16	11	17	18	5	0	1

– = Less than 0.5 per cent

Table 11.3 The 'sector' distribution of money available to boys		Sector 1	Sector 2	Sector 3	Sector 4	All sectors
	Weighted cases	999	839	517	740	3,095
	Range of money	up to 10/-	10/-$^+$–£1	£1$^+$–£2	£2$^+$	
	Percentage in this sector	32%	27%	17%	24%	100%

What the boy buys with his money and what he cannot afford

In Question I 2b each boy was asked what he spent his money on and, following this, for what kinds of things *definitely wanted by him* his pocket money was insufficient. The responses to these two questions are set out in Tables 11.4 and 11.5 below.

Table 11.4
On what do boys spend their pocket money?
(3,113 cases, weighted)

Items named	(n)	(%)
Sweets	1,484	48
Cigarettes	648	21
Food/soft drinks	662	21
Drink (where 'alcoholic' is implied)	482	16
Girls/girl friends	472	15
Dancing	337	11
Gambling	138	4
Cinema	1,416	45
Newspapers/comics/magazines	330	11
Books	335	11
Records	331	11
Football/football matches	313	10
Other sports/sports equipment (e.g. bowling, swimming, fishing, boxing gear)	682	22
Hobbies/equipment for hobbies (e.g. coin collecting, train set . . .)	642	21
Clubs/club subscription	443	14
Clothes	858	28
Car/bike/scooter	98	3
Up-keep and gear for car, motor bike, bike/scooter/petrol	342	11
Fares	454	15
Other trips/holidays	310	10
Going out (other than activities above)	637	20
Stationery	124	4
Equipment for school work other than books	88	3
For presents/to give to other people	297	10
For savings	440	14

It would dangerous to make much of the *precise* figures in Tables 11.4 and 11.5 because: (*a*) there is no guarantee that all boys who spent money on item *X* or who wanted but could not afford item *X* have volunteered this information; (*b*) to say that 48 per cent of

Table 11.5
Things boys want but cannot afford
(3,113 cases, weighted)

Items named	(n)	(%)
'Nothing'	775	25
Sweets	64	2
Cigarettes	70	2
Drinks (where 'alcoholic' implied)	42	1
Taking out girls/girls	138	4
Food	10	–
Records	176	6
Books	127	4
Tape recorder/radio/gramophone/musical equipment	232	7
Hobbies/equipment for hobbies/electrical equipment	379	12
Sports equipment/sports	246	8
Car	133	4
Motor bike/bike	384	12
Equipment for car/for bike/for motor bike	136	4
Clothes/special clothes/latest in clothes	1,148	37
Travelling/making trips/holidays	124	4
Going out	516	17
For saving	38	1

– = Less than 0.5 per cent

boys spend money on sweets does not establish sweet buying as a major activity with boys (it indicates only that about half the boys say they bought sweets from time to time).

Bearing this in mind, it is still noteworthy that certain items are sources of expenditure at least occasionally by at least the percentage of boys shown in Table 11.4, namely: alcoholic drinks (16 per cent), gambling (4 per cent), cigarettes (21 per cent), presents for others (10 per' cent). Secondly, it is perhaps noteworthy, with respect to Table 11.5, that: 25 per cent of boys denied there was anything they really wanted that was beyond what they had for spending; 37 per cent wanted but could not afford 'clothes' or 'special clothes'; 12 per cent wanted (but could not afford) sports equipment and 12 per cent equipment for hobbies; *only ten boys mentioned food.*

Of the two tables, Table 11.5 is probably the more useful in that it indicates areas of wants that cannot be satisfied by the boys' legal money and so could possibly be or become objectives of other forms of acquisition, including stealing.

Do parents help out when the boy cannot afford something?
Boys were asked:

'Do your parents help out by buying things you want but cannot afford yourself?'
    IF 'YES':
'Can you give me some examples?'

Results are set out in Table 11.6.

Table 11.6
(3,113 cases, weighted)

	(n)	(%)
Do parents help and with what sorts of purchases?		
Yes	2,003	64
No	230	7
No information	105	3
Not applicable because nothing extra wanted	775	25
What sorts of things do parents help with?		
Cigarettes	41	1
Sweets	33	1
Records/gramophones/tape recorder/radio/ musical instruments	277	9
Books/comics/magazines	132	4
Sports equipment	199	6
Equipment for hobbies	165	5
Toys or games	145	5
Clothes	1,467	47
Watch/cufflinks/	60	2
Bike/motor bike/gear for bike/car/ car insurance	317	10
Fares	39	1
Holidays/trips/travel	148	5
School equipment	67	2
Money for going out	151	5

It seems noteworthy that (*a*) most parents appear at least occasionally to help out when boys want something they cannot afford (64 per cent in all and 86 per cent of those who say they have wants that go beyond their means); (*b*) the largest figure with respect to the *kinds* of help given is 47 per cent for clothes — clothes also being a major item in the list of things boys want but cannot afford from pocket money; (*c*) 7 per cent of all boys claim that parents do not help with things they want but cannot afford.

Financial commitments and borrowings
Boys were asked if they did any saving-up, if there were some things they had to pay for regularly and if they ever borrowed to pay for what they could not afford. Details of responses are given in Table 11.7, though it must be noted that boys having no wants beyond what they can buy from pocket money were not asked all these questions.
    The indications of Table 11.7 appear to be as follows.

1 There is a considerable claim for a saving tendency amongst boys and for having a savings account.

2 Of the boys who say their pocket money will not cover all they want, about half claimed they had regular payments of some kind to make and of these, 28 per cent named hire-purchase payments.

3 In terms of borrowing by boys whose pocket money will not cover all their wants, 28 per cent of these denied they ever borrowed to pay for things wanted and *of the* 68 per cent who said they *did* borrow for such a purpose, there were many who admitted they did not always pay back, with approximately 14 per cent saying that they paid back only sometimes or never.

Thus, in spite of a marked tendency by boys to save and to claim having a savings account, there is a lot of borrowing going on and an appreciable commitment to regular payments of some kind. This situation raises the possibility that some boys will be under financial pressure of the sort that might promote stealing by them. To this important point we will be coming in the part of this Section dealing with the testing of expectations.

'Causal' and related variables analysed by characteristics and backgrounds of boys
The 'causal' or independent variable has been described here as one concerned with 'wants exceeding means'. It and related variables were subject to cross-analysis in terms of a limited number of other variables, as described in Table 11.8.

The main indications of Table 11.8 are as follows:

1 Boys whose wants exceed their personal (and legal) means (i.e. their legal spending money) tend to be drawn in more than due proportion from those wanting a great deal of fun and excitement and much less from boys who want but little fun and excitement. On the other hand, there is relatively little variation by occupational level of fathers, by nominal religion and by amount of pocket money.

2 There is some tendency for boys in the top educational and social groupings to have less spending money than others. And understandably there is enormous variation in the amount of spending money in going from the younger to the older boys and in going from those with jobs to those without jobs. We may feel, on this evidence, that boys with jobs will be better placed to meet their spending needs. But it does not necessarily follow that they will thus be less pressured to steal — for one might expect their needs or wants to increase both with age and with their having more spending power. The evidence in later parts of this report bears on this important issue.

Table 11.7
Savings accounts and borrowings and regular
financial commitments
(3,113 cases, weighted)

	(n)	Percentage on 3,113	Percentage on all asked (= 2,338)	
a *SAVINGS*				
(i) *Does the boy claim he does any saving-up?*				
Yes	2,053	66	88	
No	184	6	8	
No information	101	3	4	
Not asked because he says there is 'nothing' he wants that can't be secured through his pocket money (IQ.2c)	775	25	*	
(ii) *Does the boy claim he has a savings account?*				
Yes	1,415	45	61	
No	610	20	26	
Doesn't save or no information on previous question	285	9	12	
Not asked because 'nothing' wanted (IQ.2c)	775	25	*	
No information on this question	28	1	1	
b *BORROWINGS*				
(i) *Does he ever have to borrow to pay for the things he wants?*	(n)	(%)		
Yes	1,579	51	68	
No	649	21	28	
Not asked	775	25	*	
No information	110	4	5	Percentage on all borrowers (= 1,579)
(ii) *Does he pay it back?*				
Always	1,073	34	46	68
Often	293	9	13	19
Sometimes	201	6	9	13
Never	8	—	—	1
Not applicable because he never borrows	649	21	28	*
Not applicable because not asked*	775	25	*	*
No information	114	4	5	
c *REGULAR PAYMENTS*				
(i) *Are there things that he has to pay for regularly?*	(n)	(%)		
Yes	1,210	39	52	
No	1,020	33	44	
Not asked*	775	25	5	
No information	108	3		
(ii) *What sorts of things has he to pay for regularly?*‡			Percentage (on 1,210)	
Hire-purchase of clothes	119	4	10 } 28	
Hire-purchase of other items	221	7	18 }	
Rent	157	5	13	
Loan club	28	1	2	
Club	588	19	49	
Magazines/comics/newspapers	245	8	20	
Meals at school/work	27	1	2	
Insurance	73	2	6	

*Not asked
‡Not additive
— = Less than 0.5 per cent

Table 11.8
Relating 'causal' and related variables to the
characteristics of boys
(3,113 cases, weighted)

Characteristics and background of boys	All cases	Is his pocket money sufficient to meet his needs?					Amount of pocket money				
		More than enough	About enough/ enough	Need a little more	Need much more	No informa-tion	Q.1 (up to 10/-)	Q.2 (10/1 – £1)	Q.3 (£1+ – £2)	Q.4 (£2+ – over)	Not classified
Cases (weighted)	3,113	414	1,653	810	210	26	999	839	517	740	18
	(n)	(%)	(%)	(%)	(%)	(%)	(%)	(%)	(%)	(%)	(%)
Occupational level of father											
Professional, semi-professional, managerial	518	13	53	31	3	1	40	31	17	12	–
Highly skilled	514	10	54	27	7	1	38	29	14	18	1
Skilled	674	12	56	25	7	–	29	29	14	28	–
Moderately skilled	630	16	49	28	6	1	30	21	21	27	1
Semi-skilled	517	15	53	21	9	1	26	26	16	31	1
Unskilled	254	13	52	22	13	–	29	28	17	26	–
No information	6										
Nominal Religion											
Protestant	1,370	14	55	23	7	1	Not analysed				
Catholic	500	12	50	28	9	–					
Jewish	214	17	56	25	2	0					
None	621	11	53	29	6	1					
Other	217										
No information	15										
Total money in pocket											
Low sector (1)	999	8	59	28	5	–	Not analysed				
Sector (2)	839	15	52	25	8	1					
Sector (3)	517	19	53	21	6	0					
High sector (4)	740	15	48	28	9	–					
No information	18										
Fun and excitement wanted											
Terrific amount	463	9	44	31	16	–	Not analysed				
Quite a lot	1,102	13	51	28	7	1					
A fair bit	979	14	55	26	5	–					
Some/not much/ none	562	17	62	18	3	1					
No information	7										
Type of school											
Secondary modern	1,464	Not analysed					24	24	19	32	1
Comprehensive	549						32	25	18	23	1
Grammar	718						42	31	14	13	–
Public	257						42	37	13	9	–
Others	105										
No information	20										

When he was younger did he want lots of things he could not afford?			Is there anything he cannot buy with his existing pocket money?			Combining I.Q.2c & II.Q.3		
No	Yes	No information	Claimed nothing	Claimed something at least	No information	Wants exceed means	Wants do not exceed means	Others
1,177	1,862	74	775	2,189	149	538	749	1,826
(%)	(%)	(%)	(%)	(%)	(%)	(%)	(%)	(%)
38	61	1	31	69	1	18	23	59
32	64	3	23	72	5	19	19	62
38	60	2	26	69	5	17	26	57
39	58	3	23	71	6	17	25	58
39	60	1	22	69	9	15	24	61
43	54	3	22	77	1	18	29	53
33	64	2	25	69	5	18	23	59
43	56	1	19	74	7	18	24	57
40	58	2	38	57	5	12	28	60
41	57	2	22	74	3	18	24	59
41	56	3	27	67	4	15	26	59
35	64	1	22	73	5	20	22	58
39	58	2	29	65	6	14	26	60
37	63	—	24	75	2	20	23	57
45	54	1	16	78	6	25	24	51
40	57	3	24	71	5	17	23	60
33	63	2	28	67	4	19	23	58
38	60	2	27	69	4	9	28	64
Not analysed			Not analysed			Not analysed		

Table 11.8 (continued)

Characteristics and background of boys	All cases	Is his pocket money sufficient to meet his needs?					Amount of pocket money				
		More than enough	About enough/ enough	Need a little more	Need much more	No informa- tion	Q.1 (up to 10/-)	Q.2 (10/1 – £1)	Q.3 (£1+ – £2)	Q.4 (£2+ – over)	Not classified
Cases (weighted)	3,113	414	1,653	810	210	26	999	839	517	740	18
	(n)	(%)	(%)	(%)	(%)	(%)	(%)	(%)	(%)	(%)	(%)
Age of boy at interview											
12/13 yrs	719	Not analysed					58	28	11	2	1
14 yrs	782						39	38	17	7	–
15 yrs	754						25	27	22	26	–
16/17 yrs	856						11	17	17	55	–
Job and earning status											
Full-time job	635	Not analysed					1	4	11	85	–
Not full-time job, but he earns	1,421						28	34	25	12	0
Does not earn money	1,016						57	32	8	2	1
No information	41										

— = Less than 0.5 per cent

Some other variables analysed by the characteristics of boys who want something that their pocket money will not buy

Other information collected was analysed by the occupational level of fathers and by the amount of stealing so far done by the boys. This analysis was limited to boys who claimed that there was at least something they wanted that their pocket money would not buy (2,338 cases). Details are given in Table 11.9.

For the boys dealt with in Table 11.9, the main indications are as follows:

1 There is very little variation, by occupational level, in whether boys get parental help, in whether or not they save-up, in having regular financial commitments, in borrowing, in paying-back what was borrowed.

2 Amount of stealing done tends to be unassociated with things like 'getting help from parents with regards to things the boy could not afford'; having regular money commitments; tendency to pay-back after borrowing.

3 On the other hand, there was substantial correlation between occupational level and having a savings account. Also, there was some tendency for boys who did a lot of stealing to be less prone to save-up and more prone to borrow.

Some special analyses related to amount of money in pocket

The variable 'amount of money in pocket' was not put forward as a causal factor. In fact, the estimate of 'amount' was arrived at only as a stage in getting the respondent to consider whether his wants were in excess of what his pocket money would buy. Nonetheless, it is hard to see how amount of money in pocket can be unimportant in the general matter being considered and it seems relevant therefore to correlate it with a number of other variables. This is done in Table 11.10.

The main indications of Table 11.10 are as follows:

1 The total amount of a boy's pocket money does not appear to be related in any significant way to whether or not his wants exceed his (legal) means.

2 There is a substantial relationship between amount of a boy's (legal) pocket money and his involvement in stealing — with the greater the amount of a boy's (legal) pocket money the greater his involvement in stealing. This result, superficially surprising, is no doubt much influenced by the fact that older boys both get more pocket money and have accumulated a greater total incidence of stealing.

When he was younger did he want lots of things he could not afford?			Is there anything he cannot buy with his existing pocket money?			Combining I.Q.2c & II.Q.3		
No	Yes	No informa-tion	Claimed nothing	Claimed some-thing at least	No informa-tion	Wants exceed means	Wants do not exceed means	Others
1,177	1,862	74	775	2,189	149	538	749	1,826
(%)	(%)	(%)	(%)	(%)	(%)	(%)	(%)	(%)
Not analysed			Not analysed			Not analysed		
Not analysed			Not analysed			Not analysed		

Investigating the hypothesis

The strategy of investigation

As in all the previous checks on hypotheses reported in this volume, the basic strategy of investigation was to derive from the hypotheses a range of testable expectations and to test these. If such expectations were verified, the hypothesis would be made more tenable. If not, it would be made less tenable.

The expectations to be tested

1 Boys who say they do not get enough pocket money to meet their needs will have engaged in more stealing than boys who say they *do* get enough to meet their needs.

2 Boys who say there is nothing they definitely want that their pocket money will not buy will have been engaged in less stealing than other boys.

3 Boys who claim that when younger they wanted things they could not buy with their pocket money will tend to have been engaged in more stealing than other boys.

4 Boys who have wants that exceed the limits of their pocket money and who were similarly placed when smaller, will have been engaged in more stealing than boys who deny having been in this situation either now or when they were smaller.

5 Expectation 4 applies even when the two groups are closely matched in terms of the correlates of stealing. Expectation 5 concerns both variety of stealing and amount of stealing.

6 Expectation 5 applies to acts of theft generally rather than to some limited number of different types of theft.

7 Expectation 5 applies also to the duration of serious stealing.

8a When asked to *volunteer* how they get things they want but they cannot afford, many boys will include 'stealing' as a means employed by them.

8b When asked directly if they steal to get the things they want, a large proportion of boys will say they do.

9 When asked what it was that led them to have wants that exceed their means, boys will *not* tend to say it was stealing. This expectation relates to the possibility that it

Table 11.9
Relating various questions to occupational backgrounds of fathers and to the extent of boys' involvement in stealing
(2,338 cases, weighted)*

Characteristics and background of boys	All cases	Occupational level of fathers							Index of amount of stealing			
		Professional semi-professional managerial	Highly skilled	Skilled	Moderately skilled	Semi-skilled	Un-skilled	No information	Low score			High score
Cases (weighted)	2,338	360	398	497	483	401	196	3	0.1	0.2	0.3	0.4
	(n)	(%)	(%)	(%)	(%)	(%)	(%)	(%)	(%)	(%)	(%)	(%)
Do his parents help him when he cannot afford something?												
Yes	2,003	94	82	90	81	87	78		87	88	86	82
No	230	4	10	8	14	9	16		9	8	9	14
No information	105	1	8	2	6	4	6		4	4	5	4
Does he do any saving-up?												
Yes	2,053	88	87	91	86	85	90		94	90	88	81
No	184	7	7	6	9	11	5		3	6	7	15
No information	101	4	7	3	5	4	6		3	4	5	5
Does he have a savings account?												
Yes	1,415	71	73	60	54	52	49		61	63	64	54
No	610	22	13	34	32	34	41		32	29	26	28
No information	28	3	8	2	5	4	6		3	4	5	5
Not applicable	285	4	6	4	9	11	5		4	4	6	12
Are there some things he has to pay for regularly?												
Yes	1,210	50	50	52	56	51	51		46	52	56	53
No	1,020	48	42	46	39	46	43		50	44	39	43
No information	108	1	9	2	5	4	7		4	5	5	5
Does he ever borrow?												
Yes	1,579	74	73	66	63	71	56		62	63	72	73
No	649	23	18	32	32	26	39		33	33	24	23
No information	110	3	9	2	5	4	6		4	5	5	4
Does he pay back what he borrows?												
Never	8	0	0	1	0	0	2		—	—	1	0
Sometimes	201	14	7	9	4	8	3		5	10	7	11
Often	293	11	13	15	14	12	10		8	10	16	17
Always	1,073	50	52	41	40	53	40		49	42	49	45
No information	114	3	9	2	5	4	6		4	5	5	5
Not applicable	649	22	19	32	36	25	39		34	33	23	22

*Based solely on boys who claimed they had wants that their pocket money would not cover
— = Less than 0.5 per cent

Table 11.10
Relating money in pocket
to whether boy feels he
needs more to buy what
he wants
(3,113 cases, weighted)

Characteristics and backgrounds of boys	All cases	Total amount of money in pocket				
		Q.1 up to 10/-	Q.2 10/1–£1	Q.3 £1+–£2	Q.4 £2+	No information
Cases (weighted)	3,113	999	839	517	740	18
	(n)	(%)	(%)	(%)	(%)	
Was 'money in pocket' sufficient to meet his needs/wants?						
More than enough	414	8	15	19	14	
Enough	1,653	59	52	53	48	
Need a bit more	810	28	25	21	28	
Need a lot more	210	5	8	6	9	
No information	26	–	1	0	–	
Is there something he specially wants that his pocket money will not buy?						
Claimed nothing	775	27	22	29	24	
Claimed at least something	2,189	67	73	65	75	
No information	149	4	5	6	2	
In general, his:						
Wants exceed means	538	15	20	14	20	
Wants do not exceed means	749	26	22	26	23	
Others	1,826	59	58	60	57	
When younger, did he have wants that exceeded his means?						
Yes	1,862	56	64	58	63	
No	1,177	41	35	39	37	
No information	74	3	1	2	–	
Quartile distribution of variety of stealing						
Q.1	771	40	23	19	10	
Q.2	769	29	28	19	19	
Q.3	822	19	33	30	26	
Q.4	751	12	16	31	45	
Quartile distribution of amount of stealing						
Q.1	749	41	22	13	12	
Q.2	861	30	32	29	19	
Q.3	779	16	29	31	30	
Q.4	724	12	17	28	41	

— = Less than 0.5 per cent

was 'stealing' that led boys to have wants that exceed means rather than vice versa as hypothesized.

Testing Expectations 1 to 3

These three expectations involve the simple correlational checks presented in Table 11.11.

Expectations 1 and 2 are borne out by the evidence in Table 11.11, but Expectation 3 is not. The failure of Expectation 3, compared with the relative success of Expectations 1 and 2, raises a possibility that 'having wants that exceed one's means' tends not to relate to stealing when boys are quite young ... that it becomes an influential factor only later on.

Testing Expectation 4

This expectation was that there would be differences in terms of variety and amount of stealing between two particular groups of boys, namely: (a) those who say they do not get enough money now and in the past wanted things they could not afford; and, (b) those who say they have enough pocket money now and in the past have not wanted things they could not afford. The results of testing this expectation are set out in Table 11.12.

On the evidence of Table 11.12, Expectation 4 tends to be borne out.

Testing Expectation 5 (using unweighted sample 1,425 cases)

The expectation in this case was that Expectation 4 will still apply when boys in the second of the two named groups (the control group) are matched to boys in the first group (the qualifying group) in terms of the correlates of stealing.

The qualifying and control groups were separated out through the process detailed in Figure 11.1. Group C comprising boys who both need more money to satisfy their wants and felt this way when they were younger, is the control group and Group B, who say they have enough money to satisfy their wants and who say this was also the case when they were younger, is the qualifying group.

Both the qualifying and the control groups were split into matching sub-groups as in all previous uses of the matching technique and the controls were matched to the qualifiers in terms of these sub-groups. The results of this matching procedure are set out in Table 11.13.

The evidence in Table 11.13 tends to support

Table 11.11
Testing Expectations 1 to 3 by relating their central variables to variety and amount of stealing
(3,113 cases, weighted)

Concerning Expectation 1 Is pocket money sufficient to meet his wants?	(n)	Quartile distribution of variety of stealing				Quartile distribution of amount of stealing			
		Q.1 (%)	Q.2 (%)	Q.3 (%)	Q.4 (%)	Q.1 (%)	Q.2 (%)	Q.3 (%)	Q.4 (%)
More than enough	414	32	28	19	22	29	29	22	21
About right	1,653	28	25	25	22	27	30	23	20
Need a bit more	810	19	25	30	25	20	26	27	27
Need much more	210	10	17	34	38	9	13	36	42
No information	26								

Concerning Expectation 2 Was there anything he definitely wanted that his pocket money would not buy?	(n)	Quartile distribution of variety of stealing				Quartile distribution of amount of stealing			
		Q.1 (%)	Q.2 (%)	Q.3 (%)	Q.4 (%)	Q.1 (%)	Q.2 (%)	Q.3 (%)	Q.4 (%)
No, nothing	775	37	25	21	17	32	30	23	15
At least something	2,189	20	25	28	27	21	27	26	26
No information	149								

Concerning Expectation 3 When he was younger, did he want lots of things he could not afford?	(n)	Quartile distribution of variety of stealing				Quartile distribution of amount of stealing			
		Q.1 (%)	Q.2 (%)	Q.3 (%)	Q.4 (%)	Q.1 (%)	Q.2 (%)	Q.3 (%)	Q.4 (%)
Yes	1,862	24	25	27	24	23	29	28	21
No	1,177	27	24	25	24	26	26	22	27
No information	74								

376

Figure 11.1
Division of sample for testing Expectation 5

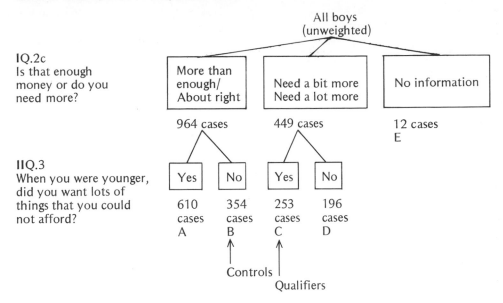

All boys
(unweighted)

IQ.2c
Is that enough
money or do you
need more?

| More than enough/ About right | Need a bit more Need a lot more | No information |

964 cases   449 cases   12 cases E

IIQ.3
When you were younger,
did you want lots of
things that you could
not afford?

Yes   No   Yes   No

610 cases A   354 cases B   253 cases C   196 cases D

↑ Controls

↑ Qualifiers

Table 11.12
Relating state of 'wants exceeding means' to the variety and amount of boys' stealing (3,113 cases, unweighted)

State of 'wants exceeding means'	(n)	Quartile distribution of variety of stealing				Quartile distribution of amount of stealing			
		Q.1 (%)	Q.2 (%)	Q.3 (%)	Q.4 (%)	Q.1 (%)	Q.2 (%)	Q.3 (%)	Q.4 (%)
Wants exceed pocket money now and did in the past	538	15	25	33	27	14	26	33	27
Wants do not exceed pocket money now and did *not* in the past	749	30	27	23	20	28	29	21	22

Table 11.13
Differences between qualifiers and controls before and after matching: variety, amount and duration of stealing

Indices of stealing	Unadjusted average score for qualifiers* a (253 cases)	Unadjusted average score for controls* b (354 cases)	Adjusted average score for controls c	Differences between qualifiers and adj. controls a−c	Difference a−c as percentage of c (%)
Averaged index of variety of stealing	15.46	12.24	12.98	2.48†	19
Averaged index of amount of stealing	107.59	84.56	92.94	14.65†	16
Duration of serious stealing	4.47	3.11	3.67	0.80†	22

*Qualifiers — boys who say they need more money to meet their wants and who felt this way when smaller
Controls — boys who say they do not need more money to meet their needs and who were similarly positioned when they were younger
†Significant at the 0.05 level

Table 11.14
Differences between qualifiers and controls before and after matching: each of the forty-four types of theft

Theft type at Level 2 and over	Unadjusted average score for qualifiers* a (253 cases)		Unadjusted average score for controls* b (354 cases)		Adjusted average score for controls* c		Differences between qualifiers and adj. controls a−c	Difference a−c as percentage of c
	(n)	(%)	(n)	(%)	(n)	(%)		(%)
1	240	94.9	299	85.7	217.87	86.2	8.7	10
2	145	57.3	176	50.4	131.24	51.9	5.4	10
3	118	46.6	125	35.8	92.71	36.7	9.9	27
4	154	60.9	163	46.7	121.01	47.9	13.0	27
5	59	23.3	68	19.5	53.74	21.3	2.0	9
6	164	64.8	188	53.9	139.16	55.0	9.8	18
7	122	48.2	139	39.8	108.01	42.7	5.5	13
8	99	39.1	105	30.1	78.42	31.0	8.1	26
9	49	19.4	47	13.5	35.84	14.2	5.2	37
10	122	48.2	123	35.2	101.03	40.0	8.2	21
11	114	45.1	110	31.5	84.41	33.4	11.7	35
12	50	19.8	51	14.6	37.45	14.8	5.0	34
13	118	46.6	120	34.4	91.72	36.3	10.3	28
14	74	29.2	67	19.2	52.95	20.9	8.3	40
15	45	17.8	36	10.3	28.30	11.2	6.6	59
16	123	48.6	146	41.8	109.41	43.3	5.3	12
17	56	22.1	62	17.8	47.29	18.7	3.4	18
18	190	75.1	201	57.6	154.63	61.2	13.9	23
19	107	42.3	106	30.4	80.42	31.8	10.5	33
20	90	35.6	95	27.2	77.25	30.6	5.0	16
21	31	12.3	46	13.2	33.33	13.2	−0.9	−7
22	108	42.7	121	34.7	87.94	34.8	7.9	23
23	65	25.7	62	17.8	58.29	23.1	2.6	11
24	31	12.3	42	12.0	32.33	12.8	−0.5	−4
25	53	20.9	76	21.8	58.70	23.2	−2.3	−10
26	75	29.6	85	24.4	63.57	25.1	4.5	18
27	55	21.7	57	16.3	44.71	17.7	4.0	23
28	63	24.9	69	19.8	54.81	21.7	3.2	15
29	20	7.9	22	6.3	16.89	6.7	1.2	18
30	144	56.9	131	37.5	110.60	43.7	13.2	30
31	99	39.1	73	20.9	63.41	25.1	14.0	56
32	25	9.9	24	6.9	19.17	7.6	2.3	30
33	174	68.8	205	58.7	156.46	61.9	6.9	11
34	86	34.0	102	29.2	73.89	29.2	4.8	16
35	46	18.2	62	17.8	49.07	19.4	−1.2	−6
36	97	38.3	92	26.4	69.43	27.5	10.8	39
37	13	5.1	12	3.4	10.55	4.2	0.9	21
38	71	28.1	65	18.6	50.05	19.8	8.3	42
39	56	22.1	58	16.6	44.46	17.6	4.5	26
40	175	69.2	215	61.6	159.48	63.1	6.1	10
41	17	6.7	27	7.7	21.84	8.6	−1.9	−22
42	26	10.3	44	12.6	35.05	13.9	−3.6	−26
43	79	31.2	99	28.4	76.52	30.3	0.9	3
44	149	58.9	163	46.7	121.83	48.2	10.7	22

*Qualifiers = boys do not get enough money now and in the past wanted things they could not afford
Controls = boys who have enough money now and in the past have not wanted things they could not afford

378

xpectation 5. It also tends to support Expectation 7,
e. boys in the qualifying group tend to have engaged in
erious stealing over a longer period than boys in the
ontrol group.

esting Expectation 6 (using unweighted ample, 1,425 cases)

his expectation was that Expectation 5 applied gener-
ly and not just to certain classes of thefts. To test this
xpectation, the qualifying and the control groups were
ompared, before and after matching, with respect to
ach of the forty-four classes of theft involved in the
quiry. The results are set out in Table 11.14.

The evidence in Table 11.14 tends to support
xpectation 6, though there are some types of theft for
hich this is not the case.

esting Sub-Expectations 8a and 8b

hese two (related) sub-expectations were:

When asked to *volunteer* how they get things they
vant but cannot afford, many boys will include *stealing*
s a means employed by them.

When asked directly if they steal to get what they
vant, a large proportion of boys will say they do.

he questions asked of boys, as a means of testing these
wo expectations, were:

1(a) 'What do you do about getting things you want *but
can't afford*?'
'What else do you do to get them?' (WAIT FOR IT)

1(f) 'These days, do you have to do any pinching to get
he things you want?' YES/NO
   IF 'YES', 'What sort of things were they — these
hings you wanted?'
'And *how often* do you have to do some pinching for
what you want?'
   LET HIM SAY IT AND THEN OFFER CHOICE
   CARD
   (VERY OFTEN/FAIRLY OFTEN/NOW AND
   THEN/NEVER) CIRCLE CHOICE
'About how much a week would that amount to (in
money)?'

1(g) 'What about in the past — over the last few
years — did you have to pinch *then* to get things you
wanted?' YES/NO
   IF 'YES', SAY: 'What sort of things were they —
these things you wanted?'
   LET HIM SAY IT. THEN OFFER CHOICE CARD.
   (VERY OFTEN/FAIRLY OFTEN/NOW AND
   THEN/NEVER) UNDERLINE HIS CHOICE.

The response details relating to Sub-Expectations 8a and
8b are set out in Tables 11.15 to 11.17.

On the evidence of Table 11.15, Sub-Expectation 8a
is borne out to an appreciable degree.

Table 11.16 presents the evidence related to Sub-
Expectation 8b and confirms it to an appreciable degree.

Replies to Questions 1f and 1g provide further
evidence about 'stealing as a consequence of living
beyond one's means'. They relate to the kinds of things
boys say they steal when living beyond their means.
Details, based on Question 1g, are presented in Table
11.17.

Table 11.15
Showing how many boys say they steal or do other
things to get what they want
(2,338 cases, weighted)*

What does he do to get the things he wants but cannot afford?	(n)	(%)	
Direct reference to stealing	242	10	11%
Buys stolen goods (cheaper)	13	—	
Save-up	1,303	56	
Use personal savings	66	3	
Use money put aside for something else	119	5	
He sells something (not stolen property)	46	2	
Borrows from family	277	12	21%
Borrows from friends/others	130	6	
Gets it on credit	78	3	
Asks family for money for it or to get it for him	639	27	
Gets a job/works to earn money for it	497	21	
Does nothing	87	4	

*Excluding 775 who said they wanted nothing that their
pocket money would not buy
— = Less than 0.5 per cent

Table 11.16
Frequency of claimed pinching to get what was wanted
(2,338* cases, weighted)

Frequency	These days		Over the past few years	
	(n)	(%)	(n)	(%)
Very often	2	—	29	1
Fairly often	23	1	134	6
Now and then	309	13	993	42
Never	1,895	81	1,059	45
No information	109	5	123	5

*Excluding 775 who said they wanted *nothing* that their pocket
money would not buy
— = Less than 0.5 per cent

379

Table 11.17
The kinds of things boys steal when living beyond their means
(2,338* cases, weighted)

Types of things stolen	(n)	(%)
Sweets	395	17
Soft drinks	11	—
Cigarettes	109	5
Comics/magazines/newspapers	72	3
Books	150	6
Stationery/writing equipment	187	8
Toys	158	7
Tape recorder/gramophone/radio	22	1
Equipment for hobbies	67	3
Sports equipment	59	3
Clothes	142	6

*Excluding 775 who said they wanted nothing that their pocket money would not buy
— = Less than 0.5 per cent

Testing Expectation 9

It remains a possibility that the reverse of the hypothesis is true, namely that:

Boys have wants that exceed their means *because* of their involvement in stealing.

Strictly speaking, it is desirable to subject this hypothesis to the full expectation-testing procedure employed in this inquiry. In its absence, however, the boys were asked:

'Now there are some things that you want but can't afford. What led you to want these things?' PROBE FOR EXTENDED REPLY, NOTING THAT WE NEED TO FIND OUT IF HIS *PINCHING* LED HIM TO HAVING WANTS BEYOND HIS MEANS — BUT DON'T SUGGEST THIS TO THE BOY.

The distribution of replies is set out in Table 11.18. This evidence gives very little support to the hypothesis in reverse.

Table 11.18
What led the boy to want things beyond his means?
(2,338 cases, weighted)

Claimed cases	(n)	(%)
His own stealing	20	1⎫
Other people's stealing	8	—⎬1.6%
Own/other's stealing	10	—⎭
Other reasons (i.e. no reference to stealing) or no reason given	2,330	98%

— = Less than 0.5 per cent

5 SUMMING-UP ON THE INVESTIGATION OF THE HYPOTHESIS

1 This chapter is concerned with the investigation of the hypothesis:

When a boy's wants exceed his legal means, he will tend to make up the difference by stealing.

As a basis for the investigation of this hypothesis, ten propositions or expectations were derived from the hypothesis and put to the test. Nine of these related to the hypothesis as stated, while the tenth would follow if the hypothesis were true in reverse. The latter expectation was not borne out when tested. Of the other nine, eight were confirmed by test and the ninth was *not* confirmed. This non-confirmed expectation was that 'boys who claim that when younger they wanted things they could not afford will have done more stealing than other boys'. This particular finding raises the possibility that 'having wants that exceed one's (legal) means' tends not to influence stealing when boys are quite young — and that it becomes an influential factor only later on.

With that limitation, the original hypothesis is made more tenable by the inquiries reported in this chapter. Furthermore, this finding tends to apply both for stealing considered generally and for the majority (but not all) of the different sorts of stealing that boys do. The hypothesized causal process does not appear to work in reverse.

2 Whereas the majority of boys (66 per cent) agree that their pocket money is sufficient for their general needs, only 25 per cent deny that it is insufficient for certain of their (special) wants. These special wants principally involved: clothes or special clothes, sports equipment, equipment for hobbies. Less than 0.3 per cent named food in this connection.

3 Many boys have certain fixed payments to make and for 28 per cent of these boys one such fixed payment is a hire-purchase payment.

6 SOME COMMENTS AND POSSIBLE ACTION

The hypothesis that 'having wants beyond one's legal means contributes to the occurrence of juvenile stealing' is borne out by the findings, though it appears not to be functional for younger boys. Though the causal factor dealt with in the hypothesis does not, on the evidence, appear to be a specially potent one, its social relevance is increased by the fact that so many boys *do* have special wants that exceed their (legal) means.

Some of these special wants of boys are of the kind that only their parents and/or the boy himself could be expected to meet. But others may well be in the province of local authorities and/or welfare organizations and/or schools. These include: records, books, sports equipment, trips and travel. The provision of any such facilities would have to be geared to actual wants of boys as established through intensive interviewing.

Consideration should also be given to the origin of the special wants of boys, possibly with a view to giving boys some protection against the development in them of *unrealistic* wants. The extent of hire-purchase payments by the juveniles studied should also be noted with care.

The present hypothesis might be usefully modified (for any further investigation) by dropping from its expectations the reference to special interests in boys when younger.

APPENDIX 11.1

The Sub-Questionnaire used

Q.1 To find out what his present (lawful) allowance is.
Q.2 To find out how he spends his lawful allowance and what it leaves him wanting.

Q.1 His lawful allowance.

1a 'Do you earn any money by working?' YES/NO
IF 'NO' CHALLENGE WITH: '*Any* kind of work?'
IF HE HAS A JOB, ASK: 'How much a week do you get from this job?' 'How much of that do you keep for your own pocket?'
IF HE WORKS IRREGULARLY, FIND OUT WORK PERIODS
THE AMOUNT EARNED THEN
THE AMOUNT KEPT FOR POCKET

1b (Apart from that) 'Are you given any pocket money each week?' YES/NO
IF 'YES', 'How much?' (TELL HIM THAT THIS DOES NOT INCLUDE MONEY FOR FARES, OR FOR SCHOOL DINNERS OR THE LIKE)

1c 'You've told me that you get pocket money (and money from working)' (PAUSE) 'Now what other money do you get?'
PROBE AND PROMPT FOR ANY OTHER MONEY FROM ANY SOURCE: THIS INCLUDES SPORADIC EARNINGS, ETC.
GET AMOUNTS AND SOURCES. IF IRREGULAR OR SPORADIC, GIVE DETAILS. WORK HARD ON THIS QUESTION
IF HE STARTS MENTIONING *STOLEN* MONEY, TELL HIM YOU MEAN MONEY HE GOT LEGALLY
IF HE REPORTS LEGAL MONEY UNDER 1c ASK:
'Exactly how much of that do you deep for yourself — for your own pocket?'

1d ADD UP WHAT HE GETS A WEEK. SAY:
'So adding it all up, how much money would you say you had for your own pocket each week?'
CHECK AGAINST YOUR OWN ADDITION AND CHALLENGE IF MUCH DIFFERENT. PUT YOUR OWN ADDITION, IN BRACKETS, AFTER HIS ADDITION — IF THE TWO ARE CLOSELY SIMILAR.

Q2 How he spends his lawful allowance and what it leaves him wanting.

2a 'Is that enough pocket money or do you need more?'
SHOW CARD, READ OUT, CIRCLE CHOICE (MORE THAN/RIGHT/BIT/MUCH)
IF POCKET MONEY SAID TO BE 'ABOUT RIGHT' OR 'MORE THAN ENOUGH' CHALLENGE WITH:
'You mean that your pocket money of' (SAY THE AMOUNT PER WEEK) 'is enough for the things you want — that it doesn't leave you wanting things?'

2b 'What do you spend your pocket money on?' (REMIND HIM OF ITS AMOUNT) ('What else?') ('What else?')

2c 'What are the things it is *not* enough for? I mean the things you definitely *want* but can't buy with your pocket money?' (PROMPT AND RE-PROMPT WITH STATEMENTS SUCH AS: 'Anything more?' 'What about when you go out?' Cigarettes? Sweets? 'What else?' 'What else?')
IF THERE IS *NOTHING* HE WANTS UNDER 2c GO TO II,Q.3

II Q.1 How does he pay for/get what he wants but can't afford?
Q.2 Do his excessive wants grow out of his stealing?
Q.3 Did he have wants beyond his means when he was smaller?

Q.1 How does he pay for/get what he wants but can't afford?

1a 'What do you do about getting things you want *but can't afford*?'
'What else do you do to get them?' (*WAIT FOR IT*)

1b 'Do your parents help out by buying things you want but can't afford yourself?' YES/NO
IF 'YES':
'Can you give me some examples?' (PROMPT WITH: 'What else?')

1c 'Do you ever do any saving-up?' YES/NO
IF 'YES':
'Do you have a savings account anywhere?' YES/NO

1d 'Are there some things you have to pay for regularly?' YES/NO
IF 'NO', PROMPT WITH:
'What about HP/rent/club subscriptions/magazine subscriptions?'
IF 'YES':
'What are they?'
PROMPT WITH:
'What about HP, or rent, or club subscriptions or magazines?' (ENTER ALL OTHERS ENUMERATED)
IF 'YES' ON 1d
'How do you pay for these?'
'Any other way at all?'

1e 'Do you ever borrow to pay for the things you want?' YES/NO

IF 'YES':
'Do you pay it back?' (SHOW CARD AND CIRCLE
  CHOICE)
  NEVER/SOMETIMES/OFTEN/ALWAYS
  IF 'ALWAYS', 'OFTEN' OR 'SOMETIMES':
'How do you pay it back?'

1f 'These days, do you have to do any pinching to get
the things you want?' YES/NO
  IF 'YES':
'What sort of things were they — these things you
wanted?'
'And *how often* do you have to do some pinching for
what you want?'
  LET HIM SAY IT AND THEN OFFER CHOICE
  CARD
  (VERY OFTEN/FAIRLY OFTEN/NOW AND
  THEN/NEVER) CIRCLE CHOICE
'About how much a week would that amount to (in
money)?'

1g 'What about in the past — over the last few years —
did you have to pinch *then*, to get the things you
wanted?' YES/NO
  IF 'YES', SAY:

'What sort of things were they — these things yo
wanted?'
'About how often did you have to do pinching to ge
what you wanted?'
  LET HIM SAY IT. THEN OFFER CHOICE CARD
  (VERY OFTEN/FAIRLY OFTEN/NOW AND
  THEN/NEVER) UNDERLINE HIS CHOICE.

1h 'Exactly how old were you when you *first* pinchec
to get things you wanted but could not afford?
(CHALLENGE AGE).

Q 2 Do his excessive wants grow out of his stealing?

  IF HE WANTS THINGS HE CAN'T AFFORD, ASK:
'Now there are some things that you want but can't
afford. What led you to want these things?'
  (PROMPT FOR EXTENDED REPLY, NOTING
  THAT I WANT TO FIND OUT IF HIS *PINCHING*
  LED TO HIS HAVING WANTS BEYOND HIS
  MEANS — BUT DON'T SUGGEST THIS TO BOY)

Q.3 Did he have wants beyond his means when he was
smaller?

'When you were younger, did you want lots of things
you could not afford?' YES/NO

Chapter twelve
Schooling, truancy, ambition, religion

CONTENTS

1 THE COVERAGE OF THIS CHAPTER

In this chapter I have presented information related to schooling, truancy, ambition, and religion. This information was collected and processed to serve two associated purposes, the more important of which was to examine the roles of the above factors as possibly causal in the development of juvenile stealing. Such roles were expressed in the following forms:

1 Boys who play truant from school are thereby made more likely to be involved in stealing.

2a Being backward at school leads boys into greater involvement in stealing.

b Disliking school leads boys into greater involvement in stealing.

3 Being without ambition as to what one will become or do on leaving school predisposes boys to become involved in stealing.

4a A boy's nominal religion is causally related to the amount of stealing he does.

b Frequent attendance at church, chapel or synagogue reduces the amount of a boy's stealing.

The second purpose of the collected data was to provide general background information about each of the factors or conditions hypothesized as causal in character. For example, with respect to truancy we sought to establish the frequency of truancy and its distribution among the different social sectors.

2 RESEARCH PROCEDURES COMMON TO ALL THE HYPOTHESES DEALT WITH IN THE INQUIRY

The gathering of information relevant to the hypotheses about schooling, truancy, ambition and religion was done in the context of an inquiry concerned with over thirty other hypotheses. The techniques relating to the inquiry *as a whole* have been summarized in Chapter 1. That summary deals with sampling procedures; with a technique for getting boys to provide reliable information about any stealing they have done; with questioning procedures for classifying boys in terms of the variables hypothesized as causal factors in the different hypotheses (i.e. in terms of the different independent variables); with strategies for investigating the tenability of hypotheses about causal factors and processes. The reader should as necessary refer to the relevant parts of Chapter 1 in reading statements of findings in the present and subsequent chapters.

3 RESEARCH PROCEDURES APPLYING ONLY TO THE HYPOTHESES DEALT WITH IN THIS CHAPTER

Whereas many aspects of research procedure applied generally to the whole range of hypotheses under study, certain parts of it related only to the variables featured in this chapter. These 'parts' tend to be encapsulated in one of the sub-questionnaires put to boys in the course of the interview and presented in full in Appendix 12.1.

The questions used for classifying boys in terms of the different hypotheses are set out in the context of the relevant sections of this chapter.

4 METHODS AND FINDINGS RELATED TO THE INVESTIGATION OF HYPOTHESIS 1

The nature of the Hypothesis
The first of the hypotheses was as follows:

Boys who play truant from school are thereby made more likely to be involved in stealing.

The distribution of boys in terms of frequency of playing truant from school
In this section are presented: (*a*) the questions asked as bases for classifying boys in terms of truancy; and, (*b*) the distribution of boys in terms of frequency of playing truant.

The questions asked

The questions asked were:

'Do/did you ever play truant from school?' YES/NO
  IF 'NO' CHALLENGE.
  IF 'YES'
(i) 'How often' (ONCE A WEEK/ONCE A MONTH/ HARDLY EVER)
(ii) 'What do/did you do with your spare time when you were playing truant?'
(iii) 'How much pinching do/did you do when you played truant?'

Questions (ii) and (iii) were additional to what was *needed* for classifying boys in terms of frequency of playing truant, but they were meant to provide supplementary information.

Response distributions
For the sample as a whole, the distribution of responses to Question (i) was as shown in Table 12.1.

Table 12.1
Claimed frequency of playing truant
(3,113 cases, weighted)

	(*n*)	(%)	(%)
Yes	1,368		44
Once a week	331	11	
Once a month	262	8	
Hardly ever	766	25	
Frequency not given	9	—	
No or never	1,745		56

— = Less than 0.5 per cent

Truancy analysed in terms of characteristics of boys

Claimed frequency of playing truant was analysed by occupational level of boy's father, type of school last attended, attitude towards school work, how boy gets on with his teachers, frequency of church going, whether boy has an ambition, desire for fun and excitement, whether born in the United Kingdom. Details are given in Table 12.2.

The main indications of Table 12.2 are as follows:

1 Truancy is more likely to occur:

a Amongst the sons of the occupationally less skilled.

b Amongst those who attended comprehensive or secondary-modern schools.

Table 12.2
Analysis of truancy by background and characteristics of boys
(3,113 cases, weighted)

Characteristics	All cases	Does he play truant?		How often does/did he play truant?		
		Yes	No	Once a week	Once a month	Hardly ever
Cases (weighted)	3,113	1,368	1,745	331	262	766
		(%)	(%)	(%)	(%)	(%)
Occupational level of boy's father						
Professional, semi-professional, executive	518	21	79	5	5	11
Highly skilled	514	40	60	10	7	23
Skilled	674	48	52	9	11	29
Moderately skilled	630	48	52	10	11	28
Semi-skilled	517	54	46	19	8	27
Unskilled	254	54	46	15	7	32
No information	6					
Type of school attended						
Secondary modern	1,464	55	45	14	9	32
Comprehensive	549	48	52	15	10	23
Grammar	718	27	72	5	5	18
Public	257	16	84	2	3	11
Other	105					
No information	20					
How does he feel about school work?						
Dislike it very much	81	74	26	40	21	14
Dislike it	597	68	32	19	16	33
Like it	2,117	38	62	8	7	24
Like it very much	312	26	74	5	3	18
No information	6					
How does he get on with his teachers?						
Well	1,287	34	65	7	5	22
Average	1,481	45	55	9	10	26
Not very well	235	66	34	23	13	30
Badly	110	83	17	47	19	17
Frequency of church going						
Never	1,012	57	43	16	13	28
Hardly ever	774	46	54	12	9	25
Once a month	356	37	63	5	4	28
Once a week	791	26	73	4	4	18
No information	180					

Table 12.2 (continued)

Characteristics	All cases	Does he play truant? Yes	Does he play truant? No	How often does/did he play truant? Once a week	How often does/did he play truant? Once a month	How often does/did he play truant? Hardly ever
Cases (weighted)	3,113	1,368	1,745	331	262	766
		(%)	(%)	(%)	(%)	(%)
Does he claim an ambition?						
Yes	2,758	44	56	11	8	24
No	273	42	58	8	8	25
No information	82					
How much fun and excitement does he say he wants?						
A terrific amount	463	58	42	18	15	26
Quite a lot	1,102	49	51	13	10	27
A fair bit	979	39	61	6	6	26
Some	511	31	69	9	5	17
Not much	48 }	21	69	4	0	17
None	3 }					
Born in the UK?						
Yes	2,856	44	55	11	9	25
No	257	38	62	9	4	25

c Amongst those who dislike school.

d Amongst those who do not get on well with their teachers.

e Amongst those who do not attend church, chapel or synagogue.

f Amongst those who want lots of fun and excitement.

g Amongst those who were born in the United Kingdom (i.e. versus immigrants).

2 There is no appreciable relationship between the occurrence of truancy and the existence of an ambition to do something or become something after leaving school.

Investigating Hypothesis 1
The central strategy for investigating Hypothesis 1 (and indeed any of the other hypotheses to be studied) was to derive from it a series of testable *expectations* and to test these. A description of this strategy has already been made in Chapter 1.

Table 12.3
The association between incidence of truancy and amount of stealing (3,113 cases, weighted)

Claims about truancy	All cases	Quartile distribution of variety of stealing Q.1	Q.2	Q.3	Q.4	Quartile distribution of amount of stealing Q.1	Q.2	Q.3	Q.4
		(%)	(%)	(%)	(%)	(%)	(%)	(%)	(%)
Has he ever played truant?									
Yes	1,368	8	18	33	41	10	20	33	37
No	1,745	38	30	21	11	35	33	19	13
Frequency of playing truant									
Once a week	331	2	10	31	57	4	16	30	50
Once a month	262	12	16	24	48	10	18	33	39
Hardly ever	766	9	22	36	33	13	23	34	30
No/never	1,745	38	30	21	11	35	33	19	13
No information	9								

he derivation of the expectations
rom the hypothesis (i.e. that boys who play truant
rom school are thereby made more likely to be involved
n stealing), the following expectations were derived.

Boys who admit they have played truant will also
admit a greater involvement in stealing than boys who
say they have not played truant.

This relationship will hold even after the two popu-
ations concerned are closely matched in terms of the
correlates of stealing.

and 4 When asked what they do/did when playing
truant, boys will tend to volunteer 'stealing' amongst
their other activities and will also, to a greater degree,
endorse stealing as an activity during truancy *if directly
asked if they steal when truanting.*

Testing Expectation 1
The test of Expectation 1 involves establishing the
degree of association between the occurrence of truancy
and the amount of stealing done. The extent of this
relationship is shown in Table 12.3.

This evidence supports Expectation 1. Thus, not only
do boys who have *ever* played truant have a greater
involvement in stealing but *frequency* of playing truant
is also related to the amount of stealing done.

Testing Expectation 2 (using unweighted sample, 1,425 cases)
This expectation was tested on the basis of the 1,425
unweighted cases. To test it, boys were split into two
groups as follows.

Figure 12.1
Division of sample for testing Expectation 2

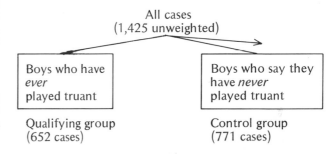

All cases
(1,425 unweighted)

Boys who have *ever* played truant	Boys who say they have *never* played truant
Qualifying group (652 cases)	Control group (771 cases)

Table 12.4
Differences between qualifiers and controls before and after matching: variety and amount of stealing

Indices of stealing	Unadjusted average score for qualifiers* a (625 cases)	Unadjusted average score for controlst b (771 cases)	Adjusted average score for controls c	Differences between qualifiers and adj. controls a–c	P	Difference a–c as percentage of c (%)
Averaged indices of variety of stealing	17.91	9.96	11.93	5.98	0.01	50
Averaged indices of amount of stealing	124.4	63.2	82.7	41.7	0.01	50

*Qualifiers = boys who have *ever* played truant
†Controls = boys who have *never* played truant

Table 12.5
Differences between qualifiers and controls before and after matching: variety and amount of stealing

Indices of stealing	Unadjusted average score for qualifiers* a (157 cases)	Unadjusted average score for controlst b (771 cases)	Adjusted average score for controls c	Differences between qualifiers and adj. controls a–c	P	Difference a–c as percentage of c (%)
Averaged indices of variety of stealing	21.52	9.96	12.58	8.94	0.01	71
Averaged indices of amount of stealing	166.10	65.56	92.91	73.19	0.01	79

*_Qualifiers_ = boys who often play truant
†_Controls_ = boys who never play truant

The controls were then matched to the qualifiers in terms of the correlates of stealing with results as shown in Table 12.4.

The details in Table 12.4 strongly support Expectation 2.

As a further check on Expectation 2, the matching operation was carried out afresh with a slightly different standard for 'qualification' in terms of the hypothesis. In this case, the qualifiers were defined as those boys who said they played truant once a week or more, and the controls were boys who said they *never* played truant. Matching was carried out in the usual way, with the results shown in Table 12.5.

Here, too, the expectation is very substantially confirmed.

Testing Expectations 3 and 4
Boys were asked to say what they did when they played truant. A randomly-drawn collection of their replies given below and this is followed by Table 12.6 based on the responses of *all* the boys.

'When my mother isn't home cause she has to go [to] work, I just stay in the house and sit there reading. [If] my mum is at home, we go out down to Woolwich – places like that.'

'Stayed in my friend's house and got into trouble.'

Boy said that when he plays truant these days it only consists of leaving school about half an hour early so that all he does is go straight home. About two year[s] ago he had a week off and stayed down his mate['s] house. One other period of two days when he and [his] mates went to cinemas in town.

'Go round the High Street shops, cafes. There's [a] Wimpy bar. (INT: 'What do you go round the shops for?') 'Just looking, clothes.'

'Usually go with some of my friends. Usually go fishing. If there was some place we wanted to go, we'd have it off. Go to exhibitions at Earl's Court. Go to the pictures.'

'Go to bed.'

'Went swimming.'

'Go home. Play football round the back with other boys.'

'Stay indoors.'

'Went up to my mate's house and listened to records.'

'There was two or three of us used to play truant. Sit around and play records and invite some girls round that we know in one of my friend's houses.'

(i) 'Went to pictures.'   (ii) 'I stayed at home.'

'Went down to cafes and wandered round. Nothing special. We used to go round to boys' houses to have coffee.'

'Nothing – probably cook the dinner.' (Boy had previously said that he had missed school in order to visit father in hospital.)

'Listened to records at home. Arranged to meet some girl. Or just go swimming. Anything to get away from school. I used to hate it. Anything rather than school.'

'We just walked around. Looked in shops.'

'My mates dared me to so I did. I played football and then just walked around.'

'I used to sit and watch the schools programmes on the TV, read some books, listen to the radio.'

Table 12.6

What boys said they did when they played truant
(3,113 cases, weighted)

Activity claimed	No. and percentage claimed	
	(*n*)	(%)
Any reference to stealing	51	2
Making a nuisance of themselves/annoying people	21	1
Destroying property/vandalism	5	—
Fighting/watching fights	3	—
Trespassing/going places where he should not go	28	1
Informal unstructured activities with or without mates (e.g. walking around/going to friends' houses)	727	23
With a girl/with girlfriend	63	2
Physically-active sport	208	7
More sedentary indoor games	63	2
Go to the cinema	194	6
Listen to radio or gramophone/watch television	147	5
Go home/stay at home/stay in bed	366	12
Doing homework/studying	70	2
Helping with household chores	27	1
Pursuing hobbies or interests	76	2
Reading	67	2
Go shopping/looking around in shops	83	3
Take part in a sport that you do in the country (e.g. golf, fishing)	62	2
Playing on a boat/looking at a boat	23	1
Went to see some place of interest (e.g. museum, art gallery, library)	81	3
Go out to visit places/make a trip	117	4
Go out on a bike/scooter	33	1
Watch sports	32	1
Go to fun fair	17	1

— = Less than 0.5 per cent

'Fishing'

'I go over my mate's house and play records. Might go up to the West End, just to look around.'

'Go to the park. Go and see my mate.'

Boy told his mother he had a cold and stayed indoors.

'Went to the park for a walk round.'

'The two times we played truant there was a football match on TV — that's all we played it for.'

'Most of the time we go to Paddington Recreation — walk there and back.'

'Go round to my sister's and tell I've been sent home from school and that Mum was not in. Go to pictures. Swimming.'

'Used to visit Madame Tussaud's in his last year at school or go for a walk in Regent's Park.'

'Go to cafe or park or museum.'

'Played in park.'

'Went to pictures or walked about with my mates.' He also went to exhibitions or to his mates' houses.

The main activities detailed in the responses for all the boys who said they played truant are set out in Table 12.6.

The indications of Table 12.6 are as follows and they give scant support to the hypothesis.

1 Only 2 per cent of the boys directly volunteered stealing as an activity during truancy.

2 The most frequently-volunteered activity (during truancy) was informal/unstructured activity with or without mates.

3 A lot of boys simply went home or stayed at home.

In testing Expectation 4, the respondent was asked directly if he did any stealing when he was playing truant. Responses are listed in Table 12.7.

The detail in Table 12.7 suggests that an appreciable amount of stealing goes on during truancy and, not surprisingly, suggests that 'stealing during truancy' occurs more often amongst those who play truant more frequently. Whereas the evidence supports Expectation 4, that support is by no means marked.

Summing-up on the investigation of Hypothesis 1

The tests of Expectations 1 and 2 were verified and provide strong support for the hypothesis. On the other hand, the test of Expectation 4 is not supportive of the hypothesis to anything like the same degree and that of Expectation 3 is hardly supportive at all.

In all likelihood the special weakness of Expectation 3 arises partly from the non-probing form of Question 4(ii), for boys *did* admit much more 'stealing while truanting' when directly asked about it in Question 4(iii) for the test of Expectation 4. But even Expectation 4 came through the testing operation with much less strength than Expectations 1 and 2.

One possible explanation of this outcome that must be faced is that there has been a methodological failure of some kind. But it seems to the writer that there is another possible explanation of an enlightening kind. *On the one hand*, Expectations 3 and 4 relate to stealing done *while* truanting — a time when boys could reasonably be expected to be trying to keep 'out of the way' as much as possible, so that they are in a situation not very conducive to the general run of juvenile thieving. Expectations 1 and 2, *on the other hand*, relate to thieving at any time and not specifically in the period of the truanting behaviour. The likelihood thus exists that truanting does not operate directly and spontaneously as a causal factor in thieving. Thus it may be that truanting (which tends to be done in company with other truants) by a given boy serves to develop his association with one

Table 12.7

Relating claimed frequency of truancy to claimed frequency of stealing while truanting

Claimed frequency of truanting Cases (weighted)	All cases 1,368	Claimed frequency of stealing while truanting					
		Never 1,006	Hardly ever 175	Now and then 36	Fairly often 54	Frequency unclear 72	No information 25
	(n)	(%)	(%)	(%)	(%)	(%)	(%)
Once a week	331	62	15	6	9	7	1
Once a month	262	68	15	3	6	6	2
Hardly ever	766	81	11	1	1	4	2
No information	9						

or more others in a context of regulation breaking — a situation that could foster thieving later on, at some more opportune time. If the boys with whom the truant teams up (for or during truancy) happen to be thieves anyhow, then we may well have a rather catalytic beginning to 'thief association' — a condition which the findings in Chapter 5, and which many criminologists suggest, is rather potent in the development of stealing.

At the methodological level, it must be remembered that when the truancy questions were asked, boys had already been through a phase of intensive questioning about their stealing and had between them made extensive and major admissions. So it is unlikely that they were being especially secretive about stealing when asked about it in the truancy context.

In the circumstances, the writer regards the evidence collected as supporting the hypothesis, but advises investigation of the particular way in which truancy promotes stealing.

5 METHODS AND FINDINGS RELATED TO THE INVESTIGATION OF SUB-HYPOTHESES 2a AND 2b

The nature of the sub-hypotheses
The sub-hypotheses dealt with in this chapter are as follows.

Being backward at school leads boys into greater involvement in stealing. (Sub-Hypothesis 2a.)

and

Disliking school leads boys into greater involvement in stealing. (Sub-Hypothesis 2b.)

The distribution of boys in terms of the variables put forward as causal in character
In this section are presented: (*a*) the questions asked as a basis for classifying boys as qualifying or not in terms of the hypotheses, and, (*b*) the distribution of boys in terms of the variables hypothesized as causal.

The 'measurement' of backwardness
The hypothesis about backwardness was not put forward as a central one or anything like it. Furthermore, the information collection system available to the project — bearing in mind all the other measurements that had to be made — did not allow for any direct measurement of 'backwardness'. What was intended, however, was to propose a fairly simple *index* of backwardness, at the same time warning that this index was not empirically developed.

To this end, the education questionnaire carried questions about:

1 'Passing' the 11-plus examination.

2 Type of school last attended.

3 Where relevant, what stream the boy was in/what part of the comprehensive system he was in.

4 Where the boy usually came in his class.

5 Whether any examinations had been passed and which ones.

In the event, it was decided that classification of boys as qualifying or not (in terms of the sub-hypotheses) should be limited to: type of school last attended; stream or sector within school where relevant; whether in higher or lower class position where relevant. Details are shown in Table 12.9.

The measure of liking/disliking school
In order to rate boys in terms of like/dislike of school, two types of questions were asked.

(i) How much he liked or disliked school work ['At . . . school, how did you feel about your school work?' (SHOW CARD AND CODE CHOICE)]

(ii) How did he get on with his teachers? ['At . . . school, how did you get on with most of your teachers.' (SHOW CARD AND CODE CHOICE)]

Table 12.8
Reactions to school work/teachers
(3,113 cases, weighted)

	(*n*)	(%)
Attitude towards school work		
Dislike very much	81	3
Dislike	597	19
Like	2,117	68
Like very much	312	10
No information	6	—
How well did he get on with teachers?		
Well	1,287	41
Average	1,481	48
Not very well	235	8
Badly	110	4
No information	0	0

The distribution of key responses
Responses to two such questions are shown in Table 12.8.

Table 12.9 repeats certain basic educational data given elsewhere in this report and provides in addition: (*a*) evidence about the claims of secondary-modern school boys concerning which educational stream they were in; and, (*b*) evidence about the claims of boys in comprehensive schools about which sector of the school

390

hey were in. These extra details should be interpreted relatively and not as absolutes, their purpose being to allow the comparison of school status in terms of theft level – rather than to provide status information in its own right.

Table 12.9
Claims about last school attended
(3,113 cases, weighted)

School last attended	(n)	(n)	(%)	(%)
Secondary-modern school		1,464		47
upper stream	435		14	
middle stream	331		11	
lower stream	361		12	
other	337		11	
No information				
Comprehensive school		549		18
Secondary modern sector	82		3	
Technical sector	69		2	
Grammar sector	164		5	
Other	234		8	
No information				
Grammar school		718		23
Public school		257		8
Other types of school		105		3
No information about school last attended		20		1

Noteworthy features of Table 12.9 are: the claim by a majority (78 per cent) that they like or liked school work; the claim by only 12 per cent that they got on 'badly' or 'not very well' with their teachers.

Some other distributions of relevance
Other of the questions asked produced the distributions of responses set out in Table 12.10.

Several of the more noteworthy indications of Table 12.10 are:

1 The denial by 56 per cent that they every played truant.

2 The tiny proportion of boys who denied liking *any* subject at school (1 per cent).

The list of subjects set out in Table 12.10 should be interpreted with care, for it reflects the *volunteering* of such subjects by boys in a long interview. In all likelihood, most of the listed subjects would get higher ratings if a checklist rating system were used. As they stand, the details presented in Table 12.10 indicate the 'topics that spring most readily to mind as liked'.

Table 12.10
Other distributions
(3,113 cases, weighted)

	(n)	(%)
Did he 'pass' the 11+ examination?		
Yes	172	6
No	1,539	49
Not taken	173	6
Not asked because boy was at grammar or public school	997	32
No information	232	7
Was he still at school at time of the interview?		
Yes	2,402	77
No	683	22
Left school aged 14–15	536	17
Left school aged 16–17	147	5
No information	28	1
How often did he play truant?		
Not at all	1,745	56
Hardly ever	766	25
About once a month	262	8
About once a week	331	11
Frequency not established	9	–
Were there any subjects he liked?		
Yes	3,059	98
No	46	1
Undecided	8	–

What subjects were liked by boys?

	Percentage volunteering subject		Percentage volunteering subject
English (language or literature)	28	Art	19
History	31	Music	4
British Constitution	1	Drama/acting	2
Modern languages	13	Crafts	2
Latin/Greek	3	Pottery	2
'Maths'	35	Technical drawing	13
Geography	27	Woodwork	17
Science (unspecified)	13	Metal work	15
Physics	12	Building	1
Chemistry	10	Engineering	3
Biology/zoology/botany	8	Religious instruction	4
Social studies/Civics	1	Physical education/gym	20
Current affairs	–	Sports	18
Economics	1	Reading	1
Commerce/office practice	1		

– = Less than 0.5 per cent

Key variables analysed in terms of the characteristics of boys
Claims about school background were analysed by occupational level of father and a large number of other

Table 12.11
Level of schooling achieved analysed by characteristics
of boys
(3,113 cases, weighted)

Characteristics of boys	Secondary modern school				Comprehensive school				Grammar school	Public school	Other or NI
	Lower stream	Middle stream	Upper stream	Other or no information	Sec. mod. sector	Technical sector	Grammar sector	Other or no information			
Cases (weighted)	361	331	435	337	82	69	164	234	718	257	125
	(%)	(%)	(%)	(%)	(%)	(%)	(%)	(%)	(%)	(%)	(%)
Occupational level of father											
Professional, semi-professional, executive	1	6	7	4	1	6	10	5	28	78	14
Highly skilled	13	16	15	8	4	32	25	17	23	15	11
Skilled	18	22	20	32	29	20	27	34	20	3	29
Moderately skilled	28	21	28	26	18	16	13	17	17	3	28
Semi-skilled	26	23	20	18	38	17	15	20	8	1	13
Unskilled	15	12	10	11	10	9	9	7	3	0	5
No information**	0	1	0	1	0	0	0	0	0	0	0
Nominal religion											
Protestant	37	38	44	50	65	52	45	58	42	39	50
Catholic	19	18	19	12	2	13	17	8	19	14	11
Other Christian	7	7	8	6	4	0	9	5	4	2	9
Jewish	0	2	–	1	0	0	2	6	17	25	0
None	29	26	19	22	23	19	18	15	14	17	25
Frequency of church attendance											
Never	49	45	29	38	44	38	42	47	18	10	31
Hardly ever	23	20	27	27	29	10	27	23	28	21	24
Once a month	10	9	10	11	12	13	9	6	13	23	7
Once a week	13	19	27	20	11	32	20	17	36	39	26
No information	5	6	7	5	4	7	2	7	5	7	12
Truancy ever?											
No	39	43	52	44	52	44	55	51	72	84	54
Yes	61	57	48	56	48	56	45	49	27	16	46
Once a week	17	16	11	12	18	12	15	15	5	2	6
Once a month	11	12	7	7	5	12	12	11	5	3	23
Hardly ever	32	28	30	37	24	33	19	23	18	11	16
Like school work?											
Dislike very much	6	5	2	3	5	0	1	3	2	0	0
Dislike	26	24	18	20	21	15	13	15	18	14	16
Like	63	65	67	65	69	77	72	74	72	69	65
Like very much	5	6	12	13	4	9	13	9	8	17	18
How does he get on with teachers?											
Well	36	31	40	41	34	51	57	33	41	60	46
Average	44	53	52	48	54	44	35	57	49	38	50
Not very well	15	7	7	10	6	6	7	6	8	2	2
Badly	6	9	2	2	6	0	1	4	2	0	2

Table 12.11 (continued)

Characteristics of boys	Secondary modern school				Comprehensive school				Grammar school	Public school	Other or NI
	Lower stream	Middle stream	Upper stream	Other or no information	Sec. mod. sector	Technical sector	Grammar sector	Other or no information			
Cases (weighted)	361	331	435	337	82	69	164	234	718	257	125
	(%)	(%)	(%)	(%)	(%)	(%)	(%)	(%)	(%)	(%)	(%)
Room of his own?											
Yes	51	47	59	55	60	60	65	57	69	79	60
No	49	51	41	43	39	40	35	41	31	21	40
No information	0	2	0	2	1	0	0	2	0	0	0
*Index of crowdedness in home**											
0.5 or less	1	6	4	6	4	2	7	10	12	16	10
0.51–0.75	15	14	23	16	9	12	24	13	30	48	21
0.76–1.00	38	31	39	26	60	35	33	38	38	27	36
1.01–1.25	9	17	10	19	13	18	14	15	7	4	2
1.26–1.50	16	18	13	14	9	22	10	7	10	4	14
1.51–2.00	8	6	4	6	2	3	8	4	3	2	9
2.01 or over	12	7	7	12	4	9	1	9	1	0	8
No information	1	1	0	1	0	0	3	3	0	0	0
Hours of homework per week†											
None	40	31	23	29	34	25	15	23	7	13	31
Up to 1 hr	14	14	5	12	4	3	6	4	1	0	2
1–3 hrs	22	17	21	12	11	7	7	17	3	1	9
3–5 hrs	7	23	16	22	20	14	12	16	11	8	20
5–8 hrs	9	6	16	9	20	22	23	21	25	15	20
8–15 hrs	4	2	13	5	10	28	28	14	43	43	15
15 hrs +	1	3	3	5	0	0	9	2	11	18	3
No information	3	4	2	5	2	1	2	4	1	2	0
Does he go out just looking for fun and excitement?											
Often	8	12	5	7	11	6	2	7	3	—	7
A fair bit	19	9	10	12	9	10	6	6	4	4	3
Now and then	24	27	25	20	6	19	16	17	15	14	20
Hardly ever	9	9	8	3	18	10	10	4	7	8	9
Never	40	42	52	57	56	55	67	66	71	74	61
No information	0	—	1	1	0	0	0	0	0	0	0
Quartile distribution of interests scores‡											
Q.1 (= Most interests)	22	21	27	30	16	28	19	34	16	28	27
Q.2	17	18	27	20	18	26	17	12	23	25	19
Q.3	26	34	20	23	33	15	34	27	31	21	26
Q.4 (= Least interests)	35	26	26	26	33	32	31	26	30	26	28

continued

Table 12.11 (continued)

Characteristics of boys	Secondary modern school				Comprehensive school				Grammar school	Public school	Other or NI
	Lower stream	Middle stream	Upper stream	Other or no information	Sec. mod. sector	Technical sector	Grammar sector	Other or no information			
Cases (weighted)	361	331	435	337	82	69	164	234	718	257	125
	(%)	(%)	(%)	(%)	(%)	(%)	(%)	(%)	(%)	(%)	(%)
Index of liking school and teachers											
Likes school work and gets on well with teachers	59	65	76	72	67	84	81	77	76	86	69
Likes school work but gets on badly with teachers	9	6	4	5	5	1	5	6	4	0	7
Dislikes school work but gets on well with teachers	20	19	16	16	18	10	12	13	14	13	20
Dislikes school work and gets on badly with teachers	12	10	5	7	7	4	3	5	6	2	3

*The smaller the index the less crowded the home
**NI = no information
†These figures must be interpreted *relatively* only — not as absolutes
‡Q.1 = boys with most interests; Q.4 = boys with least interests
— = Less than 0.5 per cent

variables as listed in Tables 12.11 and 12.12. The first of them deals with the educational status of the boys and the second with whether boys liked school work and their teachers.

The main indications of Table 12.11 appear to be as follows.

1 Not surprisingly, there is a marked tendency for occupational level of fathers to be related to the school status of their sons. For example: lower-stream boys in secondary-modern schools tend more than upper-stream boys to be the sons of the less skilled; similarly for secondary-modern school boys within the comprehensive system in relation to grammar-school boys within that system; public-school boys tend more than any other group to have fathers in the professional and semi-professional sector.

2 What is less obvious is the difference in occupational background of the fathers of boys in grammar schools *within* and *outside* the comprehensive system — the latter being of higher occupational status than the former. Also noteworthy is the great extent of the occupational difference between fathers of public-school boys and those of grammar-school boys.

3 There are differences in the religious denomination of boys of different school status, but the outstanding one relates to Jewish boys: they have only minor representation in the secondary-modern and comprehensive systems, but major representation in the grammar-school and public-school systems.

4 Frequency of church attendance is greater for upper-stream secondary-modern boys than for the middle- and lower-stream boys and is greatest of all for public-school boys. It appears also to be much greater for grammar-school boys outside of the comprehensive system than for grammar-school boys within the comprehensive system.

5 Truancy increases quite sharply in going from upper to lower status in the secondary-modern system and is lowest for public-school boys. More of the grammar-school boys in the comprehensive system claim truancy than grammar-school boys outside that system and the same tendency applies with respect to *frequency* of truanting.

6 'Liking school work' is at its lowest among the lower-stream boys of the secondary-modern system and

Table 12.12
Attitudes to school work and teachers analysed by
characteristics of boys
(3,113 cases, weighted)

Characteristics of boys	All cases	Indices of liking school				NI*
		Like school work & get on well with teachers	Like school work & get on badly with teachers	Dislike school work & get on well with teachers	Dislike school work & get on badly with teachers	
Cases (weighted)	3,113	2,280	149	482	196	6
	(n)	(%)	(%)	(%)	(%)	
Occupational level of father						
Professional, semi-professional, executive	518	18	10	13	10	
Highly skilled	514	18	10	10	16	
Skilled	674	22	27	18	18	
Moderately skilled	630	19	25	28	17	
Semi-skilled	517	15	20	21	26	
Unskilled	254	7	8	10	14	
No information	16					
Nominal religion						
Protestant	1,370	45	35	42	41	
Catholic	500	15	20	18	17	
Jewish	214	7	4	6	6	
None	621	18	27	24	28	
Other religions	217					
No information	15					
Frequency of church attendance						
Never	1,012	29	40	41	51	
Hardly ever	774	25	22	22	26	
Once a month	356	14	15	10	6	
Once a week	791	29	15	19	11	
No information	180	5	9	8	7	
Truancy ever?						
No	1,745	45	32	33	26	
Yes	1,368	35	68	67	75	
Once a week	331	6	32	18	30	
Once a month	262	6	14	17	15	
Hardly ever	766	23	22	32	29	
Frequency not known	9					
Like school work?						
Dislike very much	81	0	0	8	22	
Dislike	597	0	0	92	78	
Like	2,117	87	95	0	0	
Like very much	312	13	5	0	0	
No information	6					
How does he get on with teachers?						
Well	1,287	50	0	29	0	
Average	1,481	50	0	71	0	
Not very well	235	0	75	0	63	
Badly	110	0	25	0	37	
No information	0	0	0	0	0	

*NI - No Information.

continued

Table 12.12 (continued)

Characteristics of boys	All cases	Indices of liking school				
		Like school work & get on well with teachers	Like school work & get on badly with teachers	Dislike school work & get on well with teachers	Dislike school work & get on badly with teachers	NI
Cases (weighted)	3,113	2,280	149	482	196	6
	(n)	(%)	(%)	(%)	(%)	
Room of his own?						
Yes	1,885	60	59	62	65	
No	1,208	40	41	37	35	
*Index of crowdedness of the home**						
0.5 or less	236	7	8	7	7	
0.51–0.75	707	24	28	16	20	
0.76–1.00	1,097	36	22	36	34	
1.01–1.25	340	10	6	16	15	
1.25–1.50	369	12	17	12	10	
1.51–2.00	150	5	7	7	6	
2.01 or over	185	6	12	5	8	
No information	29					
Hours of homework per week						
None	690	17	39	33	44	
Up to 1 hr	191	5	9	7	10	
1–3 hrs	367	11	14	13	12	
3–5 hrs	451	15	17	15	10	
5–8 hrs	512	18	5	11	12	
8–15 hrs	639	24	7	13	7	
15 hrs plus	184	8	1	3	1	
No information	79	2	7	4	5	
Does he go out just looking for fun and excitement?						
Often	182	4	4	12	8	
A fair bit	260	7	7	11	15	
Now and then	605	18	28	19	29	
Hardly ever	236	8	10	6	10	
Never	1,823	62	52	52	39	
No information	7					
Quartile distribution of interests score†						
Q.1 (= Most interests)	723	27	12	18	7	
Q.2	647	21	32	19	20	
Q.3	834	26	28	30	27	
Q.4 (= Least interests)	892	26	28	34	46	
No information	17					

*The less crowded the home, the lower the index (0.5 = two persons per room)

†Q.1 = boys with most interests; Q.4 = boys with least interests

greatest amongst public-school boys. But a noteworthy feature of the findings is the similarity of the figures across the educational spectrum.

7 In terms of getting on well with teachers, public-school boys came out best and middle-stream secondary-modern school boys worst. But the grammar-school boys *within* the comprehensive system appear to get on better with their teachers than the grammar-school boys *outside* the comprehensive system.

8 Boys in the middle and lower streams of secondary-modern schools tend more than other boys to 'go out just looking for fun and excitement', but this activity is claimed by an appreciable number of boys in each of the educational levels referred to in Table 12.11.

9 The number of a boys' interests varies somewhat by educational sector, being higher among the upper-stream boys in the secondary-modern system than amongst middle- and lower-stream boys; but it was slightly lower for grammar-school boys than for secondary-modern boys.

10 Liking both schoolwork and teachers (see index) also varies somewhat by educational status, being most frequent amongst public-school boys and least frequent amongst boys in the lower stream in secondary-modern schools. But the outstanding feature of this section of data is the overall high frequency of this favourable reaction.

11 There is much variation in the amount of homework different boys claim to do, the variation being in the expected directions. What is especially noteworthy is the large proportion of boys who claim they do/did no homework at all.

Table 12.12 deals with boys' attitudes to school work and their teachers and, like the previous tables, is best studied by the reader for the extraction of those of its many indications that are of special interest to him. At a general level, however, its main indications appear to be as follows.

1 Tendency to like school and teachers is greater among the sons of the professional sector; those who go often to church or chapel or synagogue; those who say they have never played truant; those who say they do a lot of homework; those who say they never go out just looking for fun and excitement; those who say they have lots of interests.

2 There is relatively little association between attitudes to school work and teachers and the following variables: having a room of one's own; crowdedness of the home.

Relating permissiveness towards stealing to educational variables

Table 12.13 relates the two educational variables featured in this study to an index of permissiveness towards stealing. For each boy, this index is the average

Table 12.13

Backwardness at school and liking of school related to permissiveness towards stealing (3,113 cases, weighted)

	Index of permissiveness*
Position in school system	
Secondary-modern school	
Lower stream	1.9
Middle stream	2.1
Upper stream	2.0
Comprehensive school	
Secondary-modern sector	2.0
Technical sector	1.9
Grammar sector	1.8
Grammar school	1.8
Public school	1.6
Like/dislike of school	
Likes school work and likes teachers	1.8
Likes school work but dislikes teachers	2.3
Dislikes schoolwork but likes teachers	2.1
Dislikes schoolwork and dislikes teachers	2.5

*See Chapter 5 on 'Permissiveness'. The lower the index, the less permissive is the boy in relation to stealing. The Index of Permissiveness was calculated by computing the mean weighted score of a boy with respect to his rating of the goodness or badness of committing twenty-five different types of theft, where 'quite all right' = 5; 'nothing much wrong' = 4; 'a bit wrong' = 3; 'fairly wrong' = 2; 'very wrong' = 1; 'can't decide' = 3

of the twenty-five ratings he made of how acceptable or otherwise he would find it to commit certain acts of theft (twenty-five in all). Details of this rating system are given in Chapter 5 which is especially concerned with 'Permissiveness towards stealing'.

In interpreting the evidence in Table 12.13 it may be taken that a difference between two ratings of 0.3 is statistically significant and one of 0.4 is highly so.

It thus appears that:

1 Public-school boys are significantly less permissive towards stealing than are boys from secondary-modern schools especially those in the low stream.

2 Boys who dislike both school and their teachers are markedly more permissive towards stealing than boys who *like* both school and their teachers.

Investigating Sub-Hypotheses 2a and 2b

For studying these two sub-hypotheses, it was intended that two expectations be derived from each and that these be tested in the usual way. The two expectations were to have involved: (*a*) a test of the association

Table 12.14
The association between aspects of schooling and past involvement in stealing
(3,113 cases, weighted)

Aspects of schooling	All cases 3,113 (n)	Quartile distribution of variety of stealing				Quartile distribution of amount of stealing			
		Q.1 (%)	Q.2 (%)	Q.3 (%)	Q.4 (%)	Q.1 (%)	Q.2 (%)	Q.3 (%)	Q.4 (%)
School status									
Secondary-modern schooling									
Lower stream	361	13	19	35	34	16	28	27	29
Lower class position	95	13	25	36	26	24	28	31	17
Higher class position	239	12	15	35	38	14	26	26	34
Not known	27								
Middle stream	331	19	15	27	39	20	19	28	32
Lower class position	104	18	9	38	36	14	19	33	34
Higher class position	201	20	17	22	41	24	17	27	31
Not known	26								
Top stream	435	22	25	30	23	22	26	29	23
Lower class position	79	24	22	29	25	24	18	23	35
Higher class position	337	21	26	31	22	22	26	32	20
Not known	19								
No stream	203	21	18	33	28	19	24	30	28
Stream not known	134								
Comprehensive schooling									
Secondary-modern sector	82	28	22	26	24	29	17	32	22
Technical sector	69	25	10	36	29	15	26	23	36
Grammar sector	164	28	29	17	26	27	30	25	18
Other sectors/sector not known	234								
Grammar school	718	32	33	20	15	30	30	23	17
Public school	257	39	29	23	9	28	43	14	15
Other schools	105								
No information	20								
Likes/dislikes at school									
Likes school work and likes teachers	2,280	30	27	25	19	29	29	23	19
Likes school work but dislikes teachers	149	3	10	32	56	4	12	44	40
Dislikes school work but likes teachers	482	16	24	31	29	17	27	26	30
Dislikes school work & dislikes teachers	196	3	17	34	46	4	24	30	42
Whether still at school									
Aged 15 yrs									
Still at school	561	24	24	34	17	19	33	27	21
Left school	193	18	17	28	38	19	16	26	39
Aged 16–17 yrs									
Still at school	364	22	29	29	19	26	22	26	27
Left school	492	9	18	23	50	10	19	31	41

*Omitting boys who could not yet have left school (i.e. under fifteen years)

between the postulated causal factors and stealing; and, (b) an assessment of the difference between qualifying and control groups after empirical matching.

In the event, the test by matching was not made, the principal reason being the complexity of the computer processing required in the case of Sub-Hypothesis 2a combined with the shortage of funds for the matching analyses.

The expectations derived and tested were as follows.

1 *Concerning Sub-Hypothesis 2a.* The higher the educational status of boys, the less stealing they will have committed.

2 *Concerning Sub-Hypothesis 2b.* Boys who tend to like both school work and teachers will tend to have done less stealing than other boys.

The results of testing these two expectations are presented in Table 12.14 and they lend a degree of support to each expectation.

A conclusion about the result of testing *Expectation 1* depends to some degree upon the definition of 'backwardness' that is adopted. Thus:

1 If boys of *secondary-modern school background* are regarded as 'backward' in relation to grammar-school and public-school boys, then Expectation 1 is borne out. At the same time we must note that the secondary-modern boys *within* the *comprehensive* system are not much different in terms of theft level from the grammar-school boys in the comprehensive system and are much less involved in stealing than are boys in the secondary-modern system as such.

2 If we describe as 'backward' the boys in the lower and the middle streams in the secondary-modern system, then Expectation 1 is borne out — in that these boys do more stealing than boys in the top stream of the secondary-modern system. It is noteworthy, however, that there is little difference in theft level between the lower and middle streams.

3 If we define as 'backward' boys in the lower class positions within the lower stream in the secondary-modern system, then Expectation 1 is *not* borne out — in that these boys appear to do *less* stealing than those in the higher class positions in the lower stream. Indeed, they appear to do less stealing than secondary-modern boys generally and about the same as grammar-school boys within the comprehensive system.

So whether Expectation 1 is borne out by the present evidence (Table 12.14) is dependent on the definition of

'backward' adopted. Whatever is decided on that score, the fact remains that *degree* of backwardness is not correlated with theft level in the form of a straight-line relationship.

Expectation 2 is also borne out in that boys who like school work and teachers have lower than average theft 'scores' and those who dislike either teacher or school work or both have higher than average theft 'scores'. On the evidence, the more powerful of these two (linked) discriminants of theft behaviour is how the boy feels about his teacher. Thus, boys who dislike their teachers are especially prone to be involved in stealing.

What must be remembered in interpreting this evidence is that it constitutes only a single and ambiguous challenge to the two hypotheses and that in the circumstances it can serve only to render the two hypotheses *slightly more tenable*. We should note, therefore, that the two hypotheses await further challenge.

Summing-up on the investigation of Sub-Hypotheses 2a and 2b

The investigation of Sub-Hypothesis 2a was unsatisfactory in that only the first of the two expectations derived from it could be tested with the analysis facilities available. Depending upon the definition of 'backwardness' used, the hypothesis does or does not get support from the evidence collected. Thus, it gets support if we define as 'backward' boys who attend or attended a secondary-modern school. It does *not* get support if we define as 'backward' boys in the lower class positions in the lower stream of the secondary-modern system.

Hypothesis 2b gets quite a lot of support from correlational evidence gathered — though here, too, we must keep it clearly in mind that a correlation does *not necessarily* imply a causal relationship.

6 METHODS AND FINDINGS RELATED TO THE INVESTIGATION OF HYPOTHESIS 3

The nature of the hypothesis
The third hypothesis was as follows:

Being without ambition as to what one will become or do on leaving school predisposes boys to become involved in stealing.

Distribution of boys in terms of expressed ambition
In this section are presented: (a) the questions asked as bases for classifying boys in terms of 'ambition'; and, (b) the distribution of boys in terms of their responses to these questions.

The questions asked

The questions asked were:

a) 'When you *left* school, what did you want to become?'
   OR
'When you *leave* school, what do you want to become?'

b) 'Is there anything you want specially to do in your life?' YES/NO
   IF 'NO' CHALLENGE:
'Anything at all you want to do or to be?'
   IF 'YES':
(i)   'Can you tell me what it is?'
(ii) 'Anything else?'
(iii) 'Any ambition you have not told me about?'

Question (a) was for use in identifying boys who *qualified* on the hypothesis and Question (b) was supplementary in character.

Distribution of Responses
Responses were analysed in terms of whether or not the boy claimed he wanted to become anything in particular on leaving school or *do* something in life. Details are given in Table 12.15.

Table 12.15
Distribution of responses

	Yes (%)	No (%)	No information (%)
Did he say he wanted to become anything in particular on leaving school?	89	9	2
Did he claim there is anything he specially wanted to *do* in life?	80	18	2

Ambition analysed in terms of characteristics of boys
Claims about wanting to become or do something were analysed by various characteristics of the boys: occupational level of boy's father; whether boy born in the United Kingdom; last type of school attended; how the boy feels/felt about school work; how the boy got on with/gets on with his school teachers. Details are given in Table 12.16.

The principal indications of Table 12.16 are as follows.

1 There is very little tendency for boys of different occupational backgrounds to vary in terms of the proportion who claim they want to become something particular on leaving school: the figure is relatively high for all of them.

2 There is a slight tendency for 'wanting to become something in particular on leaving school' to *fall-off* in

going from secondary-modern school boys to public-school boys — and for a reverse tendency to apply with respect to there being anything the boy wants especially to 'do in life'.

3 There is a slight tendency for boys who 'very much dislike' school work to want more than other boys to 'do something' in life — though this does not apply to wanting to do something in particular on leaving school.

4 There is a slight tendency for boys who got on badly with teachers to want *less than others* to 'do something' in life.

This set of results is challenging in its departure from what one might expect. Its special import seems to be that the two indices of ambition involved in this check are basically rather different. The one on which the hypothesis was based concerns a desire to become something in particular on leaving school (a sort of 'job intention') — as distinct from 'doing something in life' and, of course, there are many other forms that ambition might take.

Investigating Hypothesis 3
Two expectations were derived from the hypothesis.

Expectation 1   Boys who deny there is anything in particular they want to become on leaving school will have done more stealing than other boys.

Expectation 2   Expectation 1 applies even after the latter boys have been matched to the former in terms of the correlates of stealing.

Testing Expectation 1
The testing of Expectation 1 involves establishing the extent of relationship between stealing on the one hand and 'ambition' on the other and details of this relationship are shown in Table 12.17.

The data in Table 12.17 do not support Expectation 1 in that those who deny having something they want to become on leaving school are involved in a smaller amount of stealing than are other boys. The situation is broadly the same for the other definition of 'ambition'.

Testing Expectation 2 (using unweighted sample, 1,425 cases)
To test Expectation 2, boys were split into a qualifying group (i.e. those who denied or could not say there was anything they wanted to become on leaving school) and a control group (i.e. boys who said there *was* something they wanted to become on leaving school). The control group was then matched to the qualifying group in terms of the correlates of stealing, with the results shown in Table 12.18.

The evidence in Table 12.18 does not support Expectation 2 to any meaningful degree.

Table 12.16
Do boys want to do or to
become something in
particular? Analysed by
characteristics and
background
(3,113 cases, weighted)

Characteristics Cases (weighted)	All cases 3,113	Does boy want to be anything in particular after leaving school?			Is there anything in particular boy wants to do in life?		
		Yes 2,775	No 274	NI 64	Yes 2,500	No 548	NI 65
		(%)	(%)	(%)	(%)	(%)	(%)
Occupational level of father							
Professional, semi-professional, executive	518	89	8	3	87	9	3
Highly skilled	514	86	11	3	82	14	3
Skilled	674	92	6	1	80	18	2
Moderately skilled	630	89	11	–	78	20	2
Semi-skilled	517	91	6	2	77	23	1
Unskilled	254	86	13	2	78	21	2
No information	6						
Born in UK?							
Yes	2,856	89	9	2	81	17	2
No	257	95	5	0	72	23	4
School last attended							
Secondary modern	1,464	91	8	1	79	20	1
Comprehensive	549	92	7	1	82	18	–
Grammar	718	86	11	3	80	15	5
Public	257	83	11	6	85	12	3
Other	105						
No information	20						
How does boy feel about schoolwork?							
Dislikes it very much	81	85	14	1	87	11	2
Dislikes it	597	87	12	2	79	18	3
Likes it	2,117	90	8	2	81	17	2
Likes it very much	312	90	8	2	73	24	3
No information	6						
How did he get on with his teachers?							
Well	1,287	91	7	2	82	15	3
Average	1,481	87	11	2	80	18	2
Not very well	235	93	7	0	81	19	0
Badly	110	87	11	2	71	29	0

– = Less than 0.5 per cent

Summing-up on the investigation of Hypothesis 3

Neither expectation was supported in any meaningful way by the tests made and the hypothesis must therefore be regarded as getting no support from the evidence. This finding does not, of course, preclude a different result for some other definition of 'ambition' — possibly one specifying some particular class of ambition.

7 METHODS AND FINDINGS RELATED TO THE INVESTIGATION OF SUB-HYPOTHESES 4a AND 4b

The nature of the sub-hypotheses

Sub-Hypotheses 4a and 4b were phrased as follows.

A boy's nominal religion is causally related to the amount of stealing he does (Sub-Hypothesis 4a).

Table 12.17
The association between 'ambition' and amount of stealing (3,113 cases, weighted)

Claims about 'ambition'	All cases	Quartile distribution of variety of stealing				Quartile distribution of amount of stealing			
		Q.1	Q.2	Q.3	Q.4	Q.1	Q.2	Q.3	Q.4
	(n)	(%)	(%)	(%)	(%)	(%)	(%)	(%)	(%)
Anything he wants to become on leaving school									
Yes	2,775	25	24	26	25	24	27	25	24
No	274	21	29	31	18	21	33	28	18
No information	64								
Anything he wants specially to do in life									
Yes	2,500	24	25	26	25	23	28	26	24
No	548	29	21	30	20	30	30	20	21
No information	65								

Table 12.18
Differences between qualifiers and controls before and after matching: variety and amount of stealing

Indices of stealing	Unadjusted average score for qualifiers* a (116 cases)	Unadjusted average score for controls b (1,283 cases)	Adjusted average score for controls c	Differences between qualifiers and adj. controls a−c	Difference a−c as percentage of c (%)
Averaged indices of variety of stealing	13.1	13.6	12.5	0.6†	5
Averaged indices of amount of stealing	87.0	91.6	80.4	6.6†	8

*Qualifiers are boys who answered: no idea/not sure/don't know/nothing in particular
Controls are boys who answered in terms of there being something in particular they wanted to become on leaving school
†Not significant at the 0.05 level

and

Frequent attendance at church, chapel or synagogue reduces the amount of a boy's stealing (Sub-Hypothesis 4b).

Distribution of boys in terms of religious identification and involvement
In this section are presented: (a) the questions asked as bases for classifying boys in terms of religious involvement; and, (b) the distribution of boys in terms of their responses to those questions.

The questions asked
The questions asked were as follows.

a 'Have you got a religion?' YES/NO
  IF 'YES':
  'What is your religion?'

b 'Do you ever go to church or chapel or synagogue?'
  IF 'YES':
  'How often do you go?' SHOW CARD AND READ ALL OUT. UNDERLINE CHOICE OF FREQUENCY. (NEVER/HARDLY EVER/ONCE A MONTH/EACH WEEK)

Response distributions
For the sample as a whole, the distributions of responses to Questions a and b were as shown in Tables 12.19 and 12.20.
  Noteworthy features of Tables 12.19 and 12.20 are as follows.

1 That about a third of the boys claimed that they never attended church or chapel or synagogue and a further 25 per cent did so 'hardly ever'.

2 That 20 per cent claimed to have no religion at all.

Table 12.19
Claimed frequency of attendance
(3,113 cases, weighted)

	(n)	(%)
Once a week	791	25
Once a month	356	11
Hardly ever	774	25
Never	1,012	33
No information	180	6

Table 12.20
Distribution of religions claimed by boys
(3,113 cases, weighted)

	(n)	(%)		(n)	(%)
Church of England	1,158	37	Christian (only)	176	6
Methodist	52	2	Greek Orthodox	77	2
Presbyterian	12	–	Jewish	214	7
Protestant	148	5	Other religions	140	4
Roman Catholic/			Claimed no religion	621	20
Catholic	500	16	No information	15	–

– = Less than 0.5 per cent

Religious background analysed by characteristics of boys

Claimed religion and attendance at church, etc. were analysed by a range of characteristics of boys. Details of this analysis are set out in Table 12.21.

The main indications of Table 12.21 appear to be as follows.

1 Boys claiming no religion are under-represented amongst those whose fathers are of the professional or semi-professional or executive sector and are slightly over-represented amongst those with secondary-modern school background.

2 Jewish boys tend much more than other boys to be drawn from the professional, semi-professional or executive sector and to have public- or grammar-school backgrounds.

3 Boys from the professional, semi-professional and executive sectors attend church more often than other boys and those from the semi-skilled sector *less* than any of the others.

4 There is a lower rate of church attendance among: the sons of the semi-skilled; those who say they sometimes go out 'just looking for fun and excitement'; those who say there are frequent rows in the family; those with

Table 12.21
Religious backgrounds analysed by characteristics of boys
(3,113 cases, weighted)

Characteristics	All cases	Religious denomination claimed					Frequency of attendance at church				
		Protestant	Catholic	Christian (only)	Jewish	None	Never	Hardly ever	Once a month	Once a week	No information
Cases (weighted)	3,113	1,370	500	176	214	621	1,012	774	356	791	
	(n)	(%)	(%)	(%)	(%)	(%)	(%)	(%)	(%)	(%)	(%)
Occupation or background of boy's father											
Professional, semi-professional, executive	518	40	14	5	24	13*	15	26	19	39	2
Highly skilled	514	43	12	5	9	23	26	25	16	23	9
Skilled	674	51	16	7	1	19	37	22	9	27	5
Moderately skilled	630	43	16	5	5	21	35	27	9	24	5
Semi-skilled	517	46	17	7	1	23	44	26	9	15	6
Unskilled	254	35	27	5	1	22	37	21	6	26	10
No information	6										
Go out just looking for fun and excitement?											
Yes	2,229	No analysis made					34	26	12	22	6
No	884						28	21	11	34	5

continued

Table 12.21 (continued)

Characteristics	All cases	Religious denomination claimed					Frequency of attendance at church				
		Protestant	Catholic	Christian (only)	Jewish	None	Never	Hardly ever	Once a month	Once a week	No information
Cases (weighted)	3,113	1,370	500	176	214	621	1,012	774	356	791	
	(n)	(%)	(%)	(%)	(%)	(%)	(%)	(%)	(%)	(%)	(%)
Rows in family											
Every day	196	No analysis					44	24	13	16	3
Most days	800						31	23	10	29	7
Once a week	917						31	23	12	27	8
Once a month	516						35	34	10	18	3
Hardly ever/never	642						31	23	12	28	5
No information	42										
From how many sources was anti-stealing teaching received (including home, school, church)											
0	224	No analysis					35	30	8	19	8
1	702						45	23	8	15	9
2	1,283						38	24	10	21	7
3	863						13	26	17	44	1
No information	41										
Type of school last attended											
Secondary modern	1,464	42	17	7	1	24	40	24	10	20	6
Comprehensive	549	55	11	5	3	18	43	24	9	19	5
Grammar	718	42	33	4	17	14	18	28	13	36	5
Public	257	39	14	2	25	17	10	21	23	39	7
Other	105										
No information	20										
Age of boy											
12–13 yrs	721	No analysis					29	24	11	31	4
14 yrs	782						34	25	12	25	4
15 yrs	754						30	25	11	28	7
16–17 yrs	856						37	26	11	20	6

*Total across will not add to 100 per cent because other categories excluded

secondary-modern and comprehensive-school backgrounds; older boys. Relatively high rates of church attendance were claimed by boys who said they received anti-stealing instruction from home *and* school *and* church.

Investigating Sub-Hypotheses 4a and 4b

The central strategy for investigating these sub-hypotheses was, as for all other hypotheses, to derive from them a series of testable expectations and to test these. A description of this strategy has already been presented in Chapter 1.

Derivation of the expectations

From these two hypotheses, the following expectations were derived.

Expectation 1 Boys of different religious denominations will have been involved in different degrees of stealing.

Expectation 2 Expectation 1 applies even when these boys are matched in terms of the correlates of stealing.

Expectation 3 Boys who attend church more often will have been less involved in stealing than other boys.

Expectation 4 Expectation 3 will apply even when those who attend infrequently are matched to the frequent attenders.

Testing Expectation 1

This test involved calculating the association between religious denomination and the extent of stealing done. Details are given in Table 12.22.

The results indicate that Jewish and Greek Orthodox boys have a marked tendency to be less involved in stealing than boys of any other denomination.

Testing Expectation 2 (using unweighted sample, 1,425 cases)

To test Expectation 2, with respect to a given denomination, boys in that denomination and all other boys were equated in terms of the correlates of stealing, with the results as shown in Table 12.23.

Table 12.22
Relating religious denomination to amount and variety of stealing done
(3,113 cases, weighted)

Religious denomination	All cases	Quartile distribution of variety of stealing				Quartile distribution of amount of stealing			
		Q.1	Q.2	Q.3	Q.4	Q.1	Q.2	Q.3	Q.4
	(n)	(%)	(%)	(%)	(%)	(%)	(%)	(%)	(%)
Protestant	1,370	23	25	28	24	23	28	22	27
Catholic	500	21	27	25	27	23	22	29	26
Christian (only)	176	25	13	27	35	21	22	34	23
Greek Orthodox	77	33	16	43	9	33	34	22	12
Jewish	214	44	33	16	7	33	35	29	3
None	621	20	26	26	28	22	27	26	25
Other religions	140								
No information	15								

Table 12.23
Differences between qualifiers and controls before and after matching: variety and amount of stealing
(1,425 cases, unweighted)

Theft indices for different religious groups	Unadjusted average score for qualifiers a	Unadjusted average score for controls b	Adjusted average score for controls c	Differences between qualifiers and adj. controls a−c	Difference a−c as percentage of c (%)
Protestant boys (n =)	(625)	(714)			
Variety of stealing	13.69	13.39	13.34	0.35	3
Amount of stealing	94.29	89.25	89.40	4.89	5
Catholic boys (n =)	(253)	(1,086)			
Variety of stealing	14.26	13.30	13.45	0.81	6
Amount of stealing	97.47	90.24	91.36	6.11	7
Greek Orthodox boys (n =)	(41)	(1,298)			
Variety of stealing	10.62	13.08	13.25	−2.63*	−20
Amount of stealing	65.69	93.02	89.29	−23.60*	−26
Jewish boys (n =)	(110)	(1,229)			
Variety of stealing	8.57	13.76	12.61	−4.04†	−32
Amount of stealing	52.98	92.90	83.97	−30.99†	−37
No religion (n =)	(320)	(1,019)			
Variety of stealing	14.29	13.29	13.49	0.80	6
Amount of stealing	95.55	90.36	94.95	0.60	6

*Significant at 0.05 level
†Significant at 0.01 level

The data in Table 12.23 indicates that Expectation 2 holds with respect to Jewish and Greek Orthodox denominations but not to any significant degree with respect to the other denominations.

Testing Expectation 3

To test Expectation 3, a study was made of the degree of association between claimed frequency of going to church and the extent of involvement in stealing. Details are given in Table 12.24.

This evidence tends to support Expectation 3 with respect to variety and amount of stealing.

Testing Expectation 4 (using unweighted sample, 1,425 cases)

To test Expectation 4, the sample was split into three groups: (a) a qualifying group, made up of boys who claimed they attended church each week; (b) a control group made up of boys who said either that they had no religion or that they never went to church; (c) the others. The controls were then matched to the qualifiers in terms of the correlates of stealing.

Table 12.25 presents the results both for total amount of stealing and for variety of stealing for each of the forty-four types of theft on which total score was based. The evidence supports the expectation.

Summing-up on the investigation of Sub-Hypotheses 4a and 4b

Sub-Hypothesis 4a was supported with respect to Jewish and Greek Orthodox denominations, but not to any meaningful degree with respect to Protestant or Catholic denominations or boys saying they have no religion.

Sub-Hypothesis 4b was supported by the evidence and thereby made more tenable. This hypothesis appears also to apply for the majority of the different types of theft dealt with.

8 SUMMING-UP ON THE INVESTIGATION OF THE FOUR HYPOTHESES

This chapter reports on the investigation of four hypotheses. Between them they postulate a causal relationship between boys' involvement in stealing and each of the following conditions:

1 Truanting from school (Hypothesis 1).

2 Backwardness at school (Sub-Hypothesis 2a).

3 Disliking school (Sub-Hypothesis 2b).

4 Lack of personal ambition (Hypothesis 3).

5 Religious denomination (Sub-Hypothesis 4a).

6 Non-attendance at religious services (Sub-Hypothesis 4b).

Hypothesis 1, concerning truancy   The evidence supports the hypothesis, but also indicates that truanting is partly indirect in its causal function. Thus, it appears from the evidence that stealing promoted through truancy does not necessarily occur during the actual period of truancy. It is hypothesized that truancy catalyses thieving behaviour by bringing the new truant into association with other truants in what is essentially a delinquent context and that thereafter that association is continued in other delinquent activities that could include stealing.

Sub-Hypothesis 2a, concerning backwardness at school This sub-hypothesis was only partly investigated because analysis facilities were not available for the rather complex matching techniques required for testing the various expectations. For some definitions of 'backwardness', the evidence available gave support to the hypothesis. But for an extreme definition of backwardness (i.e. in terms of boys in the lower class positions in the lower stream of the secondary-modern system), the evidence does not support the sub-hypothesis. The evidence available is weak because it is solely correlational in character.

Sub-Hypothesis 2b, concerning disliking school The sub-hypothesis is supported by the evidence available. Thus, boys who say they dislike(d) both school work and their teachers, had much higher theft scores than those who said they like(d) both school work and their teachers. The evidence also indicated that the disliking of teachers was more strongly associated with thieving than was disliking school work. However, as for Sub-Hypothesis 2a, the evidence available for challenging the hypothesis was only correlational in character.

Table 12.24 Relating frequency of church attendance to variety and amount of stealing (3,113 cases, weighted)	Frequency of attendance		Quartile distribution of variety of stealing				Quartile distribution of amount of stealing			
			Q.1	Q.2	Q.3	Q.4	Q.1	Q.2	Q.3	Q.4
		(n)	(%)	(%)	(%)	(%)	(%)	(%)	(%)	(%)
	Never	1,012	19	20	31	30	20	26	22	32
	Hardly ever	774	19	28	25	27	19	29	30	22
	Once a month	356	31	22	29	18	23	29	26	22
	Each week	791	35	28	22	14	34	29	23	14

Table 12.25
Differences between qualifiers and controls before and after matching: each of the forty-four types of theft (1,425 cases, unweighted)

Theft indices	Unadjusted average score for qualifiers a (328 cases)	Unadjusted average score for controls b (522 cases)	Adjusted average score for controls c	Differences between qualifiers and adj. controls a−c	Difference a−c as percentage of c (%)
Variety index average score	10.06	15.16	13.61	−3.55	−26
Amount index average score	72.79	109.12	95.00	−22.21	−23
Duration index average score	3.02	4.16	3.65	−0.63	−17

Theft type at L2	a		b		c		Diff. (a−c)	a−c as percentage of c
	(n)	(%)	(n)	(%)	(n)	(%)	(a−c)	(%)
1	289	88.1	483	92.5	294.6	90.2	−2.1	−2
2	125	38.1	310	59.4	183.7	56.3	−18.2	−32
3	105	32.0	242	46.4	138.7	42.5	−10.5	−25
4	152	46.3	285	54.6	168.5	51.6	−5.3	−10
5	53	16.2	137	26.2	77.3	23.7	−7.5	−32
6	143	43.6	320	61.3	181.4	55.5	−11.9	−21
7	97	29.6	227	43.5	126.5	38.8	−9.2	−24
8	124	37.8	155	29.7	97.17	29.8	8.0	27
9	48	14.6	84	16.1	46.0	14.1	0.5	4
10	106	32.3	222	42.5	113.9	34.9	−2.6	−7
11	92	28.0	211	40.4	121.0	37.1	−9.1	−25
12	48	14.6	97	18.6	49.8	15.2	−0.6	−4
13	98	29.9	232	44.4	127.0	38.9	−9.0	−23
14	45	13.7	150	28.7	77.1	23.6	−9.9	−42
15	33	10.1	95	18.2	48.4	14.8	−4.7	−32
16	107	32.6	273	52.3	158.4	48.6	−16.0	−33
17	36	11.0	135	25.9	67.1	20.6	−9.6	−47
18	196	59.8	358	68.6	207.3	63.5	−3.7	−6
19	113	34.5	186	35.6	103.1	31.6	2.9	9
20	89	27.1	167	32.0	92.8	28.4	−1.3	−5
21	42	12.8	74	14.2	41.3	12.7	0.1	1
22	99	30.2	227	43.5	136.8	41.9	−11.7	−28
23	49	14.9	142	27.2	68.0	20.8	−5.9	−28
24	25	7.6	83	15.9	42.6	13.1	−5.5	−42
25	68	20.7	135	25.9	74.5	22.8	−2.1	−9
26	64	19.5	186	35.6	103.2	31.6	−12.1	−38
27	51	15.5	122	23.4	69.8	21.4	−5.9	−28
28	49	14.9	149	28.5	78.8	24.1	−9.2	−38
29	15	4.6	52	10.0	24.4	7.5	−2.9	−39
30	137	41.8	248	47.5	136.6	41.8	0.0	0
31	54	16.5	171	32.8	86.0	26.3	−9.8	−37
32	16	4.9	44	8.4	22.7	7.0	−2.1	−30
33	185	56.4	365	69.9	214.1	65.6	−9.2	−14
34	91	27.7	176	33.7	104.9	32.1	−4.4	−14
35	29	8.8	130	24.9	65.8	20.2	−11.4	−56

continued

Table 12.25 (continued)

Theft indices	Unadjusted average score for qualifiers a (328 cases)	Unadjusted average score for controls b (522 cases)	Adjusted average score for controls c	Differences between qualifiers and adj. controls a–c	Difference a–c as percentage of c (%)
Variety index average score	10.06	15.16	13.61	−3.55	−26
Amount index average score	72.79	109.12	95.00	−22.21	−23
Duration index average score	3.02	4.16	3.65	−0.63	−17

Theft type at L2	a		b		c		Diff. (a–c)	a–c as percentage of c
	(n)	(%)	(n)	(%)	(n)	(%)		
36	73	22.3	183	35.1	98.6	30.2	−7.9	−26
37	7	2.1	38	7.3	16.0	4.9	−2.8	−57
38	46	14.0	156	29.9	85.9	26.3	−12.3	−47
39	51	15.5	114	21.8	60.2	18.4	−2.9	−16
40	194	59.1	347	66.5	201.5	61.7	−2.6	−4
41	23	7.0	63	12.1	29.6	9.1	−2.1	−23
42	35	10.7	66	12.6	37.0	11.3	−0.6	−5
43	59	18.0	184	35.2	102.8	31.5	−13.5	−43
44	158	48.2	291	55.7	167.7	51.4	−3.2	−6

Hypothesis 3, concerning lack of ambition   Ambition was defined in terms of there being something one wants to become on leaving school. The hypothesis did not get meaningful support from the evidence. Other definitions of ambition might, of course, be introduced into substitute hypotheses.

Sub-Hypothesis 4a, concerning religious denomination   The evidence would support a sub-hypothesis that boys' membership of the Jewish or the Greek Orthodox religions tends to reduce their involvement in stealing. The evidence would not support such a sub-hypothesis about Catholic or Protestant boys or about boys who claim they have no religion.

Sub-Hypothesis 4b, concerning attendance at religious services   The evidence supports the sub-hypothesis that attendance at religious services tends to reduce boys' involvement in stealing.

9 SOME COMMENTS AND POSSIBLE ACTION
In this chapter, thieving has been studied in the context of three aspects of schooling: how boys feel about their work at school and about their teachers; whether boys are backward; the degree to which boys commit truancy.

Backwardness at school is a matter of degree and in its extreme form it does not appear to be a causal element in relation to stealing. On the other hand, disliking school work and one's teachers does appear to promote stealing to some degree and truancy very much more.

It may well be that attitude towards schooling and teachers is linked to truancy, but research would be needed to establish that. The evidence collected in this inquiry could, if subjected to special analysis, be effectively brought to bear on that issue and it is suggested that this be done.

Truancy itself appears to operate somewhat indirectly in promoting stealing – in the sense that the stealing does not necessarily occur in the period of the actual truancy. The writer has hypothesized that one of the functions of truancy is to build-up relations between the new truant and other truants in the context of delinquent activity (truancy in this case). This in turn could lead to further delinquent activity in its own right and at a more opportune time, especially if the truant's new associates are already thieves. This and other hypotheses about the way truancy may promote stealing will need to be studied empirically for the better understanding of that process. But in the meantime, the evidence from this part of the inquiry should be taken as providing a case for stepping-up action against the occurrence of truancy.

Preventive action against truancy will be more effective if based upon the results of intensive interviews with truants designed to increase insight into the reasons for truancy and into the truant's personal strategies for 'getting away with it'. This form of preparatory study need not and should not be lengthy or costly. It should not be undertaken in a theoretical context but should be designed solely to provide practical guidelines for the effective design and administration of preventive action.

10 APPENDIX 12.1

The sub-questionnaire used

Religion, school, ambitions and others
Q.1 Age? Birthday?

Q.2 About religion

2a 'Have you got a religion?' YES/NO
IF 'YES':
'What is your religion?'

2b 'Do you ever go to church/chapel/synagogue?'
IF 'YES':
'How often do you go?' SHOW CARD AND READ ALL OUT.
UNDERLINE CHOICE OF FREQUENCY
NEVER/HARDLY EVER/ONCE A MONTH/EACH WEEK

Q 3 About school

3a 'Are you still at school full time?' YES/NO.
IF 'NO':
'How old were you when you left school?'

3b 'What sort of school are you at/were you last at?'
GET DETAILS AND ENTER THESE (E.G. SECONDARY MODERN/COMPREHENSIVE/GRAMMAR/PUBLIC/...)

3c IF SECONDARY MODERN
(i) 'Did you pass the 11 plus?' (EXPLAIN IF NECESSARY: 'Where you offered a grammar school place after the 11 plus?)' YES/NO.

(ii) 'Which stream were/are you in at your secondary modern school?' PROBE FOR A, B, C, D, OR OTHER LEVEL.

(iii) 'Where did/do you usually come in your class?'

(iv) 'How many were/are there in your class?'

(v) 'Were/are there any subjects you liked at school?'
YES/NO
IF 'YES':
'What were/are they?'

(vi) 'Did you ever pass/have you ever passed any exams at shcool?'
IF 'YES':
'What were they?' ENTER THESE BELOW (E.G. 'O LEVELS', C.S.E. SCHOLARSHIP)
AND ADD SUBJECTS AFTER EACH

(vii) 'At secondary-modern school, how did/do you feel about your school work?'
SHOW CARD, CIRCLE CHOICE: (DISLIKE VERY MUCH/DISLIKE/LIKE/LIKE VERY MUCH).

(viii) 'At secondary-modern shcool, how did you get on with most of your teachers?'
SHOW CARD, CIRCLE CHOICE (WELL/AVERAGE/NOT VERY WELL/BADLY)

(ix) 'Were you ever a prefect or head boy or anything like that?' YES/NO
IF 'YES':
'What were you?'
NOW GO ON TO Q.4.

3d IF COMPREHENSIVE
(i) 'Did you pass the 11 plus?' (EXPLAIN IF NECESSARY: 'Were you offered a grammar school place after you did your 11 plus)?' YES/NO

(ii) 'What section of the school were/are you in?' (PROBE FOR SEC. MOD/GRAMMAR/ETC.)

(iii) 'What stream were/are you in?' PROBE FOR A, B, C, D or OTHER LEVEL.

(iv) 'Where did/do you usually come in your class?'

(v) 'How many were/are there in your class?'

(vi) 'Where/are there any subjects you liked at school?'
YES/NO
IF 'YES':
'What were/are they?'

(vii) 'Did you ever pass/have you ever passed any exams at school?'
IF 'YES':
'What were they?' ENTER THESE BELOW (E.G. 'O LEVELS', C.S.E. SCHOLARSHIP)
AND ADD SUBJECTS AFTER EACH.

(viii) 'At your comprehensive school, how did/do you feel about your school work?'
SHOW CARD, CIRCLE CHOICE: (DISLIKE VERY MUCH/DISLIKE/LIKE/LIKE VERY MUCH)

(ix) 'And at your comprehensive school, how did you get on with most of your teachers?'
SHOW CARD, CIRCLE CHOICE: (WELL/AVERAGE/NOT VERY WELL/BADLY)

(x) 'Were you ever a prefect or a head boy or anything like that?' YES/NO

IF 'YES':
What were you?'
  NOW GO TO Q.4

3e *IF GRAMMAR*
(i) 'What was/is your best subject?'

(ii) 'How well did/do you do in this?' (PROBE FOR
    PLACE OR FOR SUBJECT GRADING IF THERE
    WAS NO PLACING)

(iii) 'Were/are there any subjects you liked at school?'
    YES/NO
    IF 'YES':
'What were/are they?'

(iv) 'Did you ever pass/have you ever passed any exams
at school?'
    IF 'YES':
'What were they?' ENTER THESE BELOW (E.G. 'O
    LEVELS', C.S.E. SCHOLARSHIP).
    AND ADD SUBJECTS AFTER EACH

(v) 'At grammar school how did/do you feel about your
schoolwork?'
    SHOW CARD, CIRCLE CHOICE: (DISLIKE VERY
    MUCH/DISLIKE/LIKE/LIKE VERY MUCH)

(vi) 'And at grammar school, how did/do you get on
with most of your teachers?'
    SHOW CARD, CIRCLE CHOICE (WELL/
    AVERAGE/NOT VERY WELL/BADLY)

(vii) 'Were you ever a prefect or head boy or anything
like that?' YES/NO
    IF 'YES': 'What were you?'
    NOW GO TO Q.4

3f *IF PUBLIC/BOARDING SCHOOL*
(i) 'What was/is your best subject?'

(ii) 'How well did/do you do in this?' (PROBE FOR
    PLACE OR FOR SUBJECT GRADING IF THERE
    WAS NO PLACING).

(iii)'Were/are there any subjects you liked at school?'
    YES/NO
    IF 'YES':
'What were/are they?'

(iv) 'Did you ever pass/have you ever passed any exams
at school?'
    IF 'YES':
'What were they?' ENTER THESE BELOW (E.G. 'O
    LEVELS', C.S.E. SCHOLARSHIP)
    AND ADD SUBJECTS AFTER EACH.

(v) 'At your public/boarding school how did/do you
feel about your school work?'
    SHOW CARD, CIRCLE CHOICE: (DISLIKE VERY
    MUCH/DISLIKE/LIKE/LIKE VERY MUCH)

(vi) 'And at public/boarding school, how did/do you get
on with most of your teachers?'
    SHOW CARD, CIRCLE CHOICE: (WELL/
    AVERAGE/NOT VERY WELL/BADLY)

(vii) 'Were you ever a prefect or head boy or anything
like that?' YES/NO
    IF 'YES':
'What were you?'
    NOW GO TO Q.4

Q.4 Truancy

'Do/did you ever play truant from school?' YES/NO
    IF 'NO', CHALLENGE:
    IF 'YES':
(i) 'How often?' ONCE A WEEK/ONCE A MONTH/
    HARDLY EVER

(ii) 'What do/did you do with your time when you were
playing truant?'

(iii) 'How much pinching do/did you do when you
played truant?'

Q.5 Ambitions

(a) 'When you *left* school, what did you want to
become?'
    OR
'When you *leave* school, what *do* you want to become?'

(b) 'Is there anything you want specially to do in your
life?' YES/NO.
    IF 'NO', CHALLENGE:
'Anything at all you want to do or to be?'
    IF 'YES':
(i) 'Can you tell me what it is?'
(ii) 'Anything else?'
(iii) 'Any ambition you have not told me about yet?'

Q.6 Girls

'Have you got a girl friend?' YES/NO.
    IF 'YES':
'Are you going steady with her?' YES/NO
'How often do you go out with her?'
    IF 'NO':
'Do you go out with girls?' YES/NO
    IF 'YES':
'How often?' EACH WEEK/ONCE A MONTH/LESS
    THAN THAT.

Q.7 The house

'How many rooms have you got in your home? Are you
counting the bathroom and kitchen?' YES/NO
'So not counting the bathroom and kitchen, how many
rooms are there in your house?'

.8 His personal background

a) 'Have you ever done any of these?' (CALL OUT AND CIRCLE EACH TIME HE ANSWERS 'YES'):
Been a cub or scout/played a sport/won a prize/belonged to a library/gone to a youth club/passed an exam/did some welfare work/been baptised/been to a communion/taken a trip out of England/had a fist fight/had a job during school holidays/played in the street a lot/delivered newspapers/been in a team for sport/had a talk with someone about what you want to do in life.'

Q.9 Others

'Do you ever try to get your own back on boys?'
   YES/NO
   IF 'YES':
'How often?' (OFFER CARD AND CIRCLE CHOICE)
   OFTEN/NOW AND THEN/HARDLY EVER/NEVER